Crisis in American Institutions

Eighth Edition

Jerome H. Skolnick
Elliott Currie

University of California, Berkeley

 HarperCollins*Publishers*

Sponsoring Editor: Alan McClare
Project Editor: David Nickol
Design Supervisor: Pete Noa
Text Design: Merlin Communications, Inc.
Cover Design: Ben Arrington
Cover Photo: Reginald Wickham
Production: Linda Murray
Compositor: Circle Graphics
Printer and Binder: R. R. Donnelley & Sons Company
Cover Printer: New England Book Components

Crisis in American Institutions, Eighth Edition

ISBN: 0-673-52144-3

92 93 94   9 8 7 6 5 4 3

Crisis
in American
Institutions

Contents

Preface

For this eighth edition, the plan of the book remains basically the same as in earlier editions. But we have added many new articles, reflecting the changing contours of the crisis in American institutions as we enter the 1990s.

They include analyses of the savings and loan scandals and the impact of Wall Street money on the political process; explorations of the limits of the "drug war" and the decay of America's infrastructure. We have updated and strengthened selections dealing with povery and inequality—tragically, problems that have deepened in the past few years. A new selection examines the problems facing Hispanics in American society; another offers a personal glimpse into the human realities behind the abortion debate.

As we move closer to the end of the twentieth century, the crisis of the environment looms even larger and more fateful than ever, as our new articles on global atmospheric changes and the threat of toxic air pollution demonstrate. But there are also new hopeful notes: With the end of the Cold War, another new article examines the possibility for conversion of the military economy to civilian needs.

Each edition has offered an opportunity to review the best contemporary writing on American social problems, and with each we have regretted dropping old favorites and omitting promising new writings. We invariably find far more worthwhile writing than we are able to use. After all, we survey a range of topics—from corporate power through racism, to the family and the environment—each of which could profitably occupy a lifetime of study and writing.

As always, many people helped us in many ways to make this edition a reality. At HarperCollins, Alan McClare and David Nickol helped smooth the book's transition to a new home. The Center for the Study of Law and

Society at the University of California, Berkeley, once again offered facilities and a supportive environment. Rod Watanabe, the Center's administrative assistant, as always created order whenever chaos threatened, this time aided by Kiara Jordan. We appreciate their assistance and friendship. Finally, we are most grateful to the students and teachers who have continued to teach us about each edition's strengths and weaknesses.

Jerome H. Skolnick
Elliott Currie

Introduction:
Approaches to Social Problems

When we first put this book together in the late 1960s, the American mood was very different than it is today. The United States in those days was the undisputed political and economic leader among the world's countries. American living standards had been steadily rising. Each year brought new technological wonders that seemed to promise still more abundance to come. Small wonder that many social scientists accepted the widely prevailing view that most fundamental economic and political problems had been solved in the United States—or, at least, were well on their way to a solution.

Today, all of that seems like ancient history, even to us—not to mention contemporary students, many of whom were toddlers when the first edition of this book appeared. Indeed, by the time *Crisis in American Institutions* first appeared, the superficial tranquility of postwar American society had already begun to unravel—hence our choice of title. But by now, Americans are confronted with a range of social problems whose magnitude and visibility would have seemed almost incomprehensible when we first wrote our book.

These changes have had a profound effect on the way social scientists (and other observers of American society) have thought about social problems. The study of social problems, after all—like any other aspect of social science—does not take place in the antiseptic confines of a scientific laboratory. Social theorists, like everyone else, are deeply influenced by broader trends in the society, the economy, and in the cultural and technological setting of social life. As a way of introducing the articles that follow, of placing the debates of the 1980s and 1990s in some historical and intellectual context, we want to spend a few pages outlining the way in

1

which the study of social problems has developed over time and how those larger social changes have shaped its basic assumptions and its guiding themes.

DEFECTIVES AND DELINQUENTS

The earliest writers on social problems in this country were straightforward moralists, staunch supporters of the virtues of thrift, hard work, sexual purity, and personal discipline. Writing at the end of the nineteenth century, they sought ways of maintaining the values of an earlier, whiter, more Protestant, and more stable America in the face of the new challenges of industrialization, urbanization, and immigration.[1]

This early social science usually concentrated on the problems of what one nineteenth-century textbook described as the "defective, dependent, and delinquent classes."[2] The causes of social problems were located in the physical constitution or the moral "character" of the poor, the criminal, the insane, and other "unfortunates." For these theorists, the solution to nineteenth-century social problems lay in developing means of transforming the character of these "defective" classes, in the hope of equipping them better to succeed within a competitive, hierarchical society whose basic assumptions were never questioned. Social reformers working from these theories created, in the last part of the nineteenth and the first part of the twentieth centuries, much of the modern apparatus of "social control" in the United States: reformatories, modern prisons, institutions for the mentally ill, and the beginnings of the modern welfare system.

THE RISE OF "VALUE-FREE" SOCIAL PROBLEMS

During the first decades of this century, this straightforward moralism was increasingly discarded in favor of a more subtle, ostensibly "neutral" approach to writing about social problems. By the 1930s, the idea that the social sciences were—or could be—purely "objective" or "value-free" had come to be widely accepted. From that point until the present, social problems theory has been characterized by a tortuous attempt to prove that theories and policies that serve to support the status quo are actually scientific judgments arrived at objectively. In this view, social scientists do not try to impose their own values in deciding what kinds of things will be defined and dealt with as social problems. Instead, the "scientific" student of social problems simply accepts "society's" definition of what is a problem and what is not. This approach is apparent in these statements, taken from major textbooks, on what constitutes a social problem:

> Any difficulty or misbehavior of a fairly large number of persons which
> we wish to remove or correct.[3]
> What people think they are.[4]
> Whenever people begin to say, isn't it awful! Why don't they do some-
> thing about it?[5]
> Conditions which affect sizable proportions of the population, which are
> out of harmony with the values of a significant segment of the popu-
> lation, and which people feel can be improved or eliminated.[6]
> Any substantial discrepancy between socially shared standards and ac-
> tual conditions of social life.[7]

These definitions share the common idea that social problems are
popularly defined. No condition is a problem unless a certain number of
people in a society say it is. Since we are merely taking, as our starting
point, the definitions of the problem that "other people," "society," or
"significant segments of the population" provide, we are no longer in the
position of moralizing about objective conditions.

The basic flaw in this happy scheme is that it does not make clear *which*
segments of the population to consult when defining problems or how to
decide between conflicting ideas about what is problematic and what is
not. In the real world, societies are divided along class, racial, sexual, and
other lines, and the sociologist who proposes to follow "people's" definitions of social problems in fact generally adopts one of several competing
ideologies of social problems based on those divisions. In practice, the
ideology adopted has usually been not too different from that of the
"unscientific" social problems writers of the nineteenth century.

These points are not new; they were raised as early as 1936 in an
unusually perceptive paper called "Social Problems and the Mores," by
the sociologist Willard Waller. Waller noted, for example, that discussions
of poverty in the social problems literature of the 1930s were shaped by
the unquestioning acceptance of the ideology of competitive capitalism:

> A simpleton would suggest that the remedy for poverty in the midst of
> plenty is to redistribute income. We reject this solution at once because
> it would interfere with the institution of private property, would destroy
> the incentive for thrift and hard work and disjoint the entire economic
> system.[8]

Waller's question is fundamental: What has been left out in a writer's
choice of what are to be considered as problems? What features of society
are going to be taken for granted as the framework *within* which problems
will be defined and resolved? In this case, the taken-for-granted framework is the principle of private property and individual competition. In
general, Waller argued, "social problems are not solved because people
do not want to solve them";[9] they *are* problems mainly because of people's
unwillingness to alter the basic conditions from which they arise. Thus:

> Venereal disease becomes a social problem in that it arises from our
> family institutions and also in that the medical means which could be
> used to prevent it, which would unquestionably be fairly effective, can-
> not be employed for fear of altering the mores of chastity.[10]

For Waller the definition of social problems was, in the broadest sense, a
political issue involving the opposed ideologies of conflicting groups.

Waller's points still ring true. Most social problems writers in the
United States still tacitly accept the basic structure of American society
and restrict their treatment of social problems to maladjustments *within*
that structure.

SOCIAL PROBLEMS IN THE 1950s: GRADUALISM
AND ANTICOMMUNISM

This is not to say that the literature on social problems since the 1930s has
all been the same. Books on social problems, not surprisingly, tend to
reflect the preoccupations of the time when they were written. Those
conceived in the 1950s, for example, reflect social and political concerns
that now seem bizarre. The shadow of McCarthyism and the general
national hysteria over the "Communist menace" pervaded this literature.
Consider the discussion of "civil liberties and subversion" in Paul B.
Horton and Gerald R. Leslie's textbook, *The Sociology of Social Problems*.[11]
Horton and Leslie saw the "American heritage of liberty" being attacked
from both left and right, from both "monolithic communism" and over-
zealous attempts to defend "our" way of life from it. Their position was
resolutely "moderate." They claimed a scientific objectivity; yet, they
were quite capable of moral condemnation of people whose politics were
"extreme," whether right or left:

> Most extremists are deviants. Most extremists show a fanatical preoc-
> cupation with their cause, a suspicious distrust of other people in gen-
> eral, a disinterest in normal pursuits, recreations, and small talk, and a
> strong tendency to divide other people into enemies and allies.[12]

The preference for "normal pursuits," even "small talk," over social
criticism and action was common in an age noted for its "silent generation," but it was hardly "scientific." Among the other presumably objective features of the book were the authors' "rational proposals for preserv-
ing liberty and security," including these:

> *An adequate national defense* is, needless to say, necessary in a world
> where an international revolutionary movement is joined to an aggres-
> sive major power. This is a military problem, not a sociological problem,
> and is not discussed here.
>   *Counterespionage is essential.* Highly trained professional agencies such
> as the FBI and the Central Intelligence Agency can do this efficiently

and without endangering personal liberties of citizens. If headline-hunting congressmen, Legion officials, or other amateurs turn G-men, they merely scare off any real spies and destroy the counterespionage efforts of the professionals.[13]

The military and intelligence services themselves were not considered as problems relevant for social science. Questions about the operation of these agencies were viewed as internal and technical, military rather than sociological, issues.

In a section on "Questions and Projects," the authors asked: "How have conservatives or reactionaries sometimes given unintentional assistance to the Communists? How have liberals sometimes given unintentional assistance to the Communists?"[14]

In the introduction to their book, Horton and Leslie considered the possibilities of social change and the proper role of social scientists in promoting it. They carefully adopted a middle ground between conservatives, to whom social problems were primarily problems of individual character, and "extremists" hoping for sudden or radical changes in social structure. They argued that the resolution of social problems "nearly always involves sweeping institutional changes" but also that such changes are "costly" and "difficult," and that therefore

> it is unrealistic to expect that these problems will be solved easily or quickly. . . . Basic solutions of social problems will come slowly, if at all. Meanwhile, however, considerable amelioration or "improvement" may be possible.[15]

Social change, according to these authors, must be gradual and realistic; it must also be guided by experts. The authors insisted that their own role, and that of social experts in general, was merely to show the public how to get what they already valued. But in this role it was folly for the "layman" to question the expert. Horton and Leslie wrote that "when experts are *agreed* upon the futility of one policy or the soundness of another, it is sheer stupidity for the layman to disagree."[16]

An elitist, cold-war liberalism and gradualism, a fear of extremism and of an international Communist conspiracy—all these were presented not as moral and political positions but as fundamental social scientific truths. The sturdy entrepreneurial and Protestant values described in Waller's paper of the 1930s gave way, in Horton and Leslie's book of the 1950s, to a general preference for moderation, anticommunism, and "normal pursuits."

THE 1960s: AFFLUENCE AND OPTIMISM

A different imagery dominated the social problems literature of the next decade. Robert K. Merton and Robert M. Nisbet's *Contemporary Social Problems*[17] was a product of the beginning of the 1960s, the period of the

"New Frontier," which saw a significant shift, at least on the surface, in the focus of social concern. Americans were becoming aware of an "underdeveloped" world abroad and a "disadvantaged" world at home, both unhappily excluded from the benefits of an age of general "affluence" and well-being. New agencies of social improvement were created at home and abroad. A critique of old-style welfare efforts began to develop, along with the notion of "helping people help themselves," whether in Latin America, Harlem, or Appalachia. The idea of inclusion, of participation, in the American way of life became a political metaphor for the age. From a slightly different vantage, the idea emerged as "development" or "modernization." The social problems of the 1960s would be solved by extending the technological and intellectual resources of established American institutions into excluded, deprived, or underdeveloped places and groups. An intervention-minded government combined with an energetic social science on a scale unprecedented in this country.

In this period—very brief, as it turned out—social problems were often seen as problems of being *left out* of the American mainstream: "left behind," as the people of Appalachia were described; "traditional," like the Mexican-Americans; or "underdeveloped," like most Africans, Asians, and Latin Americans. In social problems theory, these ideas were manifested in a conservative ideology that celebrated American society as a whole, coupled with a liberal critique of the conditions hindering the extension of the American way to all.

One variant of this view was given in Nisbet's introduction to *Contemporary Social Problems.* For Nisbet, social facts become problematic when they "represent interruptions in the expected or desired scheme of things; violations of the right or the proper, as a society defines these qualities; dislocations in the social patterns and relationships that a society cherishes."[18]

Nisbet's assessment of the American situation was in keeping with the exaggerated optimism of the early 1960s:

> In America today we live in what is often called an affluent society. It is
> a society characterized by imposing command of physical resources,
> high standards of private consumption, effective maintenance of public
> order and security, freedom from most of the uncertainties of life that
> plagued our ancestors, and relatively high levels of humanitarianism.
> There are also, of course, squalid slums, both urban and rural; occa-
> sional epidemics of disease; sudden eruptions of violence or bigotry,
> even in the most civilized of communities; people for whom the struggle
> for food and shelter yet remains obsessing and precarious. Thus, we are
> not free of social problems, and some of them seem to grow almost in
> direct proportion to our affluence.[19]

Nisbet was aware that America had not yet solved all its problems; indeed, that some seem to come with the generally glittering package that is America in the twentieth century. Yet, the problems were viewed as peripheral, as occasional eruptions in the backwaters of society where modern institutions had not fully penetrated.

Like earlier theorists, Nisbet sharply separated the role of the scientific student of social problems from that of other concerned people. The social scientist, as a scientist, should not engage in moral exhortation or political action but should concentrate on understanding. At the same time, the scientist is

> as interested as the next citizen in making the protection of society his first responsibility, in seeing society reach higher levels of moral decency, and when necessary, in promoting such legal actions as are necessary in the short run for protection or decency.[20]

Here the scientific stance masked a preference for vaguely defined values—"societal protection" and "moral decency"—which, in turn, determine what will be selected as social problems. In this instance, problems were selected according to whether they offended the values of social stability, that is, values associated with the conservative tradition in social thought.

Thus, problems were repeatedly equated with "dislocations and deviations";[21] they were problems of "dissensus," as if consensus might not also be a problem. Indeed, the entire book was divided into two sections, one of which dealt with "deviant behavior" and the other, with "social disorganization." The articles in the text were not all of a piece. A paper by Robert S. Weiss and David Riesman on the problems of work took a different view on what constitutes a problem; the authors declared that "social forms which tend toward the suppression or frustration of meaning and purpose in life are inferior forms, whether or not they tend toward disorganization."[22] But many of the articles simply accepted the purposes of existing institutions and defined problems in terms of combating disorganization *within* those institutions. Perhaps the clearest illustration of this tendency appeared in an essay by Morris Janowitz dealing with problems of the military establishment:

> It is self-evident that the military establishment, the armed forces, and their administrative organizations have become and will remain important institutions of United States society. The distinctive forms of military organization must be analyzed in order to understand the typical sources of personal and social disorganization found in military life.[23]

The existence of a large military establishment was defined as outside the critical concern of the sociologist. The focus was not on the effect of the military on national or international life but on the problems of maladjustment within the military apparatus. The increasing scope of military activities was noted, but it was simply accepted as a fact of modern life:

> The armed forces have also become involved in a wide variety of logistical, research, and training activities. In the current international scene,

they must take on many politico-military duties, including military assistance of allied powers.[24]

The implication was that the militarization of American society is not itself a problem for social analysis. And the acceptance of the place of the military in American society leads to the enlistment of social science in the service of military ends. Thus, in discussing changes in the requirements of military discipline, Janowitz noted that, in the 1960s, instead of employing "shock technique" to assimilate the recruit into the military, the problem had become how to foster "positive incentives and group loyalties through a team concept."[25] Janowitz didn't ask *what* the recruit is being assimilated *into*. The effect of primary-group relations on morale under cold-war conditions was extensively discussed, but the cold war itself was not.

Robert Merton's epilogue to *Contemporary Social Problems*, called "Social Problems and Sociological Theory," represented a major attempt to give theoretical definition to the "field" of social problems. Merton was well aware that different interests were present in society and therefore that definitions of social problems are likely to be contested—"one group's problem will be another group's asset"—and more specifically that "those occupying strategic positions of authority and power of course carry more weight than others in deciding social policy and so, among other things, in identifying for the rest what are to be taken as significant departures from social standards."[26]

According to Merton, however, this diversity of perspectives did not mean that sociologists must succumb to relativism or abandon their position as scientific students of society's problems. The way out of the dilemma was to distinguish between "manifest" and "latent" social problems—the latter are problems also "at odds with the values of the group" but not recognized as such. The task of the sociologist is to uncover the "latent" problems or unrecognized consequences of existing institutions and policies; in this way, "sociological inquiry does make men increasingly accountable for the outcome of their collective and institutionalized actions."[27]

The demand that social science makes people accountable for their actions was a healthy departure from the false relativism of some earlier theorists. But the distinction between manifest and latent problems did not do what Merton claimed for it: it did not make the choice of problems a technical or neutral one. Actually, Merton's approach is best seen as providing a rationale for evaluating and criticizing particular policies and structures within a presumably consensual society whose basic values and institutions are not seen as problematic.

We could easily agree with Merton that "to confine the study of social problems to only those circumstances that are expressly defined as problems in the society is arbitrarily to discard a complement of conditions that are also dysfunctional to values held by people in that society."[28] But what about those values themselves? Shouldn't they be examined and, if necessary, criticized? It seems obvious to us, for example, that it is part of the sociologist's task to study and criticize the values held by people in German society during the Nazi era or by slaveholders in the antebellum American South, rather than to confine ourselves to studying those conditions that might be "dysfunctional" in terms of those values. To do otherwise amounts to an acceptance by default; the social scientist becomes an expert at handling problems within the confines of an assumed consensus on basic goals and values.

The division of social problems into the two categories of *deviant behavior* and *social disorganization* reflected this acceptance, for both categories were defined as "disruptions" of an existing social order and did not question the adequacy of that social order itself. Thus:

> Whereas social disorganization refers to faults in the arrangement and working of social statuses and roles, deviant behavior refers to conduct that departs significantly from the norms set for people in their social statuses.[29]

It is not, as some critics have suggested, that this kind of analysis suggests that whatever is, is right. But it does imply that whatever *disturbs* the existing social system is the primary problem.

The sociologists' "expert" judgment, of course, may conflict with what people themselves feel to be their problems, and if so, according to Merton, the expert should prevail. Merton argued that:

> We cannot take for granted a reasonably correct public imagery of social problems; of their scale, distribution, causation, consequences and persistence or change. . . . Popular perceptions are no safe guide to the magnitude of a social problem.[30]

The corollary, presumably, is that the sociologist's imagery of social problems is at least "reasonably correct," even, perhaps, where segments of the public strongly object to having their problems defined, or redefined, for them. We seem to have come back to the same condescending attitude toward the public expressed by Horton and Leslie and other sociologists of the 1950s.

This kind of attitude wasn't, of course, confined to writers on social problems. It was a major theme in the social thought and government policy of the sixties, a decade characterized by an increasing detachment of governmental action from public knowledge and accountability—as exemplified in the growth of a vast intelligence apparatus, the repeated attempts to overthrow popularly elected governments overseas, and the whole conduct of the Vietnam War. This process was often excused on the ground that political decisions involved technical judgments that were out of the reach of ordinary people.

The conception of social problems as technical, rather than moral and political, issues was explicit in Merton and Nisbet's text. Thus, Merton suggested that "the kind of problem that is dominated by social disorganization results from instrumental and technical flaws in the social system. The system comes to operate less efficiently than it realistically might."[31]

If the problems are technical ones, then it was, of course, reasonable to view social scientists as technicians and to regard their intervention into social life as free from partisan interest. It is this, apparently, that renders the social scientist a responsible citizen, rather than a "mere" social critic or ideologue:

> Under the philosophy intrinsic to the distinction between manifest and latent social problems, the social scientist neither abdicates his intellectual and professional responsibilities nor usurps the position of sitting in judgment on his fellow men.[32]

It is apparent, however, that this kind of "philosophy" lends itself all too easily to an alignment of expertise and "professionalism" with dominant values and interests masquerading as societal consensus. This is apparent in the choice of topics offered in most textbooks. Merton and Nisbet— whose widely used textbook has gone through several editions—characteristically dealt with mental disorders, crime and delinquency, drug use, alcoholism, suicide, sexual behavior, the population crisis, race relations, family disorganization, work and automation, poverty, community disorganization, violence, and youth and politics. The book did not deal with (to take some examples from our own table of contents) corporate power, sexism, health care, the criminal justice system, and so on. The pattern of these differences is obvious: Merton and Nisbet focused most heavily on those who have, for one reason or another, failed to "make it" within the American system—delinquents, criminals, the mentally ill, drug users— and on disorganization *within* established institutions. Even when individual authors in their book attempted to analyze the system itself, the effort was usually relegated to a peripheral, or merely symbolic, place.

In spite of its claim to political neutrality, the social science of the 1960s typically focused on the symptoms of social ills, rather than their sources: the culture of the poor, rather than the decisions of the rich; the "pathology" of the ghetto, rather than the problems of the economy. What "socially shared standards" dictated this choice of emphasis? In the introduction to a newer edition of *Contemporary Social Problems*, Nisbet tried to answer this question. "It may well be asked," he writes, "why these problems have been chosen by the editors," rather than others, which "for some persons at least might be regarded as even more pressing to national policy."

> The answer is that this is a textbook in sociology. Sociology is a special science characterized by concepts and conclusions, which are based on

analysis and research, yielding in turn perspectives on society and its central problems. For many decades now, sociologists have worked carefully and patiently on these problems. In other words this book is concerned not only with the presentation of major social problems but with the scientific concepts and procedures by which these problems have been, and continue to be, studied.[33]

Nisbet seems to be explaining that these problems were selected by the editors because sociologists have studied them, and not others, in the past. Such an argument is hardly compelling.

Even the Merton and Nisbet view of contemporary social problems has changed somewhat with the times. Their latest editions include some chapters and revisions far more critical of the prevailing social system than was evident in previous editions. Still, as the preface points out, "the fundamental character of this book has remained constant through all editions."

THE SEVENTIES AND EIGHTIES: A HARSHER VISION

Much of the thinking about social problems in the sixties—and the public policies that flowed from it—tended to assume, at least implicitly, that most of the ills of American society were solvable; that a rich and technologically advanced society should be able to overcome problems like poverty, unemployment, and inadequate health care, if it had the will to do so. And so an active government launched a number of social programs and experiments designed to bring the American reality in closer harmony with the American ideal. In the eighties it became fashionable to say that government attempted too much in those years, throwing vast amounts of money at social problems. In fact, though we did try a multitude of programs, the amounts we spent on them were never large. Our total federal spending on job training, public job creation, and schooling programs for low-income people, for example, never rose to as much as one-half of 1 percent of our gross national product during the sixties.[34]

But the belief that government had taken on too big a role helped to usher in a harsher, more pessimistic perspective in the seventies—a perspective that has dominated social policy in the United States ever since. In the context of a deeply troubled economy, the stubborn persistence of poverty and joblessness, and frightening levels of social pathology in the cities, the moderate optimism of the sixties began to give way to a new brand of scholarly pessimism that argued that many of these problems were due to "human nature" or defective "culture"—or even genetic deficiencies. The implication was that social concern of the sixties' variety couldn't have much positive impact on social problems—and, in the view of some writers, had probably made them worse.

Writers like Arthur Jensen resurrected long-discredited hereditary theories of racial inferiority in intelligence to explain why blacks still remained at the bottom of the educational and economic ladder, in spite of all the equal-opportunity programs of the sixties. Others, like Harvard's Edward Banfield, explained the persistence of poverty and urban crime as the reflection of a distinctive "lower-class culture" that prevented the poor from thinking ahead or delaying immediate gratification. By the eighties, Charles Murray and other critics were explaining the stubbornness of poverty as the result of the demoralization of the poor through an overly generous welfare system. The growth of urban violence was similarly explained as the result of excessive leniency with criminals; and in the eighties, when years of "getting tough" with criminals left us with still frightful levels of crime and violence, some writers began looking for the roots of crime—and of poverty and other social pathologies as well—in faulty physiology or defective genes.

By the eighties, in other words, American thinking about social problems had just about come full circle; we had returned to something that looked very much like the focus on "defectives, dependents, and delinquents" that characterized late nineteenth-century social science. And the harsh social policies that flowed from this attitude were also strikingly reminiscent of the Social "Darwinism" of the late nineteenth century. The belief that many of our social problems (from school failure to juvenile delinquency to welfare dependency) can be traced to deficiencies in the minds, cultures, or genetic makeup of a hard-core few—and/or to the folly of government intervention—so comforting to the complacent thinkers of the nineteenth century, had returned with a vengeance.

As in earlier times, this outlook serves to explain away some of the most troubling expressions of the crisis in American institutions—swollen, violent prisons, the rapid descent of millions of Americans into the ranks of the poor in the past few years, minority joblessness that persists at near-Depression levels even during economic "recovery." And it helps to justify sharp cutbacks in many of the programs we've created to cope with the social problems of the last decades of the twentieth century—even very successful programs such as those in nutrition, child health care, and early education.

By now, however, this perspective has itself come under growing criticism. Its proponents, after all, have been arguing for a *long* time that the poor, the jobless, and the sick are largely responsible for their own problems and that they—along with the rest of us—would be better off with less help from government. We have, accordingly, been reducing government's role as well for a long time. But the problems haven't gone away; they have grown. And so the job of developing a fresh and creative approach to social problems is once again on the agenda.

That task is certainly an urgent one. As many of the articles in this book suggest, we have reached what seems to be a crucial turning point in our policies toward social problems. Technological and economic changes are reshaping the conditions of American life with sometimes dizzying speed, and how we choose to deal with those changes will profoundly affect the character of life in the United States for many years to come. Consider just one example: the galloping rate of technological change in the workplace. As suggested by several of the following articles (especially those by Leontieff and Currie, Dunn, and Fogarty), the growth of the new automation will deeply affect how Americans work and make a living. But whether these changes will be for better or for worse will depend on how our social and political institutions respond to them—on whether, for example, we are willing to make enough investments in training and retraining workers so that the rapid automation of industry doesn't simply bring us more joblessness and poverty, rather than abundance and leisure.

These are very big questions, and in this book we can only begin to explore them, not answer them once and for all. But we believe the articles that follow represent some of the best and most searching thinking on American social problems available today. As in earlier editions, they represent a wide range of styles and perspectives. But most of them fit comfortably within a common general vision: a critical, democratically inclined approach to social institutions that emphasizes the potential for constructive change.

Within this very broad perspective, there is plenty of room for controversy. Our authors don't necessarily share the same theoretical positions or social or political views. The editors, for that matter, don't always agree—and we think that's as it should be. We frequently argue about many of the issues covered in this book, and this debate has continued through eight editions. But we think this tension is fruitful, and we have tried to capture it in our selection of readings.

We see this book as an introductory work, useful for beginning courses in sociology, social problems, or political science. Its purpose is to raise issues, to provide students with the beginnings of a critical approach to the society they live in and will hopefully help change. It provides few definitive answers, and it leaves unresolved many basic theoretical and practical questions about the sources and solutions of the American crisis. But its purpose will be accomplished if it helps lead students to begin their own process of confronting those questions.

REFERENCES

1. C. Wright Mills, "The Professional Ideology of the Social Pathologists," in Irving L. Horowitz, ed., *Power, Politics and People: The Collected Essays of C. Wright Mills* (New York: Ballantine, 1963).
2. Charles Richmond Henderson, *An Introduction to the Study of Defective, Dependent and Delinquent Classes* (Boston: Heath, 1906).
3. Lawrence K. Frank, "Social Problems," *American Journal of Sociology*, 30 (January 1925), p. 463.

4. Richard C. Fuller and Richard R. Myers, "The Natural History of a Social Problem," *American Sociological Review,* 6 (June 1941), p. 320.

5. Paul B. Horton and Gerald R. Leslie, *The Sociology of Social Problems* (New York: Appleton-Century-Crofts, 1955), p. 6.

6. Arnold M. Rose, "Theory for the Study of Social Problems," *Social Problems,* 4 (January 1957), p. 190.

7. Robert K. Merton and Robert M. Nisbet, *Contemporary Social Problems* (New York: Harcourt, Brace and World, 1961), p. 702.

8. Willard Waller, "Social Problems and the Mores," *American Sociological Review,* 1 (December 1936), p. 926.

9. *Ibid.,* p. 928.

10. *Ibid.,* p. 927.

11. Horton and Leslie, *Sociology.* We refer here to the original edition in order to place the book in its historical context.

12. *Ibid.,* p. 517.

13. *Ibid.,* p. 520.

14. *Ibid.,* p. 523.

15. *Ibid.,* p. 12.

16. *Ibid.,* p. 19.

17. Merton and Nisbet, *Contemporary Social Problems.* Here, too, we refer to the first edition in order to consider the book in historical perspective. The general theoretical perspective in the book has changed little, if at all, as we will note later; there have been some substantive changes, however—for example, the chapter by Janowitz has been dropped, and new chapters added.

18. Robert A. Nisbet, "The Study of Social Problems," in *ibid.,* p. 4.

19. *Ibid.,* p. 5. The reader might compare C. Wright Mills' notion, developed during the same period, that the United States should be seen as an "over-developed" society; see Irving L. Horowitz, "Introduction," in Horowitz, *Power, Politics, and People,* p. 8.

20. Nisbet, "The Study of Social Problems," p. 9.

21. *Ibid.,* p. 12.

22. Robert S. Weiss and David Riesman, "Social Problems and Disorganization in the World of Work," in Merton and Nisbet, *Contemporary Social Problems,* p. 464.

23. Morris Janowitz, "The Military Establishment: Organization and Disorganization," in Merton and Nisbet, *Contemporary Social Problems,* p. 515.

24. *Ibid.,* p. 516.

25. *Ibid.,* pp. 533–534.

26. Robert K. Merton, "Social Problems and Sociological Theory," in Merton and Nisbet, *Contemporary Social Problems,* p. 706.

27. *Ibid.,* p. 710.

28. *Ibid.,* p. 711.

29. *Ibid.,* p. 723.

30. *Ibid.,* pp. 712–713.

31. *Ibid.,* p. 723.

32. *Ibid.,* p. 712.

33. Robert M. Nisbet, "The Study of Social Problems," in *ibid.,* p. 2.

34. Gary L. Burtless, "Public Spending for the Poor," in Sheldon H. Danziger and Daniel H. Weinberg, *Fighting Poverty: What Works and What Doesn't* (Cambridge, Mass.: Harvard University Press, 1986), p. 37.

Systemic Problems

I

Corporate Power

The myth of American capitalism is individual "free enterprise": the vision of the hard-working, thrifty entrepreneur competing with others and constrained by the forces of the market. But the reality of American capitalism is what Ralph Nader once called "corporate collectivism": the domination of economic life by a relative handful of giant corporations—corporations whose size and power enable them to control markets rather than be controlled by them.

Since the late 1960s, the 500 largest industrial corporations in America have consistently accounted for about two-thirds of all industrial sales, four-fifths of all industrial profits, and three-fourths of all industrial employment. The largest 50 of those corporations alone account for about one-fourth of the value of all manufactured goods in the country and employ about one in five industrial workers. Similar concentration exists in other areas of business as well—banking and finance, transportation, utilities, and communications. All told, about 1,000 corporations now produce roughly one-half of all privately produced goods and services in the United States, and those corporations are deeply entwined with government in a multitude of ways—from long-term defense contracts to massive federal "bail-outs" of big corporations in trouble.

The real issue, then, is not whether we have a "free enterprise" economy. Instead, the important questions have to do with the performance and control of the modern corporate version of capitalism: How has the concentration of corporate power affected such key economic problems as inflation and recession? How has it changed the terms on which business relates to the public and to political authorities? And how, more generally, does the growing power of the giant corporation affect the quality of social and economic life?

Mark Dowie's story of the Ford Motor Company's refusal to make minor changes in its Pinto that could have saved hundreds of lives shows, in stark relief, the ability of the large corporations to insulate themselves from public accountability or social control. When the article was written, Ford was the fifth largest industrial corporation in the world; its total sales exceeded the gross national products of all but 30 of the world's countries. The company's enormous economic power enabled it to operate with military-like secrecy, open defiance of government safety standards, and a near-total disregard for the lives of its consumers. Dowie's article has become something of a classic for our understanding of how the profit motive can lead managers and engineers to ignore the safety of the public in the interests of maximizing the black side of the balance sheet.

Sometimes, the pressures to be profitable edge business executives over the line between efficient production and dangerous production, as in the case of the Pinto. But we rarely, if ever, have serious suggestions that the automobile—when properly designed and manufactured—is not a socially desirable product.

The same claim, however, can scarcely be made for tobacco. As the Surgeon General warns on cigarette packages and advertising, "Smoking causes lung cancer, heart disease, emphysema, and may complicate pregnancy . . . smoking by pregnant women may result in fetal injury, premature birth, and low birth weight." That, in a time of increasing concern over the effects of drugs and a law enforcement "war on drugs," we permit cigarettes to be advertised and sold may be a national scandal. But what of smokeless tobacco—chewing tobacco and snuff? These products do not carry similar warnings. Whether their manufacturer knew that these products also caused cancer is the question in the case of Sean Marsee, who died of cancer at 19, after six years of heavy snuff use. The case involved U.S. Tobacco's liability for Sean's addiction to Copenhagen brand. Morton Mintz's article shows how the expert witnesses for U.S. Tobacco dissembled on the witness stand about what they knew about the relation between tobacco and cancer.

John Logue's portrait of the steel corporations' destruction of the industry in Youngstown, Ohio, illustrates how the search for fast profits can undermine even a profitable industry and the communities that depend on it. The shutdown of the Mahoning Valley steel mills wasn't primarily the result of foreign competition or declining productivity, two of the problems most often said to be responsible for industrial decline in America. Instead, Logue shows that the mills were deliberately drained of resources by their new owners—conglomerate corporations less interested in making steel than in finding other, more immediately profitable places to invest. Since Logue first wrote this article, the self-destruction of the American steel industry has continued; and, while the steel companies increasingly shift their capital into shopping malls and chemical corporations, tens of thousands of steelworkers will never work in their industry again.

When we think of corporate power and concentration, we usually think of major manufacturers of automobiles, cigarettes, and steel. We may not, however, consider the media as a prime area of corporate concentration. But, just as anyone has the legal right to begin a business in America, while few have the resources to do so, so it is with the media. Everyone has the right to freedom of speech under the First Amendment, but increasingly few have the means to participate in the "marketplace of ideas" protected by the Constitution. Here, too, as in the manufacturing businesses, myth and economic reality are at considerable odds. As Ben Bagdikian indicates, the major media are exhibiting "an extraordinary race to monopoly control." This, according to Bagdikian, results in journalistic self-censorship, pressures to support the status quo, and a loss of public knowledge about major and important events.

1

Pinto Madness

Mark Dowie

One evening in the mid-1960s, Arjay Miller was driving home from his office in Dearborn, Michigan, in the four-door Lincoln Continental that went with his job as president of the Ford Motor Company. On a crowded highway, another car struck his from the rear. The Continental spun around and burst into flames. Because he was wearing a shoulder-strap seat belt, Miller was unharmed by the crash, and because his doors didn't jam he escaped the flaming wreck. But the accident made a vivid impression on him. Several months later, on July 15, 1965, he recounted it to a U.S. Senate subcommittee that was hearing testimony on auto safety legislation. "I still have burning in my mind the image of that gas tank on fire," Miller said. He went on to express an almost passionate interest in controlling fuel-fed fires in cars that crash or roll over. He spoke with excitement about the fabric gas tank Ford was testing at that very moment. "If it proves out," he promised the senators, "it will be a feature you will see in our standard cars."

Almost seven years after Miller's testimony, a woman, whom for legal reasons we will call Sandra Gillespie, pulled onto a Minneapolis highway in her new Ford Pinto. Riding with her was a young boy, whom we'll call Robbie Carlton. As she entered a merge lane, Sandra Gillespie's car stalled. Another car rear-ended hers at an impact speed of 28 miles per hour. The Pinto's gas tank ruptured. Vapors from it mixed quickly with the air in the passenger compartment. A spark ignited the mixture and the car exploded in a ball of fire. Sandra died in agony a few hours later in

Mark Dowie, "Pinto Madness," from *Mother Jones*, Vol. II, No. VIII, September/October 1977. Reprinted by permission.

an emergency hospital. Her passenger, 13-year-old Robbie Carlton, is still alive; he has just come home from another futile operation aimed at grafting a new ear and nose from skin on the few unscarred portions of his badly burned body. (This accident is real; the details are from police reports.)

Why did Sandra Gillespie's Ford Pinto catch fire so easily, seven years after Ford's Arjay Miller made his apparently sincere pronouncements—the same seven years that brought more safety improvements to cars than any other period in automotive history? An extensive investigation by *Mother Jones* over the past six months has found these answers:

Fighting strong competition from Volkswagen for the lucrative small-car market, the Ford Motor Company rushed the Pinto into production in much less than the usual time.

Ford engineers discovered in pre-production crash tests that rear-end collisions would rupture the Pinto's fuel system extremely easily.

Because assembly-line machinery was already tooled when engineers found this defect, top Ford officials decided to manufacture the car anyway—exploding gas tank and all—*even though Ford owned the patent on a much safer gas tank.*

For more than eight years afterwards, Ford successfully lobbied, with extraordinary vigor and some blatant lies, against a key government safety standard that would have forced the company to change the Pinto's fire-prone gas tank.

By conservative estimates Pinto crashes have caused 500 burn deaths to people who would not have been seriously injured if the car had not burst into flames. Burning Pintos have become such an embarrassment to Ford that its advertising agency, J. Walter Thompson, dropped a line from the end of a radio spot that read, "Pinto leaves you with that warm feeling."

Ford knows the Pinto is a firetrap, yet it has paid out millions to settle damage suits out of court, and it is prepared to spend millions more lobbying against safety standards. With a half million cars rolling off the assembly lines each year, Pinto is the biggest-selling subcompact in America, and the company's operating profit on the car is fantastic. Finally, in 1977, new Pinto models have incorporated a few minor alterations necessary to meet that federal standard Ford managed to hold off for eight years. Why did the company delay so long in making these minimal, inexpensive improvements?

Ford waited eight years because its internal "cost-benefit analysis," *which places a dollar value on human life,* said it wasn't profitable to make the changes sooner.

Before we get to the question of how much Ford thinks your life is worth, let's trace the history of the death trap itself. Although this particular story is about the Pinto, the way in which Ford made its decision is typical of the U.S. auto industry generally. There are plenty of similar stories about other cars made by other companies. But this case is the worst of them all.

The next time you drive behind a Pinto (with over two million of them on the road, you shouldn't have much trouble finding one), take a look at the rear end. That long silver object hanging down under the bumper is the gas tank. The tank begins about six inches forward of the bumper. In late models the bumper is designed to withstand a collision of only about five miles per hour. Earlier bumpers may as well not have been on the car for all the protection they offered the gas tank.

Mother Jones has studied hundreds of reports and documents on rear-end collisions involving Pintos. These reports conclusively reveal that if you ran into that Pinto you were following at over 30 miles per hour, the rear end of the car would buckle like an accordion, right up to the back seat. The tube leading to the gas-tank cap would be ripped away from the tank itself, and gas would immediately begin sloshing onto the road around the car. The buckled gas tank would be jammed up against the differential housing, which contains four sharp protruding bolts likely to gash holes in the tank and spill still more gas. The welded seam between the main body frame and the wheel well would split, allowing gas to enter the interior of the car.

Now all you need is a spark from a cigarette, ignition, or scraping metal, and both cars would be engulfed in flames. If you gave the Pinto a really good whack—say, at 40 mph—chances are excellent that its doors would jam and you would have to stand by and watch its trapped passengers burn to death.

This scenario is no news to Ford. Internal company documents in our possession show that Ford has crash-tested the Pinto at a top-secret site more than 40 times and that *every* test made at over 25 mph without special structural alteration of the car has resulted in a ruptured fuel tank. Despite this, Ford officials denied having crash-tested the Pinto.

Eleven of these tests, averaging a 31-mph impact speed, came before Pintos started rolling out of the factories. Only three cars passed the test with unbroken fuel tanks. In one of them an inexpensive light-weight metal baffle was placed so those bolts would not perforate the tank. (Don't forget about that baffle, which costs about a dollar and weighs about a pound. It plays an important role in our story later on.) In another successful test, a piece of steel was placed between the tank and the bumper. In the third test car the gas tank was lined with a rubber bladder. But none of these protective alterations was used in the mass-produced Pinto.

In preproduction planning, engineers seriously considered using in the Pinto the same kind of gas tank Ford uses in the Capri. The Capri tank rides over the rear axle and differential housing. It has been so successful in over 50 crash tests that Ford used it in its Experimental Safety Vehicle, which withstood rear-end impacts of 60 mph. So why wasn't the Capri tank used in the Pinto? Or, why wasn't that baffle placed between the tank and the axle—something that would have saved the life of Sandra Gillespie and hundreds like her. Why was a car known to be a serious fire hazard deliberately released to production in August of 1970?

Whether Ford should manufacture subcompacts at all was the subject of a bitter two-year debate at the company's Dearborn headquarters. The principals in the corporate struggle were the then-president Semon "Bunky" Knudsen, whom Henry Ford II had hired away from General Motors, and Lee Iacocca, a spunky young turk who had risen fast within the company on the enormous success of the Mustang. Iacocca argued forcefully that Volkswagen and the Japanese were going to capture the entire American subcompact market unless Ford put out its own alternative to the VW Beetle. Bunky Knudsen said, in effect: let them have the small-car market; Ford makes good money on medium and large models. But he lost the battle and later resigned. Iacocca became president and almost immediately began a rush program to produce the Pinto.

Like the Mustang, the Pinto became known in the company as "Lee's car." Lee Iacocca wanted that little car in the showrooms of America with the 1971 models. So he ordered his engineering vice president, Bob Alexander, to oversee what was probably the shortest production planning period in modern automotive history. The normal time span from conception to production of a new car model is about 43 months. The Pinto schedule was set at just under 25.

Design, styling, product planning, advance engineering and quality assurance all have flexible time frames, and engineers can pretty much carry these on simultaneously. Tooling, on the other hand, has a fixed time frame of about 18 months. Normally, an auto company doesn't begin tooling until the other processes are almost over. *But Iacocca's speed-up meant Pinto tooling went on at the same time as product development*. So when crash tests revealed a serious defect in the gas tank, it was too late. The tooling was well under way.

When it was discovered the gas tank was unsafe, did anyone go to Iacocca and tell him? "Hell no," replied an engineer who worked on the Pinto, a high company official for many years, who, unlike several others at Ford, maintains a necessarily clandestine concern for safety. "That person would have been fired. Safety wasn't a popular subject around Ford in those days. With Lee it was taboo. Whenever a problem was raised that meant a delay on the Pinto, Lee would chomp on his cigar, look out the window and say 'Read the product objectives and get back to work.' "

The product objectives are clearly stated in the Pinto "green book." This is a thick, top-secret manual in green covers containing a step-by-step production plan for the model, detailing the metallurgy, weight, strength and quality of every part in the car. The product objectives for the

Pinto are repeated in an article by Ford executive F. G. Olsen published by the Society of Automotive Engineers. He lists these product objectives as follows:

1. TRUE SUBCOMPACT
   • Size
   • Weight
2. LOW COST OF OWNERSHIP
   • Initial price
   • Fuel consumption
   • Reliability
   • Serviceability
3. CLEAR PRODUCT SUPERIORITY
   • Appearance
   • Comfort
   • Features
   • Ride and Handling
   • Performance

Safety, you will notice, is not there. It is not mentioned in the entire article. As Lee Iacocca was fond of saying, "Safety doesn't sell."

Heightening the anti-safety pressure on Pinto engineers was an important goal set by Iacocca known as "the limits of 2,000." The Pinto was not to weigh an ounce over 2,000 pounds and not to cost a cent over $2,000. "Iacocca enforced these limits with an iron hand," recalls the engineer quoted earlier. So, even when a crash test showed that that one-pound, one-dollar piece of metal stopped the puncture of the gas tank, it was thrown out as extra cost and extra weight.

People shopping for subcompacts are watching every dollar. "You have to keep in mind," the engineer explained, "that the price elasticity on these subcompacts is extremely tight. You can price yourself right out of the market by adding $25 to the production cost of the model. And nobody understands that better than Iacocca."

Dr. Leslie Ball, the retired safety chief for the NASA manned space program and a founder of the International Society of Reliability Engineers, recently made a careful study of the Pinto. "The release to production of the Pinto was the most reprehensible decision in the history of American engineering," he said. Ball can name more than 40 European and Japanese models in the Pinto price and weight range with safer gas-tank positioning. Ironically, many of them, like the Ford Capri, contain a "saddle-type" gas tank riding over the back axle. *The patent on the saddle-type tank is owned by the Ford Motor Co.*

Los Angeles auto safety expert Byron Bloch has made an in-depth study of the Pinto fuel system. "It's a catastrophic blunder," he says. "Ford made an extremely irresponsible decision when they placed such a weak tank in such a ridiculous location in such a soft rear end. It's almost designed to blow up—premeditated."

A Ford engineer, who doesn't want his name used, comments: "This company is run by salesmen, not engineers: so the priority is styling, not safety." He goes on to tell a story about gas-tank safety at Ford:

Lou Tubben is one of the most popular engineers at Ford. He's a friendly, outgoing guy with a genuine concern for safety. By 1971 he had grown so concerned about gas-tank integrity that he asked his boss if he could prepare a presentation on safer tank design. Tubben and his boss had both worked on the Pinto and shared a concern for its safety. His boss gave him the go-ahead, scheduled a date for the presentation and invited all company engineers and key production planning personnel. When time came for the meeting, a total of two people showed up—Lou Tubben and his boss.

"So you see," continued the anonymous Ford engineer, "there *are* a few of us here at Ford who are concerned about fire safety." He adds: "They are mostly engineers who have to study a lot of accident reports and look at pictures of burned people. But we don't talk about it much. It isn't a popular subject. I've never seen safety on the agenda of a product meeting and, except for a brief period in 1956, can't remember seeing the word safety in an advertisement. I really don't think the company wants American consumers to start thinking too much about safety—for fear they might demand it, I suppose."

Asked about the Pinto gas tank, another Ford engineer admitted: "That's all true. But you miss the point entirely. You see, safety isn't the issue, trunk space is. You have no idea how stiff the competition is over trunk space. Do you realize that if we put a Capri-type tank in the Pinto you could only get one set of golf clubs in the trunk?"

Blame for Sandra Gillespie's death, Robbie Carlton's unrecognizable face and all the other injuries and deaths in Pintos since 1970 does not rest on the shoulders of Lee Iacocca alone. For, while he and his associates fought their battle against a safer Pinto in Dearborn, a larger war against safer cars raged in Washington. One skirmish in that war involved Ford's successful eight-year lobbying effort against Federal Motor Vehicle Safety Standard 301, the rear-end provisions of which would have forced Ford to redesign the Pinto.

But first some background:

During the early '60s, auto safety legislation became the *bête-noire* of American big business. The auto industry was the last great unregulated business, and if *it* couldn't reverse the tide of government regulation, the reasoning went, no one could.

People who know him cannot remember Henry Ford taking a stronger stand than the one he took against the regulation of safety design. He spent weeks in Washington calling on members of Congress, holding press conferences and recruiting business cronies like W. B. Murphy of Campbell's Soup to join the anti-regulation battle. Displaying the sophistication for which today's American corporate leaders will be remembered, Murphy publicly called auto safety "a hula hoop, a fad that will pass." He was speaking to a special luncheon of the Business Council, an organization of 100 chief executives who gather periodically in Washington to provide "advice" and "counsel" to government. The target of their wrath in this instance was the Motor Vehicle Safety Bills introduced in both houses of Congress, largely in response to Ralph Nader's *Unsafe at Any Speed*.

By 1965, most pundits and lobbyists saw the handwriting on the wall and prepared to accept government "meddling" in the last bastion of free enterprise. Not Henry. With bulldog tenacity, he held out for defeat of the legislation to the very end, loyal to his grandfather's invention and to the company that makes it. But the Safety Act passed the House and Senate unanimously, and was signed into law by Lyndon Johnson in 1966.

While lobbying for and against legislation is pretty much a process of high-level back-slapping, press-conferencing and speech-making, fighting a regulatory agency is a much subtler matter. Henry headed home to lick his wounds in Grosse Pointe, Michigan, and a planeload of the Ford Motor Company's best brains flew to Washington to start the "education" of the new federal auto safety bureaucrats.

Their job was to implant the official industry ideology in the minds of the new officials regulating auto safety. Briefly summarized, that ideology states that auto accidents are caused not by *cars*, but by people and highway conditions.

It is an experience to hear automotive "safety engineers" talk for hours without ever mentioning cars. They will advocate spending billions educating youngsters, punishing drunks and redesigning street signs. Listening to them, you begin to think that it is easier to control 100 million drivers than a handful of manufacturers. They show movies about guardrail design and advocate the clear-cutting of trees 100 feet back from every highway in the nation. If a car is unsafe, they argue, it is because its owner doesn't maintain it properly.

In light of an annual death rate approaching 50,000, they are forced to admit that driving is hazardous. But the car is, in the words of Arjay Miller, "the safest link in the safety chain."

Before the Ford experts left Washington to return to drafting tables in Dearborn they did one other thing. They managed to informally reach an agreement with the major public servants who would be making auto safety decisions. This agreement was that "cost-benefit" would be an acceptable mode of analysis by Detroit and its new regulators. And, as we shall see, cost-benefit analysis quickly became the basis of Ford's argument against safer car design.

Cost-benefit analysis was used only occasionally in government until President Kennedy appointed Ford Motor Company President Robert McNamara to be Secretary of Defense. McNamara, originally an accountant, preached cost-benefit with all the force of a Biblical zealot. Stated in its simplest terms, cost-benefit analysis says that if the cost is greater than the benefit, the project is not worth it—no matter what the benefit. Examine the cost of every action, decision, contract, part, or change, the doctrine says, then carefully evaluate the benefits (in dollars) to be certain that they exceed the cost before you begin a program or pass a regulation.

As a management tool in a business in which profits count over all else, cost-benefit analysis makes a certain amount of sense. Serious problems arise, however, when public officials who ought to have more than corporate profits at heart apply cost-benefit analysis to every conceivable decision. The inevitable result is that they must place a dollar value on human life.

Ever wonder what your life is worth in dollars? Perhaps $10 million? Ford has a better idea: $200,000.

Remember, Ford had gotten the federal regulators to agree to talk auto safety in terms of cost-benefit. But in order to be able to argue that various safety costs were greater than their benefits, Ford needed to have a dollar value figure for the "benefit." Rather than coming up with a price tag itself, the auto industry pressured the National Highway Traffic Safety Administration to do so. And in a 1972 report the agency determined that a human life lost on the highway was worth $200,725 [Table 1]. Inflationary forces have recently pushed the figure up to $278,000.

Furnished with this useful tool, Ford immediately went to work using it to prove why various safety improvements were too expensive to make.

Nowhere did the company argue harder that it should make no changes than in the area of rupture-prone fuel tanks. Not long after the government arrived at the $200,725-per-life figure, it surfaced, rounded off to a cleaner $200,000, in an internal Ford memorandum. This cost-benefit analysis argued that Ford should not make an $11-per-car improvement that would prevent 180 fiery deaths a year.

This cold calculus [Table 2] is buried in a seven-page company memorandum entitled "Fatalities Associated with Crash-Induced Fuel Leakage and Fires."

The memo goes on to argue that there is no financial benefit in complying with proposed safety standards that would admittedly result in fewer auto fires, fewer burn deaths and fewer burn injuries. Naturally, memoranda that speak so casually of "burn deaths" and "burn injuries" are not released to the public. They are very effective, however, with Department of Transportation officials indoctrinated in McNamarian cost-benefit analysis.

All Ford had to do was convince men like John Volpe, Claude Brinegar and William Coleman (successive Secretaries of Transportation during the Nixon-Ford years) that certain safety standards would add so much to the price of cars that fewer people would buy them. This could damage the

Table 1. What's Your Life Worth? Societal
Cost Components for Fatalities, 1972
NHTSA Study

Component	1971 Costs
Future productivity losses	
Direct	$132,000
Indirect	41,300
Medical costs	
Hospital	700
Other	425
Property damage	1,500
Insurance administration	4,700
Legal and court	3,000
Employer losses	1,000
Victim's pain and suffering	10,000
Funeral	900
Assets (lost consumption)	5,000
Miscellaneous accident cost	200
Total per fatality: $200,725	

Here is a chart from a federal study showing how
the National Highway Traffic Safety Administration has calculated the value of a human life. The
estimate was arrived at under pressure from the
auto industry. The Ford Motor Company has used
it in cost-benefit analyses arguing why certain
safety measures are not "worth" the savings in
human lives. The calculation above is a breakdown
of the estimated cost to society every time someone
is killed in a car accident. We were not able to find
anyone, either in the government or at Ford, who
could explain how the $10,000 figure for "pain and
suffering" had been arrived at.

auto industry, which was still believed to be the bulwark of the American
economy. "Compliance to these standards," Henry Ford II prophesied at
more than one press conference, "will shut down the industry."

The Nixon Transportation Secretaries were the kind of regulatory officials big business dreams of. They understood and loved capitalism and
thought like businessmen. Yet, best of all, they came into office unin-
formed on technical automotive matters. And you could talk "burn injuries" and "burn deaths" with these guys, and they didn't seem to envision children crying at funerals and people hiding in their homes with
melted faces. Their minds appeared to have leapt right to the bottom
line—more safety meant higher prices, higher prices meant lower sales
and lower sales meant lower profits.

So when J. C. Echold, Director of Automotive Safety (chief anti-safety
lobbyist) for Ford, wrote to the Department of Transportation—which he

Table 2. Benefits and Costs Relating to Fuel Leakage Associated with the Static Rollover Test Portion of FMVSS 208

Benefits
Savings: 80 burn deaths, 180 serious burn injuries, 2,100 burned vehicles.
Unit cost: $200,000 per death, $67,000 per injury, $700 per vehicle.
Total benefit: 180 × ($200,000) + 180 × ($67,000) + 2,100 × ($700) = $49.5 million.

Costs
Sales: 11 million cars, 1.5 million light trucks.
Unit cost: $11 per car, $11 per truck.
Total cost: 11,000,000 × ($11) + 1,500,000 × ($11) = $137 million.

still does frequently, at great length—he felt secure attaching a memorandum that in effect says it is acceptable to kill 180 people and burn another 180 every year, *even though we have the technology that could save their lives for $11 a car.*

Furthermore, Echold attached this memo, confident, evidently, that the Secretary would question neither his low death/injury statistics nor his high cost estimates. But it turns out, on closer examination, that both these findings were misleading.

First, note that Ford's table shows an equal number of burn deaths and burn injuries. This is false. All independent experts estimate that for each person who dies by an auto fire, many more are left with charred hands, faces and limbs. Andrew McGuire of the Northern California Burn Center estimates the ratio of burn injuries to deaths at ten to one instead of the one to one Ford shows here. Even though Ford values a burn at only a piddling $67,000 instead of the $200,000 price of life, the true ratio obviously throws the company's calculations way off.

The other side of the equation, the alleged $11 cost of a fire-prevention device, is also a misleading estimation. One document that was *not* sent to Washington by Ford was a "Confidential" cost analysis *Mother Jones* has managed to obtain, showing that crash fires could be largely prevented for considerably *less* than $11 a car. The cheapest method involves placing a heavy rubber bladder inside the gas tank to keep the fuel from spilling if the tank ruptures. Goodyear had developed the bladder and had demonstrated it to the automotive industry. We have in our possession crash-test reports showing that the Goodyear bladder worked well. On December 2, 1970 (*two years before* Echold sent his cost-benefit memo to Washington), Ford Motor Company ran a rear-end crash test on a car with the rubber bladder in the gas tank. The tank ruptured, but no fuel leaked. On January 15, 1971, Ford again tested the bladder and again it worked. The total purchase and installation cost of the bladder would have been $5.08 per car. That $5.08 could have saved the lives of Sandra Gillespie and several hundred others.

When a federal regulatory agency like the National Highway Traffic Safety Administration (NHTSA) decides to issue a new standard, the law usually requires it to invite all interested parties to respond before the standard is enforced—a reasonable-enough custom on the surface. However, the auto industry has taken advantage of this process and has used it to delay lifesaving emission and safety standards for years. In the case of the standard that would have corrected that fragile Pinto fuel tank, the delay was for an incredible eight years.

The particular regulation involved here was Federal Motor Vehicle Safety Standard 301. Ford picked portions of Standard 301 for strong opposition back in 1968 when the Pinto was still in the blueprint stage. The intent of 301, and the 300 series that followed it, was to protect drivers and passengers *after* a cash occurs. Without question the worst postcrash hazard is fire. So Standard 301 originally proposed that all cars should be able to withstand a fixed-barrier impact of 20 mph (that is, running into a wall at that speed) without losing fuel.

When the standard was proposed, Ford engineers pulled their crash-test results out of their files. The front ends of most cars were no problem—with minor alterations they could stand the impact without losing fuel. "We were already working on the front end," Ford engineer Dick Kimble admitted. "We knew we could meet the test on the front end." But with the Pinto particularly, a 20-mph rear-end standard meant redesigning the entire rear end of the car. With the Pinto scheduled for production in August of 1970, and with $200 million worth of tools in place, adoption of this standard would have created a minor financial disaster. So Standard 301 was targeted for delay, and, with some assistance from its industry associates, Ford succeeded beyond its wildest expectations: the standard was not adopted until the 1977 model year. Here is how it happened:

There are several main techniques in the art of combating a government safety standard: a) make your arguments in succession, so the feds can be working on disproving only one at a time; b) claim that the real problem is not X but Y (we already saw one instance of this in "the problem is not cars but people"); c) no matter how ridiculous each argument is, accompany it with thousands of pages of highly technical assertions it will take the government months or, preferably, years to test. Ford's large and active Washington office brought these techniques to new heights and became the envy of the lobbyists' trade.

The Ford people started arguing against Standard 301 way back in 1968 with a strong attack of technique b). Fire, they said, was not the real problem. Sure, cars catch fire and people burn occasionally. But statistically auto fires are such a minor problem that NHTSA should really concern itself with other matters.

Strange as it may seem, the Department of Transportation (NHTSA's parent agency) didn't know whether or not this was true. So it contracted with several independent research groups to study auto fires. The studies took months, often years, which was just what Ford wanted. The completed studies, however, showed auto fires to be more of a problem than Transportation officials ever dreamed of. A Washington research firm found that 400,000 cars were burning up every year, burning more than 3,000 people to death. Furthermore, auto fires were increasing five times as fast as building fires. Another study showed that 35 per cent of all fire deaths in the U.S. occurred in automobiles. Forty per cent of all fire department calls in the 1960s were to vehicle fires—a public cost of $350 million a year, a figure that, incidentally, never shows up in cost-benefit analyses.

Another study was done by the Highway Traffic Research Institute in Ann Arbor, Michigan, a safety think-tank funded primarily by the auto industry (the giveaway there is the words "highway traffic" rather than "automobile" in the group's name). It concluded that 40 per cent of the lives lost in fuel-fed fires could be saved if the manufacturers complied with proposed Standard 301. Finally, a third report was prepared for NHTSA. This report indicated that the Ford Motor Company makes 24 per cent of the cars on the American road, yet these cars account for 42 per cent of the collision-ruptured fuel tanks.

Ford lobbyists then used technique a)—bringing up a new argument. Their line then became: yes, perhaps burn accidents do happen, but rear-end collisions are relatively rare (note the echo of technique b) here as well). Thus Standard 301 was not needed. This set the NHTSA off on a new round of analyzing accident reports. The government's findings finally were that rear-end collisions were seven and a half times more likely to result in fuel spills than were front-end collisions. So much for that argument.

By now it was 1972; NHTSA had been researching and analyzing for four years to answer Ford's objections. During that time, nearly 9,000 people burned to death in flaming wrecks. Tens of thousands more were badly burned and scarred for life. And the four-year delay meant that well over 10 million new unsafe vehicles went on the road, vehicles that will be crashing, leaking fuel and incinerating people well into the 1980s.

Ford now had to enter its third round of battling the new regulations. One the "the problem is not X but Y" principle, the company had to look around for something new to get itself off the hook. One might have though that, faced with all the latest statistics on the horrifying number of deaths in flaming accidents, Ford would find the task difficult. But the company's rhetoric was brilliant. The problem was not burns, but . . . impact! Most of the people killed in these fiery accidents, claimed Ford, would have died whether the car burned or not. They were killed by the kinetic force of the impact, not the fire.

And so once again, the ball bounced into the government's court and the absurdly pro-industry NHTSA began another slow-motion response.

Once again it began a time-consuming round of test crashes and embarked on a study of accidents. The latter, however, revealed that a large
and growing number of corpses taken from burned cars involved in rear-
end crashes contained no cuts, bruises or broken bones. They clearly
would have survived the accident unharmed if the cars had not caught
fire. This pattern was confirmed in careful rear-end crash tests performed
by the Insurance Institute for Highway Safety. A University of Miami
study found an inordinate number of Pintos burning on rear-end impact
and concluded that this demonstrated "a clear and present hazard to all
Pinto owners."

Pressure on NHTSA from Ralph Nader and consumer groups began
mounting. The industry-agency collusion was so obvious that Senator
Joseph Montoya (D-N.M.) introduced legislation about Standard 301.
NHTSA waffled some more and again announced its intentions to pro-
mulgate a rear-end collision standard.

Waiting, as it normally does, until the last day allowed for response,
Ford filed with NHTSA a gargantuan batch of letters, studies and charts
now arguing that the federal testing criteria were unfair. Ford also argued
that design changes required to meet the standard would take 43 months,
which seemed like a rather long time in light of the fact that the entire
Pinto was designed in about two years. Specifically new complaints about
the standard involved the weight of the test vehicle, whether or not the
brakes should be engaged at the moment of impact and the claim that the
standard should only apply to cars, not trucks or buses. Perhaps the most
amusing argument was that the engine should not be idling during crash
tests, the rationale being that an idling engine meant that the gas tank had
to contain gasoline and that the hot lights needed to film the crash might
ignite the gasoline and cause a fire.

Some of these complaints were accepted, others rejected. But they all
required examination and testing by a weak-kneed NHTSA, meaning
more of those 18-month studies the industry loves so much. So the
complaints served their real purpose—delay; all told, an eight-year delay,
while Ford manufactured more than three million profitable, dangerously
incendiary Pintos. To justify this delay, Henry Ford II called more press
conferences to predict the demise of American civilization. "If we can't
meet the standards when they are published," he warned, "we will have
to close down. And if we have to close down some production because we
don't meet standards we're in for real trouble in this country."

While government bureaucrats dragged their feet on lifesaving Standard 301, a different kind of expert was taking a close look at the Pinto—
the "recon man." "Recon" stands for reconstruction; recon men recon-
struct accidents for police departments, insurance companies and lawyers
who want to know exactly who or what caused an accident. It didn't take
many rear-end Pinto accidents to demonstrate the weakness of the car.

Recon men began encouraging lawyers to look beyond one driver or another to the manufacturer in their search for fault, particularly in the growing number of accidents where passengers were uninjured by collision but were badly burned by fire.

Pinto lawsuits began mounting fast against Ford. Says John Versace, executive safety engineer at Ford's Safety Research Center, "Ulcers are running pretty high among the engineers who worked on the Pinto. Every lawyer in the country seems to want to take their depositions." (The Safety Research Center is an impressive glass and concrete building standing by itself about a mile from Ford World Headquarters in Dearborn. Looking at it, one imagines its large staff protects consumers from burned and broken limbs. Not so. The Center is the technical support arm of Jack Echold's 14-person anti-regulatory lobbying team in World Headquarters.)

When the Pinto liability suits began, Ford strategy was to go to a jury. Confident it could hide the Pinto crash tests, Ford thought that juries of solid American registered voters would buy the industry doctrine that drivers, not cars, cause accidents. It didn't work. It seems that citizens are much quicker to see the truth than bureaucracies. Juries began ruling against the company, granting million-dollar awards to plaintiffs.

"We'll never go to a jury again," says Al Slechter in Ford's Washington office. "Not in a fire case. Juries are just too sentimental. They see those charred remains and forget the evidence. No sir, we'll settle."

Settlement involves less cash, smaller legal fees and less publicity, but it is an indication of the weakness of their case. Nevertheless, Ford has been offering to settle when it is clear that the company can't pin the blame on the driver of the other car. But, since the company carries $2 million deductible product-liability insurance, these settlements have a direct impact on the bottom line. They must therefore be considered a factor in determining the net operating profit on the Pinto. It's impossible to get a straight answer from Ford on the profitability of the Pinto and the impact of lawsuit settlements on it—even when you have a curious and mildly irate shareholder call to inquire, as we did. However, financial officer Charles Matthews did admit that the company establishes a reserve for large dollar settlements. He would not divulge the amount of the reserve and had no explanation for its absence from the annual report.

Until recently, it was clear that, whatever the cost of these settlements, it was not enough to seriously cut into the Pinto's enormous profits. The cost of retooling Pinto assembly lines and of equipping each car with a safety gadget like that $5.08 Goodyear bladder was, company accountants calculated, greater than that of paying out millions to survivors like Robbie Carlton or to widows and widowers of victims like Sandra Gillespie. The bottom line ruled, and inflammable Pintos kept rolling out of the factories.

In 1977, however, an incredibly sluggish government has at last instituted Standard 301. Now Pintos will have to have rupture-proof gas tanks. Or will they?

To everyone's surprise, the 1977 Pinto recently passed a rear-end crash test in Phoenix, Arizona, for NHTSA. The agency was so convinced the Pinto would fail that it was the first car tested. Amazingly, it did not burst into flame.

"We have had so many Ford failures in the past," explained agency engineer Tom Grubbs, "I felt sure the Pinto would fail."

How did it pass?

Remember that one-dollar, one-pound metal baffle that was on one of the three modified Pintos that passed the pre-production crash tests nearly ten years ago? Well, it is a standard feature on the 1977 Pinto. In the Phoenix test it protected the gas tank from being perforated by those four bolts on the differential housing.

We asked Grubbs if he noticed any other substantial alterations in the rear-end structure of the car. "No," he replied, "the [baffle] seems to be the only noticeable change over the 1976 model."

But was it? What Tom Grubbs and the Department of Transportation didn't know when they tested the car was that it was manufactured in St. Thomas, Ontario. Ontario? The significance of that becomes clear when you learn that Canada has for years had extremely strict rear-end collision standards.

Tom Irwin is the business manager of Charlie Rossi Ford, the Scottsdale, Arizona dealership that sold the Pinto to Tom Grubbs. He refused to explain why he was selling Fords made in Canada when there is a huge Pinto assembly plant much closer by in California. "I know why you're asking that question, and I'm not going to answer it," he blurted out. "You'll have to ask the company."

But Ford's regional office in Phoenix has "no explanation" for the presence of Canadian cars in their local dealerships. Farther up the line in Dearborn, Ford people claim there is absolutely no difference between American and Canadian Pintos. They say cars are shipped back and forth across the border as a matter of course. But they were hard pressed to explain why some Canadian Pintos were shipped all the way to Scottsdale, Arizona. Significantly, one engineer at the St. Thomas plant did admit that the existence of strict rear-end collision standards in Canada "might encourage us to pay a little more attention to quality control on that part of the car."

The Department of Transportation is considering buying an American Pinto and running the test again. For now, it will only say that the situation is under investigation.

Whether the new American Pinto fails or passes the test, Standard 301 will never force the company to test or recall the more than two million pre-1977 Pintos still on the highway. Seventy or more people will burn to death in those cars every year for many years to come. If the past is any indication, Ford will continue to accept the deaths.

According to safety expert Byron Bloch, the older cars could quite easily be retrofitted with gas tanks containing fuel cells. "These improved tanks would add at least 10 mph improved safety performance to the rear end," he estimated, "but it would cost Ford $20 to $30 a car so they won't do it unless they are forced to." Dr. Kenneth Saczalski, safety engineer with the Office of Naval Research in Washington, agrees. "The Defense Department has developed virtually fail-safe fuel systems and retrofitted them into existing vehicles. We have shown them to the auto industry and they have ignored them."

Unfortunately, the Pinto is not an isolated case of corporate malpractice in the auto industry. Neither is Ford a lone sinner. There probably isn't a car on the road without a safety hazard known to its manufacturer. And though Ford may have the best auto lobbyists in Washington, it is not alone. The anti-emission control lobby and the anti-safety lobby usually work in chorus form, presenting a well-harmonized message from the country's richest industry, spoken through the voices of individual companies—the Motor Vehicle Manufacturers Association, the Business Council and the U.S. Chamber of Commerce.

Furthermore, cost-valuing human life is not used by Ford alone. Ford was just the only company careless enough to let such an embarrassing calculation slip into public records. The process of willfully trading lives for profits goes back at least as far as Commodore Vanderbilt, who publicly scorned George Westinghouse and his "foolish" air brakes while people died by the hundreds in accidents on Vanderbilt's railroads.

The original draft of the Motor Vehicle Safety Act provided for criminal sanction against a manufacturer who willfully placed an unsafe car on the market. Early in the proceedings the auto industry lobbied the provision out of the bill. Since then, there have been those damage settlements, of course, but the only government punishment meted out to auto companies for non-compliance to standards has been a minuscule fine, usually $5,000 to $10,000. One wonders how long the Ford Motor Company would continue to market lethal cars were Henry Ford II and Lee Iacocca serving 20-year terms in Leavenworth for consumer homicide.

This article was published in September of 1977, and in February 1978 a jury awarded a sixteen-year-old boy, badly burned in a rear-end Pinto accident, $128 million in damages (the accident occurred in 1973 in Santa Ana, Calif.). That was the largest single personal injury judgment in history.

On May 8, 1978, the Department of Transportation announced that tests conducted in response to this article showed conclusively that the Pinto was defective in all respects described in the article and called for a recall of all 1971 to 1976 Pintos—the most expensive recall in automotive history.

2

The Artful Dodgers

Morton Mintz

The story of Sean Marsee is familiar to millions of Americans. They saw it on "60 Minutes," and read about it in *Reader's Digest* and newspapers around the country. Marsee was the 12-year-old closet "snuff dipper" from Oklahoma. He was habituated or addicted to the Copenhagen brand, which is made from moist smokeless tobacco and which has very high levels of nicotine. His mother, a nurse, discovered what he was doing, but he told her that smokeless tobacco couldn't hurt his lungs as cigarettes would. It mattered very much to him that he not damage his lungs because he wanted to, and did, become a medal-winning high school track star. Besides, if snuff weren't safe, the cans would carry warnings, as do cigarette packs, and professional athletes wouldn't promote it.

In 1983, when Sean was 18, he was found to have cancer in the middle third of his tongue near the groove on the right side of his mouth where he had kept his quid of Copenhagen. He underwent three increasingly mutilating rounds of surgery, and in February 1984, when he was 19, he died.

Later when Sean's mother, Betty Marsee, was living in Ada, Oklahoma, she told her son's story to Dania Deschamps-Braly, a local attorney. The result was a David-and-Goliath product-liability lawsuit that pitted Betty Marsee against United States Tobacco Company, the 476th-largest industrial corporation in America.

Morton Mintz, "The Artful Dodgers," reprinted with permission from *The Washington Monthly*, October 1986. Copyright 1986 by The Washington Monthly Co., 1711 Connecticut Avenue, NW, Washington, DC 20009. (202) 462–0128.

In previous smoking lawsuits, judges have sealed documents obtained in pretrial discovery that showed that cigarette executives knew about tobacco-related disease, marketing strategies, and other major issues, and when they knew it. The Marsee trial was different. Dania Deschamps-Braly and her husband and legal partner George Braly not only obtained and reviewed an estimated 800,000 pages of documents from U.S. Tobacco, which had also once manufactured cigarettes, but also exposed the papers—many of them devastating—to public scrutiny.

A jury of four women and two men tried the case for 22 days last May and June in the U.S. District Court in Oklahoma City. The Bralys argued that Copenhagen is far richer than any other consumer product in nitrosamines, extremely potent carcinogens that have caused cancer—including tongue cancer—in about 40 separate species of laboratory animals. Defense counsel Alston Jennings Sr., a famed trial attorney from Little Rock, Arkansas, countered that it hasn't been "scientifically established" that tobacco, whether smoked or held in the mouth, causes disease. Moreover, he pointed out, no abnormality at all was found in the tip of Sean's tongue, which he used to position the quid, nor in the cheek and gum tissue that were directly and almost constantly exposed to the quid. The plaintiff's experts, including world-renowned scientists, blamed Sean's cancer on his use of snuff; the defense experts, some of them equipped with minor-league credentials and suspect motives, tried to exonerate tobacco.

Goliath won. On June 20, the jury found for U.S. Tobacco, deciding that a preponderance of the evidence did not show that Sean's six-year, heavy use of Copenhagen had caused his tongue cancer. Having made that decision, the jury, as instructed, did not consider other issues, such as the conduct of the company and the credibility of some of its witnesses, particularly Louis F. Bantle, chairman and chief executive officer of U.S. Tobacco, and Dr. Richard A. Manning, vice president for research and development.

Moreover, in numerous pretrial and trial rulings, U.S. District Judge David L. Russell barred important plaintiff's evidence, and these rulings will be the foundation of an appeal. Had the jury considered such issues and evidence, it might have severely jolted U.S. Tobacco because, for the first time in a tobacco product-liability case, the jury was allowed to set punitive damages.

Did Bantle, Manning, or others testifying on behalf of U.S. Tobacco commit perjury by hiding behind a wall of alleged ignorance despite overwhelming evidence that the product they produce kills people? Does their testimony say something about our own cynicism, about our tolerance for disingenuousness and our willingness to accept it from top corporate officials hoping to guard the bottom line? The jury couldn't rule on these questions. You can.

ROBINSPEAK

U.S. Tobacco manufactures Copenhagen and Skoal, the world's best-selling brands of snuff. In 1985, in this country alone, U.S. Tobacco sold 480.8 million cans of these and other brands of snuff—17.3 million more than in 1984 and 54.9 million more than in 1983. Sales were $480 million, with smokeless tobacco, cigars, and pipe tobacco accounting for 86 percent of the total. In four years profits had more than doubled to $93.5 million, or 19.5 percent of sales—the highest rate among the Fortune 500. For this financial performance, chairman and CEO Bantle received compensation of more than $1.1 million. He, his wife, and their children own about 172,000 shares of company stock worth about $7 million.

Such data provide a context for troubling questions. Suppose snuff causes mouth cancer, gum disease, and tooth loss. Suppose also that these sales increases and high profits are significantly attributable to marketing techniques that were intended to, and do, hook children and youths. Suppose, too, that a U.S. Tobacco official is realistic enough to know the suppositions to be truths. Finally, suppose he knows that admitting what he knows would probably ruin U.S. Tobacco, causing the loss of investment, of thousands of jobs, and of his executive compensation. Would you expect him, under oath, to tell the whole truth?

In Oklahoma City, issues of this very kind confronted Bantle, Manning, other U.S. Tobacco executives, and several well-paid scientific experts. All swore the answers they gave were the whole truth.

Louis Bantle swore that "I am not aware that anyone has said that snuff causes cancer." Like a number of company officials, Bantle refused to attend the trial and, under court rules, he couldn't be compelled to do so. George Braly managed to get, instead, Bantle's testimony in a sworn deposition that he videotaped and played before the jury in Oklahoma. In the deposition Bantle testified that he didn't know of a statement by the National Cancer Advisory Board in February 1985 that "there is sufficient evidence for a cause-and-effect relationship between smokeless-tobacco use and human cancer." He said that "I have not heard of" the International Agency for Research on Cancer, which is funded by the World Health Organization, and which, in September 1985, found "sufficient evidence that oral use of snuff . . . is carcinogenic to humans."

An advisory panel on smokeless tobacco appointed by the Surgeon General said in a much-publicized report last March: "The scientific evidence is strong that the use of snuff can cause cancer in humans." Bantle said he did know of this report, but hadn't read it. He gave this testimony ten days after the report was issued and five weeks after President Reagan signed legislation that requires rotating warnings on smokeless tobacco products.

One of Bantle's partners in sworn ignorance was Hugh W. Foley, the company spokesman to whom all health inquiries about smokeless tobacco were referred from February 1981 to the spring of 1985, when he was promoted to vice president for corporate affairs. The National Cancer Advisory Board resolution that found "sufficient evidence for a cause and effect relationship between smokeless tobacco use and human cancer" had been adopted in February 1985 during his watch. Was he even aware that the International Agency for Research on Cancer had considered the issue? "No sir, I am not." Like Bantle, Foley gave his videotaped deposition a few days after the press reported that the Surgeon General's advisory panel had found strong scientific evidence "that the use of snuff can cause cancer in humans." Did Foley know of this? "No sir, I was not aware of that statement."

Why should a U.S. Tobacco executive bother himself with such matters when, as Bantle told George Braly, he doesn't believe the scientific evidence warrants a health warning on the cans, or even a statement that a controversy exists about the safety of smokeless tobacco? Besides, he pointed out in testimony, he subscribes even today to a joint statement, which his own and other tobacco companies published as an advertisement in 1954, that "an interest in public health is a basic responsibility paramount to every other consideration in our business." Had it ever "entered your mind?" that a health warning might have hurt U.S. Tobacco's soaring sales, Braly asked. "No, sir," Bantle replied. "Not at all?" "No, sir." For some years, the smokeless tobacco U.S. Tobacco has shipped to Sweden has carried a warning saying in part that it "contains nicotine causing a strong dependency equal to that of tobacco smoking. Mucous membranes and gums may be damaged and require medical attention." Asked about why his company warned Swedes but not Americans, Bantle said, "Well, it's the law in Sweden."

In May 1974, T.C. Tso, a tobacco scientist with the Agricultural Research Service, sent W.B. Bennett, then U.S. Tobacco's director of research and development, a copy of a report that one might expect to have set off alarm bells, a report that *Science* would publish the following October. The report, mainly by Drs. Dietrich Hoffman and Stephen S. Hecht, stated that N-Nitrosomornicotine (NNN), a "potential carcinogen, has been positively identified" in smokeless tobacco at levels of "between 1.9 to 88.6 parts per million, one of the highest values of an environmental nitrosamine yet reported. The amount in food and drink rarely exceeds 0.1 part per million. This compound is the first example of a potential organic carcinogen isolated from tobacco."

When silence is golden

Frequently, a corporation or trade association dumps an executive or hireling, but buys his silence with a wad of cash. Only rarely do the terms of the deal surface. But surface they did in the Marsee case concerning the eternal silence about smokeless tobacco of one Gerald V. Gilmartin.

In 1957, Gilmartin went to work in Peekskill, New York, for Allied
Public Relations, Inc., which represented U.S. Tobacco and three other
snuff makers. In 1965, he shifted those accounts to his own company,
Prudential Public Relations, Inc. Fifteen years later these accounts were
again shifted, this time to the Smokeless Tobacco Council (STC), which
shared offices with Prudential and employed Gilmartin as its executive
vice president and secretary-treasurer. After some undisclosed disagree-
ments developed, the STC asked Gilmartin to leave. He did so in June
1984.

Under the termination agreement, signed by James W. Chapin, chairman of the STC and general counsel of U.S. Tobacco, the STC bought a
$257,000 annuity for Gilmartin. The owner of the annuity was listed as
the STC, c/o Jacob, Medinger & Finnegan. The annuity might be viewed
as generosity, because Gilmartin did not have an ongoing contract that
had to be bought out; he served at will and could be let go at any time.
"I was told," Gilmartin testified, that the annuity "was in payment for
many years of faithful and productive service."

But, as Braly showed, the termination agreement provided for "forfei-
ture of all amounts payable" under the agreement and the $257,000 an-
nuity if "Gilmartin shall at any time make any statement (written or
oral) which is disparaging or inimical to the STC, its member companies, or any tobacco products."

" . . . have you ever made any statements that were disparaging or
inimical to the Smokeless Tobacco Council?" Braly asked.

"No," Gilmartin answered.

—M. M.

The company's reaction was, and remained, cool. "Our initial approach
was to attempt to discredit the claims," according to a September 1975
memo by Richard Manning, who would succeed Bennett in 1980 before
becoming vice president for R&D. U.S. Tobacco "made a judgment" that
no action be taken, Bantle testified a decade later.

A major concern about smokeless tobacco is its promotion to children
under 18, who commonly start with a low-nicotine brand, become
hooked, and are "graduated" to Copenhagen, the richest in nicotine. In
answers to interrogatories, Vice President Wuchiski said: " . . . defendant has always maintained a strict and explicit company policy forbidding the giving of free samples of smokeless tobacco to minors." Similarly, Bantle swore that under "written policies dating way back into the
thirties, we never have—and we never will—market tobacco to persons
under 18."

However, in January 1968, when Bantle was vice president for marketing, he attended a two-day meeting in New York on "the future of the
company's orally utilized tobacco products." The minutes quote him as
having said: "We must sell the use of tobacco in the mouth and appeal to
young people . . . we hope to start a fad." Confronted with the quote by
Braly, Bantle did not dispute it. Braly also quoted from a 1977 *Chicago*

Tribune article in which Bantle said, "We've gotten excellent sales growth from young people." "I don't remember that statement," Bantle testified. "But I don't deny it."

Bantle also conceded that certain U.S. Tobacco marketing methods could reach boys. An example cited by Braly was an offer of free snuff samples to anyone who mailed in a coupon in advertisements in magazines such as *Sports Illustrated*, which, Bantle acknowledged, are read by those under 18. But the people who processed the coupons "reviewed the signatures," Bantle testified. "If they looked like they were coming from young people, they were not answered."

S. David Schiller, an assistant United States attorney in Richmond, Virginia, has described the evasive testimony about blatant violations of court bankruptcy orders by several executives of the A.H. Robins Company as "Robinspeak," which he defined as: "I don't know," "I don't recall," "I have no present recollection," "We had no definitive discussion," "I probably said," "I would have said." Were the answers of Louis Bantle the whole truth and nothing but? Or were the answers of the professedly ignorant CEO merely Robinspeak on tobacco road?

WHAT CARCINOGENS?

Dr. Richard Manning, vice president for R&D, joined U.S. Tobacco in 1969 as a senior research chemist. Because of his position, his testimony left many courtroom observers incredulous. It's easy to see why. For starters, he and George Braly had this exchange:

Q. "What is the range of nicotine found in tobacco?"
A. "I don't know."
Q. "Did you tell the jury you are a tobacco chemist?"
A. "Yes, sir. . . . "
Q. "No information on that subject?"
A. "No."

Per Erik Lindqvist, senior vice president for worldwide marketing, followed Manning's lead in obscuring the importance of nicotine in hooking snuff dippers. Looking toward the development of new smokeless tobacco products, Lindqvist wrote the president of the tobacco division in June 1981: "Flavorwise we should try for innovation, taste, and strength. Nicotine should be medium, *recognizing the fact that virtually all tobacco usage is based upon nicotine, 'the kick,' satisfaction.*" (My emphasis.) Was this a recognition by Lindqvist "that virtually all tobacco usage is based upon nicotine?" George Braly asked. "No," the executive swore. "What I am saying in this paragraph is that it is important that the consumer can feel the tobacco satisfaction."

Q. "Don't you, in fact, use the following precise words, 'recognizing the fact that virtually all tobacco usage is based upon nicotine'?"
A. "Satisfaction."
Q. "Yes."
A. "Nicotine satisfaction."
Q. "Yes."
A. "That is what I am saying."
Q. "Virtually all tobacco usage is based upon nicotine satisfaction; is that what you are telling the jury?"
A. "That's what this document says. . . . "
Q. "The United States Tobacco Company had for years planned different tobacco products around different levels of nicotine satisfaction; isn't that correct?"
A. "No, I can't answer that question. I don't know what you refer to here."
Q. "Do you deny that that is true?"
A. "I don't deny it and I don't admit it. I don't recall."

The next exchange with Manning led more eyebrows to rise:

Q. "What are carcinogens?"
A. "What do you mean by carcinogens?"

Timothy M. Finnegan of Jacob, Medinger & Finnegan in New York, U.S. Tobacco's principal law firm, interjected: "The witness is entitled to have a question that he understands. I ask you to clarify."

Q. "Doctor, my question is what are carcinogens?"
A. "I really don't know what you mean by carcinogens."

After Manning gave the same answer a third time:

Q. "I will tell you that what I understand the word carcinogen to mean is something that causes cancer. Do you understand it any differently?"
A. "It causes cancer in what, sir?"
Q. "Animals."
A. "What is cancer in animals? I am an organic chemist. I am not a pathologist. I am not an oncologist. I am not a medical doctor and, no, I cannot answer that question because I don't know."

Three times Braly asked: "Is there anybody that works for the United States Tobacco Company that knows more about this particular subject of carcinogens than you do?" Manning's first answer was, "I didn't say I knew about this particular subject of carcinogens." His second answer was, "Is your question is there somebody that knows more than nothing?"

Q. "About carcinogens."
A. "I don't know."
Q. "So if there is such a person that works for the U.S. Tobacco Company, you don't have any idea who it is?"
A. "Correct."
Q. "And you admit to this jury that you know nothing about that subject?"

Immediately, there followed exchanges, twice interrupted by Finnegan, in which Manning tried to deny his admission that he was a total ignoramus about carcinogens. Finally:

Q. "My question was didn't you just tell the jury that you didn't know of anybody in the company that knew more than nothing about carcinogens?"
A. "I think you are telling me I just said that."
Q. "I am asking you. Didn't you just say that a few minutes ago?"
A. "Right now, I don't remember."

Later:

Q. "What research has been carried out by the United States Tobacco Company in connection with the safety of snuff used by human beings?"
A. "I don't know what you mean by the use of the word safety in that context, either."
Q. "Has the United States Tobacco Company ever carried out any research to determine whether or not its snuff products are dangerous for human beings to use?"
A. "I don't know what you mean by dangerous in that concept—or context."

There was much more of the same kind of grappling over issues such as whether the company has researched or hired others to research whether snuff is carcinogenic or mutagenic. And, to end, there was this:

Q. "What is a low concentration of nitrosamines?"
A. "I do not know what a low concentration of nitrosamines is."

Braly told the jury he had a word for Manning's testimony: "Snuffspeak."

After the verdict, a juror told me this about the executives' testimony: "They stonewalled it. It was very obvious to everybody. Dr. Manning pretended he didn't know anything at all. The chairman was even worse than Manning." But the same juror, asking not to be identified, said that deposition testimony taken in advance of a trial is like "a game plan" in sports, i.e., a strategy to be held close to the vest, is therefore not taken as seriously as live testimony in the courtroom. It didn't faze the juror, who spoke as if this notion was widely shared in this buckle of the Bible Belt, when I pointed out that both kinds of testimony are given under an identical oath.

ARRANT EXPERTS

It's easy for cash-rich corporate law firms to find academicians to provide helpful testimony. It was particularly easy in the Marsee case because of the foresightedness of U.S. Tobacco. In August 1974, R&D chief Bennett wrote a letter, with a copy to Bantle, in which he said that "cigarette companies have built up quite a stable of experts in these fields related to their products, but we are not in too good a shape in this respect." How they got in shape is exemplified by their recruitment of Dr. William H. Binnie, chairman of pathology at Baylor College of Dentistry in Dallas.

In early 1984, Binnie went to an oral pathology meeting in Holland. So did Janet S. McClendon of Jacob, Medinger, the U.S. Tobacco law firm, which for several years also represented R.J. Reynolds Tobacco Company, the big cigarette maker. Within a few minutes in the trial, Binnie gave George Braly two differing accounts of the origin of his availability to Jacob, Medinger and the smokeless tobacco industry.

Initially, he said "I was approached" by McClendon. Then he said he had "sought out" the lawyer. "Here was this lady sitting in our meeting and I was just curious to find out who she was," Binnie said. "I didn't even know she was an attorney." Braly asked Binnie whether McClendon "travels around to all these medical meetings hunting for doctors that will testify for the tobacco industry?" The doctor replied, "No comment."

Braly asked Binnie if he had "testified on behalf of the smokeless tobacco industry before Congress about a year ago?" "No," he said, "I submitted a document." In it, he expressed the belief that smokeless tobacco does not cause oral cancer. At whose request had he given his opinion to Congress? "I had seen the proposed bill [to require health warnings on smokeless tobacco products] and the law firm asked if I wanted to see what I thought of it."

> **Q.** "And, I take it, you think that tobacco doesn't cause oral cancer?"
> **A.** "Correct."

Braly reminded him that at least 90 percent of the victims of head and neck cancers are tobacco users and asked if this had "any significance to you?" "No," Binnie said. Indeed, he was so protective of all tobacco use that, when asked whether cigarette smoking is "a cause of lung cancer," he replied, "I don't know that."

Then Braly asked the witness if he was the same W.H. Binnie who had published an article in the *Journal of Oral Pathology* in 1983—a year before the McClendon recruitment in Holland. Binnie said he was. In the article he had written: "The method of smoking notwithstanding, there is ample evidence to support the premises of tobacco consumption as a dose/time related entity in the etiology of intra-oral cancer."

> **Q.** "But have you changed your mind now?"
> **A.** "No, I haven't."

On January 10, 1983, ABC television aired a piece on snuff that disturbed the peace of Chairman Bantle. Two days later, he sent a memo to Executive Vice President Barry Nova: "What is the downside of Monday's broadcast? 'The Surgeon General warning snuff dipping may cause cancer'? It's possible it could trigger such a suggestion. We should develop a strategy for such a possibility, or better, for seeing that it does not happen." A few days later the company's Task Force on Regulatory/Political Environment came up with an unsigned memo listing numerous "preliminary strategy recommendations." One of them was only three words, the second word of which is an adjective that, dictionaries say, often modifies "knave": "Develop arrant doctors." Braly inquired, "Are you one of the arrant doctors that they have recruited?" Binnie said he was not.

YOU DIRTY RAT

So, how, with all this dubious testimony, could the jury rule in favor of U.S. Tobacco? The witness who decisively influenced them to conclude that snuff hadn't been shown to have killed Sean Marsee was Dr. Arthur Furst, immediate past president of the American College of Toxicology. Although an organic chemist, the impressively credentialed Furst is a full professor in the pharmacology department at Stanford University Medical School and is the author of about 220 professional papers in the fields of cancer research, chemistry, and toxicology.

From 1965 to 1969, while he was at the University of San Francisco, Furst conducted smoking studies paid for in full or in part by the Council for Tobacco Research U.S.A., which is funded by the cigarette industry. In 1981, when the Smokeless Tobacco Research Council was formed, Furst became a member of its scientific advisory board. He testified that the 1974 "stable of experts" letter was "news to me." "Isn't the Council the 'stable' for the smokeless tobacco industry?" George Braly asked. "Absolutely not," Furst replied.

Furst acknowledged at the trial that he hadn't published an article on the subject of tobacco and cancer for probably 20 years. He testified that he was aware that the Surgeon General, on the advice of a large number of the country's most prestigious scientists, had listed five criteria to be taken into account in determining whether there is "a sufficient basis to form a judgment of causality." But when asked "if you have any recollection of what they are?" he replied, "At the moment, no." He went on to "disagree, absolutely," with the criteria and claim that "the scientists" do not agree either.

As one would expect, the positions Furst took on the relationship between tobacco and disease were echoes of the views of the cigarette and smokeless tobacco industries, and rejections of views of the majority of the medical and scientific community. "[A]re cigarettes a cause of lung cancer in human beings?" Braly asked. "[T]he answer would be no because it has not been proven," Furst said. Similarly, he dismissed all of the authoritative warnings by the Surgeon General and others that snuff can cause mouth cancer.

Furst's testimony was seductive. Yes, he said, nitrosamines are carcinogens in animals. But he had happy news: in snuff, they are counteracted by "anti-cancer agents." In asserting this, he relied heavily on an experiment in which snuff components caused cancer in rats, while snuff itself did not. "There must be some anti-cancer activity in that snuff," he testified.

Once again, George Braly's cross-examination was shattering, even if it didn't strike the jury that way. Furst admitted he had not made the simple calculations that would have established the comparative exposures to NNN, in terms of body weight, of the rats in the experiment on which he relied, and of Sean Marsee. These calculations, which Braly did on the spot, showed that Sean, by consuming four cans of Copenhagen a week for six years, had been exposed to nine to ten times as much NNN as the rats.

Moreover, Furst said he believed it to be "absolutely" important to have hands-on experience in scientific experiments, but admitted he had never tested nitrosamines in animals. Few, if any, scientists know more about or have more hands-on experience with nitrosamines than Dr. William Lijinsky of the Cancer Research Center in Frederick, Maryland. Lijinsky had done his own study in which NNN caused tongue cancer in animals, and U.S. Tobacco attorney Jennings had told Furst of this. But, Furst testified, Jennings had not told him (or other defense experts) of the most salient fact, revealed in this exchange:

Q. "Did they tell you that this was the experiment that had been done at the lowest dose levels ever tested on nitrosamines?"
A. "Obviously not, no, sir."

Furst also disclosed that he had not been told that Lijinsky had testified at the trial about the dose levels in his tongue-cancer study. "I just learned about this today," Furst told Braly during cross-examination. "I won't argue with that."

He did not, however, change his position.

SILENT OATHS

If, in 1986, the chairman and CEO of the leading snuff company is "not aware that anyone has said that snuff causes cancer," and if the vice president for R&D doesn't know what a "carcinogen" is, or what "safe" or "dangerous" are, do they know what an oath is? What the "whole truth" is? I believe they do.

Probably I'm naive, but I have to say I'm repelled by the sight of platoons of corporate executives, on Capitol Hill as well as in the courts, who swear to tell—but who tell nothing like—the truth, the whole truth, and nothing but the truth. And I'm appalled when they tell nothing like the truth about conduct that has exposed dozens, hundreds, or even tens of thousands of human beings to avoidable disease, injury, and death.

To be blunt, I am talking about conduct that, when engaged in on the street, is universally recognized as manslaughter, or, if the conduct was knowing and willful, as murder. Maybe it's also naive to wonder why it is that when corporate executives who engage in such conduct violate a solemn oath to tell the truth, "so help you God," they rarely, if ever, elicit even a tut-tut from mainline editorialists and columnists, or the wrath of mainline clergymen, or such telegenic hellfire preachers as Jerry Falwell and Jimmy Swaggart.

But maybe the public oath these executives mouth is not the silent oath they obey. The silent oath, as I imagine it, would run like this: "I do solemnly swear to tell the truth, the whole truth, and nothing but the truth, so long as I reveal no truth that could hurt my corporation or me, so help me CEO."

3

When They Close the Factory Gates: How Big Steel Scrapped a Community

John Logue

J ust west of the Pennsylvania border lies the Mahoning Valley, once the second-leading steel producing area in the United States. In Youngstown and in its industrial suburbs, mills line both sides of the river. For generations their noise has muted the Mahoning, but in recent times the furnaces have gradually been banked, and one by one the mills have closed. In a matter of months, the sounds of the river will be audible again.

Youngstown is a microcosm of the problems of the aging industrial towns of the Northeast: the predatory conglomerate, systematic disinvestment, the flight south, the trained labor force suddenly unemployed, the collapse of the community tax base, and the obsolescence of the saving their plants and jobs depended on increasing production. They succeeded, but the gates still closed.

In the long run, labor force dedication cannot replace modernization. And modernization simply did not occur in Youngstown. The steel companies took millions out of the valley over the last decades and returned little to the plants.

The lack of reinvestment in the Mahoning Valley had a variety of causes. One is geographic: Inland mills lack cheap water transportation, a notable

John Logue, "When They Close the Factory Gates," from *The Progressive* (August 1980). Copyright © 1980, The Progressive, Inc. Reprinted by permission from The Progressive, Madison, WI 53703.

handicap for traditional mills (though not for those with modern electric furnaces which use a higher proportion of scrap). More crucial was the changing industrial structure. Merger activity hit steel—and Youngstown—hard. Lykes, the New Orleans-based shipping conglomerate, acquired Youngstown Sheet and Tube in the late 1960s. Sheet and Tube was more than six times the size of Lykes at the time of acquisition but the smaller fish swallowed the bigger. Lykes was less interested in Sheet and Tube's dies and presses than in its large cash flow, which could be diverted into financing other acquisitions. Plant maintenance diminished from the day Lykes took over, and investment in modernizing steel facilities slowed notably. Similarly, Jones and Laughlin Steel (J & L) was absorbed by the LTV corporation, a Dallas-based conglomerate.

Systematic disinvestment by the conglomerates is a symptom of the deeper problem: International competition in steel is intense, and profits are lower than in other industries. Emerging from World War II with its facilities intact, the American steel industry prospered while its foreign competition was prostrate. In time, the German and Japanese mills were reconstructed with more advanced technology, but American management rested on its laurels, in large measure because of the conviction that the new technology being pioneered abroad (derived, ironically, from foreign studies of American plants) was inappropriate for the huge scale of the American domestic market. New investment went instead into advanced versions of technologically antiquated production processes. By the late 1960s, foreign steel companies were making major inroads into the American market, while American investment had lagged so far behind the growth in demand that American producers were no longer able to meet peak domestic requirements.

Wages play a subsidiary role to investment. American steelworkers are among the best-paid industrial workers in the country, but the same can be said of Western European steelworkers. Japanese wage rates, long below those in other industrial countries, have moved up rapidly. But new plants now coming on line in such Third World countries as Brazil and South Korea will benefit not only from a low-wage labor force but also from the anti-union policies of those governments.

The obvious answer is to encourage unionization, and efforts to aid union organizers in Third World countries have met limited success. The principal problem is pressuring Third World governments to permit union organizing. Unions in western nations have had occasional successes: The threat of a boycott on unloading Chilean exports wrung a few concessions from that government in allowing union activity in Chile. But what is really needed is governmental pressure, and for all the human rights campaign, the Carter Administration has done little in this area.

Not all American steel firms have been slow to modernize. Some smaller companies, like Armco's Western Steel division, which has installed electric furnaces in all its plants, are fully modern, highly competitive, and profitable. But the industry giant, U.S. Steel—which last year grossed $12 billion, equal to the gross national product of Egypt—has lagged so far behind that cynical outsiders suspect it of deferring capital spending and allowing foreign inroads into its markets in order to compel the Government to provide tax breaks for the industry.

Instead of modernizing their mills, many American steel firms are diversifying—diverting profits from steel into investment in other areas. The conglomerates that now own Youngstown Sheet and Tube and J & L do this as a matter of course. But even U.S. Steel is turning its back on the industry, channeling an increasing portion of its investment dollars into the chemical industry, oil, gas, and uranium exploration, and real estate development. U.S. Steel's latest annual report is illustrated with pictures of a company-developed shopping mall.

If Youngstown's problems were typical of the industry's, its response was not: Workers and community have fought stubbornly and imaginatively to save the valley's economic backbone. It is this struggle that has projected Youngstown into the national consciousness.

The fight began with Lykes's surprise shutdown of Sheet and Tube's Campbell works. Campbell local union presidents first learned of the impending disaster when they were called into management offices one Monday morning in September 1977 to receive the press release announcing the closure; the first layoffs began three days later. Initially accepting management's explanation that the plant was a victim of pollution control rules and Japanese imports, ten of thousands signed petitions asking the Government to invoke import restrictions and relax environmental protection standards.

But public outrage grew as the real reasons for the closure became clear: New Orleans executives had plundered Sheet and Tube to invest elsewhere, leaving Youngstown with a silent mill and 5,000 unemployed. The formation by religious leaders of the Ecumenical Coalition of the Mahoning Valley provided a focal point for organization. Its goal quickly became a worker–community-run steel mill—a suggestion first made by Gerald Dickey, a steelworker at the Brier Hill works and recording secretary of the union local. The proposal called for a community corporation that would combine worker, community, and private investment. After a study by Gar Alperovitz and the Center for Economic Alternatives established that a community mill was potentially viable, the Ecumenical Coalition asked the Federal Government for $245 million in loan guarantees—guarantees of the sort provided to other steel producers, such as Wheeling-Pittsburgh, for modernizing aging plants. Reaction was initially favorable, but in March 1979 the Government rejected the request, killing the Campbell plan. (See "Must Youngstown Roll Over and Die? How 'Big Steel' Got to Jimmy Carter," *The Progressive*, October 1979.)

By this time, the Justice Department had compounded Youngstown's problems by suspending antitrust rules that would probably have prevented the merger of Lykes, the owner of Youngstown Sheet and Tube (the nation's eighth-largest steel producer), and LTV, which owned Jones and Laughlin (the seventh-largest). Overruling staff recommendations, Attorney General Griffin Bell approved the merger under an imaginative application of the "failing business doctrine," otherwise reserved for firms in or near bankruptcy. Bell cited a desire to save jobs at Sheet and Tube, but that wasn't one of the results of the merger. Sheet and Tube's Brier Hill mill was superfluous to the integrated company and was closed in December 1979.

The U.S. Steel shutdown, announced November 27, 1979, was less surprising than the earlier closures. The Ohio and McDonald works were among the most marginal facilities the company owned; they had been close to getting the ax before. Yet to a community organized on the issue of plant closings, the shutdown was the final straw: Keeping the plants open or selling them to the employes was an issue to be pushed in the streets as well as in the courts. Irate steelworkers seized U.S. Steel's district headquarters on January 28 to underline their view.

The aborted plan for a community takeover of the Campbell works was readily adapted to U.S. Steel's Youngstown works. This time the plan called for a small infusion of local capital, a $60 million Federally guaranteed loan, and a substantial reduction in labor costs by deferring incentive payments and writing off accumulated pension and vacation benefits. Plans called for running the mills "as is" until the regular capital market could be tapped—possibly with Government loan guarantees—for modernization funds. The plan called for cutting labor costs by 21 per cent, but this time it was hoped that labor's sacrifice would save the mill jobs permanently.

"We have a much better chance than ever existed for reviving the Campbell works," said Bob Vasquez, chairman of the Ohio Works local. "The labor force is in place. The management is in place. Our customers have not turned to other suppliers yet."

There was just one problem: U.S. Steel refused to sell the mills to any group which sought Federal loan guarantees—a proviso that would exclude sales to several of U.S. Steel's competitors as well as to former employes. Ironically, the company's stand was announced at a press conference in conjunction with the steel industry's request for new tax deductions which would cost other taxpayers some tens of billions of dollars.

The leadership of the steelworkers' locals at U.S. Steel's McDonald and Ohio Works in Youngstown are not radicals. They seemed more discomfited than the company itself by the temporary occupation of U.S. Steel's Youngstown headquarters, preferring to place their hopes in reviving the mills under community ownership. That required the cooperation of the

Carter Administration, not notable for its enthusiasm for plant occupations. They sought redress in the courts, suing U.S. Steel for breaking what they alleged was an oral agreement to keep the mills open as long as they broke even, and for anti-trust violations in refusing to sell the mills to Community Steel.

"We are not talking about a local bakery shop, a grocery store, a tool-and-die shop, or a body shop in Youngstown that is planning to close and move out," Federal District Judge Thomas Lambros declared in granting the restraining order that prevented the planned March 10 shutdown. "U.S. Steel cannot leave the Mahoning Valley and the Youngstown area in a state of waste." In agreeing to hear the case, the judge said he chose to "view the law not as something static but in terms of the modern-day conditions." And he moved the trial to Youngstown to enable the plaintiffs to subpoena U.S. Steel executives from Pittsburgh.

William Roesch, president of U.S. Steel since April 1979, told the crowded courtroom of studies that had been undertaken to determine whether there was a "viable fit" between Jones and Laughlin and Youngstown Sheet and Tube, and whether a merger would improve the profitability of the two.

What about the "fit" between Sheet and Tube's Brier Hill works in Youngstown and J&L's seamless operation at Aliquippa, Pennsylvania? asked Staughton Lynd, attorney for the steelworkers.

"I didn't see that as a problem," Roesch responded. There were murmurs from the audience, most of whom were free to attend the trial because of what the "fit" had done to the Brier Hill works in December.

David Roderick, chairman and former president of U.S. Steel, making his first trip to Youngstown since 1977, testified that when the decision was made to shut down the Youngstown works on November 27, 1979, U.S. Steel officials had performance figures for Youngstown showing profitable operation on the first half of the year and a cumulative loss of only $300,000 for the first ten months (Roderick's salary in 1979 was $360,000). It was on the basis of future projections that U.S. Steel acted, Roderick said.

What projections? Lynd demanded. He said U.S. Steel's own figures, from plant management, showed a projected 1980 *profit* on fixed expenses. Roderick said he had no knowledge of that report.

Roderick's answers seemed surprisingly thin on facts, but he spoke categorically on policy topics. U.S. Steel would not sell the plants to its employes or any other group with a Government-guaranteed loan.

"Are you closing the door?" Lynd asked. Roderick affirmed his belief in free enterprise and the market place.

"Is there anything that the USW locals and the community can do to reopen U.S. Steel's consideration of the closures?" Lynd asked. "I cannot foresee such circumstances," the company chairman replied. His answer had a ring of finality.

The judge also heard from William Kirwan, general superintendent of the Youngstown works. Kirwan did not talk of free enterprise but of producing steel profitably—of the fact that the Youngstown works turned a $10 million profit on fixed expenses in 1978 and $4 million in 1979, with the projection of a tiny profit in 1980. He recalled how, in February 1979, Youngstown had produced half the profits in U.S. Steel's Eastern Division, and how production records were broken time and time again despite the antiquity of the equipment.

Kirwan spelled out the details of his "Kirwan plan," which he had pushed on the unreceptive U.S. Steel hierarchy, for massive new investment in the Youngstown works, and for building a new mill on the site of the old works. The audience applauded this glimpse of what community control is all about.

Judge Lambros's decision favored the company. The last heat of iron was tapped at the Ohio works within hours after the decision was handed down. Judge Lambros dismissed the employes' antitrust case three weeks later, ruling that despite Community Steel's offer of $20 million for the Youngstown works, the steelworkers had not demonstrated "any ability to purchase, [and] therefore no one has denied them anything."

A legal victory by the steelworkers might have brought a delay of one or two years in the shutdown. But the Youngstown issue goes deeper than that: What is a corporation's responsibility to employes and the community and what influence should employes have on investment decisions?

The Youngstown shutdowns and community opposition to them have drawn national attention. The United Steel Workers, whose national leaders have done little to help save the Youngstown mills, have now introduced plant shutdowns as a national bargaining issue.

Pending before the Ohio legislature is a bill requiring advance notification, severance pay, and payment to a community readjustment fund in the event of closures of major plants. Similar legislation has been proposed in Oregon, Michigan, Massachusetts, Pennsylvania, and New York, and in Congress. Milder plant closing laws are already on the books in Maine and Wisconsin.

Such moves deal with effects, not causes. Employe influence on investment decisions is more crucial; it was the decision not to reinvest in Youngstown, made in the 1960s and early 1970s, that led to the shutdown. Employes now have some influence in other countries—in Sweden and in Germany, for example—and few would maintain that the plants are the worse run for it. Swedish employers are required to provide full information to their employes and to negotiate all major investment decisions with the union. Full disclosure requirements would probably improve the quality of information in the hands of managers when they make important decisions. Perhaps the most astonishing point in Roderick's testimony in the Youngstown trial was the paucity of his company's knowledge of the profitability of the Youngstown works when the decision was made to shut them. He had never heard of the "Kirwan plan" to modernize the works.

Though the plant closing legislation under consideration confers no powers on employes or communities, it does raise the cost of shutting marginal facilities rather than modernizing them. Currently the tax law weights the balance on the other side. The economics of massive closures are more attractive to corporate executives because the public pays most of the tab. The company takes a one-year bath of tax losses (which can be written off against future income) and ends the drain on current earnings. Its executives gain a reputation for acting decisively to "turn the company's profits around."

But the cost to the taxpaying public for shutting marginal mills is heavy. Of the roughly $200 million loss, charged against future taxable income, that U.S. Steel took in the Youngstown shutdown, other taxpayers will eventually pick up 46 per cent, or almost $100 million. In addition, the direct cost in unemployment compensation, retraining, and other benefits for workers idled by the shutdown is estimated at $70 million over the next three years. Add in the state and Federal governments' losses in taxes, the waste in underutilization of Youngstown schools, roads, water and sewage plants, and the sum of losses absorbed by the public would far exceed $200 million—about the cost of Kirwan's modernization program.

Perhaps the greatest irony is that Youngstown employes were unable to use their considerable financial clout. The assets of U.S. Steel's manual employes pension plan are *double* the value of the corporation's stock. Were the equity of the fund subdivided, Youngstown workers would be entitled to about $100 million. But far from following the interests of its normal owners, the company-controlled pension fund has sunk (as of 1976) a half billion dollars into the stock of predominantly non-union and, in some cases, blatantly anti-union firms. Conceivably, many of the beneficiaries would have preferred to see some of that fund invested in saving jobs by modernizing the mills instead of being pumped into non-union companies investing in the South or farther afield in Taiwan, South Korea, or Brazil. But the company controls the fund.

At issue in Youngstown, then, was the question of economic power. Do the rights of property ownership include the right to scrap jobs, mills, an entire town? The answer of the Youngstown community was a resounding No. While community control has been invoked as a last resort, Community Steel could have provided the vehicle to save Youngstown's steel industry by taking over the mills as Sheet and Tube, J&L, and U.S. Steel shut them down. Stabilizing the Youngstown steel industry under community control would also have cost jobs, but nothing like the 10,000 that now have disappeared.

The decision was not up to Youngstown. It rested with the steel companies and the courts, which ruled, albeit reluctantly, that the privileges of ownership included the right to scrap a community and its people.

From family firm to mini-conglomerate

Small, family-owned companies have been hit hard by the merger wave of the 1960s and 1970s, with countless hundreds of locally owned firms falling into new hands. The A. C. Williams Company in Ravenna, Ohio, about thirty miles west of Youngstown, is a case in point.

Founded in 1844, A. C. Williams is among the oldest foundries in the country, and until 1976 it was still owned and managed by the family that founded it. The firm's two plants in Ravenna—together the town's second-largest private employer—had been unionized since the mid-1930s, and while wages were hardly munificent, the atmosphere was decent, the work steady, and the stress less than at the higher-paid assembly line jobs in the region. Union local president Jim Boyle described labor relations as average to good; in the twenty-one years he had worked at A. C. Williams, there had been only one strike, and that had lasted less than a day.

Four years ago, a group of investors bought the firm, and quickly used the assets to acquire three other Ohio foundries. As it happened, two of the new plants were non-union. So it was hardly surprising that the new management was willing to take a strike at A. C. Williams when the old contract expired in January 1980. Management did not even appear at the bargaining table; it sent only its attorney.

In the third week of the strike, the company bought a non-union foundry in Tennessee and announced its intention to move machinery from one of the struck plants to the new one, where production could be resumed. What followed could have been a scene out of a Grade B 1930s strike film.

Shortly after midnight on Thursday, February 14, a convoy of eleven trucks drove full speed through the picket line, along with a car and a van carrying twelve men equipped with pistols, shotguns, mace, nightsticks, and riot helmets. The pickets were forewarned of the arrival of the "movers" (who, according to Boyle's queries, specialize in such operations and have moved 192 plants under comparable circumstances) because the convoy got lost and radioed the police for directions. The police charged the eight pickets with aggravated riot, but they did not search the trucks for armaments. Only after the trucks were on the road did the police have a look in the remaining vehicle—the van—to find some disassembled shotguns and a fully assembled pistol.

The story has a happy ending. Although production did begin at the Tennessee plant, a decent contract was finally signed in Ravenna, raising wages, improving pensions, and leading to the rehiring of three employes previously fired. The old machinery stayed in Tennessee, but new machinery was brought in from yet another plant bought during the strike. The union chalked it up as a victory.

But the nature of the company and its relations with the employes had been fundamentally changed. Four years ago, A. C. Williams was part of the community; today, it is free to shift work among union and non-union plants, or even out of state.

"When I went to work there twenty-one years ago," Boyle says, "the manager was Harry Beck. He knew the wife's name, the names of your children, whether they played baseball or football, when they were sick. All that's gone now. This president don't give a damn whether he operates in Ravenna or someplace else."

A few months after the end of the strike, the company proved Boyle right by shutting one of its two Ravenna plants indefinitely for economic reasons and laying off half the work force. It was the first shutdown within memory; A. C. Williams had weathered other recessions and the Great Depression by reducing the work week rather than shutting down.

As in Youngstown, the power has moved out of the community, and with it has gone the old sense of security. Community loyalty and 130 years of tradition mean little in the new world of the mini-conglomerate.

4

Missing from the News

Ben H. Bagdikian

Almost weekly we read of yet another great media merger. Time-Warner attempts to form the largest media conglomerate in the world, or Rupert Murdoch adds another major segment to his global empire. We are witnessing an extraordinary race toward monopoly control. In 1982, fifty corporations had half or more of all the business in the major media of the United States. Today, that number is less than twenty-five and shrinking.

Among our 1,600 daily newspapers, for example, about a dozen corporations now control more than half the circulation. Among our 11,000 individual magazine titles, a half dozen corporations have most of the revenue. Among our four television networks and 900 commercial stations, three corporations have most of the audience and revenue. There are at least 2,500 book-publishing companies, but a half dozen corporations have most of the sales in the book industry. Three major studios have most of the movie business.

What these giants seek is control or market domination not just in one medium, but in all the media. The aim is to control the entire process from an original manuscript to its use in as many forms as possible. A magazine article owned by the company becomes a book owned by the company, then becomes a television program owned by the company, then becomes a movie owned by the company. The movie is then shown in theaters owned by the company, and the movie's sound track is issued by a record label owned by the company. Obviously, the company will not be enthusiastic about outside ideas and productions that it does not own. More and more, we will be dealing with closed circuits.

The leading owners of our daily newspapers include Gannett, which owns *USA Today* and eighty-eight other dailies, or about six million in total daily circulation; International Thomson, with 116 papers and two million circulation; Knight-Ridder, with three million; Newhouse, and about eight others.

The chief owners of magazines dealing with the general news will be dominated by Time-Warner, which will control more than 40 per cent of the country's magazine business. Other major owners are Rupert Murdoch, Hearst, and Newhouse, though not all issue general news. *Newsweek*, which does carry news, is owned by the Washington Post Company.

In broadcasting, despite some loss of audience, the three networks, ABC, CBS, and NBC, still have most of the television viewers and business. In books, some of the major owners are Gulf + Western, owners of Simon & Schuster; Time-Warner; Reader's Digest Association; Bertelsmann, a German firm; Maxwell, a British firm; Hachette, a French firm; and Thomson, a Canadian firm.

How well do these major owners of the news and knowledge serve the public?

The good news about American reporting is that in some technical matters, it is the best in the world. Its journalists are the best educated, far better educated than any earlier generation of American journalists. They operate under higher professional ethics than journalists elsewhere and higher than at any time in the past. They lie less than journalists elsewhere, fictionalize less, and, on the whole, take seriously their individual duty to provide the public with accurate information. Collectively, they issue an extraordinary volume of news every day.

But if things are so good, why are they so bad? The problem lies with the institutions and the conventions of standard American journalism. Most reporters in the standard media can say, truthfully, "No editor tells me to lie." But most reporters are told every day what to write *about*.

There are 50,000 print reporters and 50,000 broadcast reporters in the country, and each day, each week, each month they are pointed toward particular tasks, particular stories, particular personalities, particular government activities, particular foreign scenes, particular series. In the resulting mass of stories, there are often articles of importance and distinction, and there is a daily volume of routine, factual, essential local and national information.

The problem lies in something beyond the mass of useful items.

Each day, editors necessarily select some stories for emphasis, some for deemphasis, and some for the waste basket. Certain kinds of stories, certain public figures, certain social data, certain analysts of social and political events are regularly on the network evening news and the front page, while other stories, spokespersons, and analysts are mentioned obscurely if at all. The main problem in the news today is not what is false, but what is missing.

The pattern begins when owners appoint executive editors and producers. Owners seldom appoint someone who is likely to be interested in emphasizing those events and interpretations that undermine the owners' political and economic interests. Some editors do so, and there is a steady record of their being fired or resigning to protest restrictions.

In 1980, members of the American Society of Newspaper Editors were asked whether they would feel free to publish news harmful to the parent corporation of their newspaper. One-third said they would not feel free to do so. Given how offensive the very idea is to professional journalists, I think we're safe in assuming that 33 per cent is a conservative figure.

The consequences, I believe, are clear. In foreign affairs, the main news of the country follows the official national policy. This does not mean that there is never any reporting contrary to officialdom. But it does mean that information that contradicts governmental versions gets into the news with greater difficulty and only briefly compared to the official view. It is not done by official censorship, but by self-censorship.

If journalists are as much improved as I think they are, it's fair to ask what causes this self-censorship. One reason is the awareness by the top editors and executive producers that stories seriously affecting their owners' interests will cause the editor problems. Such stories do appear, but infrequently. And they usually focus on those developments that are, in effect, unavoidable.

The recent departure of William Kovach as editor of the *Atlanta Constitution & Journal* illustrates the editor's dilemma. He had been told to be fearless and make his paper the best in the country. He took this literally, and his paper began publishing stories about problems in Atlanta— problems of race, of commercial development, and of flaws in the establishment. He was squeezed out, and it took no memorandum from the publisher to let the staff know that stories of that kind will get reporters and their editors in trouble with the owners.

Several years ago, a reporter and editor at the *Dallas Morning News* did a documented story about a bank in serious trouble. The reporter was fired, and so was the editor who passed the story. The bank did fail, and the story was confirmed. But no memorandum has to instruct that news staff or others around the country that stories disclosing flaws in specific banks will get them into trouble. As we all know, there are no problems with banks and savings-and-loan associations in the state of Texas, or anyplace else.

Self-censorship also comes from a basic strategy of American news. Since most of the revenues of the news media are derived from advertising and there is an incentive to maintain an audience of as many affluent people as possible, news policies are designed not to offend the political sensibilities of the advertising target-audience.

This is done in two ways. One is to attribute every fact and judgment to as high an authority as possible, so that no one can accuse a journalist of selective reporting. The other method is to give the news a kind of political tone-deafness, an appearance of neutrality without political, social, or economic context. When you give the context of events, you begin to be political. Accurate reports of events, with interpretation by high officials, is much safer.

But the result is not neutral. If you strain out independent political and economic contexts, if you do not pursue the likely causes and consequences of events, if you emphasize or rely exclusively on the words and ideas of the highest officials, public and private, you have presented a picture of an uncontested and inevitable status quo. When you add to that the Cold War and the nature of anticommunism in American politics, it is always safer to swing to the Right than to the Left. The status quo, in politics and in corporate life is, of course, sharply skewed to the conservative side. It resists significant change in society.

Finally, self-censorship in the standard news media comes from twenty years of accusations against American journalists by neoconservative intellectuals and academics and conservative political leaders who have branded journalists, individually and as a group, for being biased against the established order and conservative politics.

These charges, when they are based on anything at all, are based on surveys of journalists who, when asked whether they tend to be Democrats or Republicans, say they tend more to be Democrats than Republicans, or tend to be more liberal than conservative. That this is precisely the pattern of the American electorate seems not to make any difference. While recent Presidential elections have gone Republican, countrywide voting for Congress and for state and local office continues to be heavily Democratic. But the accusations by conservatives have had the effect of making many journalists lean over backward to favor conservatives to show that they are not biased.

These pressures to support the status quo happen to conform with the politics and economics of the major media owners. If the breaking news is noticeably embarrassing for conservatives, the question regularly asked within news organizations is whether the reporting is really being fair to the conservatives. I have never heard of similar questions of fairness being raised in regard to the treatment of Ralph Nader, Common Cause, labor unions, and other forces on the other side.

Public knowledge of events in Nicaragua and El Salvador has suffered from an astonishing failure of the mainstream news media to do continuous reporting from the field, though Central America remains the center of White House attention and activities, and the closest we have been to a new war. The main body of news coverage has never checked out assertions about events in those countries in any systematic way. For years the news media took official declarations at face value, often when there was overwhelming evidence to the contrary.

Recent examples include the case of Raymond Bonner, a correspondent for *The New York Times,* who was withdrawn from El Salvador because he reported that a real civil war existed in that country, and that atrocities were committed on both sides, including the side supported by American aid. His recall did not require a printed order to other correspondents warning them that departing from the official line in Washington or at the American embassies can get them in trouble with their editors.

The Iran-contra exercise, in violation of the Constitution and contrary to the word of our highest officials, was exposed fairly early by the alternative press in this country and finally was blown open by an obscure publication in Beirut, not a mainstream American news organization.

In domestic affairs, there is a steady pattern of looking the other way, of avoiding obvious causes and consequences, so as not to disturb or threaten the status quo.

President Reagan's program of supply-side economics, with huge military spending accompanied by large tax cuts, had enormous support in corporate America. But people with perfectly respectable expert credentials saw it from the start as a formula for disaster. Nevertheless, for years, most of the judgments reported in the news came from organizations and individuals who were beneficiaries of those economic policies. Even after David Stockman, one of the architects of the idea, went on record to say it was all really a cover to shift wealth from the poor to the rich, the mainstream media continued to quote almost exclusively these same beneficiaries, as though Stockman and serious economists had never spoken. If criticism ever was aired, it was in the seventeenth paragraph.

We have had massive deregulation of our economy, with some good results and some bad. But for more than ten years, the news media were close to silent on the bad results. One is tempted to say that some of the serious negative effects of deregulation finally broke into the standard news only when corporate officials themselves began to worry about the safety of the airplanes they were riding in. To this day, there is a zone of silence on the negative effects of mergers, acquisitions, leveraged buyouts, ominous levels of corporate debt, and monopolistic levels of market domination, including those in the news business.

We have turned our economy on its head by eliminating the progressive income tax, the only sane and fair way to build our public institutions, but the media have turned a deaf ear to those who say so.

The causes and consequences of some public acts are seldom made clear. For example, in the miles of newsprint and hours of television reporting on fantastically high real-estate prices for the middle class and the millions of homeless, how often has this been placed in the context of a number of rather clear causes: (1) in the 1970s, 200,000 low-cost housing units were built each year with Federal help, and in the 1980s only 17,000 a year; (2) the increase in the homeless population can be directly related to that reduction and to cuts in Social Security and other benefits during the 1980s; (3) it is clearly connected to the growing separation in this country between the rich and the poor, thanks to changes in tax and welfare policies; (4) it comes from tax advantages to the builders of commercial property even if it remains empty and has replaced urban residential housing.

A regular story on the economy is the need for greater productivity in the workplace. This has been accompanied by dramatic coverage of strikes and union activities, with corporate sources regularly citing unions as the problem. How often have you seen in such stories the established data, true for years, that show productivity has increased in unionized activities and decreased at managerial and administrative levels?

The whole society, including government and corporations, suffers in the long run because accountability and correction of faulty policies require good information that simply isn't available. Damaging or ineffective policies continue longer than they should. Positive opportunities are lost.

The spectrum of allowable context in the news runs vaguely from right to center. One of the major networks recently had a brief announcement of proposed economic policy and followed it with three commentaries: fifteen seconds from the chair of a House committee, twelve seconds from a spokesperson for the American Enterprise Institute, a conservative think tank, and eleven seconds from a spokesperson from the Heritage Foundation, a right-wing group. By keeping the news tone-deaf, but weighted heavily toward facts and spokespersons from the centers of power, the media render the national discourse more sterile each year. Ideas for solution to problems are not aired, alternatives to present policies fade, and the status quo seems unchangeable.

The effect of the homogenized, narrow spectrum of information and context in American news is profound. A country whose major news media are oriented around the centers of power will soon have national politics also homogenized around centers of power. That is what we have today. Our national political discourse is sterile in ideas for necessary change, deficient in its confrontation with the realities of social injustice, and therefore narrow in plausible alternatives held out to the public.

When masses of people are bedeviled by problems but see no possibility of significant change, the result is hopelessness and apathy. Many who have no hope become destructive. It is not surprising that each year since 1960, the percentage of eligible voters who go to the polls has declined. And when the cause of suffering remains mysterious, people find scapegoats. When we look for scapegoats, we move to the Right and we move to race hatred.

Our mainstream news media have fine figures to prove what the world looks like from the standpoint of policymakers in Washington, from the interplay of lawyer-lobbyists and legislators, from the opinions of conservative think tanks, the board rooms of corporations, and the floors of stock exchanges. But that is a long way from the compelling realities in which most of our citizens live.

There is another reality, in our streets where millions sleep in doorways; where most children can no longer expect to live in families with one income or buy a house or go to a university; where the poor are getting poorer and the rich richer; where ever-more-lavish skyscrapers and luxury hotels cast shadows on deteriorating schools and libraries; where air and water are increasingly unhealthy; where thirty-seven million people have no health-insurance coverage; where millions of children in hopeless neighborhoods with hopeless schools and no hopes for good jobs are killing themselves with drugs—drugs often imported from countries we favor because their governments call themselves anticommunist.

All this in a rich society, still full of vitality and with millions willing to work for policies that will improve their lives. But the ideas for plausible policies to take advantage of this vitality, the ideas to produce change, must enter the national discussion. And this cannot happen unless these ideas and possible solutions enter our mainstream news media, not as abstracted verbiage in the dialogue between Wall Street and Washington and the ten-second television slogans of election campaigns, but in the reporting about our whole society, directed clearly and primarily to the realities in our cities and towns.

That, in essence, is what is missing in our main media, and, therefore, in our politics.

II

Economic Crisis

Economic troubles remain a harsh fact of life in America in the last years of the twentieth century. The specific form they take changes rapidly, often confusingly; inflation waxes and wanes in severity, and the unemployment rate rises and falls as we oscillate giddily between recession and "recovery." But some things seem to have changed, perhaps irrevocably, from the days when the American economy was thought to be a virtually invincible source of abundance, stability, and material well-being. The level of unemployment we consider to be "normal" is far higher than it used to be; our status as the undisputed leader of the world's economies has been shattered by the performance of Japan and other competitors; and some of our largest, most traditional industries are declining with brutal speed, taking with them hundreds of thousands of jobs and the livelihoods of whole communities.

Today, there isn't much serious disagreement that what we once described as the "affluent" society is facing an economic crisis of unprecedented proportions—and one that has changed the face of American society in fundamental ways. The articles in this chapter explore some of the dimensions, probable causes, and possible outcomes of this change.

Despite considerable economic growth during the 1980s and 1990s, for example, unemployment remains a persistent and stubborn problem, especially, but not exclusively, in minority communities. But why—in a society that is ostensibly devoted to the "work ethic"—do we continue to tolerate high levels of joblessness? In "The Specter of Full Employment," Robert Lekachman makes the startling case that unemployment, however painful it may be to the workers who suffer it, also has its uses—at least for some employers. A pool of jobless workers puts a damper on the expectations of those workers who have jobs, frightens people into clinging to jobs that are dangerous, demeaning, and badly paid, and thus helps keep wages low and profits high.

Barry Bluestone and Bennett Harrison's article, "Boomtown and Bust-town," looks at the other side of the economic crisis—the costs and pains of economic growth or, at any rate, of the kind of growth that the American economy has undergone in recent years. Focusing on the problems emerging in the "Sunbelt" of the Southern and Southwestern states, Bluestone and Harrison show that unregulated growth has had highly disruptive consequences for American communities—ranging from urban sprawl and congestion to high rates of crime and frustratingly unyielding levels of poverty and unemployment. The implication of their analysis is that simply trying to spur "growth," of whatever kind and by whatever means, is—by itself—no real answer to the human and social problems of the American economy.

By the late 1980s, indeed, many of the "boomtowns" described by Bluestone and Harrison had "gone bust," especially in Texas and other states of the Southwest. The collapse of that shaky economic "boom" is part of the backdrop for what, by all accounts, is the most massive single financial disaster in American history—the scandal-ridden collapse of a large part of the savings and loan industry. Though that collapse may cost Americans half a *trillion dollars* in the coming decades, its growth and causes have been hard for most Americans to comprehend—in part because its financial roots are so complex, but also because the depth of the impending crisis was systematically covered up by a complaisant government. Some of the roots of the savings and loan crisis are described in "The Bonfire of the S & Ls," written by staff reporters of *Newsweek* magazine. The causes are diverse, but at bottom the savings and loan debacle is a reflection of the same freewheeling climate of heedless economic deregulation that Bluestone and Harrison describe.

Another manifestation of that economic free-for-all in the 1980s was the surge of financial mergers and "buyouts" of companies that add little if anything to the productivity of the economy—and may well reduce it—while enriching the investment bankers and lawyers who undertake these "deals." The most spectacular examples in recent years have been multi-billion dollar "leveraged buyouts," in which relatively small amounts of money are used to "leverage" huge amounts of debt in order to buy large corporations. These buyouts divert vast resources from more productive pursuits, and they may leave the targeted company floundering in a sea of debt from which it may not be able to escape. Given the negative effects of these deals on the economy, why doesn't government step in to regulate them? In their article, Max Holland and Viveca Novak offer a troubling answer; the ability of Wall Street corporations to funnel large amounts of money to elected officials has virtually insured that little federal action will take place. Their description of the extraordinary influence of corporate financial contributions over the political process illustrates the sense in which America's economic crisis represents a crisis of its political institutions as well.

5

The Specter of Full Employment

Robert Lekachman

Men and women want to work. Work, private and public, is there to be done. How come, a wandering rationalist might ask, the work and the workers are not happily married? Well, as the radicals of my youth were wont to intone, it is no accident that we tolerate as a nation years of 7, 8, even 9 percent general unemployment and horrifying rates of teenage joblessness which among urban blacks exceed, by some estimates, 50 percent.

The brutal fact is that unemployment at "moderate" rates confers a good many benefits upon the prosperous and the truly affluent. If everyone could be employed, extraordinarily high wages would have to be paid to toilers in restaurant kitchens, laundries, filling stations, and other humble positions. Whenever decent jobs at living wages are plentiful, it is exceedingly difficult to coax young men and women into our volunteer army. Without a volunteer army, how can the children of the middle and upper classes be spared the rigors of the draft?

Unemployment calms the unions and moderates their wage demands. . . . When people are scared about losing their jobs, they work harder and gripe less. In more dignified language, absenteeism declines and productivity ascends.

Better still, factory and office workers, alert to potential layoffs and plant shutdowns, are unlikely to nag unions and employers to make work more interesting, and less menacing to health and personal safety. It cannot be mere coincidence that in Sweden, where job enrichment and plant democracy have had their greatest success, unemployment is practically zero and astute management of their economy protected Swedes even from the worldwide economic crisis of 1973–75. The new government, elected on the fortuitous issue of nuclear safety, has promised to extend even further the social benefits for which Sweden has become celebrated. American employers preserve themselves from Swedish experiments in good part by keeping the industrial reserve army plentifully manned.

Nor is this quite the end of the tale. The hunger of communities and regions for jobs and tax revenues has allowed large corporations to extort an endless assortment of valuable concessions from local and state governments, either as blackmail to keep existing installations or bribes to lure new ones. Few major corporations pay their fair share of property taxes. Propaganda by oil, steel, chemical, and paper industries has noticeably slowed the pace of regulation to protect the environment. . . .

By contrast, full employment on a sustained and assured basis (the system can stand a spell of full employment so long as all parties understand that it is temporary) presents an embarrassment to the movers and shapers of American plutocracy. To begin with, full employment is the most efficient agent of equitable income redistribution which is at all politically feasible in the United States. Full employment sucks into the labor force men and women who now struggle on welfare, food stamps, Social Security, and unemployment compensation. It pushes up the wages of low-paid people whose position is scarcely less precarious than that of the unemployed. It is an especial boon to blacks, Hispanics, teenagers, and women—last hired and first fired in expansion and recession alike. A long spell of full employment would substantially narrow existing wide differentials between the earnings of these groups and those of white males. In a time of layoff and business contraction, affirmative action is a mockery, but when there is full employment the cry for justice is heard more sympathetically by members of [the] majority whose own security is not threatened.

These repercussions are severe enough to alarm gentlemen in their clubs and boardrooms. The threat, I suspect, is still more grave. For men of property the charm of the 1970s lies in the way economic adversity . . . cooled the campuses and shoved American politics, already the most conservative in the developed world, still further right; one only has to look at Gerald Ford of all people, after Watergate and the Nixon pardon, and in the middle of a messed-up economy, very nearly winning the Presidential election. This could not have happened without general apprehension and dampened expectations of the efficacy of action by any national administration. As one comedian commented upon the stock-market decline which preceded the election, investors were selling out of deadly fear that one of the candidates would win. Lift the burdens of apprehension and apathy from the psyches of ordinary folk and—who knows?—they might entertain radical thoughts of inviting the rich to share rather more of their capital gains and inheritances.

It goes without saying that it is scarcely respectable for the rich and their mercenaries, lawyers, economists, politicians, public-relations types, and so on, to openly proclaim their affection for unemployment, although among friends they tend to be more candid. One requires a respectable rationale, a convenient theory that combines apparent concern about the sufferings of the unemployed with actual capacity to avoid any action realistically calculated to alter their status.

My colleagues (I am an economist, but I am confessing, not boasting) have risen to the challenge. As their apologetic runs, we can't proceed sensibly toward universal job guarantees, even in the cautious, timid shape of the Humphrey-Hawkins Full Employment Bill, a revival of the 1945 original effort to write a serious job guarantee into law, because of the horrifying menace of more inflation. That menace is among economists embodied in a marvelous construction interred in the textbooks under the rubric of the Phillips curve.

The provenance of this notion that democratic societies must choose between inflation and unemployment deserves a paragraph. The late A. W. Phillips, a British economist who taught for much of his career in Australia, published in 1958 an article catchily entitled "The Relationship between Unemployment and the Rate of Change in Money Wage Rates in the United Kingdom, 1862–1957." Phillips's data appeared to demonstrate that, as unemployment rose, wages increased less and less rapidly. The man said nothing at all about prices, price inflation, or the manner in which rising wages might or might not be translated into commensurate increases in the cost of living. Nevertheless, his findings were rapidly extended in statements like this typical textbook pronouncement: "Low rates of unemployment tend to be associated with high rates of inflation and, conversely, price stability or low rates of inflation tend to be associated with high rates of unemployment." Triumphant conclusion: "There seems to be a trade-off between employment and the price level."

Economists shifted from Phillips's cautious conclusions about unemployment and wage rates to the words just cited very simply. After all, wages and salaries, including those of executives and other overpriced folk, amount to about 70 percent of business costs. Wherever competition reigns, employers have no choice except to pass along plumper labor costs to their customers in the shape of higher prices. The line of causation is direct: low unemployment stimulates wage demands, higher wages enlarge business costs, and these in turn lead to higher prices. It's an indisputable pity, but if we are to restrain demand inflation, we simply must operate the economy at what an MIT economist, Robert Hall, has recently labeled the "natural" rate of unemployment. A bit hard on those selected to serve their country by losing their jobs, but their patriotic sacrifice is nothing less than a valuable public service.

Let us absolve A. W. Phillips of blame for the intellectual sins committed in his name and look calmly, on its merits, at the Phillips curve in its modern guise. It is to start with an embarrassingly inaccurate explanation of recent stagflation—the malignant combination of persistent inflation and high unemployment. To those untutored in economics, the causes of a good part of current inflation have nothing at all to do with the Phillips curve. Out there in a world mostly beyond American control, OPEC has been busy quintupling petroleum prices, the Russians have been bidding up the cost of food in American supermarkets by vast grain purchases, and the world market for American farm products, temporary fluctuations aside, has been exerting steady upward pressure upon domestic food supplies.

These external shocks initiated an inflationary surge in 1973 and 1974. In spite of the sharpest recession (1974–75) since the 1930s, that inflation continued, somewhat abated in 1976, and gave ominous signs of spurting once more by the end of that year. Here is the real embarrassment for Phillips curve groupies. Their mechanism has simply failed to work. Unemployment has escalated and stuck at the highest recorded levels since the Great Depression. Wages have risen more slowly than the cost of living. Productivity is improving. Nevertheless, prices continue to rise. It has proved perfectly possible to suffer simultaneously from severe inflation and still more severe unemployment and factory underutilization.

As it happens, there is a reasonable explanation at hand for events so baffling to partisans of inflation-unemployment trade-offs. Clearly, inflation is not a simple matter of translation of higher wages into higher prices. Rather, it is an aspect of the distribution and concentration of market power among suppliers and sellers, abroad and here at home, who are in a position, within generous limits, to set their own prices for the goods and services that they sell. In both recession and expansion, sellers with market power have chosen to charge more, even if, as a result, they sell less. Businessmen and respectable mainstream economists who judge full employment to be inflationary are utterly correct. It is only their reasons that are wrong.

Prices rise during both phases of the business cycle because in recession businessmen who enjoy monopoly or quasimonopoly power over their markets push prices upward in order to maintain their profit margins. When better times come, businessmen seize the opportunity to improve their profit margins. As fair example, recall that during 1974 and 1975, two of the auto industry's worst years since the 1950s, General Motors and its amiable rivals marked up auto sticker charges an average of $1,000 per car, even though the customers were reluctant to buy. The rarer the customers, the larger the profit that needed to be attached to the selling price of each unit. Now that sales are behaving more wholesomely, prices continue to rise. Why not get more when the customers are willing to pay more? As in autos, so in steel, aluminum, and a long list of other industries in which one, two, three, or four dominant corporations set prices and conduct orderly markets unblemished by unseemly price rivalry. The manufacturers have company. In the delivery of health services, a pleasant cartel of health insurers, hospitals, medical societies, and complaisant federal authorities has propelled medical costs higher at twice the pace of general inflation. The television monopolies have raised the charges for network time, and the university professors who lecture and consult have done rather better than the inflation rate. Lawyers have long judged advertising and price competition two serious breaches of legal ethics. Food prices rise partly because of the widening profit margins of food processors.

WORSE THAN THE DISEASE

The diagnosis dictates the choice of remedies. One is as old as the 1890 Sherman Antitrust Act: break up the monopolies and end price-fixing in restraint of trade. The remaining true believers in antitrust would cheerfully fragment the large corporations, which, either by themselves or in combination with one or two peers, dominate many markets. Alas, the nonprogress of former Sen. Philip Hart's oil divestiture bill in the last Congress and its dim prospects in the new one are the latest evidence of the political futility of this tactic. Although no technical reasons justify the size of Exxon or General Motors, the public is yet to be persuaded that small is beautiful.

The only feasible alternative is control of key prices and profit margins in the very large proportion of the economy where old-fashioned competition is celebrated only by banquet speeches. Such controls were imposed during World War II and the Korean War. It is a historical curiosity that John Kenneth Galbraith, who was a price administrator, and Richard Nixon, who briefly served as a compliance attorney, drew diametrically opposite conclusions from their respective experience. Galbraith continues to believe that price control is both necessary and feasible. Nixon preached the wickedness of interference with private markets, but nevertheless suddenly froze prices August 15, 1971, and followed the ninety-day freeze with a year or so of more flexible but astonishingly successful wage- and price-hike limitations. As the Nixon experience suggests, wage controls generally accompany price controls. There recently has been the rub. The wage controls in 1972 and 1973 were considerably more effective than the price controls, for two excellent reasons. The Nixon controllers, pro business to a man, were far more eager to check union demands than to interfere with business earnings, and employers gladly cooperated with Washington to police the wage-rise limits. Seldom did patriotism pay better.

The fact is that in the United States (England is, of course, quite a different matter) mandatory price controls over concentrated industries and the health sector, together with voluntary wage guidelines, would probably work very well for a time. American unions are, after all, both weak and conservative. The path to full employment without inflation is impossible without a firm incomes policy and the statutory authorization of price controls administered by individuals who believe in what they are doing.

Does the political will to shape a national full employment policy exist? It is difficult to answer yes to that question. . . . For, as has been noted, full employment means diminishing long-standing inequalities of income, wealth, and power; inviting the black, brown, young, and female to the American celebration; and controlling the rapacity of doctors, lawyers, giant corporations, and other reputable extortionists. After full employment who will iron Russell Long's shirts, clean up after the Lutèce diners, and do the world's dirty work? Settle the job issue once and for all, and even American unions will begin to entertain dangerous thoughts about job redesign, codetermination, and similarly radical Swedish and German nonsense.

The fine Christian (and occasionally Jewish) men whom the good Lord has placed in the seats of authority and the halls of the mighty know that there are far worse phenomena than unemployment. One of them is full employment. . . .

A genuine commitment to sustained full employment demands a good deal more than a temporary tax cut or a brief loosening of the federal purse strings. The United States will move toward a coherent high-employment economy at the same time as it becomes politically feasible to diminish the power of greater wealth and reduce inequalities of income and wealth.

The fate of George McGovern in 1972 and Fred Harris in 1976, two brave souls who rose to the perils of open discussion of such political dynamite, makes it depressingly plain that Americans continue to admire the people and institutions that make life harder for them than it need be. As Prof. Walter Burnham of MIT pointed out last year, the missing 45 percent of the American electorate who don't turn up on Election Day, in Europe vote Labor, Socialist, or Communist.

All my life my country has suffered from the absence of significant political left. As I trudge through middle age toward the golden years of senior citizenship, I glimpse even less hope of the emergence of a democratic socialist party than I did during the late 1930s and early 1940s when, at least in Manhattan, revolution was in the air.

Until a credible left rises in the United States, unemployment will be a little higher when the Republicans are in the White House, a little lower when the Democrats take their turn. Genuine full employment, decent jobs at decent wages for every man, woman, and youth interested in working, has been a myth, is a myth, and will stay a myth so long as every four years voters choose between one party minimally to the right of dead center and a second minimally to the left.

6

Boomtown and Bust-town

Barry Bluestone and Bennett Harrison

F ew people, and certainly not those who have spent any time in cities like Youngstown and Detroit, or in towns like Anaconda, Montana, would deny that deindustrialization is an agonizing experience for the families and communities that must contend with it. Yet the belief lingers that disinvestment is somehow a necessary precondition for the constant renewal and reinvigoration of the economy. It is part of the grand scheme of creative destruction—a reminder that omelettes can be made only by cracking eggs.

The omelettes, in this case, are presumably cities like Houston, the southern metropolis that *U.S. News & World Report* claims is "bursting out all over." Houston is not a city, it declared,

> It's a phenomenon—an explosive, roaring urban juggernaut that's shat-tering traditions as it expands outward and upward with an energy that surprises even its residents. . . . Absorbing capital, people and new cor-porations like a sponge, Houston is constantly being reshaped—physi-cally by the wrecking ball and new construction and culturally by newcomers with fresh ideas and philosophies.

In a twenty-page special advertisement in *Fortune*, Houston recently paid tribute to itself as the new international city of America. The statistics are indeed impressive. By the end of 1980, Houston led the nation in "almost every economic indicator," including growth in population, em-ployment, retail sales, and per capita income. It was first among the nation's cities in residential construction, and in the latter part of the 1970s, in overall construction. Office space tripled during the decade; bank deposits quadrupled. Office towers went up by the dozen, while millionaires were turned out as though on an assembly line. The spirit of prosperity lost elsewhere in the country seems to be incarnate in Houston. As one leading Texas architect put it, "People still think big and act big here. They have the confidence that the rest of the country seems to lack."

THE QUINTESSENTIAL BOOMTOWN

In part, Houston is what *re*industrialization is all about. This exploding metropolis and cities like it have been able to attract billions of dollars of investment in practically no time at all. Between 1971 and 1978 alone, ninety-nine large firms moved into the city followed by thousands of smaller supplier establishments. This created so many jobs that despite population growth of more than half a million residents during the 1970s, unemployment rates have generally remained below 4 percent. In 1979 the area's economy generated 79,000 new jobs, driving the jobless rate down to an extraordinary 2.6 percent. The nationwide unemployment rate was nearly three times larger.

By the middle of this decade, Houston will surpass Philadelphia in population, making it the nation's fourth largest city. Only New York, Los Angeles, and Chicago will be bigger; this will give each of the four census regions of the country its own natural "capital city." Houston's 45 percent population boom during the last ten years contrasts with Frostbelt declines of 27 percent in St. Louis, 24 percent in Cleveland, and 23 percent in Buffalo. More than 1,000 new residents arrive every week, many making the same cross-country trek as Houston's founders—the Allen brothers from New York who bought the land site for $10,000 in 1836.

Houston is perhaps not exactly typical of all the new boomtowns in America, but its evolution illustrates how reindustrialization is supposed to work. What has attracted capital and people to the city is its energy industry. It is a city built on oil. Thirty-four of the thirty-five largest U.S. petroleum companies have their headquarters there, or have major divisions for exploration, production, research, and marketing. Four hundred other oil companies and more than 1,600 suppliers and manufacturers of oil-related equipment have settled in the surrounding area, as have hundreds of marine service enterprises, drilling contractors, seismic companies, and pipeline installers. About 40 percent of the nation's oil is refined in Houston and the nearby Texas Gulf Coast. Altogether the area manufactures about 60 percent of the country's basic petrochemicals. Based on this incredible wealth, the financial community has attracted foreign bankers from Germany, England, France, Saudi Arabia, Switzerland, Brazil, and Hong Kong. More than forty-five foreign banks are represented in the city.

Unabashedly the city boasts that "it is not just lukewarm towards business, it is *pro-business*" (emphasis theirs). Its advertisements placed in business journals to attract even more capital remind potential investors that "Texas is virtually a tax haven." It is one of only four states in the nation without an income tax on corporate earnings and is one of just six states with no personal income tax. As a result, according to the U.S. Census Bureau, Houston's per capita tax burden is a mere $175 compared with New York City's $841 and Boston's $695. To add to its attractiveness, its workers' compensation costs are among the lowest in the nation, and it is one of the so-called right-to-work states that have outlawed the union shop.

With a pro-business climate to attract investment, the city's public relations office has only the job of convincing corporate executives—those who manage these investment dollars—that, despite the heat and humidity, Houston is a charming place to live. One advertisement, aimed particularly at those in the North, claims "everything is dehumidified and air conditioned" with a housing selection to meet every need. With ballet, opera, concerts, and theater, seven four-year colleges, and the largest medical complex in the world, the city's backers believe they have rounded up everything necessary to create "the good life" and to continue to attract capital and labor.

Houston is not alone in the burgeoning Sunbelt. Rapid economic growth has meant that family incomes in the South are quickly catching up with those in the rest of the country. Between 1953 and 1978 median family income, adjusted for inflation, rose by two thirds in the Northeast, the North Central states, and the West. But in the South, family incomes nearly doubled. Whereas southern incomes averaged only 73 percent of those elsewhere in the country in 1953, by the dawn of the 1980s, they approached 90 percent. Moreover, between 1973 and 1978 while real incomes were actually falling outside the South, they were rising in the Sunbelt. The median family in the Northeast received 3.5 percent *less* real income in 1978 while the average southern family—despite double digit inflation—was able to enjoy a modest (2.3 percent) improvement over its 1973 income.

The standard of living in the South is actually better than these numbers indicate because living costs are so much lower. The Bureau of Labor Statistics estimates that in 1979 a family of four needed $19,025 to maintain an "intermediate" standard of living in Houston. To maintain the same standard in Boston cost $24,381 and in New York, $23,856. The median family income in the South is 14.6 percent lower than that in the Northeast, but the budget requirement is 22 percent less in Houston. As a result, the typical family in this Sunbelt metropolis—despite its lower *money* income—enjoys 7.4 percent more real purchasing power than the

median family in Beantown and 5.6 percent more than the same family in
the Big Apple. For the wealthy in cities like Houston, the cost of living
differential is even greater, proving what many boomtown residents
already know—that it is cheaper to live high off the hog in Texas than in
New York, Boston, or other northern cities. Excluding Anchorage and
Honolulu, the cities of New York, Boston, and Washington, D.C. are the
most expensive to live in (if you can afford an intermediate- or higher-
budget standard of living) while three of the leading Sunbelt cities, Dallas,
Atlanta, and Houston, are the cheapest. At an intermediate budget level,
food costs in Houston are 8 percent lower, transportation costs are 13
percent lower, and housing costs and personal income taxes are less than
half what they are in Boston. Boomtown growth seems to be the yellow
brick road in the nation's otherwise gloomy economic landscape.

THE "DOWNSIDE" OF THE BOOMTOWN STORY

Indeed the economic juices of the nation seem to be flowing swiftly to
areas like Houston, and millions of transient families are following the
flow. Youngstown's loss seems to be Houston's gain, so that on average
the nation prospers.

But does it? A closer look at America's new boomtowns suggests that
not all is well there either. The movement of capital imposes enormous
social costs on the "winners" just as it does on the "losers." Like the
boomtowns of the nineteenth-century Wild West, much of the glitter is
true gold, but not everyone in town is overjoyed with the social conditions
that accompany its discovery.

No one can deny the fact that explosive economic growth in the Sunbelt
has brought "the good life" to many of the region's residents and to those
who have migrated to the area. Yet this is only one side of the Sunbelt
story. To leave off here would be to totally ignore the other side of the
"boomtown syndrome"—the often-destructive consequences of unplanned rapid development.

With a deliberate policy of enacting no zoning laws and doing practically no planning, Houston and other boomtown cities have been virtually overrun by the influx of capital. Growth has occurred so rapidly and
haphazardly that boomtown metropolises now paradoxically exhibit
many of the same urban woes that plague northern central cities. To most
city planners, "Houston's sprawling growth represents how not to do it.
In Houston, developers can build what they want, when they want,
where they want. While such laissez faire certainly engenders boomtown vitality, it also creates boom-town problems."

Among these are highway congestion, air pollution, water shortages,
overcrowded schools, and a housing crisis marked by some real estate
prices that have tripled in a matter of a few years. Twenty-five percent of

the city's streets remained unlighted, 400 miles were unpaved, and 29 percent of the poor lived in substandard housing—even as recently as 1978. Every day nearly 200 newly registered cars join the armada that clog Houston's freeways. As a result, a commute that took thirty minutes five years ago takes an hour today. And there is no alternative way to get to work. What passes for the bus system, according to *Newsweek*, is "a joke"; the more charitable *Wall Street Journal* calls it merely "decrepit." Only eighty-two buses—four fifths of them paid for by the federal government—serve Houston's 400,000 residents. This situation is typical of many Sunbelt cities built during the age of the internal-combustion engine. In neighboring Albuquerque, New Mexico, 95 percent of all trips in and around the metropolitan area are done by car.

Other city services suffer as well. Annexation of suburban communities, combined with successful attempts at limiting property-tax levies to lure yet more industry, leave many a boomtown with inadequate revenues for even the most basic social services. This is certainly true in Houston where there is only one policeman for every 600 people and the average police response time to an emergency call is twenty-six minutes. (This amounts to one third of the police protection of Philadelphia and less than half of that found in other big cities.) The frighteningly slow emergency response time in Houston is almost surely due to the fact that a total of only seven police stations service the city's 556 square miles!

Yet perhaps the worst legacy of uncontrollable boomtown expansion is not in poor social services but in the violence done to a community's social fabric. As a consequence of the hyper-investment boom, the disparity between rich and poor is becoming increasingly evident throughout the Sunbelt, creating a dualism reminiscent of the pre-Civil War South. In 1978 the richest 5 percent of the Sunbelt population enjoyed a far larger share (16.4 percent) of income than the top 5 percent in any other region, and the bottom 20 percent have less (only 4.8 percent) than anywhere else. The wealthiest one fifth of the southern population has nearly nine times the aggregate income of the poorest fifth. Outside the South, that differential is 7.4 to 1.

Reflecting on these data, Georgia State Senator Julian Bond fears "the creation of a permanent underclass in the new South." *Fortune* magazine, a champion of Sunbelt development, admits that the black population (16 percent of the Sunbelt) has "scarcely shared in the economic upsurge." Again the statistics tell a gloomy story. In spite of boom conditions all around them, over *one third* (35.1 percent) of all blacks in the South—more than 4.8 million—were still below the official poverty line in 1980. More than a quarter (27.3 percent) of what the Census Bureau calls the "Spanish origin" population shared the same fate. In Houston the poverty has been described in particularly graphic terms:

> Left behind in Houston's headlong flight toward growth and eco-
> nomic success are an estimated 400,000 people who live in a 73-square-

mile slum that, says a college professor, has an infant mortality rate "that would have embarrassed the Belgian Congo."

As a partial consequence of extreme income inequality, acutely visible in the juxtaposition of new industrial wealth and old rural squalor, the new boomtowns are experiencing a crime wave. In 1979, reports the FBI, Houston distinguished itself with one of the highest murder rates in the country: 40.4 killings per 100,000 residents, two thirds higher than New York City's homicide record. It is at least partly for this reason that the Commission on the Future of the South—made up of bankers, a judge, college presidents, and regional politicians—concluded that the South is a "time bomb" ready to go off. The unmet need for services for new residents is so staggering that the whole urban system may be on the brink of an explosion. The Fantus Company, which helps businesses select new plant locations, has even gone so far as to lower its official assessment of Houston's business climate, precisely because of poor public services. The city's own residents agree. In a recent University of Houston survey, only 26 percent of those who live in the city now think the impact of rapid growth has been "good."

Houston's problems are not unique. In many ways, they can be found in all of the boomtowns that have become the victims of too much unplanned development too fast. Atlanta has even sorrier stories to tell. And so do many of the cities in Florida. Every six minutes, the equivalent of a family of four moves to the Sunshine State seeking jobs or a retirement home. The new residents require housing, roads, schools, sewers, and water. Given the extremely fragile ecology of Florida, fresh water is a real problem—as it is in the booming Southwest. The Florida aquifer, the water table underlying the state, is down to its lowest level in recorded history. Fresh-water wells are being destroyed by salt-water seepage and some lakes are down by as much as 12 feet. Air pollution is killing Dade County's palm trees, while the state's rivers are dying of chemicals, sewer waste, and algae. The water and sewage system is simply overloaded and many experts fear a real environmental calamity. A leading Florida newspaper editor summed up his assessment of the situation to a group of state planners saying, "[Florida] is going to die of thirst or choke to death on a glut of people, exhaust fumes, concrete, and sewage unless the public wakes up."

Silicon Valley, California, the bustling home of the computer "chip" in Santa Clara County, suffers from the same boomtown syndrome. At the end of World War II, Santa Clara County was known for its fruit orchards and Stanford University. Today, it is blanketed with 500 electronics firms that make components for everything from the cruise missile to Space Invader computer games. Between 1960 and 1975, employment in the valley grew by 156 percent—three times the national rate and twice that of California. High-tech workers flocked into the area the way that retirees headed for Florida. And with the influx came the same problems.

By 1980 there were over 670,000 jobs, but only 480,000 housing units in the county. As a result the *average* price for a house soared to well over $100,000. Cheaper houses were bid up in price so rapidly that low-income families were displaced in the process. With no viable mass transit, the freeways became jammed and the average commuting time reached three hours or more for workers living in the southern parts of the county. Federal air-quality standards are now violated at least 10 percent of the time. With land prices out of control and the air spoiled, the fruit orchards have entirely disappeared.

This drama of industrialization that has gone haywire seems quite ubiquitous across the Sunbelt. University of California regional economist Ann Markusen estimates that between 5 and 15 million Americans are now involved in rapid-growth boomtowns in the Southwest and Mountain states alone. In many of the thousands of smaller communities, particularly where new capital-intensive energy investment is leading to exaggerated boom-bust cycles, long-time residents are finding themselves evicted from their homes, and the competition for land is resulting in the direct displacement of agricultural and tourist related jobs. The newly introduced production techniques and skill requirements often mean that the higher-wage jobs created in the capital-intensive sector are not available to those who lose their jobs in more traditional lines of work. Indeed, . . . much of this high-tech development often leads to job creation for technicians and managers brought into the area by the companies, *not* for local residents. This population influx places added stress on a city or town's existing school, water, and sanitation services—usually at the expense of those same local citizens who could not obtain the jobs.

There has never been a comprehensive or systematic cost-benefit analysis of the boomtown syndrome. But economists and sociologists have at least devoted some attention to particular case studies of economic expansion. From these we can hazard some generalizations about the costs of rapid economic development. One group of sociologists, led by Gene Summers of the University of Wisconsin, has recently compiled evidence from 186 case studies of what they term the "industrial invasion of nonmetropolitan America." They found that the net gains from boomtown development are not anywhere near as great as most people imagine. In the majority of cases only a small proportion of the new jobs created are filled by previously unemployed persons. In thirteen studies that examined this specific question (excluding one special case in which the Area Redevelopment Administration stipulated the hiring of unemployed workers as a *quid pro quo* for federal grant support), the proportion of jobs filled by the previously unemployed was less than 11 percent. What employment opportunities are created by the establishment of a new plant are often taken by workers from outside the immediate area, both commuters and immigrants. "Possessing more education, better skills, or the 'right' racial heritage, these newcomers intervene between the jobs and the local residents, especially the disadvantaged."

Of course, other jobs are created in the process of new plant location through the ripple effect. . . . These are mostly in wholesale and retail trade and in services. But even there the net gain is not as great as normally imagined, for in half of all the case studies of new industrial development, the estimated employment multiplier is below 1.2. That is, ten new jobs in a new manufacturing firm generate, in the majority of cases, less than two new *local* jobs in other sectors. Part of the reason for the low local multiplier effect is that new establishments that are part of a larger firm or conglomerate tend to use the services of suppliers that are already doing business with the home office rather than ones from the local community. Another reason is that commuters tend to patronize retail establishments in their home towns rather than where they work. Moreover, in many communities where the process of industrialization is just beginning, there is surplus capacity in the retail trade and service sector that can absorb some of the new growth.

One surprising finding is how often new industrial development fails to reduce measured unemployment at all. To be sure, in two thirds of the case studies unemployment rates declined after new industry came to town. But in most cases the impact on unemployment was less than 1 percentage point. Regional experts believe this is due to the fact that the perceived promise of new jobs slows the rate of outmigration, causes local labor-force participation to increase, and attracts immigrants who take a disproportionate share of the new opportunities.

In light of these private sector impacts, it is useful to consider the net gain to the public sector. Here the sociologists are in near agreement. New industry clearly is associated with an increase in the public sector costs of delivering basic services to residents. Utilities, especially water and sewage, appear to be the primary source of increased local cost. The need for new roads, schools, and police and fire protection is also important. What makes matters worse is that since industry is often attracted through the provision of tax holidays and other incentives, the revenue generated by new establishments is often not sufficient to pay for the increased service needs. As a result, the overall net gain of boomtown growth is often small, and sometimes even negative.

The unrealized burden of boomtown expansion goes beyond that which is easily measured. Paradoxically, both the physical and emotional health consequences of boomtown developments turn out to be similar to those found in communities like Youngstown and Akron that experience acute capital loss. El Dean V. Kohrs, for example, finds that unplanned expansions

> always seem to leave in their wake the grim statistics of mental depression, family disorganization, emotional damage, alcoholism, delin-

quency, and dissipation. These boomtown crises are not new to rural America, but the social consequences are becoming clearer today, and they are being felt in more parts of the country . . .

A growing segment of the population in the Sunbelt now recognizes the immense social costs that accompany unplanned and anarchic hyper-investment. They are being forced to pay for some of these costs through rapidly rising tax rates, although until recently they were getting the federal government to pick up a large share. With the new Reagan "federalism" forcing local communities to shoulder more of the fiscal burden, the contradictions of boomtown growth are becoming more evident. "Deep inside," notes Juan de Torres, an economist for the Conference Board, "the people of the South simply don't want their areas to grow any larger." The boomtown expansion has simply been too rapid for the city's public services, the environment, and the people themselves.

7

Bonfire of the S and Ls: How Did It Happen?

Steven Waldman and Rich Thomas

L ike a huge storm in the financial stratosphere, the great savings and
loan scandal has been raging for years without really touching most
Americans. Rogues and swindlers paraded across the business pages and
through the courts, accused of looting astronomical sums. Inept state and
federal regulators fumbled to figure out what was going on, and bum-
bling politicians resolutely looked the other way, all the while accepting
millions in campaign contributions. Like the sums involved, the scandal
was too big and abstract for most people to grasp. But in recent weeks, the
storm has dipped down to blast the earth—or at least to bring an uneasy
chill. Does the spreading slump in housing prices have something to do
with the S&L problem? Is the bailout, so painfully crafted last year, itself
in trouble? What does the huge loss mean in real money, and how can it be
repaid? What's all this talk of a credit crunch, maybe a recession? How is it
going to affect *me?*

The answers are depressing, and getting worse as the price tag ratchets
up. The scandal was by any measure the worst in U.S. history, a 10-year
loss estimated by *Newsweek* at $250 billion that was stolen or wasted and
must be repaid. That's $1,000 for every man, woman and child in Amer-
ica, not counting the interest that we will go on paying for the next 40
years. It is an unfair drain on honest citizens to pay the piper for knaves
and fools, and it will hit the young and poor harder than the old and rich.

We will almost surely avoid financial disaster, but the bill is a drag on the economy and could trigger recession. Recession or no, it will curb our standard of living. We will feel it most in choices we must forgo: roads and clinics unbuilt, educational programs untried, job retraining that won't happen. And the victims are all of us, from the low-income residents evicted from a Phoenix housing project to the unborn children who will still be paying the tax bill four decades hence.

Worse yet may be to come: the S&L scandal is only part of a mountain of bad debt that lawmakers have allowed to pile up in recent decades. There is an additional $100 billion to $150 billion to be written off in government-guaranteed loans to millions of private interests. . . . Worst of all, the nation's commercial banks may be next in line. Like the $945 billion in S&L deposits, their $2.5 trillion deposits are unconditionally guaranteed by Uncle Sam. Many banks are playing out a script remarkably like the follies of the S&Ls, to much the same official indifference. If their watchdog, the Federal Deposit Insurance Corp., were to close all the ailing banks it is now permitting to operate, its $14 billion insurance fund might be exhausted overnight. Official Washington scoffs there's nothing to worry about—"The FDIC is not in question," a Treasury aide told *Newsweek*—but outside experts dispute that. "The administration and Congress just don't want to acknowledge the problem," says R. Dan Brumbaugh, the Stanford economist who first predicted the S&L collapse. "This is *déjà vu* all over again. You can't believe it's happening, but there it is." . . .

WHAT $250 B COULD BUY

The huge sums destined to be sucked down the drain by the S&L crisis could easily fund some of the country's biggest wish lists.

Defense: Cover cuts slated for the next five years or buy 132 B-2 bombers, 40 Aegis cruisers and 100 Seawolf submarines.

Education: Fully fund every existing government program—from preschool through college—for the next four years.

Health care: Provide universal insurance *and* long-term care for the elderly and disabled for nearly four years.

Environment: Fund a 20-year coast-to-coast project to tackle the country's mounting hazardous–waste problem.

Infrastructure: Overhaul the nation's water systems, repair all bridges and have money left over to start fixing the highways.

How could the savings and loan crisis *possibly* have happened? How could the government inadvertently lose $250 billion—an amount approaching the cost of the Vietnam War? "This is the single most grievous legislative error of judgment this century," says Republican Rep. Jim Leach of Iowa, a House Banking Committee member who warned in vain about the problem for years. "It's the single greatest accounting misjudgment this century. It's the largest lapse on the part of the press. It's the single greatest regulatory lapse of this century. It's the single greatest indicator of the defer-at-all-costs approach to government in this century."

It would be comforting to think the scandal occurred because of a conspiracy of unusual forces, the political equivalent of a rare planetary alignment. But actually the forces that caused the S&L problems to fester for so long are familiar parts of American political culture. The warped campaign-finance system, failures to police white-collar crime, ethical permissiveness—all contributed to the S&L crisis and all could, without dramatic reform, cause the next scandal.

A FAILURE OF (DE)REGULATION

Before the 1980s, S&Ls were the most boring businesses in America. They loaned money to individuals to buy houses. Period. No loans for office buildings, none for breathtaking shopping malls or brash oil ventures. The motto was 3-6-3: offer 3 percent on savings, lend at 6 percent, and hit the golf course by 3 o'clock. The staid life changed with the high inflation of the late '70s as depositors pulled funds out of S&Ls to take advantage of higher-yield possibilities like money-market funds. The S&Ls were left holding long-term mortgages that paid them little. That left Congress with a choice: shrink the industry or let it fly free in the winds of deregulation. They chose the latter course—and the industry quickly became a lot more aggressive.

Congress took three key steps to revitalize the industry, all of which contributed to the fiasco. In 1980 it allowed S&Ls to pay much higher interest rates. The effect: S&Ls competed by offering savings-account rates as high as 13 percent. But to make up for the money they lost by paying more interest, they needed to generate extra income from investments. So in the early 1980s, Congress and many states allowed thrifts to invest in anything they wished. Effect: the thrifts bought everything from palatial estates for their owners to an Iowa plant that converted manure to methane. The government also permitted investors to open an unlimited number of accounts, each insured up to $100,000. That brought in more deposits—and gave irresponsible S&L managers more Monopoly money to spend. Together, these steps gave the industry the money and the freedom to fly high. "All in all," said Ronald Reagan when signing the 1982 deregulation act, "I think we've hit the jackpot."

Unfortunately, that "we" included a lot of high rollers with vivid imaginations. Don Dixon, head of Vernon Savings and Loan in Vernon,

Texas, took his wife on a "gastronomique fantastique" tour of fancy European restaurants. But he defended the junket as a scouting trip for investments. "You think it's easy eating in three-star restaurants twice a day six days a week?" he protested.

Such behavior was allowed to persist because of a profound flaw in the Reagan administration's thinking about deregulation: that markets should be liberated not only by writing new laws but by weakly enforcing existing ones. Officials did this at other agencies, like the Occupational Safety and Health Administration, but the financial cost was greatest at the Federal Home Loan Bank Board, which regulated S&Ls. The three other regulatory bodies that oversee banks hired more examiners to monitor commercial banks, which had been partially deregulated in the early 1980s to compete with other financial markets. But while those agencies could pay for new cops by increasing fees on banks, S&L regulators had to go cup in hand to ask the White House budget office. The White House turned them down flat.

Adding insult to bureaucratic injury, the other financial agencies then picked off some of the Bank Board's most talented examiners. That wasn't hard: in 1983 the starting salary for an accountant at the Comptroller of the Currency, which regulates federally chartered banks, was $26,000; at the Bank Board it was $14,000. In the early '80s, the S&L overseer lost about half of its veteran examiner staff. Those who remained were told by Reagan's first S&L regulator, Richard Pratt, to adopt new accounting procedures that let thrifts pretend to be solvent until they worked their way back—or so they hoped—to real health. These gimmicks made things seem better, but in the same way a doctor can make a patient appear better by whiting out a tumor on an X-ray.

THE IMPACT OF POLITICAL MONEY

Debates about the role of money in politics often make the need for reform seem either abstractly moralistic ("an affront to democratic values") or oddly trivial ("we're trying to eliminate not wrongdoing but the *appearance* of impropriety"). The S&L scandal shows clearly the dangers of having legislators depend so heavily on campaign funds from interest groups and businessmen with dealings before the federal government. Quid pro quos can rarely be proven but we do know this: never has so much money gone to such key legislators who worked so hard for measures that cost taxpayers so dearly.

The biggest politician to fall was Jim Wright, who resigned as speaker of the House in 1989 as the House Ethics Committee zeroed in on his attempts to bully regulators on behalf of thrift operators. Tony Coelho, the House majority whip who raised hundreds of thousands of dollars from thrift owners for the Democratic Congressional Campaign Committee, also retired that year under fire for a deal with Columbia S&L. Fernand St. Germain, former chairman of the House Banking Committee, lost his bid for reelection after disclosures he was using the credit card of the U.S. League of Savings Institutions for his personal entertainment. Now the Senate Ethics Committee is investigating the Keating Five, a group of powerful senators (Alan Cranston, John Glenn, Donald Riegle, John McCain and Dennis DeConcini) who received a total of $1.4 million in contributions from Charles Keating, head of the Lincoln S&L. That's not too mention the $131,000 Keating gave to Arizona state politicians and the $255,000 he gave to politicians in the Phoenix area, according to a PBS "Frontline" documentary. Near Phoenix, Keating built the Phoenician, a lavish hotel with gold-leaf ceilings and $12 million in Italian marble.

Mostly what the S&Ls got from these politicians was delay. In 1986 Wright sat on a key piece of reform legislation that would have raised $15 billion in desperately needed bailout funds. During the ensuing delay, the bailout's price tag rose several billion dollars. The Keating Five helped push regulators into putting off action against the Lincoln S&L. The senators deny wrongdoing, but after their intervention the Bank Board waited another two years before shutting down Lincoln—a postponement that may have cost taxpayers millions more.

Responding to questions about whether his money had influenced the senators, Keating said, "I want to say in the most forceful way that I can, I certainly hope so." All five senators denied the money swayed them and Cranston said, "I never did anything to derail any investigation of anybody." Glenn argues that there's a difference between pressure and questioning: "I learned very quickly that as a senator I can ask any question that I want. How [the regulators] answer is their decision." The senators also say part of their job is to help constituents—whether it's Aunt Sally with her social-security check or Keating with his S&L. Yet as William Black, a top Bank Board enforcer, puts it, "there were lots of constituents that needed protecting. But the one constituent who put up more than a million bucks in contributions to the five senators is the only one that got the protection." The pressures of the campaign-finance system tempt legislators to define the "public interest" as the sum of narrow special interests—too often the special interests with the most money.

THE HIRED-GUN SYNDROME

Follow the bouncing buck. Regulators eased off Charles Keating after intervention from the senators. The senators say that they interceded on behalf of Keating because they were persuaded by a letter written by

Alan Greenspan, now chairman of the Federal Reserve and then a private consultant, vouching for Lincoln's health. And Greenspan was paid to write the letter by a law firm that was representing . . . Charles Keating.

Greenspan claims he genuinely thought, as he wrote, that Lincoln's management was "seasoned and expert" and that the S&L itself was "a financially strong institution that presents no foreseeable risk." He says Lincoln was regarded as a sound thrift when he wrote his endorsement and he is now "surprised and distressed" by the S&L's demise. Financial consultant Bert Ely, who has studied the case, says that if Greenspan had objectively studied the existing data "there's no way he could have reached those conclusions. It was clearly an inappropriate letter."

Keating was also helped because Arthur Young, a big-eight accounting firm, diagnosed his S&L as sound and accused the government of harassment. DeConcini cited the Arthur Young study in his meeting with regulators, asking, "You believe they'd prostitute themselves for a client?" Michael Patriarca, chief thrift regulator in San Francisco, answered: "Absolutely; it happens all the time." Jack Atchison, the accountant who gave Lincoln a glowing report, soon afterward joined Keating's firm at a salary of more than $900,000. Atchison declined to comment. Arthur Young officials say the firm carefully considered regulators' arguments at the time but concluded they were wrong.

Other hired guns contributed to the mess. "Professional" real-estate appraisers valued a parcel of California land at $30 million even though most of it was on a sloped, completely undevelopable piece of mountainside. Margery Waxman, a lawyer in the Washington law offices of Sidley & Austin, helped get the Bank Board to take the Keating investigation out of the hands of the San Francisco office, which was leading the charge. "As you know," she wrote Keating, "I have put pressure on [then Bank Board chairman M. Danny] Wall to work toward meeting your demands and he has so instructed his staff." Waxman declined to comment last week, but a Sidley & Austin spokesman told Legal Times that the firm holds her "in high regard."

Lobbyists, corporate lawyers and consultants often compare their work to that of the noble public defender toiling in a grimy municipal court. Their point: society doesn't chastise a criminal-defense lawyer for representing a murderer—it's part of our adversary system, after all—so it shouldn't blame an advocate for representing an unpopular business client. But campaigning for government benefits should not enjoy the same moral standing as protecting constitutional rights. When professionals become, in effect, political lobbyists, they should be held accountable if their efforts succeed. That would force them to make some independent judgments about what they're advocating and provide an important check on irresponsible behavior.

SUICIDE BY FOUNTAIN PEN

Cosigning someone else's loan is known in private business as "suicide by fountain pen." It is a simple problem of human nature: people are less careful if they know someone else will pick up the pieces after the crash. If Uncle Sam pays off any deposits if an S&L goes under, the depositors may be less careful about where they put their money. That is why the government's decision to allow large investors to open unlimited numbers of guaranteed $100,000 accounts is considered one cause of the catastrophe. Savvy investors started putting money in the S&Ls with the highest interest rates, which gave men like Charles Keating the money with which to build their dreams. Meanwhile, "the gamblers at least could reassure themselves that depositors wouldn't suffer," says Northwestern University economist Haskel Benishay. And the deeper in trouble the owners became, the less they had to lose by gambling some more.

This "moral hazard," as economists call the effect of government guarantees, has plagued other programs as well. Congress will soon have to spend $100 billion to $150 billion *on top of* the S&L bailout to cover losses from programs ranging from student loans to flood insurance to commercial banking. Ironically, Congress loves these programs because they seem so cheap. The cost becomes clear only years later, when the loan goes bad or the disaster happens.

Even though these programs often cover bad risks, they get lax scrutiny because they are off-budget. "Nobody dreamed we'd have to raise $120 billion to bail out savings and loan depositors," say Rep. J. J. Pickle. "Nobody dreamed we'd have to put up $4 billion for the Farm Credit System. Nobody dreamed. Why, all of a sudden we realize that there's a tremendous risk. We've handed credit cards to these folks without ever watching what happened."

THE CULTURE OF FINANCIAL CRIME

Picture the following scene: five senators sit in a room with a local district attorney who is prosecuting an accused bank robber. The senators charge the D.A. with harassing the bank robber and a few help a Senate employee, friendly with the accused, to be appointed the new D.A. Even the most cynical observer cannot fathom this happening. Yet five senators didn't view inquiries on behalf of Keating to be improper—even though the Bank Board's investigation was attempting to protect taxpayers from huge losses and, as it turns out, alleged fraud.

In the private sector, people who would be outraged to see a thief snatch an old woman's purse become numb to the implications of a senior being ripped off through fraud. Such a double standard is reinforced by the criminal-justice system: an unarmed bank robber who steals $100,000 will get a sentence between 51 and 63 months. Someone who commits a $100,000 fraud gets between 15 and 21 months.

Political and corporate culture can include pockets of permissiveness about crime just as ghetto subcultures can incubate violent crime. Until the insider-trading crackdown, Wall Street financial crime often went unpunished because it was so complicated—and in some cases so routine. The same sort of lapse in ethical standards lay at the heart of the HUD scandal, as Housing and Urban Development officials gave out grants on the basis of political ties instead of merit. People seem to forget that their gain comes at someone else's expense.

As part of his reform efforts, Rep. Henry Gonzalez, chairman of the House Banking Committee, required that regulators log contacts from congressmen. The S&L meddling suggests a further step: a ban on lawmakers privately lobbying regulators about the solvency problems of an individual bank or company.

THE BIG DENIAL

Adolf Hitler theorized that "the big lie" would work because human beings have a limited capacity to fathom deception on a grand scale. The S&L scandal provides a corollary that might be called "the big denial." When the facts present a situation so extraordinarily bad, human beings will devise brilliant ways to avoid reality. Congress and the regulators didn't face the S&L crisis early in part because they just couldn't believe it was as bad as people thought. The same has been true with problems like nuclear-waste disposal at the Department of Energy facilities, which will require an additional $150 billion in taxpayer funds to correct.

Facts weren't faced for more mundane reasons as well. To do so would have meant paying for a bailout earlier, which might have required an unpopular tax increase. Thrift watchers charge that Wall continually downplayed the size of the thrift problem to keep it from becoming an issue in the 1988 presidential election campaign, a claim Wall denies. Examiners within the Home Loan Bank Board feared that if they pushed too hard they would incur the wrath of their bosses who, in turn, were being browbeaten by the politicians.

The failure to confront the S&L crisis made a bad problem into the worst financial scandal in American history. The sicker S&Ls became, the more their managers threw good money after bad. If Congress had confronted the problem in 1984 it would have cost $40 billion, estimates consultant Bert Ely—a lot of money but a small fraction of what we'll end up paying. "It's like the government has been borrowing from a loan shark," Ely says. So if it depresses you to think of how much we'll be paying now that we're confronting the problem, think of how much we're saving by dealing with it now instead of in 1995.

8

Buyouts: The LBO Lobby Makes Its Move On Washington

Max Holland and Viveca Novak

N o matter what the weather report says, January 12th may have been the coldest day of the year in the gusty canyons of lower Manhattan.

It was no less a staunch Republican than George Bush who sent shivers up Wall Street's collective spine that day. At a pre-inaugural press conference, Bush indicated that he might be willing to cut back on a tax deduction that helps make leveraged buyouts (LBOs) the best game going for the Street's brash new stars.

The unprecedented $25 billion LBO of RJR Nabisco last fall had sparked public furor and the threat of congressional investigations; but this evidence of top-level discussion of the issue among even Republicans steeped in laissez-faire economics was worse news. Buyout artists, banking on continuing the ideological harmony of the Reagan years, had invested heavily in the 1988 Bush campaign, with LBO king Henry Kravis of premier buyout firm Kohlberg, Kravis, Roberts (KKR) setting a furious pace. Kravis personally contributed at least $112,000 to the Bush effort (most of it in "soft" money), arranged a Wall Street lunch that took in more than $500,000 for the candidate and was named finance co-chairman for the Bush New York campaign.

The buyout community began breathing easier when, two weeks later, Treasury Secretary Nicholas Brady—a longtime Wall Streeter himself, though from a more conservative line—testified on LBO mania before two congressional panels. His statement was a mild replay of a common criticism of LBOs, that they are simply financial devices designed for the outrageous profit of a few investors with little regard for the long term. "I have a gnawing feeling that we are headed in the wrong direction," said Brady, "when so much of our young talent and the nation's financial resources are aimed at financial engineering while the rest of the world is laying the foundation for the future." Yet despite his disapproval, which Wall Street knew came from the heart, Brady offered Congress no proposals for change.

And by the time Treasury again went before the House Ways and Means Committee, nearly four months later, Wall Street was finding the administration as comfortable as an old shoe. A Brady emissary not only failed to offer specific suggestions on how to curb the LBO trend but rejected those of the committee as well. Dan Rostenkowski (D-Ill.), chairman of the powerful tax-writing panel and one of many who thought Brady's testimony had opened the door a crack for congressional action, was fuming: "The best you can do is tell us you are monitoring and you are concerned. . . Why has Secretary Brady changed his position?"

And so goes the tale of how Washington backed off from tackling an issue that, nearly a year ago, had promised to bring a kind of public reckoning of Wall Street's increasingly speculative, debt-ridden ways.

Policymakers haven't sat still for lack of popular support. In a February public opinion poll taken for the *National Law Journal*, 84 percent of the respondents said they believed mergers and acquisitions take place in a corrupt environment, and two-thirds singled out LBOs for stiffer government regulation. But public backing was no match for the riches and personal ties of Wall Streeters with Washington, their constant generation of confusing economic data and their ability to feed the dread, especially in Congress, of triggering another Black Monday.

As one critic, economist Robert Reich, observes, "Congress and the administration were simply afraid to act, and the inhibitory mechanism was primarily Wall Street's connections with Washington"—not the least of which, of course, is money. A *Common Cause Magazine* analysis of contributions by 239 of the individuals most active in LBOs, along with 54 wives and offspring who also gave, attests to their generosity: In 1987–88 practitioners at well-known buyout boutiques, as well as some of the key executives and buyout artists at larger houses like Salomon Brothers, gave a total of $3.5 million to presidential candidates, members of Congress, Republican and Democratic party committees and PACs. And that doesn't come close to reflecting the total contributions by Wall Streeters and those in the securities industry generally, many of whom profit through business generated by the buyout deals.

The return for the LBO community wasn't votes—there was nothing to vote on. That, in fact, was the goal: inaction by both Congress and the executive branch—a prize the buyout community valued as highly as any affirmative government handout.

THE RJR CATALYST

Popular among those who master-mind corporate mergers and acquisitions, LBOs are financed almost wholly with debt, or leverage. Investors, often including a company's managers and a small group of investment bankers, use the company's assets as collateral on some package of loans and high-interest "junk" bonds they put together, along with a small equity contribution of their own, to buy up the firm's public stock.

Almost immediately, the new owners must begin slashing costs to whittle down the debt. Often parts of the company are sold to raise cash. Capital expenditures and research and development outlays frequently are cut. Critics say workers often pay a price through layoffs, frozen wages or other forced concessions. Witness the recent dismissal of more than 1,600 workers at RJR in Durham, N.C.—a layoff that analysts attribute as much to the effects of the buyout as to the decreased demand for tobacco products.

If the leveraged company brings its debt under control a few years down the line, the owners take it public again by selling the stock. Assuming all goes well, it's the "pot of gold" they've been waiting for, and can mean a return of as much as 10 to 20 times their initial investment.

Fans say LBOs are an antidote to the conglomeration trend of past years and that they pare clumsy, outsized firms down to streamlined, efficient units. It's sometimes true. Highly leveraged companies, though, court disaster if threatened by a recession or other unforeseen development; dismemberment or bankruptcy may be the only escape. Some deals can run into trouble even in the absence of a downturn. In mid-August, Seamen's Furniture Co., a New York firm, and SCI Television Inc., both KKR buyouts, announced they couldn't make their debt payments.

LBOs, and the marketing of junk bonds to finance them, increased at a spectacular rate during the mid-1980s, thanks in part to the prowess of junk-bond magician Michael Milken, recently indicted for insider trading and numerous other securities law violations. Yet it wasn't until the RJR buyout that Washington took serious notice. The sheer size of the deal guaranteed attention; at $25 billion, it was more than triple the largest previous LBO. But added to the huge price tag were some particularly unsavory features.

There was, for example, the fact that RJR head Ross Johnson had put his own company into play and proposed an LBO that would have enriched him by more than $100 million. There was the widely publicized braggadocio of Kravis: Soon after hearing of Johnson's bid, Kravis vowed to do the deal to protect KKR's status as No. 1 LBO agent. And when the dust

settled, there were some disturbing numbers. KKR reportedly was putting up only $15 million of its own money to leverage a $25 billion deal—
the equivalent of putting down $60 on a $100,000 house—and earned $75
million in fees for engineering the deal. Ultimately KKR is expected to
earn even more in fees by selling off parts of RJR and taking the company
public again.

All this gave substance to the widespread belief that LBOs were being
driven by greed. And there was no telling when the buyout binge was
going to stop. "All but a few of the largest [American] corporations may be
candidates for an LBO," concluded a Salomon Brothers study in the wake
of the RJR deal.

Sensing popular discontent, key members of Congress spoke out immediately following the bidding war for RJR. In early November, Senate
Minority Leader Robert Dole (R-Kan.) told an American Stock Exchange
conference that corporate buyouts did not contribute to the U.S. economy
and that LBO loans fed on loopholes in the tax code. Then-House Speaker
Jim Wright (D-Texas) told reporters in late November that the government
should act swiftly to stem LBOs, saying the "intensification and concentration of economic wealth into the hands of fewer and fewer have begun
to erode the broad base of the American economy." Shortly afterward,
Sen. Lloyd Bentsen (D-Texas), chairman of the Senate Finance Committee, scheduled hearings, saying leveraged buyouts "have gotten out of
hand."

By New Year's Day no fewer than nine congressional committees had
announced they would hold hearings. On Wall Street a few investment
bankers who had qualms about some of the deals quietly welcomed the
scrutiny. But the toughest players on the Street were prepared to do battle
because of their huge stakes in the lucrative system.

As one investment banker has acknowledged, "Never before have so
many people made so much money for doing so little." While traditional
Wall Street is in a slump (more than 17,000 employees have lost their jobs
since October 1987), the kingpins of mergers, LBOs and junk bonds still
pull in staggering salaries. Most can't match the $550 million pay of junk
bond czar Milken in 1987, but senior buyout engineers at KKR each took in
about $50 million last year, according to *Financial World*. Today more than
150 buyout boutiques and departments of long-established Wall Street
firms are doing LBOs—up from half-a-dozen in 1981—and their deals
totaled more than $65 billion in 1988.

The fever that's seized Wall Street has completely changed the rules of
the financial world. The new crowd views old-fashioned stock and bond
traders as drudges and says traditional corporate indicators like net earnings don't count for much anymore. A corporation is prized more for its
breakup value and cash flow, because the higher a company's cash flow,
the more a buyout artist can borrow to buy it. Stocks are increasingly

bought and sold solely according to whether a firm is likely to attract a bid. "What's going on," says Louis Lowenstein, a professor of finance and law at Columbia University, "is that people are trying to guess the next takeover target."

Put another way, "There's pervasive greed going on," says Rep. Byron Dorgan (D-N.D.), one of the Ways and Means members pushing hardest to curb the buyout binge. With the fees, profits and environment that make these deals attractive at risk, the buyout barons were hardly going to sit idly by while Washington threatened.

A LEVERAGED ADMINISTRATION

While most of the criticism was coming from Congress, both Wall Street and Capitol Hill knew that any effort not supported by the administration would be tough going, if only because of the LBO interests' economic and political clout. Everyone realized it "would stir up very powerful political forces—very powerful and well-financed forces," as Jamie Heard, a consultant to institutional investors, notes. But there was another reason why the Democrat-controlled Congress was wary about pursuing the complex issue without executive branch leadership.

Back in the fall of 1987, with the stock market rising on a seemingly inexhaustible pyramid of speculation and creative debt, Ways and Means approved a measure that would have slowed down takeovers and buyouts by limiting the deductibility of interest for debt incurred in such transactions. Less than a week later, Black Monday brought the biggest one-day plunge in the history of the stock exchange, and some observers say that the proposal was at least a trigger. A study released last May by the Securities and Exchange Commission's Office of Economic Analysis suggested that the bill's restrictions "were a fundamental economic event" that helped precipitate the crash.

The Democrats could have used the episode as proof that the market was riding on sheer speculation rather than sound economics. Instead, they became defensive and backed off. Being blamed for the crash "is a factor," says Rep. Sander Levin (D-Mich.), "even though I don't think we had much to do with it."

If the administration's position was pivotal, then the LBO community had every reason to believe it was at least holding several aces, if not all the cards. First, there's a certain traditional coziness between the financial community and the parts of the executive branch that bear most closely on its interests—especially under Republican administrations. Brady was cochairman of the Dillon, Read investment banking house until he was tapped by Reagan and then Bush to head Treasury. Pete Peterson, a founding partner of one of the largest LBO firms, the Blackstone Group, was secretary of Commerce under Nixon, and David Stockman, director of the Office of Management and Budget in the early '80s, went first to Salomon Brothers and then to Blackstone.

And during the campaign, Bush had pushed all the right buttons with Wall Street by proclaiming himself heir to the pro-market, anti-regulatory economic environment nurtured under Reagan. The buyout interests had responded by going all out financially for the Bush campaign, apparently banking on the hope that if elected, he would keep America safe for deals.

The high-flying financiers of Wall Street with their European suits, Armani ties and (as writer Tom Wolfe would put it) "masters of the universe" egos are in an exalted league when it comes to their relationships with Washington policymakers. Small in number, big in clout, Wall Streeters, and particularly some of the prominent LBO artists, are profligate political spenders.

The support of buyout interests for Bush was plain early on—witness the Kravis fundraising lunch only six weeks after the stock market meltdown. More than $1.3 million in individual contributions went to the Bush campaign from 239 of those prominent in the buyout world and their families. Those individuals gave at least $103,300 directly to Bush, compared with $30,450 for Dukakis. But the big bucks, often in contributions as large as $100,000 each, went to "soft" money accounts—at least $1.2 million to Bush, compared with $269,000 to Dukakis. (Soft money allows large donors to skirt the $1,000 per candidate per election contribution limit. Ostensibly earmarked for party-building activities, soft money is in fact generally given and used to support the presidential candidates. Each party has voluntarily disclosed some, but not all, of its soft money receipts.) Another $516,900 went to Republican national committees, as against $141,650 to comparable Democratic committees.

Only Hollywood and the Oil Patch rival Wall Street's ability to raise political money from wealthy individuals. As Ed Zuckerman, editor of the newsletter *PACs & Lobbies*, has noted, "the real money [from Wall Street] is going through the personal checkbook." Wall Street partners "tithe Washington," says Bart Naylor, a former investigator for the Senate Banking committee, much as some Americans give to the church of their choice.

The impact of just one buyout boutique, KKR, is impressive. Kravis and his partner George Roberts each gave at least $100,000 to the Bush soft money drive, thereby earning a place on "Team 100." KKR has only 19 professionals, but they and a few of their wives managed to give a total of $418,200 to the Bush presidential bid and various political committees. Other $100,000 donors included Nicholas and Theodore Forstmann and Brian Little of Forstmann, Little; Stephen Schwarzman of the Blackstone Group; and Frank Richardson and Raymond Chambers from Wesray. Some of the firms themselves gave soft money to the Bush effort. Wesray anted up with at least $100,000, as did Paine Webber (which does a number of things besides buyouts); Blackstone gave at least $90,000. Not all the money went to Republicans, of course—Jerome Kohlberg, a founding partner of KKR who left to start another firm, Kohlberg & Co., was a managing trustee of the Democrats' soft money Victory Fund, meaning he pledged to raise $500,000 for Dukakis. But the GOP was clearly favored.

The clout of the buyout industry, moreover, is not limited to the artists themselves. There are also the contributions of the mammoth commercial banks and insurance companies that finance these deals, and especially the small, tight circle of Wall Street law firms retained whenever "premium dealwork" promises to yield millions of dollars in legal fees. The runaway favorite of many buyout artists, Skadden, Arps, Slate, Meagher & Flom, reportedly lobbied on its own behalf when LBOs were under fire.

Financial generosity goes hand-in-hand with becoming part of the Washington scene. "Obviously the people who give want to be invited to the party, the White House, the lunch, the dinner," says veteran political consultant David Garth. "They're doing nothing but trying to get some access." And high-level entrée is enjoyed by major donors. In late June, for instance, Kravis and his fashion designer wife, Carolyne Roehm, helicoptered down to Washington for dinner at the home of top Bush fundraiser and Commerce Secretary Robert Mosbacher and his wife Georgette, where they mingled with the likes of Republican National Committee chairman Lee Atwater, House Speaker Tom Foley (D-Wash.) and Michael Boskin, chairman of the president's Council of Economic Advisers.

Still, administration support wasn't a fait accompli. Before his January testimony, the Treasury secretary himself, despite his Wall Street background, was viewed as a potential obstacle. One of the most intriguing divisions on Wall Street pits old money, in the person of Treasury's Brady, against the new, cocky and frequently ostentatious buyout entrepreneurs who now reign. Brady is a man of caution. Uncomfortable with the speculative excesses that LBOs represent, he had avoided using junk bonds while at Dillon, Read—and even wrote and testified against their use.

His unease, in part, reflects his concern about where most of the cash needed to pay for LBOs is coming from—the federal government's shrinking coffers. "The substitution of tax-deductible interest charges for [taxable] income is the mill in which the grist of takeover premiums is ground," Brady told Congress in late January. Under the tax code, companies can write off interest payments on debt. Nearly every leveraged company pays no income taxes during the first two years or so after a buyout. Some even get large refunds because the interest write-offs can be applied against past taxes. RJR Nabisco, for example, may get back a substantial chunk of the $1 billion it paid in taxes in the three years prior to the buyout.

NEUTRALIZING CONGRESS

The focus on the administration didn't mean buyout interests ignored Capitol Hill. Although key players in the buyout world overwhelmingly favor the Republican Party and its presidential candidates, they are more pragmatic than partisan when giving to members of Congress—particularly when it comes to members on the banking and tax-writing committees. Democrats, who control both houses, received $517,500 from the 239 buyout activists and their families, versus $440,000 to Republicans in 1987–88. The top 10 Banking and Finance recipients in the Senate—far more popular than the House with this group—took in $222,000 in individual contributions from LBO players. While PACs connected with firms with LBO funds give negligible amounts to presidential contenders, they donated a generous $255,197 to the top 10 Senate Banking and Finance recipients. Two of the 10 senators weren't up for reelection in that cycle.

Both of New York's senators, Democrat Daniel Moynihan (who sits on the Finance Committee) and Republican Alfonse D'Amato (on Banking) are widely perceived as being well disposed to Wall Street's perspective. The latter is considered more than sympathetic. "They own D'Amato," says critic Louis Lowenstein. In 1985, when D'Amato chaired a Senate securities subcommittee, he killed a junk bond amendment opposed by Drexel Burnham Lambert, which pioneered the financing mechanism, during a period when he received more than $41,000 in political contributions from Drexel partners, according to the *Wall Street Journal*. In 1987–88 D'Amato, who wasn't up for reelection, took in more than $30,000 from LBO interests, including their PACs. Moynihan received more than $50,000.

Members of the leadership are also favorite money targets. In March 1988, when Rep. Foley was House majority leader, 41 executives of the securities firm Salomon Brothers (which has many interests, including a growing LBO fund) attended a $500-per-person breakfast fundraiser for him or sent in their checks. In all, Foley took in at least $27,500 from Salomon executives in 1987–88.

The largest amount, however, went to Sen. Bill Bradley (D-N.J.), a smart, economically conservative member of the Finance Committee. Bradley is not up for reelection until 1990, but is considered possible presidential material. In 1987–88 he took in at least $96,000 from individuals in the buyout community, including more than 60 individual contributions of $1,000 each from employees of just two firms that are heavily into buyouts, Wesray and Hambrecht & Quist. William Hambrecht and his wife and children alone gave Bradley $14,000, some of it at a fundraiser Hambrecht held for the candidate at his California home in February 1987. Bradley's staffer on the issue says the senator isn't sure there is a buyout problem or how to fix it if there is one.

Supplementing Wall Street money are the skill and PAC contributions of its trade group, the Securities Industry Association (SIA). The current SIA chairman, Hardwick Simmons, is also vice chairman of Shearson Lehman Hutton and personally lobbies members of Congress. "The SIA has been very active," Simmons says. "We've tried to play the role of wise counselor."

Add the lobbying of powerhouse law firms like Cadwalader, Wickersham & Taft or Davis, Polk & Wardwell and it makes for a formidable interest group. The connections of these firms are telling. Cadwalader's J. Roger Mentz, for instance, a lobbyist for leading buyout firm Clayton & Dubilier, is former deputy assistant secretary of Treasury for tax policy. Former Senate Finance Committee staff director William Diefenderfer's firm, Wunder & Diefenderfer, registered to lobby for KKR in February. To show how quickly the door can spin, he's now back in government as deputy director at the Office of Management and Budget.

"Access is available to those who pay lobbyists, who make contributions," says Jon Sheiner, a staffer to Ways and Means Committee member Rep. Charles Rangel (D-N.Y.). "Money makes a difference—it creates the access, the camaraderie." Sheiner says Rangel met with Kravis because "he knew the lobbyist representing him."

Some argue that Wall Street's contributions haven't been especially significant on the LBO issue. Says Rep. Levin, "There are so many hoops, you never know which one is decisive. In this case, if [Wall Street's contributions] are a hoop, it's a small hoop. The main reason we haven't done anything is there's tremendous uncertainty."

DIVERSIONARY TACTICS

But by using its relatively easy access, the LBO gang was able to effectively exploit that uncertainty and cultivate confusion. Armed with data and a host of reports prepared or paid for by the industry itself, Wall Street sought to prevent Congress from arriving at a consensus on how to approach the LBO issue.

At a Ways and Means hearing in early February, after more than a day of testimony pro and con, Levin went to the heart of the matter, asking respected economist Henry Kaufman whether Congress needed to move even in the absence of an administration position. "If you were here, instead of where you are," Levin queried Kaufman, "would you act this session?" Replied Kaufman, "If I were there, which is a difficult place to be, I would, based on my recommendations, certainly act."

The suggestions of Kaufman and others included imposing an excise tax on the fees earned in these types of transactions; penalizing short-term capital gains; prohibiting federally insured banks and pension funds from making LBO loans; and eliminating the deductibility of interest for takeover- and buyout-related debt, or in some other way equalizing the tax treatment of equity and debt (the current system does not allow corporations to deduct dividends paid to shareholders, which provides one incentive for going into debt).

But befuddlement and fear had eroded December's blustery congressional front. The buyout interests had come up with two refrains. First, they said, buyouts are good for the economy. Second, they warned, if there is something wrong, the cure could be worse than the disease.

To document the first contention, some of the top firms prepared their own studies. The first and most important was a KKR report released in January, when Congress was hearing a drumbeat of mostly critical news reports about LBOs. KKR claimed outstanding results, not only for investors, but the economy as a whole. According to its study, KKR's buyouts increased employment, led to more research and development, yielded higher taxes to the government and kept capital spending high.

Independent confirmation—or refutation—of these claims was hard to come by because once a buyout target goes private it usually stops reporting to the Securities and Exchange Commission. This added to the KKR report's impact, as did its selective distribution. Most of the press was shut out, but key members of Congress, especially friendly ones, were given copies. Once, after AFL-CIO chairman Lane Kirkland finished his testimony before the Senate Finance Committee, Sen. Robert Packwood (R-Ore.) held up the study and said it contradicted Kirkland's testimony—KKR claimed its buyouts had added 37,000 jobs to the economy. Kirkland was of course unable to refute a figure based on information he wasn't privy to.

Not everyone on the Hill swallowed the report, of course. But only the House Subcommittee on Telecommunications and Finance asked some of the buyout firms for detailed data on their deals. The request, made of KKR, Merrill Lynch and Shearson Lehman Hutton, was met with howls of protest. One buyout lobbyist labeled the request a "witch-hunt."

Weeks passed, and most of the information never came. Meanwhile, though, the telecommunications subcommittee, chaired by Rep. Ed Markey (D-Mass.), had another hearing. This time, Bill Long, a former Federal Trade Commission economist who was researching buyouts at the Brookings Institution, took apart the KKR study's methodology, arguing that the report proved only that its LBOs yielded high profits to investors. Nearly all the other claims were misleading, Long argued; the study's avowed increases in R&D, employment and capital spending rested not on actual figures but optimistic projections.

But Long's testimony came late—in May—well after the KKR study was accepted on Capitol Hill as "self-serving but solid," in the words of financial columnist Jerry Knight of *The Washington Post*.

Meanwhile the LBO lobby fed the Democrats' nagging fear of being blamed for Black Monday. In a June full-page ad in *Roll Call*, a Capitol Hill newspaper, under the headline "A word to those who would limit LBOs through tax proposals," Merrill Lynch warned that limiting the interest deduction for debt "could have a serious negative effect on the stock market, just as many concluded that similar proposals had in October 1987."

The buyout crowd also frequently pointed out that attempts to limit interest deductions would give foreign bidders an advantage over U.S. bidders in acquiring American corporations. Congress generally missed the hypocrisy: Buyout artists often sell off parts of their acquisitions to foreign purchasers, who are increasingly Japanese, to help reduce their debt on deals. And the Japanese own significant chunks of some of the buyout firms themselves, including Blackstone, the Lodestar Group and Wasserstein, Perella & Co.

Their arguments, however, were almost never made publicly. When House Banking Committee Chairman Henry Gonzalez opened his hearings, he asked leading commercial and investment banking houses to testify. All said no. "This desire by both groups to be silent clearly says volumes," Gonzalez observed. His committee was not the only one that was having trouble rounding up key witnesses. At 17 days of hearings over five months, only two buyout boutiques agreed to testify, and they weren't from the top 10 buyout firms.

Instead, the top buyout people like Kravis, Forstmann and Kohlberg and their lobbyists made their rounds at private meetings on Capitol Hill. In addition to visiting most members of the Senate Finance Committee, Kravis sought out some of the harshest critics of buyouts. "The big guys come around here and get in to see everybody," says Rep. Dorgan.

Even in private the buyout artists set some limits. At one point Rostenkowski wanted to arrange a breakfast seminar for committee members, one that would feature Kravis, the no-holds-barred LBO advocate; Forstmann, a Kravis rival who differs with him on some LBO financing techniques; and Lowenstein, a prominent critic of the whole game. But Kravis would not agree to be in the same room with the others, and the powerful Rostenkowski accommodated him. Kravis came with his partner Roberts to one breakfast, and Forstmann and Lowenstein debated at another.

THE SOBERING FINALE

If Congress started out intent on doing something, the absence of leadership from the executive branch coupled with a tenacious and intimidating lobby dulled its impulse. Currently the only congressional proposals that would directly affect buyouts and are viewed as having a chance of passing are one from Sen. Bentsen to stop leveraged companies from getting refunds on taxes paid before the deal; and one from Ways and Means, similar to the administration's only proposal, to disallow interest deductions on certain types of financing instruments. Most experts believe both proposals, while they might marginally affect the pricing of buyouts, would do little to hamper the deals themselves.

Economist Kaufman predicts that LBOs will become a more potent political issue when a recession hits and hundreds of companies with weakened financial structures prove unable to service their bloated debts. A downturn like that of 1981–82, according to some estimates, could double the number of corporate bankruptcies, and the government would be pressured to bail out failing companies. Worse still, the crisis could spill over to banks, pension funds and insurance companies involved in the buyout mania, requiring further federal intervention. Washington's delay in dealing with the corporate debt situation, exemplified by LBOs, suggests sobering parallels to Third World debt and the S&L crisis.

"I think we're very much thrashing around," says Rep. Levin. "All is far from well."

III

Inequality

In the 1950s and 1960s many social scientists described the United States as an "affluent" society—one in which most people could expect a steady improvement in their standard of living, great disparities in income and wealth were fast disappearing, and true poverty was soon to be a thing of the past. These perceptions were based on some undeniable facts. On average, Americans' incomes did rise substantially after World War II, and during the 1960s millions of the poor were lifted above the official poverty line. It was natural to believe that these trends would continue.

But even in the expanding economy of the 1950s and 1960s, there were important limits to what some believed was a steady march toward greater equality. For one thing, even the progress in raising the overall standard of living had virtually no impact on the *distribution* of income and wealth in America—the gap between rich and poor. Throughout most of the period since World War II, the upper one-fifth of income earners received roughly 40 percent of the country's total personal income; the bottom fifth, about 5 percent. And, although poverty was sharply reduced in many rural areas, it proved to be much more stubborn in the inner cities.

More recently the trends have become much more discouraging: the limited postwar progress toward economic equality has been reversed. By the early 1980s, the spread of income inequality in the United States had begun to increase as the share of the most affluent began a slow but perceptible shift upward and the share of the poor fell correspondingly: At the beginning of the 1990s, income inequality had reached its most extreme level since World War II. Poverty, too, rose sharply from the late 1970s onward. And, under the impact of recession, inflation, and slower economic growth, the living standards of many American families began a steady decline.

As the article by Elliott Currie, Robert Dunn, and David Fogarty shows, that decline has struck unevenly among different sectors of the population, creating new and complex patterns of inequality. Broad changes in the economy have deeply affected living standards, work, and family life in the United States and have profoundly altered what many Americans can expect from the future. Currie, Dunn, and Fogarty argue that currently fashionable policies designed to boost the overall economy will not restore the American dream of equality in abundance. If anything, they may aggravate existing inequalities and contribute to the impoverishment and desperation of millions of Americans. For this edition of *Crisis in American Institutions*, Currie, Dunn, and Fogarty have added a postscript describing the changes—and similarities—in the "New Inequality" since the early 1980s.

Currie, Dunn, and Fogarty see new kinds of poverty emerging in the United States along with new kinds of affluence. Unfortunately, recent events bear out their prediction. In an earlier edition of this book, we wrote that "the size of the poverty population has remained depressingly unchanged for a decade." Today we cannot make that statement, for things are even more depressing. The proportion of Americans living below the poverty line has increased dramatically since the end of the 1970s: between 1979 and 1988, close to 9 million people joined the ranks of the poor.

Perhaps the most tragic aspect of this increase in poverty is that it has been fastest for America's children. Today more than one child in five in the United States is living below the federal government's poverty line. Many people are aware that childhood poverty is widespread in this country; fewer realize that it is much more prevalent here than in most other industrial societies. As Timothy Smeeding and Barbara Boyle Torrey show in their article, "Poor Children in Rich Countries," only Australia among other rich countries comes close to our rate of poverty among families and children. Their research also makes it clear that this gap between the United States and other nations doesn't simply reflect the often discussed breakdown of the American family and the rise of the single-parent household. Sweden, with a higher proportion of single-parent families, has a far lower percentage of children who are living in poverty.

Poverty is more than a matter of income alone. One of the most devastating, and most visible, consequences of rising poverty (among other causes) has been the growth of homelessness in the United States. Peter Rossi's article, "Why We Have Homelessness," which is based on original research on Chicago's homeless population, carefully disentangles the multiple roots of homelessness. Though many forces contribute to the problem—including high levels of mental and physical disability—Rossi reminds us that, in the final analysis, the spread of homelessness means that our housing market is simply failing to provide sufficient shelter that the poor can afford.

The final article in this chapter, "Hunger in America: The Growing Epidemic," written by a group of physicians who recently toured the country to witness the problem firsthand, illustrates even more starkly the real-life consequences of rising poverty. In this excerpt from their report, the doctors describe some of the shocking conditions they discovered—ironically enough—in America's traditional "breadbasket," the Midwest. They found people in Chicago living on dog food, mothers watering down their babies' formula so it would last through the month, elderly people so inured to starvation that they no longer felt hungry. In the Declaration of Independence, "life" is enshrined as one of the three "inalienable rights" that flow to Americans by virtue of having been "created equal." The threat of starvation in the midst of great wealth surely violates that right—and mocks the most basic American ideals.

9

The Fading Dream: Economic Crisis and the New Inequality

Elliott Currie, Robert Dunn, and David Fogarty

In the 1980s, no one any longer doubts that the United States is in the midst of a deep crisis in expectations. In the 1950s and 1960s, most Americans were led to believe in a future of indefinite economic expansion. Rising living standards, it was said, had made most people feel part of the "middle class." Real economic deprivation, to the extent that it was acknowledged at all, was presumed to be confined to the margins of the "affluent" society.

The combination of economic stagnation and high inflation—"stagflation"—in the 1970s replaced that rosy vision with the sense that the United States was slipping rapidly into economic decline. Suddenly the celebrated American standard of living seemed to be falling precipitously, and the easy optimism was quickly displaced by gloom and anxiety about the future. Faith in the "American Dream" disintegrated with dizzying speed, bringing fear, resentment, and a widespread demand to "turn the country around" at whatever cost. Today, some variant of a program for economic "revitalization" is on everyone's agenda, at all points on the political spectrum.

But beyond the sense of crisis and the urgent call for change, there is remarkably little agreement about the degree to which the era of "stagflation" has actually damaged American standards of living or clouded the prospects for the future. *Fortune* magazine recently described, with

Elliott Currie, Robert Dunn, and David Fogarty, "The Fading Dream " from *Socialist Review*, No. 54, November/December 1980. Reprinted by permission.

considerable accuracy, the national pessimism about the state of the economy:

> Of all the changes in American society during the Seventies, none was more fundamental than the erosion of faith in the future. By the end of the decade, the conviction that the material aspects of life will get a little bit better each year had given way to the bleakness of spirit known as diminishing expectations. It seems that most people nowadays aspire to little more than holding on to what they've already got, and many become downright despondent when they contemplate the world their children will inherit.

Fortune hastened to assure us, however, that such "dour resignation" was "out of phase" with the "upbeat outlook" for family income in the 1980s and also exaggerated what really happened during the 1970s. Many groups "did a lot better in the 1970s than is generally appreciated." The real problem, *Fortune* insisted, was psychological; people's expectations had been too high to begin with, so they "didn't *think* they were doing particularly well."

The disagreement has been sharpest over the impact of inflation. The business-oriented Committee for Economic Development, for example, describing inflation as a "pernicious addiction," declared that "the damage inflation does to the fabric of both our economic system and our society is so great that it must not be allowed to proceed unchecked." On the other hand, others have argued, with the economist Robert Heilbroner, that whatever dangers inflation may hold for the future, its impact on current living standards has been "much less than we commonly believe." "Despite our sense of being impoverished by inflation," Heilbroner writes, inflation has not "substantially" affected the "national standard of well-being and comfort."

Which of these views is accurate? As with so many social issues, the answers we get depend greatly on the kinds of questions we ask. In what follows, we want to delve beneath the conventional statistics on income and earnings to ask a different, and broader, set of questions about the way the economic crisis has affected social life and living standards in the United States.

In particular, we want to address two crucial problems in the usual statistics and the debates based on them: (1) They tell us nothing about the measures people have had to take in order to cope with recession and inflation, and (2) they are *averages* that tell us nothing about how *different groups* have fared under the impact of economic crisis.

The answers to these questions are crucial to an understanding of the social impact of the current economic crisis and, consequently, for evaluating policies that claim to confront it. We will look at the way inflation and recession have affected work and family life, patterns of saving and debt, and the availability of housing and jobs, and will argue that neither the relatively optimistic view—that the crisis has had only a mild effect on living standards—nor the more drastic vision of a massive economic decline adequately conveys what has happened to American life under the impact of "stagflation."

The real picture is more complicated. Developments in the economy have brought a complex sorting of the population into "winners" and "losers"—a recomposition, or reshuffling of the deck, rather than a uniform decline. On the one hand, many American families have maintained living standards, if at all, only by working harder, sacrificing leisure and family life, and/or mortgaging their futures and those of their children. Those hardest hit by the economic crisis, and with the least resources to cope with it, have suffered real decline; poverty-level styles of life have appeared among people who once thought of themselves as part of the "middle class." Some of the basics of the "American Dream"—the home of one's own, the successful job as the reward for education and effort— have moved, for all practical purposes, beyond their reach. At the same time, at the other end of the scale is a new affluence for the relative "winners" in the restructuring of social and economic life in America.

Increasingly, one's chances of affluence or poverty, comfort or insecurity, are crucially determined by a complex web of conditions that includes not only one's sex, color, and age, but also family composition, position in the housing market, and much more. One implication of this complex trend—as we will see—is that policies of economic "renewal" designed to stimulate the economy as a whole through such means as cuts in taxes and social spending may only accelerate the re-sorting of the American population into affluent "winners" and impoverished "losers." And the destruction of the social programs that have traditionally cushioned the blows suffered by those "losers" can only hasten the process.

THE PLIGHT OF THE THREE-JOB FAMILY

How we define the contours of a problem depends crucially on the way we choose to measure it. Measured in terms of overall family income, the rapid growth in living standards that fed rising expectations throughout postwar America came to an abrupt halt in the early 1970s. The median income for all American families approximately doubled (in constant dollars) between 1950 and 1973. But it fell—by over a thousand dollars— during the recession of the mid-1970s and by 1979 had inched back no further than its level of six years before.

Some economists dispute the relevance of these figures, arguing that real living standards actually *rose* even at the height of the mid-1970s "stagflation." This view is based on the argument that *per capita* income— total personal income divided by the number of people—is a much better measure, since it allows us to take account of the statistical impact of population changes. For example, since families are smaller, on the average, than they used to be, measures of overall family income will give a misleading picture of trends in how well-off families are: What we need to know is the income available per person, which may have increased even while total family income has stagnated. As Lester Thurow argues, "from 1972 to 1978, real per capita disposable income rose 16%. After accounting for inflation, taxes, and population growth, real incomes have gone up, not down. The average American is better off, not worse off."

What this argument ignores is that behind the soothing figures on per capita income is the grinding reality that, for many families, that income has been achieved only by sending more people to work. The clearest evidence of this fact comes when we look not simply at income per family or per person, but per *worker*. Thus discretionary income—basically, disposable income minus expenditures for necessities and transfer payments—declined by about 5 percent between 1973 and 1979. But this figure ignores one of the most striking features of the 1970s—the great increase in the number of people working. As *Business Week* points out, "Adjusting discretionary income for the huge recent increases in employment, to reflect the sweat that goes into producing that income, shows that discretionary income per worker over the past six years declined by 16%." These figures show that families increasingly need two—or more—workers just to keep up, much less to "get ahead." Statistics on the trend of family incomes in the 1970s bear this out: the incomes of families with only one earner fell about 7 percent behind the cost of living from 1969 to 1978; those of two- (and three-) earner families came out about 6 percent above it.

This trend has given the family a crucial—and somewhat paradoxical—role in the contemporary economy. On the one hand, the material support of other family members is often all-important as a protection against the erosion of living standards. Such support is especially crucial for women, given the pervasive discrimination they face in the labor market. This difference is most apparent in what has been called the "feminization of poverty"; single women, especially those with young children, have become the most predictably impoverished group in America. But at the same time, increased labor places severe strains on many dual-earner families. The need for two incomes in such families means that three jobs are now being done for the price of one—two in the paid labor force, one unpaid—the household and child-rearing tasks done in the home. As the work time needed to keep up with living costs increases, something has to give. And there is considerable evidence that often what is "giving" is the quality of family life.

On the one hand, the tasks of child-rearing and housework are often being pushed out of the home—usually to the private sector—as working people, if they can afford to, consume more and more day care, fast food, and even paid housekeeping. (One result is the rapid growth of low-wage, quasi-domestic "service" occupations that both cater to the needs of the multiearner household and often supply what passes for job opportunities for the second earner.) On the other hand, especially for those who cannot afford outside services, modern family life often means a decline in the possibility of real leisure—or, what amounts to the same thing, an increase in the pace of life, a kind of social "speedup" resembling the deliberately increased pace of an industrial assembly line. With an extra job to do and little public provision for domestic services, many people wind up routinely cutting corners, compressing their lives, and feeling "hassled" much of the time they are supposedly "off the job." While this situation has always been the fate of many lower-income working families, it is now becoming a predictable aspect of the lives of many who once saw themselves as part of the "middle class."

But—like other effects of the rising cost of living—the burden of this "social speedup" has not been evenly distributed among working people. Instead, it has served to widen the gap between men and women and between income groups, in ways that are obscured by the conventional statistics on income and earnings.

Most of the extra work brought by the "speedup" has fallen on women—both because they are most of the second earners in the paid labor force and because paid work has not freed most women from unpaid work in the home. Instead, the extra job that women do has most often been coupled with continuing responsibility for running the household. As Willard Wirtz, head of the National Commission on Working Women, puts it,

> For a great many women, taking a job outside the home isn't a matter of substituting one kind of work for another; what it means is double duty. . . . If limited opportunities on the new job away from home are part of the problem, the rest of it is the unchanging terms and conditions of the job at home. When all the old duties still have to be performed, body and mind sag under the double burden.

Much of that burden involves child care. A 1978 study by the University of Michigan's Survey Research Center found that nearly half of women working in the paid labor force, versus only 13 percent of men, reported spending 3½ hours or more—*on working days*—with their children. Forty-four percent also reported spending an additional 3½ hours on other household chores.

It is remarkable, in fact, how closely the overall working time of typical two-earner families matches the time requirements of three full-time jobs—and what a large proportion of the "third job" falls to women. Another recent study found that among working couples, the men spent an average of about 9 hours a week on family care, the women an average of about 29 hours. At the same time, the men averaged 44, to the women's

40, hours of paid work (because men were more often in jobs with frequent overtime). Put together, this amounts to an average of 69 hours of work a week for women, 53 for men, or 122 altogether for a family—the equivalent of three full-time jobs.

For many women, then, entering the labor force to keep the family standard of living intact has meant more work, less leisure, and a more harried family life. What one critic has called the "overwhelming poverty of time" in these families is given abundant testimony in a national survey of women wage-earners undertaken by the National Commission on Working Women. An astonishing 55 percent of the women surveyed reported having *no* leisure time; 39 percent had no time to pursue education. Only 14 percent were able to say that job and family life did not seriously interfere with each other.

There is, of course, another side to this increase in women's work. It is doubtless true that moving into the paid labor force has provided many women with wider options and may have helped undermine the traditional subordination of women in many families. But because of the persistence of the sexual division of labor in the home and the lack of adequate public support services, it has also meant that women have shouldered a disproportionate—though often hidden—share of the burdens imposed by the economic crisis. And the potential benefits in greater independence for women have also been constrained by the rising cost of living—especially in housing—which, in some areas, has made "coupling" almost an economic requirement.

Obviously, the effects of entering the labor force are different for the grocery clerk's wife who gets a job as a telephone operator than for the lawyer's wife who becomes a stockbroker or psychotherapist. And this difference illustrates one of the most striking trends of the stagflation era. For women who have the resources to enter well-paying and rewarding jobs, and to afford the costs of the private-sector "industrialization" of domestic services, the "two-paycheck" family can represent an enviable and liberating way of life. At the other end of the scale, it can mean a virtually unrelieved round of dull, rote work, in and out of the home. And the distance between these two ways of life is growing—in part because an increasing proportion of the wives entering the paid labor force comes from more affluent families, with the result that, as a Labor Department study puts it, "the gap between above-average income families and below-average income families will widen" in the coming years.

As access to extra work becomes more and more important in maintaining or improving standards of living, we can expect this gap to widen for another reason as well. Not everyone has the *opportunity* to take on more work—even relatively unrewarding work—in response to threats to their living standards. In a survey of how different kinds of families coped with recession and inflation, David Caplovitz found that about two out of five tried to handle inflation by working more—either sending more family members to work or taking on overtime or an extra job. But poorer people, often lacking access to even *one* job, were less often able to exercise those options.

The "new impoverishment"—of time as well as income—of many American families, then, is only one side of the coin; the other is the growing affluence of some families. Between 1970 and 1977, when average family incomes barely improved at all and many families' living standards fell sharply, the proportion of families with incomes above $25,000 (in constant dollars) jumped by about 23 percent. The rise in the number of relatively affluent families was even sharper for blacks, at the same time as many blacks suffered even greater stagnation or decline in living standards.

At one end of the new scale of living standards is what *Fortune* has gushingly termed the "superclass"; those two-income families with the additional "formidable advantages of connections, intelligence, and education," whose incomes may reach six figures. At the other end is a broad stratum of the poor and nearly poor—single parents, one-earner families with low incomes, and people on fixed incomes. Somewhere in the middle are the broad ranks of two-earner families with middling incomes who must cope with the escalated costs of necessities and the increased need for domestic services, for whom even two paychecks barely cover expenses from one week to the next.

MORTGAGING THE FUTURE

Conventional data on living standards, then, obscure the enormous increases in labor—and the resulting changes in family life—that have gone into keeping up with the rising cost of living. Something similar happens with the conventional picture of working people's consumption. The fact that levels of buying and spending have, on the whole, remained remarkably high in the stagflation era is often taken as evidence that things can't be as bad as we might think. Again, though, this conclusion ignores what working people have *done* in order to maintain consumption. For many families, stagflation has meant sacrificing the future to pay for the present, making the future a source of anxiety and dread—a situation most clearly visible in the changing patterns of savings and debt.

As recently as the fourth quarter of 1975, the rate of personal saving—the proportion of people's income put away for the future—stood at 7.1 percent. By the fourth quarter of 1979, it had dropped to 3.3 percent, less than half its level only four years before. This general figure masks much lower rates of saving at the lower levels of the income ladder and among younger people, but the inability to save afflicts even many middle-class families that have otherwise been able to weather inflation's attack fairly well. As Caplovitz's survey discovered, "Even if they are able to maintain their standard of living within limits, many white collar families find for the first time that they are unable to save money."

Along with reduced saving has come rising consumer debt. The average American consumer now holds only about $3 in assets for every dollar of debt owed, compared with about $5 in the 1950s. Installment credit as a proportion of disposable income rose by about 42 percent between 1960 and 1978.

Like the increase in labor, the growth of debt has struck some people much more severely than others—in this case, particularly lower-income and younger people. Debt repayments as a percentage of disposable income were 25 percent for the lowest income fifth in 1977, only 6 percent for the highest fifth. And that disparity has been increasing steadily; the proportion rose from 19 percent for the lowest-income fifth since 1970, while it dropped slightly for the most affluent.

The result is that low-to-moderate income families have become even more highly "leveraged," in financial jargon, and hence ever more precarious financially. As a leading student of debt patterns in the United States notes, "As measured by the ratio of debt payment commitments to income, vulnerability to recession has increased, especially among the lowest 20 percent of the income distribution." Debt use is also most frequent among the young—especially younger families.

Why has debt grown—and savings evaporated—so rapidly while average family incomes have remained relatively stable? Part of the answer is that, as research by the National Center for Economic Alternatives has shown, costs for the necessities—food, energy, housing, health care—have risen much faster than the Consumer Price Index as a whole in the past few years. This rise in the cost of necessities seriously undermines the value of income even when it is measured in "real" terms—that is, adjusted for rises in the overall cost of living. Hence the sharp rise in the debt burden of families at the lower end of the income scale, where necessity costs already take a larger chunk of total income.

But there is a more subtle and less measurable reason for the growth of debt: more expenses become necessary as inflation creates its own set of escalated needs. Thus sharply rising housing prices may force a family out of easy commuting range to jobs and services, raising transportation and energy costs, perhaps requiring a second car. Paying for the extra car and the extra gas may require a second job. The second job in turn increases transportation costs still further; it may also create the need for more paid day care, and probably changes eating habits in a vastly more expensive direction—more eating out, less careful food shopping, and less economical food preparation. Thus the changes in family living patterns we noted above lead not only to increased labor, but to escalating expenses as well. At the extreme, the new expenses may cancel out most of the benefits of increased work, in an inflationary "Catch 22."

Greater "leveraging" of family income to cope with these inflation-induced "needs," as well as the rising cost of necessities, is hard to avoid, given the insufficiency of public services that could cushion the need for ever-higher individual expenditures. But this "leveraging" means that some families—again, especially younger and poorer ones—may not be able to provide for a reasonably secure future. They won't be able to send their kids to college, cope with emergencies like major illnesses or deaths, or add savings to their pensions to help ensure a decent retirement.

These issues have become especially keen because of the specter of disintegration of the traditional systems of support for old age. Although Social Security benefits have so far kept up with inflation, the entire system's funding is increasingly in jeopardy—and reduction in benefits is now on the political agenda. Living on Social Security benefits alone, in any case, is a sure ticket to poverty; and private pensions, the most common alternative support, are rarely adjusted for increases in the cost of living.

The need to sacrifice security to keep up with essentials can only have a devastating psychological impact on the quality of life. It not only makes the present more frightening, but is one reason why many can no longer look forward to the ideal of a decent old age as the reward for a lifetime of labor—and why opinion polls show that Americans, for the first time in memory, think that their children will live in conditions worse than the present. In 1979, according to a *Washington Post*/ABC News poll, 66 percent of respondents still believed that their children would be "better off" than they were, whereas 18 percent thought their children would be worse off. By March 1981, only 47 percent thought their children would be better off, and 43 percent now believed their children would lead worse lives than their own.

THE VANISHING PROSPECT FOR HOME OWNERSHIP

Coping with "stagflation," then, has meant cutting deeply into savings and going further into debt, as well as greatly increasing labor—for some people much more than others. But even with these adaptations, there are aspects of the traditional American Dream that many working people— especially the young—may never achieve, given the peculiar contours of the economic crisis. One of them, as we'll see in a moment, is the good job with reasonable chances for achievement—or at least good pay. Another is a home of one's own.

What has happened to housing represents a drastic change from traditional expectations. Decent housing, even rental housing, is fast becoming an unrealistic goal for all but a dwindling fraction of young Americans. Between 1972 and 1978, the price of an average one-family new home increased 72 percent nationally, 86 percent in the West, and much more in some high-demand metropolitan areas, while median family income increased only 40 percent. The Department of Housing and Urban Development estimates that in 1970 half of the American people could have afforded a median-priced new house (then costing $23,400), using the standard rule of thumb that no more than a fourth of pretax income should be spent on mortgage costs. In 1979, by the same standard, only 13 percent could afford new-home ownership (the median price then being $62,000), and 38 percent of all actual new-home buyers were ignoring the prudent rule of thumb.

The "affordability crisis" has hit renters as well, and today both owners and renters are overspending in order to put a roof over their heads. American families are now paying an average of almost 36 percent of disposable income for housing and housing-related expenses, double the average of only ten years ago. For low-income households the situation is much worse; by 1977, some 5.8 million households—4.2 million renters and 1.6 million owners—were paying over half of their incomes for shelter, and the problem has worsened considerably since then.

For many of these families, the cost of housing has meant stretching their budgets beyond the point where they can pay for other necessities and has made them terribly vulnerable to recession-caused disasters— either forced sale, default, or learning to live with poverty-level habits in all other realms of life.

Rising housing costs, moreover, have priced some groups out of the housing market altogether—notably low-income families, young couples, singles, and minorities. In 1975, a couple earning $16,650 could have bought a median-priced California home for $41,000; They would have made a 20 percent down payment of $8,000, and their monthly mortgage payment—including insurance, interest and taxes—would have been $347. By the end of 1979, the same home cost $88,300. A buyer had to earn over $35,000 to qualify for a loan, put down $17,750 as a 20 percent down payment, and pay out $878.42 per month.

At those rates, a broad segment of American working people—especially those now coming of age and those who, for whatever reasons, have delayed entry into the housing market for too long—may never have a chance to own a home. The fading dream of home ownership represents a crucial change in living standards—not only because it condemns some people to inferior housing, but perhaps even more importantly, because it eliminates one of the only tangible assets traditionally available to people without high incomes. The fact that roughly two-thirds of American families own their own homes today suggests how far down the income scale home ownership has extended in postwar America. Without the home as asset, the material security of these people will drop precipitously, again suggesting that ordinary income and wealth data greatly underestimate the real "losses" stagflation has caused for some groups.

Meanwhile, those who already have a strong foothold in the housing market have seen their homes appreciate wildly in value and their relative mortgage costs decline, often dramatically, because of inflation. The benefits of inflation for people who already own their homes should not be exaggerated, however, for other costs—maintenance and taxes, particularly—have risen dramatically in the decade. For people with limited or fixed incomes, these costs can tip the balance between being able to keep a home or being forced back into the rental market. Still, the crisis in housing has created one of the deepest and most powerful divisions between "winners" and "losers" in the stagflation era.

THE OUTLOOK FOR JOBS

The divisions between winners and losers multiply and deepen when we look at what recent changes in the American economy have meant in terms of the kinds of jobs that will be available in the future. For, like housing, the job outlook is changing—in ways that will mean intensified competition for a shrinking proportion of good jobs. The losers in that competition may face a lifetime of poorly paid, dull, and unstable work.

Some point to the rapid growth of overall employment, even during the recessionary 1970s, as evidence of the fundamental health of the economy. Nearly 13 million new jobs were created between 1973 and 1979. The American economy, in fact, produced new jobs at a rate much faster than its chief economic competitors, West Germany and Japan. What is striking, however, is that the economy stagnated, and living conditions flattened, in *spite* of all those new jobs. Why, with all those people newly at work, did only a minority of families see their standard of living rise?

The answer lies partly in the nature of the new jobs themselves—and it bodes ill for the future. For the new jobs have overwhelmingly been in those parts of the economy that offer the poorest pay, the fewest chances for advancement, and the least possibility of providing an adequate livelihood. And it is precisely these jobs that are expected to continue to grow in the future, while those that have traditionally offered a ticket to higher living standards will correspondingly decline.

By the end of the 1970s, well over two-fifths of all American workers in the private, nonagricultural economy were employed in just two sectors: retail trade and "services." More significantly, over 70 percent of all *new* jobs created in the private economy between 1973 and 1980 were in those two sectors. What kinds of jobs are these? Labor Department economists estimate that by 1990 there will be over 4 million new jobs in various private medical-care services—nursing homes, hospitals, blood banks, and medical laboratories. Another fast-growing sector is "miscellaneous business services," including janitorial, photocopying, and temporary office help. Over 5 million new jobs are expected in retail trade, mainly in fast-food restaurants, department stores, and food stores.

The jobs in these expanding fields are notoriously low-paying. In 1979, workers in manufacturing industries averaged about $232 a week in spendable earnings. Workers in service industries averaged $162, and in wholesale and retail trade, $155. Part of the reason for these low average earnings is that these jobs are often part-time, as is illustrated by the short—and declining—work weeks in service and retail trade. The average work week in retail trade was almost 40 hours in 1959, had dropped to 33 hours by 1977, and is expected to drop to 30 hours by 1990. Workers in manufacturing, as Emma Rothschild points out, had an average work week (in 1979) of about 40 hours, while workers in eating and drinking places, one of the fastest-growing sectors of the economy, averaged just 26 hours a week.

In the 1950s and 1960s social critics often worried that technological changes in the economy were on the verge of eliminating work. A whole literature about the "postindustrial" society emerged, in which the problem of what to do with the predicted increase in leisure was a primary concern. But the reality today is not quite what these critics expected. Technological change has not so much eliminated jobs, in the aggregate, as it has changed the mix of jobs available—and with it, the relative chances that work will bring economic security. The prediction of a "postindustrial" or "service" economy has been partly realized—and will become even more so during the remainder of this century. But—as we've already seen—the rise of the "service society" has not brought greater leisure—but, in many cases, the opposite; not increased freedom from toil—but, often, an ever-faster race to stay in one place.

The impact of these changes is already ensuring that youth are one of the greatest casualties of the economic crisis. Men and women under twenty-four are earning less today, in real terms, than their counterparts did in 1967. Even *Fortune* magazine, in its generally "upbeat" rendering of the income picture during the 1970s, notes that the combination of the "bulge" of baby-boom workers and a declining job market has played havoc with youth's life chances. Men aged fifty-five to sixty-four, the magazine points out, enjoyed a real income increase of nearly 18 percent between 1969 and 1977; those twenty-five to thirty-four saw their incomes rise less than 3 percent, while men eighteen to twenty-four suffered a slight decline. The cumulative effect has been dramatic: "By the end of the Seventies," *Fortune* notes, "the baby boomers had effectively lost about ten years' income growth relative to the group just ahead of them. One of the biggest uncertainties about income in the Eighties is whether they will be able to make up that lost ground." The division between those with a clear shot at the dwindling proportion of good jobs, and those who may never rise out of the poorly paid, unstable work force in the spreading retail and service sectors will become increasingly important in the coming years.

That division will probably be intensified by the wholesale destruction of many blue-collar jobs under the impact of the decline and restructuring of key industries like auto, steel, and rubber. Traditionally, these industries provided high-wage jobs that often offered a path into relative affluence (though that affluence was always threatened by job instability). Until the late 1970s workers in these industries (as well as certain others, like coal mining) fared best in terms of real income. By 1977, nearly a third of all American families making between $25,000 and $50,000 a year were officially classified as "blue collar." But these jobs, of course, are threatened with elimination as those industries either shut down, move away, or automate in response to intense competition. According to recent estimates, for example, by late 1980 the crisis in the American auto industry had cost the jobs of close to 300,000 workers in the industry itself and another 600,000 in related industries. And it is clear that—even if the industry does ever regain its past level of production—it will do so with a work force that is considerably smaller, replaced as much as possible by new, superefficient "robots."

To the extent that these and other well-paying blue-collar jobs are obliterated, the result will be a still greater split between a relatively few high-level professional and technical jobs on the one hand, and a growing array of poorly paid, rote jobs on the other. This split will strike hardest at younger workers' expectations for a decent job in the future, especially young minority workers, for whom industrial blue-collar jobs have long been a main route to a decent standard of living.

THE NEW INEQUALITY AND ECONOMIC POLICY

Two themes stand out most strongly from the strands of evidence on changes in work and family life, expectations for jobs and housing, and patterns of spending, saving, and debt.

First, it is true that—as *Business Week* magazine puts it—"the American credo that each generation can look forward to a better life than its predecessor has been shattered." What's more, it has been shattered in particularly threatening ways, for what have been most powerfully assaulted by the changes in the economy are the most fundamental expectations and most basic courses of stability and security—the quality and character of home and family life, the security of one's future, and the fate of one's children.

At the same time, these burdens have been felt very differently by different groups. The lineup of "winners" and "losers" in this redistribution of life-chances is complicated and sometimes unexpected. Traditional differences, like sex, race, and age, have been widened and redefined, while newer ones based on family composition, position in the housing market, or—increasingly—participation in specific industries have arisen or become more important. The brunt of stagflation's impact on living standards, patterns of labor and family life, and job prospects has been borne by a few especially hard-hit groups. Others, better endowed with the appropriate resources, have coped more than adequately, carving out new kinds of affluence in the midst of economic "decline."

What do these trends tell us about the social and economic policies that could reverse the harshest effects of the new inequality? It would take another article to do justice to such a large, and freighted, question. But a few general points seem clear.

Most importantly, our analysis suggests that the kind of economic "revitalization" so fashionable among the legions of the "New Right"—and given political momentum by the Reagan administration—is more likely to aggravate the trends we've outlined than to alter them. At the core of the "conservative" program is a set of incentives designed to fuel economic expansion by stimulating private investment. These incentives include across-the-board tax cuts, "deregulation" of industry, and drastic reductions in public spending on social programs (coupled, of course, with massively increased spending for defense). According to the new conventional wisdom of "supply-side" economics, these policies would both fight high inflation and "get America moving again" by "unleashing" private enterprise.

At bottom, the "supply-side" vision is the most recent (and most drastic) variant of the longstanding argument that the way to increase jobs, income, and well-being throughout the society is to allow them to "trickle down" from an expanding private economy. By shifting the balance of social resources upward and improving the "business climate," society as a whole—including its poorest members—should benefit.

Whether such a program can, in fact, cause a spurt of economic growth—as measured by a rising Gross National Product or a higher rate of productivity—is a question we won't venture to answer. For our purposes, it is the wrong question. The more important one is not whether we can generate *some* kind of economic growth—but whether the growth we produce will be translated into better lives and greater opportunities across all sectors of society. And this is where the "supply-side" program seems badly out of touch with the reality of modern society.

The "supply-side" program assumes, at least implicitly, that the problem we face is a general economic decline—a decline that can be reversed by providing sufficient lures to ever-greater investment. But the notion of a *general* economic decline, as we've demonstrated, is misleading. Something far more complex has been taking place. Rather than a simple, overall stagnation, we are witnessing a complicated process of recomposition and "restratification," bringing new sources of affluence along with new forms of poverty. Economic shifts have been translated into complex changes in work, family, and other social institutions. Policies of "revitalization" that fail to take account of those changes—of the institutional structure that necessarily forms the context of economic life—will only deepen present inequalities, worsening the situation of those "losing" and accelerating the advance of those already "winning" in the social and economic reshuffling we've described.

Illustrations are not hard to come by. How will an economic "boom," fueled by tax cuts for the wealthy, help an unskilled single mother find economic security—especially when the same policies are, with the other hand, taking away public funds for child care that would enable her to take a job—if a job were there? How will growth in nursing homes and hamburger stands help a skilled blue-collar worker whose $20,000-a-year job has been lost to a more "productive" industrial robot? How will the expansion of defense industries in the Southwest help a young minority couple facing the runaway housing market in New York? Or an unemployed 18-year-old in Chicago's ghetto?

Dealing effectively with the new forms of impoverishment will require policies targeted directly to those groups most at risk in the modern economy—and to those sectors of the economy where inflation and recession have taken their worst toll. A program to confront the new inequality cannot simply bank on the "trickling down" of jobs and income from expanding private investment, but must involve active intervention in economic life toward explicit social goals.

Addressing these problems will require *more* "government intervention," not less; a larger (if more efficient) public sector, not a diminished one; more "planning," not less. We know that these strategies go strongly against the stream. But we believe that without them the alternative scenario is clear: a sharper division between the newly affluent and the newly poor; for the young, fast-vanishing opportunities for good jobs and decent housing; and continued inflation with its devastating pressures on home and family. The choice is clear. We will either decide to engage in serious, democratic public planning to redress the social imbalances generated by economic development or we will watch helplessly as an uncontrolled "revitalization" brings greater insecurity, desperation, and misery in its train.

STAGFLATION, INEQUALITY, AND THE POLITICAL CULTURE

What are the prospects for that kind of democratic social planning? At first glance, the outlook seems less than hopeful. In the face of the injuries inflicted by the economic crisis, there have been some encouraging expressions of public mobilization and concern. But, at least as often, the crisis has seemed to generate cynicism and political withdrawal, epitomized by the fact that the winner of the 1980 presidential election came into office on only 26 percent of the potential popular vote. Contemporary politics—and contemporary American culture as a whole—often seem mired in narrow interest-group concerns and a spirit of individual indulgence.

And these responses—negativism, cynicism, withdrawal from social concern—are themselves partly rooted in the changes we have already described. The heightened insecurity that economic crisis has brought to personal life in America—the receding prospects for decent jobs and housing, the looming threat of downward mobility and of a pauperized old age—helps explain the resurgence of broader cultural themes of competition and individual survival. ("Tomorrow only the fit will survive," declares an ad for a new magazine for "entrepreneurs," "and only the *very* fit will flourish.") And it also offers fertile soil for the desperate focus on the "self" that Barbara Ehrenreich has aptly called a "psychological version of the 'lifeboat ethic' "—the "me-first" character of life lived mainly in the present because the future seems less and less certain or worth building toward. Given the particularly harsh effects of the economic crisis on family life, it isn't surprising that political campaigns narrowly focused on the "defense" of the traditional family—like the campaign against the Equal Rights Amendment—have enjoyed especially wide appeal in the era of "stagflation."

All of these tendencies have been reinforced by the increasing *fragmentation* we have described. When relative prosperity or impoverishment may hang on the timing of a house purchase or the fact of working in (say) the aerospace rather than the auto industry or having been born in 1940 rather than 1950, the sense of commonality of experience and needs disintegrates. Individual (or, at best, familial) solutions to social and economic problems can easily come to seem the only alternatives available, the only visible avenues to security and well-being.

This individualization is aggravated by the growing split between the newly affluent and other working people—what we might call the "Brazilianization" of the American class structure. Working people see some enjoying considerable success—"making it" in highly visible ways—while others sink; some buying second homes in the mountains, speedboats, and Cuisinarts, while others descend into the ranks of the welfare poor. Those differences act both as a spur to individual striving and as a demonstration that the proper management of personal life can bring significant rewards—that it can put you, as *Fortune* pants, on "a fast track to the good life." And for those at the upper reaches of the scale, it provides a sharp and nagging incentive to hold on more tightly to what they have.

These trends—fragmentation, individualization, the narrowing of political concern to family and personal life—are not the only ones now evident in the United States. As Michael Harrington has pointed out, the American people seem to be moving in several different ideological directions at once. There is a new theme of narrow self-seeking in American culture; but there is also—as public opinion polls reveal—a growing support for guaranteeing jobs through public programs and for accepting wage and price controls in response to runaway inflation. There is, in some quarters, a new reverence for private gain and the forces of the "market"; but there is also evidence of a growing concern for what the psychologist Urie Bronfenbrenner has called the "human ecology"—a recognition of the connectedness of the fabric of social life and a rejection of the periodically fashionable idea that human life should be left to the not-so-tender mercies of the "free market." Which trend will prevail depends crucially on the seriousness and energy with which we build a broad movement for democratic planning and control of economic life.

POSTSCRIPT—1990

When we wrote this article in the late 1970s, we associated the decline in American living standards, and the sense of diminished expectations that went with it, with the effects of "stagflation"—the unprecedented combination of high inflation with high unemployment—which so preoccupied both economists and the American public at that time. Today, the effect of falling oil prices rippling through the economy combined with the tight money policies of the Reagan and Bush administrations has brought the overall rate of inflation down considerably. But that overall drop masks continuing rises in the costs of housing, medical care, and college tuition—among other expenses. And it has not affected the main economic and social trends we discussed: the loss of well-paying industrial jobs and the multiplication of low-paying ones in the service sector; the stagnation of average family income even with more and more families having two earners to support them; an increasingly unequal income distribution, leading to more of the very rich and many more of the very poor; a declining rate of homeownership combined with greater housing costs for both renters and owners; and a level of public and private indebtedness that threatens the very basis for future economic growth. A great deal of research published since we first wrote has shown that these trends have continued and even intensified in the 1980s.

The continued weakening of America's international economic position has steadily aggravated the loss of jobs in industries like steel, auto, and now even semiconductors. As recently as 1979, for example, the United States steel industry accounted for 400,000 production workers; by 1986 it employed only 200,000. Severe job losses have affected many white-collar and service industries as well, as companies have "restructured" and "downsized" in an increasingly tough economic environment.

By the end of the 1980s the spread of income inequality was wider than at any point since World War Two. After taxes, between 1977 and 1990, the poorest fifth of American families suffered a drop in income of 14 percent. The next-poorest fifth lost 10 percent, and the middle fifth lost 7 percent. The top one percent of families enjoyed an increase of *110 percent* in after-tax income. The ranks of the rich, according to the economists Sheldon Danziger, Peter Gottschalk, and Eugene Smolensky, have more than doubled since the early 1970s (their study defined the rich as earning more than $95,000 a year in 1987). In the past, as Danziger and his colleagues point out, economic inequality has generally increased in periods of recession but *diminished* in times of economic recovery. What is perhaps most troubling about the "new" inequality of the eighties and nineties is that it has continued to rise during a several-year-long recovery.

The sources of the continuing growth of inequality are, as we suggested, complex. Some of it is attributable to government policies that have reduced spending for low-income people while simultaneously reducing taxes for the affluent—resulting, as Barbara Ehrenreich has put it, in the government's "first major upward distribution of wealth since World War Two." Despite the much-touted tax reform of 1986, ostensibly designed to make the tax structure more progressive, the wealthy now pay a proportionately lower share of their income in taxes than they did in the late 1970s. Between 1977 and 1990, according to the House Ways and Means Committee, the most affluent one percent of the population enjoyed a startling 85 percent rise in real pretax income—and a 23 percent *drop* in their tax rate. The poorest fifth of Americans, meanwhile, suffered a 12 percent loss in income and saw *their* tax rate increase by 3 percent. Overall, as the Congressional Budget Office has shown, nine out of ten American families now pay a larger proportion of their incomes in federal taxes than they did before the "tax cuts" of the late 1970s and early 1980s. Only the wealthiest tenth has actually seen their rates go down as a proportion of income. These shifts are due in part to reductions in personal income tax rates and large cuts in corporate income taxes for the wealthy, on the one hand, and steady increases in Social Security taxes for working people on the other.

Other causes were underway well before President Reagan took office in 1981, and are therefore probably rooted in a longer-term decline in the competitive position of the American economy and the way this has affected the labor market.

Barry Bluestone, Bennett Harrison, and Chris Tilly have recently shown that this "sharp U-turn" toward inequality can be dated to sometime in the years 1975 to 1978, with the distribution of wage and salary income becoming steadily more unequal ever since. They conclude that "the sense of relative deprivation, of frustrated expectations, of falling behind, of being badly-paid—this is becoming the common experience of a growing number of Americans. They are white as well as persons of color. They are men as well as women. Having a full-time, year-round job is no longer a guarantee of being sheltered from this experience."

Nor, as we suggested, does the future look any brighter, since most of the new jobs now being created in the "service" economy are low-paying and often unstable. Other research by Bluestone and Harrison shows that, between 1963 and 1978, only about a fourth of all new jobs paid poverty- or near-poverty-level wages; but of the new jobs created between 1978 and 1984, almost half did so.

Research by the Senate Budget Committee has shown that the burden of the shifting job market has fallen heaviest on the young. Between 1979 and 1987, the quality of jobs available to workers under 35 dropped sharply; the number of jobs for younger workers that paid middle-level wages fell by more than 1.5 million, while the proportion paying low wages correspondingly rose. For workers over thirty-five, the proportion of high-level jobs actually increased slightly in those years. In our original article, we noted that the young were already among the "greatest casualties" of the emerging economic crisis. As we'll see, that has become even more true since we wrote.

Other writers, notably Robert Kuttner and Lester Thurow, have called this erosion in the number of people earning middle-level wages a "decline of the middle class" in the United States. If we take the "middle class" to be those families earning between $20,000 and $49,999, in 1984 dollars, then the middle class did indeed decline in recent years, while the proportion of both low- and high-income families increased. According to Katharine Bradbury, an economist for the Federal Reserve Board of Boston, the proportion of American families earning less than $20,000 increased by over 4 percent between 1973 and 1984, while the proportion earning $20,000 to $50,000 dropped by more than 5 percent.

Although these numbers don't sound very dramatic, before 1973 the income distribution pattern in this country had changed only glacially since the Census Bureau began collecting statistics in 1947; so this is a remarkable shift. Taken in combination with the stagnation of real incomes over the same period, it means that millions of American families have been unable to achieve the living standards they had expected to attain at their current stage in life.

The only real disagreement about the "decline of the middle class" is over *why* it is occurring. Some economists, notably Robert Lawrence of the Brookings Institution, say that the problem isn't economics, but demographics. He thinks that the baby-boom generation made up of people born between 1946 and 1964 has flooded the labor market, temporarily increasing the competition for jobs and bringing down wage levels. As fewer young workers enter the labor market, and as the baby boomers reach prime earning age, wage levels will increase and the "middle class" will expand again. In other words, we don't need any change in social or economic policy, because the problem will correct itself in good time.

But Katharine Bradbury recently tested this theory and found it to be incorrect. Using Census data, she demonstrated that "the fraction of families with middle-class incomes declined within virtually all demographic groups." It declined within all regions, within all age ranges, and within all family types except families in which the head was 65 or over. But not surprisingly, given the declining job opportunities for younger workers we've just noted, the decline in living standards has struck hardest at younger families, especially those with young children. Between 1973 and 1987, according to the Children's Defense Fund, those families suffered an average income decline of almost 25 percent.

That decline has been concentrated at the lower end of the income scale. But even for middle-income people, relatively stagnant wages combined with rising housing costs have meant (as we predicted) that fewer young families can afford to buy their own home, the major single element of the American Dream. In a 1985 study for the Joint Economic Committee, Frank Levy and Richard Michel showed that in 1973 the typical 30-year-old man could make the payments required to purchase a median-priced house with only 21 percent of his salary. By 1984, he would need to spend 44 percent of his salary for the house, since the cost of housing had risen much more rapidly than the average salary for that age group. Similarly, a 1986 study by the Joint Center for Housing Studies of MIT and Harvard concluded that "unless young adults achieve substantial income growth or unless the cost of homeownership declines to more traditional levels, many more young families than in the past will find themselves unable to purchase a home." The study found that in the period 1981 to 1985 alone, the percentage of homeowners dropped from 20.7 to 17.4 among those under 25; from 41.7 to 37.7 in the 25–29 age bracket; and from 59.3 to 54.7 in the 30–34 age group. And the shrinking chances for homeownership are only one aspect of the housing pressure on young families, many of which are trapped in a rental housing market that is itself escalating drastically. The median rent burden for young lower-income house-holds—that is, rent payments as a proportion of income—went up by 50 percent between 1974 and 1987, and there is no relief in sight.

With their income stretched precariously to meet stratospheric mortgage payments, and most or all of their assets locked into housing, young families are now terribly vulnerable to catastrophe if their income falls. In parts of the country now undergoing economic slowdowns after the long housing "boom" of the eighties, disaster has already struck many overextended families. According to the *New York Times*, for example, in New Jersey, Connecticut, and on Long Island, "housing foreclosures, delinquent mortgage payments and personal bankruptcy filings are rising." The economic crunch is taking its toll on personal and family life; "As a result of financial pressures caused largely by high housing costs . . . psychologists and social workers say they are treating many more cases of stress, depression, spouse and child abuse and marital strife."

Our article pointed out that, squeezed between stagnant wages and rising outlays for housing and other costs, families had two main methods to maintain their living standards: sending an additional family member to work (usually the wife), and buying more things on credit. But, as Frank Levy has pointed out, the potential of the first method is nearly exhausted because more than two-thirds of young married couples now rely on two earners, and "there is no third earner in reserve to keep consumption growing." There is also evidence that American households can no longer continue to support the rising burden of consumer debt.

Consumer installment credit outstanding has more than *tripled* since 1976 and didn't stop growing even during the 1981–1982 recession. With almost one-third of average monthly cash household income now allocated to debt payments, many economists fear that this burden will inevitably put a brake on consumer spending and sharply limit future economic growth.

Two groups are already suffering noticeable effects from indebtedness: small farmers and college students. In large part because of farmers' inability to meet debt payments, the number of farms with less than $20,000 in annual sales fell by 60 percent between 1975 and 1985. Thirty percent of all farms are now owned by people over 65, and only 6 percent by people under 35, indicating a severe erosion in the number of future farm families. And student loan programs that originated in the 1960s as a convenience to the middle class have turned into a necessity for millions of college students as a result of sharply rising tuition costs and simultaneously declining federal grants for tuition aid.

By 1986, borrowing under the Federal Guaranteed Student Loan Program had soared to nearly $10 billion a year, with the total amount of loans outstanding exceeding $50 billion. The College Board estimates that about half of the nation's 10 million undergraduates are now leaving school with some debts, but for those who go on to graduate or professional school, the amount owed easily grows so large that it inevitably shapes personal and professional decisions. With new doctors now owing an average of $30,000 on graduation, few can afford to become rural general practitioners; and new lawyers, who now owe an average of $25,000, will think twice before deciding to practice public interest law.

The rise in debt and decline in homeownership are part of a major trend toward concentration of wealth in the United States, as shown by a study for the Joint Economic Committee released in July 1986 and based on data collected in 1983 for the Federal Reserve Board and other government agencies. The report defined wealth as "stored-up purchasing power . . . measured by the value of what could be purchased if all a family's debts were paid off and the remaining assets turned into cash." By this measure of net assets, the group the report called the "Super Rich"—the top one-half of 1 percent of the population—held an astonishing 35.1 percent of the nation's total wealth in 1983. Between 1963 and 1983, the share owned by the top one-half of 1 percent of the population increased by 38 percent while the share owned by every other group declined. The "Everyone Else" category, which includes 90 percent of the population, suffered the greatest decline. By 1983 the 419,590 households classified as "Super Rich" owned average holdings worth $8.9 million, and some held many times more than that. The 75 million households in the "Everyone Else" category had average holdings worth $39,598. The disparities would be even greater if the JEC study had broken down the Everyone Else category into the lower 50 percent of the population or the lowest 20 percent. Unless they own substantial equity in their home, most families have little or no net wealth.

Just how thin the financial safety net is for many American families is illustrated in a more recent study by the sociologists Thomas Shapiro and Melvin Oliver. If we subtract equity in homes and cars, for example, 67 percent of black and 30 percent of white households have zero or negative "net financial assets"; that is, what they owe is equal to or greater than what they have saved in cash, stocks and bonds, or other assets. What this means is that almost any sudden economic misfortune—loss of a job, a big medical expense—could put the assets they do have, especially their homes, in jeopardy. Again, the financial safety net is thinnest for younger families; over half of households headed by someone under 35, versus 30 percent of those between 35 and 64, have no or negative financial assets.

But perhaps even more than the new pressures on the middle and the rising fortunes of the rich, it is the precipitous decline at the bottom that has most transformed the social and economic landscape in America. Writing in the late 1970s, we anticipated that the adverse shifts in jobs and income would bring new kinds of poverty to the United States. We did not anticipate how massive and rapid the impoverishment of lower-income Americans would be. About 8 million people have joined the ranks of the poor since we wrote, 3 million of them children. And while poverty widened its grip on Americans, it also deepened; about 2 out of 5 of the poor had less than *half* the poverty-level income in 1987, the highest proportion in a decade. Poverty has also "hardened" in the United States over the last several years; according to the University of Michigan's Panel Study of Income Dynamics, the chances of "exiting" from poverty decreased substantially after the early 1970s.

Nor do the official poverty figures alone adequately capture the disaster that has afflicted the low-income population since the start of the 1980s. The deepening income poverty has been brutally compounded by the erosion of public services—including health and mental health care, subsidized housing, and resources for the public schools. In many inner cities and hard-hit rural areas, the most basic human needs are now routinely unmet in the 1990s. It's no exaggeration to say that we may be witnessing the emergence of two distinct classes of citizenship in America, based not only on growing differences in income but on sharply diverging access to the fundamental means of participation in economic, social and political life.

That widening gap may help to shed light on the perplexing *political* question we noted in the original article. If living standards have declined since the early 1970s, and if the country has moved much further toward inequality in income and wealth, why haven't the victims of this process demanded more egalitarian social and economic policies? Voters have, of course, shown some discontent around economic issues, but on the whole, unrest around "pocketbook" concerns has been mobilized much more successfully by the right than the left. In particular, the right has offered voters some economic relief through property tax "revolts" and

President Reagan's cuts in the personal income tax, although the right's traditional constituency, the wealthy, has been the main beneficiary of these reductions.

In our original article we suggested the troubling possibility that the trends toward greater inequality and insecurity might be self-perpetuating. The growing fragmentation of experience and the gnawing sense of an unsure future seemed, to us, to be pitting Americans against each other in an individualistic struggle for constricting rewards—not spurring them toward common action in pursuit of larger social and economic goals. The decline of the sense of commonality is surely exacerbated by the very real deterioration at the bottom—the resurgence of violent crime and hard drugs, the abrasive visibility of the homeless.

That kind of individualism, of course, isn't new to the United States; as Robert Bellah and his coauthors remind us, in their noted book *Habits of the Heart*, "it is individualism, and not equality, as Tocqueville thought, that has marched inexorably through our history." But we think that a number of recent institutional changes may have exacerbated the atomization of American political culture and further eroded the potential for a strong, unifying movement built around egalitarian concerns.

Historically, for example, two of the most important channels for the political expression of those concerns have been the labor movement and the Democratic party. But many of the same forces that have fostered the new inequality have also weakened the influence of organized labor: the shift from traditional blue-collar industry to services, the displacement of jobs overseas, the resulting growing power of management to wring concessions on pay and working conditions from labor. In 1984, according to the AFL-CIO, the labor movement organized about 350,000 new workers—but *lost* about 700,000 members from plant closings, layoffs, and decertification elections. Just to maintain their current membership, then, unions would have to double their rate of organizing victories. At the same time, as the *Washington Post* political reporter Thomas Edsall has shown, *both* political parties have come to be increasingly dominated by the affluent—to the detriment of the concerns of the other 60 percent of the American population. In both cases, the result has been a vacuum of leadership and organizational support for a more genuinely democratic political and economic agenda. Whether that vacuum can be filled and a new, more cohesive political vision created, in the face of increasing pressures toward social fragmentation, is one of the most important social questions of our time—and one we cannot yet answer. As we said over a decade ago, the quality of our collective future will depend on the "seriousness and energy" with which we work to build a movement for social change.

10

Poor Children in Rich Countries

Timothy M. Smeeding and Barbara Boyld Torrey

The industrial countries in the world have a higher standard of living than at any time in history, but within the wealthy countries, there are still a number of children who live in poverty. The United States, which is the wealthiest country of six studied, had the highest poverty rate among children and the second highest poverty rate among families with children.

From 1970 to 1987, the poverty rate for children in the United States increased from 15 to 20 percent. This occurred at the same time that the poverty rate for the elderly in the United States decreased from 25 to 12 percent (1). This reversal in the economic status of the young and old in the United States occurred without an explicit government policy favoring one group over the other. The reversal was not expected at the beginning of the 1970s, and the divergence of the two groups was not carefully documented until the 1980s (2, 3).

Many of the countries studied provide similar amounts of income benefits to their poor families as are provided in the United States. The other countries, however, reduce the percentage of families in poverty more than does the United States. Because patterns of poverty and poverty reduction result from complex interactions among economic and social trends in each country, conclusions about social programs in one country cannot be automatically applied to another. But international comparisons may reveal universal patterns of poverty as well as problems specific to each country.

From *Science*, Vol. 242, November 11, 1988. Copyright 1988 by the American Association for the Advancement of Science. Reprinted by permission.

In this article data from the Luxembourg Income Study (LIS) are used to compare the poverty rates of families with children in six industrial countries (Australia, Canada, Sweden, United States, United Kingdom, and West Germany) for the years 1979 and 1981. First, the post-tax and transfer poverty rates (defined below) of children are examined, and then the poverty rates of families with children before they receive income and tax benefits are described. Next the correlations of sources of income and family structures with pretax and transfer poverty are discussed, poverty rates of these families after they receive taxes and transfers are compared, and the effect of participation and benefit levels on these rates are examined. Because of their growing numbers and high level of economic disadvantage, single-parent families with children are highlighted as a group of particular interest.

DEFINITION OF INCOME AND POVERTY

Two definitions of income are used: pretax and transfer income, which is earned income and property income before payment of taxes or receipt of government benefits, and post-tax and transfer income, which is the income after paying taxes and receiving government benefits. Post-tax and transfer income includes the cash value of food stamps in the United States and housing allowances in the United Kingdom and Sweden (4). Income estimates (both pre- and post-tax and transfer income) also are adjusted for differences in family size and composition with the use of the U.S. poverty line equivalence scale (5, 6).

Poverty can be defined in relative or in absolute terms. For ease of comparison, the definition we use is the absolute definition of poverty used by the U.S. government. In 1979, the U.S. poverty line for a family of three was $5763. Families with lower adjusted incomes were in poverty. The dollar amount of the U.S. poverty line was converted into the currencies of the other countries by using the purchasing power parities developed by the Organization for Economic Cooperation and Development (OECD) (6, 7). These equivalent poverty lines vary from 39.4 percent of adjusted median income in Canada to 55.8 percent in Germany; the U.S. poverty line is 42.1 percent of the median income in the United States (Table 1).

Other family and income definitions, equivalence scales, and currency conversion techniques could be used. Different definitions and adjustment scales would change the level of poverty rates in most countries. But, the United States had more poor children and more poor families with children than virtually every other country in the study regardless of the definitions and adjustments made (6, 8).

Income measures provide only a partial description of the conditions of poverty. Noncash income components, such as health care, may be as

Table 1. Post-tax and transfer poverty rates among children (Children are persons 17 years or under.)

Measure	Australia (1981)	Canada (1981)	West Germany (1981)	Sweden (1981)	United Kingdom (1979)	United States (1979)
			Rate (%)			
	Poverty rates of all children					
All families	16.9	9.6	8.2	5.1	10.7	17.1
One-parent families	65.0	38.7	35.1	8.6	38.6	51.0
Two-parent families	12.4	6.8	4.9	4.5	9.5	9.4
Extended families	10.6	5.5	12.1	0.5	1.5	16.2
	Below 75 percent of poverty line					
Poor children	43.1	45.8	30.8	42.4	35.2	57.7
All children	7.3	4.4	2.5	2.2	3.8	9.8
U.S. poverty line as a percentage of adjusted median income	51.4	39.4	55.8	50.1	52.9	42.1

important as money income in describing the true social condition of the poor (9). But if noncash income factors were included in these comparisons, they would be unlikely to improve the relative position of the United States because most countries provide more noncash benefits to their children than does the United States.

The sources of the LIS data are national household income surveys taken by the governments of each country between 1979 and 1981. Because the data from these surveys are adjusted for definitional differences in income and household composition, the level and composition of families and their incomes across countries can be compared accurately (10).

POVERTY AMONG CHILDREN

The United States and then Australia have the highest rates of poverty among children of the countries studied (Table 1). This poverty rate measures the number of children who are living in families who are poor even after receiving income and tax benefits from the government. Child poverty rates vary enormously by the structure of the child's family. In every country, child poverty rates are at least twice as high, and usually much higher, in single-parent families than in two-parent families. Australia has the highest poverty rates in both kinds of families, but the

United States has the highest rate among children in extended family structures. These extended families are usually a young, single parent with children living in a relative's home. Perhaps the most striking figures are those that show the percentage of all children and of all poor children who are living in families with incomes below 75 percent of the U.S. poverty line. Here we find that U.S. poor children are the worst off of children in any country, including Australia, with almost 10 percent existing at an income level at least 25 percent below the official U.S. poverty standard.

Government programs give income support to families, not to children. Therefore, in order to understand the patterns of poverty among children, the poverty of families, particularly single-parent families, and governments' response to this poverty are examined.

FAMILY POVERTY RATES BEFORE TAXES
AND INCOME TRANSFERS

The magnitude of the problem faced by governments in addressing the poverty of children is described by the pretax and transfer poverty rates and gaps. The pretax and transfer poverty rate measures how many families with children have incomes below the poverty line before they receive government benefits or pay taxes; the poverty gap measures how far below that poverty line the families are. (Family-based measures of child poverty may differ from child-based measures because poor families may be larger or smaller than all families with children.)

The United States has the highest pretax and transfer poverty rate for families with children, except Australia, which has the lowest median family income of the countries studied (Table 2). Germany has less than half the poverty rate of the United States. The pretax and transfer poverty gap (the poverty gap is expressed as the difference between the income and the poverty line as a percentage of the poverty line) for the families who are poor in these countries was more similar than their rates. Australia, Canada, Sweden, and the United States all had similar poverty gaps, between 59 and 68 percent of their poverty lines.

One group of particular interest in both the United States and in the other countries studied is single parents and their children (11, 12). These families have poverty rates and gaps that are much higher than those in other families. Although the rates are indeed higher for single parents, before taxes and transfers, U.S. single-parent families had near average poverty rates and gaps, below those in Australia and close to those in the United Kingdom and Canada.

There are a number of possible explanations for the differences in the pretransfer poverty rates and gaps among the countries and groups. Two important factors that vary by country and were correlated with pre-

Table 2. Pretax and transfer poverty rates and gaps for all families with children and for single-parent families with children (The gap is the difference between the average income of poor families and the poverty line divided by the poverty line. Single-parent families with children are those with only one adult present. Group averages are the simple mean of the estimates for the six countries.)

Measure	Australia (1981)	Canada (1981)	West Germany (1981)	Sweden (1981)	United Kingdom (1979)	United States (1979)	Group averages
	All families with children						
Poverty rate	17.6	13.6	7.9	10.4	14.1	16.6	13.4
Poverty gap	68	59	50	63	47	63	58
	Single-parent families with children						
Poverty rate	67.6	48.0	37.2	33.1	53.1	49.3	48.1
Poverty gap	84	77	68	60	72	74	73

transfer poverty are the level of average earnings and transfers and the structure of poor families. Another possible explanation is related to population heterogeneity within and across countries.

The earned and transfer income of poor families. At the time of these surveys, the United States had a lower unemployment rate than most of the other countries, and its real wage level was generally higher. Both factors should have given the poor families in the United States an advantage. Yet, the average earnings of poor families in the United States were only about two-thirds those in Germany, Sweden, and the United Kingdom (Table 3). In Australia earnings were two-thirds the level in the United

Table 3. Source of income for families with children who were poor before taxes and income transfers (Source of income is in 1979 U.S. dollars. Distribution of transfers is a percentage of the total amount of transfers.)

Measure	Australia (1981)	Canada (1981)	West Germany (1981)	Sweden (1981)	United Kingdom (1979)	United States (1979)
	Source of income (1979 U.S. dollars)					
Earnings	1,210	2,075	2,593	2,760	2,766	1,902
Income transfers less taxes	2,593	2,766	2,420	4,944	2,864	2,237
	Distribution of transfers (percentage)					
Social insurance						
Employment-related	0	39	69	44	37	29
Child-related	13	13	20	19	24	0
Welfare	87	48	11	37	39	71
Total	100	100	100	100	100	100

States. Australia and the United States had the lowest level of earnings among their poor families; they also had the highest poverty rates.

Poor families have more earnings in countries that rely more on social insurance benefits than on welfare benefits to relieve their poverty. Social insurance programs are either universal, such as child-related benefits that go to all children, or related to work, such as unemployment insurance. Welfare programs are related to economic need and therefore are reduced when beneficiaries increase their income from earnings. This reduction of welfare benefits with increases in earned income creates an implicit tax rate on earned income, which tends to reduce labor force participation and hours worked (*13, 14*).

Among the six countries studied, there are considerable differences in the reliance on social insurance and welfare programs. Three countries (Germany, Sweden, and the United Kingdom) provide more than 60 percent of their transfer income to poor families through social insurance programs; Canada relies equally on social insurance and welfare programs to provide benefits. The United States and Australia provide most of their benefits to poor families through welfare programs.

One might expect that in countries that have child-related benefits, such as children's allowances and maternity grants (or parents' allowances), these benefits would be an important source of income for poor families with children. But, in fact, although these benefits are universal, they also are relatively small. The levels of child benefits vary from 6 to 13 percent of the U.S. poverty line for families with children in the five countries that provide them. In Germany child benefits are larger than welfare benefits for families with children, but in no country are they a major source of income for poor families with children (Table 3). They are large enough to help remove some families from poverty and to help reduce the poverty gap, but they are not large enough to solve the child poverty problem in any country. On the other hand, employment-related social insurance benefits—unemployment, sickness, accident, and disability—are much more important in every country than are child-related benefits in those countries that have both. Employment-related and child-related benefits combined are the most important government benefits to poor families in every country but Australia and the United States.

Low earnings among poor families with children are not only correlated with the structure of the income transfer system, they are related to the structure of poor families. Single-parent families have lower earnings than two-parent families in every country. And the United States has more children in single-parent families than the other countries, except Sweden.

Family structure. In every country, poverty rates vary by the structure of the family. Children in single-parent families have poverty rates that are much higher than those in two-parent families in every country (Tables 1 and 2). Single-parent families begin with higher pretax and transfer poverty rates and higher poverty gaps (the latter in every country but Sweden; Table 2). And after tax and transfers, single-parent families still have higher poverty rates than other families (Table 4). On this basis the United States has the second highest poverty rate and the highest remaining poverty gap for single-parent families among the countries.

The high percentage of children in single-parent families in the United States, together with the high U.S. single-parent poverty rate, does contribute to the high child poverty rates in the United States. If the other countries had the same percentage of children in single-parent families as the United States in 1979 (14.7 percent), but their own actual poverty rates by family status, the poverty rate for children of the other countries would increase everywhere but in Sweden. However, in the other countries, except Australia, the increase in child poverty would still leave those countries well below U.S. child poverty rates. (If Australia had the same fraction of children in single-parent families as the United States, it would have a higher overall child poverty rate than the United States.) Although the proportion of U.S. children who are in single-parent families is somewhat higher than in other countries, except Sweden, what appears to distinguish the U.S. and Australian situation is that single-parent families are so much more economically vulnerable (as measured by their poverty rates) than in other countries.

Heterogeneity. If poverty rates vary by race or ethnic groups as they do in the United States, then countries with a more diverse population, such as Australia, Canada, and the United States, may have higher poverty rates

Table 4. Post-tax and transfer poverty rates and gaps for all families with children and for single-parent families with children. (The gap is the difference between the average income of poor families and the poverty line divided by the poverty line. Single-parent families with children are those with only one adult present. Government transfers are measured as a percentage of the pretax and transfer poverty gap. Group averages are the simple mean of the six country estimates.)

Measure	Australia (1981)	Canada (1981)	West Germany (1981)	Sweden (1981)	United Kingdom (1979)	United States (1979)	Group averages
All families with children							
Poverty rate	15.0	8.6	6.9	4.4	8.5	13.8	8.4
Poverty gap	32	32	24	28	21	38	29
Government transfers	71	85	106	176	117	64	64
Single-parent families with children							
Poverty rate	61.4	35.3	31.9	7.5	36.8	42.9	36.0
Poverty gap	31	33	28	30	23	40	31
Government transfers	70	75	84	203	90	58	97

than more homogeneous countries. The Australian, Canadian, and U.S. surveys described in this article collected data on separate minority sub-groups within those populations. Sweden and the United Kingdom do not make much differentiation, whereas the German data set excludes foreign-born heads of households.

In the United States, black families with children are particularly eco-nomically disadvantaged relative to white (nonblack and non-Hispanic) families. The poverty rates among black children are three times as high as the rates of white children. Poverty rates of Hispanic children in the United States are double those of white children as well (*15*). But the poverty rate of U.S. white children is still 11.4 percent. This poverty rate of white children in the United States alone is higher than the poverty rate of all children in the other countries except in Australia (Table 1). The poverty rate of nonminority and minority populations in Canada (both 9.6 percent) is lower than that of U.S. white children alone. The Austra-lians, on the other hand, have more poverty among the native-born and foreign-born population than the United States does among its white population.

Heterogeneity does matter; poverty rates are different for different populations and U.S. poverty rates are high, due in part to its social and ethnic diversity. But this diversity does not matter enough to explain fully the high poverty of U.S. children in general, or even white children in particular.

FAMILY POVERTY RATES AFTER TAXES AND INCOME TRANSFERS

Tax and transfer benefits reduce the poverty of families with children in every country studied, but none of these countries has eliminated poverty among families with children entirely (Table 4). In fact, the difference in poverty rates among the six countries was larger after accounting for government taxes and transfers than the differences in poverty rates before taxes and transfers. The post-tax and transfer poverty rates for families with children in Australia and the United States remain the highest of the countries studied, both for single-parent families and for all families. Transfers in every country reduced the poverty gap of the fami-lies that remained in poverty. But the poverty gap after transfers was largest in the United States for both family types. On average U.S. income transfers represent 64 percent of the pretax and transfer poverty gap for all families and 58 percent for single-parent families. These are a smaller percentage of the poverty gap than in any country, including Australia (Table 4). This helps explain why the pretax and transfer poverty rates and gaps for both kinds of families improved relatively less in the United States than in other countries after taxes and transfers (Tables 2 and 4).

Overall, the U.S. transfer system reduces the pretransfer poverty population by 17 percent. But government programs reduce the number of people in poverty twice as much on average in the other countries as in the United States. Again, there are a number of possible explanations for why the U.S. transfer programs reduce poverty less than in other countries. Two important factors are the level of participation in income transfer programs and the income support these programs provide.

Participation in income transfer programs. One of the reasons why many children in the United States are poor is that 27 percent of all poor families with children and 23 percent of single-parent families receive no public income support from the programs studied. In every other country at least 99 percent of both types of families that were defined as poor by the U.S. poverty line definition received some type of income support. In every country except the United States and Australia the participation rate in child allowances or other social insurance programs was higher than in welfare programs. All the countries, except the United States, have child allowances that reach at least 80 percent of poor children. Social insurance programs other than child allowances are based on employment history. All countries studied but Australia have these types of programs. Among the U.S. pretax and transfer poor, only 25 percent received social insurance as compared to at least 40 percent in the other four countries with such programs.

Welfare program rules in the United States restrict participation of poor families. For example, two-parent families in 27 states still are not eligible for cash income transfers. Even in programs where all families with children are eligible for benefits, such as food stamps, welfare program rules may discourage some people who are eligible from applying. One reason the U.S. social insurance and welfare programs decrease pretax and transfer poverty less than in other countries is simply because they reach a smaller percentage of the poverty population.

The poverty rates of children would decline if all families with poor children in the United States received income support. If we assume that the 27 percent of poor families with children currently without benefits in the United States receive some type of support, and that because of this support 17 percent of the new recipients were removed from poverty (which is the same rate of poverty reduction in current U.S. transfer programs), then the U.S. poverty rate among families with children could be reduced from 13.8 to 13.1 percent. This would reduce the difference in poverty rates between U.S. families with children and the average of the four countries with lower poverty rates by about 10 percent.

Taken together, the differences in family structure, racial heterogeneity, and the differences in participation rates may explain 64 percent of the difference between the post-tax and transfer poverty rate of children in the United States and of the average poverty rate in the four other countries with lower poverty rates (*16*). Increased earnings by the U.S.

pretransfer poor would reduce the difference still further. And most of the remaining difference may be explained by the differences in levels of government income benefits provided to families with children in general and the poor in particular.

Amount of income support provided. The level of income support to poor families in U.S. dollars is shown in Table 3. Sweden provides almost twice the transfers net of taxes as the other countries provide to their poor families with children. For the other five countries, total government transfers minus taxes are within $627 of each other. The level of average transfers to poor families are more similar among the countries studied, except Sweden, than their after-transfer poverty rates. For instance, Canada provides on average only $500 more to their poor families than does the United States, but reduces the pretransfer poverty rate 37 percent compared to the 17 percent reduction rate of the United States. This suggests that Canadian transfer benefits may be better targeted on poverty; 99 percent of poor families with children in Canada get government transfers, and these transfers appear to be more efficiently distributed than in the United States. But another reason why the United States does less well with almost the same level of transfers is because the poverty gap is larger in the United States than in Canada and the other countries. The larger the poverty gap the more income is needed to remove a family from poverty. And the United States, which has the biggest gap for these families, provides the least income support per family.

Income support as a percent of gross domestic product (GDP). If we compare how much income support is provided to poor families as a percentage of GDP instead of in absolute dollar amounts, the difference among countries increases. The OECD has recently estimated family income benefits, including both universal and means-tested benefits for children, and has separately estimated tax credits and tax relief for children (17). Combining the two calculations provides a composite estimate of the two forms of income support for children. These estimates are presented as a percentage of GDP; the nature of the calculations, however, means that they should not be treated as precise measures of government support, but rather as relative orders of magnitude.

Canada and the United States distribute about 0.5 percent of GDP in income transfers to children, about half of what the four other countries provide. This understates the U.S. and Canadian efforts since it does not take into account their benefits provided through the tax system. When tax benefits are added to transfers, Canada's share increases considerably to 1.6 percent, but the U.S. resource allocation only rises to 0.6 percent of GDP, still half or less the allocation of Sweden, the United Kingdom, Australia, and Canada. If these estimates of transfers and taxes as a percentage of GDP allocated to children are adjusted by the percentage of the population 0 to 17 years of age relative to the United States, the differences between the United States, which has a relatively young population, and the other countries would increase still further.

The OECD also has estimated educational expenses as a percentage of GDP. And in educational expenses, the United States spends a higher percentage of its GDP than Germany and the same as the United Kingdom (5.3, 4.6, and 5.3, respectively). Canada, Sweden, and Australia spend at least 5.9 percent of GDP on education. The relative difference in the percentage of GDP spent on education among the six countries is much less than the differences for income transfers. Separate estimates for health care expenditures developed at LIS indicate even less variance in health care expenditures per child across these six countries, with the range being from 1.1 to 1.7 percent of GDP and with the United States at 1.4 percent, the average of the six countries studied. It appears, therefore, that although the United States is as willing to provide education and health care to families with children, as are the other nations examined here, we are less willing to provide direct income support to families with children.

CONCLUDING REMARKS

Child poverty rates in the United States have increased from 16 percent in 1979 to 20 percent in 1987 (*18*). A great deal has now been written about the reluctance of the U.S. public to support public assistance to families with poor children. Moynihan has described U.S. policy as one more focused on individuals than on families (*19*). This focus encourages us to help the individual child through education but not the family of the child through income support. Jencks *et al.*, however, have warned that we cannot depend exclusively on our educational system to provide equal economic opportunity for all children (*20*).

International comparisons across many countries may be instructive, but they are not necessarily proscriptive. Every country's welfare and other tax-transfer programs reflect their own cultural and social philosophies, just as differences in child poverty rates across countries reflect individual country differences in family structure and population heterogeneity. Any changes in tax and transfer policies must be done within the national context of the country's social philosophy. But international comparisons of the poverty of today's children raise long-term questions. To the extent that poverty of children is related to their poverty as adults (*21, 22*), the quality of our future work force may be affected by the present poverty of our children. And the poverty of our children today may affect our long-term competitiveness with other wealthy countries who tolerate much less child poverty than does the United States.

REFERENCES AND NOTES

1. Bureau of the Census, *Curr. Popul. Rep.*, *Ser. P-60* (no. 161) (1988), table 16.
2. S. Preston, *Demography* **21**, 435 (1984).
3. J. Palmer, T. Smeeding, B. B. Torrey, Eds., *The Vulnerable* (Urban Institute Press, Washington, DC, 1988).
4. Because our income definition includes food stamps and subtracts income and payroll taxes, it differs slightly from the official U.S. poverty definition, even though LIS uses the exact same data base, family definition, and poverty definitions as does the U.S. Bureau of the Census. These differences are relatively small. For instance, in 1979, the U.S. Bureau of the Census (*1*) estimated that 16.0 percent of U.S. children were in families with incomes below the poverty line. Our estimate (Table 1) shows 17.1 percent poor.
5. Adjusted income is calculated by dividing the income of a given size family unit by the relative number of equivalent adults in that unit, normalized to a family of size three. A single mother and one child's income is divided by 0.84, a couple with one child (or a single parent with two children) has its disposable income divided by 1.0, a couple with two children by 1.28, and so on. Once income is adjusted and normalized in this way, it can be compared to any three person poverty line.
6. T. Smeeding, B. Torrey, M. Rein, in (*3*), pp. 89–119.
7. M. Ward, *Purchasing Power Parities and Real Expenditures in the OECD* (OECD, Paris, 1985), p. 117.
8. B. Buhmann et al., *Rev. Income Wealth* **34**, 115 (1988).
9. C Jencks and B. Torrey, in (*3*), pp. 229–273.
10. The LIS data base currently includes ten countries, the six studied here and Israel, Netherlands, Norway, and Switzerland. Previous analyses [for instance, Smeeding, Torrey, and Rein (*6*) and Buhmann, Rainwater, Schmaus, and Smeeding (*8*)] indicate that including these countries would not affect the results shown below. Therefore, in the interest of space we restricted our analysis to those countries that provided the most contrast and also the most insights in comparison with the U.S. situation.
11. I. Garfinkel and S. McLanahan, *Single Mothers and Their Children* (Urban Institute Press, Washington, DC, 1986).
12. R. Hauser, *European Econ. Rev.* **31**, 138 (1987).
13. R. Haveman, *Poverty Policy and Poverty Research* (Univ. of Wisconsin Press, Madison, 1987).
14. B. Wolfe et al., *Kyklos*, **37**, 609 (1984).
15. Table 5.9 in (*6*) and table 16 in (*1*).
16. The difference in poverty rates of all U.S. families and the average poverty rates of all families in Canada, Germany, Sweden, and the United Kingdom is 6.7 percentage points (13.8 percent minus 7.1 percent). If we consider the poverty rates of only two-parent white families in each country, then the difference shrinks to 2.8 percentage points (8.8 percent minus 6.0 percent). This is a 58 percent reduction in the original differences between the United States and the other countries. If we assume that increasing participation in income transfer programs would reduce U.S. two-parent white families in poverty by the same amount as we estimated for all families (4.6 percent), this

would further reduce the difference between the United States and other countries another 0.4 percentage points (8.8 × 0.046) to 2.4 percentage points. This represents a 64 percent reduction from the original differences in poverty rates (6.7 minus 2.4 divided by 6.7).

17. M. O'Higgins, in (3), pp. 201–228.
18. See data in (1), table 16.
19. D. P. Moynihan, *Family and Nation* (Harvest/Harcourt Brace Jovanovich, New York, 1987), p. 5.
20. C. Jencks *et al. Inequality* (Harper & Row, New York, 1977), p. 7.
21. S. J. McLanahan, *Demography* **25**, 1 (1988).
22. G. Duncan, M. S. Hill, S. D. Hoffman, *Science*, **239**, 467 (1988).
23. Supported in part by grants from the Ford Foundation, the Sloan Foundation, and the National Science Foundation. We gratefully acknowledge L. Rainwater and G. Schmaus for their considerable contribution to the development of the LIS data; B. Buhmann for data tabulations; G. Duncan, I. Garfinkel, R. Hauser, S. McLanahan, S. Preston, P. Ruggles, F. Torrey, M. Wolfson, and the referees for their comments on the manuscript.

11

Why We Have Homelessness

Peter H. Rossi

HOUSING AND HOMELESSNESS

In discussing the distinguishing characteristics of homeless Americans, it is easy to lose sight of the fact that the essential and defining symptom of homelessness is lack of access to conventional housing. Clearly, if conventional housing were both everywhere abundant and without cost, there would be no homelessness except for those who preferred to sleep in the streets and in public places.[1] That there are homeless people in fairly large numbers means that our housing market is not providing appropriate housing abundantly at prices the homeless can afford. Nor is it providing affordable housing for the extremely poor, who must double up with others.

To be sure, there is no way any housing market dominated by private providers can offer housing at an "affordable price" for those who have close to zero income. But market-offered housing is not the only option. Most of the extremely poor are domiciled, and their housing chances are affected by the supply of low-cost housing generally, a market factor that affects the households they live with. There is abundant evidence that homelessness is related both directly and indirectly to the shortage of

---

[1]Many commentators and researchers on homelessness claim they have talked to homeless people who said they preferred homelessness to conventional housing. I have no doubt that such statements have been made. I also have little doubt that when offered an option under realistic conditions, few homeless people would make such a choice.

From Peter H. Rossi, *Down and Out in America: The Origins of Homelessness*, University of Chicago Press, 1988.

inexpensive housing for poor families and poor unattached persons that began in the 1970s and has accelerated in the 1980s.

The decline in the inexpensive segment of our housing stock has been precipitous in the largest cities, such as New York and Los Angeles, but it also has characterized cities of all sizes (Wright and Lam 1987). The Annual Housing Survey, conducted by the Census Bureau for the Department of Housing and Urban Development, has recorded in city after city declines in the proportion of housing renting for 40% or less of poverty-level incomes. These declines ranged from 12% in Baltimore between 1978 and 1983 to 40% in Washington D.C. for 1977 to 1981 and 58% in Anaheim, California, in the same period. In twelve large cities surveyed between 1978 and 1983, the amount of inexpensive rental housing available to poor families dropped precipitously, averaging 30%. At the same time, the number of households living at or below the poverty level in the same cities increased by 36%. The consequence of these two trends is that in the early 1980s a severe shortage occurred in housing that poor households could afford without bearing an excessive rent burden. Note that these calculations assume that such affordable housing rents for 40% or less of the poverty level, a larger proportion of income than the customary prudent 25% for rent.

Most of the housing I have discussed so far consists of multiroom units appropriate to families. If we restrict our attention to that portion of the housing stock that is ordinarily occupied by poor unattached single persons, then the decline is even more precipitous. Chicago's Planning Department estimated that between 1973 and 1984, 18,000 single-person dwelling units in SRO hotels and small apartment buildings—amounting to 19% of the stock existing in 1973—were demolished or transformed for other uses (Chicago Department of Planning 1985).[2] In Los Angeles a recent report (Hamilton, Rabinowitz and Alschuler, Inc. 1987) indicated that between 1970 and 1985 more than half of the SRO units in downtown Los Angeles had been demolished. Of course there is nothing wrong per se with the demolition of SROs; most were certainly not historical landmarks or examples of any notable architectural style. Nor can they be said to have been of high quality. The problem is that units comparable in function or price were not built or converted in sufficient volume to replace them. . . .

In 1958 about 8,000 homeless men were accommodated in such units in Chicago; by 1980 all the cubicle hotels had been removed.[3] In New York,

---

[2]At the same time, 11,000 subsidized senior citizens' units had been added to the stock, and 8,500 section 8 senior citizens' housing vouchers were issued. Provision was made for replacing housing stock, but only for a portion of the single-person housing, that used by persons sixty-five and over.

[3]In 1980 the last two Chicago cubicle hotels, the Star and the Major, were demolished to be replaced by Presidential Towers, a 1,200-unit luxury apartment complex.

by 1987 only one of the cheap hotels that dominated the Bowery in the 1960s remained (Jackson 1987).[4] Similar changes have occurred in other large cities. Of course it is difficult to mourn the passing of the often dirty and always inadequate cubicle hotels. Like the SROs, they had little or no symbolic or aesthetic value. But only the emergency dormitory shelters have replaced the housing stock they represented. There are virtually no rooms in Chicago today that can be rented for $1.80 to $2.70 a night, today's dollar equivalent of the 1958 rents. The emergency dormitory shelters are arguably cleaner than the cubicle hotels, but they are certainly not much closer to decent housing. Indeed, the old Skid Row residents regarded the mission dormitory shelters as considerably inferior to the cubicle hotels, lacking in privacy and personal safety (Bogue 1963).[5]

The decline in inexpensive housing influences homelessness both directly and indirectly. Indirectly, the effect can be felt through the increased financial housing burden placed on poor families, whose generosity toward their dependent adult members becomes more difficult to extend or maintain. Housing prices partially reflect the amount of housing involved, with larger units commanding higher prices. Faced with declining real income, poor families may have had to opt for smaller dwellings, restricting their ability to shelter adult children.

The direct effects are upon the homeless themselves, putting inexpensive housing, such as SRO accommodations, beyond the reach of most of the new homeless. For example, in a study of SROs in Chicago, Hoch (1985) found that the average monthly rental for SRO hotels in Chicago in 1984 was $195 if rented by the month or $240 ($8 a day), if rented day to day. For most of the homeless, with median monthly incomes of $100, renting an SRO room steadily was out of the question.

Because rents were so high relative to income, the tenants of Chicago's SROs were forced to spend a very large proportion of their income on housing. When some out of the ordinary expense occurred, many had to resort to the shelters and the streets. According to Hoch, about one in ten of the SRO tenants had been homeless for some period during the previous year, apparently too short of funds to pay the rent. Hoch does not tell us whether these SRO tenants lived in shelters or on the streets when they became homeless. But in our survey of the Chicago homeless, both the shelter and the street samples claimed they spent about 10% of their nights in rented rooms, presumably in SRO hotels.

Some of the homeless people we interviewed on the streets or in the shelters ordinarily spent most nights in SRO hotels and were just tempo-

---

[4]Jackson's essay on the history of the Bowery relates that by 1987 gentrification had begun to convert land to upscale condominiums.

[5]The dormitory shelters in the old Skid Rows were those offered by the religious missions. At least part of the old Skid Row men's dislike for the shelters centered on the typical requirement that they attend religious services in return for access to the dormitory beds.

rarily homeless.[6] Others occasionally spent a night or two in an SRO, perhaps when they received a windfall. Apparently there is a considerable interchange between the homeless and the SRO populations, the latter being a cut above the former in income. Similarly, Piliavin and Sosin (1987–88) found that homeless people in Minneapolis typically moved between having homes and being homeless several times a year.

High rents relative to income also forced some of the SRO tenants to overspend on housing and, accordingly, to skimp on other expenditures. Hoch reports that many SRO residents resorted to the food kitchens, to the medical clinics set up for homeless persons, and to the clothing depots. In a study of the homeless in downtown Los Angeles, one out of every three persons in the soup-kitchen lines was renting a room in an SRO (Farr, Koegel, and Burnham 1986). Further confirmation can be found in Sosin's 1986 study of persons using Chicago food kitchens and day centers (Sosin, Colson, and Grossman 1988), which found that about half were living in SROs and apartments.

The impact of the housing market on homelessness in the aggregate was shown dramatically in a recent analysis by Tucker (1987). There are several deficiencies in Tucker's procedures; nevertheless, some of his findings are both useful and relevant. Using the HUD estimates[7] of the number of homeless in each of fifty cities to compute a homelessness rate for each city,[8] Tucker was able to show a fairly strong negative correlation, −.39, between housing vacancy rates in 1980 and homelessness rates in 1984 across cities. In other words, the higher the vacancy rate in a city, the lower its homelessness rate. Tucker also showed that the vacancy rate is highly sensitive to the presence of rent control measures, but that need not concern us here. The point Tucker's analysis drives home is that the tighter the housing market from the buyer's (or renter's) point of view, the greater the housing burden on poor families and the more difficult it becomes for the extremely poor to obtain housing, and consequently the easier it is to become homeless.

In a perfect unrestricted housing market, the range of housing offered by sellers at equilibrium would supply all buyers who can enter bids. But this statement is more a matter of faith than of fact. The American housing

[6]This information comes from interviewers' comments on the filled-out questionnaires. Unfortunately, we did not ask shelter residents for enough detailed information to estimate the prevalence of this pattern of intermittent homelessness.

[7]These estimates are simply averages of what informed persons in the cities studied thought were the total number of homeless people there. Although no one can gauge their accuracy, it is likely that they reflect well the differences among cities in amount of homelessness. Note that these intercity differences in homelessness are the focus of Tucker's analysis.

[8]HUD analysts related the number of homeless people in each city to the population for the Rand McNally metropolitan area in which the city was situated, a strategy that was heavily criticized. Tucker computed his rates by using only the populations for the central cities.

market is neither unfettered nor perfect. Nor would we have it any other way. Our building codes are designed to ensure that the housing industry provides accommodations that meet minimum standards of public health and safety. Zoning laws attempt to regulate the externalities surrounding existing structures. Occupancy laws discourage overcrowding of dwelling units. These regulations also accomplish other ends, some undesirable to many citizens: for example, zoning laws designed to ensure that structures occupy no more than some given proportion of urban land plots, a desirable aesthetic amenity, also make neighborhoods socioeconomically homogeneous. In some cities rent control is an additional restriction whose burden falls heavily on households entering the market and provides a bonus in the form of cheaper rents to long-term residents. These regulations are not the only factors restricting the amount of "affordable housing" available to the poor, but they certainly drive up the prices of even minimum standard housing.

However, there can be no market where there is no effective demand. The market cannot provide affordable housing for the homeless because their incomes are so low and variable that their demand is too weak to stimulate housing providers. The housing market was not always unresponsive to the demand of poor people. The Skid Rows of the nation were such responses, but the old cubicle hotels of the 1950s and 1960s were responding to a much stronger demand. Recall that the constant-dollar income of the Skid Row residents in 1958 was at least three times the income of the current homeless. Even so, as Bogue and the other social researchers observed in the 1950s and 1960s, the cubicle hotels were experiencing high vacancy rates.

The records are silent on whether the cubicle hotel owners and operators welcomed or fought the exercise of eminent domain in the urban renewal of Skid Row areas. Perhaps they welcomed the bulldozers as a way to recover some of the equity they had sunk into an increasingly unprofitable business.

In the past, when the housing industry was unable (or unwilling) to provide homes for the extremely poor they sometimes built their own. In the Great Depression of the 1930s, "shantytowns" consisting of shacks cobbled together out of scrap materials were built on New York's riverfronts and even in Central Park. Similar settlements were erected on Chicago's lakefront, in Washington's Anacostia Flats, and on vacant sites in other cities. In the 1980s no comparable settlements have appeared, unless one counts the cardboard and wooden packing cases used as living quarters by a few of the homeless. It may be that vacant land is not as available now or that law enforcement officials are quicker to respond.[9]

[9]Indeed, in 1987 when homeless people in Los Angeles built a "tent city" on a vacant downtown parcel, the mayor ordered the police to tear it down. Temporary shacks and tents have been built in Washington's Lafayette Park, but they must be removed every evening.

Whatever has caused the difference, the self-help response of the homeless to market failure has not been as strong as in the past.

As the rents the homeless could afford declined with their incomes during the 1970s and 1980s, housing providers found them an increasingly unattractive set of customers, especially in contrast to others. There is no mystery about why no housing is offered on the unsubsidized market that is affordable to the homeless. If there is a question, it is why local, state, and federal government have not intervened in the market to ensure that such housing is supplied. . . .

THE LABOR MARKET AND HOMELESSNESS

A major factor in the 1960s and 1970s decline of the Skid Rows was the shrinkage of the casual labor market in urban economies. This decline in labor demand is carefully documented in Barrett Lee's (1980) analysis of the trends in Skid Row populations in forty-one cities from 1950 to 1970, showing that as the proportion of each city's labor force employed in unskilled labor and unskilled service occupations declined in that period, so did the population of its Skid Row.

In earlier decades, urban employers needing muscle power to wrestle cargo apparently put up with the low productivity of the Skid Row inhabitants because they could hire them as needed for low pay. Apparently, materials-handling equipment such as forklifts put both the homeless and Skid Row out of business. Cause and effect are almost hopelessly muddled here. As Skid Row populations declined, employers may have been motivated to invest in equipment that lowered their need for casual labor, and at the same time the lowered need for such labor meant that Skid Rows were populated more and more by persons out of the labor force (e.g., pensioners either retired or disabled).

The lack of demand for unskilled labor contributes to contemporary homelessness and helps account for the poor employment and earnings records of the extremely poor and the homeless. Labor market factors are especially important in understanding the sharp decline in the average age of the extremely poor and the homeless over the past three decades. Between 1955 and 1985 there was a drastic increase in unemployment among young males in general and blacks in particular. Unemployment reached catastrophic proportions in 1985 with 40% rates among black males under twenty-five (Freeman and Holzer 1986). Freeman and Holzer showed that young black males were considerably more likely to be employed only for short periods and were more likely to be fired.

The demographic processes at work during the post—World War II period also help explain the declining average age of the homeless. Recent decades have seen a bulge in the proportion of persons in our population who are between twenty and thirty-five, an outcome of the postwar baby boom. This excess of young people, especially males, depressed the earnings level for young adults and elevated the unemployment rate. As Easterlin (1987) has shown, the earnings of workers under thirty-five declined between 1968 and 1984 to about 80% of the 1968 level, computed in constant dollars. In contrast, the real wages of workers forty-five to fifty-five rose in the same period to 125% of their 1968 levels. Easterlin showed similar trends in the unemployment rate. At the beginning of the period under study, unemployment rates for young men below thirty-five were under 5% and rose to a high of 15% in 1980, declining to 13% in 1984. Older workers did not show such fluctuations.

The point of this analysis of the labor market is to show that the employment opportunities for young men has been extremely poor over the same period when the homeless population has increased and its composition has changed, with a time lag of five to ten years. As usual, the burdens of a poor labor market fall disproportionately upon precisely those groups we find overrepresented among the homeless—the disabled and minorities.

The impact on females of labor market and demographic trends since 1965 is a little more subtle. Easterlin's analysis shows that young women did not suffer as much from increased unemployment and decreased earnings as young men, although their positions on the labor market certainly showed no improvement over time. In comparison with those of young men, their earnings did not show as radical a decline in real dollars, and unemployment rates did not rise as dramatically.

But there is also an indirect effect on household formation that did affect the proportion of women with children who are married and thus contributed to what has been called the feminization of poverty. . . . Homeless women are younger than homeless men—on the average five to ten years younger. Almost all the homeless heads of households were female. The abrupt rise in female-headed households from 1968 to 1984 in part reflects the uncertain economic fate of young men, who thereby become less attractive as mates, less willing to become household heads, and less able to fulfill the economic role of husband and father when marriage does take place.[10] In this respect it is significant that almost all the families housed in New York's welfare hotels are black or Hispanic female-headed households. Likewise, almost all the young homeless women we studied in Chicago were black, and almost all the homeless families were headed by black females.

In short, the uncertain labor market and earnings fates of young black men jeopardized family formation among young blacks. The consequence is that young black women became heads of extremely poor households

[10]Although few of the homeless men had married and those that had were divorced or separated, a majority (60%) claimed to be fathers. It is tempting to speculate how many of the fathers of the children in the homeless female-headed households are to be found among the homeless men.

with high risk of becoming periodically homeless. In his analysis of poverty among blacks in Chicago, Wilson (1987) attributes much of the rise in female-headed households to the lack of marriageable black males. Owing to their catastrophically high unemployment rates, few young black men were able to make economic contributions to the households formed by the mothers of their children, let alone be the major providers.

THE LIMITS OF KINSHIP OBLIGATIONS

It is an easy wager that there are few if any readers of this book whose families and kin would allow them to sink into literal homelessness. It is another easy wager that few if any readers would allow a family member or a near relative to become homeless. At least that would be our initial reaction to someone close to us who had become destitute through disabling illness, severe alcoholism, or an episode of mental disturbance. We would certainly offer financial help and even make room in our homes. American norms concerning obligations owed to kin support strongly such actions.[11] But how long could we keep it up? One would not begrudge support over a few weeks or months or even a year, but imagine having to supply maintenance and food for several years and, in addition, to share crowded housing.

Sharing might not be too hard for those of us who have room to spare in our houses and apartments and who have some discretionary income left after we finance a reasonably good standard of living. The generous impulse would be harder to extinguish if the dependent family member or kin was well behaved and did nothing bizarre or in poor taste. Even so, it would be hard to put up with. Doubtless we all know, and admire, people in our circles of kin, friends, and acquaintances who have made such sacrifices for fairly long periods. . . .

In 1987 2.6 million extremely poor adult children aged twenty-two to fifty-nine were living in their parents' homes, and an additional 677,000 were living with siblings or grandparents. Of course many, if not most, of their families could sustain the additional burden: the household incomes of the supportive families were slightly above average. In addition, some families subsidized their impoverished adult members without taking them into their homes. Unfortunately, the Current Population Survey does not provide enough information so we can estimate the extent of such cash subsidies: we do know that there are at least 3.5 million impoverished dependent adults who are being subsidized by their parents and possibly as many as 6.5 million.

[11]In a recent study of kinship norms, Alice Rossi and I found that almost all of a sample of metropolitan Boston adults acknowledged strong obligations to provide financial help to primary kin (parents, children, and siblings) who were suffering from the effects of illness, psychological difficulties, or unemployment.

But now imagine the situation of poor parents, living at the poverty level or below in cramped quarters, on whom the responsibility for supporting an impoverished unemployed adult family member has fallen. How long could they keep it up? Imagine, in addition, that this dependent adult child has a serious alcohol or drug problem or has been in prison or exhibits the bizarre thinking or behavior of the chronically mentally ill.

It appears from our . . . data that the average life of tolerance and help under such conditions is about four years, the period that the homeless were without steady work before becoming homeless. For that length of time they were presumably supported by their families' and friends' sharing housing, food, and maintenance. In addition, keep in mind that the families and friends are also poor and all those necessities are in short supply. Indeed, it is also a euphemism to talk about families, since many of the homeless come from single-parent households: their mothers and siblings may have been all there was to the "family" they relied on for support.[12] Piliavin and Sosin (1987) and Sosin, Colson, and Grossman (1988) comment that many of the homeless grew up in foster homes and may have had no parents at all or ones who were unable to fulfill their parental responsibilities.

There is good evidence that many of the homeless have worn out their welcome as dependents of their parents or as recipients of aid and funds from their friends. . . . striking differences [exist] between the extremely poor unattached persons in the General Assistance population and the homeless. . . . the groups are almost equally destitute, but most of the GA recipients are not living in shelters or out on the streets.

There are other important differences between the two groups that go along with their living arrangements. First, the levels of disability among GA clients are much lower on every indicator we can find in the data. Chronic mental illness, alcoholism, serious criminal records, and physical illnesses are far less prevalent among the domiciled. Second, the GA recipients largely manage to get by because their family and friendship support networks subsidize them, either by providing housing and maintenance or by supplementing their income.

Recall also that the GA recipients are on the average six years younger than the homeless men, suggesting that they have not yet worn out their welcome in their parents' households. Their much lower levels of alcoholism and chronic mental illness may also mean it is more acceptable to share housing with them. At least some of the GA recipients may thus simply be younger versions of the homeless and may wear out their acceptance if their dependence goes on too long. The demoralizing and debilitating effects of long-term unemployment undoubtedly also play a role: the longer a person goes unemployed, the more likely it is that the

[12]Many of the mothers may also have been on AFDC during much of the time the sons were growing up and in their late teens or early adulthood. The Chicago AFDC study showed that 10% of AFDC recipients had children over eighteen living in their households.

disabilities of depression, mental illness, and even alcoholism will take their toll.

I suggest that the poverty of the families the homeless come from and their levels of disability both contribute heavily to their being homeless. Generosity may come up against the constraints of poverty when disability makes it difficult to exercise that virtue.

THE EROSION OF PUBLIC WELFARE BENEFITS

We have seen that at least part of the burden of supporting extremely poor unattached persons is borne by poverty-stricken households who stretch their meager resources to house and maintain dependent adult children and sometimes friends. We can see national trends in young people living with their parents, especially among the poor. Indeed, black young men are especially likely to live in their parents' households. According to the census, in 1970, 39% of both black and white young men aged eighteen to twenty-nine lived with their parents. By 1984, 54% of black young men lived with their parents while only 41% of white men of comparable age did so.

Evidence for the extent of the burden on poor families is difficult to come by, since we do not know much about the households the homeless come from. But we do know that those households are poor and that many are supported by welfare—in particular, AFDC payments. Strong indicators of the declining positions of poor families can be found in the downward trends of transfer payments from 1968 to 1985. The level of welfare benefits also directly affects the capacity of the extremely poor to take care of themselves without the help of their parents. It is obvious that at the heart of homelessness and extreme poverty are the extremely low incomes of those groups. Among those states that have programs of income support to unattached persons, none provides enough to reach $4,000 a year. In addition, there are many states—for example, Texas, Alabama, and Tennessee—that have no income support programs at all for this segment of the population.

The importance of income support in alleviating extreme poverty is obvious. What is not obvious is that income support programs that cover unattached people below retirement age have undergone a severe deterioration in value over the past decade and a half, exacerbating the erosion of the life chances of the poor caused by labor and housing market trends. . . .

On the national level, in 1985 AFDC payments declined to 63% of their 1968 value. Illinois AFDC payments declined to 53% of 1968 value in the same period. An even more drastic decline occurred in Illinois's General Assistance payments, the program most often available to homeless persons and to unattached persons generally: 1985 General Assistance payments in Illinois were only 48% of 1968 payments in constant dollars. The major drop in value of these two transfer programs occurred in the five years between 1975 and 1980, reflecting the ravages of inflationary trends that were not sufficiently compensated for by raising payment levels.[13] As the burden of supporting unemployed adults fell upon families who in turn were dependent on AFDC or GA payments, such poor families entered the 1980s with considerably diminished financial capability and hence reduced capacity to help.

In addition, the reduction in the real value of AFDC payments contributed directly to the appearance of female-headed households among the homeless. Female-headed households dependent on AFDC surely must have had a hard time meeting housing and other expenses on payments that barely covered average rents for small apartments. Living so close to the edge of financial disaster and often slipping into crisis, households headed by young females understandably often become literally homeless. Indeed, it is difficult to understand how the typical Illinois AFDC household composed of a mother and her 1.5 children managed to get by on $4,014 a year in direct cash payments and $798 in food stamps. More than a third of the AFDC households received help from other persons (presumably relatives) over a year's time. The Chicago AFDC study provides considerable evidence that AFDC families had a tenuous hold on their housing, with close to one in four experiencing problems over the previous year.

Illinois's AFDC payment schedule in 1985 and 1986 was among the ten most generous state plans. AFDC households in Illinois fared much better than comparable households in, say, Alabama or Texas, where payments averaged under $2,000 a year. Indeed, a major reason the extremely poor female-headed households were concentrated in the southern regions was that even with AFDC payments total annual income rarely reached $2,000.

The similar drop in the dollar value of General Assistance payments also influenced homelessness. General Assistance payments in 1968 were generous enough to cover SRO rent, with a bit left over for other types of consumption. In addition, in 1968 unattached adults on General Assistance had enough income from their benefits to make significant contributions to the income of a household, possibly making their dependence more palatable to their hosts. By 1985, with General Assistance payments

---

[13]Of course there were some compensatory increases in other programs for which unemployed persons became eligible. Food stamps in 1985 could provide an additional $70 in food purchases, a benefit of dubious value to the homeless. Medicaid coverage was also extended in some states (Illinois, for example) and provided for most medical needs. Although food stamps and housing subsidies compensate in a very direct way for low income, Medicare or Medicaid is more questionable: you cannot pay the rent or eat with Medicaid coverage.

more than cut in half, GA clients could neither make large contributions to host households nor get by on their own.[14]

The low levels of GA benefits may help explain why so few homeless applied for and received them. Such benefits were not enough to allow recipients to leave the homeless state and were difficult to obtain. Applying for GA benefits in 1984, as described by Stagner and Richman (1986), involved at least three interviews with Illinois Department of Public Aid caseworkers, a determination of employability, and an assignment either to an unemployable class or to a "jobs" program in which a person had to sustain eligibility by applying for work to at least eight employers a month. A person assigned to the jobs program who did not find employment within sixty days was assigned either to the unemployable class or to a public service workfare task. Keeping to the complex schedule of interviews and reporting requirements must have been difficult for the homeless.

Table 7.1 also contains clues to why so few aged persons are found among the homeless and the extremely poor in the 1980s. Fewer than 2% of the Chicago homeless were sixty-five or over. Only 500,000 of the extremely poor persons in the 1987 Current Population Survey were sixty-one or older with incomes under $4,000. Old age Social Security retirement benefits increased by 162% from 1968 to 1985, thanks to favorable changes in the benefit levels in 1972 plus the indexing of such benefits by tying them to the consumer price index. The constant-dollar value of the average old age pension in Illinois in 1968 was slightly below the value of General Assistance payments, but by 1985 it had increased by 164% and was 3.3 times the value of General Assistance.

Note also that the absolute amount of Illinois average monthly old age pension payments in 1985, $511, was enough to rent accommodations at the bottom portion of the conventional housing market and certainly sufficient for the subsidized senior citizens' housing developments.

The sharply enhanced economic well-being of the elderly is one of the great program success stories of the twentieth century. Throughout the century, until the 1970s, the elderly were greatly overrepresented among

---

[14]Contributions toward rent reported by the GA recipients were more than half of the benefit level received, as shown below:

Living Arrangements	Average Monthly Rent or Contribution
Living alone	$159
Living with nonrelatives	$122
Living with relatives	$ 97

Note that GA recipients living alone paid more in rent, on the average, than they received in GA payments. Most (84%) GA recipients living alone also received help from their relatives. (Unfortunately the survey did not ascertain either the kind or the amount of help received. It is a fair presumption, however, that financial help must have loomed large.)

the poor; today, for the first time in our history, the poverty rate for persons aged sixty-five and over is less than that for the rest of the population. How this was accomplished says a lot about how the problem of homelessness will have to be solved, if indeed it ever is. We virtually wiped out poverty among the aged by providing generous benefits. Public spending on the elderly, through Social Security pensions, Medicare, and housing subsidies, dwarfs every other item in the federal human services budget.[15]

There are two main lessons to be drawn from the past decade's decline in welfare. First, our policies have undermined the income positions of the extremely poor and the capacity of poor families to care for their dependent adult members. In every state, income support programs for unattached persons are not generous enough to support minimum standard housing and diet. In addition, by allowing welfare payments to be eaten away by inflation, we have reduced the capacity of families to care for their dependent adult members. Second, we have not sufficiently assimilated the lessons of the recent history of the Social Security retirement program. By providing decent payment levels, this program has virtually wiped out homelessness and extreme poverty among the aged.

AN INTERPRETATION OF HOMELESSNESS

Throughout this book I have described the characteristics of the current homeless, highlighting those that mark off this population from that of the old Skid Rows and from the current domiciled poor. Drawing these various threads together, we can now begin to weave an explanation both of why some people are more likely to be found among the homeless and of why homelessness has apparently increased over the past decade.

First of all, it is important to distinguish between the short-term (episodic) homeless, and the long-term (chronic) homeless who appear likely to remain so. Most of what I have to say . . . concerns the latter group; the former consists primarily of people in the lower ranks of the income distribution who meet short-term reversals of fortune. This is not to deemphasize the problems of the short-term homeless but simply to say that their problems are different.

The "dynamics" of episodic homelessness are distressingly straightforward. So long as there is a poverty population whose incomes put them at the economic edge, there will always be people who fall over that edge into homelessness. Small setbacks that those above the poverty line can absorb may become major disruptions to the very poor. Several homely

---

[15]In 1984 the total federal social welfare expenditure was $419 billion. Social Security pensions and Medicare expenditures alone amounted to $302 billion, 72% of the total social welfare expenditure. See *Statistical Abstract of the United States: 1987* (Washington, D.C.: U.S. Department of Commerce, 1986, table 574).

examples illustrate this point. The failure of an old refrigerator or stove and a subsequent repair bill of $50 can make the nonpoor grumble about bad luck, but for someone whose monthly income is under $500 and whose rent is $300, the bill represents one-fourth of the monthly resources used to buy food, clothing, and other necessities. For a poor person who depends on a car to travel to work, a car repair bill of a few hundred dollars may mean months of deprivation. Renting an apartment increasingly means paying one month's rent in advance and perhaps a security deposit as well and is often why poor people remain in substandard housing. In many states welfare programs make provision for such emergency expenses, but the unattached person who is not eligible for welfare may experience wide swings of fortune, with the downsides spent among the homeless.

The solution is to be found in extending the coverage of the social welfare system and incorporating provisions that would cushion against short-term economic difficulties.

What about the long-term or chronic homeless? Their critical characteristic is the high level of disabilities that both impair their earning capacity and reduce their acceptance by their families, kin, and friends. These are the people who are most strongly affected by shortages of unskilled positions in the labor force, lack of inexpensive housing, and declines in the economic fortunes of their families, kin, and friends. Under these unfavorable conditions, unattached persons with disabilities have increasing difficulty in getting along on their own. And as the living conditions of poor households decline, those disabled by chronic mental or physical illnesses or by chronic substance abuse are no longer tolerated as dependents.

Note that I am using the term disabled in this context to mark any condition that appreciably impairs the ability to make minimally successful connections with the labor market and to form mutually satisfactory relationships with family, kin, and friends. This definition goes beyond the usual meaning of disability to include a much wider set of conditions—for example, criminal records that interfere with employment chances or chronic problems with drinking, as well as physical and psychiatric impairments.

Let me emphasize that this interpretation is not "blaming the victim." It is an attempt to explain who become the victims of perverse macrolevel social forces. If there is any blame, it should be placed on the failure of the housing market, labor market, and welfare system, which forces some people—the most vulnerable—to become victims by undermining their ability to get along by themselves and weakening the ability of family, kin, and friends to help them. . . .

The resurgence of extreme poverty and homelessness in the past two decades should remind us that the safety nets we initiated during the Great Depression and augmented in the 1960s are failing to prevent destitution. The Reagan administration did not succeed in dismantling any significant portion of the net, but it made the mesh so coarse and weak that many fall through. Those who are disabled by minority status, chronic mental illness, physical illness, or substance abuse are especially vulnerable. All the very poor suffer, but it is the most vulnerable who fall to the very bottom—homelessness.

The social welfare system has never been very attentive to unattached, disaffiliated men, and now it appears to be as unresponsive to unattached females. Likewise, the social welfare system does little to help families support their dependent adult members. Many of the homeless of the 1950s and early 1960s were pushed out or thrown away by their families when they passed the peak of adulthood; many of the new homeless are products of a similar process, but this one commences at age twenty-five or thirty rather than at fifty or sixty.

As a consequence, homelessness now looms large on our political agenda, and there is anxious concern about what can be done. I have suggested a number of measures to reduce homelessness to a more acceptable level. These include compensating for the failure of our housing market by fostering the retention and enlargement of our urban low-income housing stock, especially that appropriate for unattached persons; reversing the policy that has put personal choice above institutionalization for those so severely disabled that they are unable to make decisions that will preserve their physical well-being; enlarging our conception of disability to include conditions not purely physical in character and, in particular, recognizing that chronic mental illness and chronic substance abuse are often profound disabilities; restoring the real value of welfare payments to the purchasing power they had in the late 1960s; and extending the coverage of welfare benefits to include long-term unemployed, unattached persons.

There is considerable public support in the United States for a social welfare system that guarantees a minimally decent standard of living to all. Homelessness on the scale currently being experienced is clear evidence that such a system is not yet in place. That homelessness exists amid national prosperity without parallel in the history of the world is likewise clear evidence that we can do something about the problem if we choose to. I have stressed that public policy decisions have in large measure created the problem of homelessness; they can solve the problem as well.

12

Hunger in America: The Growing Epidemic

Physician Task Force on Hunger in America

O ne cannot help but appreciate the special irony of hunger in America's breadbasket. The prolific crops which spring from the fertile land produce hundreds of thousands of tons of grains and other food products, so much that each year millions of excess tons are stored in underground caves. Yet American citizens living within a short distance of this productive system are hungry.

The huge, overwhelming complex of buildings known as Cook County Hospital is located right in the middle of Chicago, the nation's third-largest city. It is an unlikely place to find kwashiorkor and marasmus, the Third World diseases of advanced malnutrition and starvation, which were reported to us in south Texas. As our team of doctors listened, joined by the Administrator of the hospital and the Chief of Internal Medicine, Dr. Stephen Nightingale, we learned that these conditions do exist in urban America: "They say we don't see kwashiorkor and marasmus in this country, but we do. I see 15–20 cases every year in my hospital."

The person speaking was Dr. Katherine K. Christoffel, Chair of the Committee on Nutrition of the Illinois Chapter of the American Academy of Pediatrics. The hospital about which she spoke is Children's Memorial Hospital, where she is Attending Pediatrician in the Division of Ambulatory Services.

Despite her impressive credentials, members of the visiting team of physicians remained skeptical until her report was corroborated by yet another Chicago doctor with his own impressive credentials and experience.

Dr. Howard B. Levy is Chairman of Pediatrics at Mount Sinai Hospital, and previously was Chief of Pediatric Nephrology at the Walter Reed Army Medical Center in Washington, D.C. A member of the American Academy of Pediatrics and the American Medical Association, Dr. Levy joined us to express concern about what he is seeing: "We too are seeing kwashiokor and marasmus, problems which I have not seen since I was overseas. Malnutrition has clearly gone up in the last few years. We have more low-birth-weight babies. We are seeing so much TB that my house staff is no longer excited by it; it excites me that they are not excited by this trend."

Dr. Levy underscored the significance of what he was reporting: "clear, measurable, methodological phenomena" which demonstrate that the health of the patients is getting worse. More and more patients, Dr. Levy observed, have inadequate money to purchase food necessary to prevent growth failure and other nutrition-related problems among the pediatric population.

Well-known Chicago pediatrician Effie Ellis concurred with this observation: "We have a problem here of serious proportions. Social service agencies are having to provide medicines, and hospitals and clinics are having to give out food."

Cook County Hospital gives out food itself and is asked regularly for more by hungry patients. Dr. Nightingale, the Internal Medicine Chief, said that he admits 20 people a day whose problems stem from inadequate nutrition. Pediatric social worker Brenda Chandler has patients come to her saying, "Do you have anything I could eat?" Dietitian Mary Jo Davis sees hunger among "patients" who are not really admitted to the hospital. "Almost every day we have people looking around trying to find out where the hospital leaves its garbage," she reported. Elaborating, she added: "Our hospital patients can't worry about special diets; they do well just to have food in their homes. Sometimes we do dietary recalls over the past three to four days for patients and find that the pages are entirely blank!"

The Chicago Department of Human Services reported that applicants for emergency food have increased 900% in the last two years, a phenomenon seen by social service and religious organizations in the city. The Salvation Army presented statistics showing hunger up significantly for 1984 over 1983, and other agencies, such as the Association House, state that hunger is their number one problem.

Betty Williams of Chicago United Charities placed the mounting hunger problem in a unique perspective: "Our agency is over 100 years old, and this period is as bad as many of us can recall." According to Joel Carp,

Chairman of the Mayor's Task Force on Hunger, at least 600,000 Chicago residents are hungry or likely to be hungry every month. These are people of all ages living well below the federal poverty line: people, he said, "like the old folks on the North Side whom we found living on dog food."

Later that day, some of our team of doctors would confirm this report during their visit to the Marillac House, a large Catholic settlement house in the city. In discussions with the director and her staff, as well as home visits conducted in a housing project, we learned that it is not uncommon for elderly people, living alone in apartments with no cooking facilities, to consume an evening meal of a tin of cat food and a raw egg.

The mayor's office reported that at least 224,000 residents seek emergency food assistance each month, and that the actual number may be twice as high. To respond to the increasing demand, the number of soup kitchens in the city jumped over 80% in the last two years, and now serve 11,500 meals a week. The number of church-related food pantries increased 45% in the same period of time. . . .

The Chicago Health Systems Agency presented survey data to the mayor's office showing food distribution in the city between 1981 and 1983, as part of the city's Emergency Food Program. Approved requests for food assistance rose from 19,312 the first year to 223,500 the last year.

Another barometer of food assistance to the hungry is the Greater Chicago Food Depository, which distributes 400% more food today than it did two years ago. . . . Increasing need is one variable at which we looked. Another is the profile of the hungry and the impact of hunger on their lives. In southwest Chicago our inquiry into the situation faced by laid-off steelworkers at the Wisconsin Plant could have taken place at the Armco Plant in Houston. Frustrated and angry, unemployed workers and their families stand in line for a 5-pound block of cheese and a loaf of bread. Frank Lumkin, president of the Save Our Jobs Committee, explained the dimensions of the problem. "It's having 100 bags of food to give to the families and finding 500 people show up, already in line, at 7:00 A.M."

The hungry are also the elderly. There are 8,000 poor elderly in need of food who are not being served, according to Chicago Office for Senior Citizens. Director Robert Ahrens points out that it is believed that this figure is considerably under the number who are in need of food.

The hungry in Chicago are the families seen by the Visiting Nurse Association, whose district offices have been forced to open food pantries to respond to the lack of food among their patients. "These babies are hungry," implored executive director Margaret Ahern. But, according to her, not only babies. She cited many instances of parents and the elderly also going hungry, some whose caloric intake is as low as 550 calories and 24 grams of protein. "In the prison camps of Germany," she noted, "the daily ration was 800 calories and 40 grams of protein."

The hungry are the patients at the South Lawndale Health Center. The medical director, Dr. Alvarez, and the clinic staff report that health problems related to poor nutrition are not uncommon. Some 10% of their pediatric patients have iron-deficiency anemia, and pulmonary tuberculosis is seen in young people they serve, itself often a result of compromised nutrition. Health workers note that, when they do home visits, they find families unable to purchase adequate food. Children often consume only coffee and an egg for a meal.

The hungry, according to other Chicago agencies, are the undocumented workers whose fear of being deported prevents their even standing in line for cheese. Hector Hernandez sees the realities faced by these families, who come through the Immigrant Services branch of the Traveler's Aid office. Hernandez says that the families often have very little to eat and receive no help as a general rule. Many of them, he explained, have children born in the United States. Yet, if parents seek help such as emergency food assistance, they stand the risk of being reported to Immigration. Immigration may well attempt to deport the parents of the children who are U.S. citizens, thereby breaking apart the family. In this fundamental sense, he explained, the ability of some American children to eat brings with it the likelihood that they will lose their parents.

Hunger in Chicago is the faces, young and old, black and white, of people living on the margins, and many who live beyond the margins of a full stomach:

- The 81-year-old man and his wife who come for a meal at the Uptown Ministries, who live on $293 monthly in social security benefits and $24 in food stamps. They eat mostly grits and oatmeal, sometimes rice and beans.
- The 30-year-old woman whose acknowledged racism was turned around when she saw more people suffering who are white, as she is, than blacks and Spanish. "I used to go without food just so my kids could eat, but now they often go without also."
- The patient in a hospital who, along with her three children, stuffed food into their mouths by hand. They had had nothing to eat for three days.
- The mothers whom doctors find diluting their infant's formula in order to make it last the month.

These American citizens are hungry. They are the "anecdotes" which together reflect and comprise a large problem in this city—people without adequate food to eat. They are the individuals behind the numbers which Dr. Howard Levy and his medical colleagues in the city tabulate: increasing low-birth-weight rates, 50% anemia rates, and the high proportion of children failing to grow, which other doctors noted in a recent study.

"These people are human beings," Charles Betcher reminded us when we visited the soup kitchen at the Uptown Baptist Church. "You can't live long on two pieces of bread a day." Both the center at which Betcher works and this church are among the many agencies in the area trying to feed the hungry, a task that is getting bigger, not smaller.

It is perhaps what Jack Ramsey, director of Second Harvest, umbrella organization for food banks around the nation, had in mind when he observed: "When you see government agencies making referrals to small food pantries that are running out of resources, that's an American tragedy."

Ramsey was not the only person to see the extent of hunger in this major city as a tragedy. Psychiatrist Gordon Harper, a physician who has examined hunger in other regions of the nation, visited a soup kitchen run by the Missionaries of Charity, the order started by Mother Teresa in Calcutta. Reported Dr. Harper: "We observed the spectacle and the tragedy of Missionaries of Charity coming from Calcutta to the West Side of Chicago to provide food for the hungry in America." . . .

Throughout the breadbasket region of southern Illinois, agencies feeding the hungry report increasing need. In June, 1984, the Salvation Army conducted a telephone survey of ten food pantries located in various counties in downstate Illinois. . . . Selected randomly to present a representative picture of pantry experience, the agencies were asked to compare caseloads (however they maintained their records) this year and last. Only one pantry, the Salvation Army in West Frankfort, reported a slight decline in need, a factor attributed to a union and other churches in the town opening food facilities. All the rest report increasing hunger.

The Salvation Army survey reflects the data reported by others whose records we examined. The Friendship House in Peoria, which went from feeding 400 families in 1982 to 2,400 in 1984, perhaps depicts the dimensions of the problem in that city, where hunger is of unusual proportions. Zack Monroe, Peoria welfare director for some 32 years, sat before statistical tables piled on his desk as he analyzed trends over recent years: "Things are getting worse, not better. Even in the Depression there weren't as many people in need of help as now."

"I grew up in the Depression," reported a woman at an elderly feeding site. "I never thought I'd see this again." But there is evidence of Depression-like hunger and suffering in this area. At the Labor Temple in Peoria, we met with unemployed workers and their families. "Thank you for coming," the business manager said as he welcomed our group of doctors, "and for trying to understand the pain and suffering in our lives."

A 30-year-old woman, neatly dressed and self-confident, spoke first. Employed until her factory closed, she and her son now live on AFDC and food stamps, a total income of $368 monthly. "I don't like coming here to reveal my personal life in front of everyone," she admitted, "but I got to because of my son. I'm willing to work, I always have. Just try me."

Among numerous others speaking was a 53-year-old Army veteran, a painter out of work for two years. A tanned, lined face and light hair reflected the features of many in this region of the nation. Now with no income, no car insurance, and his children studying by candlelight since his electricity was shut off, he and his family frequently go hungry. "I was reluctant to apply for food stamps," he says. "The politicians keep saying there aren't enough to go around, so you think someone else needs them more than you. You keep hoping the phone will ring."

Another worker, sitting silently until prodded by his wife, who reported that her husband is a good man and tries hard to provide for his family, told his plight. He can't find work, and his family cannot live on what income he does receive. "You keep thinking you'll progress to middle-class, but instead you get poorer. My mother got us through the last Depression, and now I somehow got to get us through this one."

Peoria, Illinois, the all-American city. Southern Illinois, heart of American agricultural production. We found substantial hunger in this region of the nation, suffering reminiscent, as so many of the residents reminded us, of the Depression some 50 years ago.

In the 1930s, American farms produced more inconsistently. Today, they produce enough, some say, to feed the world. Yet many people who used to work those farms, and the workers who once built the machinery by which others farm, are now hungry.

Eighty-six-year-old Effie Alsop is hungry, but only sometimes. As the doctors talked to her in the living room of her modest home in the southern Missouri town of Caruthersville, Mrs. Alsop was a picture of emaciation:

Q: What did you eat today?
A: Nothing.
Q: You've had nothing all day?
A: No.
Q: You must get hungry.
A: I get hungry when food is in the house, but when I don't have any I'm not hungry. Isn't that funny, doctor?

IV

Racism

During the 1960s, the successful struggle for legislation to enforce equal opportunity for minorities—in jobs, housing, and education—created the hope that government action would effectively remove the most important barriers to racial equality in American society. This sense of optimism was enhanced by the expectation of an ever-expanding economy, which seemed to promise that there would be room for everyone to have a chance at the good life in America.

To some extent, these expectations were borne out—for a while. Blacks and other minorities made significant social and economic progress, particularly in the 1960s, as a result of civil rights protest, government action, and an expanding economy. But the urban riots of the sixties also showed a more ominous side of the racial picture and revealed that some aspects of racial disadvantage in the United States were relatively impervious to both economic growth and the expansion of civil rights. And during the 1970s and early 1980s, some of the gains made by minorities in earlier years began to be reversed. Minority income fell behind as a proportion of white income, and minority poverty—especially in the inner cities—increased sharply. A combination of unfavorable economic trends, a less generous public policy, and a waning commitment to the vigorous enforcement of civil rights laws have taken their toll on minority progress in the past several years.

At the same time, a series of ugly and tragic incidents—at Bensonhurst and Howard Beach in New York City, and on a number of college campuses—revealed all too clearly that the most virulent and dangerous forms of racial animosity were still deeply entrenched in America. Race, in short, still matters very much in the United States, as the articles in this section illustrate in various ways.

In 1989, the government-funded National Research Council pulled together much of what social scientists had learned about the progress of black Americans in recent decades. In this excerpt from their report, "Blacks and American Society," the Council shows that in every area of American life—from education, to jobs, to housing, and more—blacks remain disadvantaged relative to whites 25 years after the passage of the Civil Rights Act. There has been considerable improvement, to be sure—a good part of it resulting from strong antidiscrimination measures. But the historic gap between black and white Americans "has only been narowed; it has not closed." Worse, the recent problems of the American economy—and the sharp reductions in many social programs—may portend shrinking opportunities to narrow that gap in the future.

The Council's study lays out the current status of black Americans in dense, authoritative statistics. Phillip Hoose's account of a team of young black swimmers, in "A New Pool of Talent," shows us something about what race and racism mean beyond the statistics—in the lives of young people engaging in what should be a very ordinary activity, competitive sports. In fact, until very recently, blacks almost never reached the upper levels of competitive swimming—a situation sometimes "explained" on the grounds that they lacked sufficient "buoyancy" or had the wrong kind of ankles or muscle fibers. Hoose shows that, historically, the cards have been stacked against black swimmers in a variety of ways, including segregated pools and inadequate facilities (or none at all) in inner-city neighborhoods. The story of how one black swim club is helping to change all this is both inspiring in its portrayal of dedicated coaches and determined young athletes, and sobering in its depiction of the persistence of stereotypical attitudes.

The 20 million Hispanic residents in the United States, according to Rafael Valdivieso and Cary Davis in "U.S. Hispanics: Challenging Issues for the 1990s," suffer not only from high rates of poverty, underemployment, and dropping out of school but also from a kind of invisibility that hobbles effective policies to deal with those problems. Even the term "Hispanic" itself is a kind of catchall that blurs important distinctions among different groups. But, as Hispanics move into the schools and the labor force in ever-greater numbers, the need to address the causes of their disadvantage, especially through better education and job training, and attacking discrimination in hiring and promotion at work, becomes ever more urgent.

In the face of the continuing—and in some ways worsening—situation of some American minority groups, there has been a resurgence of theories attempting to blame this outcome on some deficiency of culture or motivation in the groups themselves rather than on adverse forces in the larger society. If other groups have "made it" in America despite obstacles, the typical refrain goes, "why can't they?" But, as Stanley Lieberson shows in "A Piece of the Pie," what this rather self-righteous argument ignores is that the experience of different groups can't be so simply equated. Though some other ethnic groups faced considerable discrimination and prejudice in the American past, the barriers faced by blacks have been uniquely formidable, and we won't understand the current situation of different groups without taking that difference into account.

13

Blacks and American Society

National Research Council

Just five decades ago, most black Americans could not work, live, shop, eat, seek entertainment, or travel where they chose. Even a quarter century ago—100 years after the Emancipation Proclamation of 1863—most blacks were effectively denied the right to vote. A large majority of blacks lived in poverty, and very few black children had the opportunity to receive a basic education; indeed, black children were still forced to attend inferior and separate schools in jurisdictions that had not accepted the 1954 decision of the Supreme Court declaring segregated schools unconstitutional.

Today the situation is very different. In education, many blacks have received college degrees from universities that formerly excluded them. In the workplace, blacks frequently hold professional and managerial jobs in desegregated settings. In politics, most blacks now participate in elections, and blacks have been elected to all but the highest political offices. Overall, many blacks have achieved middle-class status.

Yet the great gulf that existed between black and white Americans in 1939 has only been narrowed; it has not closed. One of three blacks still live in households with incomes below the poverty line. Even more blacks live in areas where ineffective schools, high rates of dependence on public assistance, severe problems of crime and drug use, and low and declining employment prevail. Race relations, as they affect the lives of inhabitants of these areas, differ considerably from black-white relations involving

From National Research Council, *Blacks and American Society*, Washington, DC, National Academy of Sciences Press, 1989. Reprinted by permission. Portions of the original have been omitted.

middle-class blacks. Lower status blacks have less access to desegregated schools, neighborhoods, and other institutions and public facilities. Their interactions with whites frequently emphasize their subordinate status—as low-skilled employees, public agency clients, and marginally performing pupils.

The status of black Americans today can be characterized as a glass that is half full—if measured by progress since 1939—or as a glass that is half empty—if measured by the persisting disparities between black and white Americans since the early 1970s. Any assessment of the quality of life for blacks is also complicated by the contrast between blacks who have achieved middle-class status and those who have not.

The progress occurred because sustained struggles by blacks and their allies changed American law and politics, moving all governments and most private institutions from support of principles of racial inequality to support of principles of racial equality. Gradually, and often with much resistance, the behaviors and attitudes of individual whites moved in the same direction. Over the 50-year span covered by this study, the social status of American blacks has *on average* improved dramatically, both in absolute terms and relative to whites. The growth of the economy and public policies promoting racial equality led to an erosion of segregation and discrimination, making it possible for a substantial fraction of blacks to enter the mainstream of American life.

The reasons for the continuing distress of large numbers of black Americans are complex. Racial discrimination continues despite the victories of the civil rights movement. Yet, the problems faced today by blacks who are isolated from economic and social progress are less directly open to political amelioration than were the problems of legal segregation and the widely practiced overt discrimination of a few decades past. Slow overall growth of the economy during the 1970s and 1980s has been an important impediment to black progress; in the three previous decades economic prosperity and rapid growth had been a great help to most blacks. Educational institutions and government policies have not successfully responded to underlying changes in the society. Opportunities for upward mobility have been reduced for all lower status Americans, but especially for those who are black. If all racial discrimination were abolished today, the life prospects facing many poor blacks would still constitute major challenges for public policy. . . .

Blacks and whites in a changing society

Two general developments in the status of black Americans stand out; each is reflective of a near-identical development in the population at large. First, for the period 1940–1973, real earnings of Americans improved steadily, but they stagnated and declined after 1973. Similarly, over these same periods, there was a clear record of improving average material status of blacks relative to whites-followed by stagnation and decline. Second, during the post-1973 period, inequality increased among Americans as the lowest income and least skilled people were hurt most by changes in the overall economy. Similarly, there were increasing differences in material well-being and opportunities among blacks, and they have been extremely pronounced.

These developments may be understood as consequences of four interdependent events that have altered the status of blacks, relative black-white status, and race relations in the United States. These events were the urbanization and northern movement of the black population from 1940 to 1970; the civil rights movement that forced the nation to open its major institutions to black participation during the same three decades; the unprecedented high and sustained rate of national economic growth for roughly the same period; and the significant slowdown in the U.S. economy since the early 1970s.

The civil rights movement, blacks' more proximate location near centers of industrial activity, and high economic growth enabled those blacks best prepared to take advantage of new opportunities to respond with initiative and success. Increases in educational opportunities were seized by many blacks who were then able to translate better educations into higher status occupations than most blacks had ever enjoyed. Black incomes and earnings rose generally, with many individuals and families reaching middle-class and even upper middle income status. . . . The new black middle class moved into better housing, frequently in the suburbs, and sometimes in desegregated neighborhoods. Despite much confrontation between whites and blacks as blacks abandoned traditional approaches to black-white relations, race relations eventually advanced closer to equal treatment.

At the same time, many blacks were not able to take advantage of the new conditions that developed: some were still located in areas relatively untouched by the changes; some lacked the family support networks to provide assistance; for some, better opportunities simply did not arise. Those who were left behind during the 1960s and 1970s faced and still face very different situations than poor blacks immediately before that period.

A major reason is the performance of the economy. Real weekly earnings (in constant 1984 dollars) of all American men, on average, fell from $488 in 1969 to $414 in 1984; real weekly earnings of women fell from $266 in 1969 to $230 in 1984. For the first time since the Great Depression of the 1930s, American men born in one year (e.g., 1960) may face lower lifetime real earnings than men born 10 years earlier. . . . Among the myriad and complex responses to these economic conditions have been rising employment rates among women, but falling rates among men, while the unemployment rates of both men and women have been on an upward trend for three decades. . . .

A generation ago, a low-skilled man had relatively abundant opportunity to obtain a blue-collar job with a wage adequate to support a family at a lower middle class level or better. Today the jobs available to such men—and women—are often below or just barely above the official poverty line for a family of four. For example, black males aged 25–34, with some high school but no diploma, earned on average $268 weekly in 1986; in 1969, black male dropouts of that age had averaged $334 weekly (in constant 1984 dollars). For white men of the same age and education, work conditions have been better, but changes over time cannot be said to have been good: in the years 1969 and 1986, mean weekly earnings were $447 and $381. Thus, among men who did not complete high school, blacks and whites had lower real earnings in 1986 than in 1969.

Obtaining a well-paying job increasingly requires a good education or a specific skill. Many young blacks and whites do not obtain such training, and the educational system in many locations is apparently not equipped to provide them. Recent reports on the state of American education sound great alarm about the future status of today's students. One in six youths dropped out of high school in 1985, and levels of scholastic achievement are disturbingly low by many measures. Young men with poor credentials, finding themselves facing low-wage job offers and high unemployment rates, frequently abandon the labor force intermittently or completely. Some choose criminal activity as an alternative to the labor market.

Greater numbers of people are today susceptible to poverty than in the recent past. With some year-to-year variation, the percentage of Americans living in poverty has been on an upward trend: from 11.2 percent in 1974 to 13.5 percent in 1986. In addition, the poor may be getting poorer in the 1980s: the average poor family has persistently had a yearly income further below the poverty line than any year since 1963.

More and more of the poor are working family heads, men and women who are employed or seeking employment but who cannot find a job that pays enough to prevent their families from sliding into or near poverty. For the more fortunate, reasonably secure from the fear of poverty, such middle-class advantages as a home in the suburbs and the ability to send their children to the best college for which they qualify are goals that were reached by their parents but may be unattainable for many of them.

Perhaps the most important consequences of the stagnating U.S. economy have been the effects on the status of children. Many members of the next generation of young adults live in conditions ill suited to prepare them to contribute to the nation's future. In 1987, 1 of 5 (20 percent) American children under age 18—white, black, Hispanic, Native American, and Asian-American—were being raised in families with incomes below official poverty standards. Among minorities the conditions were worse: for example, 45 percent of black children and 39 percent of Hispanic children were living in poverty. During the 1970s, approximately 2 of every 3 black children could expect to live in poverty for at least 1 of the first 10 years of their childhood, while an astounding 1 of 3 could expect at least 7 of those 10 years to be lived in poverty.

We cannot emphasize too much the gravity of the fact that in any given year more than two-fifths of all black children live under conditions of poverty as the 1980s draw to a close. As fertility rates decrease, the total youth population of the United States will contain a larger proportion of comparatively disadvantaged youths from minority ethnic and racial groups. This change may in turn lead to major changes in labor markets, childbearing, the armed forces, and education.

Under conditions of increasing economic hardship for the least prosperous members of society, blacks, because of their special legacy of poverty and discrimination, are afflicted sooner, more deeply, and longer. But the signs of distress that are most visible in parts of the black population are becoming more discernible within the entire population. This distress should be viewed in the context of the underlying changes within American society that affect not only black-white differences, but all disadvantaged blacks and whites who face the difficult economic conditions of the late 1980s. . . .

Attitudes, participation, identity, and institutions

Large majorities of blacks and whites accept the principles of equal access to public institutions and equal treatment in race relations. For whites this is the result of a long upward trend from a low base in the 1940s; blacks have favored equality since survey data have been collected. Yet there remain important signs of continuing resistance to full equality of black Americans. Principles of equality are endorsed less when they would result in close, frequent, or prolonged social contact, and whites are much less prone to endorse policies meant to implement equal participation of blacks in important social institutions. In practice, many whites refuse or are reluctant to participate in social settings (e.g., neighborhoods and schools) in which significant numbers of blacks are present; see Figures S.1, S.2, and S.3.

Whether one considers arts and entertainment, religious institutions, public schools, or a number of other major institutions, black participation has increased significantly since 1940 and since 1960. Yet increased black participation has not produced substantial integration. An exception is the U.S. Army, where a true modicum of integration—significant numerical participation on terms of equal treatment—has been accomplished. The other three military services, although generally ahead of the civilian sector, have not attained the level of equality found in the Army. Although large-scale desegregation of public schools occurred in the South during the late 1960s and early 1970s—and has been substantial in many small and medium-sized cities elsewhere—the pace of school desegregation has slowed, and racial separation in education is significant, espe-

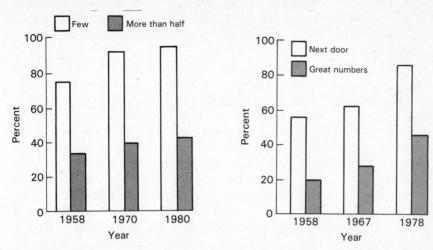

Figure S.1 left Whites with *no* objection to sending their children to a school in which a few or more than half of the children are black. Figure S.2 right Whites who would *not* move if black peolple came to live next door or in great numbers in the neighborhood.

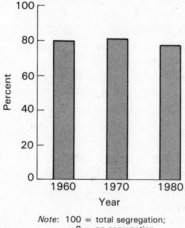

Note: 100 = total segregation;
0 = no segregation.

Figure S.3 Median residential segregation in 29 metropolitan areas with the
largest black populations.

cially outside the South. And residential separation of whites and blacks in large metropolitan areas remains nearly as high in the 1980s as it was in the 1960s.

These findings suggest that a considerable amount of remaining black-white inequality is due to continuing discriminatory treatment of blacks. The clearest evidence is in housing. Discrimination against blacks seeking housing has been conclusively demonstrated. In employment and public accommodations, discrimination, although greatly reduced, is still a problem. . . .

The long history of discrimination and segregation produced among blacks a heightened sense of group consciousness and a stronger orientation toward collective values and behavior than exists generally among Americans, and group consciousness remains strong among blacks today. . . . Contemporary conditions in the United States reinforce a recognition of group identity and position among blacks, who continue to be conspicuously separated from the white majority. This separation is manifested in a range of specific findings: two findings of special importance are separation of blacks and whites in residential areas and public schools. The residential separation of blacks and whites is nearly twice the rate of white and Asian-Americans, and it is often much greater than residential separation between Hispanic Americans and whites in many cities. . . .

These past experiences and current conditions have important consequences for the status of blacks and the manner in which they attempt to improve their status. Blacks overwhelmingly believe in values such as individual responsibility and free competition, but they are more likely to disapprove of the ubiquity of individualism and market autonomy throughout American society than are whites. This disapproval has appeared primarily in black support, at levels higher than whites, of such federal policies as guaranteed full employment, guaranteed income floors, and national health care. . . .

Given blacks' history, the sources of this desire for change are not difficult to identify. Data show that blacks generally believe that basic social institutions are biased in favor of whites and against blacks. . . . Many blacks believe that their relative position in society cannot be improved without government policies to intervene with social institutions on behalf of minorities and the disadvantaged. In contrast with whites, blacks have highly favorable views of the high activity years of government policy intervention of the 1960s.

As a consequence of their heightened group consciousness, their belief that racial discrimination remains a major deterrent to black progress, and their history of collective social expression, black Americans vote at the same or higher rates than whites of comparable socioeconomic status, support redistributive policies more often than do whites, and participate in a wider variety of political activity.

This political participation has had some important effects on American politics. After the legislative and judicial successes of the civil rights movement during the 1960s, there have been continuous struggles to enforce laws and administrative measures aimed at eliminating discrimination and improving opportunities. As a result, blacks' right of access to public facilities and accommodations is now widely accepted. Arbitrary harassment and intimidation of blacks by legal authorities, by organized antiblack organizations, and by unorganized individuals have greatly diminished, although there are regular reports of such incidents.

The changes since 1940—and particularly since the 1960s—have had important effects on the nature of black communities. The organizations and institutions created by blacks, as well as changing concepts of black identity, were two crucial foundations on which the achievement of sweeping improvements in blacks' legal and political status were attained. Changes in black social structure have resulted from the rising incomes, occupations, and educations of many blacks. The exit of higher status blacks from inner cities has accentuated problems of increasing social stratification among blacks. The service needs of poorer blacks have placed strains on many black institutions, including schools, churches, and voluntary service organizations. These strains have resulted in a proliferation of activities devoted to the material needs of poor blacks by black organizations. . . .

Other effects on black institutions and organizations have been produced by the civil rights movement. Greater access to majority white institutions by higher status blacks has led to alterations in black leadership structure, problems of recruitment and retention of black talent by black organizations, and reduced participation in many spheres of black life by those blacks. As a result, the often well-knit, if poor and underserviced, black communities of the past have lost some of their cultural cohesion and distinct identity. However, most blacks retain a high degree of racial pride and a conscious need to retain aspects of black culture as a significant component of their American identity. Because of these desires and needs, black institutions continue to play important roles in the lives of most blacks.

Political participation

Until the 1960s, black political activity was primarily directed toward the attainment of basic democratic rights. Exclusion of black Americans from voting and office holding meant that blacks had to seek political and civil rights through protest and litigation. The civil rights movement arose out of long-standing grievances and aspirations. It was based on strong networks of local organizations and given a clear focus and direction by articulate leadership. Because most blacks were unable to vote, move freely, or buy and sell property as they wished, their efforts were directed to the objective of attaining these basic rights of citizenship. During the civil rights movement, civic equality and political liberty came to be viewed by increasing percentages of Americans as basic human rights that blacks should enjoy. By the 1960s, the federal executive branch and a congressional coalition backed by a sufficient public opinion was finally able to legislate black civil equality.

Active participation by blacks in American political life has had a major impact on their role in the society. Figures S.4 to S.7 highlight some of the effects. The number of black elected officials has risen from a few dozen in 1940 to over 6,800 in 1988. However, blacks comprise only about 1.5 percent of all elected officials. The election of black officials does result in additional hiring and higher salaries for blacks in public-sector jobs and more senior positions for blacks in appointive public office. The black proportion of federal, state, and local public administrators rose from less than 1 percent in 1940 to 8 percent in 1980; even so, it was less than blacks' 13 percent proportion of the U.S. population. As measured by the proportion of delegates to the national party conventions, black participation in the political party organizations has increased dramatically among Demo-

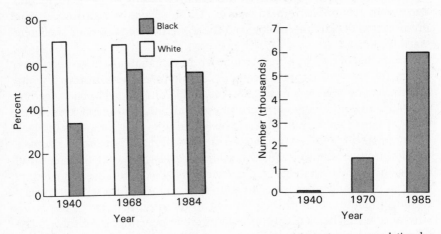

Figure S.4 left Reported voter participation as a percentage of the voting-age population, by race. Figure S.5 right Black elected officials.

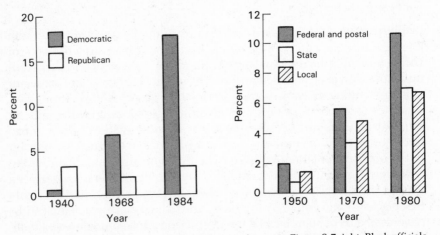

Figure S.6 left Black national convention delegates, by party. Figure S.7 right Black officials and administrators, by level of government.

crats since 1940, while black participation in Republican party affairs, after declining during the 1960s and 1970s, has returned to be about the same level as in 1940.

Blacks' desires for political rights were not merely based on abstract principles of equality, but also on the practical fruits of political participation. Blacks sought democratic rights because they believed that direct access to political institutions through voting, lobbying, and office holding would lead to greater material equality between themselves and the rest of society. However, changes in blacks' socioeconomic status, although complex, have not attained levels commensurate to black-white equality with respect to civil rights. But black influence in the political sector has been an important factor in determining many of the important gains that have occurred. In particular, the extensive development of equal opportunity law has improved the status of blacks (as well as that of women and other minorities) in the areas of education, occupations, health care, criminal justice, and business enterprise. Blacks have also benefited from increased public-sector provision of job training, health care, Social Security, and other cash and in-kind benefit programs.

Although political participation has not been the only important determinant of changes in black opportunities, resulting alterations in American politics have had influence in many areas of life. A review of blacks' status shows that increased civil rights have been important in all areas of society.

Economic status

Changes in labor market conditions and social policies of governments have had many beneficial effects on the economic status of black Americans. Yet the current economic prospects are not good for many blacks. Adverse changes in labor market opportunities and family conditions—falling real wages and employment, increases in one-parent families with one or no working adults—have made conditions especially difficult for those blacks from the most disadvantaged backgrounds. However, among blacks, changes in family structure per se have not been a major cause of continuing high poverty rates since the early 1970s.

Black-white differences are large despite significant improvements in the absolute and relative positions of blacks over the past 50 years. After initial decades of rising relative black economic status, black gains stagnated on many measures after the early 1970s. Lack of progress in important indicators of economic status during the past two decades is largely a consequence of two conflicting trends: while blacks' weekly and hourly wages have risen relative to whites, blacks' relative employment rates have deteriorated significantly. Figures S.8 to S.11 present some key data.

In terms of per capita incomes, family incomes, and male workers' earnings, blacks gained relative to whites fairly steadily from 1939 to 1969;

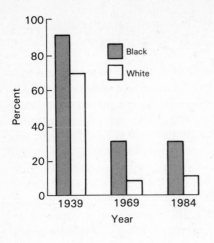

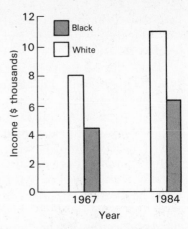

Note: Per capita income is calculated in 1984 constant dollars.

Figure S.8 left Persons below the poverty level, by race. Figure S.9 right Per capita income, by race.

measures of relative status peaked in the early to mid-1970s and since have remained stagnant or declined. Women earn much less than men, but the gap between black and white women decreased steadily throughout the period until, by 1984, black women had earnings very close to those of white women. Employment rates of adult black men and women have been falling relative to those of white men and women throughout the period; black unemployment rates remain approximately twice those of white rates. The proportion of working black men and women in white-collar occupations and in managerial and professional positions increased throughout the period, but these gains show signs of slowing in the 1980s.

Uneven change in the average economic position of blacks has been accompanied, especially during the past 25 years, by accentuated differences in status among blacks. An important aspect of the polarization in the incomes of black families has been the growth of female-headed black families since 1960. It is among such families that the incidence of poverty is highest. It is no exaggeration to say that the two most numerically important components of the black class structure have become a lower class dominated by female-headed families and a middle class largely composed of two-parent families. The percentage of both blacks and whites living in households with incomes below the poverty line declined during the 1939–1975 period. But poverty rates have risen in the past decade, and black poverty rates have been 2 to 3 times higher than white rates at all times.

The major developments accounting for black gains in earnings and occupation status from 1939 to 1969 were South-to-North migration and concurrent movement from agricultural to nonagricultural employment,

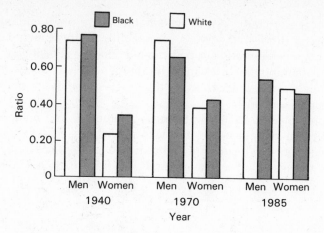

Figure S.10 Employment to population ratios, by race.

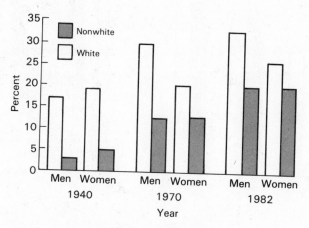

Figure S.11 Employed workers holding professional or managerial jobs, by race.

job creation, and national economic growth. After 1965, major factors
responsible for improvements in blacks' status have been government
policies against discrimination, government incentives for the equal employment opportunity of minorities, general changes in race relations,
and higher educational attainment.

Schooling

Substantial progress has been made toward the provision of educational
resources to blacks. Yet black and white educational opportunities are not
generally equal. Standards of academic performance for teachers and

students are not equivalent in schools that serve predominantly black students and those that serve predominantly white students. Nor are equal encouragement and support provided for the educational achievement and attainment of black and white students. Figures S.12, S.13, and S.14 highlight some of the effects of the progress that has been made and the gaps that remain.

Measures of educational outcomes—attainment and achievement—reveal substantial gaps between blacks and whites. Blacks, on average, enter the schools with substantial disadvantages in socioeconomic backgrounds and tested achievement. American schools do not compensate

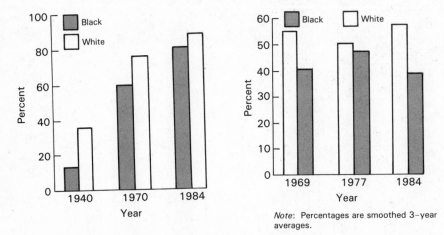

Figure S.12 left High school graduates aged 25–29, by race. Figure S.13 right High school graduates enrolled in college, by race.

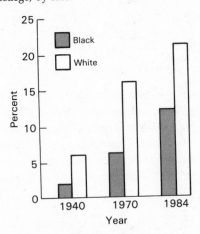

Figure S.14 College graduates aged 25–29, by race.

for these disadvantages in background: on average, students leave the schools with black-white gaps not having been appreciably diminished.

There remain persistent and large gaps in the schooling quality and achievement outcomes of education for blacks and whites. At the pinnacle of the educational process, blacks' life opportunities relative to whites' are demonstrated by the fact that the odds that a black high school graduate will enter college within a year of graduation are less than one-half the odds that a white high school graduate will do so. College enrollment rates of high school graduates, after rising sharply since the late 1960s, declined in the mid-1970s; while white enrollment rates have recovered, black rates in the 1980s remain well below those of the 1970s. The proportion of advanced degrees awarded to blacks has also decreased. While we cannot conclude with certainty that the cause has been the decline in (real) financial aid grants to students, other reasonable hypotheses can explain only a negligible component of this change.

Segregation and differential treatment of blacks continue to be widespread in the elementary and secondary schools. We find that school desegregation does not substantially affect the academic performance of white students, but it does modestly improve black performance (in particular, reading). When several key conditions are met, intergroup attitudes and relations improve after schools are desegregated. And desegregation is most likely to reduce racial isolation as well as improve academic and social outcomes for blacks when it is part of a comprehensive and rapid desegregation plan.

Differences in the schooling experienced by black and white students contribute to black-white differences in achievement. These differences are closely tied to teacher behavior; school climate; and the content, quality, and organization of instruction. Early intervention compensatory education programs, such as Head Start, have had positive effects on blacks' educational performance. Among the most recent cohorts to complete their education—people born in the late 1950s and early 1960s—blacks have a median education close to that of whites, 12.6 years, compared with 12.9 years for whites. But a remaining substantial gap in overall educational attainment is noncompletion: high school dropout rates for blacks are double those for whites.

Changes in academic achievement test scores show that, while black students' average scores remain well below white students' average scores, black performance has improved faster, and black-white differences have become somewhat smaller. . . .

Crime and criminal justice

Among black Americans, distrust of the criminal justice system is widespread. Historically, discrimination against blacks in arrests and sentencing was ubiquitous. Prior to the 1970s, very few blacks were employed as law enforcement officials, but in the 1980s, the percentage of blacks in police forces has increased to substantial levels. Black representation among attorneys and judges has also increased, although it is not as high as that in the police.

Blacks are arrested, convicted, and imprisoned for criminal offenses at rates much higher than are whites. Currently, blacks account for nearly one-half of all prison inmates in the United States; thus, blacks' representation in prisons is about 4 times their representation in the general population. Compared with the total population, black Americans are disproportionately victims of crime: they are twice as likely to be victims of robbery, vehicle theft, and aggravated assault, and 6 to 7 times as likely to be victims of homicide, the leading cause of death among young black males. Blacks also suffer disproportionately from injuries and economic losses due to criminal actions.

Most black offenders victimize other blacks. But offenders and victims are often in different socioeconomic strata: most offenders are poor; many victims are not. Consequently, middle-income and near-poor blacks have greater economic losses due to criminal acts than the black poor or than whites at any income level.

The role of discrimination in criminal justice has apparently varied substantially from place to place and over time. Some part of the unexplained differences in black-white arrest rates may be due to racial bias and the resulting differential treatment. Current black-white differences in sentencing appear to be due less to overt racial bias than to socioeconomic differences between blacks and whites: people of lower socioeconomic status—regardless of race—receive more severe sentences than people of higher status. An important exception may be bias in sentencing that is related to the race of the victim: criminals whose victims are white are on average punished more severely than those whose victims are black.

As long as there are great disparities in the socioeconomic status of blacks and whites, blacks will continue to be overrepresented in the criminal justice system as victims and offenders. And because of these disparities, the precise degree to which the overrepresentation reflects racial bias cannot be determined.

Children and families

Changes since the mid-1960s among both blacks and whites have brought higher rates of marital breakup, decreased rates of marriage, rapidly rising proportions of female-headed households, and increasing proportions of children being reared in single-parent families. The changes have been much greater among blacks than among whites. Some characteristics of families are shown in Figures S.15, S.16, and S.17.

Birthrates for both the white and black populations have fallen since the baby boom of the 1950s, and fertility rates have declined for women of all ages. By the mid-1980s, the lifetime fertility rates were similar for black and white women. Contrary to popular myth, birthrates among black teenagers—although still an important problem—have declined significantly during the past two decades.

In 1970, about 18 percent of black families had incomes over $35,000 (1987 constant dollars); by 1986 this proportion had grown to 22 percent. The increase in well-to-do families was matched by an increase in low-income families. During the same 1970–1980 period, the proportion of

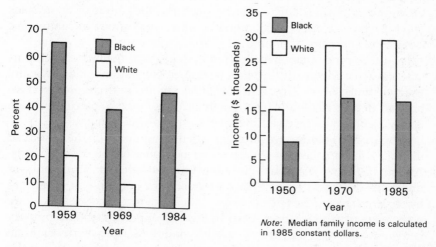

Figure S.15 left Children in poverty, by race. Figure S.16 right Median family income, by race.

Note: Median family income is calculated in 1985 constant dollars.

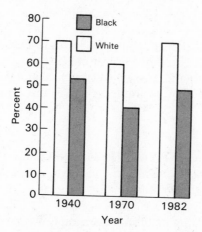

Figure S.17 Childless women aged 20–24, by race.

black families with incomes of less than $10,000 grew from about 26 to 30 percent. After declining during earlier decades, the percentage of black and white children in poverty began to increase in the 1970s. In 1986, 43 percent of black children and 16 percent of white children under age 18 lived in households below the poverty line.

Black and white children are increasingly different with regard to their living arrangements. As we noted above, a majority of black children under age 18 live in families that include their mothers but not their fathers; in contrast, four of every five white children live with both parents. (Although some fathers who are not counted as household members may actually aid in child rearing, there are no data to estimate the number, and it is believed to be small.) In the course of their childhood, 86 percent of black children and 42 percent of white children are likely to spend some time in a single-parent household.

The greater inequality between family types among blacks has important consequences for the welfare of future generations. Black female-headed families were 50 percent of all black families with children in 1985, but had 25 percent of total black family income, while 70 percent of black family income was received by black husband-wife families.

The data and analyses we have examined throw doubt on the validity of the thesis that a culture of poverty is a major cause of long-term poverty. Although cultural factors are important in social behavior, arguments for the existence of unalterable behaviors among the poor are not supported by empirical research. The behaviors that are detrimental to success are often responses to existing social barriers to opportunity. The primary correlates of poverty are macroeconomic conditions of prosperity or recession and changes in family composition. However, increases in female-headed families have had only negligible effects on increasing black poverty rates since the mid-1970s. Importantly, attitudes toward work and the desire to succeed are not very different among the poor and the nonpoor.

Black-white differences in family structures result from a complex set of interrelated factors. The most salient are black-white differences in income and employment, greater (relative) economic independence of black women, and a more limited pool of black men who are good marriage prospects.

THE FUTURE: ALTERNATIVES AND POLICY IMPLICATIONS

Blacks' status in the near future

In assessing the status of black Americans, we have asked what roles blacks play in the nation today and what role they are likely to play in the near future. Our conclusion is largely positive, but it is mixed. The great majority of black Americans contribute to the political, economic, and social health of the nation. The typical black adult—like the typical white adult—is a full-time employee or homemaker who pays taxes, votes in public elections, and sends children to school. Blacks make important contributions to all forms of American life, from the sciences and health care, to politics and education, to arts and entertainment.

However, this role is not available to a sizable minority of black—and of a small but growing group of white—Americans. The evidence for this assessment is clear. High school dropout rates among young black adults have risen, and attaining high standards of academic competence seems unavailable to millions of poor black youths attending school systems that are not able to teach them. During the 1980s, thousands of young black men who were not enrolled in school have also not been active participants in the labor market. Many of these men are incarcerated or have dropped out of society into the escape offered by alcohol and drug addiction. And, on the basis of the fertility rates of 1986, 170 of 1,000 black females become mothers before the age of 20, often disrupting or discontinuing their secondary educations. These young mothers are likely to be poor as they establish households, and they will frequently have to receive family assistance benefits. These alarming developments are mirrored by similar, if more modest, trends among whites.

Barring unforeseen events or changes in present conditions—that is, no changes in educational policies and opportunities, no increased income and employment opportunities, and no major national programs to deal directly with the problems of economic dependency—our findings imply several negative developments for blacks in the near future, developments that in turn do not bode well for American society:

- A substantial majority of black Americans will remain contributors to the nation, but improvements in their status relative to whites are likely to slow even more as the rate of increase of the black middle class is likely to decline.
- Approximately one-third of the black population will continue to be poor, and the relative employment and earnings status of black men is likely to deteriorate further.
- Drugs and crime, teenage parenthood, poor educational opportunities, and joblessness will maintain their grip on large numbers of poor and near-poor blacks.
- High rates of residential segregation between blacks and whites will continue.
- The United States is faced with the prospect of continued great inequality between whites and blacks and a continuing division of social status within the black population.
- A growing population of poor and undereducated citizens, disproportionately black and minority, will pose challenges to the nation's abilities to solve the emerging economic and social problems of the twenty-first century.

14

A New Pool of Talent

Phillip Hoose

After the plane touched down at Cleveland Hopkins Airport, six young black athletes straightened their blue-and-gold team parkas and started toward the baggage claim area. As they strode through the corridor with their parents and coach, a black woman squinted from behind the Avis counter at the "PDR Swimming" insignia on their backs and hustled out to catch them. "You all *swimmers?*" she asked, her face bright. "So's my son. You here for the nationals? Well, all right. Lookin' good."

Throughout the following week, coaches, officials, fans and competitors attending the Junior National Championship meet in Cleveland last month took special notice of the black swimmers whose attire bore the letters PDR, for Philadelphia Department of Recreation. This was something new. While there have been a scattering of black individuals competing on a national level in the past, the PDR squad, coached by Jim Ellis, was by all accounts the largest contingent of black swimmers ever to appear at a national meet. To many, they are a harbinger of things to come.

One of those watching was Chris Martin, a tall, 30-year-old black man who coaches a predominantly white prep school team in New Jersey. To Martin, who as a youngster competed as the only black on a prep school squad, the presence of a team of inner-city black swimmers at an elite national meet was little short of revolutionary. "By the force of his will, Jim

Ellis has turned swimming into a *normal* experience for black kids in the city of Philadelphia," Martin said. "And he's 90 percent of the way to making it normal for the people watching them at this meet. You can see it. . . . Not 100 percent, but getting there."

Throughout the nation, black athletes from urban areas, many trained by black coaches like Ellis, are beginning to prove themselves as competitive swimmers. Last year, an Arkansas teen-ager named Matt Twillie, who, at 6-feet-3 and 195 pounds, gave up several sports for swimming, turned in the nation's fastest time in the 100-yard butterfly for the 15-to-16-year-old age group. In 1987, a Cleveland teen-ager named Byron Davis, another versatile athlete now at University of California, Los Angeles, recorded the fastest time in United States history for his age group in the 50-yard freestyle event.

The City of Atlanta Dolphins, a huge, publicly financed and almost entirely black squad, now features several of Georgia's top-ranked swimmers.

In Chicago, thousands of black kids from 87 park district teams compete in the summer. The Chicago South Swim Club includes four black swimmers who have posted times among the top 10 statewide for their events.

But best of all are the PDR swimmers from Philadelphia. Among the program's 175 swimmers are three—14-year-old breast-stroker Michael Norment, 12-year-old breast-stroker Atiba Wade and 15-year-old back-stroker Jason Webb—whose times place them among the top six nationally in their events, as well as eight other swimmers who are regionally ranked in the top 10. In 1988, a boys' 10-year-and-under relay team from PDR set a national record. Behind these children are a host of 8-year-olds, who, Ellis claims, will make everyone forget about their elders. "I am blessed with talent in all age groups," Ellis says. "We haven't even scratched the surface here yet."

There is no sport, except perhaps for skiing, in which black Americans have been so rare at elite levels as swimming. United States Olympic teams have included black figure skaters, cyclists, gymnasts, wrestlers, judo wrestlers, volleyball players, weight lifters, fencers, even an oarswoman. But according to all available records, it took until 1984—nearly a century after the resumption of the modern Olympic Games—for the first black American swimmer even to reach the Olympic trials. And while black swimmers have competed from other nations—most notably Anthony Nesty, who won a gold medal for the tiny Republic of Suriname in the 1988 Games—no black swimmer has ever made the United States Olympic team.

Whites have long been content to explain the scarcity of black competitive swimmers by supposing Americans of African ancestry to be, as a race, engineered to drown. As the former Los Angeles Dodger executive Al Campanis put it in his now infamous 1987 appearance on ABC's

"Nightline": "Why are black men or black people not good swimmers? Because they don't have the buoyancy."

Over the years, it has been said that blacks are aquatically limited by, among other supposed design flaws, heavy bones, dense muscles, hair that retains water, skin that repels it and pores that release carbon dioxide too slowly. "There was a theory that blacks had thicker skulls than whites and that was the problem," Buck Dawson, now executive director emeritus of the International Swimming Hall of Fame, said two years ago. "There was a theory about ankles. It's not a flexible ankle. . . . Everyone called them 'sinkers.'"

Given the discouragement blacks have faced, the current crop is something of a miracle. Quality indoor pools in the inner city are scarce, as are swim teams in inner-city high schools. There are only a handful of black coaches with the technical expertise to work with champions, and virtually no role models on the order of a Michael Jordan. It is rare enough to find a black swimmer who grew up with swimmers in the family or whose parents even knew how to swim. "I never even thought of swimming," says Verner Webb, father of 15-year-old Jason Webb, who last year had the nation's fastest 100-meter backstroke time for his age group. "I'm a typical black person. I can dog paddle but that's about it. I grew up in Arkansas and Chicago. The pools were segregated. When the coach said Jason had potential as a swimmer, I said, 'What's a swimmer? I saw Mark Spitz on TV but that's about it."

For most of this century, whites sought desperately to avoid contact with blacks in swimming pools. Until the 1950's, and in some areas even through the mid-60's, municipalities maintained separate pools for blacks and whites, kept separate schedules for the races, or excluded blacks altogether. "What it was, really, was sexual taboos," says Andrew Young, the former Atlanta Mayor and an ex-Howard University freestyler whose administration last year spent $1.25 million in an effort to make swimming available to inner-city residents. "Swimming is the sport that you do with the least amount of clothes on. It's the sport where, especially in swimming pools, males and females are likely to come in the closest contact."

During the civil rights movement, leaders organized "Wade-ins" and "Swim-ins" to gain access to pools and beaches. One memorable incident occurred in 1964, when a racially mixed group of seven demonstrators leaped together into a white-owned motel pool in St. Augustine, Fla. Horrified, the owner poured gallons of muriatic acid, a chemical used to clean the pool, into the water. When the demonstrators remained, the police jumped in and forced them out.

When, gradually, pools became available, few blacks felt at home in them. "D.C. Parks and Recreation only had two pools before 1961," recalls Lorn Hill, chief of the Aquatics Division of the District of Columbia Department of Recreation and Parks. "But then in the next nine years we built 45 pools. I was a lifeguard then. We were pulling out 10 to 12 people every day. Nobody knew how to swim."

Through the years, blacks competed mainly on Y.M.C.A. and Y.W.C.A. teams—segregated throughout much of the century—or on city recreation department teams, in black colleges and in the armed services. A few excellent swimmers were recruited by predominantly white universities. But while black athletes began to break into other sports, the shabby facilities, intramural competition and scarcity of black coaches who could train international competitors kept black swimmers out of the Olympics. It was frustrating. "No colored swimmers in the last Olympic Games, none in the ones before that or before those," lamented The California Eagle, a black-owned newspaper, in 1934. "Well isn't it high time we showed the world that we can swim as well as sprint, jump and box."

It took another half-century for the first black swimmer, Chris Silva, a freestyler, even to compete in the Olympic trials. The current inner-city blossoming has been spurred in part by Silva's highly visible bid for the 1984 and 1988 United States Olympic teams. The 1988 effort was financed in part by Silva's barnstorming, pass-the-hat clinics throughout the country. One group of inspired black Atlanta children organized The Silva Bullets Booster Club to help pay for his training expenses and to keep him on the road.

Now inner-city teams are sprouting up everywhere, many of them coached by the black pioneer swimmers of a generation ago, men and women who are determined to make competitive swimming available for everyone. One coach, a 39-year-old former backstroker named Clarence E. (Moby) McLeod 3d, is now in his 20th year of coaching black boys and girls from downtown Cleveland. McLeod moonlights as an all-night tow-truck driver, and begins practice for his Cleveland Barracudas swim team only when the kids can bang loudly enough on the pool door to wake him up.

"Without someone besides their parents and grandparents to help them," he says, "I can see some of them not making it to their 18th birthday. Or the girls not making it to 21 without having children. If you can make it as a swimmer you can make it at anything."

Last February, more than 300 black swimmers from teams in eight cities gathered in Washington for the fourth annual Black History Invitation Swim Meet. It was a family affair, a Woodstock of black swimmers who usually swim against whites, and of coaches like McLeod who volunteer their time. They conceded that competitive swimming, still a sport with little black tradition and no professional tour, remains a hard sell in the inner city. As one T-shirt seen at the Black History meet put it, "Bo May Know Weights . . . Bo May Know Football . . . But Bo Don't Know Swimming."

But for the increasing number who are stepping onto the blocks and beginning to taste success, the rewards are obvious. Vanessa Patterson, a lean, 14-year-old backstroker from the PDR team who qualified for the United States Junior National meet this year, spends 18 hours a week in a pool. Nine years of chlorine has given her hair a slightly reddish tint. She doesn't regret a minute of it. "At the lunch table my friends tell me about things they shouldn't be doing, like with their boyfriends," she says. "Going to swim practice does more for me than just sitting there with my boyfriend. I get to meet new people and see new places. I'm off the street. Once you start this commitment, you don't want to stop."

Every Tuesday and Thursday, when a morning workout is added to the daily afternoon regimen, 30 or so PDR parents get up and drive their children through the dawn to meet Jim Ellis at the Marcus Foster Recreation Center, a bleak, two-room building in a depressed section of central Philadelphia called Nicetown.

They rarely know what to expect when they get there. One morning they discovered a boy curled up and sleeping in the heating ducts. Two weeks later a custodian reported that all the steel parts to their filtration system had been removed overnight, presumably stolen and sold for scrap. For much of the winter there was no heat at all.

According to the United States Swimming Office, which regulates amateur swimming in this country, most Olympians come from one of the nation's approximately 2,500 competitive swim clubs. Typically, clubs are formed by an entrepreneurial coach who rents the local country club or college pool and who draws a salary by charging for lessons and collecting monthly dues from team parents.

One elite national club, Club Mission Bay, in Boca Raton, Fla., recruits top athletes by providing what its brochure describes as "a total life style" for the entire family. The Mission Bay Aquatic Center, home of the Mission Bay Makos swim team, is the centerpiece of a 565-acre development devoted to competitive swimming, which includes two adjacent 50-meter pools, a diving complex, two condominium parks, office buildings, a mall, a Montessori school and two Olympic team coaches.

Jim Ellis's situation is radically different. A junior high school math teacher by day, Ellis, 42, becomes an $18,000-a-year "Water Safety Instructor II" at a neighborhood recreation center by night. This gives him morning and after-school access to a deteriorating 25-yard-long pool (less than half the distance of pools used in the Olympic meets). He charges his 80 or so families annual dues of $100. They pay for expenses by holding pizza sales, swimathons and raffles. Having little, they scavenge materials and use them in innovative ways. Ellis has long taught his backstrokers the proper techniques of turning and spinning by placing them on a large scrap of slippery green matting that once lay beneath the artificial turf at Philadelphia's Veterans Stadium.

There are few seats for spectators at Marcus Foster, and the deck surrounding the pool is too narrow for anything more than dual meets. Sometimes they have to practice seven swimmers to a lane. But it's home. "This is my Mission Bay," Jim Ellis shouts above the churning water of a morning practice. "I got six lanes of fast water. And we *are* on a mission here. We want to go to the Olympic trials in 1992. Most exceptional black swimmers have been recruited by major white clubs. And they'll go, thinking there's not a black coach able to get them to a national level. I believe swimmers can come out of the urban community with a black coach. I have the key to this building. For now, that's enough."

Ellis recruited most of his swimmers by advertising free swimming lessons at day-care centers and elementary schools. He has known them since they were barely out of diapers. "I've had to grow my own team, starting with little children," he says. "Where was I going to find black kids in Philly who were going to walk in with technique?"

Ellis, who had been a free-styler at Westinghouse High School in Pittsburgh in the early 1960's, attended Cheyney State College and swam there his freshman year; then the coach quit when he was a sophomore and the team was dissolved. In 1971, still in school, he took a job as a water safety instructor at the Sayre Community Recreation Center in West Philadelphia. His first swimmers were proud if they could put their faces in the water and flail the 10 yards that earned them a Red Cross pin. He pitted them against one another, and goaded them to bring in their big brothers. Soon they wanted to race Ellis. "Everyone wanted to beat me," he recalls. "I told them to do that they'd have to be on a team."

Weeks later, the Sayre Sea Devils trundled off to a meet in Delaware for children 8 years and under. "My wife laughed at me all the way out the door," he recalls. "But I told her, 'We have to start somewhere.' We came home with one little brown ribbon, for 15th place."

From the start, he decided to pit his young athletes against strong competitors in the Philadelphia and Delaware suburbs. Seeing five or six Sea Devils approaching, locals would sometimes assume they were basketball players and point out the gym. The parents and officials he met told him constantly, as if the observation made his day, that the kids were exceptionally well behaved.

Some of the original Sayre Sea Devil families dropped out after a few excursions into the suburbs. "Some of them felt inferior, like they didn't belong," Ellis recalls. "We'd go on a trip, and the father would buy a bottle and stay in his room." But Ellis knew that for the children to feel genuinely comfortable in the white world of club swimming, a large number of parents would have to travel with the team. He could well remember his own experience as a teen-ager when a group of white swimmers surrounded and threatened him before a major indoor meet. The only other black person present that day, as usual, had been his mother.

In the mid-70's, one of Ellis's swimmers, an 8-year-old named Trevor

Freeland, began to win regularly against stiff regional competition. At first, Ellis recalls, Freeland seemed hopelessly awkward, a churner with little innate feel for finding what Ellis calls "the good water" on a given stroke. What he did have, though, was an appetite for hard work and a hunger to excel.

Ellis saw in Freeland the national-caliber swimmer that could anchor a team, and the pursuit of training information became an obsession for the coach. "He was always asking, 'What are the things I need to know to move a swimmer up to the next level?'" recalls Mark Bernardino, head coach of the University of Virginia men's swimming team. "He raided our library. He met every great teacher and coach out there and grabbed their tricks and brought them back."

From George Haines, who coached four different United States Olympic teams, Ellis learned to shave the hair from his swimmers' bodies before a big meet. "Haines saw my swimmers at a meet one day and asked why I didn't shave them," Ellis recalls "I told him, 'Hey, black people don't have a lot of body hair. Why shave off what little we have?' He sat me down and explained:

"'Your kids come to a meet and everybody else is in there shaving, putting on linaments and getting rubdowns. And your kids aren't doing it. They're going to get up there on the blocks, thinking, "The others are doing something extra we didn't do."'" It stuck with me. So I started talking it up, saying. 'This is going to help you.' And they believed it. I could shave the kid and not do anything else different in training and he'd go faster."

Much of what he learned had to do with giving black children positive expectations, the sense that, even though they trained in a small neighborhood pool, they were limited only by their desire to excel. When it became obvious that the best swimmers lifted weights, they filled coffee cans with cement and devised a program. He gave them metric-conversion tables to carry in their wallets and purses so that they would begin to think internationally.

When Trevor Freeland began to establish national-caliber times, Ellis tore the local pool record off the wall, which he then papered with a listing of the best 100 times for each age group in United States history. Now his swimmers have six entries on that list.

With Freeland as a role model, more and more parents began to bring their children in for lessons. Many of the parents, Ellis observed, were teachers, disciplined by nature and holding high expectations for their children. They were, he thought, perfect.

In the mid-1980's, Ellis moved to the Marcus Foster center and changed the team's name simply to PDR. His swimmers begged him to let them be dolphins or sharks or swimming cobras but he told them that they were lucky PDR meant nothing. That way, he said, you have the chance to make it mean something.

Now the PDR swimmers convoy up and down the mid-Atlantic coast with a battalion of parents, friends and alumni, often including several of the 25 swimmers for whom Ellis has found college scholarships. A regular attendee is Trevor Freeland, who, after an exceptional swimming career at the University of Virginia, last year won two events at the Corporate Superstars Swim meet, representing a D.C.-based engineering firm.

They arrive early and drape a blue-and-gold PDR banner in a conspicuous place. The parents sit front and center and Ellis assumes a command position on the deck. He huddles with each swimmer before a race, forcing him or her to visualize every component of the swim, every length, every turn, the start, the kick, the stroke and the finish. Then comes the standard benediction. "O.K.," he says. "It's showtime. Swim funky."

Success has brought changes in the way the PDR swimmers are regarded. Mostly, people seem amazed. "The swimmers say, 'I didn't know you could swim that good,'" says Vanessa Patterson. "I think it's just because we're black that they say that, to distract us." The parents agree that the question they hear most commonly from white onlookers now is, "What do you feed those kids?" Nate Norment, Michael's father, usually says chitlins. Others say greens. "It depends on who's doing the asking," says Ellis. "If it seems like they're just trying to make us sound different, I tell them the truth: chlorine, three meals a day."

Beyond PDR, successful black swimmers in general—many of whom compete in short-distance races—are beginning to hear a different tune, not that they can't swim but that they had an advantage all along. The highly influential and recently retired Indiana University swimming coach James (Doc) Counsilman wrote in 1975: "The black athlete excels because he has more white muscle fibers, which are adapted for speed and power, than red fibers, which are adapted for endurance."

The first successful black American runners, more than a half century ago, were sprinters, and it was long accepted as gospel that black runners tired after a mile or so. Now that black African athletes, especially Kenyans, have come to the forefront as long-distance runners, theories have surfaced explaining that there have really been *two* kinds of black people all along: those of East African ancestry, whose muscle fibers are adapted for endurance, and those of West African ancestry, whose muscles contain fibers that deliver oxygen rapidly, producing explosive power.

The discussion baffles even some scientists. "We create, we imagine a physiology," Dr. David Pearson has said. Pearson is a longtime staff member at the Human Performance Laboratory at Ball State University in Muncie, Ind., which has conducted thousands of muscle biopsies on subjects of all races since 1966 and has found no differences in muscle fibers by race. "It's as if they're saying, 'Let's hide our myth deeper and deeper in science so that fewer and fewer people can understand it.'"

Jim Ellis finds the discussion absurd. "The black sprinter is a stereo-type," he says flatly. "I think the white world looks at us as sprinters. My first kids wanted to race fast all the time, like track. So I went with it, and we developed some great sprinters. I'm out to develop middle-distance and distance athletes as well. Now we are winning 200- and 400-meter races. We're just attacking the 1,000 this year."

His swimmers are hampered, he says, only by the shortness of the Marcus Foster pool, whose walls prematurely interrupt their strokes. PDR's best distance swimmer is Valerie Patterson, Vanessa's twin, who has won freestyle events in regional meets in distances up to 1,650 meters. Ellis works with Valerie on her pace, which he says is almost eerily consistent. "Ask her for a 32-second lap, and she'll give it to you, lap after lap," he says. "Take it down to 31 and she knows exactly where that is. Her potential is unlimited."

As Ellis's reputation grows, parents of black swimmers throughout the nation are beginning to find him. After observing the PDR team at an all-star meet in Buffalo, Nate Norment moved to Philadelphia from Long Island to give his son a chance to swim for PDR. Whites, too, are becoming interested. About a year ago, David Goodner, a physician who is the father of two well-known young swimmers around the Philadelphia area, passed over Team Foxcatcher, a well-heeled private club that placed two swimmers on the 1988 United States Olympic team, and asked Ellis for a chance with PDR. "I'd go to these big meets and see Jim," Goodner recalls. "He so obviously loves kids. He treated them with respect and love. I wanted that for my kids." Both Goodner children, Blake, 15, and Alyson, 11, now swim for PDR.

After a recent article about the team in a Philadelphia newspaper, Ellis received five calls from other parents of white swimmers. An unantici-pated byproduct of his success, it continues to cause him some thought. "It's something I have to deal with—as a coach, as a person, as a black man," he says.

As it turned out, the PDR delegation did not blow away the rest of America's young swimmers at the junior national meet. It was the first major national competition for five of the six swimmers, and the nervous-ness showed. Only Jason Webb, the lone veteran of national competition, finished in the top half of his field in an event. Jim Ellis noticed that his kids seemed to swim well in the straightaways, but lost ground when they thrust against the walls to change direction, a sign to him that they need more weight training.

But while most meets, like the junior nationals, offer lessons and disappointments, some moments shine through like beacons, vindicating all the dawn practices and the sacrifices the families have made. For Jim Wade, Atiba's father, such a moment came in the summer of 1988. On the recommendation of a coaching friend, Jim Ellis had accepted an invitation for the team to swim at a major regional meet in Greensboro, N.C.

Like Ellis, Jim Wade did not know what to expect. It was their first meet ever in the South. He had grown up in Coosawhatchie, S.C., a town in which every public facility had been segregated. On the bus ride down, he spoke to the kids in small groups, telling them of his childhood. They listened politely.

When they got there, Jim Ellis, himself nervous, told the kids to walk confidently from the bus into the facility and take their rightful place in the practice pool. They did. Wade took a seat in the bleachers to watch, wondering if he and Ellis had perhaps made them overwrought. "They tore that meet up," Wade recalls, laughing. "Almost everybody swam their best time. People were *amazed*. But I'll tell you when I knew we were getting somewhere. It was in the 100-meter butterfly. One of our swimmers, Akida Stephens, was the only black swimmer in the race.

"When they got to the 50-meter mark, Akida and a white girl were neck and neck. I was sitting behind two white ladies. One turned to the other and said, 'My God, they're tied.' After 75 it was, 'My God, she's *ahead*.' When Akida won, it was as if that woman's view of the world had turned upside down in a 100 meters. For me, it was like a victory. I hadn't even been able to swim in the pool in my town. I said to myself, 'Thank God I have lived to see this moment.'"

15

U.S. Hispanics: Challenging Issues for the 1990s

Rafael Valdivieso and Cary Davis

The number of Hispanic residents in the United States reached 20 million in 1988. After blacks, they are the nation's largest minority. Most Americans know that the number of Hispanics is increasing rapidly, but few really know much about the Hispanic community or appreciate the diversity among Latino groups. Nor do they realize the impact the Hispanic population will have on the nation's schools and labor force in the future.

The very term "Hispanic" is a label with a nebulous meaning, applied by the general population to an ever-changing group of U.S. residents. The terms Hispanic or Latino generally refer to individuals whose cultural heritage traces back to a Spanish-speaking country in Latin America, but also include those persons with links to Spain, or from the southwestern region of the U.S., once under Spanish or Mexican control.

Hispanics are found in every U.S. state, in every type of profession, and may be of any race—but the tendency to generalize about them as a group is fueled by the fact that the majority speak Spanish, live in the Southwest, and occupy the lower end of the social hierarchy.

Many Hispanics face similar problems which—because of their increasing numbers—U.S. policymakers must address. High dropout rates, low salaries, and job discrimination have plagued many Latinos, ensnaring them in a cycle of poverty, alienation, and underachievement. Public

Rafael Valdivieso and Cary Davis, "U.S. Hispanics: Challenging Issues for the 1990s," Population Reference Bureau, Inc., Washington, D.C., 1988. Reprinted by permission.

policies and programs dealing with education, welfare, and labor relations can help Hispanics lead more productive, independent lives. In addition, because at least one-third of U.S. immigrants in the 1980s are from Latin America, federal immigration laws and enforcement guidelines affect the Hispanic community.

HOW MANY HISPANICS?

Since the first European settlers arrived in the New World in the 17th century, the composition of the U.S. population has never remained stable for very long. While most of the U.S. population growth has been due to natural increase (the excess of births over deaths) immigration has always been an important component. During the late 1980s, nearly one-third of annual U.S. population increase has been due to immigration.

The Western European settlers to the continental United States were superseded by Northern and then Southern and Eastern Europeans in the late 19th and early 20th centuries. As the centuries of origin for immigration shift over time, with new immigration streams opening while older ones wither away, our self-image as a nation is transformed. This process continues today. In the late 20th century, the "new immigrants" come from Asian, African, and Latin American countries.

Using U.S. Census Bureau definitions, which have evolved over time, the Hispanic population grew from 4 million in 1950, when they were 2.7 percent of the total population, to 14.6 million in 1980, 6.4 percent of the total. In March 1988, there were an estimated 19.4 million U.S. Hispanics, accounting for 8.1 percent of the total U.S. population. . . . The number of Hispanics increased 34 percent between 1980 and 1988, compared to only a 7 percent increase in the general population.

The key factors responsible for this impressive growth are heavy immigration to the U.S. from Latin America and relatively high birth rates among U.S. Hispanic residents. These two factors contributed equally to the 5 million increase in the U.S. Hispanic population between 1980 and 1988.

YOUTHFUL AGE STRUCTURE

Immigration and high birth rates contribute to the young age structure of Hispanics, relative to the U.S. as a whole. In 1988, the median age in the U.S. was 32.2 years, compared to only 25.5 years of age among Hispanics.

High fertility keeps a population young because of the continuous influx of increasing numbers of births. Immigration also leads to a low average age because migrants are likely to be young adults, just entering the ages for starting a family.

What is the significance of a young age structure? From a public policy perspective, a young population will require day care, education, and jobs, for example, rather than pensions, retirement planning, and geriatric health care. To the extent that Hispanic and non-Hispanic populations differ in age structure, there may be conflicting priorities for public and private spending.

From a strictly demographic perspective, the Hispanics' young age structure means that Latino youth form a greater proportion of U.S. young people. Latinos accounted for 8 percent of the total U.S. population in 1988, but 11 percent of those under age 15. Society's effort to educate and nurture the next generation will be directed increasingly at an Hispanic audience.

The young age structure also contains a built-in momentum for further growth because a greater percentage of the population has yet to reach childbearing age. Even without additional immigration the Hispanics would grow relative to non-Hispanics. With high fertility and low mortality rates, Hispanics contribute an increasing proportion of the natural increase of the U.S. population.

International immigration is the second major factor in the remarkable growth of the Hispanic population. The Immigration and Naturalization Service (INS) recorded 2.7 million Latin American immigrants to the U.S. between 1960 and 1970, and many have remained here. (Puerto Ricans, who are U.S. citizens, are not included in this count.) According to Census Bureau estimates, a net figure of over 2 million Hispanic immigrants (including undocumented) entered between 1980 and 1988.

The immigration of Latinos to the U.S. is expected to remain high for the foreseeable future. In many sending countries in Latin America, the high international debt and economic disarray combined with an unprecedented number of new job seekers guarantees a growing pool of potential migrants. Continuing political unrest in countries such as El Salvador and Nicaragua will augment the flow. No provision in existing INS regulations or in recently proposed legislation is likely to seriously slow the flow of Hispanics into the U.S.

STARK CONTRASTS: HISPANIC POPULATION GROUPS

The growing Hispanic presence in the U.S. has blinded many Americans to the real diversity that exists within this community. The categories of "Hispanics" used by the Census Bureau largely reflect the countries of origin for recent migration streams: Mexicans; Puerto Ricans; Cubans; Central and South Americans; along with the catchall "Other Hispanics."

Latinos of Mexican ancestry have long been the largest U.S. group covered by the umbrella term Hispanic. In 1988, Mexicans accounted for 62 percent of all Hispanic Americans. About 13 percent of U.S. mainland Hispanics were Puerto Rican in 1988; 5 percent were Cuban; 12 percent Central and South American; and 8 percent "Other Hispanic." Except for the "Other" category, all the groups have made their major numerical impact on the U.S. since World War II.

The point of entry for each Hispanic group has largely determined its current geographic distribution. Mexican Americans are concentrated in the Southwest, particularly in California and Texas. In 1980, only about one-quarter of them were foreign-born, underscoring the fact that they are among the oldest Hispanic groups residing in the United States.

Puerto Ricans, the second largest subgroup, are clustered heavily in the New York metropolitan area. Waves of Puerto Ricans entered the U.S. when inexpensive air traffic opened up between Puerto Rico and New York in the 1950s. As natives of a U.S. Commonwealth, Puerto Ricans may enter or leave the U.S. mainland at will. In 1980, about one-half of those residing on the U.S. mainland had been born on the island of Puerto Rico.

The Cuban migration stream has flowed primarily into Florida, the point of entry for Cuban refugees fleeing the Fidel Castro regime in the 1950s and 1960s. Remarkably, Dade County, Florida, still contains about one-half of the 1 million Cuban Americans. According to the 1980 Census, three-fourths of U.S. Cubans were foreign-born. However, this number does not reflect the influx of 125,000 Cuban refugees during the 1980 Mariel Sealift.

The Central and South Americans are among the most recent of the major immigrant streams. In 1980, about 80 percent were foreign-born. The majority live in California, a favorite entry point, but large communities also exist in large eastern urban areas. New York contains sizable communities of Dominicans and Colombians, for example, and many Central Americans have flocked to the Boston and Washington, D.C. metropolitan areas.

"Other Hispanics" are heavily concentrated in the Southwest, particularly New Mexico and Arizona. The group includes some Americans who immigrated recently from Spain, and others who came centuries ago. Many are from families that have been here so many generations they no longer identify themselves with Spain or a specific Latin American country but still consider themselves to be "of Hispanic origin." The vast majority (80 percent) were born in the U.S., according to 1980 Census figures.

Although Latinos reside in every state, 89 percent live in one of nine states, five of these in the Southwest. Because most immigrants enter the U.S. through California or Texas, the Hispanic presence in these states has grown. More than one-half of U.S. Hispanics live in California and Texas; another 8 percent live in the neighboring states of Arizona, New

Mexico, and Colorado. Over 14 percent of all Hispanics reside in New York and New Jersey, 8 percent in Florida, and 4 percent in Illinois. . . . Only 11 percent of the total live in the other 41 states.

DISADVANTAGED MINORITY

Latinos have many characteristics that set them apart from other Americans, but which are also common to other disadvantaged minorities and to earlier immigrant groups. In general, Hispanics have less education, lower incomes, and higher rates of unemployment and poverty than the general population. They have been painted with a broad brush of ethnic stereotyping—hated for their differences and feared because of their growing presence.

Because many Hispanics have darker skin than the average non-Hispanic, and because most speak Spanish, they are an easy target for discrimination. Public concern and misinformation about illegal immigration has tarnished the image of all Hispanics because most illegals are from Latin America. Many blame Hispanics for the flow of illegal drugs from Latin America.

Hispanics have faced discrimination in schools and housing, and in obtaining jobs and promotions. They have suffered harassment by police and been discouraged from political participation. Many earlier immigrant groups suffered from similar injustices. However, in part because substantial immigration from Latin America is still occurring, Hispanics continue to experience ethnic discrimination.

Slow educational progress

Low educational achievement has been a major barrier to the advancement of Hispanics in U.S. society. Hispanics have made modest gains in educational attainment since 1970, yet education still stands out as one of the quality-of-life indicators most at odds with the non-Hispanic population. More than 3 out of 5 (62 percent) Latinos age 25 to 34 had completed four years of high school by March 1988, but a much higher proportion (89 percent) of non-Hispanics had completed high school. . . .

Although good schools can break the cycle, research consistently shows that the success of children in school can usually be predicted from the educational status of their parents. The Latino adults most likely to have school-age children are in the 25-to-34 age bracket. In 1988, this group was over three times as likely to have not completed high school as other Americans.

Some U.S. Latino groups are more likely than others to have high school diplomas. In 1988, nearly 83 percent of Cuban Americans age 25 to

34 had completed high school compared to only 67 percent of Puerto Ricans and 54 percent of Mexican Americans.

Only 12 percent of Hispanics in the 25-to-34 age bracket had completed four or more years of college, less than half the percentage of non-Hispanics. The range within Hispanic groups is even more striking, from a low of 8 percent of Mexican Americans to a high of 24 percent of Cuban Americans with four or more years of college.

Although many Hispanic students are handicapped by a limited knowledge of English, this alone does not explain poor academic performance. Among Hispanics, Cuban students are the most likely to speak Spanish at home, yet have the highest educational levels. Clearly, for these students the benefits of the middle class, professional background of the majority of U.S. Cuban parents outweigh the "disadvantage" of having to learn English as a second language.

While college attendance is crucial for overall advancement of Hispanics, increasing the percentage who finish high school is a necessary first step. The high dropout rate not only hurts Hispanics, it constitutes a massive waste of human resources sorely needed in this era of keen international economic competition. Moreover, because educational attainment is strongly associated with social and economic status, the high dropout rate is certain to contribute to Latino poverty in the future.

Low-paying jobs

In 1988, Hispanics made up only 7 percent of the U.S. civilian labor force. The Hispanic share, however, is likely to increase as the non-Hispanic population ages and the number of working-age Hispanics continues to grow.

Hispanic men, indeed, are more likely to be employed or seeking work than other American men, 79 percent versus 74 percent, although only about 71 percent of Puerto Rican and Other Hispanic males are in the labor force.

Hispanic women, and Puerto Ricans in particular, are less likely to be working than other women. Only 51 percent of female Hispanics, and 40 percent of Puerto Rican women, were in the labor force in 1988 compared to 56 percent of non-Hispanic women. Some observers feel that this difference reflects the traditional Latin American disapproval of women working outside the home. However, this gap may be closing: The percentage of younger Hispanic women who are working exceeds that of young non-Hispanics.

Because of their relatively low educational levels and language problems, Hispanics tend to enter poorly-paid jobs with little chance of advancement. In 1988, only 28 percent of Hispanic men were in the upper-level managerial, technical, and administrative categories compared to 48 percent of non-Hispanic men. Cuban men are an exception to this; 51 percent held higher-status positions.

Not only are Hispanics overrepresented in low-paying, semi-skilled jobs but they work in economic sectors vulnerable to cyclical unemployment and in some industries, like manufacturing, that are threatened with a long-term decline. Hispanics are as likely as non-Hispanics to be in the labor force, yet they are more likely to be unemployed. In 1988, 8.5 percent of Hispanics were out of work compared to only 5.8 percent of other Americans.

High poverty rates

The low-status occupations and high unemployment among Hispanics translate into low incomes and high poverty rates. Median family income for Hispanics in 1987 was only $20,300, two-thirds of the non-Hispanic median income of $31,600. In real dollars, this income gap between Hispanics and other Americans actually grew between 1978 and 1987, primarily because Hispanics still have not recovered from the economic recession of 1980 and 1981.

Within the Hispanic community, income levels reveal marked differences. Cuban family income in 1987, at $27,300, approached the non-Hispanic median. Puerto Rican families, at the other extreme, had average annual incomes of only $15,200, one-half of the non-Hispanic median and more than $5,000 less than the next highest Hispanic group.

Since Hispanic families are relatively large, these incomes must support more household members. The average family size for non-Hispanics in 1988 was 3.1, compared to 3.8 for all Hispanics and 4.1 persons for Mexican Americans.

Also, Hispanic families are less likely than others to be headed by a married couple and much more likely to be headed by a single parent, usually the mother. Consequently, fewer Hispanic families have the potential earning power provided by two working parents. Married-couple families account for only 70 percent of all Hispanic families, compared to 80 percent of non-Hispanic families. Nearly one-quarter, 23 percent, are headed by an unmarried or separated woman, while 16 percent of non-Hispanic families are female-headed. A whopping 44 percent of Puerto Rican families are headed by single females, double the Hispanic and almost triple the non-Hispanic average.

These statistics highlight the handicaps faced by many Latino children. With large families, low incomes, and a high proportion of single-parent families, the success of a significant proportion of the next generation is at risk. In 1987, 26 percent of all Hispanic families had incomes below the poverty threshold, compared to only 10 percent of non-Hispanic families. In single-parent families headed by an Hispanic female, over half (52 percent) were below the poverty line, exactly equal to the proportion of black families headed by a single female in poverty. . . .

Within Hispanic groups, poverty rates range from a high of 38 percent for Puerto Rican families to a low of 14 percent for Cuban. Perhaps most discouraging, two-thirds of female-headed Puerto Rican families were poor in 1987.

Poverty rates for Hispanics actually increased between 1978 and 1987, while rates for white and black Americans have decreased. The number of poor Hispanics grew from 2.9 million in 1979 to 5.5 million in 1987, a 90 percent increase.

Poor Hispanics are less likely to benefit from federal welfare programs than poor black Americans, but more likely than non-Hispanic whites. The percentage of poor Hispanics served by federal welfare programs fell slightly between 1980 and 1988, partly as a result of federal budget cuts. The only major program that reaches a majority of poor Hispanics is the subsidized school lunch program, received by 92 percent of poor Hispanic children in 1988. In the same year, only 30 percent of poor Hispanics received cash assistance; 13 percent lived in public housing; 49 percent received food stamps; and 42 percent received Medicaid. . . .

High poverty rates are likely to persist among Hispanics in the 1990s. Actions to curb the high poverty levels must deal primarily with:

• Education and job training;
• Discrimination in hiring and promotion; and
• Access to welfare programs by the Hispanic poor, especially single-parent families.

Each of these issues requires the attention of policymakers and community leaders from the national to the local level. . . .

As we enter the 1990s, U.S. Hispanics constitute an increasing share of our school children and entry-level job seekers; yet they remain a disadvantaged minority. The Latinos' growing presence suggests that policymakers should seek ways to:

• Ease their transition into mainstream society;
• Ensure their maximum productivity through improved education and training; and
• Encourage their participation in the decision-making and political processes.

Perhaps the recognition that improving the position of Hispanics is in the best interest of all Americans offers policymakers the best incentive to focus more attention on Hispanic concerns.

16

A Piece of the Pie

Stanley Lieberson

T he source of European migrants to the United States shifted radically toward the end of the last century; Northwestern Europe
declined in relative importance, thanks to the unheralded numbers arriving from the Southern, Central, and Eastern parts of Europe. These
"new" sources, which had contributed less than one-tenth of all immigrants as late as 1880, were soon sending the vast majority of newcomers,
until large-scale immigration was permanently cut off in the 1920s. For
example, less than 1 percent of all immigrants in the 1860s had come from
Italy, but in the first two decades of the twentieth century more migrants
arrived from this one nation than from all of the Northwestern European
countries combined. These new European groups piled up in the slums of
the great urban centers of the East and Midwest, as well as in the factory
towns of those regions, and in the coal-mining districts of Pennsylvania
and elsewhere. They were largely unskilled, minimally educated, poor,
relegated to undesirable jobs and residences, and life was harsh.

The descendants of these South-Central-Eastern (SCE) European
groups have done relatively well in the United States. By all accounts,
their education, occupations, and incomes are presently close to—or even
in excess of—white Americans from the earlier Northwestern European
sources. To be sure, there are still areas where they have not quite "made
it." Americans of Italian and Slavic origin are underrepresented in *Who's
Who in America*, although their numbers are growing. Every president of

the United States has thus far been of old European origin. Likewise, a study of the 106 largest Chicago-area corporations found Poles and Italians grossly underrepresented on the boards or as officers when compared with their proportion in the population in the metropolitan area. There is also evidence of discrimination in the upper echelons of banking directed at Roman Catholics and Jews, to say nothing of nonwhites and women generally. For example, as of a few years ago there were only a handful of Jews employed as senior officers in all of New York City's eight giant banks and there were *no* Jews employed as senior officers in any of the nation's 50 largest non-New York banks.

Nevertheless, it is clear that the new Europeans have "made it" to a degree far in excess of that which would have been expected or predicted at the time of their arrival here. It is also equally apparent that blacks have not. Whether it be income, education, occupation, self-employment, power, position in major corporations, residential location, health, or living conditions, the average black status is distinctly below that held by the average white of SCE European origin. Numerous exceptions exist, of course, and progress has occurred: There are many blacks who have made it. But if these exceptions should not be overlooked, it is also the case that blacks and new Europeans occupy radically different average positions in society.

Since the end of slavery occurred about 20 years before the new Europeans started their massive move to the United States and because the latter groups seem to have done so well in this nation, there are numerous speculations as to why the groups have experienced such radically different outcomes. Most of these end up in one of two camps: either blacks were placed under greater disadvantages by the society and other forces outside of their control; or, by contrast, the new Europeans had more going for them in terms of their basic characteristics. Examples of the former explanation include: the race and skin color markers faced by blacks but not by SCE Europeans; greater discrimination against blacks in institutions ranging from courts to unions to schools; the preference that dominant whites had for other whites over blacks; and the decline in opportunities by the time blacks moved to the North in sizable numbers. Interpretations based on the assumption that the differences in success reflect superior new European attributes include speculations regarding family cohesion, work ethic, intelligence, acceptance of demeaning work, and a different outlook toward education as a means of mobility. Not only is it possible for both types of forces to be operating but that their relative role could easily change over time, since a period of about 100 years is long enough to permit all sorts of feedback processes as well as broad societal changes which have consequences for the groups involved. Hence the problem is extremely complex. As one might expect, those sympathetic to the difficulties faced by blacks tend to emphasize the first factor; those emphasizing the second set of forces tend to be less sympathetic.

The answer to this issue is relevant to current social policies because an understanding of the causes would affect the ways proposed for dealing with the present black-white gap. In addition, there is the related issue of whether the SCE groups provide an analogy or a model for blacks. Finally, the historical causes of present-day circumstances are of grave concern to all those who are enmeshed in these events. Is the relatively favorable position enjoyed by the descendants of new European immigrants to be seen as purely a function of more blood, sweat, and tears such that easy access to the same goodies will in some sense desecrate all of these earlier struggles—let alone mean sharing future opportunities with blacks? If, on the other hand, the position held by blacks vis-à-vis the new Europeans is due to their skin color and the fact that blacks experience more severe forms of discrimination, then the present-day position of blacks is proof of the injustices that exist and the need to redress them.

Because there is a big stake in the answer, not surprisingly a number of scholars have addressed the question already. But as we will see, many of the answers have been highly speculative. It is one thing to note the sharp present-day differences between the new European groups and blacks and then to speculate about the causes of these differences. A far different task is the search for data that might help one determine in at least a moderately rigorous way what was going on earlier in this century and at the tail end of the last. Indeed, there are moments when I empathize with both the frustrations and challenges archaeologists must feel as they try to piece together events from some ancient society.

RACE AND DISCRIMINATION

The obstacles faced by the new Europeans were enormous and in some cases, such as the development of political power . . . , comparable to the black experience in the North. However, a massive body of evidence indicates that blacks were discriminated against far more intensely in many domains of life than were the new Europeans. Witness, for example, the disposition of both employers and labor unions . . . This fact cannot be glossed over as it is central to any explanation of group differences in outcome. This raises two questions about race. If blacks did have greater obstacles, to what degree were these due to race? Second, if race did play an important role, how does one reconcile this interpretation with the fact that such other nonwhite groups as the Chinese and Japanese have done so well in the United States (to be sure only after a rocky start)?

Among those recognizing the fact that other nonwhite groups did better in the United States, there are several variations of the same basic theme, namely, that these other groups had certain characteristics that blacks lacked. For example, there may have been special institutional forces and advantages that these groups had. Or, we return to the speculations about norms, values dispositions, and the like. Another variation of this emphasizes the heritage of slavery and the damaging effects of slavery, obstacles that did not exist for the other nonwhite groups. In any case, it leads to conclusions that the gaps were not really due to race after all, at least as an immediate cause as other nonwhite groups did alright.

There is another way of thinking about these racial gaps, one that emphasizes differences in the social context of contact. This perspective leads one to conclude that much of the black disadvantage was due to neither race nor certain personality characteristics. Rather, it is the structure of the situation that was so radically different for blacks and these other groups.

Let us recognize at the outset that there are certain disadvantages that blacks and any other nonwhite group would suffer in a society where the dominant white population has a preference for whites over nonwhites. This disadvantage is one blacks share with Japanese, Chinese, Filipinos, American Indians, and any other nonwhite group. These groups were more visible and more sharply discriminated against than were various white ethnic groups. The disposition to apply the same levels of legal protection and rights was weaker than that directed toward white populations. (This is possibly due to white predispositions stemming from the earlier slavery period as well as the fact that the SCE groups were at least European.) However, it is not impossible that whites have a hierarchy with respect to nonwhites such that blacks and Africans generally rank lower than Asian groups. In the early 1930s 100 Princeton University undergraduates were asked to characterize various racial and ethnic groups. Consider how radically different were the characterizations of blacks, Chinese, and Japanese shown in [Table 1]. Particularly impressive is the list of characteristics listed for the Japanese, almost all of which would be considered "desirable" by most Americans. By contrast, the list of black characteristics is striking both because of its almost uniform lack of any favorable attributes and also because, I suspect, the emphasis would be quite different now.

To be sure, one might argue that these stereotypes reflect real differences between these groups and hence serve to prove that the Japanese and Chinese levels of success were a reflection of important personality differences. However, given the relatively small number of Japanese in the United States and their concentration on the Pacific Coast during the 1930s, it is unlikely that the responses of these Princeton students reflect much in the way of actual contact experience. Hence these results show radical differences in the way nonwhite groups were perceived by whites.

The reader may wonder if all of this is a bit too pat; rather than simply concluding that blacks had less of the necessary characteristics for making it in the United States, it is claimed that they did not do as well as other nonwhite groups because they faced even more severe disadvantages.

Table 1 Characteristics Most Commonly Used by 100 Princeton Students [to Describe Various Ethnic and Racial Groups], 1932

Chinese		Japanese		Negroes	
Characteristic	Number of respondents agreeing	Characteristic	Number of respondents agreeing	Characteristic	Number of respondents agreeing
Superstitious	34	Intelligent	45	Superstitious	84
Sly	29	Industrious	43	Lazy	75
Conservative	29	Progressive	24	Happy-go-lucky	38
Tradition-loving	26	Shrewd	22	Ignorant	38
Loyal to family ties	22	Sly	20	Musical	26
Industrious	18	Quiet	19	Ostentatious	26
Meditative	18	Imitative	17	Very religious	24
Reserved	17	Alert	16	Stupid	22
Very religious	15	Suave	16	Physically dirty	17
Ignorant	15	Neat	16	Naive	14
Deceitful	14	Treacherous	13	Slovenly	13
Quiet	13	Aggressive	13	Unreliable	12

Source: Daniel Katz and Kenneth W. Braly, "Verbal Stereotypes and Racial Prejudice," in Guy E. Swanson, Theodore Newcomb, and Eugene L. Hartley (eds.), *Readings in Social Psychology* (2nd edition). New York: Holt, Rinehart & Winston, 1952.

Why would blacks suffer more? This is the heart of the matter. In my estimation, there are two key features that distinguish blacks from other nonwhite groups in the United States and which help explain their different outcomes. First, an exceptionally unfavorable disposition toward blacks existed on the part of the dominant white society due to the slave period and the initial contact with Africans. Blacks enter into competition as free people, but they are unable to shake off easily the derogatory notions about them and the negative dispositions toward blacks which go back to the slavery era. Of course, this was not a problem for the other nonwhite groups. Second, the threat of Asian groups was not anywhere as severe because migration was cut off before their numbers were very large. The response of whites to Chinese and Japanese was of the same violent and savage character in areas where they were concentrated, but the threat was quickly stopped through changes in immigration policy. This meant that Asian groups had more time to develop special mobility niches (see the discussion below) and that they have been of less *actual* (as opposed to *potential*) threat to whites than blacks. The cessation of sizable migration from Asia for a number of decades on the one hand indicates how quickly threatened whites were by Asian groups. On the other hand, this very cessation made it possible for those who were here to avoid eventually some of the disadvantages that would occur if there were as many of their compatriots in the country as there were blacks.

For those unconvinced, have patience because the problem is too complicated to be quickly resolved by a simple data set. Rather the answer must rest on satisfactorily weaving together the various threads of evidence and theory so that they make sense from a single perspective. Later, after analyzing the consequences that follow from a cessation of immigration, it will be possible to consider further whether the main source of black disadvantage was neither race nor their internal characteristics. At the moment, one can speculate that the comparison between Asian groups and blacks in the United States, although unfavorable to the latter in recent decades, may be due to the distinctive context of their contact with whites and the incredible threat that blacks posed. However, the contrast with other nonwhites does show that being a nonwhite was not an insurmountable obstacle.

OCCUPATIONAL OPPORTUNITIES

It is difficult to overstate the direct importance of occupation and income as well as their indirect consequences for other long-run gaps between blacks and the new Europeans. Thanks to an excellent set of 1900 occupational data from the Census Bureau, one can draw some important conclusions about the situation these groups faced in the urban North at the beginning of the century. As one might guess, neither the new Europeans nor blacks held many of the specially desirable jobs at that time so there were not sharp differences at the upper end of the scale. But there were substantial differences in some areas, particularly in the service jobs where blacks were more concentrated and in the manufacturing jobs where the new Europeans held the edge. There was some evidence, even in 1900, that the new Europeans were in a more favorable position, even if they were still lower on the queue than were the older white groups. There is also strong evidence that the black pattern in the North resembled very much the same pattern found in the urban South after compositional differences are taken into account. . . .

Other data . . . also indicate that earlier in this century blacks were disadvantaged in the urban North relative to the new Europeans. The antipathy toward blacks among labor unions displayed a striking interaction between discrimination by employers, employees, and customers, lower-wage levels among blacks, and strike breaking. However, the net effect is to see much more severe discriminatory forces operating against blacks in the labor market, with important feedback consequences on other domains of black–new European differences. As noted earlier, there is just no way of avoiding the fact that blacks were more severely discriminated against in the labor market and elsewhere. By contrast, there is strong evidence that new European participation in the labor market was not greatly affected by ethnic membership after one takes into account their lower origins. At least this is the case for a number of recent generations. Hence, the new Europeans were close enough to the intergenerational mobility rates for whites generally, and the rates were sufficiently open, that the SCE groups could do very well in relatively short order whereas this was not the case for blacks.

FURTHER ANALYSIS OF RACE

Returning to a theme suggested earlier . . . , I believe there is further reason for speculating that race was not as crucial an issue as is commonly supposed for understanding the black outcome relative to the new Europeans. In order to avoid being misunderstood by the casual reader, let me reiterate that such a conclusion does not mean that other nonwhite groups or the new Europeans possessed certain favorable characteristics to a greater degree than did blacks. There is an alternative way of interpreting these events, namely, a substantial source of the disadvantage faced by blacks is due to their position with respect to certain structural conditions that affect race relations generally. Having been reviewed in this chapter, one should now make sense of black–new European gaps, but what about comparisons of blacks with other nonwhites? There are eight important factors to consider.

1. Although hard quantitative data are not available, there is every reason to believe that the response to Chinese and Japanese in the United States was every bit as severe and as violent initially as that toward blacks when the latter moved outside of their traditional niches.
2. There was a cessation of sizable immigration from Japan and China for a number of decades before these groups were able to advance in the society.
3. The cessation was due to the intense pressures within the United States against Asian migration, particularly by those whites who were threatened by these potential competitors.
4. This meant that the number of these groups in the nation is quite small relative to blacks. In the 1970 census there were 22,580,000 blacks recorded compared with 591,000 Japanese and 435,000 Chinese.
5. Because of factors 2 and 4 above, the opportunity for these Asian groups to occupy special niches was far greater than for blacks. Imagine more than 22 million Japanese Americans trying to carve out initial niches through truck farming!
6. Because of factor 2 there has been less negative effect on the general position of these groups due to recent immigrants (a situation that is now beginning to change somewhat for the Chinese).
7. Ignoring situations generated by direct competition between Asians and whites such as existed in the West earlier, there is some evidence that the white disposition toward blacks was otherwise even more unfavorable than that toward Asians. This is due to the ideologies that developed in connection with slavery as well as perhaps the images of Africa and its people stemming from exploration of the continent. Whatever the reason, one has the impression that whites have strikingly different attitudes toward the cultures of China and Japan than toward those of blacks or of Africa.
8. The massive economic threat blacks posed for whites earlier in the century in both the South and North was not duplicated by the Asians except in certain parts of the West.

I am suggesting a general process that occurs when racial and ethnic groups have an inherent conflict—and certainly competition for jobs, power, position, maintenance of different subcultural systems, and the like are such conflicts. Under the circumstances, there is a tendency for the competitors to focus on differences between themselves. The observers (in this case the sociologists) may then assume that these differences are the sources of conflict. In point of fact, the rhetoric involving such differences may indeed inflame them, but we can be reasonably certain that the conflict would have occurred in their absence. To use a contemporary example, if Protestants in Northern Ireland had orange skin color and if the skin color of Roman Catholics in that country was green, then very likely these physical differences would be emphasized by observers seeking to explain the sharp conflict between these groups. Indeed, very likely such racial differences would be emphasized by the combatants themselves. No doubt such physical differences would enter into the situation as a secondary cause because the rhetoric would inflame that difference, but we can be reasonably certain that the conflict would occur in their absence. In the same fashion, differences between blacks and whites—real ones, imaginary ones, and those that are the product of earlier race relations—enter into the rhetoric of race and ethnic relations, but they are ultimately secondary to the conflict for society's goodies.

This certainly is the conclusion that can be generated from the classic experiment . . . in which a homogeneous group of children at camp were randomly sorted into two groups and then competition and conflict between the groups was stimulated. The experiment resulted in each of the groups developing all sorts of images about themselves and the other group. Yet, unknown to them, the groups were identical in their initial distribution of characteristics.

In order to avoid a misunderstanding of a position that is radically different from that held by most observers, whether they be black or white, oriented toward one group or the other, let me restate this part of my thesis. There is powerful evidence that blacks were victims of more severe forms of discrimination than were the new Europeans—although the latter also suffered from intense discrimination. Much of the antagonism toward blacks was based on racial features, but one should not interpret this as the ultimate cause. Rather the racial emphasis resulted from the use of the most obvious feature(s) of the group to support the intergroup conflict generated by a fear of blacks based on their threat as economic competitors. If this analysis is correct, it also means that were the present-day conflict between blacks and dominant white groups to be resolved, then the race issue could rapidly disintegrate as a crucial barrier between the groups just as a very profound and deep distaste for Roman Catholics on the part of the dominant Protestants has diminished rather substantially (albeit not disappeared).

THE GREAT NON SEQUITUR

The data comparing blacks and the new Europeans earlier in this century lead one to a rather clear conclusion about the initial question. The early living conditions of the new Europeans after their migration to the United States were extremely harsh and their point of entry into the socio-economic system was quite low. However, it is a non sequitur to assume that new Europeans had it as bad as did blacks or that the failure of blacks to move upward as rapidly reflected some ethnic deficiencies. The situation for new Europeans in the United States, bad as it may have been, was not as bad as that experienced by blacks at the same time. Witness, for example, the differences in the disposition to ban openly blacks from unions at the turn of the century . . . , the greater concentration of blacks in 1900 in service occupations and their smaller numbers in manufacturing and mechanical jobs . . . , the higher black death rates in the North . . . and even the greater segregation of blacks with respect to the avenues of eminence open to them. It is a serious mistake to underestimate how far the new Europeans have come in the nation and how hard it all was, but it is equally erroneous to assume that the obstacles were as great as those faced by blacks or that the starting point was the same.

V

Sexism

The 1960s were known as a decade of civil rights struggles, black militancy, antiwar protests, and campus disturbances. It seemed unlikely that yet another social movement could take hold and grow, but the consciousness of women's oppression could, and did grow, with enormous impact over remarkably few years.

Black militancy, the student movement, the antiwar movement, youth militancy, and radicalism all affirmed freedom, equality, and liberation, but none of these was thought to be particularly necessary or applicable to women, especially by radical men. Ironically, it was political experience with radical men that led radical women to the consciousness of women as a distinctly oppressed group and, therefore, a group with distinctive interests.

The feminism that emerged in the 1970s was in fact both novel and part of a long and often painful series of movements for the liberation of women. Women's rights proposals were first heard over a century ago. According to Peter Gabriel Filene, the movement for the equality of women ground to a halt around 1932, the darkest year of the Depression, beginning a period he calls "The Long Amnesia," when the emergencies of the Depression and World War II pushed aside feminist concerns. With victory, both sexes gratefully resumed the middle-class dream of family, security, and upward mobility. These years of the late 1940s and early 1950s were the years of "The Feminine Mystique," when the *domestic* role of women dominated American culture.

When women began, in the 1970s, once again to reassert themselves and claimed to be able to be doctors and lawyers and bankers and pilots, they were met with derision. The "Long Amnesia" had taken hold and stereotyped woman's roles into those of the 1940s and 1950s. People, especially men, had come to regard female domesticity almost as a natural phenomenon. Nevertheless, women persevered, and, in what was historically a brief period, it became inconceivable to see no female faces broadcasting the news, granting loans, and training to be jet pilots at the U.S. Air Force Academy.

The idea of sexual equality has surely made progress since the 1950s, but the struggle is hard, for reasons suggested by the readings. Although the idea of male supremacy may be on the way out in industrialized nations, female equality is not necessarily a social reality—in part because, as Carol Tavris and Carole Offir suggest in "The Longest War," conceptions of equality vary, depending on a country's history and its definitions of political, economic, and social needs, and in part because, no matter what the ideology, traditional roles with respect to women's work and relations to family seem to persist.

Some of these continuities are seen in the article by Victor Fuchs, an economist whose article examines "The Balance Sheet of Economic Well-Being" as between men and women. When women marry and have children, they tend to do more actual work than men. Women tend to take on more household responsibilities than men. So, if we count housework as part of the work burden, women do more than their share. On balance, as between genders, Fuchs finds that (albeit with some exceptions and qualifications), despite the revolutionary changes of the past quarter century, the economic inequality of men and women has scarcely been remedied. But this conclusion applies differently to different *subgroups* of women. Unmarried, young, white women have fared well economically as compared to men. But other women, especially black women and those with children, have been much less successful.

Of all the gender questions affecting women, a women's right to have an abortion will likely be the most controversial and contested question of the 1990s. How did this happen? In 1960, the Supreme Court declined to overturn a Connecticut law providing for a fine and imprisonment for any person who used or advised in the use of a contraceptive. Just five years later, partly because of a change in the Court's composition and partly because of a shift in perceptions of sexual morals, the Court introduced the right of privacy into constitutional jurisprudence. It decided that the government violated the privacy rights of married couples when it had the authority to enter the marital bedroom to find out whether couples used contraceptives. The case, *Griswold v. Connecticut,* effectively affirmed the right of married couples to have sex without conception, thus denying a potential life to be born.

It was not until 1971 that the Supreme Court extended this right to unmarried persons. "If the right of privacy means anything," Justice Brennan wrote, "it is the right of the individual, married or single, to be free of unwarranted governmental intrusion into matters so fundamen-

tally affecting a person as the decision whether to bear or beget a child."
This case, *Eisenstadt v. Baird,* in effect promised that a woman who chose
to abort a pregnancy would be constitutionally protected. The promise
was fulfilled when in 1973 the U.S. Supreme Court in *Roe v. Wade* decided,
with only two justices dissenting, that the constitutional right to privacy
was "broad enough to encompass a women's decision whether to terminate her pregnancy."

To the surprise of the Court, *Roe v. Wade* was enormously controversial
and gave rise to a major "right-to-life" social movement, which helped
elect both Ronald Reagan and George Bush to the presidency. Those who
subscribe to the "right-to-life" position oppose a woman's right to choose
to terminate a pregnancy. Essentially, they believe that there is no physical and hence moral distinction between a fetus and a child, although
some "right to lifers" make exceptions—as where the pregnancy is the
result of rape or incest, or threatens the life of the mother.

In 1989, the Supreme Court was asked to overturn *Roe v. Wade* by the
Bush administration's Department of Justice, but it did not. The Court
did, however, draw back from the relatively clear "right-to-choose" decision in *Roe v. Wade.* In *Webster v. Reproductive Health Services,* the Supreme
Court invited the states to impose significant restrictions on abortion
rights. The decision largely shifted the abortion choice controversy from
the courts to the legislatures.

No one on either side of the abortion controversy denies the intensity of
feelings surrounding it. Unlike arguments involving economic decisions—How much funding should be allocated to the defense budget and
how much to child care?—this debate involves the deepest human emotions, as illustrated in Sarah Mills' article, "Abortion Under Siege," which
describes her own abortion. Mills wanted her fetus to be born, but, if she
had continued taking her required medication for a chemical imbalance,
her baby would likely have been born deformed. In this article, Mills
describes her frightening experience in an abortion clinic undergoing an
aggressive anti-abortion demonstration.

The idea of "fetal rights" has other implications as well. Should a
woman be required to undertake unwanted medical procedures—for
example, a Caesarean section—in the interest of the health of the fetus?
Assuming that a woman wishes to have a child, rather than to abort a
pregnancy, how much should the state "police" her pregnancy? Suppose
she smokes, drinks alcohol, or uses drugs? Should she be monitored or
imprisoned? Katha Pollitt argues in "Fetal Rights: A New Assault on
Feminism," that the new "fetal-rights" movement offers yet another
illustration of, and opportunity for, the subordination of women.

17

The Longest War

Carol Tavris and Carole Offir

"**M**ale supremacy is on the way out in all industrialized nations," says Marvin Harris. "Male supremacy was just a phase in the evolution of culture." Harris, an anthropologist, makes his matter-of-fact assertion by taking the long view with an evolutionist's eye. In the twentieth century, for the first time in human history, conditions have permitted societies to experiment with equality. Birth control means that women can decide when and even whether to have babies. Overpopulation means that families must get smaller. Industrialization has brought affluence to millions and provided them with the leisure time to consider less traditional life styles. Warfare is largely mechanized, and males have no particular edge over females at pushing buttons to launch a deadly battle. The radically and rapidly altered conditions of life in this century suggest, says Harris, that male supremacy is just a long first act in a show that is not yet over.

Attempts at egalitarianism in this century have crossed national and ideological boundaries. In some countries, such as Sweden, a more equal division of labor between the sexes simply evolved, and political philosophy followed. Other efforts, such as the Israeli kibbutz, started from scratch as attempts to put theory and dreams into practice. Some nations, such as the Soviet Union and the People's Republic of China, went through complete revolutionary overhauls that brought millions of feudal peasants into the twentieth century in the flicker of an eyelid. By taking a look at how these experiments are turning out, and at how ideology and reality differ, we can get an idea of the barriers to equality and of the prospects for overcoming them.

We can also see what the idea of "equality" means in different countries, and how it relates to a country's particular needs, history, and economic and political system. Equality can mean getting women out of the home and into the work force, or assuring women of political power, or breaking down all personality and task differences based on sex, or getting rid of archaic laws designed to keep women barefoot and pregnant. Some cultures are so far from equality by any definition that it is remarkable if women are allowed to show their faces or choose their husbands. In others, the term implies equal opportunity at all levels. As New York's State Education Commissioner put it, "Equality is not when a female Einstein gets promoted to assistant professor; equality is when a female schlemiel moves ahead as fast as a male schlemiel." Your evaluation of a country's efforts at equality will depend on your definition and your values.

CASE 1: THE SOVIET UNION

In every society, wrote Marx and Engels, "the degree of emancipation of women is a natural standard of the general emancipation." The Soviet Union was the first country to try to put this belief into practice; one of the first orders of business after the 1917 revolution was to change the laws affecting women. Women quickly got the right to work alongside men, to have abortions on demand for unwanted pregnancies, and to end unhappy, arranged marriages with easy divorces. During the first heady years after the revolution, reformers were optimistic that socialism, having destroyed the economic basis of inequality, would automatically bring the demise of the patriarchal bourgeois family and liberate women. Women would take their rightful place as "productive" members of society, doing work that benefited the nation as a whole and not just the individual or the family. The state would take over the service work, childcare, and household chores. As Engels wrote, "The modern individual family is based on the open or disguised domestic enslavement of the woman; private housekeeping should become a social industry." Communal dining rooms, government-run nursery schools, and professional laundries would solve the age-old problem of who does the dirty work.

In terms of the "productive work" part of this blueprint, the country's economic needs coincided with ideology. For most of this century the Soviet Union has suffered an acute shortage of men, because so many died during the revolution, a civil war, two world wars, periods of famine, and political upheavals. Before the revolution the ratio of women to men was about equal, but by 1938 it was 103.7 women for every 100 men. And the country Rumania outlawed most abortions and stopped importing contraceptives the same year.[1]

The course of liberation, like love, never runs smooth. The clearest rumple in the socialist blueprint concerns ideology about the family. Somehow, no one in the Soviet Union ever got around to solving the logistical problems of providing millions of families with professional laundry service, food delivery, and childcare; doing so would have required shifting funds and energies away from more pressing problems. As a result, guess who does the housework and childcare?

The domestic side of life is still regarded by both sexes as the woman's responsibility. Although many children go to state-run nursery schools, the nurseries are not free and not yet available to every child. So most mothers rely on friends or relatives to help them with childcare, and in a crisis it is usually the mother, not the father, who compromises the job for the family. It is usually the mother, not the father, who interrupts a career for a few years and in an effort to juggle the needs of children, household, and job. And it is usually the mother, not the father, who stands in long lines at the market, prepares meals without benefit of fancy appliances, and cleans the house. The men "help out"—evoking a few sarcastic reactions from women:

> No one who has followed the painful efforts to modernize socialist housework over the past three decades can fail to be struck by the way this is inevitably presented as "the debt we owe our women," as though women were responsible for all the wash that is dirtied and were the sole beneficiaries of clean windows and floors and ate all the potatoes that are lugged home.
>
> There's a bachelor I knew in three periods of his life. First when he was married and, by his own words, didn't know how to put a teapot on to boil, never mind eggs. . . . Then he got divorced. A miracle followed. He could have been a professor of homemaking. His room wasn't simply clean, it was downright sterile, and the dinners he made for friends were beyond praise. . . . Then he remarried. And immediately stopped cooking dinners, making pickles, and it took an argument for his wife to get him to go down for bread.

Lenin had berated men for shirking their domestic duties. "Very few husbands, not even the proletarians, think of how much they could lighten the burdens and worries of their wives, or relieve them entirely, if they lent a hand in this 'woman's work.' But no, that would go against the privilege and dignity of the husband. He demands that he have his rest and comfort." That he does. Soviet writers have considered many ways to lighten woman's burden: giving women less strenuous jobs, arranging part-time work for women or shorter working days, distributing better household appliances, building more childcare facilities, and so on. But they seem to be overlooking Lenin's observation that the handiest labor-saving device is a husband.

CASE 2: THE PEOPLE'S REPUBLIC OF CHINA

Before the revolution of 1949, the Chinese say, all people carried three mountains on their backs—feudalism, capitalism, and imperialism—but women had a fourth burden, male supremacy. A proverb sums up the treatment of women in prerevolutionary China: "A woman married is like a pony bought—to be ridden or whipped at the master's pleasure." Women had no rights—not over their property, their bodies, or their marriages. Fathers sometimes drowned their infant daughters and sold their surviving daughters as concubines and prostitutes. Husbands could beat or even kill their wives with impunity, and landlords could rape them. When a women married she became subject to the wishes of her husband's family forever; divorce was almost impossible, and widows were forbidden to remarry.

The emancipation of Chinese women started in the nineteenth century, when capitalism began to break up the feudal system that had existed for thousands of years. Industrialization provided women with jobs in the port cities, and although both sexes labored from dawn to dusk for slave wages, women's small incomes did give them a measure of power in the family. Educational and professional opportunities for women increased slightly and feminist movements were organized, though these developments affected only a tiny minority of women. During the first half of this century the official policy of the government (the Kuomintang) was inconsistent. At times it reacted with cruel repression; in 1927, for instance, the Kuomintang executed several hundred women for wearing short haircuts, a symbol of liberation. At other times it became more liberal, at least on paper; in 1931 the Kuomintang gave women the rights to marry freely and to inherit property—though this change was never publicized, much less put into practice.

Long before it came to power, the Communist Party showed concern for the low status of women.[2] Party workers (cadres) discovered an effective way to rally women to their cause, to make women understand that their pains and burdens were shared and were not an inevitable part of being female. The cadres would go into a village and get the women to sit together and talk about their lives—nothing political at first, just their lives. Slowly, painfully, then bitterly, the stories came out: the beatings, the humiliations, the defeats. These sessions, which became known as Speak-Bitterness meetings, taught the Chinese women that they were not alone, that their experiences were the experiences of all women. And like consciousness-raising groups in the United States, the Chinese groups taught that in unity there is strength.

Then came 1949, Communist victory, and a series of sweeping reforms intended to clear away all the lingering feudal cobwebs. The new government quickly gave women property rights, a free choice in marriage, the right to vote, the right to divorce. It abolished polygamy, prostitution, wife-buying, and female infanticide. It declared that women were economically equal to men and would get the same pay for the same work. It wasn't easy to enforce all of these measures because of deep resistance from peasant males and even from loyal Communist males. Husbands did not want their wives going to Speak-Bitterness meetings before the revolution, and they were not happy about female equality after it. Some female activists who were sent to rural villages to explain the new rights of women were murdered by men who felt that their authority in the family and the community was under attack (as indeed it was). But gradually the measures gained acceptance, and attention turned to mobilizing women for productive work.

China today has had even less time than the Soviet Union to overturn centuries of feudalism and female subordination. Yet in twenty-eight years, scarcely a generation, extraordinary changes have taken place in the status of Chinese women. Ninety percent of them work outside the home, and there is a fairly extensive network of nurseries and daycare centers attached to the factories, hospitals, housing projects, and businesses where the parents work. As in Russia, women have entered jobs formerly reserved for men. They drive trucks, fly planes, and wield picks. (In 1957, China had a squadron of jet fighters run entirely by women.) They are doctors, teachers, engineers.

Of course, the entrance of women into the work force has not been steady and uncomplicated. Work for women has depended on the country's economic growth and on its shifting economic policies, as in Russia. Katie Curtin believes that an industrial slump in the mid-1950s was behind propaganda praising home life and the contributions of the housewife. (Similarly, a postwar slump in the United States evoked the "feminine mystique" that glorified large families and the joys of homemaking.) But when China developed an acute need for labor in 1958, and subsequently launched the "Great Leap Forward," the government proclaimed the liberating, patriotic effects of being a working woman. It set up daycare centers to make it possible for women to enter the work force in large numbers. The program was so successful that today a Chinese "housewife" is virtually an anachronism. In many places wives have gotten together to organize what they call "housewife factories," local enterprises that produce everything from embroidered pillows to insulation materials.

The Chinese Communists never were as concerned as the Russians about changing the basic nature of the family and sexual relations. The Chinese see no incompatibility between the family and female liberation; indeed, they believe the family is bedrock. Although a wave of divorces followed the revolution, ending thousands of brutal marriages, today divorce is more difficult to get, and a Chinese couple goes through considerable discussion and persuasion from colleagues and family before they make it to the divorce court. Further, the Chinese see no link between female liberation and sexual liberation. On the contrary. The Chinese are quite Victorian in their views: before marriage, the sexual rule is "all for none and none for all," and they will tell you seriously that their young people are too busy working for a socialist society to think of sex. Sex, the adolescents learn, saps your strength. Abortion and birth control are available to all women. The purpose, though, is not to make them sexually free but to keep the population down and the females working.

Although the Chinese have tried to strengthen, not eliminate, the family, they do believe it is unfair and uncommunist to expect women to handle all the domestic work as well as a job. How to right this common wrong, however, has not been figured out. When C. T. visited China in 1973, most of the people she talked to claimed to have egalitarian marriages, the political ideal. Whichever spouse came home first got the groceries (an easy task, since markets are attached to most housing clusters) and prepared the dinner. Both did the cleaning and cared for the children, when they were not in school or daycare or with grandparents (everyone's favorite babysitters, even in modern China). Women explained to her, with smiles and lots of stories, that a husband can't get away with male-chauvinist attitudes any more. If he persists in his "feudal" ways, the local Women's Association may decide to reeducate him, and so will his comrades at work, his in-laws, his neighbors, and his union. On the other hand, members of the Committee of Concerned Asian Scholars got other answers to the same question. When they asked who does the cooking, cleaning, shopping, washing and childcare, the usual reply was, "The wife, of course."

The discrepancy is probably a result of the size of the country and the size of the gap between policy and practice. Policy says that women will be equal and men will do housework, that families should have only two children and that girls are as good as boys, that women get equal pay for equal work. But in practice the old ways haven't changed overnight or for everyone. In much of the countryside, families still prefer sons.[3] On communes, which are huge agricultural collectives of up to 50,000 people, a system of work points determines a person's share of the collective income. The more physically strenuous the job, the more points one gets. Women earn fewer work points than men because they don't do the hardest work, because they tend to work shorter days in order to do housework (which is not regarded as productive labor), and because they don't get points for maternity leave or for days off during the menstrual period if they take them. In the cities, men still seem to wind up doing different work from women, even in the same factory, and getting more money—although wage differences by sex are nowhere near as great as they are in this country.

Some occupations are still regarded as "women's work" in China; almost all teachers in primary school, nurses, daycare attendants, and flight attendants are women. All visitors observe that fathers and grandfathers have a warm and tender relationship with their young relatives and spend much time with them, but there have been no efforts to get men to work professionally with children. "Women have more patience, after all," C. T. was told. "They are more gentle." Conversely, women are still a tiny minority in top political circles, even though the number of women accepted into the Communist Party is increasing steadily (20 percent of the delegates to the Tenth Party Congress in 1973 were women). In the prestigious People's Liberation Army (PLA), which produces the top political leaders, women work in separate battalions at service tasks such as running canteens, staffing offices, and giving medical aid. When C. T. asked why the PLA was segregated she was told, "Men are stronger, after all." This explanation was not convincing, because women get rigorous military training alongside men in the local militia units, where they have no apparent trouble learning to handle rifles, grenades, and machine guns.

To the Chinese, whatever remnants of male chauvinism still exist are mere trifles compared to what has been accomplished in the liberation of women. Because the majority of the population remembers the starvation, illness, and social problems that were so widespread before the revolution, the Chinese convey a spirit of optimism and strength. They believe they can solve whatever minor problems remain, and they are desperately determined to avoid the pitfalls that they believe entrapped the Soviet Union: a regression to capitalist competitiveness, renewed inequality between the sexes, and a premature complacency about the success of the revolution. Under Mao Tse-tung, who was unwavering in his fight against complacency, the Chinese believed that constant "revolutions" were necessary to keep a country from backsliding. Whether they will hold to that belief under the new leadership, and what priorities will be assigned to sexual equality in the future, is anybody's guess.

CASE 3: THE SCANDINAVIAN COUNTRIES, ESPECIALLY SWEDEN

Sweden and her sister countries are good examples of nations that are reaching sex-role equality through evolution, rather than revolution. In Sweden, industrialization began much sooner than it did in the U.S.S.R., and it brought a decrease in the proportion of children and an increase in the proportion of city dwellers. Twenty years ago, Sweden faced certain issues and economic problems that are only now coming to the fore in the United States. In the mid-fifties two sociologists, Alva Myrdal and Viola Klein, wrote *Women's Two Roles: Home and Work,* a book that explored the difficulties of combining those roles and suggested some solutions. The ideology of sex-role equality that is still struggling for acceptance in the United States came to Sweden years ago.

But in Scandinavia, as in China and elsewhere, ideology is one thing and daily life is another. Today in the Scandinavian countries only about one third of all married women work (in Russia, Finland, Poland, and Hungary, the figure is 50 percent; in the United States it is 43 percent). Scandinavian women are less likely to enter "masculine" professions than women in Eastern European nations, although they make up one-fifth to one-third of the physicians and lawyers and have taken over the fields of pharmacy and, especially in Denmark, dentistry. There are numerous government-sponsored nursery schools, though not enough for the children of all working women.

Because taxes and some legislation favor the two-income family, husbands and wives are redefining the division of labor in the household. Both partners are expected to share housework and childcare when both work, and—most radical innovation of all—husbands as well as wives have the option to stay home or work part-time. Sweden may be one of the few countries in the world in which a househusband is socially accepted. He may not be universally admired, but at least he need endure no snickers, and his masculinity is not questioned.

The role of Swedish women in the work force, like that of women elsewhere, has fluctuated with economic conditions. Between 1930 and 1946 droves of women left the labor force in what has been called a "mass flight" into marriage. "Aha," observers said. "See? Women are happier as housewives." However, their flight coincided with what a Swedish sociologist called an "enormously woman-hostile labor market during the Depression." After the Depression the economic standard was high enough for many women to afford to stay home, which has not been the case in the Soviet Union and Finland, for example. In the 1960s, a shortage of labor meant that Sweden needed its women in the work force. Accordingly, official policy shifted, childcare facilities were improved, and a national educational campaign for sex-role equality began. The defeat of the social-democrat system in 1976, and the apparent return to capitalism after forty-four years of socialist programs, make it hard to predict whether Sweden's need for working women, or its efforts toward equality, will continue.

Elina Haavio-Mannila compared the efforts of three neighboring nations—Sweden, Finland, and the Soviet Union—to liberate women from housework. The three countries have different ideologies about sex roles and different industrial histories, to say nothing of political philosophies. Haavio-Mannila's study was based on interviews with 430 Soviet families in three cities (Leningrad, Moscow, and Pensa); 271 families in Helsinki, Finland; and 442 families in Uppsala, Sweden. She found no differences among these countries in the families' division of labor. It didn't matter whether the women had outside jobs or not, or how actively the government encouraged them to join the labor force or stay at home. In 70 percent of the households, only the wife bought food, made breakfast, fed the children, and washed the dishes; in 80 percent she cooked dinner. As shown in Table 1, the men were more likely to fix things around the house—and that's all. Househusbandry may be an approved way of life in Sweden, but it is far from a popular practice.[4]

As these case studies illustrate, most modern nations have made great

Table 1 Division of Household Tasks in Russian, Finnish, and Swedish Cities, 1966[a]

Household task		Wife	Both spouses	Husband
Feeding the family				
Buying the food	Three Soviet cities	70%	18%	4%
	Helsinki	74	20	2
	Uppsala	71	17	5
Preparing breakfast	Three Soviet cities	72	10	3
	Helsinki	72	16	8
	Uppsala	76	9	8
Preparing dinner	Three Soviet cities	80	5	1
	Helsinki	85	9	2
	Uppsala	86	5	2
Washing the dishes	Three Soviet cities	64	20	1
	Helsinki	70	20	4
Cleaning and washing				
Daily cleaning	Three Soviet cities	67	14	4
	Helsinki	73	18	1
	Uppsala	80	12	2
Washing the windows	Helsinki	51	32	6
	Uppsala	76	9	5
Washing clothes	Three Soviet cities	90	2	0
(Helsinki: men's shirts and stockings)	Helsinki	80	4	11
Family finances				
Paying regular bills	Three Soviet cities	47	13	28
	Helsinki	32	19	48
	Uppsala	29	18	49
Repairing				
Fixing things around the house	Three Soviet cities	50	6	27
	Helsinki	6	7	82
	Uppsala	10	13	70
Childcare				
Feeding the children (if small children in the family)	Helsinki	74	20	0
	Uppsala	70	17	0

[a]Horizontal percentages do not add to 100 because in some cases a third person does the task.

strides in their efforts to unravel the work and family knot. To get women into the labor force, they have used a variety of approaches to enable women to combine "their" responsibilities of home and job. In one summary review, Constantina Safilios-Rothschild studied the male-female division of labor in twenty-three countries at all levels of economic development and noted four patterns.

1. *The Soviet Union, Poland, Hungary, Finland:* Women work, many in formerly male occupations, but men do not do women's work. State-supported nursery schools and daycare and a national ideology that favors communal child-rearing help women work but require no changes on the part of husbands.
2. *Scandinavian countries:* Fewer women work, though the ideology favors complete equality. Men are encouraged to split housework and childcare equally, though there are many fewer househusbands than housewives.
3. *Argentina, Austria, Japan, Greece, Turkey:* About one-third of the women work, and an even smaller proportion of wives. None of these countries provides daycare centers or nursery schools, except a few understaffed ones for working-class women. Wealthy wives can combine work and family because maid service is cheap and available and the extended family still thrives. Grandmothers often do housework and babysit for their working daughters.
4. *The United States, Canada, and to some extent England, France, West Germany, and Australia:* In these countries the cultural values are at odds with the realities. While many women work (at least one-third of all women, ranging to half), the reigning ideology is that childcare is a full-time occupation and that children need their mothers. These nations provide no system-wide professional help or daycare for working mothers, who are left to work out a solution on an individual basis. Partly because so many women in these countries must wait until their children are in school before they can work full-time, women have not entered traditionally male occupations in significant numbers.

In most of these countries women are steadily (though in some, slowly) being absorbed into the work force, doing a great number of jobs. Some countries make it harder, but none has succeeded in getting men to share domestic work equally. And in no nation are women 50 percent of the key politicians and leaders.

Perhaps it seems that equality on a national level would be more difficult and complicated to achieve than equality in a small, manageable unit. For this reason the example of the Israeli kibbutz is an important story.

CASE 4: THE ISRAELI KIBBUTZ

Perhaps no experiment in equality has been scrutinized as minutely as the kibbutz (plural: kibbutzim). Scarcely had the idea been planted before researchers began pulling it out by the roots to see how it was doing. The kibbutz is especially fascinating today because it seems to provide clear evidence that equality is doomed, that left to their druthers men and women will lapse into the traditional division of roles, power, and labor.

Kibbutzim are rural communities in which members collectively own all property. The first kibbutzim were founded early in this century by young socialist emigrants from Russia and Europe, who wanted to escape what they considered the stifling atmosphere of traditional urban Jewish life. They had read Marx and Freud and were determined to set up an alternative community that would represent the best of both. The founders therefore rejected the nuclear family, which they regarded as patriarchal and antifemale, a breeding ground for the Oedipus complex and sexual hostilities. They rejected the values associated with capitalism, especially competitiveness and financial ambition, and sought instead a community based on physical labor, austerity, equality, and group loyalty. There would be no salaries and no status distinctions based on wealth. Each member of the group would get the goods and services she or he needed, regardless of the work assigned.

The decision to break up the nuclear family came about for several reasons. The founders feared that family loyalties would compete with allegiance to the larger community, and in the face of harsh external conditions for survival the kibbutz could not afford much internal dissension, family squabbling, or personal ambition. Ideologically, the founders also believed that if parents dealt with their children as friendly comrades instead of as stern disciplinarians, a more democratic bond between adults and children would result. The children would be more secure as well, because they would be children of the kibbutz, nourished and loved by everyone. Finally, the founders believed that when women were free for "productive" work like plowing fields and building roads, when they didn't have to worry about cooking meals and ironing shirts, they would become equal partners with men once and for all—politically, economically, and sexually.

The kibbutz made almost all housekeeping a collective enterprise. Kibbutz members eat together in a communal dining room; they get their clothes, toothbrushes, and soap at a communal commissary; and they send their dirty linen to a communal laundry. Though they live in private apartments, the rooms are small and do not require much care. Child-rearing too is a collective procedure. Within a few days or weeks after birth, babies are brought to a special children's house, where they are cared for by a specially trained professional called a *metapelet* (nurse). Children visit with their parents in the late afternoons and on weekends, but they eat and sleep in their own quarters. A child's friends, not parents, are the primary contacts, and as a result the kibbutz child develops a strong allegiance to the peer group.

Today there are about 250 kibbutzim, with some 100,000 residents, a small, but influential proportion of the total Israeli population. They range in size from several dozen members to over 2,000; but most have a few hundred. The kibbutzniks have been remarkably successful at surviving in the face of extraordinary odds. Though life was hard and work seemed unending in the early days, today kibbutz members enjoy a standard of living that is higher than that of most Israelis. The collective principle still holds; residents together own all property and means of production.

In 1960–61 C. O. lived on a kibbutz for six months. Instead of working at a permanent job assignment she landed the job of pinch hitter, which gave her an opportunity to observe many kibbutzniks at work. Guess who was cooking meals, cleaning toilets, scrubbing floors, ironing shirts, teaching children, and caring for infants. Not for their own families, to be sure, but for the several hundred souls on the commune. A few young women labored in the fields, but none drove tractors or worked in construction. C. O. never observed a man working in the children's houses or ironing. Though both sexes were required to do a month of kitchen duty every year (washing dishes, setting and waiting tables), few men held permanent jobs in the kitchen. Some old men helped out regularly in preparing meals, doing chores like plucking chickens.

Recent studies confirm these informal observations about the sexual division of labor on the kibbutz. Lionel Tiger and Joseph Shepher studied some 16,000 women in two communes, and Martha Mednick interviewed a random sample of kibbutzniks from fifty-five settlements, 400 original settlers and 918 adults of the second generation. The women are in fact back at the service jobs in the kitchen, laundry, and schools, and those who do work in agriculture are concentrated in poultry-raising and plant nurseries. Fewer occupations are open to women than to men, and the dream of a fifty-fifty share in the work of production has vanished. As the kibbutzim prospered and the population grew, the need for support services and the desire for physical amenities increased, and the women left the fields for the household.

It might seem that a sexual division of labor could still be equitable. After all, feeding an entire community and raising loyal members of the kibbutz are as important as driving a tractor or picking apples. But that is not how it is on the kibbutz. The jobs that produce income for the community, the jobs that men do, are held in higher esteem than the jobs women do. And when members rate their own status in the community, women rate themselves lower than men.

> Work is the central value of the kibbutz. Moreover, productive work, that which results in economic gain, is valued most highly. On the other hand, services, which include the kitchen, the laundry, the clothing factory, and the dining room, are regarded as necessary, but nonproductive and therefore less valued.

Men have the political power, too, although there are no official barriers in the women's way. The kibbutz is a true participatory democracy. A general assembly of all members meets regularly to make major decisions, and each member has one vote. Yet women are not equal participants in this system. They rarely run for political office, although these positions rotate every few years; they show up in fewer numbers at the meetings; when they do attend, they are less vocal than the men. Although almost half of all kibbutz members serve on community committees, women work on those connected with education, social welfare, and cultural activities, while men dominate on the economic committee—which determines economic goals and policies, controls the budget, and wields the real power. The second-generation women, says Mednick, seem quite content to leave political matters to men. So although there are no status differences based on class and wealth, the bane of Marxist theory, there are status differences based on work and political participation. And men have the prestige.

As the kibbutzim became more successful, the "intrinsic antagonism" between the family and the community shifted in favor of the family. Most (though not all) women are enthusiastic about the trend toward traditionalism and are actively promoting it. They want larger families, and they don't want to delay having children until they have finished vocational training. Cosmetics, dresses, and beauty shops—once regarded as signs of decadent bourgeois values—are gaining acceptance. On some kibbutzim, parents are trying to reverse one of the founders' basic principles and have their children live with them, though this is permitted on fewer than 10 percent of the kibbutzim so far.

The kibbutz, then, presents us with a puzzle. Kibbutz women are even more economically independent than women in socialist countries. They do not get status from their husbands' incomes or jobs. They have total job security no matter how many children they choose to have, and they are guaranteed high-quality care and education for their children. They do not have complicated housework to contend with and they do not have to feed their families or clean up after them. Yet kibbutz women lack political power, and they don't seem to want it. They do not work in the high-prestige occupations, and they don't seem to want to. The feminine mystique has returned with a vengeance.

NOTES

1. Most of us are so concerned with the long-term consequences of overpopulation that it seems surprising that a government would want to increase its population. But a sudden drop in births can have serious short-term results— shortages of workers in critical occupations, reduced demand for consumer goods, a relative increase in the proportion of old people. Is the drop in the U.S. birth rate associated with efforts to strike down liberal abortion laws?
2. One critic argues, however, that the Communists' concern fluctuated, depend-

ing on whether they were trying to fight the Kuomintang or form an alliance with it. During efforts at accommodation, the Communists held some reforms in check, including women's rights. When Kuomintang leader Chiang Kai-shek turned them down, they returned to a more radical line.

3. The Anshan Experiment, a new Chinese method of identifying the sex of a fetus, came up with this eerie, unintended finding. Of thirty fetuses that had been intentionally aborted after the mother knew its sex, twenty-nine were female.

4. For example, Sweden has a paid paternity-leave program: fathers can take up to seven months off after the birth of a child at 95 percent of full salary. (If the mother works too, the parents can share the leave period as they wish.) Though the number of participating fathers has more than quadrupled since 1974 and is still rising, only 7 percent of fathers took paternity leaves in 1976.

18

The Balance Sheets of Economic Well-Being

Victor R. Fuchs

The fifteenth anniversary issue of *Ms.* (July/August 1987) celebrated the progress that American women have made in the past few decades and credited much of that progress to the women's movement. Gloria Steinem, a founder and editor of *Ms.*, wrote of a "quantum leap forward from fifteen years ago, when independence for women was ridiculed as the unnatural idea of a few 'bra burners.'" . . . She mentions specifically the transformation of the paid labor force in the 1970s and 1980s and the increasing representation of women in elective offices.

Other observers have been less sanguine about the effects on women of recent changes in gender roles and relationships. They point to the rise in the number of women who are divorced or never married and the increase in childlessness, although not all women consider these to be disadvantages. The failure of many divorced men to pay alimony or child support is clearly a negative phenomenon, as is the hostility of some men toward women as expressed in rape and physical abuse. There has been frequent mention of the "feminization" of poverty . . . with the implication that at least some women have been hurt economically. According to the heroine of Nora Ephron's novel *Heartburn*, "the major concrete achievement of the women's movement in the 1970s was the Dutch treat." . . .

Are women better off now than they were in 1960? Are they worse off? A

Reprinted by permission of the publishers from *Women's Quest for Economic Equality* by Victor R. Fuchs, Cambridge, MA, Harvard University Press, Copyright 1988 by the President and Fellows of Harvard College.

complete answer to this question—one that takes account of feelings of self-worth, autonomy, and other psychological dimensions—is beyond the scope of this book and is probably impossible. The sources of well-being are so numerous—love, work, health, family, friendships, religion—and their interactions so complex as to defy measurement and aggregation. Many women have testified eloquently to their enhanced feelings of self-worth, to their ability to function independently, to an enlarged sense of power and autonomy. At bottom, however, no one can ever quantify another person's misery or joy.

It is possible, however, to address a more restricted set of questions concerning *economic well-being*, which economists usually define as access to goods, services, and leisure. Here I will build on my previous discussions of employment, wages, and family in order to answer the question "Did women improve their economic position relative to men between 1960 and 1986?" Despite large structural changes in the economy and major antidiscrimination legislation, the economic well-being of women as a whole (in comparison with men) did not improve. The women/men ratio of *money income* almost doubled, but women had less leisure while men had more, an increase in the proportion of adults not married made more women dependent on their own income, and women's share of financial responsibility for children rose. One group of women, however, did achieve great gains relative to their male counterparts. They were unmarried, white, young, and well educated. . . .

ECONOMIC WELL-BEING

What determines a person's economic well-being? It obviously depends on money income, because money is needed to buy goods and services that are produced in the market. It also depends on access to goods and services produced outside the market; no one should imagine that when a man or woman substitutes a paid job for housework and childcare that the household's economic well-being increases by the full value of the money income. In addition, economists include leisure in the definition of economic well-being: a person who works 70 hours per week at $10 per hour is not twice as well off as one who works 35 hours per week at the same wage. Finally, economic well-being depends on the size and structure of the household and the extent of income sharing within that household.

The comparisons that follow focus on men and women between the ages of 25 and 64—when gender-role differences tend to be greatest. Adults at these ages are most likely to be in the labor market and most likely to be responsible for children. . . .

Hours of work

The paid work hours of women compared with men rose substantially between 1960 and 1986, primarily because the proportion of women with paid jobs jumped from 34 to 57 percent (see Table 1). A second factor was the decline in the proportion of men working at paid jobs: from 87 to 80 percent. Third, and least important, there was a slight increase in the average annual hours of those women who were employed (from 1,677 to 1,750), while hours per employed man were unchanged at 2,153 per year.

Table 1 Average annual hours of work

	Year	Paid	Housework	Childcare	Total
Women	1960	572	1,423	266	2,261
	1986	997	1,222	197	2,416
Men	1960	1,875	542	76	2,493
	1986	1,725	545	58	2,328
Women/men ratio	1960	.30	2.62	3.52	.91
	1986	.58	2.24	3.40	1.04

Housework hours fell for women while remaining virtually constant for men; childcare hours fell for both sexes. The fall in childcare hours for men may surprise some readers who know of individual families in which the father now provides as much or more care than the mother. There are probably more such families in the 1980s than there were in 1960, but two other trends work in the opposite direction. First, the proportion of men who have *no* children jumped substantially (from 27 to 47 percent at ages 25–39) between 1960 and 1986. Second, among those who do have children, the number of children per man fell from 2.4 to 1.8. Thus, hours of paternal care per child would have had to almost double in order for the *average childcare per man* in 1986 to equal that of 1960. For every married man who currently does as much housework and childcare as his wife, there is at least one divorced or never-married father who seldom sees his children, and another who has opted to have no children at all.

When the various types of work are summed, we find that women increased their total hours by almost 7 percent, while men's fell by that same proportion. As a result, by 1986 women were putting in more hours of work than men, whereas in 1960 the reverse was true. The differential change was particularly large for married couples: on average, wives increased their total work load by four hours per week while husbands decreased theirs by two and a half hours. Unmarried women work more hours (total of paid and unpaid) than unmarried men, but the differential did not change much between 1960 and 1986.

Income

The average money income received by women rose by 140 percent between 1960 and 1986, while men showed a gain of only 25 percent. . . . These are real increases because all dollar figures for 1960 have been inflated to 1985 dollars by the Consumer Price Index. The women/men ratio of money income almost doubled, primarily because of the large differential change in hours of paid work and secondarily because of an increase of about seven percentage points in the women/men wage ratio.

The women/men ratio of imputed income from housework declined, following the trend in the housework hours ratio. No income was imputed for childcare hours because they do not result in goods or services for the adult men and women whose economic well-being is being estimated. To be sure, childcare may be a source of pleasure to the adult who provides it, but that can be true of paid work as well.

Women's total income rose faster than men's, but the ratio was still only .66 in 1986, a year when the average woman worked more hours (paid plus unpaid) than did the average man.

Effective income

Almost 90 percent of women and men ages 25–64 live in households with other adults or children, or both; this affects their access to goods and services in several ways. First, larger households can usually realize *economies of scale* (make more effective use of income) through joint use of housing, durable goods, and services. Thus, the effective income resulting from any given amount of money and imputed income tends to rise with household size. Second, if there are children present, some income must be devoted to them, thus reducing the effective income available to the adult members of the household. Third, the adults in the household may, to a greater or lesser extent, share their income, thus increasing or decreasing the effective income of individuals relative to their own income.

Assuming that income is equally shared, women have almost as much as men but their relative position declined by two percentage points between 1960 and 1986. . . . This decline is primarily the result of the increase in the percentage of women who are not married and therefore not benefiting from the higher income of a husband. . . .

Effective income per hour of work

The final step in assessing economic well-being is to combine effective income (which measures access to goods and services) with leisure (time left after market and nonmarket work). One such measure that is simple to calculate and understand is effective income per hour of work (paid and unpaid). There are several other possible measures; they all yield the same qualitative conclusions. For instance, one could sum effective income and the imputed value of leisure (set equal to the imputed wage of an hour of housework). The changes in the sex ratios of this measure are similar in direction and magnitude to the changes shown below.

In absolute terms women's effective income per hour of work rose between 1960 and 1986, reflecting the general rise in economic productivity. . . . Relative to men, however, women's position fell substantially, from 1.08 to 0.92, primarily because of the increased burden of work on women who took paid jobs but still had substantial responsibilities at home. The data emphatically refute the view that women as a group have made great progress in their quest for economic equality.

Winners and losers

The failure of women *on average* to advance does not mean that each and every subgroup had the same experience. Indeed, there is one special category of women that achieved a large increase in economic well-being relative to their male counterparts. They are white, young (ages 25–44), not married, and well educated (more than twelve years of schooling). If these women perceive considerable progress toward economic equality, they are correct. If, however, they believe that women as a whole have experienced this progress, they are in error. All other subgroups of women showed losses or very small gains. . . .

In conclusion, with the exceptions and qualifications noted, the revolutionary changes of the past quarter-century did not bring women any closer to economic equality with men. It needs to be again emphasized, however, that the assessment of *economic* well-being does not capture all of the effects of the sex-role revolution. There may well have been gains in noneconomic dimensions; the data on work and income remind us that these gains have been achieved at a cost, and that the cost has varied greatly from one woman to another.

19

Abortion Under Siege

Sarah Mills

1977

My Father and I sat in companionable silence on the front porch and watched the fireflies. I was 17. Suddenly my father spoke. "Sarah," he said, sounding acutely uncomfortable. "I want you to come to me if you ever get pregnant. Don't tell your mother. Just come to me and I'll take care of it."

I knew he meant, "I'll pay for the abortion, no questions asked." Not knowing how else to respond, I simply said, "Okay." I didn't have the nerve to tell him I was already on the Pill and never expected to get pregnant by accident. But I understood his message. My mother had been faced with an unplanned pregnancy in her teens. The result was *me*. A strict Catholic, she had, over the years, helped out many pregnant teens who chose to give up their babies for adoption. Abortion was murder in my mother's eyes.

My father, on the other hand, felt that much of his youth and future had been cut short by my birth. Although he was happy to have me, he still didn't want to see me make the same mistakes he had. He was offering me an alternative.

1986

In graduate school at 26, I worked part-time as a local television reporter and kept up an active social life in between work and classes. I was constantly accused of burning the candle at both ends, a charge that took on merit when I began having irregular menstrual periods that sometimes broke through in the middle of my Pill cycle. After 10 years on the Pill, I figured it was time to take a rest and allow my body to regulate itself naturally. Besides, the fellow student with whom I'd fallen in love was leaving town for the summer. Until he left, we could simply use condoms, I reasoned.

The night before he left town, *the rubber broke,* and I knew instantly I had conceived. It had been exactly two weeks—halfway through my cycle—since my last period, and I was ovulating. Until then I had never even considered the abortion issue. I wasn't "pro" or "anti" anything, unless I could be considered pro-contraception. In 10 years of sexual activity, I had never had unprotected sex, but suddenly I was faced with the very real possibility of an unwanted and extremely dangerous pregnancy.

My body has a chemical imbalance that leads to wide mood swings: sometimes euphoria, sometimes depression. However, my illness is completely controllable by the prescription-dispensed medication lithium carbonate—which can cause severe heart defects in fetuses. If I were suddenly to stop taking the medication, I would almost certainly have to be hospitalized and, in the extreme case, probably become suicidal. I've been advised against pregnancy except under well-planned, medically supervised circumstances.

After I explained this to my boyfriend, he said resolutely, "We'll get an abortion. We can't bring a sick baby into the world. We don't even have health insurance. Who would pay the medical bills?" He was right, of course, but I felt that I had just crossed an invisible bridge and there was no turning back. We spent the rest of the night holding one another. In the morning, I made breakfast and we said good-bye for the summer.

Two weeks later, long enough for me to suspect that I'd actually missed a period, I had a blood serum pregnancy test (considered the most accurate method of determining pregnancy in its earliest stages). The results were negative, and my late period was attributed to my body's trouble readjusting after the Pill. Five weeks or so later, I still hadn't started my period and felt truly awful. I was bloated and grouchy. My breasts were tender, and my lower back ached constantly. After vomiting all morning one Tuesday, I slipped into the university health clinic for a quick examination. I learned I was two months pregnant.

Shock. Fear. Since the fetal nervous system forms during the first trimester of pregnancy, the embryonic heart was probably irreversibly damaged already. I managed to stay lucid enough to ask for the name of a reputable abortion clinic. He referred me to a large facility in the capital city.

I called in sick to work and drove home, fighting off waves of revulsion. Once inside my apartment, I headed directly to the telephone. My hands trembled as I dialed the number of the abortion clinic. Between sobs, I scheduled my abortion for the following Saturday. I hung up the phone and the dam broke. "No, this can't happen to me!" I screamed as I heaved my purse across the room, scattering the contents all over the floor. I began hurling every object within reach. Finally I sank to the floor and cradled my abdomen. "I'm sorry, baby," I cried. "Mommy's so sorry."

The next day I consulted both an obstetrician and a specialist, looking for *a chance* that my baby could be born normal, but the verdict was the same: if the baby lived, there was a probability it would be deformed; if I stopped taking the medication, I would be hospitalized.

Feeling like the loneliest person in the world, I turned to my best friend for support. To her, the issue was clear: I had no money, no insurance, and no resources to care for a handicapped child. She felt it would be horribly cruel to knowingly bring a sick baby into the world. I agreed with her, but I couldn't silence the part of me that whispered, "Murderer!"

I didn't know how I was going to pay for the abortion. I hadn't yet told my boyfriend about the pregnancy. Then, recalling our conversation nine years earlier, I decided to call my father. "Remember what you told me when I was seventeen?" I asked.

"Yes," he answered, understanding intuitively.

"Well, I need your help now," I said, my voice cracking. He asked me how much money I needed, with no other questions or demands for explanations, and promised to wire it the next day. Just before he hung up he said, "Don't ever tell your mother. It would destroy her."

Friday morning, the day before the abortion, a packet from the abortion clinic came in the mail, complete with a graphic description of the procedure itself. As I read it, nightmarish images jumped off the page: "Lidocaine is injected into the cervix at two different sites. . . . The cervix is then dilated with instruments which graduate . . . until the cervix is opened to the diameter of a piece of chalk." I broke out in a sweat as I read the rest: "You may experience a feeling similar to hard menstrual cramps. This part of the procedure takes approximately 30 seconds and is usually the most difficult part of the abortion."

Numbly I went to work for the first time that week. As I prepared my afternoon newscast, a story came across the Associated Press state wire about plans for major antiabortion demonstrations at several capital city abortion clinics. The story said that the protest leader had tried to handcuff himself to an operating table at one facility the previous fall. AP also reported bomb threats at several clinics.

I called the clinic. A calm voice assured me that several staff members planned an all-night vigil to protect the clinic. Armed guards would be stationed at all entrances, and no one would be admitted without identification. The doors leading to the clinic operating rooms would be locked at all times, the key carried only by a few select staff members. Escorts would meet patients in the parking lot with large umbrellas to shield our faces from the anticipated TV cameras. The decision to have an abortion was the most agonizing choice of my life—but the only humane alternative I felt I had. Now, in addition, I was worrying about bomb threats, right-to-life fanatics, and TV reporters.

Since my boyfriend lived in the same city as the abortion clinic, I finally called him and broke the news. I desperately needed his support and protection. The next morning, we solemnly drove to the clinic. I wore dark sunglasses and a head scarf to protect my identity from both the protesters and the television cameras. When we reached the parking lot, our car was immediately surrounded by a crowd of protesters carrying signs and shouting antiabortion slogans. My stomach turned as I saw the giant placard bearing the picture of a fully developed fetus and the words ABORTION IS MURDER.

As earlier instructed, we drove straight to the clinic entrance, where we were met by two escorts bearing large golf umbrellas. There were no TV crews yet, thank God. The escorts guided us quickly through the shouting crowd as I clung fiercely to my boyfriend. Just as we reached the clinic steps, a woman grabbed my boyfriend's arm. "Sir, it's not too late," she pleaded. "You can stop her and have a future with your baby." What future, I wondered wildly. How could I make these people understand that I would be killing my baby if I chose to continue my pregnancy? At best, my child could hope only for a life of pain, tubes, machines, and grisly infant heart operations. The woman persisted: "Please stop her. Don't kill your baby."

I froze. Shame, humiliation, and anger crept up my spine. I could actually feel the hatred hovering around us like a blanket of suffocating heat; all the agony of the past week threatened to bubble up in one great burst of bile. I lifted my head higher and walked into the clinic.

The first thing I saw made me gasp—an enormous uniformed guard standing ominously beside a closed door, a heavy gun hanging at his side. (I learned later that the door led to the clinic operating rooms.) We checked in, paid our money, and settled down to wait. We could still hear muffled shouting from outside. I was jumpy and fearful, fully expecting a bomb to explode at any moment. Most of the people in the waiting room seemed to be young girls with their mothers. Everyone spoke in whispers, adding to the feeling that we were doing something illegal. We turned to stare at the new arrivals as, one by one, they entered the clinic crying, traumatized by the right-to-life fanatics outside.

Between my blood and urine tests, I thought about how much I wanted my mother by my side at such a terrifying time in my life. I felt sad that I couldn't share my pain with her, and angry at a system that didn't allow a woman to seek medical treatment with dignity. I was disgusted with strangers who presumed they had some God-given right to "save" me. Most of all, I ached for the loss of my baby and prayed for the day I could give birth to a healthy, happy child.

Hours later, after countless routine procedures, I lay on the operating table. The doctor peered at me over a green surgical mask and asked if anyone had pushed me into having the abortion. "No," I said, and explained my medical problem and the prescription drug I took. I'll never forget the look in his eyes when he said, "If you're some kind of masochist, you can go through with this pregnancy." No other doctor had put it so bluntly. I placed my feet in the stirrups and asked for the abortion.

Expecting to be hysterical, I was surprised when I faced the operation with icy resolve. The nurse offered her hand and I squeezed it tightly, grateful for her concern. I looked away from the long, sharp needle the doctor used to numb my cervix. As he proceeded, I mentally read the clinic literature: "A small plastic tube is inserted through the cervix into the uterus and suction is used to remove the tissue from the uterine walls. You will feel movement, tugging and pulling, through this part of the procedure. You may have some cramping similar to menstrual cramps but with stronger intensity."

Finally, after only 10 minutes, the abortion was over. The nurse rubbed my stomach as the doctor declared, "You're not pregnant anymore, Sarah." I felt relief. Still fighting off imaginary demons, I asked to see the large jar containing the by-products of my abortion. Fully expecting to see tissue, or even body parts, I was reassured to find only blood.

I nearly fainted on the way to the recovery room, weak from the abortion and the emotional strain of the past few days. As a nurse placed me in a recliner, covered me with blankets, and set juice and cookies at my side, I surveyed the young women around me. Everyone looked so pale. A strange mixture of relief and misery hung in the air. Suddenly the silence was broken as a girl standing near the window shouted, "My God, TV cameras. Look, there's Channel 13!"

I am relying on others' verbal reports for what happened next, as I became too ill to move from my chair. Apparently the protesters became more violent with the added incentive of publicity. Some began blocking the clinic entrance. Women leaving the building were verbally harassed. Somehow a shoving match erupted and two people were arrested. I knew all this made for excellent TV news drama; but, as a reporter, I also knew that the news crews wouldn't leave until they could show "the other side of the story." They would do everything in their power to obtain an interview with a patient or, at least, tape close-ups of the young women leaving the clinic.

A nurse entered the recovery room; she explained that several television news crews were stationed outside and that the antiabortionists had become extreme in their verbal abuse of patients. She said we were welcome to stay inside the clinic until the TV crews left and the protest died down. The building seemed under siege, and I felt very much like a hostage. Fear magnified time—the minutes ticked by suffocatingly slowly. One heavyset, plain-looking patient restlessly paced the floor as she carried on a one-woman conversation that verbalized my own confused thoughts. "Are they gonna pay for this baby?" she asked no one in particular as she waved her hand toward the protesters down below. "My husband is laid off. I got three kids already. We can't afford another. Who's gonna give me money to raise this child?"

I felt torn. I could understand her argument, but I deeply envied her situation. She had a chance to bear a healthy baby. I knew I would have given my baby up for adoption if I'd had a choice, but who would adopt a child like mine? I'd developed a gruesome picture of my handicapped child growing up in a state institution. I battled to overcome the guilt brought on by the protesters below. Even without their cries of mortal sin, I was my harshest judge. Intellectually, even morally, I'd done the right thing, but I still had the faint fear that I would ultimately be punished for my actions.

"A child should not pay for the sins of his father," one protester had shouted. The phrase pounded in my mind as I observed a young girl recovering near me. I'd seen her earlier in the waiting room with a woman who appeared to be a social worker. From snatches of their conversation, I guessed that she'd been sexually abused by her father and, as a horrifying result, had become pregnant by him. She looked about 12 years old, a tiny child, with dull skin, vacant eyes, and stringy hair. Her bones looked as if they could snap like toothpicks.

Wasn't that young girl being punished for the sins of her sexually abusive father? Did the antiabortionists honestly think she should go through with her pregnancy? In their attacks on everyone entering the clinic, did they ever stop to think how much they could be traumatizing victims of sexual abuse and rape? Did they care? The protesters claimed to be religious, but I believe in a compassionate, understanding God. I knew I had no right to judge the women surrounding me. I couldn't see into their hearts. Yes, some of them may have chosen abortion for the wrong reasons, but they would have to answer for their own sins. Their actions were between them and God.

One black woman told me she'd had the abortion because she wanted to go to college. "I start school in the fall. No one in my family has ever gotten an education," she said. "If I'm pregnant, I can't go to college." How could those predominantly white antiabortionists outside understand a young black woman's passionate desire for an education?

Nurses came in periodically with messages from our family members and friends awaiting us, and asked each time if anyone was ready to leave. A couple of women volunteered to go home. They said they weren't ashamed of what they'd done and would no longer be subject to the right-to-lifers' terror tactics. I admired their courage, but wasn't willing to risk broadcasting my face all over the six o'clock news.

After nearly an hour of agitated rambling, the heavyset woman slowly walked over to the window and peered out pensively at the crowd below. There was an eerie quiet in the room when she finally spoke again, her fervor gone, her voice cracking. "They have no right to judge us. They never walked in our shoes."

Finally, near sunset, the siege ended. We exited the recovery room slowly, battle-weary soldiers tearfully reuniting with our nerve-racked mothers, lovers, and friends. My boyfriend and I walked to the exit. At the clinic steps, a pro-choice volunteer once more held an umbrella over my face to protect my privacy. I felt relief, anger, despair, and no closer to resolving the question of abortion than when I was 17. I would still choose contraception as the sanest solution to the entire issue. I realized, however, that as in my own case, birth control doesn't always work. Circumstances around pregnancy can endanger the mother's life or the baby's health. Women are raped. And, sometimes, they simply make mistakes.

One fact I knew with absolute certainty: the abortion clinic medical staff, counselors, and volunteers were some of the most compassionate human beings I'd ever met. Despite the antiabortionists' proclaimed Christianity, not one protester offered me nonjudgmental forgiveness or understanding. The clinic workers, on the other hand, had literally put their lives on the line to help me through the most difficult ordeal of my life.

1989

I spent six of the most frightening hours of my life at that abortion clinic. The stress I endured is beyond measure. Although it has been more than 16 years since the Supreme Court's decision in *Roe v. Wade* legalized abortion, the issue still remains emotionally charged.

The man who led the right-to-life protest outside the clinic that day was recently convicted of an attempt to bomb that same clinic. He served three months in a federal prison and is now out on five years' probation. An injunction (no longer in effect) was issued against the antiabortion demonstrators sometime after my experience there. Subsequently, too, a seven-foot stockade fence was erected around the clinic's parking lot, and the police now finally do enforce the trespass statutes that always barred the demonstrators from private property.

During a recent interview, the protest leader did not deny his involvement in the bombing incident. "Government agents set me up and trapped me," he explained. He claimed his mission in life is to "rescue the unborn." When I asked how he planned to rescue dead women and fetuses from the ruins of an exploded building, he grew hostile and accused me of being a government spy. I questioned him about medically necessary abortions, relating my own situation. "There is no middle ground," he said vehemently. "You can't be pro-choice without being pro-death." Then he used extremely abusive language for several minutes before slipping into ironic rhetoric: "Pro-lifers treat all people with tender loving care," he said before hanging up on me.

On the second anniversary of my abortion, I spoke with the clinic director about my experience. "It's never a careless, irresponsible decision when a woman chooses to have an abortion," she said, "but that still doesn't change the devastating feeling a woman gets inside when she pulls into the parking lot and has to face a crowd filled with hate. It doesn't change her decision; it just makes it harder."

20

"Fetal Rights": A New Assault on Feminism

Katha Pollitt

Some scenes from the way we live now:

- In New York City, a pregnant woman orders a glass of wine with her restaurant meal. A stranger comes over to her table. "Don't you know you're poisoning your baby?" he says angrily, pointing to a city-mandated sign warning women that drinking during pregnancy can cause birth defects.
- In California, Pamela Rae Stewart is advised by her obstetrician to stay off her feet, to eschew sex and "street drugs," and to go to the hospital immediately if she starts to bleed. She fails to follow this advice and delivers a brain-damaged baby who soon dies. She is charged with failing to deliver support to a child under an old criminal statute that was intended to force men to provide for women they have made pregnant.
- In Washington, D.C., a hospital administration asks a court whether it should intervene and perform a Caesarean section on Angela Carder, seriously ill with cancer, against her wishes and those of her husband, her parents and her doctors. Acknowledging that the operation would probably shorten her life without necessarily saving the life of her 25-week-old fetus, the judge nonetheless provides the order. The Caesarean is performed immediately, before her lawyers can appeal. Angela Carder dies; so does her unviable fetus. That incident is subsequently dramatized on *L.A. Law*, with postfeminist softy Ann Kelsey arguing for the hospital; on TV the baby lives.
- In the Midwest, the U.S. Court of Appeals for the Seventh Circuit, ruling in *UAW v. Johnson Controls*, upholds an automotive battery plant's seven-year-old

"fetal protection policy" barring fertile women (in effect, all women) from jobs that would expose them to lead [see Carolyn Marshall, "An Excuse for Workplace Hazard," April 25, 1987]. The court discounts testimony about the individual reproductive lives and plans of female employees (many in their late 40s, celibate and/or with completed families), testimony showing that no child born to female employees had shown ill effects traceable to lead exposure and testimony showing that lead poses a comparable danger to male reproductive health. The court accepts testimony that says making the workplace safe would be too expensive.

All over the country, pregnant women who use illegal drugs and/or alcohol are targeted by the criminal justice system. They are "preventively detained" by judges who mete out jail sentences for minor crimes that would ordinarily result in probation or a fine; charged with child abuse or neglect (although by law the fetus is not a child) and threatened with manslaughter charges should they miscarry; and placed under court orders not to drink, although drinking is not a crime and does not invariably (or even usually) result in birth defects. While state legislatures ponder bills that would authorize these questionable practices by criminalizing drug use or "excessive" alcohol use during pregnancy (California Senator Pete Wilson is pushing a similar bill at the federal level), mothers are arrested in their hospital beds when their newborns test positive for drugs. Social workers increasingly remove positive-testing babies into foster care on the presumption that even a single use of drugs during pregnancy renders a mother ipso facto an unfit parent.

What's going on here? Right now the hot area in the developing issue of "fetal rights" is the use of drugs and alcohol during pregnancy. We've all seen the nightly news reports of inner-city intensive care units overflowing with crack babies, of Indian reservations where one in four children is said to be born physically and mentally stunted by fetal alcohol syndrome (F.A.S.) or the milder, but still serious, fetal alcohol effect. We've read the front-page stories reporting studies that suggest staggering rates of drug use during pregnancy (11 percent, according to *The New York Times*, or 375,000 women per year) and the dangers of even moderate drinking during pregnancy.

But drugs and alcohol are only the latest focus of a preoccupation with the fetus and its "rights" that has been wandering around the *Zeitgeist* for the past decade. A few years ago, the big issue was forced Caesareans. (It was, in fact, largely thanks to the horrific Angela Carder case—one of the few involving a white, middle-class woman—that the American College of Obstetricians and Gynecologists condemned the practice, which nonetheless has not entirely ceased.) If the Supreme Court upholds the *Johnson Controls* decision, the next battleground may be the workplace. The "save the babies" mentality may look like a necessary, if troubling, approach when it's a matter of keeping a drug addict away from a substance that is, after all, illegal. What happens if the same mentality is applied to some 15 million to 20 million highly paid unionized jobs in heavy industry to "protect" fetuses that do not even exist? Or if the list of things women are put on legal notice to avoid expands to match medical findings on the dangers to the fetus posed by junk food, salt, aspirin, air travel and cigarettes?

Critics of the punitive approach to pregnant drug and alcohol users point out the ironies inherent in treating a public-health concern as a matter for the criminal justice system: the contradiction, for instance, of punishing addicted women when most drug treatment programs refuse to accept pregnant women. Indeed, Jennifer Johnson, a Florida woman who was the first person convicted after giving birth to a baby who tested positive for cocaine, had sought treatment and been turned away. (In her case the charge was delivering drugs to a minor.) The critics point out that threats of jail or the loss of their kids may drive women away from prenatal care and hospital deliveries, and that almost all the women affected so far have been poor and black or Latino, without private doctors to protect them (in Florida, nonwhite women are ten times as likely to be reported for substance abuse as white women, although rates of drug use are actually higher for whites).

These are all important points. But they leave unchallenged the notion of fetal rights itself. What we really ought to be asking is, How have we come to see women as the major threat to the health of their newborns, and the womb as the most dangerous place a child will ever inhabit? Why is our basic model "innocent" fetuses that would be fine if only presumably "guilty" women refrained from indulging their "whims"? The list of dangers to the fetus is, after all, very long; the list of dangers to children even longer. Why does maternal behavior, a relatively small piece of the total picture, seem such an urgent matter, while much more important factors—that one in five pregnant women receive no prenatal care at all, for instance—attract so little attention? Here are some of the strands that make up the current tangle that is fetal rights.

THE ASSAULT ON THE POOR

It would be pleasant to report that the aura of crisis surrounding crack and F.A.S. babies—the urge to do *something*, however unconstitutional or cruel, that suddenly pervades society, from judge's bench to chic dinner party to 7 o'clock news—was part of a massive national campaign to help women have healthy, wanted pregnancies and healthy babies. But significantly, the current wave of concern is not occurring in that context. Judges order pregnant addicts to jail, but they don't order drug treatment programs to accept them, or Medicaid, which pays for heroin treatment, to cover crack addiction—let alone order landlords not to evict them, or obstetricians to take uninsured women as patients, or the federal government to fund fully the Women, Infants, and Children supplemental feeding program, which reaches only two-thirds of those who are eligible. The policies that have underwritten maternal and infant health in most of the industrialized West since World War II—a national health service, paid maternity leave, direct payments to mothers, government-funded day care, home health visitors for new mothers, welfare payments that reflect the cost of living—are still regarded in the United States by even the most liberal as hopeless causes, and by everyone else as budget-breaking giveaways to the undeserving, pie-in-the-sky items from a mad socialist's wish list.

The focus on maternal behavior allows the government to appear to be concerned about babies without having to spend any money, change any priorities or challenge any vested interests. As with crime, as with poverty, a complicated, multifaceted problem is construed as a matter of freely chosen individual behavior. We have crime because we have lots of bad people, poverty because we have lots of lazy people (Republican version) or lots of pathological people (Democratic version), and tiny, sickly, impaired babies because we have lots of women who just don't give a damn.

Once the problem has been defined as original sin, coercion and punishment start to look like hardheaded and common-sensical answers. Thus, syndicated columnist and *New Republic* intellectual Charles Krauthammer proposes locking up pregnant drug users en masse. Never mind the impracticality of the notion—suddenly the same Administration that refuses to pay for drug treatment and prenatal care is supposed to finance all that plus nine months of detention for hundreds of thousands of women a year. Or its disregard of real life—what, for example, about the children those women already have? Do they go to jail, too, like Little Dorrit? Or join the rolls of the notorious foster care system? The satisfactions of the punitive mind-set sweep all such considerations aside. (Nor are liberal pundits immune from its spell. Around the same time Krauthammer was calling for mass incarceration, Mary McGrory was suggesting that we stop wasting resources—*what* resources?—on addicted women and simply put their babies in orphanages.)

THE NEW TEMPERANCE

While rightly sounding the alarm about the health risks and social costs of drugs, alcohol and nicotine, the various "just say no" crusades have so upped the moral ante across the board that it is now difficult to distinguish between levels and kinds of substance use and abuse and even rather suspect to try. A joint on the weekend is the moral equivalent of a twenty-four-hour-a-day crack habit; wine with meals is next door to a daily quart of rotgut. The stigmatizing of addicts, casual users, alcoholics, social drinkers and smokers makes punitive measures against them palatable. It also helps us avoid uncomfortable questions about why we are having all these "substance abuse" epidemics in the first place. Finally, it lets us assume, not always correctly, that drugs and alcohol, all by themselves, cause harm during pregnancy, and ignore the role of malnutrition, violence, chaotic lives, serious maternal health problems and lack of medical care.

SCIENCE MARCHES ON

We know a lot more about fetal development than we did twenty years ago. But how much of what we know will we continue to know in ten years? As recently as the early 1970s, pregnant women were harassed by their doctors to keep their weight down. They were urged to take tranquilizers and other prescription drugs, to drink in moderation (liquor was routinely used to stop premature labor), to deliver under anesthesia and not bother to breast-feed. Then too, studies examined contemporary wisdom and found it good. Today, those precepts seem the obvious expression of social forces: the wish of doctors to control pregnancy and delivery, a lack of respect for women and a distaste for female physiological processes. It was not the disinterested progress of science that outmoded these practices. It was another set of social forces: the women's movement, the prepared-childbirth movement and the natural-health movement.

What about today's precepts? At the very least, the history of scientific research into pregnancy and childbirth ought to make us skeptical. Instead, we leap to embrace tentative findings and outright bad science because they fit current social prejudices. Those who argue for total abstinence during pregnancy have made much, for example, of a recent study in *The New England Journal of Medicine* that claimed women are more vulnerable than men to alcohol because they have less of a stomach enzyme that neutralizes it before it enters the bloodstream. Universally unreported, however, was the fact that the study included alcoholics and patients with gastrointestinal disease. It is a basic rule of medical research that results cannot be generalized from the sick to the healthy.

In a 1989 article in *The Lancet*, "Bias Against the Null Hypothesis: The Reproductive Hazards of Cocaine," Canadian researchers reported that studies that found a connection between cocaine use and poor pregnancy outcome had a better than even chance of being accepted for presentation at the annual meeting of the Society for Pediatric Research, while studies that found no connection had a negligible chance—although the latter were better designed. While it's hard to imagine that anyone will ever show that heavy drug use or alcohol consumption is good for fetal development, studies like this one suggest that when the dust settles (because the drug war is officially "won"? because someone finally looks at the newborns of Italy, where everyone drinks moderate amounts of wine with food, and finds them to be perfectly fine?) the current scientific wisdom will look alarmist.

MEDIA BIAS

The assumptions that shape the way researchers frame their studies and the questions they choose to investigate are magnified by bias in the news media. Studies that show the bad effects of maternal behavior make the headlines, studies that show no bad effects don't get reported and studies that show the bad effects of paternal behavior (alcoholic males, and males who drink at conception, have been linked to lower I.Q. and a propensity to alcoholism in offspring) get two paragraphs in the science section. So did the study, briefly mentioned in a recent issue of *The New York Times*, suggesting that housewives run a higher risk than working women of having premature babies, stillbirths, underweight babies and babies who die in the first week of life. Imagine the publicity had it come out the other way around! Numbers that back up the feeling of crisis (those 375,000 drug-taking pregnant women) are presented as monolithic, although they cover a wide range of behavior (from daily use of cocaine to marijuana use during delivery, which some midwives recommend, and for which one Long Island woman lost custody of her newborn for eight months), and are illustrated by dire examples of harm that properly apply only to the most hard-core cases.

THE "PRO-LIFE" MOVEMENT

Antichoicers have not succeeded in criminalizing abortion but they have made it inaccessible to millions of women (only sixteen states pay for poor women's abortions, and only 18 percent of counties have even one abortion provider) and made it a badge of sin and failure for millions more. In Sweden, where heavy drinking is common, relatively few F.A.S. babies are born, because alcoholic women have ready access to abortion and it is not a stigmatized choice. In America antichoice sentiment makes it impossible to suggest to a homeless, malnourished, venereally diseased crack addict that her first priority ought to be getting well: Get help, then have a baby. While the possibility of coerced abortions is something to be wary of, the current policy of regulation and punishment in the name of the fetus ironically risks the same end. Faced with criminal charges, pregnant women may seek abortions in order to stay out of jail (a Washington,

D.C., woman who "miscarried" a few days before sentencing may have done just that).

As lobbyists, antichoicers have sought to bolster their cause by interjecting the fetus-as-person argument into a wide variety of situations that would seem to have nothing to do with abortion. They have fought to exclude pregnant women from proposed legislation recognizing the validity of "living wills" that reject the use of life support systems (coma baby lives!), and have campaigned to classify as homicides assaults on pregnant women that result in fetal death or miscarriage. Arcane as such proposals may seem, they have the effect of broadening little by little the areas of the law in which the fetus is regarded as a person, and in which the woman is regarded as its container.

At a deeper level, the "pro-life" movement has polluted the way we think about pregnancy. It has promoted a model of pregnancy as a condition that by its very nature pits women and fetuses against each other, with the fetus invariably taking precedence, and a model of women as selfish, confused, potentially violent and incapable of making responsible choices. As the "rights" of the fetus grow and respect for the capacities and rights of women declines, it becomes harder and harder to explain why drug addiction is a crime if it produces an addicted baby, but not if it produces a miscarriage, and why a woman can choose abortion but not vodka. And that is just what the "pro-lifers" want.

THE PRIVILEGED STATUS OF THE FETUS

Pro-choice activists rightly argue that antiabortion and fetal-rights advocates grant fetuses more rights than women. A point less often made is that they grant fetuses more rights than 2-year-olds—the right, for example, to a safe, healthy place to live. No court in this country would ever rule that a parent must undergo a medical procedure in order to benefit a child, even if that procedure is as riskless as a blood donation and the child is sure to die without it. (A Seattle woman is currently suing the father of her leukemic child to force him to donate bone marrow, but she is sure to lose, and her mere attempt roused *Newsday* science writer B.D. Colen to heights of choler unusual even for him.) Nor would a court force someone who had promised to donate a kidney and then changed his mind to keep his date with the organ bank. Yet, as the forced-Caesarean issue shows, we seem willing to deny the basic right of bodily integrity to pregnant women and to give the fetus rights we deny children.

Although concern for the fetus may look like a way of helping children, it is actually, in a funny way, a substitute for it. It is an illusion to think that by "protecting" the fetus from its mother's behavior we have insured a healthy birth, a healthy infancy or a healthy childhood, and that the only insurmountable obstacle for crack babies is prenatal exposure to crack.

It is no coincidence that we are obsessed with pregnant women's behavior at the same time that children's health is declining, by virtually any yardstick one chooses. Take general well-being: In constant dollars, welfare payments are now about two-thirds the 1965 level. Take housing: Thousands of children are now growing up in homeless shelters and welfare hotels. Even desperately alcoholic women bear healthy babies two-thirds of the time. Will two-thirds of today's homeless kids emerge unscathed from their dangerous and lead-permeated environments? Take access to medical care: Inner-city hospitals are closing all over the country, millions of kids have no health insurance and most doctors refuse uninsured or Medicaid patients. Even immunization rates are down: Whooping cough and measles are on the rise.

THE "DUTY OF CARE"

Not everyone who favors legal intervention to protect the fetus is anti-choice. Some pro-choicers support the coercion and punishment of addicts and alcoholics—uneasily, like some of my liberal women friends, or gleefully, like Alan Dershowitz, who dismisses as absurd the "slippery slope" argument (crack today, cigarettes tomorrow) he finds so persuasive when applied to First Amendment issues. For some years now bioethicists have been fascinated by the doctrine of "duty of care," expounded most rigorously by Margery Shaw and John Robertson. In this view, a woman can abort, but once she has decided to bear a child she has a moral, and should have a legal, responsibility to insure a healthy birth. It's an attractive notion because it seems to combine an acceptance of abortion with intuitive feelings shared by just about everyone, including this writer, that pregnancy is a serious undertaking, that society has an interest in the health of babies, that the fetus, although not a person, is also not property.

Whatever its merits as a sentiment, though, the duty of care is a legal disaster. Exactly when, for instance, does the decision to keep a pregnancy take place? For the most desperately addicted—the crack addicts who live on the subway or prostitute themselves for drugs—one may ask if they ever form any idea ordinary people would call a decision, or indeed know they are pregnant until they are practically in labor. Certainly the inaccessibility of abortion denies millions of women the ability to decide.

But for almost all women the decision to carry a pregnancy to term has important, if usually unstated, qualifications. What one owes the fetus is balanced against other considerations, such as serious health risks to oneself (taking chemotherapy or other crucial medication), or the need to feed one's family (keeping a job that may pose risks) or to care for the children one already has (not getting the bed rest the doctor says you need). Why should pregnant women be barred from considering their own interests? It is, after all, what parents do all the time. The model of women's relation to the fetus proposed by the duty of care ethicists is an abstraction that ignores the realities of life even when they affect the fetus itself. In real life, for instance, to quit one's dangerous job means to lose one's health insurance, thus exposing the fetus to another set of risks.

It is also, even as an abstraction, a false picture. Try as she might, a woman cannot insure a healthy newborn; nor can statistical studies of probability (even well-designed ones) be related in an airtight way to individual cases. We know that cigarettes cause lung cancer, but try proving in a court of law that cigarettes and not air pollution, your job, your genes or causes unknown caused *your* lung cancer.

Yet far from shrinking from the slippery slope, duty of care theorists positively hurl themselves down it. Margery Shaw, for instance, believes that the production of an imperfect newborn should make a woman liable to criminal charges and "wrongful life" suits if she knows, or should have known, the risk involved in her behavior, whether it's drinking when her period is late (she has a duty to keep track of her cycle), delivering at home when her doctor advises her not to (what doctor doesn't?) or failing to abort a genetically damaged fetus (which she has a duty to find out about). So much for that "decision" to bear a child—a woman can't qualify it in her own interests but the state can revoke it for her on eugenic grounds.

As these examples show, there is no way to limit the duty of care to cases of flagrant or illegal misbehavior—duty is duty, and risk is risk. Thus, there is no way to enshrine duty of care in law without creating the sort of Romania-style fetal-police state whose possibility Dershowitz, among others, pooh-poohs. For there is no way to define the limits of what a pregnant woman must sacrifice for fetal benefit, or what she "should have known," or at what point a trivial risk becomes significant. My aunt advised me to get rid of my cats while I was pregnant because of the risk of toxoplasmosis. My doctor and I thought this rather extreme, and my husband simply took charge of the litter box. What if my doctor had backed up my aunt instead of me? If the worst had happened (and it always does to someone, somewhere), would I have been charged with the crime of not sending my cats to the Bide-A-Wee?

Although duty of care theorists would impose upon women a virtually limitless obligation to put the fetus first, they impose that responsibility *only* on women. Philosophy being what it is, perhaps it should not surprise us that they place no corresponding duty upon society as a whole. But what about Dad? It's his kid too, after all. His drug and alcohol use, his prescription medications, his workplace exposure and general habits of health not only play a part in determining the quality of his sperm but affect the course of pregnancy as well. Cocaine dust and smoke from crack, marijuana and tobacco present dangers to others who breathe them; his alcoholism often bolsters hers. Does he have a duty of care to make it possible for his pregnant partner to obey those judge's orders and that doctor's advice that now has the force of law? To quit his job to mind the children so that she can get the bed rest without which her fetus may be harmed? Apparently not.

The sexist bias of duty of care has already had alarming legal consequences. In the Pamela Rae Stewart case cited at the beginning of this article, Stewart's husband, who had heard the doctor's advice, ignored it all and beat his wife into the bargain. Everything she did, he did—they had sex together, smoked pot together, delayed getting to the hospital together—but he was not charged with a crime, not even with wife-beating, although no one can say that his assaults were not a contributing cause of the infant's injury and death. In Tennessee, a husband succeeded in getting a court order forbidding his wife to drink or take drugs, although he himself had lost his driver's license for driving while intoxicated. In Wyoming, a pregnant woman was arrested for drinking when she presented herself at the hospital for treatment of injuries inflicted by her husband. Those charges were dropped (to be reinstated, should her baby be born with defects), but none were instituted against her spouse.

It is interesting to note in this regard that approximately one in twelve women are beaten during pregnancy, a time when many previously nonviolent men become brutal. We do not know how many miscarriages, stillbirths and damaged newborns are due, or partly due, to male violence—this is itself a comment on the skewed nature of supposedly objective scientific research. But if it ever does come to be an officially recognized factor in fetal health, the duty of care would probably take yet another ironic twist and hold battered pregnant women liable for their partner's assaults.

The Broken Cord, Michael Dorris's much-praised memoir of his adopted F.A.S. child, Adam, is a textbook example of the way in which all these social trends come together—and the largely uncritical attention the book has received shows how seductive a pattern they make. Dorris has nothing but contempt for Adam's birth mother. Perhaps it is asking too much of human nature to expect him to feel much sympathy for her. He has witnessed, in the most intimate and heartbreaking way, the damage her alcoholism did, and seen the ruin of his every hope for Adam, who is deeply retarded. But why is his anger directed only at her? Here was a seriously alcoholic woman, living on an Indian reservation where heavy drinking is a way of life, along with poverty, squalor, violence, despair and powerlessness, where, one might even say, a kind of racial suicide is taking place, with liquor as the weapon of choice. Adam's mother, in fact, died two years after his birth from drinking antifreeze.

Dorris dismisses any consideration of these facts as bleeding-heart fuzzy-mindedness. Like Hope on *thirtysomething*, Adam's mother "decides" to have a baby; like the martini-sipping pregnant woman Dorris badgers in an airport bar, she "chooses" to drink out of "weakness" and "self-indulgence."

Dorris proposes preventive detention of alcoholic pregnant women and quotes sympathetically a social worker who thinks the real answer is sterilization. Why do alcoholic Indian women have so many children? To up their government checks. (In fact, Bureau of Indian Affairs hospitals are prohibited by law from performing abortions, even if women can pay for them.) And why, according to Dorris, do they drink so much in the first place? Because of the feminist movement, which has undermined the traditional temperance of reservation women.

The women's movement has had about as much effect on impoverished reservation dwellers as it had on the slum women of eighteenth-century London, whose heavy binge drinking—and stunted babies—appalled contemporary observers. That Dorris pins the blame on such an improbable villain points to what fetal rights is really about—controlling women. It's a reaction to legalized abortion and contraception, which have given women, for the first time in history, real reproductive power. They can have a baby, they can "kill" a baby, they can refuse to conceive at all, without asking permission from anyone. More broadly, it's an index of deep discomfort with the notion of women as self-directed social beings, for whom parenthood is only one aspect of life, as it has always been for men. Never mind that in the real world, women still want children, have children and take care of children, often under the most discouraging circumstances and at tremendous emotional, economic and physical cost. There is still a vague but powerful cultural fear that one of these days, women will just walk out on the whole business of motherhood and the large helpings of humble pie we have, as a society, built into that task. And *then* where will we be?

Looked at in this light, the inconsistent and fitful nature of our concern about the health of babies forms a pattern. The threat to newborns is interesting when and only when it can, accurately or fancifully, be laid at women's doorstep. Babies "possibly" impaired by maternal drinking? Front-page stories, a national wave of alarm. A *New England Journal of Medicine* report that 16 percent of American children have been mentally and neurologically damaged because of exposure to lead, mostly from flaking lead paint in substandard housing? Peter Jennings looks mournful and suggests that "all parents can do" is to have their children tested frequently. If the mother isn't to blame, no one is to blame.

In its various aspects "fetal rights" attacks virtually all the gains of the women's movement. Forced medical treatment attacks women's increased control over pregnancy and delivery by putting doctors back in the driver's seat, with judges to back them up. The *Johnson Controls* decision reverses the entry of women into high-paying, unionized, traditionally male jobs. In the female ghetto, where women can hardly be dispensed with, the growing practice of laying off or shifting pregnant women around transforms women, whose rates of labor-force participation are approaching those of men, into casual laborers with reduced access to benefits, pensions, seniority and promotions. In a particularly vicious twist of the knife, "fetal rights" makes legal abortion—which makes all the other gains possible—the trigger for a loss of human rights. Like the divorce-court judges who tell middle-aged housewives to go out and get a job, or who favor fathers in custody disputes because to recognize the primary-caretaker role of mothers would be "sexist," protectors of the fetus enlist the rhetoric of feminism to punish women.

There are lots of things wrong with the concept of fetal rights. It posits a world in which women will be held accountable, on sketchy or no evidence, for birth defects; in which all fertile women will be treated as potentially pregnant all the time; in which courts, employers, social workers and doctors—not to mention nosy neighbors and vengeful male partners—will monitor women's behavior. It imposes responsibilities without giving women the wherewithal to fulfill them, and places upon women alone duties that belong to both parents and to the community.

But the worst thing about fetal rights is that it portrays a woman as having only contingent value. Her work, her health, her choices and needs and beliefs, can all be set aside in an instant because, next to maternity, they are all perceived as trivial. For the middle class, fetal rights is mostly symbolic, the gateway to a view of motherhood as self-sacrifice and endless guilty soul-searching. It ties in neatly with the currently fashionable suspicion of working mothers, day care and (now that wives are more likely than husbands to sue for it) divorce. For the poor, for whom it means jail and the loss of custody, it becomes a way of saying that women can't even be mothers. They can only be potting soil.

The plight of addicted and alcohol-impaired babies is indeed a tragedy. Finally, we are forced to look at the results of our harsh neglect of the welfare and working poor, and it's only natural that we don't like what we see. We are indeed in danger of losing a generation. But what about the generation we already have? Why is it so hard for us to see that the tragedy of Adam Dorris is inextricable from the tragedy of his mother? Why is her loss—to society, to herself—so easy to dismiss?

"People are always talking about women's duties to others," said Lynn Paltrow, the A.C.L.U. lawyer who successfully led the Pamela Rae Stewart defense, "as though women were not the chief caregivers in this society. But no one talks about women's duty of care to *themselves*. A pregnant addict or alcoholic needs to get help for *herself*. She's not just potentially ruining someone else's life. She's ruining her own life.

"Why isn't her own life important? Why don't we care about her?"

Institutions in Crisis

VI

The Family

Is there a crisis in the American family? Certainly it is a time of change for the family, and many believe it is also a time of trouble. Over the past two decades, the divorce rate has risen and the birth rate has decreased. The "traditional" family, with the husband as the sole source of financial support and the wife as a full-time homebody, still exists, of course, but it is now a statistical minority. Increasingly large numbers of women, married or not, have entered the labor force. Others live in unconventional intimate arrangements and contribute to the increasing diversity of American family life-styles. All of this diversity, this permissiveness, if you will, seems to many to be menacing the integrity and stability of the American family.

Still, the American family will doubtless remain with us for a long time. It may look less and less like the conventional family of suburbia in the 1950s—with its traditional male and female roles—but the family will nevertheless continue, with accompanying transformations, readjustments, and problems.

These changes do not, however, necessarily signal decline or decay—just difference. To conclude that the family is declining, one must point to a historical era when things were rosier. Certainly the ideal of home, motherhood, and apple pie is part of our romantic mythology, but the myth did not always match the experience. As one historian concludes, "There is no Golden Age of the Family gleaming at us from far back in the historical past."

Still, because of change, many Americans—men and women, husbands and wives, parents and children—are experiencing marked uncertainties and anxieties. We have known deep changes in family life and in society. But our understanding of how to interpret these changes—and to

255

deal with them—has been impaired by lack of knowledge about the relationship between family life and society, particularly about the impact of societal imperatives, structures, and constraints upon the everyday workings of family life.

The social realities of family life are made vivid in Lillian Rubin's study of working-class and middle-class families, from which "Worlds of Pain" has been taken. Rubin had two central concerns in writing her book. One was to show the complexity of the family as an institution. It is, she writes, "both oppressive and protective and, depending on the issue, is experienced sometimes one way, sometimes the other—often as some mix of the two—by most people who live in families."

Rubin's second concern is to show how other social factors—especially the relation between gender role and social class—influence the family institution. For example, as Rubin points out in her introductory chapter (not reprinted here), working-class men often hold uninteresting jobs requiring little, too little, commitment of self, while middle-class professionals hold jobs demanding too much. Each reality impinges differently on family life. The chapter we have reprinted explores aspects of such sources of strain. In it Rubin explores how working-class values and upbringing impede marital communication. Marital partners have emotional needs that are frequently undermined by the role segregation and widely differing socialization patterns of men and women, especially in the working class.

Teenage pregnancy, one of the most discussed and controversial issues of the 1980s, is a prime example of the relation between broader social factors and norms and the emergence of a "social problem." A major comparative study conducted by Elise F. Jones and others, of the Alan Guttmacher Institute (a summary of which, "Teenage Pregnancy in Developed Countries," we reprint here), shows how several different social factors influence the high pregnancy rate among both black and white American teenagers. Thus, although United States economic development is comparable to that of Western Europe, our teenage pregnancy rates resemble those of some third-world countries. Are our norms governing teenage sexuality more permissive? On the contrary, countries with low teenage pregnancy rates, like Sweden and the Netherlands, are more permissive than we are. And their teenagers engage in at least as much sexual activity. So how do we differ? We are less open about sexual matters than most countries with low teenage birthrates; we have higher levels of religiosity; we offer less sex education; and we are more restrictive of teenagers' access to contraceptives. We tend to define teenage sexual activity as the problem. Sweden, by contrast, identifies pregnancy as the problem.

Two other societal factors are noteworthy in accounting for our high rate of teenage pregnancies. Countries with lower teenage pregnancy rates have less socioeconomic inequality, and government subsidy of abortions is *not* associated with teenage fertility. All of these factors, elaborated in the article reprinted here, would seem to have significant implications for government policies regarding the American family.

As economic inequality grows in the United States, increasing numbers of children, particularly black and minority children, are being consigned to a life of poverty. In part, this is related to the high teenage pregnancy rates discussed in the preceding article. As Marian Wright Edelman also points out in "Children at Risk," adolescent parents are generally not affluent parents. They are typically unskilled, and it is their lack of marketable skills that keeps them and their children from rising out of poverty. As Edelman concludes, a disproportionate number of children will grow up unskilled and poor just when our society desperately requires healthy, educated, and productive people. This, as a recent report by a national commission concluded, is "a staggering national tragedy" facing America's future.

Is family poverty an economic or a moral problem? Does family disintegration lead to poverty, or does poverty lead to family disintegration? Which is the cause, and which the effect? More to the point, does it much matter? Obviously, poverty and family disintegration are correlated. Those who stress traditional "family values" rarely consider the need for a social system where it is possible for family values to be generated and nurtured. We do know how to help children. We know that Head Start works—not every time, nor in every instance—but on the whole. We know that prenatal care works. We know that affordable housing works. The more economic and social neglect of families and children our society tolerates, the more it must be prepared to accept the unwelcome consequences of such neglect.

In thinking about the family and its relation to society, we also need to ask a deeper question: What *is* this social formation we call the "family?" During the 1950s, sociologists studying the family entertained a vision of the nuclear family as a breadwinner father, a homemaker mother, and two or three children living in the suburbs. That vision was already becoming outdated and would become seriously so as social conceptions of gender roles shifted in the 1960s and 1970s. As we look toward the twenty-first century, it is expected that 80 percent of women will be in the work force. Today the proportion is roughly 70 percent.

But, since 1970, when the White House Conference on Children declared child care to be the most serious problem facing American families, little has been done to reach a solution to this problem, a predicament that Edward F. Zigler calls a "crisis" as increasing numbers of women flock to the job market. In "Addressing the Nation's Child Care Crisis," Zigler compares child care to education and argues that we will have to develop the same sort of commitment to universal child care that we do to education. We have learned that education is fundamental to our conception of a free society. It is both a public good and public responsibility; so, Zigler argues, is child care.

21

Worlds of Pain

Lillian Breslow Rubin

I give her a nice home, a nice car, all those fancy appliances. I don't
cheat on her. We got three nice kids—nobody could ask for better kids.
And with all that, she's not happy. I worry about it, but I can't figure
out what's the matter, so how can I know what to do? I just don't know
what she wants.

> *Twenty-nine-year-old truck driver, married nine years*

"I just don't know what she wants"—that's the plaintive and un-
comprehending cry of most working-class men, the cry that
bedevils most marriages. Sadly, she often also doesn't know what she
wants. She knows only that the dream is not being fulfilled—that she's
married, but feels lonely:

> It sounds silly, I know, but here I am in a house with three kids and
> my husband, and lots of times I feel like I might just as well be living
> alone.

. . . that life feels curiously empty:

> You wake up one day and you say to yourself, "My God, is this all
> there is? Is it really possible that this is what life is all about?"

. . . that she's often filled with an incomprehensible anger:

> I feel like I go crazy-angry sometimes. It makes me say and do things to
> Randy or the kids that I hate myself for. I keep wondering what makes
> me do those things when one part of me knows I don't really mean it.

. . . and that guilt and anxiety are her steady companions:

> I don't know what's the matter with me that I don't appreciate what
> I've got. I feel guilty all the time, and I worry about it a lot. Other
> women, they seem to be happy with being married and having a house
> and kids. What's the matter with me?

"What's the matter" with her is that, even apart from the financial
burdens incurred in buying all those goods, they add little to the emotional satisfactions of life. The advertisers' promises of instant happiness
prove to be a lie—good for the gross national product but not for the
human soul.

Sure, it's great to show those goodies off to friends and neighbors. After
all those years of poverty, it makes you feel good finally to have something
and to let people see it. Besides, they make life easier, more comfortable.
Now there's time for things other than household drudgery. But what
things? Companionship? Intimacy? Sharing? What are those things? And
how does one find them?

She has a vague idea. Television shows, the women's magazines—they
all talk about something called communication. Marriage partners have to
communicate, they say; they have to talk, to tell each other how they feel.
So she talks. And he tries to listen. But somehow, it doesn't work. He
listens, but he cannot hear. Sometimes sooner, sometimes later, he with-
draws in silence, feeling attacked:

> When she comes after me like that, yapping like that, she might as well
> be hitting me with a bat.

. . . vulnerable:

> It makes me feel like I'm doing something wrong, like I'm not a very
> good husband or something.

. . . and helpless:

> No matter what I say, it's no good. If I try to tell her she's excited over
> nothing, that only makes it worse. I try to keep my cool and be logical,
> but nothing works.

This is the dilemma of modern marriage—experienced at all class levels,
but with particular acuteness among the working-class families I met. For
once marriage is conceived of as more than an economic arrangement—
that is, as one in which the emotional needs of the individual are attended
to and met—the role segregation and the consequent widely divergent
socialization patterns for women and men become clearly dysfunctional.[1]
And it is among the working class that such segregation has been most
profound, where there has been least incentive to change.

Thus, they talk *at* each other, *past* each other, or *through* each other—
rarely *with* or *to* each other. He blames her: "She's too emotional." She
blames him: "He's always so rational." In truth, neither is blameworthy.

The problem lies in the fact that they do not have a language with which to communicate, with which to understand each other. They are products of a process that trains them to relate to only one side of themselves—she, to the passive, tender, intuitive, verbal, emotional side; he, to the active, tough, logical, nonverbal, unemotional one.[2] From infancy, each has been programmed to be split off from the other side; by adulthood, it is distant from consciousness, indeed.[3]

They are products of a disjunction between thought and feeling, between emotionality and rationality that lies deep in Western culture. Even though she complains, both honestly believe what the culture has taught them. To be rational is the more desired state; it is good, sane, strong, adult. To be emotional is the less desired state; it is bad, weak, childlike. She:

> I know I'm too emotional and I can't really be trusted to be sensible a lot of the time. I need him; he's the one in the family you can always count on to think about things right, not mixed up, like me.

He:

> She's like a kid sometimes, so emotional. I'm always having to reason with her, to explain things to her. If it weren't for me, nothing would happen very rational around here.

This equation of emotional with nonrational, this inability to apprehend the logic of emotions, lies at the root of much of the discontent between the sexes, and helps to make marriage the most difficult of all relationships.

Her lifetime training prepares her to handle the affective, expressive side in human affairs; his, to handle the nonaffective, instrumental side. Tears, he has been taught, are for sissies; feelings, for women. A *real* man is the strong, silent type of the folklore—a guy who needs nothing from anyone, who ignores feelings and pain, who can take it on the chin without a whimper. For a lifetime, much of his energy has gone into molding himself in that image—into denying his feelings, refusing to admit they exist. Without warning or preparation, he finds himself facing a wife who pleads, "Tell me your feelings." He responds with bewilderment. "What is there to tell?"[4]

When they try to talk, she relies on the only tools she has, the mode with which she is most familiar; she becomes progressively more emotional and expressive. He falls back on the only tools he has; he gets progressively more rational—determinedly reasonable. She cries for him to attend to her feelings, her pain. He tells her it's silly to feel that way; she's just being emotional. That clenched-teeth reasonableness invalidates her feelings, leaving her sometimes frightened:

> I get scared that maybe I'm crazy. He's always so logical and reasonable that I begin to feel, "What's the matter with me that I'm so emotional?"

. . . sometimes angry:

> When he just sits there telling me I'm too emotional, I get so mad, I go up the wall. Sometimes I get so mad I wish I could hit him. I did once, but he hit me back, and he can hurt me more than I can hurt him.

. . . almost always tearful and despairing:

> I wind up crying and feeling terrible. I get so sad because we can't really talk to each other a lot of times. He looks at me like I'm crazy, like he just doesn't understand a word I'm saying.

Repeatedly, the experience is the same, the outcome of the interaction, predictable. Yet, each has such a limited repertoire that they are consigned to playing out the same theme over and over again—he, the rational man; she, the hysterical woman.

But these almost wholly sociological notions—notions which speak to socialization patterns—tell only one part of the story of human development. The other part is told in the language of psychology—a language that is given its fullest and most complex expression in psychoanalytic theory. From that theory, Nancy Chodorow has presented us with a brilliant and provocative reformulation of Oedipal theory which successfully crosses the sociological with the psychological as it accounts for the dynamics of both the inner and outer world as they affect sex-role development.[5]

Her argument starts from the premise that the differences in male and female personality are rooted in the structure of the family—in particular, in the fact that women are the primary childrearers. As a result, the mother becomes the first object with which an infant—male or female—identifies, the first attachment formed. Coincident with the forming of these identifications and attachments, other developmental tasks emerge in the period between infancy and childhood—a primary one being the development of an appropriate gender identity. For a girl, that task is a relatively straightforward one—a continuous and gradual process of internalization of a feminine identity with mother as model. For a boy, however, role learning is discontinuous involving, as it must, the rejection of his early identification with his mother as he seeks an appropriate masculine identity.

Since a girl need not reject that early identification in order to negotiate the Oedipal phase successfully, feminine personality is based on less repression of inner objects, less fixed and firm ego-splitting, and greater continuity of external relationships. With no need to repress or deny their earliest attachment, girls can define and experience themselves as part of and continuous with others. Consequently, women tend to have more complex inner lives, more ability to engage in a variety of interpersonal relationships, and more concern with ongoing relational issues.

On the other hand, boys must repress these same attachments as they shift their identification from mother to father. That means that they must distinguish and differentiate themselves in a way that girls need not. In doing so, they come to define and experience themselves as more separate from others and with more rigid ego boundaries; and adult masculine personality comes to be defined more in terms of denial of connection and relations.

Such ideas present profound implications for the marriage relationship. For if it is true that their earliest experiences in the family mean that men must deny relations and connection while women must be preoccupied with them, we are faced anew with the realization—this time from the psychoanalytic perspective—that the existing structure of family relations, especially in its delegation of the parenting function solely or dominantly to the mother, makes the attainment of compatible relations between women and men extraordinarily difficult.

It hardly need be said that such relationships between men and women are not given to the working-class alone. Without doubt, the description I have been rendering represents the most common interactional pattern in American marriage. These are the behavioral consequences of the dominant sex-role socialization patterns in the culture and of the existing structure of family relations within which boys and girls internalize an appropriate identity—patterns which generate the role stereotypes that women and men bring to marriage and which effectively circumscribe their emotional negotiations.

Still, it is also true that the norms of middle-class marriage for much longer have called for more companionate relationships—for more sharing, for more exploration of feelings, and for more exchange of them. Thus, middle-class women and men have more practice and experience in trying to overcome the stereotypes. And, perhaps more important, they have more models around them for how to do so. This is not to suggest that they have done it so well, as a casual glance at the divorce rate will show; only that the demands on the marriage partners for different behaviors have been around for much longer, that there is a language that gives those demands legitimacy, and that there has been more experimentation in modifying the stereotypes.

Among working-class couples, the demand for communication, for sharing, is newer. Earlier descriptions of working-class family life present a portrait of wives and husbands whose lives were distinctly separate, both inside and outside the home—the wife attending to her household role, the husband to his provider role. He came home at night tired and taciturn; she kept herself and the children out of his way. For generations, it was enough that each did their job adequately—he, to bring home the bacon; she, to cook it. Intimacy, companionship, sharing—these were not part of the dream.[6]

But dreams change—sometimes before the people who must live them are ready. Suddenly, new dreams are stirring, *intimacy, companionship, sharing*—these are now the words working-class women speak to their men, words that turn *both* their worlds upside down. For while it is the women who are the discontented, who are pushing for change, they, no less than their men, are confused about what they are asking:

> I'm not sure what I want. I keep talking to him about communication, and he says, "Okay, so we're talking; now what do you want?" And I don't know what to say then, but I know it's not what I mean.

. . . and frightened and unsure about the consequences:

> I sometimes get worried because I think maybe I want too much. He's a good husband; he works hard; he takes care of me and the kids. he could go out and find another woman who would be very happy to have a man like that, and who wouldn't be all the time complaining at him because he doesn't feel things and get close.

The men are even worse off. Since it's not *their* dream, they are less likely still to have any notion of what is being asked of them. They only know that, without notice, the rules of the game have been changed; what worked for their fathers no longer works for them. They only know that there are a whole new set of expectations—in the kitchen, in the parlor, in the bedroom—that leave them feeling bewildered and threatened.[7] She says:

> I keep telling him that the reason people get divorced isn't *only* financial but because they can't communicate. But I can't make him understand.

He says:

> I swear, I don't know what she wants. She keeps saying we have to talk, and then when we do, it always turns out I'm saying the wrong thing.
>
> I get scared sometimes. I always thought I had to think things to myself; you know, not tell her about it. Now she says that's not good. But it's hard. You know, I think it comes down to that I like things the way they are, and I'm afraid I'll say or do something that'll really shake things up. So I get worried about it, and I don't say anything.

For both women and men, the fears and uncertainties are compounded by the fact that there are no models in their lives for the newly required and desired behaviors. Television shows them people whose lives seem unreal—outside the realm of personal experience or knowledge. The daytime soap operas, watched almost exclusively by women, *do* picture men who may be more open and more available for intimacy. But the men on the soaps don't work at ordinary jobs, doing ordinary things, for eight, ten, twelve hours a day. They're engaged either in some heroic, life-saving, glamour job to which working-class viewers can't relate or, worse yet, work seems to be one long coffee break during which they talk about their problems. Nighttime fare, when the men are home, is different, but no less unreal, featuring the stoic private eye, the brave cop, the tight-lipped cowboy.

The argument about the impact of the mass media on blue-collar workers is complex, contradictory, and largely unsatisfactory. Some observers insist that the mass media represent the most powerful current by which blue-collar workers are swept into conformity with middle-class values and aspirations;[8] others that blue-collar men especially resist exposure to middle-class manners and mores as they are presented on television—minimizing that exposure by exercising great discrimination in program choices;[9] still others that the idealized and romantic figures on television are so unreal to the average blue-collar viewer that they have little impact on their lives and little effect on their behavior.[10]

Perhaps all three of these seemingly irreconcilable perspectives are true. The issue may not be *whether* television or other mass media affect people's lives and perceptions. Of course they do. The question we must ask more precisely is: In what ways are Americans of any class touched and affected by their exposure to television? For the professional middle class, it may well be an affirming experience; for the working class, a disconfirming one since there are no programs that deal with their problems, their prospects, and their values in sympathetic and respectful ways.[11]

If their own lives in the present provide no models and the media offer little that seems relevant, what about the past? Unfortunately for young working-class couples, family backgrounds provide few examples of openness, companionship, or communication between husbands and wives:

> I don't think we ever had a good concept of what marriage was about.
> His family was the opposite of mine. They didn't drink like mine did,
> and they were more stable. Yet he feels they didn't give him a good
> concept either. There wasn't any drinking and fighting and carrying on,
> but there wasn't any caring either.

Even those few who recall their parents' marriages as good ones don't remember them talking much to one another and have no sense at all that they might have shared their inner lives:

> *Would you describe a typical evening in the family when you were growing up?*

A twenty-five-year-old manicurist, mother of two, married seven years, replies:

> Let me think. I don't really know what happened; nothing much, I
> guess. My father came home at four-thirty, and we ate right away. No-
> body talked much at the table; it was kind of a quiet affair.
>   *What about your parents' relationship? Do you remember how they behaved*
> *with each other; whether they talked to each other?*
> Gee, I don't know. It's hard to think about them as being *with* each

other. I don't think they talked a lot; at least, I never saw them talking. I can't imagine them sitting down to talk over problems or something like that, if that's what you mean.

Yes, that *is* what I mean. But that was the last generation; what about this one? *Would you describe a typical evening in your own family now?*

For some, less than half, it's better—a level of companionship, caring, and sharing that, while not all they dream of, is surely better than they knew in their past. Fathers attend more to children; husbands at least try to "hear" their wives; couples struggle around some of the emotional issues I have identified in these pages. For most, however, nothing much has changed since the last generation. Despite the yearning for more, relations between husband and wife are benumbed, filled with silence; life seems empty and meaningless; laughter, humor, fun is not a part of the daily ration. Listen to this couple married seven years. The wife:

Frank comes home from work; now it's about five because he's been working overtime every night. We eat right away, right after he comes home. Then, I don't know. The kids play a while before bed, watch TV, you know, stuff like that. Then, I don't know; we don't do anything except maybe watch more TV or something like that. I don't know what else—nothing, I guess. We just sit, that's all.

That's it? Nothing else?

Yeah, that's right, that's all. *A short silence, then angrily.* Oh yeah, I forgot. Sometimes he's got one of his projects he works on. Like now, he's putting that new door in the kitchen. It's still nothing. When he finishes doing it, we just sit.

Her husband describes the same scene:

I come home at five and we eat supper right away. Then, I sit down with coffee and a beer and watch TV. After that, if I'm working on a project, I do that for a little while. If not, I just watch.

Life is very predictable. Nothing much happens; we don't do much. Everyone sits in the same place all the time and does the same thing every night. It's satisfying to me, but maybe it's not for her, I don't know. Maybe she wants to go to a show or something once in a while, I don't know. She doesn't tell me.

Don't you ask her?

No. I suppose I should, but it's really hard to think about getting out. We'd need someone to stay with the kids and all that. Besides, I'm tired. I've been out all day, seeing different people and stuff. I don't feel like going out after supper again.

Is there some time that you two have for yourselves, to talk things over and find out how you feel about things?

The wife:

There's plenty of time; we just don't do it. He doesn't ever think there's anything to talk about. I'm the one who has to nag him to talk always, and then I get disgusted.

He'd be content just living, you know, just nothing but living for the rest of his life. It don't make no difference to him where he lives or how people around him are feeling. I don't know how anybody can be like that.

A lot of times I get frustrated. I just wish I could talk to him about things and he could understand. If he had more feelings himself, maybe he'd understand more. Don't you think so?

Her husband agrees that he has problems handling both his feelings and hers:

I'm pretty tight-lipped about most things most of the time, especially personal things. I don't express what I think or feel. She keeps trying to get me to, but, you know, it's hard. Sometimes I'm not even sure what she wants me to be telling her. And when she gets all upset and emotional, I don't know what to say or what to do.

Sometimes she gets to nagging me about what I'm thinking or feeling, and I tell her, "Nothing," and she gets mad. But I swear, it's true; I'm not thinking about anything.

Difficult for her to believe, perhaps, but it *is* true. After a lifetime of repressing his feelings, he often *is* a blank, unaware that he's thinking or feeling anything. Moreover, when emotions have been stored for that long, they tend to be feared as especially threatening or explosive. He continues:

Maybe it sounds a little crazy, but I'm afraid once I let go, I might get past the point where I know what I'm doing. If I let myself go, I'm afraid I could be dangerous. She keeps telling me that if you keep things pent up inside you like that, something's going to bust one day.

I think a lot of the problem is that our personalities are just very different. I'm the quiet type. If I have something I have to think about, I have to get by myself and do it. Elly, she just wants to talk about it, always talking about her feelings.

Yakketty-yakkers, that's what girls are. Well, I don't know; guys talk, too. But, you know, there's a difference, isn't there? Guys talk about things and girls talk about feelings.

Indeed that *is* the difference, precisely the difference I have been pointing to—"Guys talk about things and girls talk about feelings"—a difference that plagues marriage partners as they struggle to find ways to live with each other.

Again, the question presents itself: Is this just a phenomenon of working-class life? Clearly, it is not, for the social and psychological processes that account for the discrepant and often incompatible development of women and men apply across class and throughout the culture. Still, there are important class differences in the way these broad socio-cultural mandates are interpreted and translated into behavior differences that are rooted in class situation and experience. Thus, there are differences in the early childhood and family experiences of children who grow up in working-class homes and those who live in professional middle-class homes, differences in the range of experiences through their adolescence and young adulthood, and differences in the kinds of problems and preoccupations they face in their adult lives—on the job and in the family.

Whether boys or girls, children in the homes of the professional middle class have more training in exploring the socio-emotional realm and more avenues for such exploration. It's true that for the girls, this usually is the *focus* of their lives, while for the boys, it is not. Nevertheless, compared to childrearing patterns in working-class families, professional middle-class families make fewer and less rigid sex-role distinctions in early childhood.[12] As small children, therefore, boys in such middle-class homes more often get the message that it's all right to cry, to be nurturant as well as nurtured, to be reflective and introspective, even at times to be passive—in essence, in some small measure, to relate to their expressive side.

Not once in a professional middle-class home did I see a young boy shake his father's hand in a well-taught "manly" gesture as he bid him good night. Nor once did I hear a middle-class parent scornfully—or even sympathetically—call a crying boy a sissy or in any way reprimand him for his tears. Yet, these were not uncommon observations in the working-class homes I visited. Indeed, I was impressed with the fact that, even as young as six or seven, the working-class boys seemed more emotionally controlled—more like miniature men—than those in the middle-class families.

These differences in childrearing practices are expressed as well in the different demands the parents of each class make upon the schools—differences that reflect the fact that working-class boys are expected to be even less emotional, more controlled than their middle-class counterparts.[13] For the working-class parent, school is a place where teachers are expected to be tough disciplinarians; where children are expected to behave respectfully and to be punished if they do not; and where one mark of that respect is that they are sent to school neatly dressed in their "good" clothes and expected to stay that way through the day. None of these values is highly prized in the professional middle class. For them, schools are expected to be relatively loose, free, and fun; to encourage initiative, innovativeness, creativity, and spontaneity; and to provide a place where children—boys as well as girls—will learn social and interpersonal skills. The children of these middle-class families are sent to nursery school early—often as young as two and a half—not just because their mothers want the free time, but because the social-skill training provided there is considered a crucial part of their education.

These differences come as no surprise if we understand both the past experience and the future expectations of both sets of parents. Most highly educated parents have little fear that their children won't learn to read, write, and do their sums. Why should they? They learned them, and learned them well. Their children have every advantage that they had and plenty more: books, games, toys—all designed to excite curiosity and to stimulate imagination—and parents who are skillful in aiding in their use.

Working-class parents, however, have no such easy assurances about their children's educational prospects. Few can look back on their own school years without discomfort—discomfort born of painful reminders of all they didn't learn, of the many times they felt deficient and inadequate. Further, when they look at the schools their children attend now, they see the same pattern repeating itself. For, in truth, the socio-economic status of the children in a school is the best indicator of schoolwide achievement test scores—that is, the lower the socio-economic status, the lower the scores.[14]

Observing this phenomenon, many analysts and educators argue that these low achievement records in poor and working-class schools are a consequence of the family background—the lack of culture and educational motivation in the home—an explanation that tends to blame the victim for the failure of our social institutions. Elsewhere, I have entered the debate about *who* is to blame for these failures on the side of the victims.[15] Here, the major point is simply that, regardless of where we think responsibility lies, working-class parents quite rightly fear that their children may not learn to read very well; that they may not be able to do even the simple arithmetic required to be an intelligent consumer. Feeling inadequate and lacking confidence that they can pass on their slim skills to their children, such parents demand that the schools enforce discipline in the belief that only then will their children learn all that they themselves did not.

This, however, is only one part of the explanation of why the sons of the professional middle class are brought up in a less rigidly stereotypic mode than are the sons of the working class—the part that is rooted in past experience. But past experience combines with present reality to create future expectations, because parents, after all, do not raise their children in a vacuum—without some idea of what the future holds for them, some sense of what they will need to survive the adult world for which they are destined. In fact, it is out of just such understandings that parental attitudes and values about childraising are born.[16] Thus, professional middle-class parents, assuming that their children are destined to do work like theirs—work that calls for innovation, initiative, flexibility, creativity, sensitivity to others, and a well-developed set of interpersonal skills—call for an educational system that fosters those qualities. Working-class parents also assume that their children will work at jobs roughly similar to their own. But in contrast to the requirements of professional or executive work, in most working-class jobs, creativity, innovation, initiative, flexibility are considered by superiors a hindrance. ("You're not getting paid to think!" is an oft-heard remonstrance.) Those who must work at such jobs may need nothing so much as a kind of iron-willed discipline to get them to work every day and to keep them going back year after year. No surprise, then, that such parents look suspiciously at spontaneity whether at home or at school. No surprise, either, that early childhood training tends to focus on respect, orderliness, cleanliness—in a word, discipline—especially for the boys who will hold these jobs, and that schools are called upon to reinforce these qualities.

Finally, men in the professional middle class presently live in an environment that gives some legitimacy to their stirrings and strivings toward connection with their emotional and expressive side. The extraordinary proliferation of the "growth-movement" therapies, which thrive on their appeal to both men and women of the upper middle class, is an important manifestation of that development. Another is the nascent men's movement—a response to the women's movement—with its men's groups, its male authors who write to a male audience encouraging their search for expressiveness. While it may be true that numerically all these developments account for only a small fraction of American men, it is also true that whatever the number, they are almost wholly drawn from the professional middle class.

For working-class men, these movements might as well not exist. Most don't know of them. The few who do, look at their adherents as if they were "kooks," "queers," or otherwise deficient, claiming to see no relevance in them to their own lives. Yet if one listens carefully to what lies beneath the surface of their words, the same stirrings for more connection with other parts of themselves, for more intimate relations with their wives are heard from working-class men as well. Often inchoate and inarticulately expressed, sometimes barely acknowledged, these yearnings, nevertheless, exist. But the struggle for their realization is a much more lonely and isolated one—removed not only from the public movements of our time but from the lives of those immediately around them—a private struggle in which there is no one to talk to, no examples to learn from. They look around them and see neighbors, friends, brothers, and sisters who are no better off—sometimes far worse off—than they:

> We're the only ones in the two families who have any kind of a marriage. One of my brothers ran out on his wife, the other one got divorced. Her sister and her husband are separated because he kept beating her up; her brother is still married, but he's a drunk. It makes it hard. If you never saw it in your family when you were growing up, then all the kids in both families mess up like that, it's hard to know what a good marriage is like. I guess you could say there hasn't been much of a model of one around us.

Without models, it is indeed hard—hard to know what to expect, hard to know how to act. You can't ask friends because they don't seem to have the same problems, not even the same feelings. One twenty-nine-year old husband lamented:

I sometimes think I'm selfish. She's the support—the moral support—in the family. But when she needs support, I just don't give it to her. Maybe it's not just selfishness, it's that I don't know what she wants and I don't know how.

The worst thing is, I've got nobody to talk to about how a guy can be different. The guys at work, all they ever talk about is their cars or their trucks. Oh, they talk about women, but it's only to brag about how they're making it with this chick or that one. And my brother, it's no use talking to him; he don't know where anything's at. He runs around every night, comes home drunk, beats up his wife.

I know Joanie's not so happy, and I worry about what to do about it. But the guys I know, they don't worry about things like that.

Don't they? He doesn't really know because he dare not ask.

How do you know they don't worry about such things? Have you asked them?

He looks up, puzzled, as if wondering how anybody could even think of such a thing, and answers quickly:

Ask them? No! Why would I do that? They'd think I was nuts or something. People don't talk about those things; you just *know* where those guys are; you don't have to ask them.

In fact, many of those men are suffering the same conflicts and concerns—wondering, as he does, what happened to the old familiar world; fearful, as he is, that their masculine image will be impaired if they talk about the things that trouble them. But if they can't talk to brothers, friends, work mates, where do they turn?

Maybe you could talk to Joan about what you could do to make things better in your marriage?

Dejectedly, he replies:

What good would that do? She's only a girl. How would she know how a guy is supposed to act?

The women generally also suffer alone. Despite all the publicity generated by the women's movement about the dissatisfactions women experience in marriage, most working-class women continue to believe that their feelings are uniquely theirs. Few have any contact with the movement or the people in it; few feel any support for their struggle from that quarter:

They put you down if you want to be married and raise kids, like there's something the matter with you.

Nor do they want it. For the movement is still a fearsome thing among working-class wives, and their responses to it are largely ambivalent, largely dominated by the negative stereotypes of the media. "Bra-burners," "man-haters"—these labels still are often heard.

Most believe in equal pay for equal work, but even that generally is not unequivocal:

> Yes, I believe women should be paid the same as men if they're doing the same job. I meant, most of the time, I believe it. But if a man has a family to support and she doesn't, then it's different.

Few believe that women should compete equally in the job market with men:

> If a man with a wife and kids needs a job, no woman ought to be able to take it away from him.

Neither response [is] a surprise, given their history of economic deprivation and concern. Neither response [is] to be heard among the wives of professional men. Also no surprise, given their lifetime of greater financial security and the fact that they "take for granted" that their husbands will provide adequately for the family.

Beyond these two issues, one after the other the working-class women responded impatiently and with almost identical words to questions about what they know about the movement:

> I don't know anything about it, and I don't care to know either.
>   *You sound angry at the women's movement.*
> That's right, I am. I don't like women who want to be men. Those libbers, they want men and women to be just alike, and I don't want that to happen. I think men should be men and women should be women. They're crazy not to appreciate what men do for women. I like my husband to open the car door for me and to light my cigarettes. It makes me feel like a lady.

As if reciting a litany, several women spoke the same words over and over—"I like a man to open the car door and light my cigarettes." Perplexed at the repetition, at the assertion of value of these two particular behaviors, I finally asked:

> *When was the last time your husband opened a car door for you or lit your cigarette?*

Startled, the open face of the women who sat before me became suffused with color; she threw her head back and laughed. Finally recovering, she said:

> I've gotta admit, I don't know why I said that. I don't even smoke.

Of course, she doesn't know why. To know would mean she'd have to face her fears and anxieties more squarely, to recognize that in some important ways the movement speaks to the issues that plague and pain her in her marriage. If, instead, she can reach for the stereotypes, she need not deal with the reality that these issues have become a part of her own life and aspirations, that their questions are also hers, that her own discontent is an example of what so many women out there are talking about.

For her, a major problem is that it remains "out there." Unlike the experience of the women in professional families, it is not *her* sisters, *her* friends, *her* neighbors who talk of these things, but women she doesn't know, has never met; women who aren't her "kind." So she hides her pain and internalizes her guilt.

> *Do you talk to your friends about some of the things we've been discussing—I mean about your conflicts about your life and your marriage, and about some of the things you dream about and wish for?*
> No, we don't talk about those kinds of things. It's kind of embarrassing, too personal, you know. Besides, the people I know don't feel like I do, so it's no point in talking to them about those things.
> *How do you know how they feel if you don't talk about it?*
> You just know, that's all. I know. It's why I worry sometimes that maybe there's something the matter with me that I'm not satisfied with what I've got. I get depressed, and then I wonder if I'm normal. I *know* none of my friends feels like that, like maybe they need a psychiatrist or something.

It's all right to complain about money, about a husband who drinks or stays out late, even about one who doesn't help around the house. But to tell someone you're unhappy because your husband doesn't talk to you— who would understand that?

> You don't talk about things like that to friends like I've got. They'd think I was another one of those crazy women's libbers.

Yes, there is concern among these working-class women and men about the quality of life, about its meaning. Yes, there is a deep wish for life to be more than a constant struggle with necessity. The drinking, the violence, the with drawn silences—these are responses of despair, giving evidence that h pe is hard to hold on to. How can it be otherwise when so often life seems like such an ungiving, uncharitable affair—a struggle without end? In the early years, it's unemployment, poverty, crying babies, violent fights. That phase passes, but a whole new set of problems emerge—problems that often seem harder to handle because they have less shape, less definition; harder, too, because they are less understandable, farther outside the realm of anything before experienced. But if there is one remarkable characteristic about life among the working class, it is the ability to engage the struggle and to survive it—a quality highly valued in a world where life has been and often remains so difficult and problematic. With a certain grim satisfaction, a twenty-six-year-old housewife, mother of two, summed it up:

> I guess in order to live, you have to have a very great ability to endure. And I have that—an ability to endure and survive.

NOTES

1. Historian Barbara Easton (1975, 1976) presents a compelling account of the change in family ideology in America. In her fascinating work, she demonstrates the link between the technological developments that made obsolete the relationship between the household and the productive forces and the emergence of the ideology which holds women responsible for the social-emotional content of the marriage relationship and men for the economic-instrumental side. For other historical perspectives on the relationship between the family and the economy—its evolution from the public to the private sphere—and the consequent changes in the roles and responsibilities that were defined as women's, see Ariès (1962); Lasch (1974); Lazerson (1975); Shorter (1975); Zaretsky (1973).

   See also Balswick and Peek (1974), who write about the tragic consequences to modern marriage of the "inexpressive male."

2. See Broverman, et al. (1972) for an intriguing study which shows that practicing psychotherapists (both male and female) hold a different standard of mental health for women and men and that, among others, they divide on these very traits to which I refer here. The study shows that for these clinicians, the definitions of a healthy adult and a healthy male are identical; the definition of a healthy female is exactly the opposite from the other two.

3. The recent literature on sex-role socialization, both scientific and journalistic, is rich and abundant. For an excellent review as well as a fine bibliography, see Hochschild (1973). In a particularly interesting study, Johnson, et al. (1975) reexamine the expressive-instrumental distinction and distinguish between a negative and positive pole on each attribute. After examining the self-ratings of four hundred female and male college students, the authors conclude that:

   . . . men associate independence with negative expressiveness. While the women in our sample were able to incorporate positive expressiveness, positive instrumentalness, and independence in their self-pictures, the men in our sample could not include expressiveness with independence and instrumentalness. This supports the theory that development of masculinity involves the rejection of femininity. The young boy becomes a man not by accepting masculine traits but by rejecting feminine ones.

   For further development of this theme, see Stockard (1975); also Balswick and Peek (1974); Broverman, et al. (1972); Chodorow (1971).

4. See Shostak (1971, 1973) for a moving description of the bewilderment with which blue-collar husbands face these new demands from their wives.

5. Chodorow (1977 forthcoming).

6. For rich descriptions of the earlier patterns of interaction and communication between working-class couples, see Komarovsky (1962); Rainwater, Coleman, and Handel (1959); Shostak (1969, 1971).

7. Cf. Shostak (1971).

8. Bogart (1964:417).

9. Shostak (1969:188–190) writes: "In a very important way TV is essentially a confirmatory exercise. By exercising discrimination at channel-switching, blue-collarites are able to expose themselves only, or especially, to a particular brand of TV fare (a phenomenon much in effect like visiting only with

members of one's extended family or old neighborhood). . . . Undesired themes and values are screened out, the blue-collarite gaining only resonance of cultural commonplaces from a media that seems itself intent at times on deserting its own potential to challenge, stir, and inform."
10. Komarovsky (1962).
11. See U.S. Department of Health, Education, and Welfare (1973b:34–35). . . .
12. See Kohn (1959, 1963, 1969) for some of the most important work in the field on class differences in childrearing patterns. Also Bronfenbrenner (1966); Grey (1969); Pearlin and Kohn (1966).
13. See Joffe (1974) and Rubin (1972) for empirical studies showing the class differences in educational values.
14. From the famous Coleman (1966) study onward, analysts have documented this point and variations on the theme over and over again. To mention a few, Bowles (1972); Bowles and Gintis (1973); Jencks (1972, 1976); Rist (1970); Rosenthal (1973); Rosenthal and Jacobson (1968); Rubin (1972); Schafer, et al. (1970); Sexton (1964, 1967); Wilson and Portes (1975).
15. Rubin (1972).
16. Cf. Kohn (1969).

BIBLIOGRAPHY

Ariès, Philippe. *Centuries of Childhood: A Social History of Family Life*. New York: Vintage Books, 1962.

Balswick, Jack, and Charles Peek. The Inexpressive Male: A Tragedy of American Society. In *Intimacy, Family, and Society*, edited by Arlene Skolnick and Jerome Skolnick. Boston: Little, Brown, 1974.

Bogard, Leo. The Mass Medic and the Blue-Collar Workers. In *Blue-Collar World*, edited by Arthur Shostak and William Gomberg. Englewood Cliffs, N.J.: Prentice-Hall, 1964.

Bowles, Samuel. Getting Nowhere: Programmed Class Stagnation. *Society* 9 (1972):42–49.

———, and Herbert Gintis. I.Q. in the U.S. Class Structure. *Social Policy* 3 (1973):65–96.

Bronfenbrenner, Urie. Socialization and Social Class through Time and Space. In *Class, Status, and Power*, 2d ed., edited by Reinhard Bendix and Seymour M. Lipset. New York: Free Press, 1966.

Broverman, Inge K., et al. Sex-Role Stereotypes: A Current Appraisal. *Journal of Social Issues* 28 (1972):59–78.

Chodorow, Nancy. Being and Doing: A Cross-Cultural Examination of the Socialization of Males and Females. In *Woman in Sexist Society*, edited by Vivian Gornick and Barbara K. Moran. New York: Basic Books, 1971.

———. *The Reproduction of Mothering: Family Structure and Feminine Personality*. Berkeley: University of California Press, 1977.

Coleman, James, et al. *Equality of Educational Opportunity*. Washington, D.C.: U.S. Government Printing Office, 1966.

Easton, Barbara Leslie. Women, Religion, and the Family: Revivalism as an Indicator of Social Change in Early New England. Ph.D. dissertation, University of California, Berkeley, 1975.

————. Industrialization and Femininity: A Case Study of Nineteenth Century New England. *Social Problems* 23, 1976.

Grey, Alan L., ed. *Class and Personality in Society.* New York: Atherton Press, 1961.

Hochschild, Arlie Russell. A Review of Sex Role Research. *American Journal of Sociology* 78 (1973):1011–1029.

Jencks, Christopher, et al. *Inequality: A Reassessment of the Effect of Family and Schooling in America.* New York: Basic Books, 1972.

Joffe, Carole E. Marginal Professions and Their Clients: The Case of Childcare. Ph.D. dissertation, University of California, Berkeley, 1974.

Johnson, Miriam, et al. Expressiveness Reevaluated. *School Review* 83 (1975): 617–644.

Kohn, Melvin. Social Class and Parental Values. *American Journal of Sociology* 64 (1959): 337–351.

————. Social Class and Parent-Child Relationships. *American Journal of Sociology* 68 (1963): 471–480.

————. *Class and Conformity.* Homewood, Ill.: Dorsey Press, 1969.

Komarovsky, Mirra. *Blue-Collar Marriage.* New York: Vintage Books, 1962.

Lasch, Christopher. Divorce and the Decline of the Family. In *The World of Nations,* edited by Christopher Lasch. New York: Vintage Books, 1974.

Lazerson, Marvin. Social Change and American Families: Some Historical Speculations. Xerox, 1975.

Pearlin, Leonard, and Melvin Kohn. Social Class, Occupation, and Parental Values: A Cross-National Study. *American Sociological Review* 31 (1966): 466–479.

Rainwater, Lee, Richard P. Coleman, and Gerald Handel. *Working-man's Wife.* New York: MacFadden Books, 1959.

Rist, Ray C. Student Social Class and Teacher Expectations: The Self-Fulfilling Prophecy in Ghetto Education. *Harvard Educational Review* 40 (1970): 411–451.

Rosenthal, Robert. The Pygmalion Effect Lives. *Psychology Today* 7 (1973): 56–63.

————, and Lenore Jacobson. *Pygmalion in the Classroom.* New York: Holt, Rinehart and Winston, 1968.

Rubin, Lillian B. Busing and Backlash: *White against White in an Urban School District.* Berkeley: University of California Press, 1972.

Schafer, Walter E., et al. Programmed for Social Class: Teaching in High School. *Trans-Action* 7 (1970): 39–46.

Sexton, Patricia Cayo. Wife of the "Happy Worker." In *Blue-Collar World,* edited by Arthur Shostak and William Gomberg. Englewood Cliffs, N.J.: Prentice-Hall, 1964.

Shorter, Edward. *The Making of the Modern Family.* New York: Basic Books, 1975.

Shostak, Arthur B. *Blue-Collar Life.* New York: Random House, 1969.

————. Working Class Americans at Home: Changing Expectations of Manhood. Delivered at the Conference on Problems, Programs, and Prospects of the American Working Class in the 1970s, Rutgers University, New Brunswick, N.J., September 1971.

————. Ethnic Revivalism, Blue-Collarities, and Bunder's Last Stand. In *Rediscovery of Ethnicity,* edited by Sallie Teselle. New York: Harper Colophon, 1973.

Stockard, Jean, et al. Sex Role Development and Sex Discrimination: A Theoretical Perspective. Delivered at the Seventieth Annual Meeting of the American Sociological Association, San Francisco, Calif., August 25–29, 1975.

U.S. Department of Health, Education and Welfare. *Work in America*. Cambridge, Mass.: MIT Press, 1973.

Wilson, Kenneth L., and Alejandro Portes. The Educational Attainment Process: Results from a National Sample. *American Journal of Sociology* 81 (1975): 343–363.

Zaretsky, Eli. Capitalism, the Family, and Personal Life: Parts I and II. *Socialist Revolution* 3 (1973): 69–126, 19–70.

22

Teenage Pregnancy in Developed Countries

Elise F. Jones, Jacqueline Darroch Forrest, Noreen
Goldman, Stanley K. Henshaw, Richard Lincoln, Jeannie
I. Rosoff, Charles F. Westoff, and Deirdre Wulf

● ● ● **[A]** lthough adolescent fertility rates have
been declining in the United States, as
they have in virtually all the countries of western and northern Europe,
teenage fertility is still considerably higher in the United States than in the
great majority of other developed countries. There is a large differential
within the United States between the rates of white and black teenagers.
However, even if only whites are considered, the rates in the United States
are still much higher than those in most of the other countries. The gap
between the United States and the other countries is greater among
younger adolescents (for whom the great majority of births are out of
wedlock and, presumably, unintended) than it is among older teenagers.
Abortion rates are also higher among U.S. teenagers than among adolescents in the dozen or so countries for which there are data.

Two major questions were suggested by these comparisons: Why are
teenage fertility and abortion rates so much higher in the United States
than in other developed countries? And, since most teenage pregnancies
in the United States are unintended, and their consequences often ad-

From Elise F. Jones et al., "Teenage Pregnancy in Developed Countries." Excerpted from
"Teenage Pregnancy in Developed Countries: Determinants and Policy Implications,"
Adapted with permission from *Family Planning Perspectives*, Vol. 17, No. 2, March/April 1985,
pp. 53–63. Notes and some text have been omitted.

verse, what can be learned from the experience of countries with lower adolescent pregnancy rates that might be useful for reducing the number of teenage conceptions in the United States? . . .

CASE STUDIES

The five countries selected for the case studies in addition to the United States—Canada, England and Wales, France, the Netherlands and Sweden—were chosen on the basis of three considerations: Their rates of adolescent pregnancy are considerably lower than that of the United States, and it was believed that sexual activity among young people is not very different; [and] the countries are similar to the United States in general cultural background and stage of economic development. . . .

Figures 1, 2 and 3 present, for the United States and each of the five countries, 1981 birthrates, abortion rates and pregnancy rates by single year of age. The exceptional position of the United States is immediately apparent. The U.S. teenage birthrates, as Figure 1 shows, are much higher than those of each of the five countries at every age, by a considerable margin. The contrast is particularly striking for younger teenagers. In fact, the maximum relative difference in the birthrate between the United

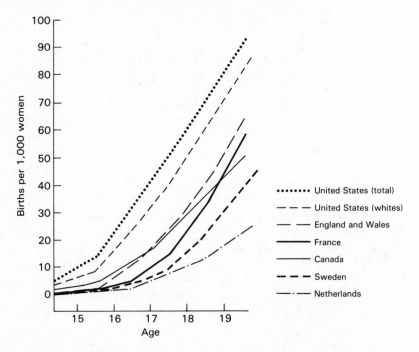

Figure 1 Births per 1,000 women under age 20, by woman's age, case-study countries, 1981

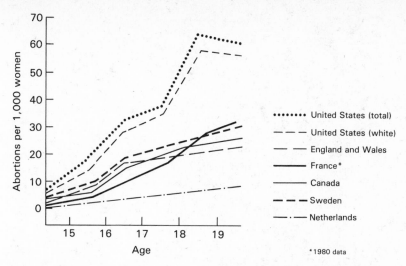

Figure 2 Abortions per 1,000 women, by woman's age, 1981

States and other countries occurs at ages under 15. With more than five births per 1,000 girls aged 14, the U.S. rate is around four times that of Canada, the only other country with as much as one birth per 1,000 girls of comparable age.

Teenagers from the Netherlands clearly have the lowest birthrate at every age. In 1981, Dutch women aged 19 were about as likely to bear a child as were American women aged 15–16. The birthrates are also very low in Sweden, especially among the youngest teenagers. Canada, England and Wales, and France compose an intermediate group. Birthrates are relatively high for Canadian girls aged 14–16, and rise gradually with age. The French rates are low among women up to age 18, but increase very sharply among older teenagers.

In 1981, as Figure 2 shows, the relative positions of the countries with respect to abortion are surprisingly close to the pattern observed for births. The United States has by far the highest rate, and the Netherlands, very much the lowest, at each age. French teenage abortion rates climb steeply with age,* while the Canadian curve is somewhat flatter. The rate for England and Wales rises relatively little after age 17. The chief difference between the patterns for births and abortions involves Sweden, which has age-specific abortion rates as high as, or higher than, those of any of the other countries except the United States.

The teenage pregnancy rates† necessarily follow the same pattern, as

*The relatively low rates among younger teenagers may be due to underreporting at those ages in France.

†Calculated as the sum of births and abortions experienced by women of a given age divided by the midyear estimate of the female population of that age.

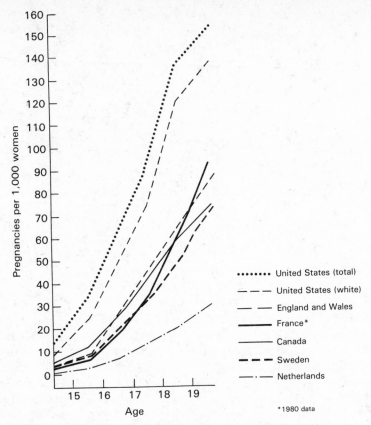

Figure 3 Pregnancy rates per 1,000 women by woman's age, 1981

Figure 3 reveals. The U.S. rates are distinctly higher than those of the other five countries; the Dutch rates are clearly lower. The French teenage pregnancy rates appear to be low among teenagers 16 and younger, and after that age, to be high. The reverse is true of Canada.

Thus, the six countries represent a rather varied experience. At one extreme is the United States, which has the highest rates of teenage birth, abortion and pregnancy. At the other stands the Netherlands, with very low levels on all three measures. Canada, France, and England and Wales are quite similar to one another. Sweden is notable for its low adolescent birthrates, although its teenage abortion rates are generally higher than those reported for any country except the United States. It is noteworthy that the United States is the only country where the incidence of teenage pregnancy has been increasing in recent years. The increase reflects a rise in the abortion rate that has not been completely offset by a decline in the birthrate. For both younger and older teenagers, the disparity between

the U.S. pregnancy rates and those for other countries increased somewhat between 1976 and 1981.

In the United States, the pregnancy rates among black teenagers are
sufficiently higher than those among whites to influence the rates for the
total adolescent population, even though in 1980, black teenagers represented only 14 percent of all 15–19-year-olds. Restriction of the international comparisons to pregnancy rates among white U.S. teenagers reduces the difference between the United States and other countries by
about one-fifth. However, the pregnancy rate for white U.S. adolescents
remains much higher than the rates for the teenage populations in the
other countries, as shown in the table [below]. What is more, some of the
other countries studied also have minority populations that appear to
have higher-than-average teenage reproductive rates (e.g., Caribbean
and Asian women in England), so that it would not be appropriate to
compare white U.S. rates with rates for the total adolescent population in
those countries.

A common approach was established for the study of the six countries
selected for close examination. Detailed information on teenage births and
abortions was collected, and a systematic effort was made to assemble
quantitative data on the proximate determinants of pregnancy—specifically, the proportion of teenagers cohabiting, rates of sexual activity
among those not living together and levels of contraceptive practice. In
addition, the investigators sought descriptive material on a number of
related topics: policies and practices regarding teenage access to contraceptive and abortion services, the delivery of those services, and the
formal and informal provision of sex education. Several aspects of teenage
life were explored to try to enhance understanding of certain social and
economic considerations that might influence the desire to bear children
and contraceptive practice. These include the proportions of young people in school, employment and unemployment patterns, the move away
from the family home, and government assistance programs for young
people and, particularly, for young unmarried mothers.

Teams of two investigators each visited Canada, England, France, the
Netherlands and Sweden for one week and conducted interviews with
government officials, statisticians, demographers and other researchers,

Pregnancy rate	15–19	15–17	18–19
U.S. total	96	62	144
U.S. white	83	51	129
England & Wales	45	27	75
France	43	19	79
Canada	44	28	68
Sweden	35	20	59
Netherlands	14	7	25

and family planning, abortion and adolescent health service providers. These interviews provided the opportunity to discuss attitudes and other less tangible factors that might not otherwise have been possible to document, and helped the investigators to identify other sources of data.

The five countries that were visited and the United States have much in common. All are highly developed nations, sharing the benefits and problems of industrialized modern societies. All belong essentially to the cultural tradition of northwestern Europe. All have reached an advanced stage in the process of demographic transition. Life expectancy is over 70 years for men and women of all the countries. Finally, all have fertility levels below that required for replacement. Yet, as Figure 3 demonstrates, teenage pregnancy rates in the six countries are quite diverse. However, the consistency of the six countries' positions in Figures 1 and 2 points to an immediate and important conclusion: The reason that adolescent birthrates are lower in the five other countries than they are in the United States is not more frequent resort to abortion in those countries. Where the birthrate is lower, the abortion rate also tends to be lower. Thus, the explanation of intercountry differences can focus on the determinants of pregnancy as the antecedent of both births and abortions.

The desire for pregnancy

Are the differences in adolescent birthrates due to the fact that in some countries, higher proportions of young women choose to become pregnant? The number of marital births per 1,000 teenagers is higher in the United States than in any other of the countries studied, and the proportion of teenagers who are married is at least twice as high in the United States as in the other countries (not shown). Data on teenagers' pregnancy intentions are available only for the United States. In 1980, 76 percent of marital teenage pregnancies and only nine percent of nonmarital teenage pregnancies were intended. On the assumption that all pregnancies ending in abortions are unintended, and that a large majority of nonmarital births are the result of unintended pregnancies (except in Sweden, where nonmarital childbearing has traditionally been free of social stigma), the distribution of pregnancy outcomes . . . sheds some light on the contribution of unintended pregnancy to the differences among the six countries. The combined fraction of all pregnancies accounted for by abortions and nonmarital births is approximately three-quarters in the United States and Canada, close to two-thirds in England and Wales and France, and only about one-half in the Netherlands. Thus, in England and Wales, France and the Netherlands, unintended pregnancy appears to constitute a smaller part of adolescent pregnancy than it does in the United States. Even more striking is the fact that the abortion rate alone in the United States is about as high as, or higher than, the overall teenage pregnancy rate in any of the other countries.

Exposure to the risk of pregnancy

Figure 4 illustrates some recent findings on levels of sexual activity (defined here as the proportion who have ever had intercourse) among teenagers in the six countries. The data should be interpreted cautiously, however, as there are numerous problems of comparability and quality. (Two potentially important aspects of sexual activity among adolescents— the number of sexual partners and frequency of intercourse—could not be examined because data on them were not available for most countries.) The most striking observation from the figure is that the differences in sexual activity among teenagers in the six countries do not appear to be nearly as great as the differences in pregnancy rates. Sexual activity is initiated considerably earlier in Sweden than elsewhere. By age 16, around one-third of all Swedish girls have had intercourse, and by age 18, four-fifths have done so. In Canada, by comparison, women may have had their first sexual experience later than the average for all six countries. At ages 16–17, only one out of five girls is sexually active. Smaller proportions of women are reported as having initiated sexual intercourse before the age of 18 in both Great Britain (England, Wales and Scotland) and France than in the United States. However, a rapid catch-up seems to take place, and in France the proportion of young women who have had

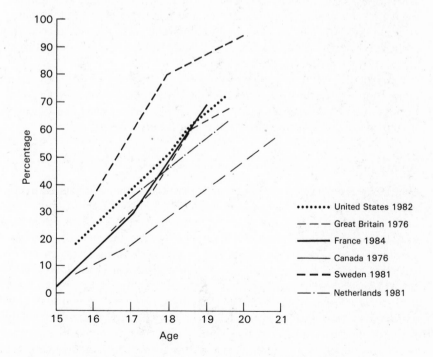

Figure 4 Percentage of women ever having had intercourse, by age

intercourse by the time they are 19 appears to be higher than that found in the United States. The median age at first intercourse is very similar for the United States, France, Great Britain and the Netherlands—something under age 18—and is about a year younger in Sweden, and may be about a year higher in Canada.

These data indicate that the variation in adolescent pregnancy rates shown in Figure 3 cannot, by and large, be explained by differences in levels of sexual experience. The examples of the Netherlands and Sweden make it clear that the postponement of first intercourse is not a prerequisite for the avoidance of early pregnancy. It does seem possible that reduced sexual exposure among younger Canadian teenagers is partly responsible for keeping their pregnancy rates relatively low. The difference in pregnancy rates between the Netherlands and Sweden may also be partly attributable to the older age at sexual initiation in the Netherlands.

Contraceptive use

The data on contraceptive practice . . . were, likewise, derived from surveys that differed widely in their design and approach to the issue. Nevertheless, it is possible to make some estimates of proportions using any contraceptive method, and proportions using the pill, at various ages. Contraceptive use among French teenagers is probably underestimated because condom use was not included in the published results of the survey. It is likely, therefore, that the United States has the lowest level of contraceptive practice among teenagers of all six countries.

In particular, pill use appears to be less widespread among U.S. teenagers than among those in the other countries. This difference suggests that American adolescents use less effective contraceptives to avoid accidental pregnancy, even if they are using a birth control method.

Access to contraceptive and abortion services

Contraceptive services appear to be most accessible to teenagers in England and Wales, the Netherlands and Sweden. In England and Wales and the Netherlands, those seeking care may choose to go either to a general practitioner (limited to their own family doctor in the Netherlands) or to one of a reasonably dense network of clinics. The Dutch clinic system is less extensive than the British one, but it is directed largely toward meeting the special needs of youth, whereas in England and Wales, there are relatively few clinics specially designed for young people. In Sweden, there are two parallel clinic systems, one consisting of the primary health care centers that serve every community, and the other consisting of a less complete network providing contraceptive care and related services to the school-age population.

Canada, France and the United States also have clinic systems, but these appear to be less accessible than those found in the other countries. (In France, however, the clinic system has expanded considerably since 1981.) The Canadian clinic system is uneven, with fairly complete coverage for adolescents in Ontario and Quebec, and scattered services elsewhere. The U.S. clinic network is reasonably accessible in a strictly geographic sense. Moreover, all family planning clinics receiving federal funds are required to serve adolescents. A basic drawback of the U.S. clinic system, however, is that it was developed as a service for the poor, and is often avoided by teenagers who consider clinics places where only welfare clients go.

Condoms are widely available in England and Wales, the Netherlands and Sweden. They not only are available from family planning clinics and pharmacies, but also are sold in supermarkets and other shops and in vending machines. In France and in many parts of Canada and the United States, condoms are less freely available.

Confidentiality was found to be an important issue in every country. Even where attitudes about sex are very open, as in the Netherlands and Sweden, the research teams were told that young people wish to keep their personal sex lives private. The need for confidential services is probably best met in Sweden, where doctors are specifically forbidden to inform parents about an adolescent's request for contraceptive services. Dutch doctors also are required to keep the visit confidential if the teenager requests it; and the services in Dutch clinics are entirely confidential. French official policy stipulates that clinic services for women under age 18 be absolutely confidential. Although the prescription of contraceptives to girls younger than 16 without a requirement that the parents be informed is now being legally contested in Britain, the practice was followed through the period covered by this study, and the British government is seeking to preserve confidentiality for young teenagers. In Canada and the United States, many individual doctors insist on parental consent before they will provide contraceptives to minors. However, most family planning clinics in Canada and the United States provide services to young women without any such restriction.

Like all medical care, contraceptive services, including supplies, are provided free of charge to young people in England and Wales and Sweden. Free services and supplies are available from clinics to French women under age 18; and for older teenagers, most of these expenses are reimbursable under social security. Contraceptive services provided by Dutch family doctors are covered under the national health insurance scheme, but the clinics charge a small fee. Until very recently, no charge was made to have a prescription filled at a pharmacy. In Canada, doctors' services are likewise covered by national medical insurance, and clinic services are free; but all patients except those on welfare have to pay for supplies obtained from pharmacies. The potential expense of obtaining contraceptive services in the United States varies considerably. Indigent teenagers from eligible families are able to get free care through Medicaid, and others do not have to pay anything because of individual clinic policy; otherwise, clinic fees are likely to be modest. On the other hand, consulting a private doctor usually entails appreciable expense, as does purchase of supplies at pharmacies.

An additional observation concerns the central role of the pill everywhere outside the United States. In each country, the research teams were told that the medical profession accepts the pill as a highly appropriate, usually *the most* appropriate method for adolescents. Moreover, a pelvic examination is not necessarily required before the pill can be prescribed in some of these countries. The emphasis on pill use emerged more clearly from the interviews than from the incomplete statistics on contraceptive use. By contrast, in the United States, there seems to be a good deal of ambivalence about pill use, both on the part of the medical profession and among potential young users. In the United States, medical protocol requires that a pelvic examination be performed before the pill can be prescribed, a procedure some young people find daunting. Whether justified or not, this requirement undoubtedly influences method selection among young women.

Postcoital contraceptive pills have been available at many family planning clinics in the United Kingdom for a number of years. Postcoital IUD insertion and oral contraceptives are available in the clinics run by both the Dutch and the French family planning associations. However, it is unlikely that these methods are sufficiently widely utilized to influence the birthrate appreciably. In Sweden, the morning-after pill is not yet permitted for general use. The federal Food and Drug Administration has not approved postcoital use of pills in the United States, and no plan exists to market them, but they are available in some college health clinics and rape treatment centers.

Geographically, abortion services are most easily accessible in the Netherlands and Sweden. Although services are theoretically in place throughout England and Wales and France, wide differences in the abortion rates by area are believed to be attributable to variation in the availability of abortion facilities. In all three countries, as in Canada and the United States, services are likely to be found in cities. In Canada, England and Wales, and France, abortions typically involve at least an overnight hospital stay.

In Sweden, there is no charge for abortion; Canadian women usually pay only a small portion of the cost; and abortions obtained under the national health service in Britain are also free. However, because of bureaucratic delays in the national health service, almost half of British women choose to pay for an abortion in the private sector. In the Netherlands, the cost of an abortion is borne by the patient but is not high. The same was true in France up until 1982, when the service became free. Most

U.S. women must pay for the abortion procedure themselves. For a second-trimester abortion, in particular, the cost may be substantial.

Sex education

Sweden has the distinction of being the first country in the world to have established an official sex education curriculum in its schools. The curriculum, which is compulsory and extends to all grade levels, gives special attention to contraception and the discussion of human and sexual relationships. Perhaps most important, there is a close, carefully established link in Sweden between the schools and contraceptive clinic services for adolescents. None of the other countries comes close to the Swedish model. Sweden established this link in 1975, following liberalization of the abortion law, because of concern that liberalized abortion access might otherwise result in a sharp rise in teenage abortion rates. In fact, adolescent abortion rates have declined dramatically since 1975, whereas the rates for adults have not changed much. (In the other countries studied, teenage abortion rates have *not* fallen during this period.) The Swedish authorities credit the combination of sex education with the adolescent clinic program for the decline.

In Canada, England and Wales, and the United States, school sex education is a community option, and it is essentially up to the local authorities, school principals or individual teachers to determine how much is taught and at what age. In England and Wales, however, there is a national policy favoring the inclusion of topics related to sex and family life in the curriculum, whereas there is no such national policy in Canada and the United States. French policy now mandates broad coverage of sexuality for all adolescents, although in practice, interpretation of this provision similarly devolves on local decision-makers.

The Netherlands is a case apart. Coverage of sex in the school curriculum is limited on the whole to the facts of reproduction in natural science classes. The Dutch government, nevertheless, encourages the teaching of contraception indirectly by subsidizing mobile educational teams that operate under the auspices of the private family planning association. At the same time, in recent years there has been an explosion of materials on contraception and other sex-related topics in the media, much of which is of a responsible and informative nature. Youth surveys show that knowledge of how to avoid pregnancy appears to be virtually universal.

In Sweden, sex education is completely accepted by the vast majority of parents, most of whom themselves had sex education while they were in school. Objections are confined to the immigrant community, for some of whom sex education represents a direct challenge to their own traditions. British law requires schools offering sex education to notify the parents. In the United States, many of the school districts that provide sex education give parents the option of excusing their children from such courses.

THE WIDER CONTEXT

Consideration was given to a number of other social, economic and political factors that appear to be related to the phenomenon of adolescent pregnancy. The investigators who visited the four European countries were struck by the fact that in those countries, the government, as the main provider of preventive and basic health services, perceives its responsibility in the area of adolescent pregnancy to be the provision of contraceptive services to sexually active teenagers. This commitment to action and the enunciation of an unambiguous social policy appear to be associated with a positive public climate surrounding the issue. Teenage childbearing is viewed, in general, to be undesirable, and broad agreement exists that teenagers require help in avoiding pregnancies and births.

Another aspect of government involvement in and commitment to contraceptive services for teenagers has to do with the rationale for such programs. In France, the Netherlands and Sweden, the decision to develop such services was strongly linked to the desire to minimize abortions among young people. In France and the Netherlands, for example, conservative medical groups had shown some reluctance to endorse the provision of contraceptives to young, unmarried women. Apparently, the alternative of rising abortion rates among teenagers helped to persuade them that such services were justified. In Sweden, the connection was made explicit by the government, and the 1975 law that liberalized abortion also laid the groundwork for the development of contraceptive services for young people, with the specific understanding that prevention of the need for abortion could best be achieved by putting safe, effective, confidential services within the reach of all teenagers. In the United States, in contrast, some powerful public figures reflect the view that the availability of contraceptive services acts as an incitement to premarital sexual activity and claim, therefore, that such services actually cause an increase in abortions.

The use of contraceptive services is obviously made simpler in the European countries, as in Canada, by the fact that medical services of all kinds are easily accessible through national health programs, and teenagers, in particular, grow up accustomed to using public health facilities or to visiting their local general practitioner as a matter of course. This combination of ease of accessibility and familiarity with the health care system probably serves to remove many of the social, psychological and financial barriers to contraceptive services experienced by young people in the United States.

There seems to be more tolerance of teenage sexual activity in the European countries visited than there is in most of the United States and in parts of Canada. Such acceptance of adolescent sexuality is unremarkable in a country like Sweden, with its long history of support for sexual freedom, and the absence there of taboos against premarital sex. However, such acceptance represents a considerable break with traditional standards in the Netherlands, France and, in Canada, Quebec. One reason for the more successful experience of the European countries may be that public attention was generally not directly focused on the morality of early sexual activity but, rather, was directed at a search for solutions to prevent increased teenage pregnancy and childbearing.

In the United States, sex tends to be treated as a special topic, and there is much ambivalence: Sex is romantic but also sinful and dirty; it is flaunted but also something to be hidden. This is less true in several European countries, where matter-of-fact attitudes seem to be more prevalent. Again, Sweden is the outstanding example, but the contrast with the United States was evident in most of the countries visited. Survey results tend to bear out this impression, although the questions asked are not directly comparable from country to country. For instance, in 1981, 76 percent of Dutch adults agreed with the statement that "sex is natural—even outside marriage," whereas in 1978, only 39 percent of Americans thought premarital sex was "not wrong at all." . . .

While the association between sexual conservatism and religiosity is not automatic, in the case of the United States the relationship appears to be relatively close. The proportion of the population who attend religious services and feel that God is important in their lives is higher in the United States than in the other case-study countries. Although England and Wales and Sweden have an established church, both countries are more secular in outlook than the United States. Moreover, in the Netherlands, France and Quebec Province, increasing secularization is believed to be an important aspect of recent broad social changes. Fundamentalist groups in America are prominent and highly vocal. Such groups often hold extremely conservative views on sexual behavior, of a sort rarely encountered in most of Western Europe. Both the nature and the intensity of religious feeling in the United States serve to inject an emotional quality into public debate dealing with adolescent sexual behavior that seems to be generally lacking in the other countries. It is notable that religiosity was found to correlate highly with adolescent fertility in the 37-country study, although the number of country observations was small.

Although all six countries included in the survey are parliamentary democracies, the nature of each country's political institutions differs, and there is considerable variation in the way in which public issues are developed and public policies formulated. The U.S. political system appears to foster divisiveness and confrontation at many levels of society, while these elements seem less salient a part of political life in the other countries. In addition, the United States is distinguished by the widespread use of private funds to mount political campaigns and create myriad pressure groups. While the American confrontational style may have its political uses, it makes the resolution of certain emotionally charged issues hard to achieve. Positions tend to become polarized, and the possibilities for creative compromise are narrowed. The most interesting country to contrast with the United States, in terms of political style, is probably the Netherlands. It has strong and diverse religious and political groups, but a complex range of formal and informal conventions exists to defuse and resolve ideological conflicts before these emerge into the open. As a result, through accommodation and negotiation, the Dutch administrations of all political tendencies have, in the past 15 years or so, been able to make birth control services available to teenagers without exacerbating divisions in the society.

Directly related to this issue is the fact that with the exception of Canada, the United States is a much larger country than any of the others, in terms of both its geographic and its population size. In smaller, more compact countries, where lines of communication are more direct, it is easier than in the United States to engage in a national debate that includes all the appropriate parties to the discussion. For example, in the early 1960s, debate within the Dutch medical community over the advisability of prescribing the pill to teenagers quickly resulted in a broad consensus. A similar process would be much harder to implement in the United States. As a result, informing concerned professionals about the terms of a debate may be as hard as keeping the general population up to date on any issue.

Another closely related facet of national life is the extent to which political and administrative power is concentrated in the national government. France is often cited as the epitome of a centralized state, and even the existence of two "nations" within England and Wales is a simple arrangement compared with the federal systems of Canada and the United States. Both countries have two-tiered government structures, with some powers delegated to the central government and some reserved to the provinces or states. This structure has two main consequences: First, major differences can develop within the country in policy-making. Second, the task of giving shape to social change, in terms of public policies and programs, becomes enormously complicated because of the many bureaucracies that must be dealt with and the sometimes indeterminate boundaries of their separate jurisdictions.

Many observers from different backgrounds have suggested that early teenage childbearing in the United States is a response to social anomie and to a sense of hopelessness about the future on the part of large numbers of young people growing up in poverty. In the course of the country visits, the investigators collected information on teenage education and employment patterns, in order to explore further the possible association between career and life opportunities for young people and their attitudes toward reproductive planning. The finding was that educational opportunities in the United States appear to be as great as, or greater than, those in other countries, except, possibly, Sweden. In

Sweden, about 85 percent of young people aged 18–19 are pursuing academic or vocational schooling. In Canada and France, most young people leave school at around 18, as they do in the United States, although a higher proportion of U.S. students go on to college. However, in the Netherlands, only about half of girls are still in school at age 18, while in England and Wales, the majority of young people end their full-time schooling at age 16.

The employment situation is difficult to compare or assess, since definitions of labor-force participation and unemployment differ from country to country. The most that can be concluded is that unemployment among the young is considered a very serious problem everywhere, and young people themselves are universally uneasy on this score. The chances of getting and keeping a satisfying or well-paying job do not appear to be worse in the United States than in other countries. To a greater extent than in the United States, however, all the other countries offer assistance to ease the problem, in the form of youth training, unemployment benefits and other kinds of support.

It is often suggested that in the United States, the availability of public assistance for unmarried mothers creates a financial incentive for poor women, especially the young, to bear children outside of marriage. Yet, all the countries studied provide extensive benefits to poor mothers that usually include medical care, food supplements, housing and family allowances. In most cases, the overall level of support appears to be more generous than that provided under the Aid to Families with Dependent Children program in the United States. Benefits in the other countries tend to be available regardless of women's marital or reproductive status, although in England and Wales and in France, at least, special supplementary benefit programs for poor single mothers also exist. In those countries, however, the existence of considerable financial support for out-of-wedlock childbearing does not appear to stimulate adolescent birthrates or explain the differences between their rates and the U.S. rates.

The final difference between the United States and the other countries that may be relevant to teenage pregnancy concerns the overall extent and nature of poverty. Poverty to the degree that exists in the United States is essentially unknown in Europe. Regardless of which way the political winds are blowing, Western European governments are committed to the philosophy of the welfare state. The Dutch and the Swedes have been especially successful in achieving reasonably egalitarian societies, but even in England and Wales and France, the contrast between those who are better off and those who are less well off is not so great as it is in the United States. In every country, when respondents were pressed to describe the kind of young woman who would be most likely to bear a child, the answer was the same: adolescents who have been deprived, emotionally as well as economically, and who unrealistically seek gratification and fulfillment in a child of their own. Such explanations are also given in the United States, but they tend to apply to a much larger proportion of people growing up in a culture of poverty. . . .

POLICY IMPLICATIONS

. . . [M]any widely held beliefs about teenage pregnancy cannot explain the large differences in adolescent pregnancy rates found between the United States and other developed countries: Teenagers in these other countries apparently are *not* too immature to use contraceptives consistently and effectively; the level and availability of welfare services does *not* seem correlated with higher adolescent fertility; teenage pregnancy rates are *lower* in countries where there is *greater* availability of contraceptive services and of sex education; levels of adolescent sexual activity in the United States are not very different from those in countries with much *lower* teenage pregnancy rates; although the teenage pregnancy rate of American blacks is much higher than that of whites, this difference does not explain the gap between the pregnancy rates in the United States and the other countries; teenage unemployment appears to be at least as serious a problem in all the countries studied as it is in the United States; and American teenagers have more, or at least as much, schooling as those in most of the countries studied. The other case-study countries have more extensive public health and welfare benefit systems, and they do not have so extensive and economically deprived an underclass as does the United States.

Clearly, then, it *is* possible to achieve lower teenage pregnancy rates even in the presence of high rates of sexual activity, and a number of countries have done so. Although no single factor has been found to be responsible for the differences in adolescent pregnancy rates between the United States and the other five countries, is there anything to be learned from these countries' experience that can be applied to improve the situation in the United States?

A number of factors that have been discussed here, of course, are not easily transferable, or are not exportable at all, to the United States: Each of the other five case-study countries is considerably smaller, and all but Canada are more compact than the United States—making rapid dissemination of innovations easier; their populations are less heterogeneous ethnically (though not so homogeneous as is commonly assumed—most have substantial minority nonwhite populations, usually with higher-than-average fertility); religion, and the influence of conservative religious bodies, is less pervasive in the other countries than it is in the United States; their governments tend to be more centralized; the provision of wide-ranging social and welfare benefits is firmly established, whether the country is led by parties labeled conservative or liberal; income distribution is less unequal than it is in the United States; and constituencies that oppose contraception, sex education and legal abortion are not so powerful or well funded as they are in the United States.

Some factors associated with low pregnancy rates that *are*, at least theoretically, transferable receive varying levels of emphasis in each country. For example, school sex education appears to be a much more important factor in Sweden than it is in the other countries: a high level of exposure to contraceptive information and sex-related topics through the media is prominent in the Netherlands; condoms are more widely available in England, the Netherlands and Sweden. Access to the pill by teenagers is probably easiest in the Netherlands.

On the other hand, although initiation of sexual activity may begin slightly earlier in the United States than in the other countries (except for Sweden), none of the others have developed official programs designed to discourage teenagers from having sexual relations—a program intervention that is now advocated and subsidized by the U.S. government. The other countries have tended to leave such matters to parents and churches or to teenagers' informed judgments.

By and large, of all the countries studied, Sweden has been the most active in developing programs and policies to reduce teenage pregnancy. These efforts include universal education in sexuality and contraception; development of special clinics—closely associated with the schools— where young people receive contraceptive services and counseling; free, widely available and confidential contraceptive and abortion services; widespread advertising of contraceptives in all media; frank treatment of sex; and availability of condoms from a variety of sources. It is notable that Sweden has *lower* teenage pregnancy rates than have all of the countries examined, except for the Netherlands, although teenagers begin intercourse at earlier ages in Sweden. It is also noteworthy that Sweden is the only one of the countries observed to have shown a rapid decline in teenage abortion rates in recent years, even after its abortion law was liberalized.

The study findings point to several approaches observed in countries other than Sweden that also might help reduce teenage pregnancy rates in the United States. These include upgrading the family planning clinic system to provide free or low-cost contraceptive services to *all* teenagers who want them, and publicizing the fact that these services are not limited to the poor; establishment of special adolescent clinics, including clinics associated with schools, to provide confidential contraceptive services as part of general health care; encouraging local school districts to provide comprehensive sex education programs, where possible, closely integrated with family planning clinic services; relaxation of restrictions on distribution and advertising of nonprescription contraceptives, especially the condom; dissemination of more realistic information about the health benefits, as well as the health risks, of the pill; and approval of the use of postcoital methods.

In sum, increasing the legitimacy and availability of contraception and sex education (in its broadest sense) is likely to result in declining teenage pregnancy rates. That has been the experience of many countries of Western Europe, and there is no reason to think that such an approach would not also be successful in the United States.

Admittedly, application of any of the program and policy measures that appear to have been effective in other countries is more difficult in the United States nationally, where government authority is far more diffused. But their application may, in fact, be as easy or easier in some states and communities. Efforts need to be directed not just to the federal executive branch of government, but to Congress, the courts, state legislatures, local authorities and school superintendents and principals—as well as to families and such private-sector and charitable enterprises as insurance companies, broadcast and publishing executives, church groups and youth-serving agencies.

Among the most striking of the observations common to the four European countries included in the six-country study is the degree to which the governments of those countries, whatever their political persuasion, have demonstrated the clear-cut will to reduce levels of teenage pregnancy. Pregnancy, rather than adolescent sexual activity itself, is identified as the major problem. Through a number of routes, with varying emphasis on types of effort, the governments of those countries have made a concerted, public effort to help sexually active young people to avoid unintended pregnancy and childbearing. In the United States, in contrast, there has been no well-defined expression of political will. Political and religious leaders, particularly, appear divided over what their primary mission should be: the eradication or discouragement of sexual activity among young unmarried people, or the reduction of teenage pregnancy through promotion of contraceptive use.

American teenagers seem to have inherited the worst of all possible worlds regarding their exposure to messages about sex: Movies, music, radio and TV tell them that sex is romantic, exciting, titillating; premarital sex and cohabitation are visible ways of life among the adults they see and hear about; their own parents or their parents' friends are likely to be divorced or separated but involved in sexual relationships. Yet, at the same time, young people get the message good girls should say no. Almost nothing that they see or hear about sex informs them about contraception or the importance of avoiding pregnancy. For example, they are more likely to hear about abortions than about contraception on the daily TV soap opera. Such messages lead to an ambivalence about sex that stifles communication and exposes young people to increased risk of pregnancy, out-of-wedlock births and abortions. . . .

23

Children at Risk

Marian Wright Edelman

Parents generally accept and even cherish the fact that each child has his or her unique personality, likes and dislikes, strengths and weaknesses, and needs. Within the family these individual differences are accepted. Most parents attempt to respond to each child's needs and welcome the child's special contributions to the life of the family. At the broader level of public policy, however, the uniqueness of each child is not recognized. Public policies, to a large degree, have yet to acknowledge that every child is special and important, not just to his or her family but also to the country. Both individual children and groups of children—by virtue of their race, family income, or other circumstances—have special needs that society must recognize and address.

Despite the inadequacy of existing public policies to meet the varied needs of children at risk, there has been some progress in defining the characteristics of children with special needs and in devising strategies for helping them. More than two decades of research, data collection, judicial activity, and restructuring state and national legislation and budgets have at least helped identify the types of children who are special and who, without a national commitment to help them, are likely to fall through the cracks to a life of poverty. The list of children at risk includes minority children, poor children, teenage parents and their children, the physically or emotionally handicapped, abused and neglected children and others in the child welfare system, and the homeless.

From Proceedings of the Academy of Political Science, Vol. 37, No. 2, 1989. Reprinted by permission.

As society changes and analyses become more sophisticated and more perceptive, the list both changes and grows. Twenty-five years ago it would probably not have included abused and neglected children. And although the child welfare system has long targeted orphans and young vagrants among those with special needs, as recently as 1985 the list would probably not have included homeless children in the sense that they are defined now—those who are still with their parents but in family units that are consigned to a nomadic, often squalid existence on the streets and in shelters that can never be a substitute for a stable family home.

But one must not oversimplify. The problem with making lists is that many children belong to several categories, increasing their jeopardy of falling into the group that has become a synonym for hopelessness—the underclass.

THE IMPORTANCE OF EVERY CHILD

The first high-school graduating class of the twenty-first century entered the first grade in September 1988. They are the country's future workers, parents, college students, taxpayers, soldiers, and leaders. Yet millions of them are already beginning to lose hope:

- One in five of them (a total of 12.4 million) is poor.
- One in five is at risk of becoming a teenage parent.
- One in five is nonwhite; among nonwhites, two in five are poor.
- One in six has no health insurance.
- One in seven is at risk of dropping out of school.
- One in two has a mother in the labor force, but only a minority have safe, affordable, quality child care.

No society that considers itself civilized or moral can condone the victimization of millions of children by discrimination, poverty, and neglect. Help should be extended to children not only because of moral obligations but also because of faith in the future of society, its progress, its values, and its traditions and because children should have every possible opportunity, as they mature, to participate in the society and contribute to it. But as the last decade of the twentieth century approaches, there are also compelling demographic reasons to reject and reverse these trends. In addition to the moral motivation of alleviating human suffering, one must add the motivation of national economic self-interest.

Because of dramatic social changes in the past century, parents no longer expect their own children to support them directly when they are elderly. Rather, they rely on Social Security, Medicaid and Medicare, tax-supported pensions, and retirement benefits financed by employers.

Many will require contributions to these programs from the next generation as a whole and from that generation's children. It is therefore in
everyone's self-interest that today's children—and their children—are
healthy, educated, productive, and compassionate. Yet the society is
aging, and the number of children and youths in relation to other age
groups in the population is declining.

The William T. Grant Foundation Commission on Work, Family and
Citizenship, which is examining the status and future of American youth,
documented these trends in its June 1987 publication, "American Youth:
A Statistical Snapshot." Among the points made by the commission:

> The number of American youth is shrinking dramatically. Between 1980
> and 1996, our youth population, ages 15–25, is expected to fall 21 per-
> cent, from 43 to 34 million. Young people as a percentage of the nation's
> population will also decline from 18.8 to 13 percent. . . .
>
> These falling numbers will drastically alter the characteristics of the
> nation's labor pool, higher education enrollments. . . .
>
> The problems facing minority youth will take on even greater impor-
> tance as they account for larger and larger proportions of America's
> youth population. . . .

Children are not only a precious resource, then, but an increasingly
scarce one. Until recently, America's youth population has been relatively
plentiful, allowing the society to survive and the economy to grow,
despite the waste of many young lives through society's neglect. That
margin for error no longer exists. The ratio of workers to retirees has
shrunk and will continue to shrink in the coming decades. And one in
three of the new potential workers is a member of a minority group.

MINORITY CHILDREN

For many blacks, recent years have been good. Black per-capita income is
at an all-time high, black purchasing power—now at $200 billion a year—
exceeds the gross national product of Australia and New Zealand combined, and there are more black elected officials than ever. Blacks head the
House Budget Committee of the U.S. Congress, the Ford Foundation, and
the marketing activities of the Xerox Corporation, and they represent the
United States on the Olympic Committee. These are important, tangible
gains of the civil rights movement. But there is another black community
for which these have not been good years—a community, in fact, where
life is getting worse.

Today, black children are more likely than in 1980 to be born into
poverty, to have been deprived of early prenatal care, to have a single
mother or no employed parent, to be unemployed as teenagers, and not
to go to college. They are twice as likely as white children to be born
prematurely, to suffer low birth weights, to live in substandard housing,

or to die in the first year of life. Black children are three times as likely as white children to be poor, to live in a female-headed family, to have no parent employed, or to be murdered between five and nine years of age. They are five times as likely as white children to rely on welfare and nine times as likely to live with a parent who has never married.

While black children's plight is the worst, the fast-growing population of Hispanic children in this country also suffers much higher rates of poverty than their white counterparts. The U.S. Bureau of the Census reported the following poverty rates for 1987: for all American children, 20.6 percent; for white children, 15.6 percent; for Hispanic children, 39.8 percent; and for black children, 48.8 percent.

Some other key indicators further tell the story of problems faced by minority children. For example, National Center for Health Statistics data on infant mortality in 1985 reveal that for all races, per 1,000 live births, there are 10.6 deaths; for whites, 9.3; for blacks, 18.2; and for nonwhite infants, 15.8. Other data show that Hispanic youths as well as blacks are less likely to be employed than whites and are more likely to become teenage parents than their white counterparts.

THE SPREAD OF POVERTY

The tide of misery that poverty breeds and that blacks have borne disproportionately throughout history has now enveloped a critical mass of white American families and children. Thirty-three million individuals— one-seventh of all Americans—are now poor as a result of economic recession, followed by slow growth, structural changes in the economy, declining real wage rates, federal tax and budget policies that favor the rich at the expense of the poor, and changing family demographics. One in every five American children lives in a female-headed household, and one in four will be dependent on welfare at some point in his or her lifetime.

Most Americans now realize that poverty is not just the result of personal inadequacy, laziness, and unworthiness, despite some national leaders' attempts to portray the poor as culpable. Iowa farmers, Detroit autoworkers, Youngstown steel workers, South Carolina textile workers, and small-business people have lost their livelihoods as a result of the economic dislocations afflicting the United States. They have been surprised to find themselves in unemployment lines or bread lines or new jobs paying a fraction of their former earnings. Of those 32.5 million poor, more than 13 million are children. Children make up the poorest age group in America. Nearly half of black children, almost two-fifths of Hispanic children, and nearly one-seventh of white children in the United States are poor. These figures are appalling.

For a growing number of Americans, moreover, working does not mean escaping poverty. The ranks of the working poor have also grown. In 1979 a parent working full-time at the minimum wage earned enough to lift a family of three above the poverty line. By 1986, a full-time, minimum-wage job yielded a paycheck equivalent to only 75 percent of the poverty-level income for a family of three and 61 percent of the poverty-level income for a family of four. (The poverty-level income for a family of four in 1986 was $11,203.) In 1986 more than a million Americans supported families on full-time, year-round jobs that did not raise them out of poverty. And fully half of the country's 7 million heads of poor households worked at least part-time in 1986.

Young parents and their children have been squeezed by changes in the economy and the job market in the past decade and a half. Young families have borne almost all of the income losses caused by the resulting turmoil. The median income for all American families declined by only 1 percent between 1973 and 1986. Among young families (those headed by persons under age thirty), however, median income dropped by 14 percent during this period. Young families with children suffered the greatest income loss—nearly 26 percent.

Not surprisingly, poverty among young families and their children has also increased far more rapidly than for older American families. The poverty rate for all young families nearly doubled between 1973 and 1986, rising from 12 percent to 22 percent. The chances of being poor are even greater for young families with children—their poverty rate jumped from 16 percent in 1973 to 30 percent in 1986. In contrast, the poverty rate for older families with children increased more gradually, from 9 percent to 13 percent. As a result of the growing economic plight of young families, one-third of all poor children in the United States now live in young families. And among the youngest families—those headed by persons under age twenty-five—a staggering 54 percent of all children are poor.

For a child of poverty, the most ordinary needs—from health care to housing—become extraordinary. Testifying in April 1988 before the U.S. House of Representatives' Select Committee on Children, Youth, and Families, twelve-year-old Yvette Diaz of New York City painted a vivid picture of the assaults on mind and body that are an integral part of daily life for her and other residents of the Hotel Martinique for homeless families. She, her mother, her sisters ages seven and nine, and her brother age three went to live in the Martinique "because my aunt's house burned down and we didn't have any place to live," she testified. "I don't like the hotel because there is always a lot of trouble there. I don't go down into the street to play because there is no place to play. . . . The streets are dangerous, with all kinds of sick people who are on drugs or crazy. My mother is afraid to let me go downstairs. Only this Saturday, my friend, the security guard at the hotel, Mr. Santiago, was killed on my floor. The blood is still on the walls and on the floor. . . . We can't cook in the apartment. The hotel warned us that if we are caught cooking in the rooms, we could be sent to a shelter."

ADOLESCENT PARENTS

Teenage pregnancy is both a cause and a consequence of poverty. In recent years a huge new group of children has been added to the list of those with special needs—adolescent parents.

A young woman testified before the House Select Committee about her life: "I would like for you to meet Robin. She is 15 years old and alone, out of school and married at 16. By the age of 21 she has no friends or family, no education, no skills. . . . She is basically alone. I guess Robin never would have been able to have seen the grave mistakes she made, if she had not been seeing her children reliving her own mistakes. . . . I am Robin." She described as eloquently as anyone could the frustrating viciousness of the cycle of teenage pregnancy, poverty, and dependency.

Adolescent pregnancy is a crisis among all races and classes of American youth today. Each day almost 2,700 girls under the age of twenty get pregnant and 1,300 give birth. Every year a million teenage girls—one in ten—get pregnant. Although these statistics include a disproportionate number of poor, minority, and urban teenagers, two-thirds of those who give birth each year are white, two-thirds do not live in big cities, and two-thirds come from families with above-poverty incomes.

Adolescent pregnancy is a crisis not because teenage birthrates are rising, as is widely believed. (In fact, both the proportion and number of adolescents giving birth generally have fallen since 1970.) It is a crisis because the society is changing and young parents are tragically unprepared to deal with the consequences of early birth in contemporary America. Both the number and rate of births to teenagers who are unmarried are rising, thereby increasing the likelihood of poverty for two generations of children—young mothers and their children. In 1950, 15.4 percent of these births were to unmarried teenagers. By 1970, the proportion had doubled. By 1986, it had doubled again—to 60.8 percent.

The costs of adolescent parenthood are enormous, and they are magnified if the mother is unmarried. Forty percent of teenage girls who drop out of school do so because of pregnancy or marriage. Only half of the young women who become parents before the age of eighteen complete high school by the time they reach their midtwenties. Furthermore, the average lifetime earnings of a woman who has dropped out of school are roughly half those of a woman who has graduated from college. In 1986, more than four out of five children living in families headed by young females were poor.

An eighteen- or nineteen-year-old man can no longer earn enough to support a family, and the average single mother of any age has never earned a decent wage in this country. Yet the birth of a child to a teenager often means that the mother will not complete her education and will be unable to secure any employment at all, let alone a job that pays well enough to support the family.

Often the father of a child born to a teenage girl is in his early twenties. As discussed in the previous section, the erosion of employment opportunities and wage levels makes it impossible for even the young men who find work to earn enough to support their families.

This trend is particularly disturbing because earnings losses among young men reduce the likelihood that young Americans will marry and form two-parent families. Research indicates a connection between unemployment or low earnings and marital instability and between joblessness and delayed marriage. The decline in real earnings and the resulting drop in marriage rates have been most severe among high-school dropouts and graduates who do not go on to college—the young people who have tended to marry and bear children earliest. While a reversal of recent earnings losses would not restore marriage rates to their previous levels, more adequate earnings would substantially increase the proportion of young adults who would be willing and able to form stable families.

CHILDREN OF ADOLESCENT PARENTS

As Robin suggested in her congressional testimony, the babies born to adolescent parents often seem condemned to repeat the mistakes and suffering of their parents. Shawn Grant, a member of a gang in Philadelphia, grew up in a single-parent household. When he testified before the House Select Committee on Children, Youth and Families, he was on intensive probation for committing a robbery. "My father has had little contact with me since I was one year old," he told the committee. "In my neighborhood, a lot of negative things go on. People sell drugs; a lot of the gang members' parents use drugs and often these guys do not see their parents. . . . When I was young I use [sic] to worry about my father. I also resented his not being involved in my life. Now I do not care. However, I think that I would not have become involved in a gang if I had had a job and if my father had had a relationship with me."

Babies born to adolescent, single parents have two strikes against them. First, they enter life with particularly high risks to their health and well-being. Babies born to single mothers are five times more likely to be poor than those born to two-parent families. Only 53 percent of all infants born to teenagers in 1985 had mothers who began prenatal care in the first three months of pregnancy. More than one in eight—twice the national average—had a mother who received either no prenatal care at all or none until the last trimester. Babies born to women who receive no prenatal care are three times more likely to die in their first year of life than infants whose mothers received comprehensive care. Children born to teenagers are also more likely than other children to grow up in poverty. Young families are two and a half times more likely than the average American family to have incomes below the poverty line.

Children who grow up in persistently poor families are far more likely to face inadequate nutrition, housing, and health care, not to be enrolled in preschool programs, to enter school less prepared than their more advantaged peers, and to be held back one or more grades. They are also more likely to drop out of school with seriously deficient academic skills that prevent them from competing in the labor market and gaining access to postsecondary education and training programs. Like Shawn, children of poor single parents may end up in a gang, committing crimes, feeling that they would prefer another kind of life but having no idea how to find it. In this way the cycle of poverty that begins with limited employment opportunities, low wages, too-early pregnancies, and low marriage rates among today's teenagers and young adults will—if society fails to intervene—be repeated and perhaps amplified in the next generation.

CHILDREN WITH OTHER SPECIAL NEEDS

While most children grow up safe, secure, and emotionally sound, a sizable minority do not. Millions of American children and adolescents endure abuse or neglect in their parental homes; others are awaiting permanent homes while in foster care; and many have unmet emotional needs. Judicial decisions and federal statutes have given handicapped children a right to education and provided a framework for state efforts to address the complex needs of children who are abused, neglected, emotionally disturbed, or in foster care. Current resources and systems, however, remain grossly inadequate to meet their growing needs.

Reports of child abuse and neglect have increased steadily since 1976, with more than a 90 percent national increase between 1981 and 1986. More than three-fifths of the states reported to the House Select Committee on Children, Youth, and Families in 1986 that the deteriorating economic conditions faced by many families were a primary contributor to the increases in child abuse and neglect since 1981. While reports of abuse and neglect escalated between 1981 and 1985, federal resources for prevention and treatment fell further and further behind, and child protective service agencies have been overwhelmed.

About 275,000 children and adolescents live in foster-family homes, group homes, residential treatment centers, and other institutions. While some have been abused or neglected, others enter care because their parents are unable to meet the demands of their disabilities or behavior problems. Still others enter because their families are homeless or too poor to support their children.

The group is varied in age and background. About one-half are minority children, who are represented disproportionately in care in many states and who tend to be in care longer, waiting for permanent homes. While youths thirteen and older account for about 46 percent of the children in foster care, very young children are also entering the system in greater numbers in some communities. Moreover, children in foster care are increasingly reported to have more special needs, such as serious medical and emotional problems, compared with the foster-care population in the past.

The foster-care system is severely challenged by increasing poverty and homelessness; the use of crack, which results in births of infants at high risk of medical and development problems; and the spread of acquired immune deficiency syndrome (AIDS), which requires more intensive supports for the children and families who are affected. Although many states report fewer children in foster care, several states—particularly those with large urban centers—report that the number of children in care is going up, not down. And virtually every state and region agrees that children in care today pose greater challenges to the foster-care system's resources. Shortages of foster homes (partly due to inadequate community support and low reimbursement rates) have propelled some states to increase out-of-state placements, a practice that impedes the reuniting of families and hampers the home state's ability to monitor the quality of care. The foster-care system also lacks the necessary resources to help children make a successful transition when they leave care. Of special concern are the tens of thousands of youths who "age out" of the system in their late teens and have no family members or friends to whom they can turn.

An estimated 7.5 million to 9.5 million children in this country have emotional or other problems that require mental-health services. Of this group, 70 to 80 percent do not receive the care they need. Even among the approximately 3 million children who suffer from serious emotional disturbances, the majority go without proper treatment. Today many of these children are being helped in a piecemeal fashion, or not at all.

Various state mental-health systems have cited growing demands and continuing deficiencies similar to those facing child-welfare agencies: the increasing severity of the problems presented by disturbed children and their families, overreliance on institutional settings and a lack of sufficient in-home and community-based support programs, the transition needs of youths aging out of mental-health programs, and the inadequate number of professionals trained to address the mental-health needs of children and adolescents.

SAVING THE CHILDREN

If it is to save itself, America must save its children. Millions of children are not safe physically, educationally, economically, or spiritually. Many of the special children described in this essay are poor or members of minority groups. On average, they are less safe than their white, more affluent counterparts. But all are at risk spiritually. The common good, truth-telling, and moral example have become devalued commodities in the United States. And all children are in danger of being corrupted by their exposure to the values reflected by the Michael Deavers, Ivan Boeskys, and Jim and Tammy Bakkers of the world. The poor black youths who shoot up drugs on street corners and the rich white youths who do the same thing in their mansions share a common disconnectedness from any hope and purpose, sense of community, and shared strivings. What one social observer has called the bug of "affluenza" has indeed bitten thousands of youths who are growing up in families that offer everything that money can buy but somehow not enough to create a purpose in life. What is done collectively to save this generation will have a major impact on how today's children and youths perform as tomorrow's adults.

SOLUTIONS DO EXIST

Despite the length and dreariness of the litany of special children and their problems, solutions are at hand. One absolutely essential avenue to pursue to save the next generation—and a generation yet unborn—is to launch a full-scale campaign to prevent teenage pregnancy.

This essay has shown how poverty and lack of education reinforce a cycle that results in underemployment or unemployment and a declining rate of marriage among young people, even when they have children. A society in which growing up with a single parent—and, worse, one who does not have the maturity, education, or resources to cope—is dangerously close to becoming the norm.

The Children's Defense Fund has been engaged since 1983 in a major initiative to prevent adolescent pregnancy. Its top priority is to prevent a teenager's first pregnancy. The second is to ensure that teenagers who have already had a child do not have a second one. The third priority is to make sure that teenage mothers get adequate prenatal care so that prematurity, low birth weight, and birth defects are not added to the hurdles already awaiting their babies as they enter this world. More specifically, it has identified six areas that are extremely important in bolstering the motivation and capacity of teenagers to prevent too-early pregnancy:

1. Education and strong basic skills. Youths who are behind a grade or have poor basic skills or poor attendance are at high risk of early parenthood. Low-income and minority teenagers have higher rates of school failure.

2. Work-related skills and exposure to work. Teenagers who perform poorly in school and become parents often have poor work-related skills and, because of lack of exposure to workplace norms, behave in ways unacceptable to employers.
3. Community service, sports, and other nonacademic opportunities for success. The potential for self-sufficiency is related to self-esteem and self-perception. For youths who are not doing well in school, nonacademic avenues for success are crucial.
4. Family life education and life planning.
5. Comprehensive adolescent health services.
6. A national and community climate that makes the prevention of teenage pregnancy a leading priority.

A decent society cannot condone any increase in child poverty, let alone the increase from 10 million to more than 12 million children between 1979 and 1987. And child poverty is not just a widening problem—it is a rapidly deepening one, as poor children become poorer.

An effective national effort must be launched to address the root cause of child poverty—inadequate family incomes. This effort requires progress on several fronts:

• Restore a strong economic base by continuing to pursue full employment, investing in productivity improvements for young workers, raising the federal minimum wage, and expanding the earned income tax credit.
• Respond more effectively to the new realities of a rapidly changing labor market by enacting the Act for Better Child Care Services, extending basic health-insurance coverage to all low-income families, and strengthening child-support enforcement and safety-net programs for poor families.
• Prepare today's children and youths for productive roles in tomorrow's economy by expanding the successful Head Start, Chapter 1, and Job Corps programs, increasing investments to help youths who are not college-bound enter the job market, and bolstering college enrollments among poor and minority youth. Only these things will provide the strong foundation that will make it possible for any child—no matter how special, no matter how many problems he or she may have—to become a proud, productive member of society.

In the long term, a service system must be established that can respond to the individual needs of children and families, regardless of the label assigned them by particular public agencies. The goal should be to develop a single system that serves vulnerable children and adolescents and has the capacity to assess, mobilize, and utilize all the resources necessary to meet their multiple needs. Such a system must have a staff that is appropriately qualified and compensated. The staff must have a system for fully addressing the needs of children and youths who need help as well as a continuum of services and other resources that can meet needs as they are indentified.

A CALL FOR ACTION

If current trends continue, a disproportionate number of children will grow up poor, uneducated, and untrained at the very time that society will need all of our young to be healthy, educated, and productive. Despite a national debt of $2.7 trillion (which children did not cause) and despite uncertainties in the national and international economies, now is the time to invest in building healthy children, self-sufficient youth and economically secure families.

Children are poor because the country has lost its moral bearings. Perverse national values, hidden behind profamily, "traditional values" rhetoric, have been manifested in budget decisions that have cut billions of dollars each year since 1980 from survival programs for poor children and families. They are creating a new American apartheid between rich and poor, white and black, old and young, corporation and individual, military and domestic needs—and abandoned millions of poor children to the furies of hunger, homelessness, abuse, and even death.

What has been missing is the moral and political urgency required to make children and families a leading national priority. The willingness to protect children is a moral litmus test of a compassionate society. If the Bush administration joins that battle, it can help make the United States a safe place for children.

24

Addressing the Nation's Child Care Crisis: The School of the Twenty-First Century

Edward F. Zigler, Ph.D.

I n 1970, the White House Conference on Children voted child care as the most serious problem facing America's families. That was two decades ago. Despite some noble attempts to deal with the matter (namely the 1971 Comprehensive Child Development Act, the Child Care Act of 1979, and the 100-plus child care bills considered by the 100th Session of Congress in 1988), our nation has not come a single step closer to providing a solution. This "serious problem" has grown so pervasive that it is now called America's child care crisis.

And a crisis it is. One brief look at current demographics will demonstrate the magnitude of the child care problem. Today in America, roughly 70% of the mothers of school-age children are in the out-of-home work force; among preschoolers, that number is approximately 60% (Shank, 1988). Most startling is the fact that slightly over half of the mothers of infants under one year of age hold jobs outside the home (Bureau of Labor Statistics, 1987) Our best prognostication is that by the year 1995, about three-quarters of all children will have a working mother (Hofferth & Phillips, 1987). What does this mean in terms of the numbers of children? If current trends continue, in 1995 there will be 14.6 million preschool children and 37.4 million school-age children who have mothers working outside the home (Hofferth & Phillips).

From *The American Journal of Orthopsychiatry,* Vol. 59, No. 4, October, 1989.

Social scientists and economists have offered much discussion and analysis as to why women are flocking to the job market. Still, there is no question that the majority of women work primarily for economic reasons. In 1989, the Select Committee on Children, Youth, and Families reported that in two-parent homes, 68% of employed mothers had husbands who earned $15–19,000 annually. Of the working mothers of preschoolers, 60% were married to men earning less than $25,000. Clearly, both husband and wife must now work to provide their family a decent standard of living.

For single-parent families, which are almost always headed by women, the situation is even more desperate. In 1986, approximately one-fifth of all single mothers had incomes below *half* the adjusted poverty line (i.e., below $3,974 for a family of three). Some 40% of these families had incomes below the adjusted poverty line *(Select Committee on Children, Youth, and Families, 1988)*. Today in the United States, approximately one in four children live with only one parent *(U.S. Bureau of the Census, 1986)*; among our black citizens, that number is more than half. These single mothers have no choice other than go to work, go on welfare, or starve. For them, child care is a particularly pressing need that will determine their children's security and future. One final statistic: it is estimated that 80% of women in the work force are of childbearing age, and that 93% of these women will become pregnant sometime during their careers *(Select Committee on Children, Youth, and Families, 1984)*.

These numbers leave no doubt that child care is a real or potential problem for the majority of American parents. From the point of view of a developmentalist, the most worrisome aspect of the problem is the impact of such widespread nonparental care on the development of our nation's children. By now researchers have reached a general consensus that child care of high quality does not harm children. (They are not so sure when it comes to infants, as reflected in the diverse range of viewpoints presented in issues 3 and 4 of the *Early Childhood Research Quarterly* in 1988.) But quality is not guaranteed in the vast nonsystem of child care in place in this country. There is little doubt that hundreds of thousands of American children are currently experiencing child care environments that are compromising their optimal development.

STANDARDS OF QUALITY

When parents select a child care setting, they are not purchasing a service that permits them to work. Rather, they are purchasing an environment where part of the rearing of their child will take place. This environment will help to shape the course of development of the child. Child-rearing environments can be arranged on a continuum of quality from good to bad. If the environment experienced by the child falls below a certain point on this continuum, optimal development will be threatened. Standards and their expression in licensing codes represent our efforts to define objectively this threshold. Actually "standards" is another misnomer because the quality of child care environments available in America is anything but standard.

Of special concern are the hundreds of thousands of settings called family day care homes. These are private homes in which a provider (usually a woman) takes care of three to nine children. Several states do not require that these homes be licensed or monitored. Even in those states that do mandate some form of registration, the vast majority of family day care providers operate underground. Estimates range up to 90% or more *(Corsini, Wisensale, & Caruso, 1988)*. Some of these settings are excellent, but there are horror stories as well *(Keyserling, 1972)*. What is most frightening about the diversity of care in the family day care system is that this is the most popular choice of parents with children under three years of age who need full-time care *(Hofferth & Phillips, 1987)*. Many parents feel that family day care is more home-like than center care, and it is often more affordable. Yet we have no assurances that these very young children are receiving care that meets the quality threshold required for healthy development.

Further evidence substantiating these concerns is presented in a recent state-by-state analysis of staff/child ratios in infant and toddler settings in this country *(Young & Zigler, 1986)*. Most experts agree that there should be no more than three infants per adult caregiver; yet in 1986 only three states met this standard. Six to one, and even eight to one, was not uncommon. No adult, no matter how well trained, can provide proper stimulation and care to six or eight infants, much less be able to evacuate them in an emergency. A staff/child ratio such as this constitutes prima facie evidence that the development of many children in child care settings is being compromised.

Allowing a caregiver to be responsible for too many children does help to keep the cost to parents down, which highlights another aspect of our current child care crisis: quality care is expensive. What has developed in America is a two-tiered system of child care. Economically advantaged families can purchase quality caregiving environments for their children. Poor, working-class, and many lower-middle-class families cannot afford quality and must settle for marginal or inadequate care. Children whose development is at risk because of economically disadvantaged life circumstances are put at even greater risk when placed in poor child care settings.

THE EDUCATION PARADIGM

There are many similarities between this two-tiered system of child care and the history of our nation's educational system. Before the advent of universal public schooling, only rich children received an extensive education. When free common schools began, children from wealthy families remained in their expensive private schools and went on to expensive universities. Gradually these inequities ended, as taxpayers and educators improved the offerings of the common school, extended free education through the high school years, and began to subsidize higher education to some extent. While students in some private schools may still receive superior educational benefits, those who go through the public school system have comparable opportunities to learn. They too may become leaders and productive members of the society. The child in a quality caregiving setting, like the educated elite of yesteryear, is likely to have his or her developmental path secured. For the child in poor quality care, however, the society may pay the price in increased social services and an unprepared labor force in the not too distant future.

We have today the knowledge to provide good quality care to every child who needs it. What is lacking in our country is the commitment and the will to do so. This is best demonstrated by a consideration of the cost of a child care system in America. No one in or out of government wishes to deal with the true dollar cost of providing good quality child care to all the children in our nation who require it. The best estimate we have been able to produce is that it will cost this country $75–100 billion a year to solve the child care problem. The fact that our federal government has no firm figure to give to policy analysts and decision makers indicates the vacuum of leadership at the national level that we have witnessed for over a decade, as the child care problem has worsened. How can anyone even begin to develop approaches to the problem until there is some sense of the dollar outlay involved in the solution? In the absence of a reasonable cost estimate, the proposals that have been put forth have tended to be unrealistic and unworkable; they include help from the private sector and from charitable organizations, and the resurrection of old child care bills.

The private sector solution was favored by the Reagan administration. That is, private business should provide or underwrite the cost of employees' child care. This has simply not happened. While some employers have moved in this direction, the fact is that out of six million U.S. employers, only 3,500 (six-hundredths of one per cent) offer some form of child care assistance *(Reisman, Moore, & Fitzgerald, 1988)*. Usually this assistance is in the form of information and referral services, which may help parents find child care but does not help them afford it. We should do all we can to get private employers to do more, but the nature of our private enterprise system guarantees the failure of this approach as a real solution. We do not directly ask business to provide children's education; why should we ask business to provide child care?

Others have suggested that we give the task of child care to a conglomeration of caring institutions: churches, YMCAs, and some other nonprofit settings. While those who run these institutions have their hearts in the right places, they have neither the money nor the personnel for such an undertaking. Some have proposed that we resurrect the 1971 Child Development Act and put into place a national network of child care settings available to all citizens (along the lines of the Swedish model). Given our federal government's precarious financial condition, this solution is unrealistic; its pursuit would likely be a waste of energy. Some have suggested expanding the Head Start program. But Head Start is designed for preschoolers, not infants and school-age children, who need quite different types of programs. Furthermore, today Head Start serves only 16% of the children who are eligible for it (*Children's Defense Fund, 1987*), so any expansion should begin with this target population.

Recently many other possible solutions have been presented in Congress. Legislators considered more than 100 of them in 1988, and that number will certainly be topped by the end of the current session. Yet even the most ambitious of these proposals, the ABC bill sponsored by Sen. Christopher Dodd with many cosponsors in both houses, provides only $2.5 billion for child care services throughout the entire country. This amount would not begin to address the magnitude of our child care problem. If the money is provided, we still do not have a coherent child care system that would enable us to put even these small funds to best advantage.

DEVELOPING A SOLUTION

Over the past years, I have developed my own plan for addressing America's child care crisis. This plan was presented before the last session of Congress, and is now being considered again in the form of two bills (one sponsored by Sen. Dodd of Connecticut and the other by Rep. Augustus Hawkins of California). My plan has taken me over a lot of intellectual terrain. I relied primarily on my own knowledge about the nature of children and their developmental needs. In the process of evolving this plan, I decided to be explicit and unwavering about certain principles and criteria that must be met for a satisfactory child care system to come about. If it does not meet these principles, then I would consider it inadequate.

The very first principle is that the child care system we create, and the child care services in that system, must be reliable and stable. We cannot wait each year to see if the federal government will appropriate the required monies. Otherwise, parents will find themselves in the same predicament they face today. The rate of caregiver turnover is very high, and providers go in and out of business frequently. This leaves parents frantic to find new arrangements, and insecure about the longevity of the setting they do find. Children suffer the most in this situation, since an important developmental need is for a consistent caregiving environment. Thus the child care system we provide must be permanent and become part of the very structure of our society. It must be tied to a major societal institution.

Child care, like education, is not mentioned in the U.S. Constitution. Therefore, like education, child care must be primarily a state-based system. There is an important federal role, however. The federal government should be funding the research that is necessary to create adequate child care and to determine its effects on children of various ages and life circumstances. The nation should also subsidize care for the most needy and the handicapped (as it currently does for education with Chapter 1 in the *Elementary and Secondary School Act and Public Law 94–142*). Through most of this decade the executive branch has been slow to provide the kind of leadership that can only come with what Theodore Roosevelt called the "Bully Pulpit."

Another principle is that there should be equal access to child care for every child who needs it. At the same time, the various ethnic and socioeconomic groups should be integrated as fully as possible. Let us not repeat the one great mistake of our nation's Head Start program, where we send poor children to one set of centers and affluent children to another.

The primary goal of the new child care system is to insure the optimal development of the children using the system, not to enable parents to work. In the past, child care has always been an adjunct to welfare reform plans, with the purpose of reducing welfare rolls by allowing recipients to enter training or gain employment. The proposed child care system must stand on its own. It must be built upon policies to meet the needs of children, not upon the politics of social services. This means we must, once and for all, mandate child care of good quality. A solid model is provided by the Federal Inter-Agency Day Care Requirements, revised in 1980 and sent to Congress by the Carter Administration.

Of course, helping parents to be able to work can contribute to the child's optimal development. Children stand to benefit when the financial status of their family improves. Yet working families may be so busy that this produces stress, which in turn may be aggravated by undependable and inadequate child care. The child care system must be sensitive to the varying needs of the children and families it serves. Thus we must appreciate the great heterogeneity of our populace. While all children will be in the same system, that system must be flexible enough to adapt to requirements of each individual child and parent.

The child care solution must be available to the child throughout all of the years of dependency. This means as early in pregnancy as possible through at least the first 12 years of life. Let us not again fall into the trap of magic periods. We are now hearing much about the first five years of life. While these are truly important years, the next five years are also important. We must remember that half the need for child care is represented by children ages 6 to 12. We must remember also that the developing child is growing from stage to stage, and that each stage requires particular environmental nutrients. These nutrients must be provided for the entire range of human development, not just for cognitive growth. We must optimize physical and mental health, and be just as concerned with the child's personality development as we are with the child's IQ. Child care programs must be committed to the optimal development of the whole child.

Another principle we have learned is that child care must be predicated on a true partnership between parents and the children's caregivers. This lesson was taught by our nation's Head Start program and by successful school programs such as the Comer project in New Haven *(Comer, 1980)*. The key ingredient in our child care plan is an adult who cares for the children while parents work. The system will never be of good quality unless the adult caregivers are skilled and dedicated. We must do everything we can to train, upgrade the pay, and increase the status of those individuals who help parents raise our nation's children. Does it make any sense that today in America, 60% of all child care workers earn less than five dollars an hour *(Reisman et al., 1988)*? In 1984, 90% of licensed family day care mothers earned less than the poverty level *(Children's Defense Fund, 1987)*. We are paying to the caregivers of our next generation about what we pay to zoo keepers, and less than we pay to janitors.

The program outlined here is a child care system of the highest quality. Although such a system will carry a high price tag, we can work to make it as cost-effective as possible without sacrificing quality. The best route toward this goal is to implement the system within the established educational structure. We will enhance already existing elementary school buildings, where formal education takes place, and create the school of the 21st century. The child care component will operate in an on-site center and provide care for children from about the age of three. The system will also have three outreach programs: (1) a family support system for first-time parents; (2) support for family day care homes within the neighborhood; and (3) information and referral services.

IMPLEMENTING THE MODEL

To start at the very beginning, the earliest child care takes place at home in the form of an infant care leave. There is a consensus today among all experts that parents should care for their children during the first few months of life. In 1983, the Yale Bush Center in Child Development and Social Policy convened a national panel of experts to study the problem and make formal recommendations to Congress. The committee recommended the provision of six months of leave, three months paid at 75% of salary. The infant care leave bills that have since been proposed have not provided this length of time or level of pay. Still, it behooves advocates for children and families to support *any* national legislation regarding infant leaves. Once a law is in place, it can be adapted over time to reach the desired length and economic benefit. In the meantime, babies will at least be guaranteed a time to begin life with the nurturance of their own parent and family.

The child care system conceptualized here would reach out to new parents through child care workers in the school. They would work with the parents of infants up to age three. This is taking place in Missouri as part of the "Parents as First Teachers" program. In this program, parents receive guidance beginning in the third trimester of pregnancy and wise counsel and support to help promote the child's development thereafter. There is an outreach program from the school building to provide this support service for all parents in the district.

Next, all family day care homes in the neighborhood of the school would be combined into a network, with the school's child care system as the hub. The school's child care staff would monitor, train, and generally support the family day care mothers. They would also connect these providers with parents of infants and toddlers who are considering going back to work. There would also be a general information/referral system to help meet other needs such as night care for children. Clearly, I am incorporating here much that has been learned from American family support groups.

Now let us look at what will happen in the school building. The on-site program will offer quality child care for preschoolers. School-age children could also receive care both before and after regular school hours, and on a full-time basis during vacations. For 3–4-year-olds, there will be developmentally appropriate child care within the school building, not formal schooling. Five-year-olds would receive one half-day of kindergarten in the formal school system; then, those children who require it could move over to the child care system for the other half of the day. The school buildings we are talking about would open two hours before formal schooling begins and remain open two or three hours after the school day.

Who would run the school of the 21st century? Formal schooling today is in the able hands of professional educators, principals and teachers. These educators are already overburdened and are working tirelessly to upgrade the quality of the American schools. It is not appropriate to ask them to take over child care as well. Also, most school personnel do not have the training or expertise necessary to work with very young children and their families. Finally, if this child care system were in the hands of formal educators, the cost to this nation would be prohibitive.

Rather, the child care system within the school building would be headed by someone with a Master's or Bachelor's degree and training in early childhood education. This person would be in charge of the overall child care system, including the outreach functions and the program in the on-site center. The day-to-day care of children would then be in the hands of Child Development Associates, fully qualified for such a role. This would require expansion of the CDA program, including subsidized tuition for those who need it. Our nation has done much to help prospective teachers gain the education they require; child care workers deserve no less.

The big question in the minds of most taxpayers is who will pay the huge cost of this system? When the percentage of working women reaches a critical mass, that is, when some 80% of all women are in the work force in the 21st century, this cost should be absorbed primarily through property taxes. Today, education is paid for by taxes; when most women are employed, we can expect that this nation will not be opposed to a tax for child care. However, during the interim period, in order to absorb costs and to keep quiescent the vocal and active minority of taxpayers who do not wish to see public monies expended to aid women's entry into the labor force, I suggest a fee system. Each family that voluntarily chooses to use a child care system in the school will be asked to pay a fee calibrated to family income. The high cost of good quality child care will demand subsidization by all levels of government, particularly in the case of the working poor who most need this service. To further offset the costs, private businesses should be induced to include child care as a conventional fringe benefit for employees.

The first step in implementing this plan would be the development of demonstration schools throughout the country (at least one in each state). The demonstration schools should be funded initially by the federal government. Then, the role of the federal government should be to help states move as quickly as possible to open more schools of this type. Bills proposing demonstration schools that encompass this model are presently before Congress. Some states have already acted on their own initiatives, however; and many others are considering similar action. The state of Missouri has implemented the 21st century school plan, and Connecticut has funded its own demonstration schools. The experiences of these states will be invaluable to our national plan.

This plan is the fruit of almost a quarter of a century of thought on this matter. The child care problem in the United States today is so massive and has been ignored for so long that it is too late to rely on Band-Aid approaches. We must institutionalize high quality child care for each and every child who requires substitute care. Our society and our place in the world depend upon the degree to which we optimize the development of every American child. We must provide our future citizens with not just a quality education, but with quality child care as well.

REFERENCES

Bureau of Labor Statistics, U.S. Department of Labor. (1987). *Employment in perspective: Women in the labor force.* Fourth Quarter, Report 749.

Children's Defense Fund. (1987). *A children's defense budget: FY 1988*. Washington, DC: Author.

Comer, J.P. (1980). *School power: Implications of an intervention project*. New York: Free Press.

Corsini, D.A., Wisensale, S.K., & Caruso, G.L. (1988, September). Family day care: System issues and regulatory models. *Young Children*. 17–19.

Hofferth, S.L., & Phillips, D.A. (1987). Child care in the United States: 1970–1995. *Journal of Marriage and the Family, 49*, 559–571.

Keyserling, M.D. (1972). *Windows on day care*. New York: National Council of Jewish Women.

Reisman, B., Moore, A.J., & Fitzgerald, K. (1988). *Child care: The bottom line*. New York: Child Care Action Campaign.

Select Committee on Children, Youth, and Families. (1984). *Families and child care: Improving the options*. Washington, DC: U.S. Government Printing Office.

Select Committee on Children, Youth, and Families. (1988). *Children and families in poverty: The struggle to survive*. Washington, DC: U.S. Government Printing Office.

Select Committee on Children, Youth, and Families. (1989). *Children and families: Key trends in the 1980s*. Washington, DC: U.S. Government Printing Office.

Shank, S.E. (1988). Women and the labor market: The link grows stronger. *Monthly Labor Review, 111* (3), 3–8.

U.S. Bureau of the Census. (1986, March). *Current population reports* (Series P-20, No. 419, Household and family characteristics).

Young, K.T., & Zigler, E. (1986). Infant and toddler day care: Regulations and policy implications. *American Journal of Orthopsychiatry, 56*, 43–55.

VII

The Environment

The tragedy of environmental destruction is all around us—a part of our daily lives that we can't ignore. We feel it—literally—with every breath we take. In recent years, there has been growing concern over the state of the environment from all quarters. But there is little agreement on the causes or cures of the environmental crisis.

One approach regards environmental destruction as a necessary, if unfortunate, "trade-off" for economic growth. In this view, the greatest danger is that, in our concern for environmental issues, we'll hobble the economy with needless regulations and weaken our ability to compete economically with other industrial countries.

A second approach takes environmental problems more seriously, arguing that they are the inevitable result of a high level of industrialization, growing population, and our craving for more and more consumer goods. From this perspective, the basic problem is *people*—too many of them, consuming too much, and making extravagant demands on the earth's limited resources. The solution is often cast in individual terms: we should recycle more, use bicycles instead of our cars, and in other ways change our life-styles to better mesh with the needs of a fragile environment.

A third approach agrees that individual change has an important place in securing our environmental future. But it also calls attention to the larger social, political, and economic forces that shape the crisis of the environment. It acknowledges that the sheer number of people, the growth of industry, and the limits of energy resources would create formidable environmental issues in any society. But it also points to such more specific forces as the nature of our economic institutions, the decisions of powerful corporations, and the frequent failure of governmental regulatory agencies as contributors to the current crisis of the environment. It views the environmental crisis, in short, not just as an individual problem or a technical, scientific one, but as a *social* problem as well. The articles in this chapter explore several of the social aspects of the environmental crisis.

In the selection from his book, *The Closing Circle*, Barry Commoner develops an argument explaining the frequent connection between pollution and the uncontrolled quest for profit. According to Commoner, the key problem is the profitability of introducing new technologies—technologies that may have a devastating impact on the natural environment and ultimately even on the functioning of the industry itself but that provide a very high rate of profit for the corporations, at least in the short run. In Commoner's view, the dramatic destruction of the environment in the years since World War II has been primarily the result of the explosion of these new technologies, which enriched the large corporations while impoverishing everyone else.

In his case study of the history of American transportation, Bradford Snell further explores the links between pollution and profit, offering a shocking story of corporate complicity in the destruction of the environment. It is well known that the automobile has been the source of much of our air pollution problem—not to mention the more general distortion of the urban and rural landscape produced by freeways, parking lots, and the other artifacts of automotive civilization. Snell shows that the rise of the private automobile and the decline of other, more efficient and less polluting means of transportation was, in large part, the result of a conscious policy by the auto and oil corporations—especially General Motors—to destroy other forms of ground transportation in order to create dependency on the automobile. His study speaks volumes about the relation between the irresponsible exercise of corporate power and the deepening destruction of the natural and social environment in the twentieth century.

The next two selections describe some of the most troubling results of our heedless approach to the natural environment. In "The Toxic Cloud," Michael H. Brown, the reporter who uncovered the massive toxic contamination at Love Canal in New York State during the 1970s, turns his attention to the growing problem of toxic chemicals in America's air. A recent government study estimates that roughly 20 pounds of some of the most dangerous substances known are released into the air over the United States each year for every man, woman, and child in the country. For some of these chemicals, there is *no* safe level of exposure; even the tiniest amount can bring cancer or other diseases. As Brown points out, one of the most disturbing aspects of this new toxic pollution is how easily these chemicals can drift from their point of origin to anywhere in the United States; no part of the country, even the most pristine, is now safe from this chemical fallout.

As frightening as it is, the pouring of carcinogenic chemicals into the air may not be our most urgent environmental problem. Even more troubling is that a range of human activities—from the production of industrial chemicals to the burning of forests in the name of economic development—is changing the basic composition of the earth's atmosphere itself. As Thomas E. Graedel and Paul J. Crutzen show, the consequences range from acid rain and the stubborn persistence of urban smog to the longer-range threats of global warming and the depletion of the ozone layer, which protects us from the extremes of ultraviolet radiation. We are learning that tampering with the chemical balance of the atmosphere may have momentous consequences, all the more worrisome because they are still "incompletely understood." Short of a global effort to alter our approach to economic development, they warn, we may face more "unwelcome surprises" further down the road.

25

The Economic Meaning of Ecology

Barry Commoner

What is the connection between pollution and profit in a private enterprise economic system such as the United States? Let us recall that in the United States, intense environmental pollution is closely associated with the technological transformation of the productive system since World War II. Much of our pollution problem can be traced to a series of large scale technological displacements in industry and agriculture since 1946. A number of the new, rapidly growing productive activities are much more prone to pollute than the older ones they have displaced.

Thus, since World War II, in the United States, private business has chosen to invest its capital preferentially in a series of new productive enterprises that are closely related to the intensification of environmental pollution. What has motivated this pattern of investment? According to Heilbroner:

> Whether the investment is for the replacement of old capital or for the installation of new capital, the ruling consideration is virtually never the personal use or satisfaction that the investment yields to the owners of the firm. Instead, the touchstone of investment decisions is profit.

The introduction of new technology has clearly played an important role in the profitability of postwar business enterprise. The economic factor that links profit to technology is *productivity*, which is usually defined as the output of product per unit input of labor. Productivity has

Barry Commoner, "The Economic Meaning of Ecology," from *The Closing Circle: Nature, Man, and Technology*. Copyright © 1971 by Barry Commoner. Reprinted by permission of Alfred A. Knopf, Inc. Portions of this book originally appeared in *The New Yorker*.

grown rapidly since World War II and, according to Heilbroner, this is largely due to the introduction of new technologies in that period of time. The following relationship seems to be at work: new investment in the postwar economy, as expected, has moved in directions that appeared to promise, and in fact yielded, increased profit; these investments have been heavily based on the introduction of new technology, which is a major factor in the notable increase in productivity, the major source of profit.

If these relationships have been operative in the technological displacements that, as we have seen, have played such an important role in generating the environment crisis in the United States, then we would expect to find, in the appropriate statistics, that production based on the new technology has been more profitable than production based on the old technology it has replaced. That is, the new, more polluting technologies should yield higher profits than the older, less polluting technologies they have displaced.

The available data seem to bear out this expectation. A good example is the pervasive displacement of soap by synthetic detergents. As it happens, United States government statistics report economic data on the combined soap and detergent industry. In 1947, when the industry produced essentially no detergents, the profit was 30 per cent of sales. In 1967, when the industry produced about one-third per cent soap and two-thirds per cent detergents, the profit from sales was 42 per cent. From the data for intervening years it can be computed that the profit on pure detergent sales is about 52 per cent, considerably higher than that of pure soap sales. Significantly, the industry has experienced a considerable increase in productivity, labor input relative to output in sales having declined by about 25 per cent. Clearly, if profitability is a powerful motivation, the rapid displacement of soap by detergents—and the resultant environmental pollution—has a rational explanation. This helps to explain why, despite its continued usefulness for most cleaning purposes, soap has been driven off the market by detergents. It has benefitted the investor, if not society.

The snythetic chemical industry is another example that illustrates some of the reasons for the profitability of such technological innovations. This is readily documented from an informative volume on the economics of the chemical industry published by the Manufacturing Chemists' Association. The chemical industry, particularly the manufacturers of synthetic organic chemicals, during the 1946–66 period recorded an unusually high rate of profit. During that period, while the average return on net worth for all manufacturing industries was 13.1 per cent, the chemical industry averaged 14.7 per cent. The MCA volume offers an explanation for this exceptionally high rate of profit. This is largely based on the introduction of newly developed materials, especially synthetic ones. For about from four to five years after a new, innovative chemical product reaches the market, profits are well above the average (innovative firms enjoy about twice the rate of profit of noninnovative firms). This is due to the effective monopoly enjoyed by the firm that developed the materials, that permits the establishment of a high sales price. After four to five years, smaller competitors are able to develop their own methods of manufacture; as they enter the market, the supply increases, competition intensifies, the price drops, and profits decline. At this point the large innovative firm, through its extensive research and development effort, is ready to introduce a new synthetic substance and can recover a high rate of profit. And so on. As the MCA volume points out: "The maintenance of above average profit margins requires the continuous discovery of new products and specialties on which high profit margins may be earned while the former products in that category evolve into commodity chemicals with lower margins." It is therefore no accident that the synthetic organic chemical industry has one of the highest rates of investment in research and development (in 1967, 3.7 per cent of sales, as compared with an average of 2.1 per cent for all manufacturing industries).

Thus, the extraordinarily high rate of profit of this industry appears to be a direct result of the development and production at rapid intervals of new, usually unnatural, synthetic materials—which, entering the environment, for reasons already given, often pollute it. This situation is an ecologist's nightmare, for in the four to five year period in which a new synthetic substance, such as a detergent or pesticide, is massively moved into the market—and into the environment—there is literally not enough time to work out its ecological effects. Inevitably, by the time the effects are known, the damage is done and the inertia of the heavy investment in a new productive technology makes a retreat extraordinarily difficult. The very system of enhancing profit in this industry is precisely the cause of its intense, detrimental impact on the environment.

It is significant that since 1966, the profit position of the chemical industry has declined sharply. Industry spokesmen have themselves described environmental concern as an important reason for this decline. For example, at recent congressional hearings, an industry official pointed out that a number of chemical companies had found pesticide manufacturing decreasingly profitable because of the need to meet new environmental demands. Because of these demands, costs of developing new pesticides and of testing their environmental effects have risen sharply. At the same time, cancellation or suspension of official pesticide registrations increased from 25 in 1967 to 123 in 1970. As a result, a number of companies have abandoned production of pesticides, although over-all production continues to increase. One company reported that it had dropped pesticide production "because investments in other areas promised better business."

Another explicit example of the impact of environmental concern on the profitability of new chemicals is NTA, a supposedly nonpolluting substitute for phosphate in detergents. Under the pressure of intense public concern over water pollution due to detergent phosphates, the industry developed NTA as a replacement. Two large firms then proceeded to construct plants for the manufacture of NTA—at a cost of about $100 million each. When the plants were partially built, the United States Public Health Service advised against the use of NTA, because of evidence that birth defects occur in laboratory animals exposed to NTA. The new plants had to be abandoned, at considerable cost to these firms. As a result of such hazards, research and development expenditures in the chemical industry have recently declined—a process which is likely to reduce the industry's profit position even more.

Nitrogen fertilizer provides another informative example of the link between pollution and profits. In a typical United States Corn Belt farm, a yield that is more than from 25 to 30 bushels per acre below present averages may mean no profit for the farmer. . . . [P]resent corn yields depend on a high rate of nitrogen applications. Under these conditions, the uptake of nitrogen by the crop is approaching saturation, so that an appreciable fraction of the fertilizer drains from the land and pollutes surface waters. In other words, under present conditions, it appears that the farmer *must* use sufficient fertilizer to pollute the water if he is to make a profit. Perhaps the simplest way to exemplify this tragic connection between economic survival and environmental pollution is in the words of one thoughtful farmer in recent testimony before the Illinois State Pollution Control Board:

> Money spent on fertilizer year in and year out is the best investment a farmer can make. It is one of our production tools that hasn't nearly priced itself out of all realm of possibility as is the case with machinery and other farm inputs. Fertilizer expense in my case exceeds $20 per acre, but I feel I get back one to three dollars for every dollar spent on fertilizer. . . . I doubt that I could operate if I lost the use of fertilizers and chemicals as I know them today. I hope adequate substitutes are developed and researched if the government decides our production tools are a danger to society.

National statistics support this farmer's view of the economic importance of fertilizers or pesticides. These statistics show that, whereas such chemicals yield three or four dollars per dollar spent, other inputs—labor and machinery, for example—yield much lower returns.

This is evidence that a high rate of profit is associated with practices that are particularly stressful toward the environment and that when these practices are restricted, profits decline.

Another important example is provided by the auto industry where the displacement of small, low-powered cars by large, high-powered ones is a major cause of environmental pollution. Although specific data on the relationship between profitability and crucial engineering factors such as horsepower do not appear to be available, some more general evidence is at hand. According to a recent article in *Fortune* magazine:

> As the size and selling price of a car are reduced, then, the profit margin tends to drop even faster. A standard United States sedan with a basic price of $3,000, for example, yields something like $250 to $300 in profit to its manufacturer. But when the price falls by a third, to $2,000, the factory profit drops by about half. Below $2,000, the decline grows even more precipitous.

Clearly, the introduction of a car of reduced environmental impact, which would necessarily have a relatively low-powered, low-compression engine and a low over-all weight, would sell at a relatively low price. It would therefore yield a smaller profit relative to sales price than the standard heavy, high-powered, high-polluting vehicle. This may explain the recent remark by Henry Ford II, that "minicars make miniprofits."

. . . [P]rominent among the large-scale technological displacements that have increased environmental impacts are certain construction materials: steel, aluminum, lumber, cement, and plastics. In construction and other uses, steel and lumber have been increasingly displaced by aluminum, cement (in the form of concrete), and plastics. In 1969 the profits (in terms of profit as per cent of total sales) from steel production (by blast furnaces) and lumber production were 12.5 per cent and 15.4 per cent, respectively. In contrast, the products that have displaced steel and lumber yielded significantly higher profits: aluminum, 25.7 per cent; cement, 37.4 per cent; plastics and resins, 21.4 per cent. Again, displacement of technologies with relatively weak environmental impacts by technologies with more intensive impacts is accompanied by a significant increase in profitability.

A similar situation is evident in the displacement of railroad freight haulage (relatively weak environmental impact) and truck freight haulage (intense environmental impact). In this case, economic data are somewhat equivocal because of the relatively large capital investment in railroads as compared to trucks (the trucks' right-of-way being provided by government-supported roads). Nevertheless, truck freight appears to yield significantly more profit than railroad freight; the ratio of net income to shareholders' and proprietors' equity in the case of railroads is 2.61 per cent, and for trucks, 8.84 per cent (in 1969).

In connection with the foregoing examples, in which profitability appears to increase when a new, more environmentally intense technology displaces an older one, it should be noted that not all new technologies share this characteristic. For example, the displacement of coal-burning locomotives by diesel engines *improved* the environmental impact of railroads between 1946 and 1950, for diesel engines burn considerably less fuel per ton-mile of freight than do coal-burning engines. Unfortunately, this improvement has been vitiated by the subsequent displacement of railroad freight haulage by truck freight, and at the same time made no lasting improvement in the railroads' economic position. It is also evident that certain new technologies, which are wholly novel, rather than displacing older ones—for example, television sets and other consumer electronics—may well be highly profitable without incurring an unusually intense environmental impact. The point of the foregoing observations is not that they establish the rule that increased profitability inevitably means increased pollution, but only that many of the heavily polluting new technologies have brought with them a higher rate of profit than the less polluting technologies they have displaced.

Nor is this to say that the relationship is intentional on the part of the entrepreneur. Indeed, there is considerable evidence, some of which has been cited earlier, that the producers are typically unaware of the potential environmental effects of their operation until the effects become manifest, after the limits of biological accommodation have been exceeded, in ecological collapse or human illness. Nevertheless, despite these limitations, these examples of the relationship between pollution and profit-taking in a private enterprise economic system need to be taken seriously, I believe, because they relate to important segments of the economic system of the world's largest capitalist power.

In response to such evidence, some will argue that such a connection between pollution and profit-taking is irrational because pollution degrades the quality of the environment on which the future success of even the most voracious capitalist enterprise depends. In general, this argument has a considerable force, for it is certainly true that industrial pollution tends to destroy the very "biological capital" that the ecosystem provides and on which production depends. A good example is the potential effect of mercury pollution from chloralkali plants on the successful operation of these plants. Every ton of chlorine produced by such a plant requires about 15,000 gallons of water, which must meet rigorous standards of purity. This water is obtained from nearby rivers or lakes, in which purity is achieved by ecological cycles, driven by the metabolic activities of a number of microorganisms. Since mercury compounds are highly toxic to most living organisms, the release of mercury by chloralkali plants must be regarded as a serious threat to the source of pure water on which these plants depend. Nevertheless, it is a fact that in this and other instances, the industrial operation—until constrained by outside forces—has proceeded on the seemingly irrational, self-destructive course of polluting the environment on which it depends.

A statistician, Daniel Fife, has recently made an interesting observation that helps to explain this paradoxical relationship between the profitability of a business and its tendency to destroy its own environmental base. His example is the whaling industry, which has been driving itself out of business by killing whales so fast as to ensure that they will soon become extinct. Fife refers to this kind of business operation as "irresponsible," in contrast with a "responsible" operation, which would only kill whales as fast as they can reproduce. He points out that even though the irresponsible business will eventually wipe itself out, it *may be profitable to do so*—at least for the entrepreneur, if not for society—if the extra profit derived from the irresponsible operation is high enough to yield a return on investment elsewhere that outweighs the ultimate effect of killing off the whaling business. To paraphrase Fife, the "irresponsible" entrepreneur finds it profitable to kill the goose that lays the golden eggs, so long as the goose lives long enough to provide him with sufficient eggs to pay for the purchase of a new goose. Ecological irresponsibility can pay—for the entrepreneur, but not for society as a whole.

The crucial link between pollution and profits appears to be modern technology, which is both the main source of recent increases in productivity—and therefore of profits—and of recent assaults on the environment. Driven by an inherent tendency to maximize profits, modern private enterprise has seized upon those massive technological innovations that promise to gratify this need, usually unaware that these same innovations are often also instruments of environmental destruction. Nor is this surprising, for . . . technologies tend to be designed at present as single-purpose instruments. Apparently, this purpose is, unfortunately, too often dominated by the desire to enhance productivity—and therefore profit.

Obviously, we need to know a great deal more about the connection between pollution and profits in private enterprise economies. Meanwhile, it would be prudent to give some thought to the meaning of the functional connection between pollution and profits, which is at least suggested by the present information.

The general proposition that emerges from these considerations is that environmental pollution is connected to the economics of the private enterprise system in two ways. First, pollution tends to become intensified by the displacement of older productive techniques by new, ecologically faulty, but more profitable technologies. Thus, in these cases, pollution is an intended concomitant of the natural drive of the economic system to introduce new technologies that increase productivity. Second, the cost[s] of environmental degradation are chiefly borne not by the producer, but by society as a whole, in the form of "externalities." A business enterprise that pollutes the environment is therefore being subsidized by society; to this extent, the enterprise, though free, is not wholly private.

26

American Ground Transport

Bradford Curie Snell

The manufacture of ground transportation equipment is one of this nation's least competitive industrial activities. . . .

Ground transport is dominated by a single, diversified firm to an extent possibly without parallel in the American economy. General Motors, the world's largest producer of cars and trucks, has also achieved monopoly control of buses and locomotives which compete with motor vehicles for passengers and freight. Its dominance of the bus and locomotive industries, moreover, would seem to constitute a classic monopoly. Although GM technically accounts for 75 percent of current city bus production, its only remaining competitor, the Flxible Co., relies on it for diesel propulsion systems, major engine components, technical assistance, and financing. In short, Flxible is more a distributor for GM than a viable competitor; virtually its sole function is the assembly of General Motors' bus parts for sale under the Flxible trade name. Likewise, in the production of intercity buses, its only remaining competitor, Motor Coach Industries, is wholly dependent upon GM for diesel propulsion systems and major mechanical components. In addition, General Motors accounts for 100 percent of all passenger and 80 percent of all freight locomotives manufactured in the United States. Such concentration in a single firm of control over three rival transportation equipment industries all but precludes the existence of competitive conduct and performance.

The distribution of economic power in this sector is remarkably asymmetrical. . . . [E]conomic power is fundamentally a function of concentration and size. In terms of concentration, the ground transport sector is virtually controlled by the Big Three auto companies. General Motors, Ford, and Chrysler account for 97 percent of automobile and 84 percent of truck production: GM alone dominates the bus and rail locomotive industries. Accordingly, the automakers have the power to impose a tax, in the form of a price increase, on purchasers of new cars to underwrite political campaigns against bus and rail systems.

In terms of size, there is an enormous divergence between the competing automotive and nonautomotive industries. Moreover, General Motors' diversification program has left only a small portion of the bus and rail industries in the hands of independent producers. As measured by aggregate sales, employment, and financial resources, therefore, the independent bus and rail firms are no match for the automakers. The Big Three's aggregate sales of motor vehicles and parts amount to about $52 billion each year, or more than 25 times the combined sales of trains, buses, subway and rapid transit cars by the four largest firms other than GM which produce bus and rail vehicles: Pullman and Budd (railway freight and passenger cars, subway and rapid transit cars); Rohr (buses and rapid transit cars); General Electric (commuter railcars and locomotives). The Big Three automakers employ nearly 1½ million workers, or more than three times as many as their four principal rivals: General Motors alone maintains plants in 19 different states. The Big Three also excel in their ability to finance lobbying and related political activities. GM, Ford, and Chrysler annually contribute more than an estimated $14 million to trade associations which lobby for the promotion of automotive transportation. By contrast, their four leading rivals contribute not more than $1 million, or less than one-tenth this amount, to rail transit lobbies. The magnitude of their sales, employment, and financial resources, therefore, affords the automakers overwhelming political influence.

It may be argued, moreover, that due to their conflicting interlocks with the motor vehicle manufacturers, these bus and rail firms would be reluctant to set their economic and political resources against them. Eighty percent of Budd's sales, for example, consist of automotive components purchased by the Big Three; Rohr, which also owns the Flxible Co., is wholly dependent upon GM for major bus components; Pullman derives more income from manufacturing trailers for highway trucks than from selling freight cars to the railroads; and General Electric manufactures a vast range of automotive electrical equipment, including about 80 percent of all automotive lamps. In sum, the independent bus and rail equipment manufacturers are probably unable and possibly unwilling to oppose the Big Three automakers effectively in political struggles over transportation policy.

Lacking a competitive structure, the group of industries responsible for providing us with ground transportation equipment fail to behave competitively. Diversification by General Motors into bus and rail production may have contributed to the displacement of these alternatives by automobiles and trucks. In addition, the asymmetrical distribution of economic and political power may have enabled the automakers to divert Government funds from rail transit to highways.

The Big Three automakers' efforts to restrain nonautomotive forms of passenger and freight transport have been perfectly consistent with profit maximization. One trolley coach or bus can eliminate 35 automobiles; 1 streetcar, subway, or rapid transit vehicle can supplant 50 passenger cars; an interurban railway or railroad train can displace 1,000 cars or a fleet of 150 cargo-laden trucks. Given the Big Three automakers' shared monopoly control of motor vehicle production and GM's diversified control of nonautomotive transport, it was inevitable that cars and trucks would eventually displace every other competing form of ground transportation.

The demise of nonautomotive transport is a matter of historical record. By 1973 viable alternatives to cars and trucks had all but ceased to exist. No producers of electric streetcars, trolley coaches, or interurban electric trains remained; only two established railcar builders (Pullman and Rohr) were definitely planning to continue production; a single firm (General Electric) still manufactured a handful of electric locomotives; and General Motors accounted for virtually all of an ever-shrinking number of diesel buses and locomotives.

There were, of course, a number of factors involved in this decline. For example, the popularity of motor vehicles, due in large part to their initial flexibility, most certainly affected public demand for competing methods of travel. On the other hand, the demise of bus and rail forms of transport cannot, as some have suggested, be attributed to the public's desire to travel exclusively by automobile. Rather, much of the growth in autos as well as trucks may have proceeded from the decline of rail and bus systems. In short, as alternatives ceased to be viable, automobiles and trucks became indispensable.

The sections which immediately follow relate in considerable detail how General Motors' diversification into bus and rail production generated conflicts of interest which necessarily contributed to the displacement of alternatives to motor vehicle transportation. A subsequent section will consider how asymmetry in the ground transport sector led to the political restraint of urban rail transit.

Before considering the displacement of bus and rail transportation, however, a distinction between intent and effect should be carefully drawn. This study contends that certain adverse effects flow inevitably from concentrated multi-industry structures regardless of whether these effects were actually intended. Specifically, it argues that structural concentration of auto, truck, bus, and rail production in one firm necessarily resulted in the promotion of motor vehicles and the displacement of

competing alternatives. Whether that firm's executives in the 1920's actually intended to construct a society wholly dependent on automobiles and
trucks is unlikely and, in any case, irrelevant. That such a society developed in part as the result of General Motors' common control of competing ground transport industries is both relevant and demonstrable.

1. THE SUBSTITUTION OF BUS FOR RAIL PASSENGER TRANSPORTATION

By the mid-1920's, the automobile market had become saturated. Those
who desired to own automobiles had already purchased them; most new
car sales had to be to old car owners. Largely as a result, General Motors
diversified into alternative modes of transportation. It undertook the
production of city and intercity motor buses. It also became involved in
the operation of bus and rail passenger services. As a necessary consequence, it was confronted with fundamental conflicts of interest regarding which of these several competing methods of transport it might
promote most profitably and effectively. Its natural economic incentives
and prior business experience strongly favored the manufacture and sale
of cars and trucks rather than bus, and particularly rail, vehicles. In the
course of events, it became committed to the displacement of rail transportation by diesel buses and, ultimately, to their displacement by automobiles.

In 1925, General Motors entered bus production by acquiring Yellow
Coach, which at that time was the Nation's largest manufacturer of city
and intercity buses. One year later, it integrated forward into intercity bus
operation by assisting in the formation of the Greyhound Corp., and soon
became involved in that company's attempt to convert passenger rail
operations to intercity bus service. Beginning in 1932, it undertook the
direct operation and conversion of interurban electric railways and local
electric streetcar and trolleybus systems to city bus operations. By the
mid-1950's, it could lay claim to having played a prominent role in the
complete replacement of electric street transportation with diesel buses.
Due to their high cost of operation and slow speed on congested streets,
however, these buses ultimately contributed to the collapse of several
hundred public transit systems and to the diversion of hundreds of
thousands of patrons to automobiles. In sum, the effect of General Motors' diversification program was threefold: substitution of buses for passenger trains, streetcars and trolleybuses; monopolization of bus production; and diversion of riders to automobiles.

Immediately after acquiring Yellow Coach, General Motors integrated
forward into intercity bus operation. In 1926, interests allied with GM
organized and then combined with the Greyhound Corp. for the purpose
of replacing rail passenger service with a GM-equipped and Greyhound-

operated nationwide system of intercity bus transportation. By mutual arrangement, Greyhound agreed to purchase virtually all of its buses from GM, which agreed in turn to refrain from selling intercity buses to any of Greyhound's bus operating competitors. In 1928, Greyhound announced its intention of converting commuter rail operations to intercity bus service. By 1939, six major railroads had agreed under pressure from Greyhound to replace substantial portions of their commuter rail service with Greyhound bus systems: Pennsylvania RR (Pennsylvania Greyhound Lines), New York Central RR (Central Greyhound Lines), Southern Pacific RR (Pacific Greyhound Lines), New York, New Haven & Hartford RR (New England Greyhound Lines), Great Northern RR (Northland Greyhound Lines), and St. Louis Southwestern Railway (Southwestern Greyhound Lines). By 1950, Greyhound carried roughly half as many intercity passengers as all the Nation's railroads combined.

During this period, General Motors played a prominent role in Greyhound management. In 1929, for example, it was responsible for the formation, direct operation, and financing of Atlantic Greyhound, which later became Greyhound's southeastern affiliate. Three years later, in 1932, when Greyhound was in serious financial trouble, it arranged for a million dollar cash loan. In addition, I. B. Babcock, the president of GM's bus division, served on Greyhound's board of directors until 1938, when he was replaced by his successor at GM, John A. Ritchie. Until 1948, GM was also the largest single shareholder in the Greyhound Corp. In short, through its interlocking interests in and promotion of Greyhound, General Motors acquired a not insignificant amount of influence over the shape of this nation's intercity passenger transportation. As the largest manufacturer of buses, it inevitably pursued a policy which would divert intercity traffic from rails to the intercity buses which it produced and Greyhound operated. Although this policy was perfectly compatible with GM's legitimate interest in maximizing returns on its stockholders' investments, it was not necessarily in the best interest of the riding public. In effect, the public was substantially deprived of access to an alternative form of intercity travel which, regardless of its merits, was apparently curtailed as a result of corporate rather than public determination.

After its successful experience with intercity buses, General Motors diversified into city bus and rail operations. At first, its procedure consisted of directly acquiring and scrapping local electric transit systems in favor of GM buses. In this fashion, it created a market for its city buses. As GM general Counsel Henry Hogan would observe later, the corporation "decided that the only way this new market for (city) buses could be created was for it to finance the conversion from streetcars to buses in some small cities." On June 29, 1932, the GM-bus executive committee formally resolved that "to develop motorized transportation, our company should initiate a program of this nature and authorize the incorporation of a holding company with a capital of $300,000." Thus was formed

United Cities Motor Transit (UCMT) as a subsidiary of GM's bus division. Its sole function was to acquire electric streetcar companies, convert them to GM motorbus operation, and then resell the properties to local concerns which agreed to purchase GM bus replacements. The electric streetcar lines of Kalamazoo and Saginaw, Mich., and Springfield, Ohio, were UCMT's first targets. "In each case," Hogan stated, GM "successfully motorized the city, turned the management over to other interests and liquidated its investment." The program ceased, however, in 1935 when GM was censured by the American Transit Association (ATA) for its self-serving role, as a bus manufacturer, in apparently attempting to motorize Portland's electric streetcar system.

As a result of the ATA censure, GM dissolved UCMT and embarked upon a nationwide plan to accomplish the same result indirectly. In 1936 it combined with the Omnibus Corp. in engineering the tremendous conversion of New York City's electric streetcar system to GM buses. At that time, as a result of stock and management interlocks, GM was able to exert substantial influence over Omnibus. John A. Ritchie, for example, served simultaneously as chairman of GM's bus division and president of Omnibus from 1926 until well after the motorization was completed. The massive conversion within a period of only 18 months of the New York system, then the world's largest streetcar network, has been recognized subsequently as the turning point in the electric railway industry.

Meanwhile, General Motors had organized another holding company to convert the remainder of the Nation's electric transportation system to GM buses. In 1936, it caused its officers and employees, I. B. Babcock, E. J. Stone, E. P. Crenshaw, and several Greyhound executives to form National City Lines, Inc. (NCL). During the following 14 years General Motors, together with Standard Oil of California, Firestone Tire, and two other suppliers of bus-related products, contributed more than $9 million to this holding company for the purpose of converting electric transit systems in 16 states to GM bus operations. The method of operation was basically the same as that which GM employed successfully in its United Cities Motor Transit program: acquisition, motorization, resale. By having NCL resell the properties after conversion was completed, GM and its allied companies were assured that their capital was continually reinvested in the motorization of additional systems. There was, moreover, little possibility of reconversion. To preclude the return of electric vehicles to the dozens of cities it motorized, GM extracted from the local transit companies contracts which prohibited their purchase of " . . . any new equipment using any fuel or means of propulsion other than gas."

The National City Lines campaign had a devastating impact on the quality of urban transportation and urban living in America. Nowhere was the ruin more apparent than in the Greater Los Angeles metropolitan area. Thirty-five years ago it was a beautiful region of lush palm trees, fragrant orange groves, and clean, ocean-enriched air. It was served then by the world's largest interurban electric railway system. The Pacific Electric system branched out from Los Angeles for a radius of more than 75 miles, reaching north to San Fernando, east to San Bernardino, and south to Santa Ana. Its 3,000 quiet, pollution-free, electric trains annually transported 80 million people throughout the sprawling region's 56 separately incorporated cities. Contrary to popular belief, the Pacific Electric, not the automobile, was responsible for the area's geographical development. First constructed in 1911, it established traditions of suburban living long before the automobile had arrived.

In 1938, General Motors and Standard Oil of California organized Pacific City Lines (PCL) as an affiliate of NCL to motorize west coast electric railways. The following year PCL acquired, scrapped, and substituted bus lines for three northern California electric rail systems in Fresno, San Jose, and Stockton. In 1940 GM, Standard Oil, and Firestone "assumed the active management of Pacific (City Lines)" in order to supervise its California operations more directly. That year, PCL began to acquire and scrap portions of the $100 million Pacific Electric system including rail lines from Los Angeles to Glendale, Burbank, Pasadena, and San Bernardino. Subsequently, in December 1944, another NCL affiliate (American City Lines) was financed by GM and Standard Oil to motorize downtown Los Angeles. At the time, the Pacific Electric shared downtown Los Angeles trackage with a local electric streetcar company, the Los Angeles Railway. American City Lines purchased the local system, scrapped its electric transit cars, tore down its power transmission lines, ripped up the tracks, and placed GM diesel buses fueled by Standard Oil on Los Angeles' crowded streets. In sum, GM and its auto-industrial allies severed Los Angeles' rail links and then motorized its downtown heart.

Motorization drastically altered the quality of life in southern California. Today, Los Angeles is an ecological wasteland: The palm trees are dying from petrochemical smog; the orange groves have been paved over by 300 miles of freeways; the air is a septic tank into which 4 million cars, half of them built by General Motors, pump 13,000 tons of pollutants daily. With the destruction of the efficient Pacific Electric rail system, Los Angeles may have lost its best hope for rapid rail transit and a smog-free metropolitan area. "The Pacific Electric," wrote UCLA Professor Hilton, "could have comprised the nucleus of a highly efficient rapid transit system, which would have contributed greatly to lessening the tremendous traffic and smog problems that developed from population growth." The substitution of GM diesel buses, which were forced to compete with automobiles for space on congested freeways, apparently benefited GM, Standard Oil, and Firestone considerably more than the riding public. Hilton added: "the (Pacific Electric) system, with its extensive private right of way, was far superior to a system consisting solely of buses on the crowded streets." As early as 1963, the city already was seeking ways of raising $500 million to rebuild a rail system "to supersede its present inadequate network of bus lines." A decade later, the estimated cost of constructing a 116-mile rail system, less than one-sixth the size of the earlier Pacific Electric, had escalated to more than $6.6 billion.

By 1949, General Motors had been involved in this replacement of more than 100 electric transit systems with GM buses in 45 cities including New York, Philadelphia, Baltimore, St. Louis, Oakland, Salt Lake City, and Los Angeles. In April of that year, a Chicago Federal jury convicted GM of having criminally conspired with Standard Oil of California, Firestone Tire and others to replace electric transportation with gas- or diesel-powered buses and to monopolize the sale of buses and related products to local transportation companies throughout the country. The court imposed a sanction of $5,000 on GM. In addition, the jury convicted H. C. Grossman, who was then treasurer of General Motors. Grossman had played a key role in the motorization campaigns and had served as a director of PCL when that company undertook the dismantlement of the $100 million Pacific Electric system. The court fined Grossman the magnanimous sum of $1.

Despite its criminal conviction, General Motors continued to acquire and dieselize electric transit properties through September of 1955. By then, approximately 88 percent of the nation's electric streetcar network had been eliminated. In 1936, when GM organized National City Lines, 40,000 streetcars were operating in the United States; at the end of 1955, only 5,000 remained. In December of that year, GM bus chief Roger M. Kyes correctly observed: "The motor coach has supplanted the interurban systems and has for all practical purposes eliminated the trolley (streetcar)."

The effect of General Motors' diversification into city transportation systems was substantially to curtail yet another alternative to motor vehicle transportation. Electric street railways and electric trolley buses were eliminated without regard to their relative merit as a mode of transport. Their displacement by oil-powered buses maximized the earnings of GM stockholders; but it deprived the riding public of a competing method of travel. Moreover, there is some evidence that in terms of air pollution and energy consumption these electric systems were superior to diesel buses. In any event, GM and its oil and tire co-conspirators used National City Lines as a device to force the sale of their products regardless of the public interest. As Professor Smerk, an authority on urban transportation, has written, "Street railways and trolley bus operations, even if better suited to traffic needs and the public interest, were doomed in favor of the vehicles and material produced by the conspirators."

General Motors' substitution of buses for city streetcar lines may also have contributed in an indirect manner to the abandonment of electric railway freight service. During the 1930's merchants relied extensively on interurban electric railways to deliver local goods and to interchange distant freight shipments with mainline railroads. The Pacific Electric, for example, was once the third largest freight railroad in California; it interchanged freight with the Southern Pacific, the Union Pacific and the Santa Fe. In urban areas, these railways often ran on local streetcar trackage. The conversion of city streetcars to buses, therefore, deprived them of city trackage and hastened their replacement by motor trucks, many of which, incidentally, were produced by GM.

General Motors also stood to profit from its interests in highway freight transport. Until the early 1950's, it maintained sizable stock interests in two of the Nation's largest trucking firms, Associated Transport and Consolidated Freightways, which enjoyed the freight traffic diverted for the electric railways. By 1951, these two companies had established more than 100 freight terminals in 29 states coast-to-coast and, more than likely, had invested in a substantial number of GM diesel-powered trucks.

GM's diversification into bus and rail operations would appear not only to have had the effect of foreclosing transport alternatives regardless of their comparative advantages but also to have contributed at least in part to urban air pollution problems. There were in fact some early warnings that GM's replacement of electric-driven vehicles with diesel-powered buses and trucks was increasing air pollution. On January 26, 1954, for instance, E. P. Crenshaw, GM bus general sales manager, sent the following memorandum to F. J. Limback, another GM executive:

> There has developed in a number of cities "smog" conditions which has resulted in Anti-Air Pollution committees, who immediately take issue with bus and truck operations, and especially Diesel engine exhaust. In many cases, efforts are being made to stop further substitution of Diesel buses for electric-driven vehicles. . . .

Three months later, in April 1954, the American Conference of Governmental Industrial Hygienists adopted a limit of 5 parts per million for human exposure to nitrogen oxides. Diesel buses, according to another report by two GM engineers, emitted "oxides of nitrogen concentrations over 200 times the recommended" exposure limit. Nevertheless, the dieselization program continued. Crenshaw reported to Limback in 1954:

> The elimination of street-cars and trolley-buses and their replacement by our large GM 51-passenger Diesel Hydraulic coaches continues steadily . . . in Denver, Omaha, Kansas City, San Francisco, Los Angeles, New Orleans, Honolulu, Baltimore, Milwaukee, Akron, Youngstown, Columbus, etc.

2. THE DISPLACEMENT OF BUS TRANSIT BY AUTOMOBILES

Diversification into bus production and, subsequently, into bus and rail operation inevitably encouraged General Motors to supplant trains, streetcars and trolleybuses with first gasoline and then diesel buses. It also contributed to this firm's monopolization of city and intercity bus production. The effect of GM's mutually exclusive dealing arrangement with Greyhound, for example, was to foreclose all other bus manufacturers and bus operating concerns from a substantial segment of the intercity market. At least by 1952, both companies had achieved their respective monopolies: GM dominated intercity bus production and Greyhound dominated intercity bus operation. By 1973, GM's only competitor, Motor Coach Industries (established in 1962 by Greyhound as the result of a Government antitrust decree) was wholly dependent on it for major components; and Greyhound's only operating competitor, Trailways, had been forced to purchase its buses from overseas. In the process, a number of innovative bus builders and potential manufacturers, including General Dynamics' predecessor (Consolidated Vultee) and the Douglas Aircraft Co., had been driven from the industry.

Likewise, in the city bus market, GM's exclusive bus replacement contracts with National City Lines, American City Lines, Pacific City Lines, the Omnibus Corporation, Public Transport of New Jersey and practically every other major bus operating company foreclosed competing city bus manufacturers from all but a handful of cities in the country and assured GM monopoly control of this market as well. Since 1925 more than 50 firms have withdrawn from city bus manufacturing including Ford, ACF-Brill, Marmon-Herrington, Mack Trucks, White Motor, International Harvester, Studebaker Twin Coach, Fifth Avenue Coach, Chrysler (Dodge), and Reo Motors. By 1973, only the Flxible Company, which had been established and controlled until 1958 by C. F. Kettering, a GM vice-president, remained as effectively a competitor-assembler of GM city buses. One other firm, AM General (American Motors), had announced its intention to assemble GM-powered city buses for delivery in late 1973. The ability of this firm, or for that matter Flxible and Motor Coach Industries, to survive beyond 1975, however, was seriously doubted by industry observers. That year a Government antitrust decree compelling GM to supply bus assemblers with diesel engines, transmissions and other major components will expire.

Monopolization of bus production and the elimination of electric street transportation has brought an end to price and technological competition in these industries. In this regard, several cities led by New York have filed a lawsuit charging that General Motors sets higher-than-competitive prices for its diesel buses and receives millions of dollars annually in monopoly profits. The suit also alleges that GM may be disregarding technological innovations in propulsion, pollution control and coach design, which would help attract patrons out of their automobiles.

In light of our dwindling petroleum supplies and mounting concerns about air pollution, the decline of technological competition in bus manufacturing is particularly unfortunate. ACF-Brill, Marmon-Herrington, Pullman-Standard, Twin Coach, and St. Louis Car once built electric buses and electric streetcars. Other firms manufactured steam-driven buses. According to a number of studies, these alternative forms of motive power would be preferable in terms of energy consumption, efficiency, pollution, noise, and durability to the diesel engine. Exclusion of these innovative firms, however, and GM's apparent disinterest in steam- or electric-powered vehicles (whose longer life, fewer parts, and easier repair would drastically reduce her placement sales), have precluded the availability of these technological alternatives today. Moreover, domination of domestic bus manufacturing by the world's largest industrial concern tends to deter entry by smaller, innovative firms. Lear Motors, for example, has developed quiet, low-pollution steam turbine buses; Mercedes-Benz, which sells buses in 160 countries, has produced low-pollution electric buses. Neither these nor any other firms, however, have been able to break into the GM-dominated American bus market. Furthermore, GM's conversion of much of this country's streetcar and interurban trackage to bus routes has precluded the survival of domestic streetcar builders and deterred entry by foreign railcar manufacturers. As a result, there remain few transit alternatives to GM diesel buses. None of the early White or Doble steam buses are still in operation. The last electric streetcars were built in 1953; only one electric bus (built in Canada) has been delivered since 1955. In 1973, only five American cities continued to operate electric buses, and eight ran a handful of ancient streetcars.

General Motors' gross revenues are 10 times greater if it sells cars rather than buses. In theory, therefore, GM has every economic incentive to discourage that effect. Engineering studies strongly suggest that conversion from electric transit to diesel buses results in higher operating costs, loss of patronage, and eventual bankruptcy. They demonstrate, for example, that diesel buses have 28 percent shorter economic lives, 40 percent higher operating costs, and 9 percent lower productivity than electric buses. They also conclude that the diesel's foul smoke, ear-splitting noise, and slow acceleration may discourage ridership. In short, by increasing the costs, reducing the revenues, and contributing to the collapse of hundreds of transit systems, GM's dieselization program may have had the long-term effect of selling GM cars.

Today, automobiles have completely replaced bus transportation in many areas of the country. Since 1952, the year GM achieved monopoly control of bus production, ridership has declined by 3 billion passengers and bus sales have fallen by about 60 percent. During that same period, GM automobile sales have risen from 1.7 million to more than 4.8 million units per year. By 1972, in a move which possibly signified the passing of bus transportation in this country, General Motors had begun converting its bus plants to motor home production. . . .

5. CURRENT PERFORMANCE OF THE GROUND
TRANSPORTATION SECTOR

Due to its anticompetitive structure and behavior, this country's ground transport sector can no longer perform satisfactorily. It has become seriously imbalanced in favor of the unlimited production of motor vehicles. Unlike every other industrialized country in the world, America has come to rely almost exclusively on cars and trucks for the land transportation of its people and goods. Cars are used for 90 percent of city and intercity travel; trucks are the only method of intracity freight delivery and account for 78 percent of all freight revenues. This substitution of more than 100 million petroleum-consuming cars and trucks for competing forms of alternately powered ground transportation is a significant factor in this sector's unacceptable level of inefficient and nonprogressive performance.

Efficiency in terms of market performance may be defined as a comparison of actual prices or costs with those that would [be obtained] in a competitively structured market. Currently, Americans pay $181 billion per year for motor vehicle transportation. In terms of high energy consumption, accident rates, contribution to pollution, and displacement of urban amenities, however, motor vehicle travel is possibly the most inefficient method of transportation devised by modern man.

More specifically, the diversion of traffic from energy-efficient electric rails to fuel-guzzling highway transport has resulted in an enormous consumption of energy. Rails can move passengers and freight for less than one-fifth the amount of energy required by cars and trucks. The displacement of rails by highways, therefore, has seriously depleted our scarce supplies of energy and has increased by several billion dollars a year the amount consumers must pay for ground transportation. It has been estimated, for example, that the diversion of passengers in urban areas from energy-efficient electric rail to gasoline automobiles results in their paying $18 billion a year more in energy cost alone. In addition, economists have found that the inefficient diversion of intercity freight from rail to trucks costs consumers $5 billion per year in higher prices for goods.

The substitution of highways for rails has also reduced efficiency by imposing higher indirect costs on the public in the form of accidents, pollution, and land consumption. Rail travel is 23 times as safe as travel by motor vehicles. The diversion to highways has cost the public an estimated $17 billion each year in economic damages attributable to motor vehicle accidents. This figure, however, cannot reflect the incalculable human costs of motor vehicle accidents: the violent deaths each year by car and truck of 55,000 Americans, more than all who died in the entire 12 years of our involvement in Vietnam, and the serious injuries to an additional 5 million of our citizens.

Likewise, the costs of urban air pollution have been greatly accentuated by the imbalance in favor of cars and trucks. Motor vehicles annually consume 42 billion gallons of petroleum within the densely populated 2 percent of the U.S. geographic area classified as urban. The consumption of this enormous quantity of fuel in urban areas produces in excess of 60 million tons of toxic pollutants, which in turn cost urban residents more than $4 billion in economic damages.

The presence of high concentrations of these motor vehicle pollutants, particularly oxides of nitrogen, in densely populated areas has also generated smog. The hazards of carbon monoxide and hydrocarbon emissions from automobiles have been widely acknowledged. Less well known are the potentially more serious effects of oxides of nitrogen produced primarily by diesel trucks and buses in high concentrations on congested city streets. When inhaled, these oxides combine with moisture in the lungs to form corrosive nitric acid which permanently damages lung tissues and accelerates death by slowly destroying the body's ability to resist heart and lung diseases. By contrast, if electric rail transportation were substituted in cities for motor vehicles, urban air pollution might be reduced substantially. Although the burning of fuels to generate this increased electrical energy would produce some pollution, it would pose a substantially less serious hazard to public health. Electric power plants can often be located in areas remote from population centers. Moreover, the increased pollution by generating facilities would be offset by a reduction in pollution due to oil refinery operations. Furthermore, the abatement of air pollution at a relatively small number of stationary power plants would represent a far easier task than attempting to install and monitor devices on 100 million transient motor vehicles.

The diversion of traffic from rail to highways has imposed a third cost on consumers—the consumption of vast amounts of taxable urban landscapes. From 60 to 65 percent of our cities' land area is devoted to highways, parking facilities, and other auto- and truck-related uses. In downtown Los Angeles, the figure approaches 85 percent. This has led to an erosion in the cities' tax base and, concomitantly, to a decline in their ability to finance the delivery of vital municipal services. Electric rail transportation, by comparison, requires less than one-thirteenth as much space as highways to move a comparable amount of passengers or goods, and in many cases can be located underground.

Progressiveness in terms of market performance is generally understood as a comparison of the number and importance of actual innovations with those which optimally could have been developed and introduced. The substitution of highways for rails has resulted in the decrease in mobility and has precluded important innovations in high-speed urban and intercity ground transportation. The decrease in mobility is most acute in urban areas. The average speed of rush hour traffic in cities dependent on motor vehicles, for example, is 12 miles per hour. Studies indicate that city traffic moved more quickly in 1890. Moreover, 20 percent of our urban population (the aged, youth, disabled, and poor) lack access to automobiles and, due to the nonexistence of adequate public transportation, are effectively isolated from employment or educational opportunities and other urban amenities. Substitution of highways for rails has also retarded innovations in high-speed urban and intercity transport. Technologically advanced rail transit systems, which currently operate in the major cities of Europe and Japan, would relieve congestion and contribute to urban mobility. High-speed intercity rail systems, such as Japan's 150-mile-per-hour electric Tokaido Express, would help to relieve mounting air traffic congestion and offer a practical alternative to slower and more tedious travel by car or truck. But the political predilections of the automakers have become the guidelines for American transportation policy. In contrast to the advanced rail transport emphasis of Europe and Japan, this country has persisted in the expansion of highway transport. As a result, America has become a second-rate nation in transportation.

There are strong indications, moreover, that due to mounting concerns about air pollution and a worldwide shortage of petroleum, our motor-vehicle-dominated transportation system will perform even worse in the future. The Environmental Protection Agency has warned that by 1977 motor vehicle emissions in major urban areas may compel a cutback in automobile, truck, and diesel bus use of as much as 60 percent. In addition, the Department of the Interior has forecast that the current petroleum crisis might cripple transportation and cause "serious economic and social disruptions." More precisely, an excessive reliance in the past on fuel-guzzling motor vehicles for transport has contributed to a crisis in energy which now threatens to shut down industries, curb air and ground travel, and deprive our homes of heating oil for winter.

Despite these adverse trends, the automakers appear bent on further motorization. Henry Ford II, for instance, has noted that notwithstanding "the energy crisis, the environmental crisis, and the urban crisis" new car sales in the United States "have increased by more than a million during the past 2 model years." General Motors' chief operating executive has predicted that soon each American will own a "family of cars" for every conceivable travel activity including small cars for trips, recreational vehicles for leisure, and motor homes for mobile living. GM is also engaged in the displacement of what little remains of this Nation's rail systems. To that end, it is developing 750-horsepower diesel engines to haul multiple trailers at speeds of 70 miles per hour along the nearly completed Interstate Highway System. These "truck trains" are slated to replace rail freight service. As substitutes for regional subway systems, GM is also advocating 1,400-unit diesel "bus trains," which would operate on exclusive busways outside cities and in bus tunnels under downtown areas. Both diesel truck trains and underground bus trains, however, would seem grossly incompatible with public concerns about petroleum shortages and suffocating air pollution.

The automakers' motorization program, moreover, is worldwide in scope. The superior bus and rail systems which flourish in the rest of the industrialized world interfere with the sale of cars and trucks by the Big Three's foreign subsidiaries. "The automobile industry put America on wheels," said GM Chairman Gerstenberg in September of 1972. "Today," he added, "expanding markets all around the world give us the historic opportunity to put the whole world on wheels."

27

The Toxic Cloud

Michael H. Brown

A warning sign could be hung somewhere in every city: Danger, Toxic Air Contamination. The poisons once thought to be a serious concern only near a place such as Love Canal are now known to be everywhere. They appear in the air of an alpine forest, or over a Pacific island. They are also in the cabinet under the kitchen sink. . . .

We live in an era during which life expectancy as a whole has increased because of better health care for conventional types of physical distress. While the majority of cancers are induced by factors other than environmental toxics, we are also at the point where cancer is contracted by 30 percent of the population. Of Americans now living, 74 million will contract the disease. The cancer death rate has increased 26 percent in just two decades. Birth defects are also on the rise. Between 1970 and 1980 there was a 300 percent increase in reported cases of displaced hips and a 240 percent increase in babies with ventricular septal defects—a hole between chambers of the heart.

Dave Haas Ewell, who used to hunt the swamps that surround his home in Louisiana, knows first-hand what pollution means to local communities. "It's unreal what they have done," he said, nodding to the refineries and chemical plants that crowd the Mississippi's banks. "And ya know what? It's our children who'll pay for it. They will."

Dave Ewell's herd of cows was poisoned by chlorinated hydrocarbons, solvents, and metals which had deluged the area years ago, scalding the cypresses and turning alligators belly-up. They came from a chemical

Adapted from Michael H. Brown, *The Toxic Cloud*, New York, Harper & Row, 1989. Reprinted by permission.

plant next to his family's plantation, and I remembered that upon my first visit there, in 1979, shiny globules of mercury oozed from the indentations my foot made in the muck near a bayou.

When the sun was hot, a thick, black sludge surfaced down by the bayou, sending an oil slick toward the Mississippi, which supplies drinking water to the city of New Orleans. There, the environment and cancer rates are such that Dr. Velma L. Campbell, a physician at the Ochsner Clinic, describes the toxic poisoning of the region as "a massive human experiment conducted without the consent of the experimental subjects."

Beginning two decades ago, the way we understand air pollution— indeed all forms of pollution—changed radically. In the 1960s and 1970s, scientists equipped with new analytical tools began identifying an array of mysterious synthetic compounds in the flesh of trout and other fish caught in the largest of the Great Lakes, that 31,700 square miles of fresh water known, with due respect, as Lake Superior. PCBs and DDT were among those found. So was another potent chlorinated insecticide called toxaphene.

In Superior's Whitefish Bay, infant birds began suffering from cataracts and edema. Their necks and heads became so swollen they could not open their eyes. Nor could some of them eat. They suffered from a defect, called "cross beak syndrome," that prevented their upper and lower bills from meeting.

In other parts of the Great Lakes, especially near Green Bay, the problem was more acute. In some spots, terns soon would be observed with club foot-like deformities that prevented the birds from being able to stand. Mink and river otters were disappearing from the south shore of Lake Ontario and around Lake Michigan. Though they had been making a comeback, by the mid-1980s bald eagles would have trouble nesting along Lake Superior. The problem, it was suspected, was their diet of chemically contaminated gulls.

There was also concern about human infants along the lakes. In one part of Michigan, some babies tested seemed to have lower birth weights and smaller head circumferences than children born to women who ate no fish. Some of the babies had what appeared to be abnormally jerky and unbalanced movements, weak reflexes, and general sluggishness.

While Lake Superior's vast shoreline could be expected to receive some chemical runoff from farms and scattered industry, the levels and character of its toxicants did not quite fit with what would be expected to enter the lake through the sewers, creeks, and rivers that drain into her.

Located at a relatively remote region between northern Michigan and southern Canada, Superior had not been plagued by the same problems that historically befell its little sister, Lake Erie. Erie's water had been starved of oxygen by phosphates which formed suds at outfall pipes and provoked wild overgrowths of algae—causing bloated fish to wash ashore. That pollution had taken no modern technical gear to detect: on

Cleveland's Cuyahoga River, fires had ignited the oil slicks into a biblical spectacle of flames shooting up from the water itself.

But several hundred miles to the northwest, Lake Superior still had the aura of purity. Nearly the size of Indiana, the lake serves as headwaters for the greatest freshwater system on earth, a system that contains 20 percent of the planet's fresh surface water.

Yet suddenly, in the 1970s, its unsullied image was compromised. The compounds being found in Superior were mostly invisible and odorless in nature, but they posed much more of a danger than the more familiar sulfides, raw sewage and oil. Among them, toxaphene—a pesticide that possesses the widely recognized capability of causing thyroid carcinomas in rodents. Though not quite as persistent as DDT, it too accumulates in the ecosystem, it too is biomagnified in animal flesh and it is every bit as toxic as DDT, if not more so. Its concentrations in the lake approached levels at which consumption of fish is banned.

The pressing question: Where was the toxaphene coming from?

In Canada it had been closely restricted, and on the American side its major use was not near the Great Lakes nor anywhere else in the Midwest—it was in two impossibly distant areas: California and the Deep South.

Had it somehow become a constituent of ambient air? Had it descended like acid rain or nuclear fallout? Looking to test an even more isolated ecosystem, scientists began journeying to Siskiwit Lake in a national park called Isle Royale. The island is situated in the northern part of Lake Superior, more than thirty miles from Ontario's Thunder Bay, the nearest community of any real proportion.

The only means of access from one part of Isle Royale to another is by foot trails. There were no outfalls, no farm runoff, no toxic dumps. Nor did nay of the tainted water of Superior flow into Siskiwit Lake, for Siskiwit's elevation, propped as it is on the island, is nearly sixty feet higher than Lake Superior's. All things considered, it seemed, there was no way at all for toxaphene to get to Siskiwit.

Yet to the shock of the investigating scientists, fish netted from Siskiwit had nearly double the PCBs that had been found in Lake Superior, and nearly ten times as much DDE—a breakdown product of DDT. One might rationalize certain levels in Lake Superior, with its vast shore and its exposure to at least some modern effluents. But, now, how did the stuff get to the isolated environs of Isle Royale in such high concentrations?

Scientists hauled up their gas chromatographs to various parts of the country and began searching for clues. One big hint was found when rain was tested at an estuary in South Carolina. Toxaphene was found in more than 75 percent of the samples. High levels also turned up in Greenville, on the lower Mississippi River. It was apparently lifting off the fields and into the wind. Tracking it northward, air samples also documented its presence in St. Louis and up in Michigan.

For those who thought such compounds remain firmly earthbound, or that what little bit does become airborne would simply disappear in the troposphere, the numbers were startling ones indeed. By the time it was 825 miles from Greenville and approaching the neighborhood of Lake Superior, the toxaphene was still at 4 percent of the Greenville level. At the same time, toxaphene was also being tracked over Bermuda and the North Atlantic, in the fish and water birds from Swedish lakes, in the North and Baltic seas, in the Tyrolean Alps and in Antarctic cod.

The conclusion seemed as obvious as it was momentous: we were no longer talking about the long-range transport of just sulphur and nitrogen but of the dreaded chlorinated pesticides—thought previously to be a crisis only in lake and river sediments. Chlorinateds, the compounds Rachel Carson worried about in her classic work, *Silent Spring*, were taking wing—in quantities great enough to threaten distant wildlife and people.

Soon, chemists tapping their computers at the University of Minnesota would start making somber estimates that would have seemed like sheer nonsense just a few years before. Perhaps 85, perhaps 90 percent of the total PCB input to Lakes Michigan and Superior was not from sewers but through the air, they said.

Whatever the number, it was a bad signal not just for cormorants and herons but also, perhaps, for the 26 million people who drink from the lakes. One 1981 estimate said about a million pounds of polycyclic aromatic hydrocarbons, a dangerous chemical produced in the generation and use of complex synthetic chemicals, were falling into the lakes each year. Also found in the lakes are substantial quantities of benzene hexachloride, a common synthetic chemical sometimes used as a fungicide, and DDT. Since it had been banned in the U.S. for a decade, the DDT, scientists conjectured, must have come over the poles from Europe and Asia, or from Mexico and parts south.

In tests in places like California, the results showed that the insecticides vaporized in great quantities right off the plants themselves. One study reported a 59 percent loss of toxaphene from a cotton field within twenty-eight days. Other experiments in closed chambers indicated that 24 percent of toxaphene turned into gas within ninety days of the last application, meaning that, in 1974, at least 142.5 million pounds of it vaporized into the American atmosphere.

That meant we were directly breathing chlorinated pesticides and PCBs, not just eating them with contaminated fish. Once the emotional reaction subsided, more questions arose. For example: If toxaphene and PCBs are so airworthy, what else is in the wild blue yonder?

With this line of study came a new understanding of airborne transport of toxic chemicals. We now know that pollution can fly in the form of tiny droplets, small pieces—or particles—of solid matter, invisible gases, or as a sort of mix of them known as the aerosol. The particulates may be washed to earth by the falling rain, or fall by simple gravity.

The gases, depending on how easily they dissolve in water, may become part of airborne moisture, moving wherever it moves, permeate vegetation, or condense into fine particulates that can be seen only with an electron microscope. Many chemicals, including chlorinated pesticides, travel both as passengers on a particle and in a gaseous state. Solvents such as benzene or toluene, by definition "volatile" compounds that easily evaporate, frequently find themselves in vapor states or dissolved in other substances. Even metals, under the right conditions, can turn vaporous. Others, such as the deadly dioxins, are not water soluble and prefer to cling to a particle.

Most large particulates remain within five or ten miles of their origin, but the smaller they are the farther they fly, and if they are small enough they can remain aloft for days or weeks. At times, if they get caught in the stratosphere, the weeks may turn to months, the months to a year. Gases, if they decay slowly enough, can travel still farther.

The question of atmospheric transport, once keen during atmospheric nuclear bomb-testing, has found greatly heightened currency in recent years with the introduction into public consciousness of acid rain. The recent specter of lake fish in Canada and upstate New York dying from acid that originates in coal-fired plants along the Ohio Valley and other parts of the industrialized Midwest has awakened us to the idea that our atmosphere is not infinite. What you place into it does not just disappear.

In the words of meteorologist and textbook author C. Donald Ahrens of California's Modesto Junior College, the atmosphere "is a thin, gaseous envelope comprised mostly of nitrogen and oxygen, with clouds of condensed water vapor and ice particles. Almost 99 percent of the atmosphere lies within eighteen miles of the surface. In fact, if the earth were to shrink to the size of a beach ball, its inhabitable atmosphere would be thinner than a piece of paper." Referring to the radioactivity tracked around the globe from the damaged reactor at Chernobyl, Dr. Kenneth A. Rahn, an atmospheric physicist at the University of Rhode Island said "It was only eleven days from Chernobyl to here. In terms of transport, this is a quite small planet."

It was in the 1950s and the 1960s that medical researchers began tracking blips that turned out to be sharp and steady upward lines on the cancer graphs of Louisiana. Since cancer is believed to take up to two decades to surface in the body, that takes us back to the 1940s when, coincidentally, the petrochemical industry was taking deep root along the lower Mississippi, drawn there by cheap feedstock gas from the oil fields, easy water transport, and lucrative tax incentives.

The government of Louisiana serviced the chemical makers as no other government did—especially those that were offshoots of the revered petroleum industry. As the older industrial states in the North began controlling the wanton pollution there, corporations looked to the South for relief from such costly regulations. Down at the mouth of the Mississippi, a manufacturing company could obtain up to ten years of exemptions from property taxes.

Soon, companies making pesticides, chlorine, rubber, antifreeze, detergents, plastics and a variety of chemical products sprouted along the river and in the swamps. Virtually every major American chemical corporation and several foreign ones have an outpost along the river. By 1986 Louisiana was ranked third nationally in chemical production, behind New Jersey and Texas.

Today, the biggest splotches of black on the nation's maps of lung cancer rates are in the south, allowing the lower Mississippi to borrow from New Jersey the nickname "Cancer Alley." While several Northeastern states still had higher rates for cancer in general in the 1970s (reflecting, perhaps, a longer exposure to industry), Louisiana lost 7,636 people to cancer in 1983 alone, and the decade before, it led the nation in lung cancer deaths with a rate of about eighty per 100,000 people—about 10 percent more than runners-up Maryland, Delaware, and Mississippi.

In one study of lung cancer among white males in three thousand American counties, thirty-eight of Louisiana's sixty-four counties (or parishes) were in the top 10 percent. In one recent period, figures showed that 30 percent of state residents could expect to develop cancer over a lifetime, including 33.1 percent of those living in New Orleans. Noted a special report to the governor in 1984, "Nearly one cancer death per hour in Louisiana is reason to be gravely concerned." The reason: There were only 4.4 million people in the state.

There are dozens of other kinds of industries that contribute to cancer, and by one estimate only 4 percent of the cancer incidents caused by airborne toxics can be laid onto the lap of chemical processors or the combination of toxics emitted by the rubber and petroleum industries. The emissions of road vehicles account for the most cases of toxicant-induced cancer.

But, for the most part, it is chemical firms that release the most troubling types of molecules into the environment. In Baton Rouge, according to company data, an Exxon Chemical plant was leaking 560,000 pounds of benzene yearly, while just south of there, according to a survey by the Sierra Club, eighteen plants in and around St. Gabriel and Geismar dumped about 400 billion pounds of toxic chemicals into the air during the first nine months of 1986 (*Editor's note: State health and environmental agencies are investigating an alarmingly high number of stillbirths in the St. Gabriel area. On August 5, Louisiana Governor Edwin Edwards, who has been criticized for gutting state environmental programs, called it "an emergency situation."*).

Add together the evaporation from oil-field pits, the volatilization from ponds of waste liquids and from storage tanks, the miasma rising from places such as Devil's Swamp, the steaming, hissing valves at petrochemical plants all the way down the Mississippi and the plumes of

refinery smoke that form their own cumulus strata across the horizon—
and the picture in southern Louisiana becomes one not of a low, lingering
smog but more that of a toxic tornado.

How can our society deal with the threat posed by toxic pollution? Much
can be accomplished, as the last decade of environmental reforms suggests, through legislation, lobbying and grassroots organizing to stem the
tide of toxic pollution. In the end, however, the solution must be pronounced at a philosophical level. In the end highly toxic chemicals must
be treated with wary respect—and isolated handling—not unlike what is
practiced with radioactive elements.

Since industry has shown itself to be indifferent to public risks it
creates, we must move toward a policy by which no company will be
allowed to make or use any compound until the firm proves that it can
either disassemble that compound into harmless, natural compounds—
destroy it completely, with no toxic residues—or proves that the compound has absolutely no health repercussions whatsoever. Those compounds that fail the test but already exist must be gradually phased out, if
not outright withdrawn.

Our society has two basic choices: to barter its health for modern
conveniences and stop worrying about this at all; or to begin ridding the
environment of compounds that threaten our immune systems, that
threaten ecosystems, that threaten the very planet itself because of their
potential to ruin protective layers of the upper atmosphere. In other
words, we must prepare to ban a great many more chemicals than have so
far been banned. And we must wean ourselves from certain conveniences—especially plastic—that cannot be made from biodegradable
products. Our selfishness, our uncaring, threaten to unravel us all.

28

The Changing Atmosphere

Thomas E. Graedel and Paul J. Crutzen

The earth's atmosphere has never been free of change: its composition, temperature and self-cleansing ability have all varied since the planet first formed. Yet the pace in the past two centuries has been remarkable: the atmosphere's composition in particular has changed significantly faster than it has at any time in human history.

The increasingly evident effects of the ongoing changes include acid deposition by rain and other processes, corrosion of materials, urban smog and a thinning of the stratospheric ozone (O_3) shield that protects the earth from harmful ultraviolet radiation. Atmospheric scientists expect also that the planet will soon warm rapidly (causing potentially dramatic climatic shifts) through enhancement of the greenhouse effect—the heating of the earth by gases that absorb infrared radiation from the sun-warmed surface of the planet and then return the radiation to the earth.

Surprisingly, these important phenomena do not stem from modifications in the atmosphere's major constituents. Excluding the widely varying content of water vapor, the concentrations of the gases that make up more than 99.9 percent of the atmosphere—nitrogen (N_2), oxygen (O_2) and totally unreactive noble gases—have been nearly constant for much longer than human beings have been on the earth. Rather, the effects are caused in large part by changes, mainly increases, in the levels of several of the atmosphere's minor constituents, or trace gases. Such gases include sulfur dioxide (SO_2), two nitrogen oxides known collectively as NO_x—

From *Scientific American*, September 1989. Reprinted by permission.

nitric oxide (NO) and nitrogen dioxide (NO_2)—and several chloro-fluorocarbons (compounds that contain chlorine, fluorine, carbon and sometimes hydrogen).

Sulfur dioxide, for example, rarely constitutes as much as 50 parts per billion of the atmosphere, even where its emissions are highest, and yet it contributes to acid deposition, to the corrosion of stone and metal and to the aesthetic nuisance of decreased visibility. The NO_x compounds, which are similarly scarce, are important in the formation of both acid deposition and what is called photochemical smog, a product of solar-driven chemical reactions in the atmosphere. The chloroflurocarbons, which as a group account for just one part per billion or so of the atmo-sphere, are the agents primarily responsible for depleting the strato-spheric ozone layer. In addition, rising levels of chlorofluorocarbons, together with methane (CH_4), nitrous oxide (N_2O) and carbon dioxide (CO_2)—by far the most abundant trace gas at 350 parts per million—are enhancing the greenhouse effect.

The hydroxyl radical (OH), a highly reactive molecular fragment, also influences atmospheric activity even though it is much scarcer than the other gases, with a concentration of less than .00001 part per billion. Hydroxyl plays a different role, however: it contributes to the cleansing of the atmosphere. Its abundance in the atmosphere may diminish in the future.

Certainly some fluctuation in the concentrations of atmospheric constit-uents can derive from variations in rates of emission by natural sources. Volcanoes, for instance, can release sulfur- and chlorine-containing gases into the troposphere (the lower 10 to 15 kilometers of the atmosphere) and the stratosphere (extending roughly from 10 to 50 kilometers above the surface). The fact remains, however, that the activities of human beings account for most of the rapid changes of the past 200 years. Such activities include the combustion of fossil fuels (coal and petroleum) for energy, other industrial and agricultural practices, biomass burning (the burning of vegetation) and deforestation.

So much is clear, but which human activities generate which emissions? How do altered concentrations of trace gases give rise to such an array of effects? How much have the problems grown, and what are their conse-quences for the planet? Although complete answers to these questions are still forthcoming, multidisciplinary efforts by chemists, meteorologists, solar and space physicists, geophysicists, biologists, ecologists and others are making good headway.

Multidisciplinary collaboration is crucial because the factors influencing the fates of the gases in the atmosphere and their interactions with the biosphere are complex and incompletely understood. For instance, the chemical reactions a gas undergoes in the atmosphere can vary depend-ing on the local mixture of gases and particles, the temperature, the intensity of the sun, the presence of different kinds of clouds or precipitation and patterns of airflow (which move chemicals horizontally and vertically). The reactions, in turn, influence how long a gas remains in the atmosphere and hence whether the gas or its end products have global or more localized effects on the environment.

Among the fruits of the investigations has been an improved understanding of the emissions produced by specific human activities. The combustion of fossil fuels for energy is known to yield substantial amounts of sulfur dioxide (particularly from coal), nitrogen oxides (which form when nitrogen and oxygen in the air are heated) and carbon dioxide. If the burning is incomplete, it also yields carbon monoxide (CO), a variety of hydrocarbons (including methane) and soot (carbon particles). Other industrial activities release additional sulfur dioxide (smelting is an example) or inject such substances as chlorofluorocarbons or toxic metals into the air.

Agricultural practices lead to the emissions of several gases as well. The burning of forests and savanna grasses in tropical and subtropical regions to create pastures and cropland yields additional large amounts of carbon monoxide, methane and nitrogen oxides. Moreover, soil exposed after forests are cleared emits nitrous oxide, as do nitrogen-rich fertilizers spread over fields. The breeding of domestic animals is another major source of methane (from oxygen-shunning bacteria in the digestive tract of cattle and other cud-chewing animals), as is the cultivation of rice, which is a staple food for many people in the tropics and subtropics.

Recent investigations have also led to a better understanding of the effects produced by increased anthropogenic emissions. For example, the much studied phenomenon of "acid rain" (by which we mean also acid snow, fog and dew) is now known to develop mainly as a by-product of atmospheric interactions involving the NO_x gases and sulfur dioxide. Through various reactions, such as combination with the hydroxyl radical, these gases can be converted within days into nitric acid (HNO_3) and sulfuric acid (H_2SO_4), both of which are dissolved readily in water. When the acidified droplets fall to the earth's surface, they constitute acid rain.

Because water droplets are removed from the atmosphere rapidly, acid rain is a regional or continental, rather than global, phenomenon. In contrast, the atmospheric lifetimes of several other trace gases, including methane, carbon dioxide, the chlorofluorocarbons and nitrous oxide, are much longer . . . and so the gases spread rather evenly throughout the atmosphere, causing global effects.

Since the beginning of the Industrial Revolution in the mid-18th century, the acidity of precipitation (as measured by the concentration of hydrogen ions) has increased in many places. For example, it has roughly quadrupled in the northeastern U.S. since 1900, paralleling increased emissions of sulfur dioxide and the NO_x gases. Similar increases have been found elsewhere in the industrialized parts of the world. Acid rain has also been detected in the virtually unindustrialized tropics, where it stems mainly from the release of the NO_x gases and hydrocarbons by biomass burning.

Wet deposition is not the only way sulfuric and nitric acids in the troposphere find their way to the earth's surface. The acids can also be deposited "dry," as gases or as constituents of microscopic particles. Indeed, a growing body of evidence indicates that dry deposition can cause the same environmental problems as the wet form.

Acid deposition clearly places severe stress on many ecosystems. Although the specific interactions of such deposition with lake fauna, soils and different vegetation types are still incompletely understood, acid deposition is known to have strongly increased the acidity of lakes in Scandinavia, the northeastern U.S. and southeastern Canada, thereby leading to reductions in the size and diversity of fish populations. Such deposition also appears to play some role in the forest damage that has been discovered in parts of the northeastern U.S. and Europe.

There is little doubt that acids deposited from the troposphere also contribute to the corrosion of outdoor equipment, buildings and works of art, particularly in urban areas—costing tens of billions of dollars each year for repairs and equipment replacement in the U.S. alone. Particles containing sulfate (SO_4^{2-}) have other effects as well. By scattering light efficiently, they decrease visibility; by influencing cloud albedo, they may have important implications for climate. . . .

In and around cities photochemical smog is another negative consequence of modern life. The term technically refers to the undesirable mixture of gases formed in the lower troposphere when solar radiation acts on anthropogenic emissions (particularly the NO_x gases and hydrocarbons from vehicle exhaust) to produce reactive gases that can be destructive to living organisms.

Ozone is a major product of such photochemical reactions and is itself the main cause of smog-induced eye irritation, impaired lung function and damage to trees and crops. The severity of smog is therefore generally assessed on the basis of ground-level ozone concentrations. In other words, the same three-oxygen molecule that is critically important for absorbing ultraviolet radiation in the stratosphere, where some 90 percent of atmospheric ozone is concentrated, is a problem when it accumulates in excess near the earth's surface.

Investigators have measured ozone levels in the atmosphere since the late 19th century, first from the ground and then within the atmosphere, aided by sophisticated airborne devices. Some of the earliest data showed that the "natural" level of ozone close to the ground at one measuring post in Europe roughly a century ago was about 10 parts per billion. Today the typical ground-level concentrations in Western Europe are from two to four times higher. Abundances more than 10 times higher than the natural level are now often recorded in Western Europe, California, the eastern U.S. and Australia.

Photochemical smog is also appearing in broad regions of the tropics and subtropics, particularly because of the periodic burning of savanna grasses; the same territories may be set afire as often as once a year. This practice releases large amounts of precursors to smog. Because solar radiation is plentiful and strong in those regions and photochemical reactions occur quickly, ozone levels can readily climb to perhaps five times higher than normal. As the populations in the tropics and subtropics grow, unhealthy air should become even more widespread there. Such a prospect is particularly worrisome because the properties of the soil in those regions may make the ecosystems there more vulnerable than the ecosystems in the middle latitudes to smog's effects.

Although a decrease in ozone near the ground would benefit polluted regions, any decrease in stratospheric ozone is disturbing, because the resulting increase in ultraviolet radiation reaching the earth could have many serious effects. It could elevate the incidence of skin cancer and cataracts in human beings, and it might damage crops and phytoplankton, the microscopic plants that are the basis of the food chain in the ocean.

So far, the extent of stratospheric ozone depletion has been most dramatic over Antarctica, where an ozone "hole," a region of increasingly severe ozone loss, has appeared each southern spring since about 1975. In the past decade springtime ozone levels over Antarctica have diminished by about 50 percent. . . . A more global assessment of the stratospheric ozone layer is still in a preliminary stage, but in the past 20 years depletions of from 2 to 10 percent have apparently begun to occur during the winter and early spring in the middle-to-high latitudes of the Northern Hemisphere, with the greatest declines in the higher latitudes.

It is now quite evident that chlorofluorocarbons, particularly CFC-11 ($CFCl_3$) and CFC-12 (CF_2Cl_2), are the major culprits responsible for ozone depletion. These anthropogenic chemicals, whose emissions and atmospheric concentrations have grown rapidly since their introduction several decades ago, are widespread as refrigerants, aerosol propellants, solvents and blowing agents for foam production, in part because they have what initially seemed to be a wonderful property: they are virtually unreactive in the lower atmosphere, and so they pose no direct toxic threat to living organisms.

Unfortunately, the very same characteristics that render chlorofluorocarbons rather inert enable them to reach the stratosphere unchanged. There they are exposed to strong ultraviolet radiation, which breaks them apart and liberates chlorine atoms that can destroy ozone by catalyzing its conversion to molecular oxygen. (Catalysts accelerate chemical reactions but are freed unaltered at the end.) Indeed, every chlorine atom ultimately eliminates many thousands of ozone molecules. Primarily because of the emission of chlorofluorocarbons, the level of ozone-destroying chlorinated compounds in the stratosphere is now four to five times higher than normal and is increasing at a rate of approximately 5 percent a year—developments that highlight the profound effect human activity can have on the stratosphere. . . .

Even if chlorofluorocarbon emissions stopped today, chemical reactions causing the destruction of stratospheric ozone would continue for at least a century. The reason is simple: the compounds remain that long in the atmosphere and would continue to diffuse into the stratosphere from the tropospheric reservoir long after emissions had ceased.

The depletion of global stratospheric ozone seems to be the handiwork primarily of a single class of industrial products—the chlorofluorocarbons—but several different emissions combine to raise the specter of a rapid greenhouse warming of the earth. Exactly how high global temperatures might climb in the years ahead is not yet clear. What is clear is that the levels of such infrared-absorbing trace gases as carbon dioxide, methane, the chlorofluorocarbons and nitrous oxide have mounted dramatically in the past decades, making added heating inevitable.

The trapping of heat near the surface of the planet by naturally emitted trace gases is a vital process: without it the planet would be too cold for habitation. Yet the prospect of a sudden temperature increase of even a few degrees Celsius is disquieting because no one can accurately predict its environmental effects, such as what the precise changes will be in precipitation around the world and in sea level. Any effects will probably be rapid, however, making it extremely difficult or impossible for the world's ecosystems and for human societies to adapt.

The extraordinary pace of the recent increases in greenhouse gases becomes strikingly evident when modern levels are compared with those of the distant past. Such comparisons have been made for several gases, including carbon dioxide—which alone accounts for more than half of the heat trapped by trace species—and methane, which is a more efficient infrared absorber than carbon dioxide but is significantly less abundant.

The histories of carbon dioxide and methane can be reconstructed on the basis of their concentrations in bubbles of air trapped in ice in such perpetually cold places as Antarctica and Greenland. Because the gases are long-lived and hence are spread fairly evenly throughout the atmosphere, the polar samples reveal the approximate global average concentrations of previous eras.

Analyses of the bubbles in ice samples indicate that carbon dioxide and methane concentrations held steady from the end of the last ice age some 10,000 years ago until roughly 300 years ago, at close to 260 parts per million and 700 parts per billion, respectively. Some 300 years ago the methane levels began to climb, and roughly 100 years ago the levels of both gases began to soar to their current levels of 350 parts per million for carbon dioxide and 1,700 parts per billion for methane. Moreover, direct worldwide measurements made by several investigators during the past decade have shown that atmospheric methane levels are growing more rapidly than those of carbon dioxide, at the remarkably high rate of about 1 percent a year.

The increases of both gases in the 20th century must be attributed in large part to the many expanding human influences on emissions. For carbon dioxide the sources are mainly fossil-fuel combustion and de-forestation in the tropics; for methane, mainly rice cultivation, cattle breeding, biomass burning in tropical forests and savannas, microbial activity in municipal landfills and leakage of gas during the recovery and distribution of coal, oil and natural gas. As the world's population grows during the next century—and with it the demand for more energy, rice and meat products—the atmospheric concentration of methane could double. The climatic warming caused by methane and other trace gases could well approach that caused by carbon dioxide.

What are the expected trends for other trace gases? We as well as several other workers have extrapolated from the past and the present to make projections for the future, taking into account such factors as estimated increases both in population and in energy consumption. The estimates indicate that increases can be expected in the atmospheric concentrations of virtually all trace species in the next 100 years if new technologies and major energy-conservation efforts are not instituted to diminish the expected dependence on high-sulfur coal, an environmentally disadvantageous fuel, as the world's major energy source.

For example, as part of a multicenter collaboration, we have looked at past sulfur dioxide concentrations over the eastern U.S. and Europe (estimated prior to the mid-1960's on the basis of emission rates) and have speculated about future levels there and over the little-industrialized Gangetic Plain of India. . . . The historical assessment for the U.S. shows a marked increase in sulfur dioxide concentrations between 1890 and 1940, paralleling the buildup of "smokestack" industries and the construction of many new power plants. The amount of sulfur dioxide then leveled off and decreased in the 1960's and early 1970's. To a great extent, the decrease reflects the increased exploitation of oil (which is low in sulfur) for energy as well as the success of clean-air legislation in curbing sulfur emissions.

The concentrations of sulfur dioxide increased over Europe between 1890 and the mid-1900's but then leveled off; they did not decline appreciably, because until recently emission-control efforts were less vigorous than in the U.S. For the Gangetic Plain, where industrialization is rather recent, sulfur dioxide concentrations over some places have climbed from almost nothing in 1890 to levels that are now approaching those over the northeastern U.S.

The average sulfur dioxide concentrations over all three large regions are expected to increase, in part because low-sulfur fuels will probably become scarcer (although extremely stringent emission controls could stabilize levels over the U.S. and Europe for a few decades). The increases could be most marked over India and other developing countries that have rapidly growing populations and access to abundant supplies of high-sulfur coal, which is relatively inexpensive. Clearly, major measures must be introduced in the energy sector to prevent sulfur dioxide concentrations from rising extremely high.

Increases may also occur in a gas we have not yet discussed in detail: carbon monoxide, which has the power to decrease the self-cleansing ability of the atmosphere. A rise in carbon monoxide concentrations is likely because its sources—fossil-fuel combustion, biomass burning and atmospheric reactions involving methane—are all expected to increase. On the other hand, a significant (but still not well-quantified) amount of the gas is formed in the atmosphere over the tropics from the breakdown of hydrocarbons emitted by vegetation, a source that human activities are removing. The future concentrations of carbon monoxide are therefore uncertain, although on balance many workers foresee a rise over the Northern Hemisphere.

Carbon monoxide undermines the self-cleansing ability of the atmosphere by lowering the concentration of the hydroxyl radical, which is an important "detergent" because it reacts with nearly every trace-gas molecule in the atmosphere, including substances that would otherwise be inert. Without hydroxyl, the concentrations of most trace gases would become much higher than those of today, and the atmosphere as a whole would have totally different chemical, physical and climatic properties.

Our projections for the future are discouraging, then, if one assumes that human activities will continue to emit large quantities of undesirable trace gases into the atmosphere. Humanity's unremitting growth and development not only are changing the chemistry of the atmosphere but also are driving the earth rapidly toward a climatic warming of unprecedented magnitude. This climatic change, in combination with increased concentrations of various gases, constitutes a potentially hazardous experiment in which everyone on the earth is taking part.

What is particularly troubling is the possibility of unwelcome surprises, as human activities continue to tax an atmosphere whose inner workings and interactions with organisms and nonliving materials are incompletely understood. The Antarctic ozone hole is a particularly ominous example of the surprises that may be lurking ahead. Its unexpected severity has demonstrated beyond doubt that the atmosphere can be exquisitely sensitive to what seem to be small chemical perturbations and that the manifestations of such perturbations can arise much faster than even the most astute scientists could expect.

Nevertheless, some steps can be taken to counteract rapid atmospheric change, perhaps lessening the known and unknown threats. For example, evidence indicates that a major decrease in the rate of fossil-fuel combustion would slow the greenhouse warming, reduce smog, improve visibility and minimize acid deposition. Other steps could be targeted against particular gases, such as methane. Its emission could be reduced by instituting landfill operations that prevent its release and possibly by adopting less wasteful methods of fossil-fuel production. Methane emission from cattle might even be diminished by novel feeding procedures.

Perhaps more encouraging is the fact that many people and institutions are now aware that their actions can have not only local but also global consequences for the atmosphere and the habitability of the planet. A few recent events exemplify this awareness: in the Montreal protocol of 1987, dozens of nations agreed to halve their chlorofluorocarbon emissions by the end of the century, and several countries and the major chlorofluorocarbon manufacturers have more recently announced their intention to eliminate the chemicals by that deadline. Some of the same nations that have been involved in the Montreal protocol are now discussing the possibility of an international "law of the atmosphere." It would be directed at limiting the release of several greenhouse and chemically active trace gases, including carbon dioxide, methane and nitrous oxide, as well as sulfur dioxide and the NO_x gases.

We and many others think the solution to the earth's environmental problems lies in a truly global effort, involving unprecedented collaboration by scientists, citizens and world leaders. The most technologically developed nations have to reduce their disproportionate use of the earth's resources. Moreover, the developing countries must be helped to adopt environmentally sound technologies and planning strategies as they elevate the standard of living for their populations, whose rapid growth and need for increased energy are a major cause for environmental concern. With proper attention devoted to maintaining the atmosphere's stability, perhaps the chemical changes that are now occurring can be kept within limits that will sustain the physical processes and the ecological balance of the planet.

VIII

The Workplace

During the past 200 years, work has held a central position in the ideas of philosophers and social scientists. Of these, the most influential and enduring commentator was Karl Marx. His analysis of the workplace during the industrial revolution was distinguished by its sympathy for the plight of the industrial worker, its analytical power, and its empirical grounding (derived from observations of the industrial workplace by British Commissions of Inquiry).

Marx wrote during the mid-nineteenth century, when manufacturing had evolved from the family cottage to the "factory"—an appropriately speeded-up word invented to describe the new industrial form. In analyzing the human effects of capitalist industry, Marx emphasized the subordination of the worker's own needs to the requirements of production for profit:

> What constitutes the alienation of labour? First, that the work is *external* to the worker, that it is not part of his nature; and that, consequently, he does not fulfill himself in his work but denies himself, has a feeling of misery rather than well-being, does not develop freely his mental and physical energies but is physically exhausted and mentally debased. The worker, therefore, feels himself at home only during his leisure time, whereas at work he feels homeless. His work is not voluntary but imposed, *forced labour*. It is not satisfaction of a need, but only a *means* for satisfying other needs. Its alien character is clearly shown by the fact that as soon as there is no physical or other compulsion it is avoided like the plague.[1]

Should work be interesting and significant, or is work simply an unpleasant task that must be done to live and to provide resources for spending on leisure activities away from the workplace? It is possible to reform work, that is, to make it less dull, less dangerous, less exhausting? All recent evidence suggests that work continues to mean a great deal to people. Despite the managerial ideology of a decline of initiative, stability, and interest in work, survey after survey shows that actual hours of work time have not declined. People want, perhaps above all, to be employed, but they are also deeply concerned about the kind of work they do. Thus, after reviewing a wide variety of studies of work and its meaning, Rosabeth Moss Kanter concludes:

> Work, then, may still be important to Americans for self-respect and meaning in life—but not just any work, and not under just any conditions. For a sizable segment of the population, work is expected to provide more than merely material rewards, and the cost of material rewards themselves should not be too high. At the very least, work should be a source of pride, and it should contribute to the realization of cherished personal values.[2]

While there is no doubt that work is important to self-fulfillment—Freud said that love and work were the basis of mental health—there is also no doubt that technological innovation reduces a society's need for workers, especially skilled ones. Nobel-prize-winning economist Wassily W. Leontief argues that technological replacement of workers is a long-term and inevitable phenomenon that badly needs consideration as a major policy issue. The problem began with the introduction of knitting machines into textile factories in nineteenth-century England. The workers—the famous Luddites—were acting on impulses familiar to later generations as their carefully honed skills were replaced—in effect, "degraded"—by mechanical or electronic devices. No easy solutions apply to the problems of technological advancement. Leontief argues that nothing short of a major revision of economic institutions and values will prove effective, although such changes can evolve through time and careful experimentation.

One result of the technological changes Leontief describes has been the loss of millions of industrial jobs (some consequences of which were explored in Chapter III). A more subtle effect has been the replacement of those lost industrial jobs with others that pay much less—often far too little to support a family in present-day America. We are often told that the United States has become a "high-tech" society in which most jobs now require considerable education and skill and are rewarded accordingly. But the reality is less bright. Our economy has indeed produced many high-skill, high-paying jobs in recent years. But it has produced a far greater number of low-level jobs paying only the minimum wage or slightly above it. Morris Thompson and Cass Peterson describe what life is like for the growing numbers of "near-poor" Americans who, unlike the much discussed urban "underclass," work year in and year out but barely rise above mere economic survival.

Another reason for the decline in well-paying jobs in the United States—in addition to the technological changes in industry described by Leontief—is that many American employers have set up plants in Third World countries, where labor is far cheaper and less often unionized than it is at home. Barbara Ehrenreich and Annette Fuentes describe the harsh and dismal working conditions prevailing in some of those overseas factories. Most of the hard-working locals on the "global assembly line" are young women, who face not only wages lower than an 11-year-old in the United States can earn with a paper route but also the increased health hazards that come with the near absence of health and safety regulations in many of these countries.

American truck drivers are also suffering the pains of an accelerated workplace. Life on the road was never easy, but, under the economic pressures of deregulation, long hours, use of amphetamines, and neglect of safety precautions have become routine. Steve Turner's article shows how a conservative economic theory—deregulation—can skid out of control.

REFERENCES

1. Quoted in Shlomo Avineri, *The Social and Political Thought of Karl Marx* (Cambridge, Eng.: Cambridge University Press, 1971), p. 106.
2. Rosabeth Moss Kanter, "Work in a New America," *Daedelus*, Winter 1978, pp. 47–78.

29

The Distribution of Work and Income

Wassily W. Leontief

My Lords: During the short time I recently passed in Nottinghamshire not twelve hours elapsed without some fresh act of violence; . . . I was informed that forty Frames had been broken the preceding evening. These machines . . . superseded the necessity of employing a number of workmen, who were left in consequence to starve. By the adoption of one species of Frame in particular, one man performed the work of many, and the superfluous labourers were thrown out of employment. . . . The rejected workmen in the blindness of their ignorance, instead of rejoicing at these improvements in art so beneficial to mankind, conceived themselves to be sacrificed to improvements in mechanism.

Wⁱᵗʰ these words Lord Byron in his maiden speech to the House of Lords in February, 1812, sought to explain, and by explaining to excuse, the renewal of the Luddite protest that was shaking the English social order. Nearly a generation earlier Ned Ludd had led his fellow workers in destroying the "frames": the knitting machines that employers had begun to install in the workshops of the country's growing textile industry. The House had before it legislation to exact the death penalty for such acts of sabotage. The Earl of Lauderdale sharpened Byron's thesis that the misled workers were acting against their own interests: "Nothing could be more certain than the fact that every improvement in machinery

Wassily Leontief, "The Distribution of Work and Income," in *Scientific American*, Volume 247, September 1982, pp. 188–90. Reprinted by permission of W. H. Freeman and Company, Publishers.

contributed to the improvement in the condition of persons manufacturing the machines, there being in a very short time after such improvements were introduced a greater demand for labour than ever before."

History has apparently sustained the optimistic outlook of the early exponents of modern industrial society. The specter of involuntary technological unemployment seems to remain no more than a specter. Beginning with the invention of the steam engine, successive waves of technological innovation have brought in the now industrial, or "developed," countries a spectacular growth of both employment and real wages, a combination that spells prosperity and social peace. Thanks as well to technological innovation, more than half of the labor force in all these countries—70 percent of the U.S. labor force—has been relieved from labor in agriculture and other goods-production that employed substantially everyone before the Industrial Revolution. It is true that the less developed countries are still waiting in line. If the outlook for the future can be based on the experience of the past 200 years, those countries too can expect to move up, provided their governments can succeed in reducing their high rate of population growth and desist from interfering with the budding of the spirit of free private enterprise.

There are signs today, however, that past experience cannot serve as a reliable guide for the future of technological change. With the advent of solid-state electronics, machines that have been displacing human muscle from the production of goods are being succeeded by machines that take over the functions of the human nervous system not only in production but in the service industries as well. . . . The relation between man and machine is being radically transformed.

The beneficence of that relationship is usually measured by the "productivity" of labor. This is the total output divided by the number of workers or, even better, by the number of man-hours required for its production. Thus 30 years ago it took several thousand switchboard operators to handle a million long-distance telephone calls; 10 years later it took several hundred operators, and now, with automatic switchboards linked automatically to other automatic switchboards, only a few dozen are needed. Plainly the productivity of labor—that is, the number of calls completed per operator—has been increasing by leaps and bounds. Simple arithmetic shows that it will reach its highest level when only one operator remains and will become incalculable on the day that operator is discharged.

The inadequacy of this conventional measure is perhaps better illustrated if it is applied to assess the effects of the progressive replacement of horses by tractors in agriculture. Dividing the successive annual harvest figures first by the gradually increasing number of tractors and then by the reciprocally falling number of horses yields the paradoxical conclusion that throughout this time of transition the relative productivity of tractors tended to fall while the productivity of the horses they were replacing was rising. In fact, of course, the cost-effectiveness of horses diminished steadily compared with that of the increasingly efficient tractors.

In the place of such uncertain abstractions it is more productive to try to bring the underlying facts into consideration and analysis. Technological change can be visualized conveniently as change in the cooking recipes—the specific combinations of inputs—followed by different industries to produce their respective outputs. Progress in electromechanical technology enabled the telephone company to replace the old technological recipe calling for a large number of manual switchboards having many operators with a new recipe combining more expensive automatic switchboards having fewer operators. In agriculture technological progress brought the introduction of successive input combinations with smaller inputs of animal and human labor and larger and more diversified inputs of other kinds—not only mechanical equipment but also pesticides, herbicides, vaccines, antibiotics, hormones and hybrid seed.

New recipes come into service in every industry by a constant process of "costing out." Some inputs included in a new recipe are at the outset too expensive, and it takes some time before improvements in their design or in the method of their manufacture bring sufficient reduction in their price and consequently in the total cost of the recipe to allow the adoption of the new technology. The decline, at the nearly constant rate of 30 percent per year for many years, in the cost per memory bit on the integrated-circuit chip has brought solid-state electronics technology first into expensive capital equipment such as telephone switchboards, automatic pilots, machine tools and computers, then into radio and television sets and powerful, low-cost computers as an entirely new category of consumer goods, then into the control systems of automobiles and household appliances and even into such expendable goods as toys. Thus the adoption of a new recipe in one industry often depends on replacement of the old by a new technology in another industry, as the vacuum tube was replaced by the transistor and its descendants in the transformed electronics industry.

Stepping back and contemplating the flow of raw materials and intermediate products through the input-output structure of an industrial system and the corresponding price structure, one can see that prices more or less faithfully reflect the state of technology in the system. With the passage of time price changes can be expected to reflect long-run technological changes going on in the various sectors. In this perspective, human labor of a specific kind appears as one, but only one, of the many different inputs, the price of which must be reckoned in the costing out of a given technological recipe. Its price, the wage rate, enters into the cost comparisons between competing technologies in the same way as the price of any other input.

In the succession of technological changes that have accompanied economic development and growth, new goods and services come on the stage and old ones, having played their role, step off. Such changes proceed at different rates and on different scales, affecting some sectors of economic activity more than others. Some types of labor are replaced faster than others. Less skilled workers in many instances, but not always, go first, more skilled workers later. Computers are now taking on the jobs of white-collar workers, performing first simple and then increasingly complex mental tasks.

Human labor from time immemorial played the role of principal factor of production. There are reasons to believe human labor will not retain this status in the future.

Over the past two centuries technological innovation has brought an exponential growth of total output in the industrial economies, accompanied by rising per capita consumption. At the same time, until the middle 1940's the easing of man's labor was enjoyed in the progressive shortening of the working day, working week and working year. Increased leisure (and for that matter cleaner air and purer water) is not counted in the official adding up of goods and services in the gross national product. It has nonetheless contributed greatly to the well-being of blue-collar workers and salaried employees. Without increase in leisure time the popularization of education and cultural advantages that has distinguished the industrial societies in the first 80 years of this century would not have been possible.

The reduction of the average work week in manufacturing from 67 hours in 1870 to somewhat less than 42 hours must also be recognized as the withdrawal of many millions of working hours from the labor market. Since the end of World War II, however, the work week has remained almost constant. Waves of technological innovation have continued to overtake each other as before. The real wage rate, discounted for inflation, has continued to go up. Yet the length of the normal work week today is practically the same as it was 35 years ago. In 1977 the work week in the U.S. manufacturing industries, adjusted for the growth in vacations and holidays, was still 41.8 hours.

Concurrently the U.S. economy has seen a chronic increase in unemployment from one oscillation of the business cycle to the next. The 2 percent accepted as the irreducible unemployment rate by proponents of full-employment legislation in 1945 became the 4 percent of New Frontier economic managers in the 1960's. The country's unemployment problem today exceeds 9 percent. How can this be explained?

Without technological change there could, of course, be no technological unemployment. Nor would there be such unemployment if the total population and the labor force, instead of growing, were to shrink. Workers might also hang on to their jobs if they would agree to accept lower wages. Those who are concerned with population growth are likely to proclaim that "too many workers" is the actual cause of unemployment. Libertarians of the "Keep your hands off the free market" school urge the remedy of wage cuts brought about by the systematic curtailment of the power of trade unions and the reduction of unemployment and welfare benefits. Advocates of full employment have been heard to propose that labor-intensive technologies be given preference over labor-saving ones. A more familiar medicine is prescribed by those who advocate stepped-up investment in accelerated economic growth.

Each of these diagnoses has its shortcomings, and the remedies they prescribe can be no more than palliative at best. A drastic general wage cut might temporarily arrest the adoption of laborsaving technology, even though dirt-cheap labor could not compete in many operations with very powerful or very sophisticated machines. The old trend would be bound to resume, however, unless special barriers were erected against laborsaving devices. Even the most principled libertarian must hesitate to have wage questions settled by cutthroat competition among workers under the pressure of steadily advancing technology. The erection of Luddite barriers to technological progress would, on the other hand, bring more menace to the health of the economic and social system than the disease it is intended to cure.

Increased investment can certainly provide jobs for people who would otherwise be unemployed. Given the rate of technological advance, the creation of one additional job that 20 years ago might have required an investment of $50,000 now demands $100,000 and in 20 years will demand $500,000, even with inflation discounted. A high rate of investment is, of course, indispensable to the expanding needs of a growing economy. It can make only a limited contribution to alleviating involuntary technological unemployment, however, because the greater the rate of capital investment, the higher the rate of introduction of new laborsaving technology. The latest copper smelter to go into service in the U.S. cost $450 million and employs fewer than 50 men per shift.

Americans might have continued to absorb potential technological unemployment by voluntary shortening of the work week if real wages had risen over the past 40 years faster than they actually have, allowing the expectation of increase not only of total annual pay but also of total lifetime take-home pay. Because of the greatly expanded opportunities to replace labor by increasingly sophisticated technology it appears that the impersonal forces of the market no longer favor that possibility. Government policies directed at encouraging a steady rise in real wages sufficiently large to induce workers to resume continuous voluntary reduction in the work week could once have been considered. Under present conditions such policies would require such a large increase in the share of total national income going to wages that it would bring decline in productive investment, which is financed largely by undistributed corporate earnings and the savings of the upper income group. This would result in an unacceptable slowdown of economic growth. There remains the alternative of direct action to promote a progressive shortening of the work week combined with income policies designed to maintain and to increase, as increases in total output allow, the real family income of wage earners and salaried employees.

Recent studies sponsored by the U.S. Department of Labor seem to indicate that the total number of working hours offered by the existing labor force might be reduced in exchange for a more flexible scheduling of work time. Indeed, some workers, depending on their age group, family status, occupation and so on, would even be prepared to forgo a certain fraction of their current income, some by extension of their annual vacation, some by earlier retirement or sabbatical leave and some by working four and a half days per week instead of five. Reducing the work day by 15 minutes proves, incidentally, to be one of the less desirable alternatives. Tentative and obviously somewhat speculative computations based on the most desirable trade-off choices for different groups developed in these studies indicate that the average U.S. worker would be willing to forgo some 4.7 percent of earnings in exchange for free time. On the basis of the 1978 work year the average employee's work time would be reduced from 1,910 work hours to 1,821, or by more than two working weeks in a year.

Although such measures certainly deserve serious consideration and, if at all possible, practical implementation, they cannot provide a final answer to the long-run question of how to enable a modern industrial society to derive the benefits of continued technological progress without experiencing involuntary technological unemployment and resulting social disruption. Sooner or later, and quite probably sooner, the increasingly mechanized society must face another problem: the problem of income distribution.

Adam and Eve enjoyed, before they were expelled from Paradise, a high standard of living without working. After their expulsion they and their successors were condemned to eke out a miserable existence, working from dawn to dusk. The history of technological progress over the past 200 years is essentially the story of the human species working its way slowly and steadily back into Paradise. What would happen, however, if we suddenly found ourselves in it? With all goods and services provided without work, no one would be gainfully employed. Being unemployed means receiving no wages. As a result until appropriate new income policies were formulated to fit the changed technological conditions everyone would starve in Paradise.

The income policies I have in mind do not turn simply on an increase in the legally fixed minimum wage or in the hourly wage or other benefits negotiated by the usual collective bargaining between trade unions and employers. In the long run increases in the direct and indirect hourly labor costs would be bound to accelerate laborsaving mechanization. This, incidentally, is the explicitly stated explanation of the wage policies currently pursued by the benevolently authoritarian government of Singapore. It encourages a rapid rise in real wages in order to induce free domestic enterprise to upgrade the already remarkably efficient production facilities of this city-state. It is perhaps needless to add that these policies are accompanied by strict control of immigration and encouragement of birth control.

What I have in mind is a complex of social and economic measures to supplement by transfer from other income shares the income received by blue- and white-collar workers from the sale of their services on the labor market. A striking example of an income transfer of this kind attained automatically without government intervention is there to be studied in the long-run effects of the mechanization of agriculture on the mode of operation and the income of, say, a prosperous Iowa farm. Half a century ago the farmer and the members of his family worked from early morning until late at night assisted by a team of horses, possibly a tractor and a standard set of simple agricultural implements. Their income consisted of what essentially amounted to wages for a 75- or 80-hour work week, supplemented by a small profit on their modest investment.

Today the farm is fully mechanized and even has some sophisticated electronic equipment. The average work week is much shorter, and from time to time the family can take a real vacation. Their total wage income, if one computes it at the going hourly rate for a much smaller number of manual-labor hours, is probably not much higher than it was 50 years ago and may even be lower. Their standard of living, however, is certainly much higher: the shrinkage of their wage income is more than fully offset by the income earned on their massive capital investment in the rapidly changing technology of agriculture. The shift from the old income structure to the new one was smooth and practically painless. It involved no more than a simple bookkeeping transaction because now, as 50 years ago, both the wage income and the capital income are earned by the same family.

The effect of technological progress on manufacturing and other non-agricultural sectors of the economy is essentially the same as it is on agriculture. So also should be its repercussions with respect to the shortening of the work day and the allocation of income. Because of differences in the institutional setup, however, those repercussions cannot be expected to work through the system automatically. That must be brought about by carefully designed income policies. The accommodation of existing institutions to the demands and to the effects of laborsaving mechanization will not be easy. The setting aside of the Puritan "work ethic," to which Max Weber so convincingly ascribed the success of early industrial society, is bound to prove even more difficult and long drawn out. In popular and political discourse on employment, full employment and unemployment, with its emphasis on the provision of incomes rather than the production of goods, it can be seen that the revision of values has already begun.

The evolution of institutions is under way as well. In the structure of the tax system and through Social Security, medical insurance, unemployment benefits and welfare payments the country is finding its way toward necessary income policies. A desirable near-term step is to reduce the contrast between those who are fully employed and those who are out of work. This is the effect of the widespread European practice of paying supplemental benefits to those who work fewer than the normal number of hours per week. In the long run, responding to the incipient threat of technological unemployment, public policy should aim at securing equitable distribution of work and income, taking care not to obstruct technological progress even indirectly.

Implementation of such policy calls for close and systematic cooperation between management and labor carried on with government support. Large-scale financial transfers inevitably generate inflationary pressure. The inflation that dogs all the market economies, some more than others, does not arise from mere technical economic causes but is the symptom of deep-seated social problems. In this country it is basically the incessant wrangling between management and labor that keeps the cost-price spiral climbing.

West Germany, a country celebrated for its successful stabilization policies, is touted also as an example of the unregulated enterprise economy. In reality the success of the Schmidt government's anti-inflation measures rests on the firm foundation of institutionalized labor-capital cooperation in the management of German industry. The "codetermination" law requires that half of the board of directors of each large corporation be elected by labor, with the stockholders represented by the other half. Among the labor members some are "outside" directors representing the national trade unions. Since wage and employment questions constitute only one problem in the broad range of problems on the agenda of these boards, their deliberations bring employers and employees into working contact at the grass roots of German industry. That relationship cannot but be of crucial importance in determining the nature of agreements reached in collective bargaining conducted between the parties at the national level.

Austria is another country that has up to now successfully resisted inflationary pressure. Relations between management and labor are mediated by institutional arrangements very similar to those in Germany. The government plays a larger and more active role in the national across-the-board wage negotiations. It does so by contributing projections, drawn from the input-output data bank of the country's bookkeeping system, that link decisions affecting the industry in question to the situation of the country as a whole. This approach was employed, for example, to model and project the impact of the new text-processing and printing technologies on the Austrian newspaper industry. That technological revolution, the occasion for months-long disputes and work stoppages in Britain, the U.S. and other countries, was carried out smoothly and expeditiously in Austria by close cooperation between management and labor in accordance with detailed plans developed by the government. Until 1980, when the tidal wave of the second oil crisis, reinforced by the recession in the U.S. economy, reached Austria, the annual rate of inflation had been held below 4 percent and unemployment below 2 percent.

Although current business publications, trade papers and the popular press abound with articles about "automation" and "robotics" and speculation on the economic impact of these developments, only the governmental and scientific agencies of Austria have produced a systematic assessment of the prospective consequences of the present revolution in laborsaving technology in a modern industrial economy and society . . .

History, even recent history, shows that societies have responded to such challenge with revision of their economic institutions and values conducive to the efficient use of changing technology and to securing its advantages for popular well-being. History shows also societies that have failed to respond and have succumbed to economic stagnation and increasing social disorder.

30

Working Hard, Getting Nowhere

Morris S. Thompson and Cass Peterson

Almost everybody knows somebody, by sight or name, like Charlie Luker. Luker, 37, a car washer in Lawrenceburg, Tenn., works long and hard. He relaxes in front of the television with a beer most evenings, goes to bed early, gets up early and does it all over again. He is part of the backbone of the U.S. economy and society, one of the many Americans who make enough to survive but not much more.

They are little noticed by politicians and policy-makers because they do not vote in large numbers or qualify for most forms of government aid. And more affluent Americans rarely consider the life, needs or thoughts of a Charlie Luker, who shined their new cars before they drove them off the lot.

The Washington Post went looking for the one-fifth of Americans, more pervasive than visible, who live above the official poverty line but below the middle-income bracket. These are the Americans who buy used cars or no cars, take few vacations, shop for clothes at discount stores, often go without health insurance and hope for the best.

According to data in the Census Bureau's 1986 Current Population Survey (CPS) of nearly 65,000 households nationwide, this group lives in households where the annual income is $9,941 to $18,700. In two-thirds of those households, it takes two wage-earners to reach that range. The members of this group are demographically so diverse that income is one of the main statistical characteristics they share.

The other is education. Except for the senior citizens, they have less of it

From the *Washington Post* National Weekly Edition, December 28, 1987. Reprinted with permission.

than the average for their age group. Throughout their lives, people with less education tend to be paid less and to be unemployed more.

But in interviews, another unquantifiable similarity emerges: Those of the same age, with about the same responsibilities, expressed remarkably similar views about the future despite vast differences in their backgrounds.

The demographic analysis suggests that the members of this nearly-poor quintile are white and black and Hispanic; married, single and divorced; working, retired or between jobs; old, young and in between.

Some, young and on their way up, may belong to the group temporarily. Others, ill or laid-off or on strike, are here suddenly and accidentally. Still others have wittingly chosen professions that will make them happy but not financially comfortable. And some, whose needs outstrip their skills, may be stuck here permanently.

Because living costs vary with family responsibilities, all of these people have to budget carefully, but some more carefully than others.

For example, the largest category of householders in the group (29 percent) is made up of persons over age 65, whose children are likely to be grown and gone.

And because the incomes of most people drop when they retire, senior citizens in this group tend to have done better during their working lives than the wage-earners now in the group. Many have accumulated such valuable assets as a paid-for house.

In fact, only 3 percent of householders older than 65 in the group list Social Security as their sole source of income. But when the workers in the group stop working, their incomes are likely to place them among the poorest of the poor.

The second-largest number of householders in the group (24 percent) are those between 25 and 34. If they are parents, they have learned that the price of children's shoes is out of proportion to their size, but those children's appetites have not yet become the black holes of adolescence.

Of the 15 percent of householders in the group between 35 and 44, many are facing the near certainty that they will never be rich and the probability that they will not be able to pay for their children's education after high school. Many others are divorced; surveys consistently find that money problems are among the leading causes of failed marriages.

The 10 percent between ages 45 and 54 are in the peak earning years for most Americans, but they find it increasingly difficult to get or keep a job, especially one that would allow them to plan for retirement.

The 14 percent between the ages of 55 and 64 have reached the stage at which persons with below-average educations who have unskilled and semiskilled jobs begin to drop out of the work force. Sometimes the years of unaffordable, and therefore neglected, health care play a role. For white-collar workers in the group, it is the age for hanging in there for their pensions.

Since more than 80 percent of the U.S. population is white, it is not surprising that most households in this group also are headed by white men like Luker, Census data show. But this group has a greater proportion of households headed by someone who is black, Hispanic, female, over 65 or unmarried than any other quintile of the population, except the poorest.

While whites in the group are worse off financially than most other U.S. whites, the median income for all black and Hispanic households in the United States falls in this $9,941 to $18,700 range. So a group often known as "working poor" is, in this land of plenty, the middle class for blacks and Hispanics.

Ray Salinas, Democrat and Roman Catholic and Chicano, a barber in teeming Houston, might seem to have little in common with Tom Price, Republican and Southern Baptist and white, a box-factory worker in tiny Lawrenceburg, Tenn.

But both are men who work hard without getting ahead, and as they speak, the differences between their backgrounds dissolve. What stands out is the similarity in their experiences of the world and the dreams they dream for their children.

Both meet life with limited means as part of America's working poor, the 17.6 million households between poverty and the middle class with incomes of $9,941 to $18,700 a year. As such, Salinas and Price seem to share an unarticulated class consciousness forged by the choices that scarcity has imposed. They struggle to feed their families, hope no one gets sick, try to figure out where the money will come from to educate the children, try not to think about what will happen when they can't work anymore.

On the threshold of middle age, they seem to accept their struggle for economic survival as a routine necessity and the world as an uncaring place in which people like them have little influence. For the sake of the children, they worry about war and hope their babies don't find the world so hard a place as they have.

In 1986, Tom Price, 37, earned about $12,000 as day manager at a local restaurant. In 1987, he earned a bit more working third shift on the gluer at a nearby box factory. Maria, his wife of almost 18 years, did not work in 1986, but was expecting to earn $6,000 or $7,000 in 1987 at a local garment factory.

Ray and Hilda Salinas each earned about $5,500 in 1986. He works six days a week on 70 percent commission as a barber, which for years was merely his moonlighting job. Hilda is paid minimum wage for a four-day week at a shirt factory. They were expecting to make an equal amount in 1986.

Theirs are families that make too much money to qualify for more than token help from the government, but too little to avoid constant financial problems.

"If I'm lucky to keep $20 in a week, I'm lucky," says Salinas, a stocky man with an easy smile. "But most, it's going to food or the car, utilities, the house note. We try, we try, but it's still a little rough."

Their personal finances have gotten worse, not better, over the past decade, an experience shared by many Americans whose raises usually come through increases in the minimum wage, which has been $3.35 an hour for nearly eight years. "Even though my wife and I are working, we're making what we were back in '77 when it was just me working," Salinas says.

Price concurs. "Right after I got out of school, around '74, I was making $10,000, $11,000 a year," he says. "Compared to what things cost, that's more than I'm making now."

In the tales Salinas and Price tell, one sees good men whose lives are constantly buffeted by forces beyond their control. As they look at the events of their time, from Vietnam to the Iran-contra scandal, their experience leads them to focus on consequences, not intentions.

Salinas looks around him and wonders how he, a high school graduate and Air Force veteran trained as a mechanical draftsman and barber, has come to live on the economic brink. "Years ago, I never thought that we were going to hit a situation like what we're in now," he says. "I thought I was always going to have a job and that I'd always be able to provide for my family."

The Salinases live in a two-bedroom house with aluminum siding in a Houston neighborhood with trees but no sidewalks. Reynol Jr., 12, and Rosa Maria, 9, occupy the other bedroom now. Fernando, 21, joined the Air Force after he finished high school in June 1986.

Like many of the working poor, Salinas has a history of jobs rather than a career. He trained as a barber after finishing high school, earning a diploma that few Hispanic men his age have received. He joined the Air Force, in 1966. At the end of his four-year hitch, Salinas took a course in mechanical drawing but couldn't find a job as a draftsman, so he worked nights at a brokerage house, processing the day's stock sales and purchases for $5 an hour.

Salinas helped support his parents and send his brother to college and law school. "Of all the family, he's the only one who got an opportunity to get a good education," Salinas says of his brother, who went on to become a U.S. Justice Department lawyer and served briefly as a judge.

Shortly after Ray Salinas' discharge, he met Hilda, an articulate, Catholic-educated Mexican woman with a young son. They were married in 1972.

Salinas supported his new family by working at anything he could get until finally landing a drafting job. He drew custom ventilators for fast-food grills for the next six years until, just before Christmas 1978, he was laid off.

At one point, jobless and facing foreclosure on the mortgage, he swallowed his pride and applied for food stamps. The application was denied because the house he was about to lose made him too wealthy. "I needed the food for my family," he says. "I ask myself, how many people are there now who get rejected who need it?" The next day, he recalls gratefully, he found a job as a janitor.

Eventually, Salinas was laid off again. He has been a full-time barber ever since. He now wistfully recalls his days as a draftsman. "I really enjoyed that kind of work," he says. "But it seems like when you get a certain age, people want a younger person."

Salinas sees signs all around him that times are hard. "I never thought in my life that I'd see Anglo kids come in the barbershop barefooted with dirty clothes," he says. "We go out and help other countries and provide for them, and it's good. But I think our government should look to the American people first."

The Prices and their children, Thomas Jr., 16, Maria, 14, Theresa, 10, and Charles 8, live on a quiet circle in quiet Lawrenceburg, population about 15,000, 50 miles northwest of Huntsville, Ala., in the rolling farmland of central Tennessee.

Price, a licensed Baptist preacher who believes that creation occurred in six days, taught mathematics and science in Christian academies after college and wishes he still could. The low pay, scant job security, skimpy fringe benefits and his family's growing needs forced him to seek a better-paying job.

"If I could find a situation where I could teach and make enough to live on, I'd do it," he says.

But Price, like Salinas, has been diverted from his druthers by his needs. "My oldest son will be graduating from high school this year," he observes. "He wants to go into engineering, with computers and robots and things like that. Maybe he'll go to Columbia State," which is nearby.

The summer after Price finished high school in 1968 in Lawrenceburg, his home town, he met his future wife, Maria, then 15 years old, at church. They were married that November and lived with Price's parents.

Tom dropped out of college before the second semester and worked for his father, a construction jobber, "digging footings, putting in septic tanks, putting in water lines."

But grief changed the direction of the Prices' lives. "We had one child who died in '75, lived a day," he says. "It sort of made us decide to devote some more to church work, because that's where we found comfort."

So the Prices moved to Chattanooga, about 130 miles to the east, where he majored in Bible at Tennessee Temple College and went on to spend a semester at Temple's seminary. He dropped out when he ran out of money, taking a job teaching junior- and senior-high school math at a Christian academy in Fort Pierce, Fla., 90 miles north of Palm Beach. It paid $8,000 a year.

There, Maria earned her high-school equivalency diploma and decided that one day she would go to college. Over the years, she has done three semesters' course work in hopes of becoming a psychologist.

Tom Price held a succession of teaching jobs. In Tallahassee, Fla., he managed to make $10,000 in 1984 by operating a backhoe on Saturdays when he was teaching seventh-grade math during the week at North Florida Christian School. He left his last teaching job in west Tennessee because he thought the principal used corporal punishment too much, including on Price's son, Tom Jr.

Price took a management-training job with Shoney's Big Boy, a regional restaurant chain. He spent four months in nearby Columbia, then was day manager in Lawrenceburg for two years.

"I got as much as $390 a week, counting the bonus, but I was working 55 to 60 hours a week," he says. "So it was fairly good money, but by the hour it wasn't a lot."

Earlier this year, the Coors Packaging plant in Lawrenceburg was hiring, and friends put in a good word for him. "I'm getting paid $7.75 an hour," he says. "I started at $5 an hour. I'll top out at $9 an hour as I get more skilled on the machines and can do more things." Free health insurance there for his family, he says, is "worth a whole lot to me."

What preoccupies these men, like many others, is not politics but their families' futures. Each speaks of his children with unequivocal pride. "That cuckoo clock?" Salinas says. "My boy Fernando sent it to us from Germany. Sometimes the cuckoo goes, 'Oh, Fernando! Oh, Fernando!'"

Says Price, "Tom Jr. is getting mostly As and Bs. You know that book 'Who's Who in American High Schools'? He's in it."

Salinas gave some advice to his elder son, Fernando. "I said to my boy, 'Take care of yourself and try to save money. Put your money into savings so the day you get married, you don't have to go through what we're struggling with.'"

In normal times, Daryl Kratochvil makes $8.20 an hour working in a Nebraska meatpacking plant, good wages by rural Midwestern standards. Janet Erks does even better—$9.25 an hour at a similar plant in South Dakota.

But Kratochvil spent most of this year doing odd jobs for whatever pay he could get—a few dollars, a bushel of sweet corn. Erks didn't draw a paycheck from the meatpacking plant from May until November. Part of that time she worked part time at a Sioux Falls, S.D., grocery store for $3.75 an hour.

Kratochvil and Erks were on strike in 1987, walking the picket line, surviving on slender checks from their union and trying not to sink deeper into the ranks of the working poor.

When the paychecks are coming in, their wages at the meatpacking plants put their families on the cusp of the second economic quintile, hovering at the $18,700-a-year cutoff that marks the entry point to the middle class. But the issue in the industry is wage concessions, not increases, and for Kratochvil and Erks the battle has an edge of desperation.

Daryl Kratochvil is 50 years old; Janet Erks, 49. Both are in what statisticians consider the peak earning years, the time when most workers are enjoying the best financial health of their lives. Too young to retire, too old to start over, Kratochvil and Erks are tied to their jobs and fighting uphill. "You never figure on going backwards," says Erks, who took a $2.44-an-hour pay cut four years ago and is trying to avoid another.

At a time when many in their age group are buying a few luxuries, planning for retirement and enjoying the economic freedom that comes of financially independent children, Kratochvil and Erks are still worrying about buying food, paying utilities and keeping the car running another year.

And there is another, constant worry: their health. As a group, they are more vulnerable to the income loss that results from an extended or debilitating illness and often lack adequate insurance against the expense of medical care.

The concern is heightened for Kratochvil and Erks, because of their age and because they work in an industry that has one of the nation's highest worker-injury rates. In a given year, three of 10 meatpacking employees can expect to be injured on the job. "That worries me all the time," says Kratochvil, who has come home twice with stitches where a steer kicked a gate into his head.

Janet Erks, a diabetic, could not afford the $216 a month it would have cost to maintain her health insurance while she was on strike. She had to cancel doctor's appointments, because she couldn't afford to go. Back then, she says, she just had to hope "the good Lord" would "take care of me."

Trust in providence is one of two recurring themes in conversations with Kratochvil and Erks. Neither wears religion on a sleeve, but it is there—an undercurrent of faith stressing perseverance more than hope, the gospel of hanging on.

The other theme is betrayal. The immediate villain is The Company, but the frustration goes deeper. Both grew up in homes with strong work ethics, guided by parents who taught them loyalty to the job and assured them that hard work would pay off. It hasn't. "The hardest part is that my father gave them 38 years of his life, and my brother gave 23," Erks says. "I gave them 30 years of my life. You work damned hard. And they have no respect for us at all."

For Kratochvil and Erks, the new watchwords of "competitiveness" and "technology" translate into lower wages, less job security and increasing despair. He is resigned; she feels duped. "When the company cut our pay last time, people believed them," she says. "We thought they needed concessions. Now they're making $28 million a year and they're paying the top man $375,000. And the politicians are saying 'Come to South Dakota, we'll give you the cheapest labor in the country.'"

Hilda Kratochvil, Daryl's wife, sits at the dinette in her small, immaculate kitchen and laughs at the question. "How would I describe us?" she says, with a merry twinkle in her eye. "We're dull."

"Dull," to Daryl and Hilda Kratochvil, means a life without credit cards, spontaneous spending or debt. Supper out is a rare treat. Vacations are planned—and paid for—months in advance. Their modest frame house in Hawarden, Iowa, a community of 2,800 about 40 miles north of Sioux City, is mortgage-free. The cars are old but wholly owned.

The television set is new, replacing the old one that lost its picture tube after 13 years. But there isn't much time to watch it. Kratochvil rises at 3 a.m. for the hour-long drive that will get him to work at the IBP meatpacking plant in Dakota City, Neb., by 5:15. Hilda spends her day babysitting for six small children. ("I've had as many as 10 at one time," she says.) From 4 p.m. to 6 p.m., both work as janitors at a local church, a job that often occupies much of their weekend as well. By 8:30 or 9 on any given night, it's lights out at the Kratochvils.

It is a regimented life, but it keeps the Kratochvils financially afloat. Rigorous frugality allows them to save for the occasional major purchase—a new television, a lower-mileage used car. More important, it allows them to put something aside for the event that keeps the Kratochvils in the stratum of the working poor: the strike.

Working 40 hours a week, Kratochvil earns just over $17,000 annually. Hilda's child-care earnings add about $2,000, and the recently acquired janitorial work contributes $4,000. It would be enough to put the Kratochvils narrowly into the middle class, except that Kratochvil is out of work for extended periods at least once every four years, when the United Food and Commercial Workers contract at IBP expires. There is always a strike.

The most recent strike started two weeks before Christmas in 1986. Kratochvil returned to work in August.

Kratochvil has worked in the stockyards at IBP for 17 years, herding cattle into the chute that leads to the killing area. The couple can accept the periodic strikes. They can be planned for. They end, sooner or later. What makes the Kratochvils apprehensive is the thought of the unexpected: an extended illness, for example, or a disabling injury.

So profound are their concerns about the cost of medical care that the Kratochvils strained their budget to take out a $160-a-month health-insurance policy while he was on strike. When the strike ended, they decided to keep the policy to supplement the coverage offered by IBP.

Retirement isn't even a topic of discussion. The union's most recent contract includes a pension plan for the first time, but Kratochvil isn't confident that it provides much for him. The plan won't become effective until 1990, by which time Kratochvil will be 53, and the size of his pension will then depend on how much profit the company makes. "I won't be able to retire at 65 because I won't be able to afford it," he says. "At the plant, they work you until they carry you out."

Janet Erks went to work at the John Morrell meatpacking plant in Sioux Falls, S.D., a week before she graduated from high school. "My father wanted me to go on to school. I wanted to go into nursing or interior decorating," she says. "But you get down there and start making what is good money for this town. . . . " Her voice trails off.

For a time, it seemed like the right decision. By the late 1970s, Erks and her husband, Don, were bringing home nearly $50,000 a year, Don working as a truck driver and Janet working in the shipping department at Morrells.

With seven children to raise—two hers from a previous marriage, four his and one theirs together—it was an adequate living but not an affluent one. They bought an old house in Lennox, S.D., and fixed it up themselves.

But in 1980, Don had to stop working because of a pulmonary ailment and arthritis. With four children still at home, Janet became the sole breadwinner. Three years later, the union's contract with Morrell expired and the company announced that it would close the plant unless workers accepted lower wages. The union conceded, and the Erkses joined the ranks of the working poor.

When meatpackers went on strike at nearby Sioux City, Iowa, Janet Erks' local walked out in a sympathy strike, fearing that their plant would be the next target for more pay cuts. For six months, the family lived on Don's disability check, her $40-a-week strike benefit from the union, and the income from a part-time job that she spent four months searching for. "Nobody would hire a Morrell striker," she says. But she says she would return to Morrell when the picket lines came down. Her pension is at stake—$15 a month for every year of service—and she is at least a year shy of qualifying for it.

Only 13-year-old Angela lives at home now. One son was killed during flight training in the Air Force. Two sons are working in Sioux Falls. Three daughters have moved away—to western South Dakota, to Michigan, to Montana.

Erks understands why her children have left. Entry-level wages for most jobs in Sioux Falls start at the minimum wage and rarely get higher than $6 an hour. To stay in Sioux Falls is to accept membership in the ranks of the working poor. "Things are so high, and wages are so low," she says. "How can you make it?"

31

Life on the Global Assembly Line

Barbara Ehrenreich and Annette Fuentes

*I*n *Ciudad Juárez, Mexico, Anna M. rises at 5* A.M. *to feed her son before starting on the two-hour bus trip to the maquiladora (factory). He will spend the day along with four other children in a neighbor's one-room home. Anna's husband, frustrated by being unable to find work for himself, left for the United States six months ago. She wonders, as she carefully applies her new lip gloss, whether she ought to consider herself still married. It might be good to take a night course, become a secretary. But she seldom gets home before eight at night, and the factory, where she stitches brassieres that will be sold in the United States through J.C. Penney, pays only $48 a week.*

In Penang, Malaysia, Julie K. is up before the three other young women with whom she shares a room, and starts heating the leftover rice from last night's supper. She looks good in the company's green-trimmed uniform, and she's proud to work in a modern, American-owned factory. Only not quite so proud as when she started working three years ago—she thinks as she squints out the door at a passing group of women. Her job involves peering all day through a microscope, bonding hair-thin gold wires to a silicon chip destined to end up inside a pocket calculator, and at 21, she is afraid she can no longer see very clearly.

Every morning, between four and seven, thousands of women like Anna and Julie head out for the day shift. In Ciudad Juárez, they crowd into *ruteras* (run-down vans) for the trip from the slum neighborhoods to the industrial parks on the outskirts of the city. In Penang they squeeze, 60 or more at a time, into buses for the trip from the village to the low,

Barbara Ehrenreich and Annette Fuentes, "Life on the Global Assembly Line," from Ms Magazine, January, 1981. Reprinted by permission of the authors.

modern factory buildings of the Bayan Lepas free trade zone. In Taiwan, they walk from the dormitories—where the night shift is already asleep in the still-warm beds—through the checkpoints in the high fence surrounding the factory zone.

This is the world's new industrial proletariat: young, female, Third World. Viewed from the "first world," they are still faceless, genderless "cheap labor," signaling their existence only through a label or tiny imprint—"made in Hong Kong," or Taiwan, Korea, the Dominican Republic, Mexico, the Philippines. But they may be one of the most strategic blocs of womanpower in the world of the 1980s. Conservatively, there are 2 million Third World female industrial workers employed now, millions more looking for work, and their numbers are rising every year. Anyone whose image of Third World women features picturesque peasants with babies slung on their backs should be prepared to update it. Just in the last decade, Third World women have become a critical element in the global economy and a key "resource" for expanding multinational corporations.

It doesn't take more than second-grade arithmetic to understand what's happening. In the United States, an assembly-line worker is likely to earn, depending on her length of employment, between $3.10 and $5 an hour. In many Third World countries, a woman doing the same work will earn $3 to $5 a *day*. According to the magazine *Business Asia*, in 1976 the average hourly wage for unskilled work (male or female) was 55 cents in Hong Kong, 52 cents in South Korea, 32 cents in the Philippines, and 17 cents in Indonesia. The logic of the situation is compelling: why pay someone in Massachusetts $5 an hour to do what someone in Manila will do for $2.50 a day? Or, as a corollary, why pay a male worker anywhere to do what a female worker will do for 40 to 60 percent less?

And so, almost everything that can be packed up is being moved out to the Third World; not heavy industry, but just about anything light enough to travel—garment manufacture, textiles, toys, footwear, pharmaceuticals, wigs, appliance parts, tape decks, computer components, plastic goods. In some industries, like garment and textile, American jobs are lost in the process, and the biggest losers are women, often black and Hispanic. But what's going on is much more than a matter of runaway shops. Economists are talking about a "new international division of labor," in which the process of production is broken down and the fragments are dispersed to different parts of the world. In general, the low-skilled jobs are farmed out to the Third World, where labor costs are minuscule, while control over the overall process and technology remains safely at company headquarters in "first world" countries like the United States and Japan.

The American electronics industry provides a classic example: circuits are printed on silicon wafers and tested in California; then the wafers are shipped to Asia for the labor-intensive process by which they are cut into tiny chips and bonded to circuit boards; final assembly into products such as calculators or military equipment usually takes place in the United States. Garment manufacture too is often broken into geographically separated steps, with the most repetitive, labor-intensive jobs going to the poor countries of the southern hemisphere. Most Third World countries welcome whatever jobs come their way in the new division of labor, and the major international development agencies—like the World Bank and the United States Agency for International Development (AID)—encourage them to take what they can get.

So much any economist could tell you. What is less often noted is the *gender* breakdown of the emerging international division of labor. Eighty to 90 percent of the low-skilled assembly jobs that go to the Third World are performed by women—in a remarkable switch from earlier patterns of foreign-dominated industrialization. Until now, "development" under the aegis of foreign corporations has usually meant more jobs for men and—compared to traditional agricultural society—a diminished economic status for women. But multinational corporations and Third World governments alike consider assembly-line work—whether the product is Barbie dolls or missile parts—to be "women's work."

One reason is that women can, in many countries, still be legally paid less than men. But the sheer tedium of the jobs adds to the multinationals' preference for women workers—a preference made clear, for example, by this ad from a Mexican newspaper: *We need female workers; older than 17, younger than 30; single and without children: minimum education primary school, maximum education one year of preparatory school [high school]: available for all shifts.*

It's an article of faith with management that only women can do, or will do, the monotonous, painstaking work that American business is exporting to the Third World. Bill Mitchell, whose job is to attract United States businesses to the Bermudez Industrial Park in Ciudad Juárez told us with a certain macho pride: "A man just won't stay in this tedious kind of work. He'd walk out in a couple of hours." The personnel manager of a light assembly plant in Taiwan told anthropologist Linda Gail Arrigo: "Young male workers are too restless and impatient to do monotonous work with no career value. If displeased, they sabotage the machines and even threaten the foreman. But girls? At most, they cry a little."

In fact, the American businessmen we talked to claimed that Third World women genuinely enjoy doing the very things that would drive a man to assault and sabotage. "You should watch these kids going into work," Bill Mitchell told us. "You don't have any sullenness here. They smile." A top-level management consultant who specializes in advising American companies on where to relocate their factories gave us this global generalization: "The [factory] girls genuinely enjoy themselves. They're away from their families. They have spending money. They can buy motorbikes, whatever. Of course it's a regulated experience too—with dormitories to live in—so it's healthful experience."

What is the real experience of the women in the emerging Third World industrial work force? The conventional Western stereotypes leap to mind: You can't really compare, the standards are so different. . . . Everything's easier in warm countries. . . . They really don't have any alternatives. . . . Commenting on the low wages his company pays its women workers in Singapore, a Hewlett-Packard vice-president said, "They live much differently here than we do. . . . " But the differences are ultimately very simple. To start with, they have less money.

The great majority of the women in the new Third World work force live at or near the subsistence level for one person, whether they work for a multinational corporation or a locally owned factory. In the Philippines, for example, starting wages in U.S.-owned electronics plants are between $34 to $46 a month, compared to a cost of living of $37 a month; in Indonesia the starting wages are actually about $7 a month less than the cost of living. "Living," in these cases, should be interpreted minimally: a diet of rice, dried fish, and water—a Coke might cost a half-day's wages—lodging in a room occupied by four or more other people. Rachael Grossman, a researcher with the Southeast Asia Resource Center, found women employees of U.S. multinational firms in Malaysia and the Philippines living four to eight in a room in boardinghouses, or squeezing into tiny extensions built onto squatter huts near the factory. Where companies do provide dormitories for their employees, they are not of the "healthful," collegiate variety implied by our corporate informant. Staff from the American Friends Service Committee report that dormitory space is "likely to be crowded, with bed rotation paralleling shift rotation—while one shift works, another sleeps, as many as twenty to a room." In one case in Thailand, they found the dormitory "filthy," with workers forced to find their own place to sleep among "splintered floorboards, rusting sheets of metal, and scraps of dirty cloth."

Wages do increase with seniority, but the money does not go to pay for studio apartments or, very likely, motorbikes. A 1970 study of young women factory workers in Hong Kong found that 88 percent of them were turning more than half their earnings over to their parents. In areas that are still largely agricultural (such as parts of the Philippines and Malaysia), or places where male unemployment runs high (such as northern Mexico), a woman factory worker may be the sole source of cash income for an entire extended family.

But wages on a par with what an 11-year-old American could earn on

"Mass hysteria" as job action?

Hysteria was supposed to have gone out with the 19th century, but it's making a comeback in today's ultramodern, high-tech electronics industry. For Malaysian women employed in the painstaking work of assembling microcircuits, mass hysteria has become a form of resistance. It starts when one young woman sees a *hantu* or *jin*, which are particularly

hideous varieties of ghosts. She falls to the floor in convulsions, scream-
ing, and within minutes the hysteria spreads up and down the assembly line. Sometimes the plant has to be closed for a week or more to
exorcise the spirits.

Western managers have tried Valium, smelling salts, and traditional
healers to combat hysteria before it paralyzes production. But Malaysian
academics who have studied the phenomenon point out that attacks are
likely to be preceded by a speedup or a tightening of plant discipline.
Since the Malaysian government does not permit labor unions, more
conventional forms of protest are hard to organize. Besides, eight or ten
hours a day spent peering through a microscope at tiny wires—for
about $2 a day pay—is enough to make anyone hysterical.

a paper route, and living conditions resembling what Engels found in
19th-century Manchester are only part of the story. The rest begins at the
factory gate. The work that multinational corporations export to the Third
World is not only the most tedious, but often the most hazardous part of
the production process. The countries they go to are, for the most part,
those that will guarantee no interference from health and safety inspec-
tors, trade unions, or even free-lance reformers. As a result, most Third
World factory women work under conditions that already have broken or
will break their health—or their nerves—within a few years, and often
before they've worked long enough to earn any more than a subsistence
wage.

Consider first the electronics industry, which is generally thought to be
the safest and cleanest of the exported industries. The factory buildings
are low and modern, like those one might find in a suburban American
industrial park. Inside, rows of young women, neatly dressed in the
company uniform or T-shirt, work quietly at their stations. There is air
conditioning (not for the women's comfort, but to protect the delicate
semiconductor parts they work with), and high-volume piped-in Bee
Gees hits (not so much for entertainment, as to prevent talking).

For many Third World women, electronics is a prestige occupation, at
least compared to other kinds of factory work. They are unlikely to know
that in the United States the National Institute on Occupational Safety and
Health (NIOSH) has placed electronics on its select list of "high health-
risk industries using the greatest number of toxic substances." If electronics assembly work is risky here, it is doubly so in countries where
there is no equivalent of NIOSH to even issue warnings. In many plants
toxic chemicals and solvents sit in open containers, filling the work area
with fumes that can literally knock you out. "We have been told of cases
where ten to twelve women passed out at once," and AFSC field worker
in northern Mexico told us, "and the newspapers report this as 'mass
hysteria.'"

In one stage of the electronics assembly process, the workers have to dip
the circuits into open vats of acid. According to Irene Johnson and Carol
Bragg, who toured the National Semiconductor plant in Penang, Ma-

laysia, the women who do the dipping "wear rubber gloves and boots, but these sometimes leak, and burns are common." Occasionally, whole fingers are lost. More commonly, what electronics workers lose is the 20/20 vision they are required to have when they are hired. Most electronics workers spend seven to nine hours a day peering through microscopes, straining to meet their quotas.

One study in South Korea found that most electronics assembly workers developed severe eye problems after only one year of employment: 88 percent had chronic conjunctivitis; 44 percent became nearsighted; and 19 percent developed astigmatism. A manager for Hewlett-Packard's Malaysia plant, in an interview with Rachael Grossman, denied that there were any eye problems: "These girls are used to working with 'scopes.' We've found no eye problems. But it sure makes me dizzy to look through those things."

Electronics, recall, is the "cleanest" of the exported industries. Conditions in the garment and textile industry rival those of any 19th-century (or 20th—see below) sweatshop. The firms, generally local subcontractors to large American chains such as J.C. Penney and Sears, as well as smaller manufacturers, are usually even more indifferent to the health of their employees than the multinationals. Some of the worst conditions have been documented in South Korea, where the garment and textile industries have helped spark that country's "economic miracle." Workers are packed into poorly lit rooms, where summer temperatures rise above 100 degrees. Textile dust, which can cause permanent lung damage, fills the air. When there are rush orders, management may require forced overtime of as much as 48 hours at a stretch, and if that seems to go beyond the limits of human endurance, pep pills and amphetamine injections are thoughtfully provided. In her diary (originally published in a magazine now banned by the South Korean government) Min Chong Suk, 30, a sewing-machine operator, wrote of working from 7 A.M. to 11:30 P.M. in a garment factory: "When [the apprentices] shake the waste threads from the clothes, the whole room fills with dust, and it is hard to breathe. Since we've been working in such dusty air, there have been increasing numbers of people getting tuberculosis, bronchitis, and eye diseases. Since we are women, it makes us so sad when we have pale, unhealthy, wrinkled faces like dried-up spinach. . . . It seems to me that no one knows our blood dissolves into the threads and seams, with sighs and sorrow."

In all the exported industries, the most invidious, inescapable health hazard is stress. On their home ground United States corporations are not likely to sacrifice productivity for human comfort. On someone else's home ground, however, anything goes. Lunch breaks may be barely long enough for a woman to stand in line at the canteen or hawkers' stalls. Visits to the bathroom are treated as privilege; in some cases, workers must raise their hands for permission to use the toilet, and waits up to a half hour are common. Rotating shifts—the day shift one week, the night shift the next—wreak havoc with sleep patterns. Because inaccuracies or failure to meet production quotas can mean substantial pay losses, the pressures are quickly internalized; stomach ailments and nervous problems are not unusual in the multinationals' Third World female work force. In some situations, good work is as likely to be punished as slow or shoddy work. Correspondent Michael Flannery, writing for the AFL-CIO's *American Federationist*, tells the story of 23-year-old Basilia Altagracia, a seamstress who stitched collars onto ladies' blouses in the La Romana (Dominican Republic) free trade zone (a heavily guarded industrial zone owned by Gulf & Western Industries, Inc.):

> A nimble veteran seamstress, Miss Altagracia eventually began to earn as much as $5.75 a day. . . . "I was exceeding my piecework quota by a lot." . . . But then, Altagracia said, her plant supervisor, a Cuban emigré, called her into his office. "He said I was doing a fine job, but that I and some other of the women were making too much money, and he was being forced to lower what we earned for each piece we sewed."
> On the best days, she now can clear barely $3, she said. "I was earning less, so I started working six and seven days a week. But I was tired and I could not work as fast as before."

Within a few months, she was too ill to work at all.

As if poor health and the stress of factory life weren't enough to drive women into early retirement, management actually encourages a high turnover in many industries. "As you know, when seniority rises, wages rise," the management consultant to U.S. multinationals told us. He explained that it's cheaper to train a fresh supply of teenagers than to pay experienced women higher wages. "Older" women, aged 23 or 24, are likely to be laid off and not rehired.

We estimate, based on fragmentary data from several sources, that the multinational corporations may already have used up (cast off) as many as 6 million Third World workers—women who are too ill, too old (30 is over the hill in most industries), or too exhausted to be useful any

Sweatshops—Made in USA

Not every manufacturer has the resources to run away to the cheap labor reservoirs of the Southern Hemisphere. An alternative is to try to duplicate in the United States the conditions that give the Third World its business appeal—substandard wages, controlled unions (if any), and the kind of no-frills work conditions that you might expect to find in Seoul or Taiwan. In the fiercely competitive light-manufacturing industries (toys, garments, artificial flowers), companies are turning to the sweatshop.

In Los Angeles, Chicago, Boston, New York, cities in New Jersey—anyplace where garment production has roots, sweatshops are springing up by the hundreds. Exact numbers are hard to come by since the shops are, by and large, unlicensed and illegal. Anyone with a few thousand dollars can start up a garment shop. All you need is a dozen sewing machines, a low-rent building, and people, usually immigrants, desperate for work. Manufacturers ("jobbers") ship out bundles of pre-cut clothes to the shop owners ("contractors") who hire workers to stitch the pieces together. A contractor in New York's South Bronx blames the jobbers for exploitation: "Do they pay enough? You got to be kidding. I pay the girls $1.25 a dress. All I get is $2.60, and I've got to run the shop, rent machines, pay for electricity."

Women are 90 percent of the sweatshop work force in this country. Here or in the Third World, women are industry's best bargain. A union organizer in Los Angeles says: "One woman I talked to this year put in a sixty-hour week and made fifty dollars." A year ago, the Department of Labor cited 85 garment shops in New York's Chinatown for violations of minimum-wage, child-labor, and overtime regulations. In many cases, a boss would punch time cards in and out for employees.

Sweatshop workers are heads of households, needing a steady, if meager, income to support their families. They are mothers without access to day-care centers who can bring their children with them to the "informal" setting of the sweatshop. Some are women who need an extra, but unreported, income to survive on welfare. And others are older women supplementing inadequate pensions.

Jobs in these garment shops are easy to get, and require little or no experience. Walk down 149th Street in the South Bronx and see one sign after another—*se necesita operadoras* (operators wanted), many with the dubious promise of *Buena Paga* (good pay). A visit to Damak Sportswear in the Bronx revealed a typical neighborhood garment operation. Thirteen Puerto Rican women were bent over sewing machines in a poorly lit room. The shop, on the third floor of an old tenement building with wooden stairs and floors, lacked fire alarms and a sprinkler system. But that's par for the course, according to Louis Berthold at the South Bronx Working Center, an ILGWU community outreach program. "One building on 161st Street had more than forty health and fire violations, and housed four shops. It wouldn't surprise me if there was another Triangle fire," he remarked.

"Homework" is another abuse spawned by the demands of industry. Women carry bundles of precut garments from the shops to stitch them at home, using their own sewing machines, paying for their own electricity, and often enlisting the help of their children to meet deadlines.

Undocumented workers, known as illegal aliens in the media, are especially vulnerable, because of their fear of discovery and deportation. Ironically, unions, industry, and the government concur in blaming "illegals" for the existence and spread of sweatshops—as if the immigrants bring the miserable conditions into this country along with their family photographs. Kurt Barnard of the Federation of Apparel Manufacturers claims that "the illegals are the cause of sweatshops and the government helps by failing to enforce immigration laws."

A study of undocumented workers in New York done by the North American Congress on Latin America (NACLA . . .) found that labor abuse was not restricted to the undocumented, but that "these are the conditions of labor that now prevail in the sectors of industry where new immigrant workers, legal or not, come to dwell." The study confirms the connection between runaway industry in the Third World and the deterioration of labor conditions at home. Charles Wang, director of New York's Chinatown Planning Council, calls on unions to become "watchdogs and take a militant stand against these conditions."

Despite their vulnerable position, women in sweatshops are beginning to organize. In 1975, 125 Chinese women at the Jung Sai garment shop in San Francisco began the longest strike in Chinese-American history; it ended nearly a year later with an ILGWU contract. In 1977, 250 workers struck the W and W Knitting Mill in Brooklyn for six months; 75 were undocumented and risked deportation to march on the picket lines. From Taiwan to New York, female labor may still be cheap, but it can't be counted on to be docile.

—A.F.

more. Few "retire" with any transferable skills or savings. The lucky ones find husbands.

The unlucky ones find themselves at the margins of society—as bar girls, "hostesses," or prostitutes.

At 21, Julie's greatest fear is that she will never be able to find a husband. She knows that just being a "factory girl" is enough to give anyone a bad reputation. When she first started working at the electronics company, her father refused to speak to her for three months. Now every time she leaves Penang to go back to visit her home village she has to put up with a lecture on morality from her older brother—not to mention a barrage of lewd remarks from men outside her family. If they knew that she had actually gone out on a few dates, that she had been to a discotheque, that she had once kissed a young man who said he was a student . . . Julie's stomach tightens as she imagines her family's reaction. She tries to concentrate on the kind of man she would like to marry: an engineer or technician of some sort, someone who had been to California, where the company headquarters are located and where even the grandmothers wear tight pants and lipstick— someone who had a good attitude about women. But if she ends up having to wear glasses, like her cousin who worked three years at the "scopes," she might as well forget about finding anyone to marry her.

One of the most serious occupational hazards that Julie and millions of women like her may face is the lifelong stigma of having been a "factory girl." Most of the cultures favored by multinational corporations in their search for cheap labor are patriarchal in the grand old style: any young woman who is not under the wing of a father, husband, or older brother must be "loose." High levels of unemployment among men, as in Mexico, contribute to male resentment of working women. (Ironically, in some places the multinationals have increased male unemployment—for example, by paving over fishing and farming villages to make way for industrial parks.) Add to all this the fact that certain companies—American electronics firms are in the lead—actively promote Western-style sexual objectification as a means of insuring employee loyalty: there are company-sponsored cosmetics classes, "guess whose legs these are" contests, and swim-suit-style beauty contests where the prize might be a free night *for two* in a fancy hotel. Corporate-promoted Westernization only heightens the hostility many men feel toward any independent working women—having a job is bad enough, wearing jeans and mascara to work is going too far.

Anthropologist Patricia Fernandez, who has worked in a *maquiladora* herself, believes that the stigmatization of working women serves, indirectly, to keep them in line. "You have to think of the kind of socialization that girls experience in a very Catholic—or, for that matter, Muslim—society. The fear of having a 'reputation' is enough to make a lot of women bend over backward to be 'respectable' and ladylike, which is just what management wants." She points out that in northern Mexico, the tabloids delight in playing up stories of alleged vice in the *maquiladoras*—indiscriminate sex on the job, epidemics of venereal disease, fetuses found in factory rest rooms. "I worry about this because there are those who treat you differently as soon as they know you have a job at a *maquiladora*," one woman told Fernandez. "Maybe they think that if you have to work, there is a chance you're a whore."

And there is always a chance you'll wind up as one. Probably only a small minority of Third World factory workers turn to prostitution when their working days come to an end. But it is, as for women everywhere, the employment of last resort, the only thing to do when the factories don't need you and traditional society won't—or, for economic reasons, can't—take you back. In the Philippines, the brothel business is expanding as fast as the factory system. If they can't use you one way, they can use you another.

There has been no international protest about the exploitation of Third World women by multinational corporations—no thundering denunciations from the floor of the United Nations' general assembly, no angry resolutions from the Conference of the Non-Aligned Countries. Sociologist Robert Snow, who has been tracing the multinationals on their way south and eastward for years, explained why: "The Third World governments *want* the multinationals to move in. There's cutthroat competition to attract the corporations."

The governments themselves gain little revenue from this kind of investment, though—especially since most offer tax holidays and freedom from export duties in order to attract the multinationals in the first place. Nor do the people as a whole benefit, according to a highly placed Third World woman within the UN. "The multinationals like to say they're contributing to development," she told us, "but they come into our countries for one thing—cheap labor. If the labor stops being so cheap, they can move on. So how can you call that development? It depends on the people being poor and staying poor." But there are important groups that do stand to gain when the multinationals set up shop in their countries: local entrepreneurs who subcontract to the multinationals; Harvard- or Berkeley-educated "technocrats" who become local management; and government officials who specialize in cutting red tape for an "agent's fee" or an outright bribe.

In the competition for multinational investment, local governments advertise their women shamelessly, and an investment brochure issued by the Malaysian government informs multinational executives that: "The manual dexterity of the Oriental female is famous the world over. Her hands are small, and she works fast with extreme care. . . . Who, therefore, could be better qualified by nature and inheritance, to contribute to the efficiency of a bench-assembly production line than the Oriental girl?"

The Royal Thai Embassy sends American businesses a brochure guaranteeing that in Thailand, "the relationship between the employer and employee is like that of a guardian and ward. It is easy to win and maintain the loyalty of workers as long as they are treated with kindness and courtesy." The facing page offers a highly selective photo-study of Thai womanhood: giggling shyly, bowing submissively, and working cheerfully on an assembly line.

Reckless, easily excited, ripe for labor agitators?

If you're a Korean factory worker, you wouldn't expect to get a free lunch, but you are likely to get a free book. Written by a man who is a former member of the Korean Central Intelligence Agency, the book explains why "Communists" and labor-reform religious groups "are very much more interested in getting women workers than men workers":

> First, women are more susceptible than men. They are emotional and less logical. They cannot differentiate between true and false or good and bad. . . . They are easily excited and are very reckless and do things hastily. . . . Third, most women workers are sentimental young girls. Fourth, women workers are so caught by vanity that they spend much more money than men workers. . . . Sixth, management, union leaders, and city administrators find it very difficult to deal with women workers when they cause trouble. The women weep and cry and behave exaggeratedly . . . and for men this kind of behavior is very troubling.

Many "host" governments are willing to back up their advertising with whatever amount of brutality it takes to keep "their girls" just as docile as they look in the brochures. Even the most polite and orderly attempts to organize are likely to bring down overkill doses of police repression:

- In Guatemala in 1975 women workers in a North American-owned factory producing jeans and jackets drew up a list of complaints that included insults by management, piecework wages that turned out to be less than the legal minimum, no overtime pay, and "threats of death." In response, the American boss made a quick call to the local authorities to report that he was being harassed by "Communists." When the women reported for work the next day they found the factory surrounded by two fully armed contingents of military police. The "Communist" ringleaders were picked out and fired.
- In the Dominican Republic, in 1978, workers who attempted to organize at the La Romana industrial zone were first fired, then obligingly arrested by the local police. Officials from the AFL-CIO have described the zone as a "modern slave-labor camp," where workers who do not meet their production quotas during their regular shift must stay and put in unpaid overtime until they do meet them, and many women workers are routinely strip-searched at the end of the day. During the 1978 organizing attempt, the government sent in national police in full combat gear and armed with automatic weapons. Gulf & Western supplements the local law with its own company-sponsored motorcycle club, which specializes in terrorizing suspected union sympathizers.
- In Inchon, South Korea, women at the Dong-II Textile Company (which produces fabrics and yarn for export to the United States) had succeeded in gaining leadership in their union in 1972. But in 1978 the government-controlled, male-dominated Federation of Korean Trade Unions sent special "action squads" to destroy the women's union. Armed with steel bars and buckets of human excrement, the goons broke into the union office, smashed the office equipment, and smeared the excrement over the women's bodies and in their hair, ears, eyes, and mouths.

Crudely put (and incidents like this do not inspire verbal delicacy), the relationship between many Third World governments and the multinational corporations is not very different from the relationship between a pimp and his customers. The governments advertise their women, sell them, and keep them in line for the multinational "johns." But there are other parties to the growing international traffic in women—such as the United Nations' Industrial Development Organization (UNIDO), the World Bank, and the United States government itself.

UNIDO, for example, has been a major promoter of "free trade zones." These are enclaves within nations that offer multinational corporations a range of creature comforts, including: freedom from paying taxes and export duties; low-cost water, power, and buildings; exemption from whatever labor laws may apply in the country as a whole; and, in some cases, such security features as barbed-wire, guarded checkpoints, and government-paid police.

Then there is the World Bank, which over the past decade has lent several billion dollars to finance the roads, airports, power plants, and even the first-class hotels that multinational corporations need in order to set up business in Third World countries. The Sri Lankan garment industry, which like other Third World garment industries survives by subcontracting to major Western firms, was set up on the advice of the World Bank and with a $20 million World Bank loan. This particular experiment in "development" offers young women jobs at a global low of $5 for a six-day week. Gloria Scott, the head of the World Bank's Women and Development Program, sounded distinctly uncomfortable when we asked her about the bank's role in promoting the exploitation of Third World women. "Our job is to help eliminate poverty. It is not our responsibility if the multinationals come in and offer such low wages. It's the responsibility of the governments." However, the Bank's 1979 World Development Report speaks strongly of the need for "wage restraint" in poor countries.

But the most powerful promoter of exploitative conditions for Third World women workers is the United States government itself. For example, the notoriously repressive Korean textile industry was developed with the help of $400 million in aid from the U.S. State Department. Malaysia became a low-wage haven for the electronics industry, thanks to technical assistance financed by AID and to U.S. money (funneled through the Asian Development Bank) to set up free trade zones. Taiwan's status as a "showcase for the free world" and a comfortable berth for multinationals is the result of three decades of financial transfusions from the United States. On a less savory note, the U.S. funds an outfit called the Asian-American Free Labor Institute, whose ostensible purpose is to encourage "free" (*i.e.*, non-Communist) trade unions in Asia, but whose actual mission is to discourage any truly militant union activity. AAFLI works closely with the Federation of Korean Trade Unions, which was responsible for the excrement-smearing incident described above.

But the most obvious form of United States involvement, according to Lenny Siegel, the director of the Pacific Studies Center, is through "our consistent record of military aid to Third World governments that are capitalist, politically repressive, and are not striving for economic independence." Ironically, says Siegel, there are "cases where the United States made a big investment—through groups like AAFLI or other kinds of political pressure—to make sure that any unions that formed would be pretty tame. Then we put in even more money to support some dictator who doesn't allow unions at all." And if that doesn't seem like a sufficient case of duplicate spending, the U.S. government also insures (through the Overseas Private Investment Corporation) outward-bound multinationals against any lingering possibility of insurrection or expropriation.

What does our government have to say for itself? It's hard to get a straight answer—the few parts of the bureaucracy that deal with women and development seem to have little connection with those that are concerned with larger foreign policy issues. A spokesman for the Department of State told us that if multinationals offer poor working conditions (which he questioned), this was not their fault: "There are just different standards in different countries." Offering further evidence of a sheltered life, he told us that "corporations today are generally more socially responsible than even ten years ago. . . . We can expect them to treat their employees in the best way they can." But he conceded in response to a barrage of unpleasant examples, "Of course, you're going to have problems wherever you have human beings doing things." Our next stop was the Women's Division within AID. Staffer Emmy Simmons was aware of the criticisms of the quality of employment multinationals offer, but cautioned that "we can get hung up in the idea that it's exploitation without really looking at the alternatives for women." AID's concern, she said, was with the fact that population is outgrowing the agricultural capacity of many Third World countries, dislocating millions of people. From her point of view, multinationals at least provide some sort of alternative: "These people have to go somewhere."

Anna, for one, has nowhere to go but the maquiladora. Her family left the farm when she was only six, and the land has long since been bought up by a large commercial agribusiness company. After her father left to find work north of the border, money was scarce in the household for years. So when the factory where she now works opened in the early 1970s, Anna felt it was "the best thing that had ever happened" to her. As a wage-earner, her status rose compared to her brothers with their on-again, off-again jobs. Partly out of her new sense of confidence, she agreed to meet with a few other women one day after work to talk about wages and health conditions. That was the way she became what management called a "labor agitator" when, six months later, 90 percent of the day shift walked out in the company's first south-of-the-border strike.

Women like Anna—or Julie K. in Malaysia—need their jobs desperately. They know the risks of organizing. Beyond that, there's the larger risk that—if they do succeed in organizing—the company can always move on in search of a still-docile, job-hungry work force. Yet thousands of women in the Third World's industrial work force have chosen to fight for better wages and working conditions. Few of these struggles reach the North American media. We know of them from reports, often fragmentary, from church and support groups:

- Nuevo Laredo, Mexico, 1973: 2,000 workers at Transitron Electronics walked out in solidarity with a small number of workers who had been unjustly fired. Two days later, 8,000 striking workers met and elected a more militant union leadership.
- Mexicali, Mexico, 1974: 3,000 workers, locked out by Mextel (a Mattel subsidiary), set up a 24-hour guard to prevent the company from moving in search of cheaper labor. After two months of confrontations, the company moved away.
- Bangkok, Thailand, 1976: 70 young women locked their Japanese bosses out and took control of the factory. They continued to make and sell jeans and floppy hats for export, paying themselves 150 percent more than their bosses had.
- South Korea, 1977: 3,000 women at the American-owned Signetics plant went on

a hunger strike for a 46.8 percent wage hike above the 39 cents an hour they were receiving. Since an actual walkout would have been illegal, they remained in the plant and held a sit-in in the cafeteria. They won a 23 percent increase.

- South Korea, 1978: 1,000 workers at the Mattel toy company in Seoul, which makes Barbie dolls and Marie Osmond dolls, staged a work slowdown to protest their 25 cents-an-hour wages and 12-hour shifts.
- South Korea, 1979: 200 young women employees of the YH textile-and-wig factory staged a peaceful vigil and fast to protest the company's threatened closing of the plant. On August 11, the fifth day of the vigil, more than 1,000 riot police, armed with clubs and steel shields, broke into the building where the women were staying and forcibly dragged the women out. Twenty-one-year-old Kim Kyong-suk was killed during the melee. It was her death that touched off widespread rioting throughout Korea that many thought led to the overthrow of President Park Chung Hee.
- Ciudad Juárez, Mexico: September, 1980: 1,000 women workers occupied an American Hospital Supply Corporation factory. They demanded better working conditions, paid vacations, and recognition of the union of their choice. The women, who are mostly in their teens and early twenties, began the occupation when 180 thugs, which the company claims were paid by a rival union, entered the factory and beat up the women's leaders. The occupation is over, but the struggle goes on.

Regarding the 1979 vigil in South Korea, Robert Snow points out: "Very few people realize that an action which began with 200 very young women factory workers led to the downfall of a government. In the 1980s Third World factory women like this are going to be a political force to reckon with." So far, feminism, first-world style, has barely begun to acknowledge the Third World's new industrial womanpower. Jeb Mays and Kathleen Connell, co-founders of the San Francisco-based Women's Network on Global Corporations . . . are two women who would like to change that. "There's still this idea of the Third World woman as 'the other'—someone exotic and totally unlike us," Mays and Connell told us. "But now we're talking about women who wear the same styles in clothes, listen to the same music, and may even work for the same corporation. That's an irony the multinationals have created. In a way, they're drawing us together as women."

Saralee Hamilton, an AFSC staff organizer of a 1978 conference on "Women and Global Corporations" (held in Des Moines, Iowa) says: "The multinational corporations have deliberately targeted women for exploitation. If feminism is going to mean anything to women all over the world, it's going to have to find new ways to resist corporate power internationally." She envisions a global network of grass-roots women capable of sharing experiences, transmitting information, and—eventually—providing direct support for each other's struggles. It's a long way off; few women anywhere have the money for intercontinental plane flights or even long-distance calls, but at least we are beginning to see the way. "We all have the same hard life," wrote Korean garment worker Min Chong Suk. "We are bound together with one string."

32

The Road Warriors

Steve Turner

"**D**o you want coffee now?"
It's a greeting reminiscent of old China, where peasants used to hail each other with the question, "Have you eaten yet?" But this is the Forty Niner Truck Plaza near Sacramento, and the person speaking is a waitress in foot-saver shoes, a white blouse and a black nylon jumper cut far above the knee. At mid-morning (as at all hours), she's equipped—like her cohorts behind the U-shaped cafeteria counters nearby—with a bulb of hot caffeine for the stream of big-rig drivers and occasional others pulling in from Interstate 80.

It's hard to hear the waitress against the background of noise, so at the slightest nod she fills the waiting plastic mugs and moves on. This is the section of the truck stop restaurant reserved for professional drivers: the side booths around the counters feature telephones for calls to company dispatchers or independent brokers to report problems or line up the next load. But the loud buzz of words is not just the sound of doing business. Truckers swill coffee the way sweathogs take water, and—released from their isolated, vibrating cabs—they talk like radios. Sitting around in jeans and wrinkled shirts, boots and work jackets, with cigarette smoke rising from underneath their cowboy hats or the duckbills with diesel and motorcycle logos, truckers bind together their common identity with tales of the daily experience. They curse and laugh about being forced to drive too many hours too fast in beat-up rigs, and revile the fast-buck "new breed" of drivers, managers and shipping brokers drawn into the trade since deregulation.

And they talk about the perils of their work.

"We were coming down from Donner Pass when the brakes failed," says trucker Sandra Martin. Sandra, called Sam and known on the CB radio as "Dallas Cowgirl," was driving. Her husband and team driver, Johnny ("Sneaky Snake"), was in the rider's seat. They were pulling 46,000 pounds of plastic wrap, bound for Modesto.

"We lost all the trailer brakes," Johnny recalls. "We only had the front brakes left. And believe me, 23 tons will *push* you down that hill."

"I headed for a turnout," says Sandra. The turnout was by the edge of a cliff. "I was standing on the brakes, and she just wasn't stopping. I said to him, 'Buddy, I think this is it. I think we're going over.'"

At the last possible moment, their tractor slewed to the left, skidded and stopped them—a development that the Martins ascribe to the grace of God. Johnny took over from a shaken Sandra, and nursed the load down the remainder of the grade with the gears and the front brakes. "You don't sit in a turnout on Donner," Sandra says. "Some other guy's going to need it, or else come by and swipe you off the edge."

At the first available rest area they called for a tow truck—a "hook." After repairs, they drove on to the Forty Niner, where they could fuel up, take showers, wash clothes, call their dispatcher back home in Missouri to line up the next load and worry in relative comfort about whether their brakes had been sabotaged at a truck stop in Nevada. "You don't come all the way from the East Coast over mountains and under mountains with perfect brakes just to have them disappear on Donner Pass," says Sandra Martin. She and Johnny believe that in the dog-eat-dog world of deregulated trucking competition, someone jealous of the big company they drive for decided to give them a hard time.

"I could do without that," says Sandra.

"Do you want more coffee now?" asked the waitress.

Under its high orange "76" ball, the Forty Niner spreads twelve acres into a flat Sacramento field like sealing wax. The nucleus is the connected series of cinderblock buildings that house the restaurant, the store, the laundromat, the showers, the motel, the repair bays, the truck wash ("If you've got a clean rig, the cops tend to leave you alone," says one driver, speaking for many) and—under a King-Kong-sized roof—the fuel pumps that yield the Unocal enterprise most of its revenue.

Around this central core lies the truck park, with diagonal slots— almost always full—accommodating 125 tractor-trailers. Big Freightliners, the authoritative Kenworths and Peterbilts, exhaust stacks aloft, carefully thread their way through the access aisles with slow dignity, like ships moving from pier berths to the sea.

For drivers on the road, truck stops are a sorry substitute for home, but it's the closest they get. The cafeteria offers something better than the peanut butter, bologna and white bread that Sandra and Johnny carry in the shelves of their sleeper cab. Here they can get traditional trucker foods such as biscuits and gravy (served in a skillet and with a spoon) or load up at a salad bar. The store sells everything from motorcycle attire and cheap porcelain to emergency truck parts—plus the white spray paint that will cover the stains smoked onto the Martins' front wheels when their brakes burned coming down off Donner Pass.

If the drivers want to escape the five- by seven-foot sleeper cab they inhabit for as long as months at a time ("We've got room to lie on our backs, side by side," says Sandra Martin), they can occupy—for $24 a night—one of the twelve motel rooms the Forty Niner reserves for truckers. In the recreation room, smoke-filled to the point of pollution alert, the drivers can shoot pool—if the television crowd hasn't overflowed to sit on the table—or play video games. And in the parking lot, especially after dark, they can get almost anything they want.

The parking slots at the farthest edges of the Forty Niner's tarmac, like those at other truck stops, are designated "party row." That's where the booze flows, drugs are done, contraband is exchanged. And that's where the Lot Lizards play. Things have gotten rougher since deregulation, everyone agrees.

It's not just rough on the lot. As Tom Schumacher, executive vice president and general manager of the California Trucking Association (CTA), an organization of owners and managers, puts it: "All sorts of weird things are happening."

Schumacher is talking about the cutthroat competition since deregulation in 1980, when minimum rates for shipping were abolished by the Congressional Motor Carrier Act. The resulting price wars have knocked a large number of trucking companies out of operation, taking union contracts down with them. Also plowed under in the business graveyard (and sometimes the real one) have been hundreds of opportunistic owner-operators who tried to beat the market by working extra hours that they—and their mortgaged equipment—couldn't handle.

In fact, the only operations benefiting from deregulation have been the largest nationwide trucking companies—which have used low pricing to gobble new contracts released by dying medium-sized outfits—and carnivorous brokers who have learned to exploit the new, brutal casino-style market.

Along with deregulation came the easing of requirements to get into the trucking business. Before 1980, the state [of California] required applicants to show probable "public convenience and necessity." Now all you need is a first-class operator's license, proof of insurance and $150 for a permit from the Interstate Commerce Commission or (for intrastate hauling) the California Public Utilities Commission. "The way it is now," says Charles Ramorino, board chairman of CTA and president of Bob Rich

Schroeder Trucking, Inc., a short-haul operation based in San Francisco, "I could set up a company with my dog Bodo as principal, and just name a human as executive secretary to sign the correspondence and answer the phone. No one would know the difference."

True to Bodo's predatory background, he would surely adopt one of the industry's new forms of business. Some corporations have "transferred risk" by compelling drivers to lease-purchase the rolling stock, the drivers thereby becoming nominal entrepreneurs instead of employees. Another kind of company has evolved that purposefully owns no trucks: They simply own the rights to lease out equipment and drivers. Both of these arrangements neatly erase anyone's responsibility for payment of employee benefits such as health protection and Social Security.

Or Bodo might become a "double-breasted trucker"—in industry parlance, a unionized firm that also has established a non-union division to avoid paying contract wages and benefits. (Union truckers make from $12 to $14 an hour, says a Teamster official; non-union drivers can expect to net $6 or $8.) A double-breasted operation works with subcontractors, deemed "subhaulers," who either are independent owner-operators or are hired through leasing companies.

The other alternative for a dog in the trucking industry is to become a new-style shipping broker, another variety of truckless operator who contacts shippers and offers to get their loads delivered for sub-market rates. These bargains are then piped through computer-telephone linkups to TV monitors at truck stops, where independent truckers desperate to make their loan deadlines take them just to get some money coming in. Veteran independent drivers, who (like companies) need to get about 75 cents per mile to break even, and more than a dollar per mile to earn decent income, cringe at the result. Sub-minimum jobs mean that other shippers can, and do, hold out for lower rates. Ramorino points out, however, that consumer prices have yet to reflect these savings.

Meanwhile, the truckers who take on these uneconomic shipments usually pass through what Chuck Mack, president of Teamsters Joint Council 7 (the union's central California umbrella organization), calls the industry's "revolving door": A few times around and they're looking for other work.

"When those wonderful social tinkerers set deregulation in motion, that's what they wanted," says CTA executive Schumacher. "A free market means working for monopoly position and squeezing out the competition." The few small operators surviving in this battle zone are those who have found a specialized niche. Gary Humphrey, for instance, a burly flatbed puller from Pocatello, Idaho, hauls machinery for a select assortment of companies. He owns his own equipment, "and all I've got to offer is good service," he says. He has deadheaded (run with no load) to the Forty Niner on his way to pick up some sophisticated garbage compactors in Phoenix.

Russ Jones, another flatbed puller, drives for an Oregon company that specializes in hauling crushed cars, Christmas trees and other unusual cargo. He is waiting empty in the Forty Niner lot for another driver from his company to arrive and switch trailers with him. He will then proceed to Los Angeles.

Carolyn and Ricky Hilburn, married "team drivers" from Gilmer, Texas, pull a "reefer" (refrigerated unit) belonging to a three-truck company, usually hauling frozen chicken to California and taking vegetables back. Both have worked in the oil fields before, but petroleum price cuts have made that a dead issue. "Sure, I'd rather be at home," says Ricky. "But everything there is at minimum wage. You've got to make the sacrifice for something."

The Hilburns have been laid over at the Forty Niner for two days with no return load. They're foremost in the small group of anxious drivers staring at the TV monitor that pipes in listings of cut-price loads in the region. They need something (cleared with their company) that will pay at least for the fuel on the return trip.

"There's a job up there on the screen for $3,000 to Montreal," says Ricky, disgusted. "That's about a dollar a mile; but look at what it means. They've just had a big snow up there, which is going to add maybe a day to the trip. And at the border you've got to pay the customs, or pay a [Canadian] guy $150 to pull it across."

The net, says Ricky, is below the 75 cents per mile his company has to make to break even. Gary Humphrey, operating at the entrepreneurial margin, figures his break-even point at 72 cents per mile. Neither of them will take the load. But both are painfully aware that someone else will.

"There was a young guy come in at a truck stop back in Ohio," recalls Johnny Martin, "and he was dressed to the nines: cowboy shirt, tight jeans, boots, all of it. And he looked on the screen and there was a job for 600 miles at 50 cents a mile. He got excited and wanted to take it. Said it was the best rate he'd had yet. I told him, 'Boy, I don't want to get smart with you, but I think you ought to get out of trucking right now.'"

The squeeze is being felt all down the line. Teamster official Chuck Mack claims that many trucking companies have survived deregulation by "chiseling and cheating to increase production," sending out overweight and over-length loads, giving drivers arrival schedules that require speeding and illicit extra hours at the wheel. Trucks are being driven harder, but CTA figures show that industry outlays for maintenance are decreasing. At issue, finally, is safety.

"One time I drove until I was all used up," says one trucker for a small company. "I was going to Fort Worth, and when I got there I realized I didn't remember going through Dallas. I got out and looked for paint scratches, afraid I might have run over someone."

"It happens to every driver," agrees another. "If they deny it, it's a lie."

The equation is simple, and sometimes deadly: Truckers have to make more trips, faster, just to earn a living. They drive longer hours, and they more frequently drive tired. Truck-at-fault accidents are on the increase, and at least one study shows that more than 40 percent of such accidents are caused by driver fatigue.

Drivers are limited to ten hours a day behind the wheel in interstate hauling (the California PUC allows twelve for intrastate work). Log books, available to any cop who asks, are supposed to register all hours of work and distances traveled and keep truckers within the limits.

"Log book," snorts a driver from the Midwest with the CB handle "Wild Child," "We call that the lie book."

"The comic book," says "Stick," a black trucker from southern California.

Like cooks offering favorite recipes, the drivers describe their methods of faking the log. "The simplest way," says "Wisconsin," "is you just keep two: one for the company, so you can get paid for all your work, and one for the cops that's different."

And then there's the trucker's friend, amphetamines. Most truckers get upset at the idea of drivers using recreational drugs and alcohol on the job. But when it comes to uppers, the tune changes. "Sure, I use them," says a freight-puller from Mississippi. "And I'll tell you, when I'm in a turn on a two-lane road at night, I'd rather meet someone that's using them than someone that's not." What about drug testing? "Look, regarding pep pills," confides one driver, "all you got to do is get a prescription for diet pills."

Truckers freely admit that speeding and extra driving are safety problems, but they feel trapped. Chuck Mack puts it this way: "Drivers have a choice between safety and economic survival, and most times they choose survival."

"What are you going to do?" says Wisconsin. "You got to eat."

Ricky and Carolyn Hilburn are team drivers—a trend in the trucking industry and a legal way to beat the time and distance rules. A driving team can move a truck twice as far in 24 hours as a solo driver, and a married team offers a stability—and trust—not available with just any old set of folks at the wheel. If you're married, however, it's drive or divorce.

"We do okay on that," says Carolyn Hilburn. At 37, she looks like an attractive schoolteacher, or the loan officer you want to see at a bank. But she's been driving trucks for the last ten years. She has hauled tanks of flammables in the oil fields and jockeyed trailers around city streets for local deliveries. Now she is part of an increasing presence of females driving the long haul—a phenomenon that has necessitated the rearrangement of some of the facilities at truck stops like the Forty Niner. Manager Mike Gentry reveals that the Forty Niner once featured a "Queens' Room" for women who arrived at the wheel or otherwise. Laundry facilities then were in the men's toilet; showers were in an open area like high school.

The Hilburns have carried the future one step further: They travel with their five-year-old son, Justin. The sleeper compartment in their new Kenworth "anteater" (the first big diesel truck to sport an aerodynamically sloped hood) has a lot of head room, allowing for a fold-down upper bunk for the child. "Sometimes we get a motel room," says Carolyn, "so we can just spread out." The sleeper cab also features a television and a small refrigerator.

Justin is not unique on the road: "Every truck stop we hit," says Carolyn, "I see one or two [trucker] families, mom and dad and the kids." But when it comes to two-day layovers like this one, once is more than enough. "I want to tell you," says Carolyn, "with a five-year-old on your hands, hanging around a truck stop gets old pretty fast."

But there are compensations. Like many truckers, the Hilburns like the fact that, as Ricky puts it, "There's no boss looking over your shoulder." And, again echoing their colleagues, they think of themselves as "professional tourists." Says Carolyn, "Justin is getting to see things most kids never will see."

Cut to two A.M. at the Forty Niner. At night a truck stop parking lot becomes a kind of sprawling, raunchy motel of sleeper cabs. Most drivers hitting a truck stop simply fuel, park, eat, shop, void, sleep and go. But for the minority otherwise inclined, there is sex for sale, and drugs, and contraband of all sorts. There is theft, and even (as the Martins will suggest) sabotage. Take away their core of bright lights and tireless, cheery waitresses (candidates for Oscars), and truck stops are like little Gomorrahs of the road map.

At the U-shaped section of cafeteria counter that's open all night, six truckers are talking with the waitress and a reporter. "Look," says "Magoo," a flatbed puller from Salem, Oregon, wryly shaking his head. "You can get on the CB out there and get anything you want. Generators, tires, anything." Where does the merchandise come from? Increasingly, they say to their chagrin, it's coming from the drivers themselves. Magoo, while parked and sleeping on the shoulder of the access road outside the truck stop when the lot was full, had an $800 tarpaulin cut off his trailer. As he tells his story, a young, carefully coiffed driver from the East comes in. The newcomer reveals that someone has just nabbed the chromed silhouettes of naked women he had affixed to his truck.

"It's a shame," says Wisconsin, a man with owlish glasses and white streaks in his beard. "Drivers never used to steal from each other. They'd steal from loads, and stores, and from cars, sure. But never from each other."

There are nods of agreement all around the counter. The conversation shifts to other aspects of the trucker's life, such as how to run some of California's new 24-hour weigh scales. Go by at night at the shift change time, says one trucker, and stay in the outside lane. There's also the matter of carrying licenses from at least two states, so that if you get points off for speeding or safety-check tickets, you'll still be able to drive. There's talk about how if the independent truckers ever want to strike again to force up shipping rates, the first thing they have to do is get the produce haulers shut down, so that supermarkets, especially in the frost belt, will run out of food. . . .

Trucking executives and Teamsters alike believe that the only way to end the chaos in the trucking industry is to re-regulate. Not as stringently as before, Charles Ramorino hastens to explain, not entirely in the same ways. But put some rules back in the game so that the players stop wiping each other out (and taking some of the rest of us along in the bargain).

"[Federal Secretary of Transportation] Elizabeth Dole says the jury is still out on deregulation," says Tom Schumacher. "That may be true, but do you want to share the highway with big trucks while it's still out?"

In 1986 the California Public Utilities Commission, finally becoming aware of the wave of trucking company bankruptcies, reestablished a rate floor for the industry. But the minimum set was just 10 percent above shipping rates at the time of deregulation six years ago, a level outpaced now by inflation. Moreover, the measure contained provisions that enable wildcat truckers to continue knocking themselves and others out of the game by charging below that level.

The CTA is pressing for a system that would let owner-operators and companies charge whatever rate they wanted to so long as they first proved that that rate would be profitable. The Teamsters union is pushing for incorporation in any new rate-setting plan of a decent income standard for drivers as part of the evaluation of a company's profitability. "We don't believe they should take the cost of deregulation out of the workers' hides," says Mack.

The CTA also is seeking a ruling that any trucking company licensed by the PUC will have to own actual rolling stock—a provision that would blow many of the rate-cutting sharks out of the industry.

In the meantime, however, drivers will still be telling the hair-raising stories and griping the gripes that tally the human cost of deregulation.

Back at the Forty Niner, the lot lizards still play, the nation's freight keeps on pulling through. Trucks come, trucks go. The waitresses keep on asking, "Do you want coffee now?" The drivers unwind in their chosen ways, waiting for the situation to improve. Waiting for their dispatchers to tell them where to go next. Waiting to head on out to the next truck stop, somewhere down the road.

IX

Health and Welfare

The social stratification of health and illness is one of the most devastating inequalities in American society. Despite our enormous wealth and technological potential, the United States still lags behind most other advanced industrial societies on many measures of health and access to health care. Americans have lower life expectancies and higher rates of infant death than citizens of many other developed countries; and some groups—including the urban and rural poor—still suffer shockingly high levels of preventable diseases and inadequate health care services. In 1967 a National Advisory Commission on Health Manpower noted that the health statistics of these groups "occasionally resemble the health statistics of a developing country."[1] Unfortunately, the same statement could still be made. Almost 20 years later, another commission found growing numbers of Americans suffering from hunger, in the midst of what we were pleased to call an economic "recovery" (see Selection 12); and rates of infant mortality began creeping upward in areas of the country hard hit by economic decline and reductions in social services.

One of the most striking differences between the United States and almost every other advanced society is our lack of any comprehensive system of national health insurance that makes adequate health care available to all citizens as a matter of right. In "The Mirage of Reform," Paul Starr explores some of the historical reasons for this difference. In the early part of the twentieth century, many progressive reformers in the United States tried to put a European-style health insurance system on the agenda. But, Starr argues, they were defeated by a combination of ideological and political forces—including the absence of a tradition of government intervention, the related absence of a strong political movement to spur government into social reforms, and the opposition of both business and parts of organized labor.

The resulting absence of accessible health care for all Americans, as Drs. Colin McCord and Harold P. Freeman point out in "Excess Mortality in Harlem," is one reason for the shockingly high rates of disease and death in many poor and minority communities. While health conditions have generally improved in recent years for most Americans, they have lagged behind—and sometimes deteriorated—in places like Harlem, where male life expectancy is lower than it is in Bangladesh. McCord and Freeman call for a "major commitment" to attack both the poverty and the inadequate health care that underlie these troubling statistics.

McCord and Freeman's statistics may indeed *underestimate* the amount of "excess mortality" in Harlem, since they were gathered before the twin epidemics of AIDS and "crack" cocaine struck the inner cities. During the 1980s, they note, AIDS became the leading cause of death for young adults in Harlem and across New York City. That AIDS is now closely connected with intravenous drug use, especially among the minority poor, reminds us that this most frightening of modern medical problems is also, in the deepest sense, a *social* problem. In "AIDS: The Epidemic and the Society," Mary Catherine Bateson and Richard Goldsby, an anthropologist and a biologist, show some of the many ways in which the spread of AIDS has followed the "fault lines of our society." Thus, our failure to address the problems of "marginalized" people, both in the Third World and in America's inner cities, has allowed the AIDS virus to "trickle up" from the most disadvantaged; our cultural inhibition against the frank dissemination of information about sex (and drugs) has hindered our ability to control the spread of the disease by changing the behavior of those at risk. Some of the authors' specific recommendations for social policy toward AIDS are controversial, but their central point—that the AIDS epidemic forces us to examine our social institutions critically—is undeniable.

The gaps in American health care that these three articles describe are one manifestation of a broader pattern that shapes most social services in the United States. In our society, human welfare has traditionally been seen as largely dependent on individual effort. The idea that society as a whole should have responsibility for the welfare of its members is relatively undeveloped in American society. For most of us, such basic human needs as health care, shelter, and the care of children are things that we have to acquire on our own, if we can. For those who can't, government programs do exist to provide basic social services—but all too often they are provided skimpily and inhumanely. And, as we've seen so sharply in the recent past, our social services are among the first casualties of governmental budget slashing in the name of economic "renewal."

A central theme of the welfare system, since its beginnings in the puritanical mentality of seventeenth-century England, has been the division of the poor into the categories of "deserving" and "undeserving"—the former including the aged and disabled, the latter comprising those who are presumably physically able to work. Most of our current programs for the poor, as well as recent government proposals for welfare reform, tend to treat them as "undeserving." Benefits are contingent on a host of special restrictions applying only to those "on welfare." In return for providing support, the welfare system assumes the authority to demand of the poor behavior that is not demanded of anyone else. In this way, a "dual system of law" has developed—one for the poor and another for everyone else.

If, as many people have argued, this system is cruel and unjust, why has it persisted? In "The Relief of Welfare," Frances Fox Piven and Richard A. Cloward argue that the deeper purpose of the welfare system is to regulate the behavior of the labor force. The puny and demeaning levels of assistance and the tendency to throw people off the welfare rolls for "immoral" behavior are means of enforcing low-wage work during times when labor is needed, but, under conditions of massive unemployment, the welfare rolls are expanded in order to forestall disorder. Thus, the persistence of a degrading welfare apparatus, for Piven and Cloward, is linked to the most fundamental requirements of an essentially unstable economic system. As long as we are unwilling to provide ample and decently paid work, there must be a system to enforce work by making "nonwork" degrading and painful.

REFERENCE

1. Report of the National Advisory Commission on Health Manpower, quoted in R. M. Titmuss, "Ethics and Economics of Medical Care," in *Commitment to Welfare* (New York: Pantheon, 1968), p. 268.

33

The Mirage of Reform

Paul Starr

W hoever provides medical care or pays the costs of illness stands to
gain the gratitude and good will of the sick and their families.
The prospect of these good-will returns to investment in health care
creates a powerful motive for governments and other institutions to
intervene in the economics of medicine. Political leaders since Bismarck
seeking to strengthen the state or to advance their own or their party's
interests have used insurance against the costs of sickness as a means of
turning benevolence to power. Similarly, employers often furnish medical
care to recruit new workers and instill loyalty to the firm. Unions and
fraternal societies have used the same means to strengthen solidarity. On
more narrowly commercial grounds, insurance companies also gain advantage from serving as middlemen. To be the intermediary in the costs of
sickness is a strategic role that confers social and political as well as strictly
economic gains.

From the viewpoint of physicians, all such intermediaries, whether
governmental or private, represent an intrusion and potential danger.
Prior to the rise of third parties, doctors stood in direct relation to their
patients as healers and benefactors. According to traditional ideals, which
are not entirely fictitious, doctors gave care according to the needs of the
sick and regulated fees according to the patients' ability to pay, which
was, in effect, the doctors' ability to charge. This system did not always
provide economic security for the physician, much less for the patient, but
it meant that doctors did not face any larger and more powerful organiza-

tion that could dictate their income and conditions of practice. And many physicians valued this freedom from hierarchical control more than the stable income that an organized system of payment or health insurance might have arguably provided.

The changing organization of economic life upset these simple arrangements. The demand for health insurance originated in the breakdown of a household economy, as families came to depend on the labor of their chief wage earner for income and on the services of doctors and hospitals for medical treatment. In individual households, sickness now interrupted the flow of income as well as the normal routine of domestic life, and it imposed unforeseen expenses for medical care. These were not merely private problems. In the economy as a whole, illness had an indirect cost in diminished production as well as a direct cost in medical expenditures. The politics of health insurance revolve around these four sorts of cost: (1) individual losses of income; (2) individual medical costs; (3) the indirect costs of illness to society; and (4) the social costs of medical care. In the last century, these have given rise successively to different interests in reform. Initially, insurance advocates emphasized the importance of spreading the risks of lost income to working-class families and reducing the loss of productive efficiency to society. After the 1920s, the rising individual risks of high medical costs created difficulties even for middle-class families and generated a new basis of interest in health insurance. And, most recently, reform has been preoccupied by the burden that rising medical costs impose on the society as a whole..

In America health insurance first became a political issue on the eve of the First World War, after nearly all the major European countries had adopted some sort of program. The rapid progress that workmen's compensation laws made in the United States between 1910 and 1913 encouraged reformers to believe that if Americans could be persuaded to adopt compulsory insurance against industrial accidents, they could also be persuaded to adopt compulsory insurance against sickness, which caused poverty and distress among many more families. The enactment of health insurance legislation in other Western capitalist countries suggested there was no fundamental reason that America could not do the same. Reformers believed as well that health insurance would not only benefit American workers; it would yield handsome returns for employers by creating a healthier and more productive labor force. So when they launched a national effort to enact compulsory health insurance, they anticipated broad support and believed it would, most likely, be the "next great step in social legislation." As would happen repeatedly in the next several decades, advocates of reform had the impression that victory was close at hand, only to see it vanish like a mirage.

This [essay] explores why a government health insurance program eluded reformers—why there is, to this day, no national health insurance in America. . . .

A COMPARATIVE PERSPECTIVE

The origins of social insurance

Financial protection against the costs of sickness, long a concern of voluntary associations, became a concern of politics in the late nineteenth century. In 1883 Germany established the first national system of compulsory sickness insurance. Organized through independent sickness funds, the program originally applied only to wage earners in some industries and trades. Besides medical attendance, it provided a cash benefit to make up for lost wages during sickness. Similar systems were set up in Austria in 1888 and in Hungary in 1891. Then in a second wave of reform, Norway adopted compulsory sickness insurance in 1909, Serbia in 1910, Britain in 1911, Russia in 1912, and the Netherlands in 1913.

Other European countries subsidized the mutual benefit societies that workers formed among themselves. France and Italy, which required sickness insurance only in a few industries such as railroads and shipping, gave relatively small subsidies, though the French expanded their program in 1910. On the other hand, Sweden, beginning in 1891, Denmark in 1892, and Switzerland in 1912 gave extensive state aid to voluntary funds and provided other strong incentives for membership. By 1907 the proportion of the population covered by sickness insurance in Denmark actually exceeded the proportion in Germany (27 compared with 21 percent).

But in the United States during this period, the government took no action to subsidize voluntary funds nor to make sickness insurance compulsory. In the years between the adoption of compulsory insurance by Germany in 1883 and by England in 1911, the issue was hardly discussed in America. This long neglect and indifference require some explanation: Why did the Europeans adopt health insurance while Americans ignored it?

The European countries that instituted compulsory sickness insurance did so as part of a general program of social insurance against the chief risks that interrupted continuity of income: industrial accidents, sickness and disability, old age, and unemployment. We associate health insurance with the financing of medical care, but its original function was primarily income stabilization. Many early voluntary funds and some governmental programs included only a sickness benefit, or "sick pay," to compensate for lost wages; paying for medical care came later, or was distinctly secondary. The governmental programs were not universal because they were originally conceived as a means of maintaining the incomes, productive effort, and political allegiance of the working class. Participation was limited to wage earners below a given income and usually did not include their dependents, agricultural workers, the self-employed, or the middle and upper classes. These groups were considered either too difficult to cover (because of high administrative costs) or not in need of income protection.

Social insurance represented a new stage in the management of destitution in capitalist societies. From the rise of national economies to the emergence of industrial capitalism—that is, between the sixteenth and late eighteenth/early nineteenth centuries—the poor received assistance in their own parishes. Industrialization, however, generated growing complaints about the effects of local poor relief on the free circulation of labor and incentives for work. In what Gaston Rimlinger calls the "liberal break" with paternalism, governments abolished the traditional system of poor relief, restricted public assistance to almshouses where it would be available only under the most demeaning conditions, and forced the able-bodied poor to work or to emigrate. While the older forms of social protection survived in the mutual societies of artisans and skilled workers, liberalism reduced the government's role as the guardian of welfare.

The advent of social insurance at the end of the nineteenth century signified a return to social protection. Social insurance departed from the earlier paternalism, however, by providing a right to benefits instead of charity. In this sense, it constituted an extension to social welfare of liberal principles of civil and political rights. On the other hand, social insurance departed from liberalism by expanding the role of the state and demanding compulsory contributions. Consequently, it represented an extension of obligations as well as freedom. In this regard, it was no different from many other modern reforms. The right to a primary education, for example, typically entails an obligation to attend school, at least until some minimum age. The right to benefits under sickness insurance, while not requiring the sick to see a physician, typically has limited the insured to use of licensed practitioners and hence has extended social control of medical practice. Social insurance, moreover, required contributions from employers as well as workers. Hence, it represented an intrusion by the state into the prerogatives of businessmen in setting wages. Where liberalism had its greatest hold and where private interests were strong relative to the state, social insurance made the slowest headway. So, contrary to the modern view of the welfare state as a "liberal" reform (in the current American sense), social insurance was generally introduced first in authoritarian and paternalistic regimes, like Germany, and only later in the more liberal and democratic societies, like England, France, and the United States. Partly because Germany industrialized later and faster, its traditional forms of social protection had partly survived when it faced the challenge of socialism. Perhaps as a result, it made a more direct transition to the social protection of the welfare state.

Political discontent precipitated the introduction of social insurance in both Germany and England. The German monarchy in the 1880s faced a growing challenge from the German Social Democratic Party. In 1875 the

Socialists had been strengthened by a coalition between the followers of Marx and Lassalle. After outlawing the Social Democratic Party, Bismarck was still convinced that repression was insufficient and sought a "welfare monarchy" to assure workers' loyalty.

In England labor unrest also preceded the introduction of social insurance in the early 1900s, but the political conditions were somewhat different. England was a parliamentary democracy in which the Liberals were attempting to hold on to their working-class support by championing social reform. In Germany, Bismarck introduced social rights to avoid granting wider political rights; in Britain, Lloyd George sought social rights within the context of existing rights to political participation. But both were basically defensive efforts to stabilize the political order by integrating the workers into an expanded welfare system. The proponents of social insurance also expected that it would increase industrial productivity and military power by diminishing class antagonism and creating a healthier labor force and army. As Lloyd George later put it in a memorable phrase, "You can not maintain an A-1 empire with a C-3 population."

Germany and England may also have been predisposed toward social insurance programs by strong preexisting mutual benefit funds, which were notably active in providing sickness benefits. In Germany, various guilds, trades, industries, and mutual societies operated *Krankenkassen* ("sickness funds"). In England, even before 1911, nearly half the adult males—generally the conservative artisans and respectable, self-supporting workers rather than the very poor—belonged to friendly societies, which were powerful national organizations; voluntary sickness insurance covered about 13 percent of the population. Although these preexisting funds represented obstacles to state control of social insurance, they also reflected a widespread awareness among workers of the value of insuring against the costs of sickness.

Why America lagged

In the United States, the political conditions and preexisting institutions were altogether different. America was the country where classical liberalism had most thoroughly shaped the relations between state and society. As of 1900, American government was highly decentralized, engaged in little direct regulation of the economy or social welfare, and had a small and unprofessional civil service. Strengthening government became one of the central concerns of Progressive reform at the turn of the century, but its impact was limited. At the national level, government had little to do with social welfare, and in health its activities were minor. Congress had set up a system of compulsory hospital insurance for merchant seamen as far back as 1798 (following European precedents), but this was an altogether exceptional measure to deal with a group that was commercially and epidemiologically strategic because of its role in foreign commerce. Congress approved aid to mental hospitals in 1854, only to see the bill vetoed by President Pierce. It created a National Board of Health in 1879 but abolished it in 1883. In two stages in 1902 and 1912, it expanded the Marine Hospital Service into the U.S. Public Health Service but gave it few functions and little authority. The federal government continued to leave such matters to state and local government, and the general rule at those levels was to leave as much to private and voluntary action as possible. Although general hospitals in Europe became primarily governmental and tax supported, in America they remained mainly private. A system of government that followed such principles was not likely to be an early convert to compulsory health insurance.

Nor was there a challenge to political stability in America comparable to the challenge in Europe. In the 1890s, America experienced depression and unrest, but much of the unrest was agrarian and populist, and social insurance would not have responded to farmers' concerns. Socialism emerged as a political force only after the turn of the century, and even then the Socialist Party was nowhere near the political threat its counterparts were in Europe. At its height, in the elections of 1912 and 1916, the party attracted only 6 percent of the vote; this was, as it happens, precisely the time the health insurance campaign began. After a shaky start, American unions had begun to grow—membership, less than half a million in 1897, was up to 2 million by 1910 and 5 million by 1920—but this growth occurred under a conservative labor leadership suspicious of political reformers. The breach between the conservative trade unions and the Socialist Party prevented the emergence of powerful working-class support for social insurance.

Finally, voluntary sickness funds were less developed in the United States than in Europe, reflecting less interest in health insurance and less familiarity with it. At the turn of the century, European immigrants established numerous small benevolent societies in American cities offering sickness benefits to their members, but the more established fraternal orders, composed of older ethnic stock, mainly provided life insurance. Some local lodges of national orders gave assistance in sickness, but it was more fragmentary than in Europe. Similarly, when unions provided sickness benefits, the locals generally did so, not the national organizations.

American unions oscillated in their attitude toward benefit programs. The first trade unions in the early nineteenth century had been as concerned with mutual aid as with jobs and wages. By the Civil War, however, they turned more toward bargaining with employers and discouraged benefits, since high dues might deter workers from membership. But after the war they began to adopt the theory that benefits promoted membership. In 1877 the Granite Cutters adopted the first national sick benefit plan. Still, unions had to weigh the gains in solidarity from benefits against the deterrent effects of high dues, and this limited their capacity to provide protection against the costs of sickness.

Commercial health insurance was as yet little developed. Around 1850 several health insurance companies were established, but they quickly went bankrupt. However, a related form of insurance, protection against losses from accidental injury and death, did gain a firm footing in the second half of the nineteenth century. Beginning about 1896, firms engaged in this business started offering insurance against specific diseases and gradually broadened their policies to cover all disability from sickness or accident. Such policies were expensive because of administrative costs and were carried mainly by the middle class. There was also a small amount of health and accident insurance sold to workers, but because of overhead and profits, only about 30 to 35 percent of premium income was returned in benefits to subscribers. Frauds were common, and the larger, more respectable firms stayed away from the business. John F. Dryden, who briefly experimented with sickness benefits when he founded the Prudential Insurance Company in 1875, commented in 1909 that conservative business practice dictated that an industrial insurance company had to limit itself to benefits payable at death. "[T]he assurance of a stipulated sum during sickness," he wrote, "can only safely be transacted, and then only in a limited way, by fraternal organizations having a perfect knowledge of and complete supervision over the individual members." But while fraternal groups could remedy some difficulties that insurance companies encountered, they had problems of their own. Often they were improperly managed and too small to be actuarially sound; as their membership aged, their reserves frequently proved insufficient.

Because most sickness benefits were provided by small immigrant benefit societies and local chapters of fraternal orders and unions, early researchers found it hard to assemble accurate statistics regarding sickness insurance. But it seems likely that such insurance was less extensive in America than in England and Germany before governmental programs were introduced in those countries. In Illinois, Ohio, and California, where state commissions studied the problem around 1918, the proportion of industrial workers enjoying some form of sickness benefit—usually very minimal—was estimated at one third. The percentage would have been much lower if computed over the entire population. In the country as a whole, only a small fraction of the population can have had any protection against loss of earnings, and even fewer received any medical care or coverage of medical expenses through insurance.

Yet American workers did spend a great deal of money for insurance to protect themselves against one related hazard. In the early twentieth century, commercial insurance companies enjoyed enormous success selling "industrial" life insurance policies to working-class families. The lump-sum payments provided by these policies generally paid for funerals and the expenses of a final illness. This business was the backbone of two companies, Metropolitan Life and Prudential, that had risen to the top of the insurance industry by collecting 10, 15, and 25 cents a week from millions of American working-class households. But because the premiums were paid on a weekly basis and lapses were frequent, these policies had to be marketed by an army of insurance agents, who visited their clients as soon after payday as possible. The administrative costs of industrial insurance were staggering; subscribers received in benefits only about 40 percent of what they paid in premiums. The rest went to the agents and the companies. Yet the fear of a pauper burial was so great that Americans bought $183 million of such insurance in 1911—about as much as Germany spent on its entire social insurance system.

GRAND ILLUSIONS, 1915–1920

The democratization of efficiency

In America, reformers outside government, rather than political leaders, took the initiative in advocating health insurance. The idea did not enter political debate under antisocialist sponsorship, as it often did in Europe. Indeed, the Socialists in 1904 were the first American political party to endorse health insurance. At the center of the movement, however, was the American Association for Labor Legislation (AALL), founded in 1906, a group of "social progressives" who sought to reform capitalism rather than abolish it. The association's membership was small and primarily academic, and it included such notable figures as the Progressive economists John R. Commons and Richard Ely of the University of Wisconsin and Henry R. Seager of Columbia. The AALL's chief initial concern was occupational disease, and its first major success came in the campaign against "phossy jaw," a disease common among workers in match factories that could be prevented by eliminating phosphorus from the production process. The association was prominent in the drive for workmen's compensation. It sought the prohibition of child labor and also supported unemployment relief through public works, state employment agencies, and unemployment insurance. Officially, it took no position on unions, but many of its members supported unions and the association originally included several prominent labor leaders.

The AALL's campaign for health insurance had the misfortune of getting under way just as Progressivism began to recede. As a political force, Progressivism reached its peak in the election of 1912, when the Progressives bolted from the Republican Party and nominated former President Theodore Roosevelt as their candidate. Much like Lloyd George and Winston Churchill, Roosevelt supported social insurance, including health insurance, in the belief that no country could be strong whose people were sick and poor. But his defeat in 1912 by Woodrow Wilson postponed for another two decades the kind of leadership that might have involved the national government more extensively in the management of social welfare. In America compulsory health insurance would not have the kind of national political sponsor it enjoyed in Germany and England.

In the December after the 1912 election, the AALL voted to create a committee on social insurance, and in June 1913 it organized the first national conference on the subject. Despite its broad mandate, the committee decided to concentrate on health insurance, and the following summer it drew up a model bill, the first draft of which was published in 1915.

The AALL's bill followed European precedent in limiting participation to the working class, though it gave medical coverage not just to workers but also to their dependents. Its program applied to all manual workers and to others earning less than $1,200 a year, except for domestic and casual employees. Benefits were of four kinds: (1) medical aid, including all physicians', nurses', and hospital services; (2) sick pay (at two thirds of wages for up to twenty-six weeks; at one third of wages during hospitalization); (3) maternity benefits for the wives of insured men as well as insured women; and (4) a death benefit of $50 to pay for funeral expenses. The costs, estimated at 4 percent of wages, were to be divided among employers and workers, each to pay two fifths, and the state, which would contribute the fifth remaining. The employers' share increased for the lowest-income workers. A worker earning $600 a year, the AALL estimated, would pay 80 cents out of a monthly premium of $2.

The reformers formulated the case for health insurance in terms of two objectives. They argued it would relieve poverty caused by sickness by distributing the uneven wage losses and medical costs that individual families experienced. And, second, they maintained it would reduce the total costs of illness and insurance to society by providing effective medical care, creating monetary incentives for disease prevention, and eliminating wasteful expenditures on industrial insurance. This mixture of concerns was typical of the social Progressives. On the one hand, in emphasizing the relief of poverty, they made an appeal to moral compassion; on the other, in emphasizing prevention and increased national efficiency, they made an appeal to economic rationality. Combining social meliorism with the ideal of efficiency fitted perfectly into Progressive ideology. It also reflected the political conditions of a democratic capitalist society, which made it incumbent upon reformers to gain the support of both the public and powerful business interests. Progressive health insurance was shaped by these political realities as well as by the economics of sickness and health care of the time.

Relieving poverty caused by sickness, as the reformers saw it, involved both compensating lost earnings and paying medical costs. The Progressives considered these equally important. Data from the period suggest that for individual workers wage losses were two to four times greater than health care costs, but for families as a whole, total losses of income and medical costs were roughly the same because of the additional health care expenses of dependents. A study of 4,474 workers in a Chicago neighborhood showed that in the course of a year about one in four was sick for a week or longer and, from such sicknesses, lost an average of $119 or 13.7 percent of annual wages. The proportion of families that could not "make ends meet" increased to 16.6 percent among those with serious illness, compared to 4.7 percent among those without. Advocates of health insurance also cited data from charities indicating that sickness was the leading immediate cause of poverty; a conservative estimate by the Illinois commission found it to be the chief factor in a quarter to a third of the charity cases in the state.

I. M. Rubinow, a leading authority on social insurance who was both a physician and an actuary as well as a Socialist, saw health insurance as the means to cut the "vicious circle" of disease and poverty. It would prevent the families of the sick from becoming destitute and thereby prevent further sickness. Such a program had to be compulsory, Rubinow argued, to make it universal (that is, among low-income wage earners) and to secure contributions from employers and the public, who shared responsibility for the conditions that caused sickness. American workers, he wrote, "must learn to see that they have a right to force at least part of the cost and waste of sickness back upon the industry and society at large, and they can do it only when they demand that the state use its power and authority to help them, indirectly at least, with as much vigor as it has come to the assistance of the business interests. . . . "

Yet, in advocating health insurance, most Progressive reformers spoke of stabilizing rather than redistributing incomes, and on behalf of a public interest in preventing poverty and disease rather than a special grievance of labor. Though their program had redistributive implications, they generally appealed for support on the grounds that all interests, including those of business, favored insurance.

This orientation was abundantly evident in the second half of the social Progressives' case for health insurance. As the AALL put it, health insurance had as one of its aims the "conservation of human resources," seen as analogous to the conservation of natural resources. Irving Fisher, then one of the country's most eminent economists, argued in a presidential address to the AALL in 1916 that health insurance would have its greatest value in stimulating preventive measures and hence was needed not just "to tide workers over the grave emergencies incident to illness," but also "to reduce illness itself, lengthen life, abate poverty, improve working power, raise the wage level, and diminish the causes of industrial discontent." B. S. Warren and Edgar Sydenstricker of the U.S. Public Health Service maintained that because a compulsory insurance scheme would require financial contributions from industry, workers, and the community, it would encourage them to support public health measures in order to prevent disease and save money.

In addition, compulsory health insurance, by including a funeral benefit, would eliminate the huge cost of marketing industrial insurance
policies, not to mention the profits. Hence, reformers claimed they could
finance much of the cost of health insurance out of the money wasted on
industrial insurance policies. Warren and Sydenstricker cited a 1901 Bureau of Labor study showing that 65.8 percent of 2,567 families had
expenditures for industrial insurance averaging $29.55 per family, while
76.7 percent had expenditures for sickness and death averaging $26.78
per family. In effect, instead of paying insurance agents to visit them
weekly to make collections, wage-earning families could pay for doctors
and nurses to visit them when they were sick. So the inclusion of funeral
benefits was not an idiosyncratic choice of Progressive reformers; it was
part of their general program for increased social efficiency.

The arguments for health insurance reflected a great confidence among
Progressive reformers in the capacity of public health and medical care to
prevent and cure disease. The achievements of medicine, Rubinow said in
a defense of health insurance, exceeded the wildest dreams of a half
century earlier. "If there was a rational basis for a certain medical nihilism
so popular then, it has vanished long ago. No reasonable being will doubt
the tremendous efficiency of competent medical aid." The democratic
view, instead of demanding that every man be his own physician, now
insisted that the services of physicians be available to all. After reviewing
the evidence that from a quarter to two fifths of the sick were not receiving
any medical care, a commission in Ohio observed that all facts pointed to
the need for a "democratization of medical service," which meant wider
distribution, not lay control.

As ardent believers in the value of medical care and the legitimate basis
of professional authority, Progressive reformers had no basic quarrel with
physicians. Consequently, the AALL in 1914 sought to involve the leaders
of the medical profession in formulating the model health insurance bill.
Anticipating some resistance by private practitioners, they tried to be
flexible about provisions that would affect doctors. To their pleasant
surprise, they found that prominent physicians not only were sympathetic but wanted actively to help in securing legislation. Among these
cooperative physicians were some of the leaders of the AMA, including
George H. Simmons, the editor of its *Journal*, and Frederick R. Green,
secretary of its newly created Council on Health and Public Instruction,
who wrote to the AALL's secretary, John Andrews, "Your plans are so
entirely in line with our own that I want to be of every possible assistance." He proposed setting up a three-man committee to work with the
AALL. In February 1916, the AMA board approved the committee, and
the Socialist I. M. Rubinow was hired as its executive secretary. The
committee was located in the same building in New York City as the
AALL, and its chairman, Alexander Lambert, Theodore Roosevelt's personal physician, was the AALL's medical advisor. At this point, the AMA
and the AALL formed a united front on behalf of health insurance.

Yet there were points of tension between the reformers and the physicians, especially where the Progressive search for efficiency conflicted with the doctors' defense of their income and autonomy. Some reformers saw health insurance as an opportunity to subordinate medical practice to public health, to encourage the growth of group practice, and to change the method of payment from fee-for-service to salary or capitation (that is, per patient per year). These changes the doctors would not accept.

The relation of health insurance to public health was one issue on which the AALL was prepared to give way to the doctors. Public health officers, arguing that preventive medicine ought to be the overriding concern, wanted to make health departments the administrative agencies for health insurance. But Lambert, speaking for both the AALL and the AMA at a conference in 1916, noted that the physicians would be unwilling to submit to "absolute control" by public health authorities, and the doctors' preferences had to be respected.

Other reformers like Rubinow wanted to use health insurance to promote a shift from individual general practice to specialized group practice under governmental control. The initially positive response of AMA leaders in 1915 encouraged Michael M. Davis, Jr., then director of the Boston Dispensary, to hope that America might be able to "improve on" Britain and Germany in the organization of services. In a letter to the AALL's John Andrews, Davis wrote that they ought to be careful not to tie health insurance "to a system of individualized private practice without creating a definite opening for . . . cooperative medical work in diagnosis and treatment." Davis added that he had "a good many ideas on organization" since visiting the Mayo Clinic. But most physicians were unlikely to be enthusiastic about such ideas, which threatened to subordinate them in a bureaucratic hierarchy, and the most the AALL could do was to include a provision allowing local insurance committees to contract with group practices as well as with individual doctors.

Undoubtedly, the most serious point of tension was the method of paying physicians under health insurance. Reformers were reluctant to adopt any method that would cause serious financial problems for the insurance system, and European experience had clearly indicated that paying doctors for each service they performed was more likely to cause budgetary problems than if they were paid per capita, that is, according to the number of patients who signed up on their list for the year. Consequently, reformers recommended that doctors be paid on a capitation basis rather than by visit. Physicians, however, strongly objected to any form of contract practice as a result of their experience with fraternal lodges and industrial firms that forced them to bid against each other for group business. Trying to mediate the conflict, Lambert proposed paying doctors by visit out of a budget for physicians' services determined by the number of people insured in a local area.

The AMA's initial cooperation with the AALL did not necessarily reflect any widespread enthusiasm among its membership. Two state medical societies, Wisconsin and Pennsylvania, had quickly endorsed the principle of compulsory health insurance, but others were apathetic. A survey of secretaries of state medical societies in late 1916 showed that the vast majority had not yet discussed health insurance. At the AALL's annual meeting in late 1916, several physicians commented that the great majority of practitioners were probably opposed to health insurance, but expressed confidence that this was primarily because of ignorance. No doctor who had given it careful study was against it, commented Frederick Green of the AMA, but it would not be long before Green himself denied he had ever favored the measure.

Although the Progressive Party broke up in the 1916 election after endorsing the Republican nominee, reformers could take some satisfaction in the early response that year to the proposal for health insurance. The Commission on Industrial Relations, created by President Wilson in the wake of labor violence, recommended health insurance in its final report. The labor committee of the U.S. House of Representatives held hearings on a resolution introduced by its sole Socialist member to create a national social insurance commission. Though the proposal failed to gain approval, several states established investigative commissions. Organizations of public health officers and nurses endorsed the measure. In short, health insurance seemed to be gaining support and moving toward public approval.

Labor and capital versus reform

Yet there were also signs of trouble. To the chagrin of reformers, the American Federation of Labor (though not all its member unions or state federations) opposed the program. Samuel Gompers, president of the AF of L, repeatedly denounced compulsory health insurance as an unnecessary, paternalistic reform that would create a system of state supervision of the people's health. In an acrimonious debate with Rubinow at the 1916 congressional hearings on a national commission, Gompers assailed the Socialist's belief that government had to be called in to ensure workers' welfare and gave a ringing defense of the success of trade unions in raising workers' standard of living.

This view was characteristic of Gompers and the AF of L, which at that time opposed legislation to establish a minimum wage, unemployment insurance, old-age pensions, or even an eight-hour day. Gompers insisted that workers could rely only on their own economic power, not the state, to obtain higher wages and benefits. He worried that a government insurance system would weaken unions by usurping their role in providing social benefits.

Gompers' central concern was maintaining the strength of the unions. As Selig Perlman writes in his classic *Theory of the Labor Movement*, the "overshadowing problem" of American unions was "staying organized" because of the "lack of class cohesiveness in American labor." All previous attempts in the United States to build unions had been wrecked during economic depressions. Early in his career, Gompers wrote that the most intelligent workers would remain members of a union in times of adversity, but the others, who had "no inclination or ability or time" to see its advantages, should find their interests made "so inseparable from the union as to make it a direct and decided loss to them to sever their connection. . . . I know of no better means than to make our unions beneficial and benevolent as well as protective." As a young leader of the cigarmakers in New York, he had proposed in 1879 that the union provide sickness and death benefits. The measure was adopted, and in one year his local increased its membership from 300 to 3,000. "Gompers," writes a biographer, "believed that the phenomenal increase in the membership of Local 144 was due to the introduction of those benefits." Explaining the AF of L's rejection in 1902 of a proposal for federal old-age pensions, Gompers wrote that "the unions desired to develop their own system of protection against all the vicissitudes of life as a means of gaining recruits. Social security would deprive them of that function."

But, in fact, American trade unions had not much developed their own systems of welfare protection. They were increasingly gaining a stable membership, not by offering welfare benefits, but by controlling job opportunities. Gompers' views were based on the expectation that benefits would prove useful rather than any extensive use of them. Although his views prevailed in the national organization, other AF of L leaders, including Vice President William Green, saw less of a threat to labor solidarity from a governmental program and favored health insurance. Ten of the largest state federations within the AF of L, including California, New York, Massachusetts, Pennsylvania, and Wisconsin, supported health insurance proposals in their states. Only in New York, however, was organized labor a leading force in the campaign.

Employers generally saw compulsory health insurance as contrary to their interests, despite some early business reaction that was tentatively sympathetic. A committee of the National Association of Manufacturers (NAM), a hard-line antiunion organization, reported in 1916 that voluntary insurance would be the "higher and better method," but it recognized that compulsory insurance might be necessary and, if so, all occupations ought to be included. This report was only accepted, not adopted, by the NAM, and like other business groups it soon joined the opposition to compulsory health insurance.

Spokesmen for American business typically rejected the argument that health insurance would add to productive efficiency. The National Industrial Conference Board, a research organization established by major industrial trade associations, agreed that sickness was a serious handicap to the "social well-being and productive efficiency of the nation," but argued that direct investment in public health would have a higher return than cash benefits for the sick. Compulsory health insurance would not "materially reduce the amount of sickness"; the incentives for prevention would not work because the responsibility for most sickness could not be fixed. Indeed, days lost from work might increase because sick pay encouraged malingering; the conference board cited statistics indicating that days lost from work on account of sickness had increased in Germany after insurance was enacted. Nor would health insurance greatly reduce poverty. The figures suggesting sickness caused poverty ignored other causes. Also, many of those seeking charity would not have had health insurance because they were casual workers, self-employed, or unemployed. The large sums spent on health insurance, therefore, would benefit only part of the population; in New York, the board calculated, the insurance bill would cover only one third of the population.

Even the most liberal elements of business, represented in the National Civic Federation (NCF), generally opposed compulsory health insurance. The civic federation, founded in 1901 by journalist Ralph Easley to bring together the leaders of capital, labor, and the public in the interest of social harmony, included the more moderate big businessmen who were willing to recognize organized labor as a legitimate partner in American capitalism, at least outside of their own factories. The NCF had been an ally of the American Association for Labor Legislation in the campaign for workmen's compensation, and it had some overlapping members, including Gompers, who served as a vice president of both groups. But even though the two organizations sought peaceful labor reform within the framework of capitalism, they grew increasingly estranged as the health insurance conflict unfolded. The AALL was composed mainly of academic reformers who saw themselves as pursuing the interests of the public rather than those of any class, while the civic federation sought a mutual accommodation between the interests of organized labor and those of big business. The social Progressives in the AALL were inclined to rely upon the judgment of professionals and the power of government, whereas organized labor and big business favored private bargaining outside the purview of the state. Gompers resigned from the AALL in 1915 in part over the association's frequent call for impartial experts and high-minded commissions to resolve social problems. Such experts Gompers distrusted as a distinct class with interests of their own. On the other hand, he remained in the National Civic Federation despite repeated attacks by left-wing labor leaders for collaborating with big business. The leaders of the AF of L, unlike many of the Progressives, accepted big business as inevitable and viewed unions as the necessary counterweight to protect the interests of workers. As has often been pointed out, American labor leaders resembled American businessmen in priding themselves on being practical, cynical about politics, and distrustful of intellectuals and their abstract schemes. Furthermore, in regard to social insurance, neither unions nor big business at that time wanted any competition from government in social welfare programs that could potentially increase workers' loyalty to either of them. Thus health insurance, rather than pitting labor unions against capital, pitted both of them against the reformers.

In 1914 the civic federation sent a committee to England to study recent social insurance legislation, and two years later it set up a social insurance department. At first, the federation criticized specific provisions of American insurance proposals. By 1917, however, it was spearheading the opposition, charging that health insurance was a failure in Europe that impractical reformers wanted to foist upon workers in the United States even though labor—witness Gompers and the AF of L—had no desire for it.

One segment of business, well represented in the civic federation, played a particularly active role in fighting compulsory health insurance—the insurance industry. Other commercial interests in health care, such as pharmaceutical companies, assailed health insurance, but none so relentlessly as the insurance firms. Where reformers mounted campaigns for health insurance, the insurance industry aroused the opposition. Particularly active were representatives of the two firms, Prudential and Metropolitan Life, whose industrial life insurance business was directly threatened by the reformers' inclusion of a funeral benefit. As of 1915 Prudential held 38 percent and Metropolitan 34 percent of industrial business. Nor were their interests alone at stake; both firms were closely linked through their investments and boards of directors with other large corporations. The reformers, in their innocent enthusiasm for efficiency, were threatening to eliminate an important source of profit for the insurance industry and of investment capital for American business. As a result, they unwittingly brought down upon themselves the concerted opposition of big business. The chief spokesman for the insurance industry was Frederick L. Hoffman, a respected actuary who was vice president of Prudential and a member of the AALL until 1917, when he resigned over the health insurance issue and became the reformers' most indefatigable critic. Nearly all the propaganda against compulsory health insurance, John R. Commons later suggested, could be traced back to Hoffman, and this was only a slight exaggeration. Another insurance company vice president, Lee K. Frankel of Metropolitan, chaired the National Civic Federation's social insurance committee and prepared its response to health insurance. Yet a third key critic was P. Tecumseh Sherman, a lawyer for insurance interests also active in the civic federation. These ties helped solidify the opposition of insurance companies and employers to health insurance. On the other hand, the unions were divided among themselves and at odds with the political organizations advocating reform.

Defeat comes to the progressives

In 1917 two developments changed the entire complexion of the health insurance debate. The first was growing opposition from physicians. Though the AMA House of Delegates in June 1917 approved a final report from its social insurance committee favoring health insurance, this action did not reflect sentiment in state medical societies. In New York, the state council of the medical society had endorsed the model health insurance bill in December 1916, but meetings in county societies in January and February saw a groundswell of opposition. In March the state council met again and withdrew its earlier approval. The source of this opposition, according to Ronald L. Numbers, was "almost entirely economic in nature." When legislative hearings were held in March, the doctors who testified were nearly all opposed to health insurance. In Illinois a committee of the state society reported in May that an insurance bill it had been prepared to fight in the legislature had never materialized: "We feel that the active opposition of the medical profession prevented its introduction."

The second key development of 1917, the entry of America into the war in April, proved a major turning point in the insurance movement. Many physicians went into the service; the AMA closed down its committee on social insurance and I. M. Rubinow took another job. In Massachusetts, debate was suspended on a bill that had the support of prominent Boston physicians and progressive social and political leaders. Anti-German feeling rose to a fever, the government's propaganda bureau commissioned articles denouncing German social insurance, and opponents of health insurance now assailed it as a Prussian menace inconsistent with American values.

The one public referendum on health insurance took place in this climate of wartime hysteria. In early 1917 the California social insurance commission recommended health insurance, and as a first and necessary step it proposed an enabling amendment to the state constitution. Some leaders of the state medical society favored the plan and kept the society neutral, but a large group of doctors formed an independent League for the Conservation of Public Health to oppose the measure. "What is Compulsory Social Health Insurance?" asked one of the league's pamphlets. "It is a dangerous device, invented in Germany, announced by the German Emperor from the throne the same year he started plotting and preparing to conquer the world." To doctors the league wrote that the state commission was "wholesaling medical services at bargain counter prices" and that two thirds of the population would be divided up among panel doctors "whose compensation would be fixed, and whose services would be supervised by political appointees." Also prominent in the opposition were Christian Scientists, who operated through an agency financed by the insurance industry. In November 1918 the health insurance referendum went down to a thunderous defeat—358,324 to 133,858.

Another promising effort failed in New York, where the State Federation of Labor and the AALL jointly sponsored a health insurance bill with the support of Governor Alfred E. Smith and a coalition of Democrats and Progressive Republicans. In 1919 the Senate passed the bill by a vote of thirty to twenty, but it died in the House, which was dominated by conservatives. In Ohio that year the insurance commission reported in favor of compulsory health insurance, but no action was taken; in Pennsylvania, the health insurance commission made no recommendation; and in Illinois, where the state commission had conducted the most thorough investigation, it voted seven to two against any health insurance proposal.

The war, though only eighteen months long for Americans, proved to be the graveyard of an already faltering Progressive movement. It diverted attention from social reform, channeled the enthusiasm for doing good into a crusade abroad, and divided the old nationalist Progressives like Roosevelt from the more pacifist and isolationist elements of the movement. In the red scare immediately after the war, when the government attempted to root out the last vestiges of radicalism, opponents of compulsory health insurance associated it with Bolshevism and buried it in an avalanche of anticommunist rhetoric. Then, along with most other Progressive causes, health insurance vanished in the complacency of the 1920s.

Why did Progressive proposals for health insurance fail? Clearly the war cannot provide the whole explanation. The opposition was growing even beforehand. The early optimism may have been an illusion caused partly by the time it took opponents to organize a concerted response. Reformers themselves, conceding their own political naiveté, later looked back on their defeat as the work of special interests, mainly the doctors and the insurance companies. Writing in 1931, Rubinow recalled that reformers had been "intoxicated" by their success with workmen's compensation and failed to appreciate the opposition that employers, insurers, and others would raise. "Nothing can be more damaging in a military campaign than the failure to appreciate the strength of the enemy," Rubinow wrote, "except it be the failure to recognize the allies the enemy might acquire." Workmen's compensation had proved to be more expensive than reformers had anticipated, and health insurance would have cost employers, Rubinow admitted, "many times as much."* Businessmen could see on which side of the balance sheet such costs would go; they could not see the gains, which were indirect. The insurance

---

*The AALL had estimated the cost of its program, including sick pay, medical aid, and maternity and funeral benefits, at only 4 percent of wages, but in its Chicago survey, the Illinois commission found it would cost 7.5 percent of payroll just to cover lost wages and medical care.

companies "suddenly realized the tremendous possibilities of the field for themselves"; the inclusion of the funeral benefit was "a grave, tactical error because of the implied threat to the gigantic structure of industrial life insurance." The doctors got "panicky." Minor but vocal groups, such as Christian Scientists, entered the opposition out of fear that a government program would limit religious and medical freedom. "All these fears, some justified, some exaggerated, and some altogether fanciful, produced such a confusion of group conflicts that only a clear recognition of the need by the millions of American workmen might have overcome it, and that clear recognition was lacking."

But the view that interest groups killed health insurance—true enough as a description of what happened—neglects the prior question of why these and other groups interpreted their interests as they did. Some historians treat these interests as if they were self-evident. But the three main opponents—the medical profession, labor, and business—all had conflicting and ambiguous interests that made them initially uncertain and divided about what position they ought to take. That the AMA could have initially approved health insurance, while the AF of L opposed it, suggests how complex the identification of group interests may be. Some doctors believed health insurance would increase their incomes, and some labor leaders believed it would inhibit working-class organization. While these interpretations of their groups' interests were ultimately rejected, they were not self-evidently mistaken. Moreover, in European countries the interest groups analogous to the opponents in America often turned out to benefit materially from government health insurance programs. For example, the insurance industry in England ended up profiting from a health insurance system that permitted private firms to play a major role in carrying cash benefits. Employers benefited from the greater political stability and diminished labor turnover that health insurance helped bring about. It is not difficult to imagine how American state legislators might have passed a health insurance program that would have enriched both insurance companies and doctors and, in the long run, strengthened the economic system. So it is not at all clear why doctors, insurance companies, and employers interpreted their interests as requiring the defeat of health insurance, when by its modification they might have satisfied those same interests.

Ideology, historical experience, and the overall political context played a key role in shaping how groups identified and expressed their interests. These factors are readily apparent if we compare the failure of health insurance in America with its earlier successes in Europe.

In neither Germany nor even Britain was the idea of compulsory health insurance fundamentally contested when it was originally proposed. The opposition did not suggest, as in America, that health insurance would subvert individual initiative and self-reliance. Many of the same groups as in America criticized the plans, but they concentrated on amending provisions that threatened to alter established relations of power. In Germany, the opposition, including conservatives and businessmen as well as socialists, resisted Bismarck's efforts to use social insurance to enhance the power of the state; and in its final form, health insurance was operated by decentralized sickness funds, rather than the imperial insurance office.

The establishment of compulsory insurance in Britain also required compromise with private interests. The insurance companies and the doctors objected to the privileged role that Lloyd George's original plan gave the friendly societies. The insurance firms were worried that the friendly societies would gain an edge in selling life insurance, and the doctors had long chafed under the power the friendly societies exercised in the provision of medical service. So, splitting the program in two, Lloyd George satisfied the objections of the insurance companies by allowing them to carry cash benefits, and he met the objections of the doctors by placing control of medical benefits in the public sector under local committees on which the physicians were given representation. Thus the shift of medical care into the public sector in Britain arose partly because of the doctors' desire to liberate themselves from a form of client control. Dealing with educated civil servants may have been more palatable than dealing with the working-class officers of friendly societies. Moreover, as an incentive for cooperation, Lloyd George gave the doctors a large boost in income by increasing their rates of compensation. Even so, the British Medical Association, out of touch with its membership, called a last-minute strike against the government. But the revolt fizzled as long-impoverished general practitioners found they could increase their incomes an average of 50 percent by signing up on panels to care for the insured.

American doctors faced no dominating purchaser, like the friendly societies, from whom a government program might offer escape. The doctors' experience with contract practice and workmen's compensation was sufficient, however, to persuade them that any financial intermediary would like nothing better than to pay them as little as possible. So their own past strongly biased them against any extension of organized financing. "My own experience in speaking to physicians," wrote the chairman of the California commission in a private letter in 1918, "is that the only questions they ask are questions of detail . . . how much money they would get, whether they would have to get up nights at the demand of whoever called them. . . . " Progressive proposals, furthermore, caught the physicians in transition to more secure economic status; during the war, their incomes rose significantly. Any positive economic incentive they might have had for favoring health insurance was diminishing.

The structure of government and the demands of politics, however, were of overriding importance in shaping the strategy of the opposition. In America, there was no comparable unification of political authority to compare with the power of Lloyd George or Bismarck. Even if an American president had wanted health insurance, he would not have had the leverage to force the opposition to compromise. Only a more serious threat to political stability in America could have so changed the terms of debate as to force interest groups to work within the framework of reform instead of against it. In the absence of such a threat, employers saw the immediate costs but not the distant and less certain gains, and their opposition, particularly through the National Civic Federation, was probably decisive. Workmen's compensation had won approval only after employers had found the liability system too erratic and unpredictable in its costs to serve their interests. Had there been more of a socialist challenge, employers might have revised their views of the possible benefits of other social insurance programs, including health insurance. The physicians would have understood that some reform was unavoidable and worked to secure as favorable a plan as they could. Indeed, this was their initial reaction, but the more uncertain the passage of health insurance became, the more categorical became their opposition. Defeating health insurance in toto by opening up the ideological issues left uncontested in England and Germany was a safer strategy for the opponents than working within the framework of reform in the hope of turning it to their advantage.

34

Excess Mortality in Harlem

Colin McCord, M.D. and Harold P. Freeman, M.D.

Mortality rates for white and nonwhite Americans have fallen steadily and in parallel since 1930. . . . Lower rates for non-whites have been associated with an improved living standard, better education, and better access to health care.[1,2] These improvements, however, have not been evenly distributed. Most health indicators, including mortality rates, are worse in the impoverished areas of this country.[3-9] It is not widely recognized just how much certain inner-city areas lag behind the rest of the United States. We used census data and data from the Bureau of Health Statistics and Analysis of the New York City Health Department to estimate the amount, distribution, and causes of excess mortality in the New York City community of Harlem.

THE COMMUNITY

Harlem is a neighborhood in upper Manhattan just north of Central Park. Its population is 96 percent black and has been predominantly black since before World War I. It was the center of the Harlem Renaissance of black culture in the 1920s, and it continues to be a cultural center for black Americans. The median family income in Harlem, according to the 1980 census, was $6,497, as compared with $16,818 in all New York City, $21,023 in the United States, and $12,674 among all blacks in the United

From *The New England Journal of Medicine*, Vol. 322, pp. 173–77, 1990. Copyright 1990 Massachusetts Medical Society. Reprinted by permission.

States. The families of 40.8 percent of the people of Harlem had incomes below the government-defined poverty line in 1980. The total population of Harlem fell from 233,000 in 1960 to 121,905 in 1980. In the same 20-year period the death rate from homicide rose from 25.3 to 90.8 per 100,000.

The neighborhood is not economically homogeneous. There is a middle-to-upper-class community of about 25,000 people living in new, private apartment complexes or houses, a less affluent group of 25,000 living in public housing projects, and a third group of about 75,000 who live in substandard housing. Most of the population loss has been in the group living in substandard housing, much of it abandoned or partially occupied buildings.

The pattern of medical care in Harlem is similar to that reported for other poor and black communities.[10, 11] As compared with the per capita averages for New York City, the rate of hospital admissions is 26 percent higher, the use of emergency rooms is 73 percent higher, the use of hospital outpatient departments is 134 percent higher, and the number of primary care physicians per 1000 people is 74 percent lower.[12] . . . For our analysis, we calculated age-, sex-, and cause-specific death rates for Harlem using the recorded deaths for 1979, 1980, and 1981 and population data from the 1980 census. . . .

The reference death rates we used to calculate the standardized mortality ratios (SMRs) are those of the white population of the United States, as published in *Vital Statistics of the United States, 1980*.[13] To calculate the SMRs, the total number of observed deaths in 1979, 1980, and 1981 for each age group, sex, and cause was divided by the expected number of deaths, based on the population of each sex and age group and the reference death rate. . . .

RESULTS

Since 1950, when the New York City Health Department began to keep death records according to health-center district, Central Harlem has consistently had the highest infant mortality rate and one of the highest crude death rates in the city. In 1970 and 1980, age-adjusted mortality rates for Harlem residents were the highest in New York City, much worse than the rates for nonwhites in the United States as a whole, and they had changed little since 1960. . . . This lack of improvement in the age-adjusted death rate reflected worsening mortality rates for persons between the ages of 15 and 65 that more than offset the drop in mortality among infants and young children. . . .

Figure 1 shows the survival curves for male and female residents of Harlem, as compared with those for whites in the United States and those for the residents of an area in rural Bangladesh. Bangladesh is categorized by the World Bank as one of the lowest-income countries in the world. The

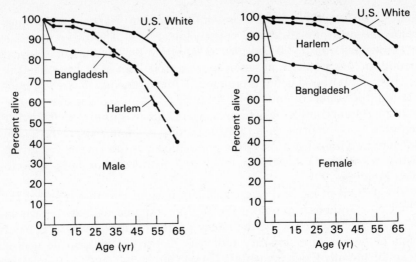

Figure 1 Survival to the Age of 65 in Harlem, Bangladesh, and among U.S. Whites in 1980.

Matlab demographic-study area is thought to have somewhat lower death rates than Bangladesh as a whole, but the rates are typical for the region. Life expectancy at birth in Matlab was 56.5 years in 1980, as compared with an estimated 49 years for Bangladesh and 57 years for India in 1986.[9, 16] For men, the rate of survival beyond the age of 40 is lower in Harlem than Bangladesh. For women, overall survival to the age of 65 is somewhat better in Harlem, but only because the death rate among girls under 5 is very high in Bangladesh.

The SMRs for Harlem . . . were high for those of all ages below 75, but they were particularly high for those between 25 and 64 years old and for children under 4. In the three years 1979 to 1981, there were 6415 deaths in Harlem. If the death rate among U.S. whites had applied to this community, there would have been 3994 deaths. Eighty-seven percent of the 2421 excess deaths were of persons under 65.

Table 1 compares the numbers of observed and expected deaths among persons under 65, according to the chief underlying causes. A large proportion of the observed excess was directly due to violence and substance abuse, but these causes did not account for most of the excess. Cirrhosis, homicide, accidents, drug dependency, and alcohol use were considered the most important underlying causes of death in 35 percent of all deaths among people under 65, and in 45 percent of the excess deaths.

For people between the ages of 65 and 74 the SMRs in Harlem were much lower than those for people younger than 65. For residents of Harlem 75 years old or older, overall death rates were essentially the same as those for U.S. whites. . . . Disease-specific SMRs for people over the

Table 1 Causes of Excess Mortality in Harlem, 1979 to 1981.*

Cause	Observed Deaths (No.)	Standardized Mortality Ratio	Annual Excess Deaths Per 100,000	% of Excess Deaths
Cardiovascular disease	880	2.23	157.5	23.5
Cirrhosis	410	10.49	120.4	17.9
Homicide	332	14.24	100.2	14.9
Neoplasm	604	1.77	84.9	12.6
Drug dependency	153	283.1	49.5	7.4
Diabetes	94	5.43	24.9	3.7
Alcoholism	73	11.33	34.6	3.2
Pneumonia and influenza	78	5.07	20.3	3.0
Disorders in newborn	64	7.24	17.9	2.7
Infection	65	5.60	17.3	2.6
Accident	155	1.17	17.2	1.1
Ill defined	44	2.07	17.4	1.1
Renal	26	4.54	6.6	0.9
Chronic obstructive pulmonary disease	35	1.29	2.6	0.4
Congenital anomalies	23	1.21	1.3	0.2
Suicide	33	0.81	−2.5	—
All other	181	3.13	40.0	6.0
All causes	3250	2.75	671.2	100.0

*The calculations are based on the deaths of all persons—male and female under the age of 65. The reference death rates are those for U.S. whites in 1980.

age of 65 were below those of younger age groups in almost every category. In several categories (notably cardiovascular disease in Harlem residents 75 or older), they were lower than in whites. This may represent the survival of the fittest in this area of excess mortality.

DISCUSSION

An improvement in child mortality in Harlem between 1960 and 1980 was accompanied by rising mortality rates for persons between the ages of 25 and 65. There was therefore no improvement in overall age-adjusted mortality. Death rates for those between the ages of 5 and 65 were worse in Harlem than in Bangladesh.

We have not attempted to calculate SMRs since 1981, because the 1980 census is the most recent reliable estimate of the population of New York City, but all available evidence indicates that there has been very little change since then. The total number of deaths in Harlem from 1985 through 1987 was 1.6 percent higher than from 1979 through 1981. According to the New York City Planning Department, the decline in Harlem's population stopped in 1980 and the total population has been growing at the rate of 1 percent per year since then.[18] If this estimate is accepted, there has been a slight drop in the crude death rate for Harlem since 1980, but not large enough to affect any of our conclusions. Since 1980 the number of deaths of persons 25 to 44 years of age has increased considerably (31 percent), and the acquired immunodeficiency syndrome (AIDS) has become the most common cause of death in this age group in Harlem and in all New York City. The number of deaths from AIDS is expected to continue to rise.

The situation in Harlem is extreme, but it is not an isolated phenomenon. We identified 54 health areas (of 353) in New York City, with a total population of 650,000, in which there were more than twice as many deaths among people under the age of 65 as would be expected if the death rates of U.S. whites applied. All but one of these health areas have populations more than half composed of minority members. These are areas that were left behind when the minority population of the city as a whole experienced the same improvement in life expectancy that was seen in the rest of the United States.[19] Similar pockets of high mortality have been described in other U.S. cities.[3, 20] Jenkins et al. calculated SMRs for all deaths in Roxbury and adjacent areas of Boston that were almost as high in 1972–1973 as those reported here.[20] This area of highest mortality in Boston was the area with the highest proportion of minority groups.

It will be useful to know more about the circumstances surrounding premature deaths in high-risk communities to determine the relative importance of contributing factors such as poverty, inadequate housing, psychological stress, substance abuse, malnutrition, and inadequate access to medical care. But action to correct the appalling health conditions reflected in these statistics need not wait for more research. The essential first steps are to identify these pockets of high mortality and to recognize the urgent severity of the problem. Widespread poverty and inadequate housing are obvious in Harlem and demand a direct attack wherever they are present. . . .

Those responsible for implementing health programs must face the reality of high death rates in Harlem and the enormous burden of disease that requires treatment in the existing facilities. The health care system is overloaded with such treatment and is poorly structured to support preventive measures, detect disease early, and care for adults with chronic problems. At the same time, the population at highest risk has limited contact with the health care system except in emergencies. Brudny and Dobkyn reported that 83 percent of 181 patients discharged from Harlem Hospital with tuberculosis in 1988 were lost to follow-up and did not continue treatment.[21] New approaches must be developed to take preventive and therapeutic measures out of the hospitals, clinics, and emergency rooms and deliver them to the population at highest risk.

Intensive educational campaigns to improve nutrition and reduce the use of alcohol, drugs, and tobacco are needed and should be directed at children and adolescents, since habits are formed early and the death rates begin to rise immediately after adolescence. Education will have little effect unless it is combined with access to adequate incomes, useful employment, and decent housing for these children and their parents. Education can help in controlling epidemic drug use and associated crime only if it is combined with effective and coordinated police and public action. AIDS in Harlem is largely related to intravenous drug use and is not likely to be controlled until drugs are controlled, but effective education about this disease is also urgently needed.

Knowledge of the history of previous efforts to improve health in Harlem does not lead to optimism about the future. The Harlem Health Task Force was formed in 1976 because Harlem and the Carter administration recognized that death rates were high. An improved system of clinics, more drug-treatment centers, and active community-outreach programs were recommended. The recommendations have been implemented to varying degrees, but funding has been limited. The preventive and curative health care system is essentially unchanged today. Drug use has increased, and the proportion of the population receiving public assistance has increased. There has been no decrease in the death rates.

In 1977 Jenkins et al. pointed out that the number of excess deaths recorded each year in the areas of worst health in Boston was considerably larger than the number of deaths in places that the U.S. government had designated as natural-disaster areas. They suggested that these zones of excess mortality be declared disaster areas and that measures be implemented on this basis.[20] No such action was taken then or is planned now. If the high-mortality zones of New York City were designated a disaster area today, 650,000 people would be living in it. A major political and financial commitment will be needed to eradicate the root causes of this high mortality: vicious poverty and inadequate access to the basic health care that is the right of all Americans.

REFERENCES

1. Manton KG, Patrick CH, Johnson KW. Health differentials between blacks and whites: recent trends in mortality and morbidity. Milbank Q 1987; 65:Suppl 1:125–99.
2. Davis K, Lillie-Blanton M, Lyons B, Mullan F, Powe N, Rowland D. Health care for black Americans: the public sector role. Milbank Q 1987; 65:Suppl 1:213–47.
3. Kitagawa EM, Hauser PM. Differential mortality in the United States: a study in socioeconomic epidemiology. Cambridge, Mass.: Harvard University Press, 1973.

4. Woolhandler S, Himmelstein DU, Silber R, Bader M, Harnly M, Jones A. Medical care and mortality: racial differences in preventable deaths. Int J Health Serv 1985; 15:1–22.
5. Savage D, Lindenbaum J, Van Ryzin J, Struening E, Garrett TJ. Race, poverty, and survival in multiple myeloma. Cancer 1984; 54:3085–94.
6. Black/white comparisons of premature mortality for public health program planning—District of Columbia. MMWR 1989; 38:33–7.
7. Freeman HP, Wasfie TJ. Cancer of the breast in poor black women. Cancer 1989; 63:2562–9.
8. Cancer in the economically disadvantaged: a special report prepared by the subcommittee on cancer in the economically disadvantaged. New York: American Cancer Society, 1986.
9. Demographic surveillance system—Matlab. Vital events and migration tables, 1980. Scientific report no. 58. Dhaka, Bangladesh: International Centre for Diarrheal Disease Research, 1982.
10. Davis K, Schoen C. Health and the war on poverty: a ten-year appraisal. Washington, D.C.: Brookings Institution, 1978.
11. Blendon RJ, Aiken LH, Freeman HE, Corey CR. Access to medical care for black and white Americans: a matter of continuing concern. JAMA 1989; 261:278–81.
12. Community health atlas of New York. New York: United Hospital Fund, 1986.
13. Vital statistics of the United States 1980. Hyattsville, Md.: National Center for Health Statistics, 1985. (DHHS publication no. (PHS) 85–1101.)
14. Vital statistics: instructions for classifying the underlying cause of death, 1980. Hyattsville, Md.: National Center for Health Statistics, 1980.
15. The international classification of diseases, 9th revision, clinical modification: ICD-9-CM. 2nd ed. Washington, D.C.: Department of Health and Human Services, 1980. (DHHS publication no. (PHS) 80–1260.)
16. The state of the world's children 1988 (UNICEF). New York: Oxford University Press, 1988.
17. Fay RE, Passel JS, Robinson JG. Coverage of population in the 1980 census. Washington, D.C.: Bureau of the Census, 1988. (Publication no. PHC 80-E4.)
18. Community district needs, 1989. New York: Department of City Planning, 1987. (DCP publication no. 87-10.)
19. Summary of vital statistics, 1986. New York: Bureau of Health Statistics and Analysis, 1986.
20. Jenkins CD, Tuthill RW, Tannenbaum SI, Kirby CR. Zones of excess mortality in Massachusetts. N Engl J Med 1977; 296:1354–6.
21. Brudny K, Dobkyn J. Poor compliance is the major obstacle in controlling the HIV-associated tuberculosis outbreak. Presented at the Fifth International Conference on Acquired Immune Deficiency Syndrome, Montreal, June 8, 1989.

35

AIDS: The Epidemic and the Society

Mary Catherine Bateson and Richard Goldsby

A previously unknown life form, the virus that causes AIDS, is now making its way through the human population, spreading around the world with devastating and accelerating effects. That virus has become a part of the biological context of our lives, one of the many life forms that actually live inside of human beings rather than around them. All of these can potentially be known and at least partially controlled but the needed thinking about AIDS has just begun, and it is already clear that it raises the most basic questions about the human condition, about human biology, and about the mechanisms of social life.

The AIDS epidemic, as it moves around the planet, is posing new questions about justice and teaching us new ways of thinking about human learning and human suffering. It throws certain characteristics of society into sharp relief, just as radioisotopes, moving through the body, can be used to highlight physiological processes for diagnosis. At one level the movement of the epidemic reflects communication and travel. At another it belies out habitual self-deceptions, tracing activities that would otherwise be secret: drug addiction and sexual practices that most people have preferred not to know about—extramarital sex, homosexuality, prostitution. AIDS has made us newly aware of human diversity. In our own society it forces us to acknowledge bisexuality, a pattern of sexual preference that most Americans, who like their distinctions clear, have

From Mary Catherine Bateson and Richard Goldsby, *Thinking Aids*, Menlo Park, CA Addison-Wesley, 1989. Reprinted by permission.

tended to ignore, and is making us more aware of middle-class intra-venous drug use. It will probably increase awareness of the sexual use of children, of sex in prisons, of sex and drugs in the peacetime army.

AIDS highlights processes of social change: urbanization and monetary economies in Africa that send men to the cities for cash earnings while their wives stay in the villages to farm; changed sexual mores for hetero-sexuals as well as homosexuals; the economic dislocations and prejudice that are increasingly turning some minority communities in America into an underclass. The history of failure to heed the early warnings of the epidemic is a statement of our priorities as a society. Now that we know how to prevent the disease from spreading, its continued spread must advertise the ways in which, in this interconnected and interdependent world, we fail to communicate to individuals the very knowledge they need to survive. AIDS moves along the fault lines of our society and becomes a metaphor for understanding that society. . . .

Once in a while, beyond the terrifying numbers projected for the future, one hears the statement that unless there are major medical breakthroughs the AIDS epidemic could bring the end of Western civiliza-tion. This is surely an exaggeration, but it is useful to clarify exactly what it might mean. Three scenarios need to be considered.

1. *Population loss*. AIDS will cause increasing numbers of casualties until the rate of spread is reversed. In the process the death rate could theo-retically come to exceed the birth rate, leading to steady population shrinkage. In the countries of Africa where prevalence is highest, the population doubles in twenty-five years or less: birth rates are so high that actual shrinkage could not become a factor unless the epidemic continued unchecked for several generations. Death rates in Africa are still shaped by a whole flock of endemic diseases, and it is projected that death from AIDS could not exceed 20 percent of the total. AIDS could not solve the African population problem—but it could subvert all regional efforts to find solutions.

The demographics are different in the industrialized countries, where general health factors probably ensure slower spread in the non-drug-using heterosexual population; but within specific communities they may be worse, and the demographic impact of AIDS will be sharpest in the great cities that are also our cultural centers. The end of civilization is not going to come about through simple loss of population due to the AIDS virus. Arguably, indeed, Europe benefited from the Black Death, which hastened the decay of medieval institutions and opened the way for the Renaissance. AIDS is similar to warfare in that the toll is highest on those in the prime of life; but functioning societies can recover remarkably quickly from massive population losses, and there are good reasons why epidemics tend to be self-limiting, as this one will surely prove to be. Diseases are rarely uniformly lethal, so the portions of the population that survive are those with natural resistance of some kind. We do not yet know for certain whether there are individuals whose own immune systems can withstand or resist HIV infection indefinitely, but there probably are. In addition, AIDS presents the possibility of behavioral immunity: anyone can make the decision to be immune by avoiding high-risk behavior, and many follow traditional patterns that already protect them. Societies have choices of how to respond, however, that may affect them long after demographic perturbations are over.

2. *Resource depletion.* AIDS will cause major economic disruption and painful choices in resource allocation which might cripple a given society or make it vulnerable to other kinds of attack. Health care costs are already a source of economic instability in the United States and the care of a single AIDS patient approaches $100,000, while the number of patients is increasing steadily. As the resources of more and more individuals are drained, more of this will become a public charge, adding to deficits. The carefully planned profitability of the health insurance industry is threatened—and so is the belief that any private industry can solve public problems like those of health care with a modicum of fairness. There will be needs for personnel and hospital facilities as well, needs that might prove to be transient. Money spent on AIDS may increase public deficits or force hard choices of taxation or reductions in other expenditures. Because the sums will be so large, major decisions of priorities will be needed. It will not be sufficient to reallocate available funds within the category of public health or human services.

This is a problem that may appear to weigh more heavily on affluent societies, where expected standards of health care are very high, than on the less developed countries, but that contrast is delusory. Officials of the United Nations Children's Fund point out that the epidemic will cause the death of more children through the diversion of resources from other public health programs than will die of AIDS. It is important to consider the cost of what does *not* happen because of the epidemic, such as the lost earnings and participation of those who die in the prime of life and opportunities missed. The AIDS epidemic may be the final straw for societies unable to establish self-sustaining economies.

In the developed world, the economic threat of AIDS will cause a certain amount of disruption in some industries and profit in others. The problem comes as always in decision making: What is the public priority on easing the pains of the dying? What are the relative values of therapy and prevention? How important is research on the immune system's defense of the body compared to research on space defense? Both will benefit basic science and have massive spinoffs, but different groups of individuals will draw the primary profit. How about drug interdiction and the immense profits of the illicit drug industry?

The concept of *triage* is a way of thinking about resource allocation on matters of life and death that originated on the battlefield. The nurse at the emergency room desk, who makes decisions about the order in which patients are seen or the need to call additional help, is called a triage nurse because of her role in sorting out need in relation to resources, but the term goes back to situations in which resources were so scarce that some patients could not be treated at all. On the battlefield, the wounded were divided into three groups: those who were so severely wounded that they would probably die even if treatment were given, those whose wounds were so slight that they would recover without treatment, and those for whom treatment would make the difference between recovery and death. In real scarcity, the third group must take priority, but we live in an affluent society that expects to be able to provide the convenience and reassurance of care for many who probably don't need it, as well as offering heroic measures for those who are close to death. AIDS is going to put major strains on resources, however, and it seems certain that new standards of care for patients with brief life expectancies will develop, including appropriate levels of intervention that will be applied to cancer patients and to the very old.

In principle, triage is ethical when it reflects real limitations and is consistently applied, but it can easily be converted, even in the emergency room, into a form of discrimination based on ideas of differences in human worth. Still, redefinitions of appropriate care can lead to improved care as well as to the withdrawal of care. Many people with only a few months left of life would prefer to spend the time peacefully becoming used to the approach of death rather than undergoing one violation after another. The AIDS epidemic could lead to improved home care, improved hospice care, and improved psychological support for the dying. It could also confirm and extend in us habits of treating groups as expendable and callously ignoring human suffering.

The AIDS epidemic will amplify the effect of past choices and priorities, and the choices we make now will leave a continuing mark on society. The adverse effect of AIDS on the economy will be more a matter of ill-chosen priorities and bad planning than of direct costs.

3. AIDS will cause *psychological and social reactions that may change the character of human social life.* If the epidemic were to induce us to give up travel or international communication or were to sabotage our tenuous capacity for global cooperation, it would quite literally be undermining civilization. It also has the potential for creating political instability in third world societies where public order is already precarious, particularly in cities, and such instability can spread.

More narrowly, if reactions to the epidemic compromise basic values too pervasively, the epidemic could destroy the more recent and potentially more vulnerable institutions of democracy. If AIDS drives us into coercive and repressive social policies, it will have tempted us away from the basic commitments of our society. It could benefit society for individuals to become more aware and selective in their sexual practices, but a wave of puritanism or repression would work against creativity. Like the Black Death in Europe, AIDS could trigger religious movements embracing ignorance, massive scapegoating, or paranoia, a failure of hope or of compassion. It could in a generation subvert the fragile structures of dedication in the medical profession.

It is this third kind of danger, danger to the way society is organized, that is the basic threat of the AIDS epidemic. Thus it is that a consideration of how to respond to the AIDS epidemic directs us back to our own values. Our view is that many ways of reacting that might be effective would represent a compromise of those values, but that if those values were more effectively realized, our danger would be reduced. The AIDS epidemic cannot help but be a source not only of self-knowledge but also of self-determination, a way of understanding the choices that make us who we are and clarifying our priorities as a society. Just as it is possible to ask what the characteristics were of gay liberation in the 1970s that made the gay community so effective in amplifying the epidemic, so it is possible to ask about the characteristics of national policy in the 1980s that have made it so difficult to respond, and about the characteristics of a future society able to deal with the disease. The society must respond to the epidemic while maintaining basic constancies—that is, without compromising identity or fundamental value commitments. This capacity can be thought of as the immune system of society.

There are real choices to be made at a national level, choices that reflect quite different premises about human beings. So far, responses have been inconsistent, reflecting sometimes one way of thinking and sometimes another. Different national styles have been clearly visible: the Swedes displaying huge posters of condoms in the streets and the Unites States avoiding even the word on television, the Soviets deporting seropositive foreign students and some developing countries denying that the disease even exists. Even New York and California have shown visibly different cultural styles, while national policy has fluctuated and waffled.

It is possible to argue that there are two contrasting ways of dealing with the epidemic, each of which might be successful, each of which would leave its mark on the societies that adopted it.

On the one hand, it is possible to respond to the epidemic by reaching for a more open, just, and intercommunicating society and world in which no one is disenfranchised and individuals have the information to make appropriate decisions. Thus if we were able, as a society, to talk openly about matters related to sex and to feel compassion equally for all of our neighbors, the AIDS epidemic would probably be under control by now. Instead, we are in a situation where help has been withheld because of unstated ideas about who is and is not deserving, where essential information is not imparted to those who need it, and where many lack the trust and self-esteem needed to use the information available to them. The perennial problems of our society and of the world, which we have not had the resolution or imagination to address, are the principal source of vulnerability.

It is clear that the disease proliferated first in populations that have every reason to suspect they will be treated unfairly, and that the existence of prejudice is the main continuing barrier to communication. Homosexuality, extramarital sex, and I-V drug use are still stigmatized as antisocial or sinful behaviors by many, and the health problems that accompany them are sometimes seen as divine punishment. The same residues of prejudice give others a false sense of security. Racial and other minorities are sensitive to the possible "good riddance!" of the larger society and justifiably sensitive to the possibility that those who have discriminated against them for so long will find the epidemic a good excuse to do so again. The epidemic flourishes on discrimination and exclusion. Furthermore, stigmatized populations are burdened by a partial acceptance of external views. "Internalized homophobia" and "low self-esteem" make individuals value their own lives and health less, leave them with less hope for the future.

Internationally, the unequal distribution of resources and concern creates the setting for the proliferation of the disease. If health care in central Africa were comparable to that in industrial societies and part of a worldwide communicating network on the lines of the U.S. Centers for Disease Control, the epidemic might have been stemmed at a local level. In a genuinely interconnected and intercommunicating world, monitoring of health problems must be international. On the other hand, it is hard to imagine an effective shift in health delivery systems without substantive changes in other conditions, including the conditions that make so many people dependent on a living earned in migratory labor. There is no way of knowing for sure where the epidemic originated, but we do know that African populations suffer so many scourges that a new disease can proliferate unseen. The entire planet is vulnerable when certain areas are neglected.

Nationally and internationally, disease and drug use thrive on poverty and inequality. In America, the epidemic developed in a period when government was withdrawing from social programs, cutting budgets in all nonmilitary areas, and using the machinery of regulation to promote economic productivity rather than individual welfare. Disease also thrives on ignorance. Programs to control the spread of HIV can be blocked by unwillingness to talk candidly about sex. How many deaths will result from the refusal to use the word *condom* on television? Reluctance to use the word *semen* apparently led to the unfortunate euphemism *bodily fluids*, which escalated public anxiety by suggesting that HIV is likely to be transmitted by sweat or saliva or tears in casual and domestic contact. People have been driven from their homes as a result of such artificially maintained ignorance.

Each of the issues mentioned here is connected to other severe social problems, ranging from famine in Africa to teenage pregnancy to the increase in homelessness and malnutrition that accompanied government withdrawal from supporting social programs. The notion that afflu-

ence will spread through the society from the privileged to the underpriv-
ileged is called the "trickle-down theory." The reality that the result of
allowing the AIDS epidemic to develop among marginalized groups will
be its spread into the mainstream might be called the "trickle-up theory."

But this is the liberal point of view, the belief that social problems can be
addressed by education and that behavior can be improved by equity. An
alternative point of view would reflect other kinds of social agendas: If the
society had more effective control over sexual and other private behavior,
perhaps it could simply prevent promiscuity. If the concern for human
rights had not been so expanded, it would be possible to deal with the
epidemic by isolating it, to test everyone and intern all carriers, extruding
them from society as was once done with lepers. If we were not burdened
by concern for individual welfare there would be no need to struggle to
prolong life for those already infected, no high insurance costs, no painful
decisions about schooling. If police powers were expanded, borders could
be effectively closed, drug traffic interdicted, and traffickers shot. It does
indeed seem probable that the epidemic would be easier to deal with if we
were a less open and caring society. Compassion can be expensive, and
certainly the costs of the epidemic are increased by the desire to alleviate
suffering. So far, the Soviet bloc seems to be less affected than the West,
and Islamic fundamentalism does provide a model for one way of reducing homosexuality and other kinds of sexual activity: by treating them as
capital crimes.

In general, there is a mirror-image quality to the costs and benefits of
particular social institutions. The blood bank industry and the bathhouse
industry both resist regulation within the ideology of capitalism, and the
Bill of Rights protects beliefs we deplore as well as those we adhere to,
allowing both information and misinformation to spread.

Against this background, we believe that policies based on openness
and equity have the best chance of success, providing a framework for
policy recommendations for reacting to the epidemic domestically and
internationally. The proposals that will be made here are idealistic in their
goals, but this is because of our conviction that survival under threat must
mean the maintenance of the basic premises of the society, premises that
have a certain biological as well as social logic. These proposals are not
based on the assumption of universal altruism, but rather on the assumption that we as a society can recognize this as a situation in which the
general welfare benefits from care for individuals and from empowering
individuals to care for each other.

Policy must be thought through place by place. There are tasks to be
done in every school and corporation, every town and city. AIDS policy is
often treated like a hot potato, passed from person to person and from
agency to agency. More painfully, individuals with AIDS are often routed
from place to place or hospital to hospital, even deported from country to
country. Because the private challenges of developing a personal behav-

ioral immunity to AIDS must be faced everywhere, it is necessary that the public challenges be faced consistently, so that the visible institutions of society support molecular change. The following, then, are some of the places where change is needed.

In the schools and communications media   The handling of sex education represents a major philosophical inconsistency in American society: the belief that the social good is best achieved by enforcing ignorance of possible options rather than by informed choice. There are many who are more comfortable with that way of doing things. Recent lawsuits brought by some fundamentalist groups about textbooks have protested against any stimulation of the imagination through fairy tales and mythology as well as exposure to different belief systems and aspects of scientific knowledge. There is also an inconsistency in the argument that children can be exposed to violence and weapons with impunity, but will be corrupted by exposure to information about sexuality. Furthermore, the ignorance we conserve is never total. Children not taught about sex pick up misinformation from their classmates. We cannot afford to conserve ignorance about sex. The alternative is to present it so early that it is clear that the information is not an invitation to immediate action.

The management of the classroom has always been important in public health education, alongside actual lessons. Particularly in the lower grades, children pick up ideas of nutrition and sanitation from school practices like hand washing and discarding dropped food and the reactions when a child is hurt. School management should be based on the possible presence of students who are knowingly or unknowingly seropositive, and this in itself is an important lesson for adult living.

Once we manage to clarify what knowledge is necessary for a responsible adaptation to a world that contains the AIDS virus, and once a commitment is made to information in preference to ignorance, it follows that the media should provide specific and candid information and corrections to misinformation—and this should take precedence over considerations of taste. The effort will be long, and hard to maintain in focus. Much can be done by including safer sex in story lines, just as smoking has been progressively excluded and interracial casts have become routine.

In the workplace   It is the task of all managers and all those making administrative decisions on the organization of work to maintain a workplace in which transmission of infection is prevented—part of a general effort to maintain health and prevent industrial accidents—and to be sure that misinformation does not lead to discrimination. No one should lose his or her job because of false beliefs about how AIDS is transmitted. Similarly, no qualified person should be denied a fair chance for a job because of the possibility of developing AIDS—this is comparable to refusing to employ women because they may eventually have children.

No employer welcomes the complexities of dealing with disability but no equitable hiring policy can avoid it. An open and matter-of-fact policy toward the disease and the distribution of information are ways of promoting realistic prevention. Discrimination goes with magical thinking about one's own safety.

In the streets   There are two issues here. First, America cannot afford to maintain an underclass that is chronically impoverished and alienated. The despair of unemployed youth in the ghettos often leads directly to I-V drug use, but it should be addressed in its own right, not because it promotes the spread of AIDS. Treatment should be easily available for all addicts, with the possibility of methadone support and even government-supplied heroin and hygienically run public shooting galleries. Addicts should not have to rent needles because carrying their own might lead to arrest. But these are half measures unless people are given alternatives: quality education, real access to employment, reason to aspire toward the future. Even the classic escape of the disinherited through the armed forces is now often closed, as the military services become increasingly selective. We need to offer every girl and boy a life that is more attractive than drug addiction.

Similar arguments apply to prostitution, which has been a major factor in the spread of AIDS in Africa and will probably be increasingly important elsewhere. The sex industry resembles I-V drug use in that you cannot make something safe if you pretend it isn't there. Many countries, such as the Netherlands, regulate prostitution and carefully supervise health in order to control venereal disease. Again, this is a necessary first step, but it needs to be combined with programs that will increase the options available to women in the sex industry, many of whom are also afflicted with problems of low self-esteem and many of whom have been long-term victims of exploitation and molestation. "The world's oldest profession" is not likely to go away, but women who choose to remain in it could benefit from better control of their own conditions of work, just as addicts who remain addicted are better off with safer and cheaper drugs.

Second, America cannot afford the massive enrichment of drug dealers and their destructive effect on the lives of youth. Drugs are a multimillion-dollar international industry so large that it threatens political stability in many regions of Latin America. There are estimated to be over a million intravenous drug users in the United States, which was a tragedy of major proportions before AIDS, contributing to a whole range of other social problems. In some cities, 60 to 80 percent of heroin users are already seropositive, and here the group that is perhaps hardest to contact and persuade has to be persuaded to change both sexual and needle-sharing behavior. The largest numbers of infants born with AIDS are the children of this population, largely black and Hispanic.

Many proposals to make the drug-using population more accessible involve partial decriminalization of some kinds of drug abuse. The criminalization of any behavior creates the motivation to support it and makes it difficult to reach those who are involved. Whatever hesitations we might have about the government supporting drug addiction or the sale of sexual services are minor compared to the cost of criminalization. In fact much of the pressure against partial or complete decriminalization of many crimes probably comes from those who see the connection between profitability and illegality.

In the drugstore   Someone should design a hypodermic needle that cannot—mechanically—be reused, and it should be available as cheaply and easily as Kleenex. Failing that, handy portable bottles of bleach solution for cleaning needles and syringes are needed. Condoms are another product that should be available as cheaply and easily as Kleenex, not only in stores but in vending machines in multiple locations and along with the free shampoo in hotel rooms.

In the marriage office   Gay rights provide the best path to gay responsibility. We need both. We need to create an environment that is accepting and supportive of gays precisely so that they will feel like full members and participants in the society, with all the responsibilities that entails. You cannot selectively approve and disapprove aspects of someone's behavior by starting from a blanket condemnation. We cannot expect those with homosexual preferences to fit into social expectations of sustained relationships unless we treat gay and lesbian relationships as equivalent in value to heterosexual relationships. Marriage is hard enough to maintain in a society that approves of it and values it. This would mean finding ways to register and celebrate new commitments, permitting gay couples to adopt, preventing discrimination in housing, and treating same-sex companions as legal spouses. Saint Paul was speaking of heterosexual marriage when he said that it is better to marry than to burn. There seems to be no question that the voluntary concentration of gays in a few urban neighborhoods has provided a breeding ground for disease, but it would be reduced if gays were not made to feel uncomfortable elsewhere. We know that the gay community has produced many of the heroes of the epidemic so far, and men who were at one time involved in impersonal sex have nursed their loves selflessly while others have given all their resources to help the community, setting extraordinary examples for the rest of the society.

Stable relationships are valuable to society for many reasons, not just to prevent the spread of AIDS, and this means that all policies and legislation that work against them should be altered. This is especially true of welfare, since the need for welfare often forces couples to live separately and drives them apart.

In the clinic and the ward   Policy toward those who are actually sick should deal with individuals in ways that express society's value commitments and elicit their cooperation and trust. This will mean changes in society's response to illness of all kinds, not only to AIDS, which will involve public expenditures and more flexible policies. One common form of medical discrimination practiced implicitly in our society is to give more and better care to people who are felt to have no responsibility for their diseases, and this kind of inequality needs to be addressed. It will not be acceptable, however, to make massive diversions of health funding, and so it seems likely that the AIDS epidemic will cause a long-overdue rethinking of the American health system. This may involve some reductions in available health care, for there is certain to be a demand for controlling medical costs by reducing heroic medical interventions at public expense that will make no more than a few days' or weeks' difference, and if this is implemented throughout the system without discrimination, it seems reasonable. Experience in the AIDS ward of San Francisco's General Hospital suggests that when patients are in an environment where they are deeply convinced that every effort is being made to sustain quality of life, there is less insistence on futile and expensive interventions.

Although many patients live for considerable periods—even several years—after developing Kaposi sarcoma, and many recover from a bout of Pneumocystis pneumonia and are able to lead normal lives, there comes a time when multiple opportunistic infections converge and medications begin to conflict, a final slide toward death. Fortunately, there is a gradually emerging ethic, represented by the hospice and home care movements, that values making that final period as peaceful and comfortable as possible. It is not reasonable to expect the society to subsidize forms of care that are regarded as ineffectual. This applies to all patients, not just AIDS patients. It is unethical to prescribe massive doses of medication or expensive treatments to support the illusion of activity.

Individuals with full-blown AIDS will make choices that, while not putting other people at risk, are widely disapproved of, and here there seems to be a great deal to be gained from tolerance. Some will pursue therapies that the medical profession regards as valueless but that the victim experiences as helpful. Some will wish to commit suicide, and are being helped to do so responsibly in some European countries. Logically, it makes sense to try to dissuade individuals from suicide after a first diagnosis, when a considerable period of nearly normal living is still available without risk to others, but this epidemic may become the occasion for a reconsideration of the individual's right to end his or her own life. Voluntary euthanasia probably promotes more careful consideration and even postponement than the need some feel to achieve suicide before they become incapable of independent action, trapped in a hospital bed, and some suicidal improvisations are dangerous to others or lead to costly and unwanted emergency procedures. Because so many victims are at the prime of life, AIDS will probably be the focal point of thinking about death and dying over the next decade, and all Americans may be the beneficiaries of the increased sensitivity and realism it engenders.

AIDS patients also differ from other groups close to death in their concern for self-determination, including making their own decisions on treatment. Currently this is leading to a form of guerrilla medicine, unsupervised self-care and experimentation with unproved therapies. The solution is a greater partnership and respect between providers and patients, including respect of patient acceptance of experimentation and risk.

Hospital administrations will have to deal with fears of infection in their personnel. The numbers suggest that these fears are very much affected by public hysteria. There are 6.8 million people working in health care, and so far there have been nine cases of AIDS directly attributable to occupational accidents, occurring mostly when recommended precautions were not being observed. Hospital administrations have a two-sided task: at the same time that they must make sure health care workers do not neglect AIDS patients, they need to persuade workers actually to observe standard precautions. Supporting the morale of health care workers and protecting them from burnout and the impact of repeated failure will also increase willingness to work with AIDS patients.

Another kind of publicly supported medical investment is needed for better care of conditions that are not life-threatening but can be co-factors of AIDS, including all of the sexually transmitted diseases.

In the research lab   Medical research and drug approval will also call for restructuring. There is a demand for relaxing some of the restrictions on experimental drugs and permitting their use with patients who are clearly terminal. AIDS-related research is of many different kinds. The search for a vaccine has been immensely popular among drug companies but offers less promise of controlling the epidemic than do education and social change—there are huge theoretical and delivery problems to be surmounted before AIDS could go the way of smallpox and polio. The very concept of vaccine may be inapplicable because of HIV's use of the immune system itself. However, only medical research and treatment can address the problems of those actually infected with the virus, controlling or ending its ravages, treating opportunistic infections, and ultimately reconstituting the immune system. There are also issues about the coordination of research, since in some areas close coordination is most useful while in others a thousand flowers should bloom. Perhaps secrecy and duplications of effort motivated by the desire for a Nobel Prize or for huge manufacturing profits should be regarded as opportunistic infections of

AIDS research, but the scientific community seems to do much of its most creative work under the spur of competition.

Implementation of policies like those just discussed is necessarily a piecemeal process, with decisions and procedures being taken at hundreds of different points. But human behavior is not generated piecemeal; rather, it expresses basic premises carried from one context to another and specifics learned by analogy. The best way to persuade individuals to behave differently in the bedroom is to create a consistent climate that is expressed in those more public places that are more easily influenced by public policy: in the classroom and in the boardroom, on the street corner and on the evening news.

Each of these proposals addresses an area where individual decisions are not likely to be adequate and public policy making is needed, but each needs to be complemented by new kinds of caution in all groups, personal decisions balanced and supported by public commitment. The same general principles hold, however, for both public and private behavior: responsible choices rest on genuine freedom; fear is a poor teacher; delay means loss of lives. If the population at large does not alter its sexual behavior until it has experienced the depth of loss and direct contact with suffering that the gay community has experienced, it will be too late to change.

Can we then visualize a society voluntarily arrived at in which all drug addicts and prostitutes are reformed and responsible members of society, all teenagers are cautious about sex, and all gays are semi-monogamous? Of course not. The vision here is of a society in which these choices are genuinely accessible, supported, and valued, and, because the choices are open, more aspects of behavior will be accessible to influence. But there is no such thing as a society in which every member is responsible.

Each of these proposals, phrased here in relation to the United States, needs rethinking and rephrasing to make it applicable in other parts of the world. It seems clear that any measures that combat ignorance and illiteracy and poverty will be helpful if the basic thrust is to give people genuine choice in protecting their own lives. AIDS drives home the message of global interdependence and demonstrates that sharp differences in quality of life are a source of instability. At the same time, rather basic information about the dangers of infection can make a difference in behavior, provided the individual has a sense of having choices. Those who are addicted to drugs feel that they have no choice; those who can barely buy food will not pay for condoms; those who do not know the alternatives cannot choose among them. The AIDS epidemic proposes a new commitment at a global level to literacy and economic opportunity.

It will not happen overnight. The first goal is a society in which the epidemic will cease to spread, and this means a society in which on the average each person infected with AIDS will transmit the disease to no more than one other person, over an apparently healthy infectious lifetime of five years or more. The next step must be to force the epidemic to recede. The number of people with full-blown AIDS will continue to rise for a decade unless there are major medical breakthroughs, and will level off five to ten years after the rate of new infection levels off. The rate of transmission per infected person has probably begun to slow, but the numbers of new infections are still rising.

What about costs? Every one of the proposals mentioned here requires social investment that will save money later. We live in a society that spends money lavishly on military preparedness under the rubric of "defense," but in this situation we should read a new meaning into that term. Talk about epidemics is always full of metaphors from warfare, metaphors of invasion and defense and infiltration, and in the area of expenditure at least, a military metaphor is useful. The most useful model for the kind of scientific mobilization needed to combat the AIDS epidemic may be the Manhattan Project. The most useful model for the social response to the epidemic is surely the response of urban Londoners to the Blitz: defense based on calm realism and mutual concern.

Outside the economic area, these warlike metaphors are flawed by the same simple assumption of competition that pervades most evolutionary discussion. Once in a while it is reasonable to speak of the total defeat of a disease, as in the eradication of smallpox. More often, the task of public health is an adjustment of mutual boundaries and niches that lowers the toll of disease. It may be that ultimately it will be possible to defeat AIDS. But in the meantime, it should be possible to learn to live with AIDS— possibly, indeed, to live better.

Warfare is an activity with only a single purpose, an activity in which priorities are simplified and energies are focused on a single goal of victory. But the proposals laid out here have multiple goals. Safer sex can control most sexual transmission of disease, and provide an effective option of family planning to whole populations. A genuine effort to improve conditions for minorities can bring all the benefits of full social participation, flowing in both directions. AIDS is a powerful reminder that ignorance and injustice are themselves insidious diseases that endanger the entire world community.

36

The Relief of Welfare

Frances Fox Piven and Richard A. Cloward

A id to Families with Dependent Children (AFDC) is our major relief
program. It has lately become the source of a major public controversy, owing to a large and precipitous expansion of the rolls. Between
1950 and 1960, only 110,000 families were added to the rolls, yielding a rise
of 17 percent. In the 1960's, however, the rolls exploded, rising by more
than 225 percent. At the beginning of the decade, 745,000 families were
receiving aid; by 1970, some 2,500,000 families were on the rolls. Still, this
is not the first, the largest, or the longest relief explosion. Since the
inauguration of relief in Western Europe three centuries ago, the rolls
have risen and fallen in response to economic and political forces. An
examination of these forces should help to illuminate the meaning of the
current explosion, as well as the meaning of current proposals for reform.

Relief arrangements, we will argue, are ancillary to economic arrangements. Their chief function is to regulate labor, and they do that in two
general ways. First, when mass unemployment leads to outbreaks of
turmoil, relief programs are ordinarily initiated or expanded to absorb and
control enough of the unemployed to restore order; then, as turbulence
subsides, the relief system contracts, expelling those who are needed to
populate the labor market. Relief also performs a labor-regulating function in this shrunken state, however. Some of the aged, the disabled, and
others who are of no use as workers are left on the relief rolls, and their

treatment is so degrading and punitive as to instill in the laboring masses a fear of the fate that awaits them should they relax into beggary and pauperism. To demean and punish those who do not work is to exalt by contrast even the meanest labor at the meanest wages. These regulative functions of relief are made necessary by several strains toward instability inherent in capitalist economics.

LABOR AND MARKET INCENTIVES

All human societies compel most of their members to work, to produce the goods and services that sustain the community. All societies also define the work their members must do and the conditions under which they must do it. Sometimes the authority to compel and define is fixed in tradition, sometimes in the bureaucratic agencies of a central government. Capitalism, however, relies primarily upon the mechanisms of a market— the promise of financial rewards or penalties—to motivate men and women to work and to hold them to their occupational tasks.

But the development of capitalism has been marked by periods of cataclysmic change in the market, the main sources being depression and rapid modernization. Depressions mean that the regulatory structure of the market simply collapses; with no demand for labor, there are no monetary rewards to guide and enforce work. By contrast, during periods of rapid modernization—whether the replacement of handicraft by machines, the relocation of factories in relation to new sources of power or new outlets for distribution, or the demise of family subsistence farming as large-scale commercial agriculture spreads—portions of the laboring population may be rendered obsolete or at least temporarily maladjusted. Market incentives do not collapse; they are simply not sufficient to compel people to abandon one way of working and living in favor of another.

In principle, of course, people dislocated by modernization become part of a labor supply to be drawn upon by a changing and expanding labor market. As history shows, however, people do not adapt so readily to drastically altered methods of work and to the new and alien patterns of social life dictated by that work. They may resist leaving their traditional communities and the only life they know. Bred to labor under the discipline of sun and season, however severe that discipline may be, they may resist that discipline of factory and machine, which, though it may be no more severe, may seem so because it is alien. The process of human adjustment to such economic changes has ordinarily entailed a generation of mass unemployment, distress, and disorganization.

Now, if human beings were invariably given to enduring these travails with equanimity, there would be no governmental relief systems at all. But often they do not, and for reasons that are not difficult to see. The regulation of civil behavior in all societies is intimately dependent on stable occupational arrangements. So long as people are fixed in their work roles, their activities and outlooks are also fixed; they do what they must and think what they must. Each behavior and attitude is shaped by the reward of a good harvest or the penalty of a bad one, by the factory paycheck or the danger of losing it. But mass unemployment breaks that bond, loosening people from the main institution by which they are regulated and controlled.

Moreover, mass unemployment that persists for any length of time diminishes the capacity of other institutions to bind and constrain people. Occupational behaviors and outlooks underpin a way of life and determine familial, communal, and cultural patterns. When large numbers of people are suddenly barred from their traditional occupations, the entire network of social control is weakened. There is no harvest or paycheck to enforce work and the sentiments that uphold work; without work, people cannot conform to familial and communal roles; and if the dislocation is widespread, the legitimacy of the social order itself may come to be questioned. The result is usually civil disorder—crime, mass protests, riots—a disorder that may even threaten to overturn existing social and economic arrangements. It is then that relief programs are initiated or expanded.

Western relief systems originated in the mass disturbances that erupted during the long transition from feudalism to capitalism beginning in the sixteenth century. As a result of the declining death rates in the previous century, the population of Europe grew rapidly; as the population grew, so did transiency and beggary. Moreover, distress resulting from population changes, agricultural and other natural disasters, which had characterized life throughout the Middle Ages, was now exacerbated by the vagaries of an evolving market economy, and outbreaks of turbulence among the poor were frequent. To deal with these threats to civil order, many localities legislated severe penalties against vagrancy. Even before the sixteenth century, the magistrates of Basel had defined twenty-five different categories of beggars, together with appropriate punishments for each. But penalties alone did not always deter begging, especially when economic distress was severe and the numbers affected were large. Consequently, some localities began to augment punishment with provisions for the relief of the vagrant poor.

CIVIL DISORDER AND RELIEF

A French town that initiated such an arrangement early in the sixteenth century was Lyons, which was troubled both by a rapidly growing population and by the economic instability associated with the transition to capitalism. By 1500 Lyons' population had already begun to increase. During the decades that followed, the town became a prosperous commercial and manufacturing center—the home of the European money market and of expanding new trades in textiles, printing, and metalworking. As it thrived it attracted people, not only from the surrounding countryside, but even from Italy, Flanders, and Germany. All told, the population of Lyons probably doubled between 1500 and 1540.

All this was very well as long as the newcomers could be absorbed by industry. But not all were, with the result that the town came to be plagued by beggars and vagrants. Moreover, prosperity was not continuous: some trades were seasonal and others were periodically troubled by foreign competition. With each economic downturn, large numbers of unemployed workers took to the streets to plead for charity, cluttering the very doorsteps of the better-off classes. Lyons was most vulnerable during periods of bad harvest, when famine not only drove up the cost of bread for urban artisans and journeymen but brought hordes of peasants into the city, where they sometimes paraded through the streets to exhibit their misfortune. In 1529 food riots erupted, with thousands of Lyonnais looting granaries and the homes of the wealthy; in 1530, artisans and journeymen armed themselves and marched through the streets; in 1531, mobs of starving peasants literally overran the town.

Such charity as had previously been given in Lyons was primarily the responsibility of the church or of those of the more prosperous who sought to purchase their salvation through almsgiving. But this method of caring for the needy obviously stimulated rather than discouraged begging and created a public nuisance to the better-off citizens (one account of the times describes famished peasants so gorging themselves as to die on the very doorsteps where they were fed). Moreover, to leave charity to church and citizen meant that few got aid, and those not necessarily according to their need. The result was that mass disorders periodically erupted.

The increase in disorder led the rulers of Lyons to conclude that the giving of charity should no longer be governed by private whim. In 1534, churchmen, notables, and merchants joined together to establish a centralized administration for disbursing aid. All charitable donations were consolidated under a central body, the "Aumone-Generale," whose responsibility was to "nourish the poor forever." A list of the needy was established by a house-to-house survey, and tickets for bread and money were issued according to fixed standards. Indeed, most of the features of modern welfare—from criteria to discriminate the worthy poor from the unworthy, to strict procedures for surveillance of recipients as well as measures for their rehabilitation—were present in Lyons' new relief administration. By the 1550's, about 10 percent of the town's population was receiving relief.

Within two years of the establishment of relief in Lyons, King Francis I ordered each parish in France to register its poor and to provide for the "impotent" out of a fund of contributions. Elsewhere in Europe, other townships began to devise similar systems to deal with the vagrants and mobs cast up by famine, rapid population growth, and the transition from feudalism to capitalism.

England also felt these disturbances, and just as it pioneered in developing an intensively capitalist economy, so it was at the forefront in developing nationwide, public relief arrangements. During the closing years of the fifteenth century, the emergence of the wool industry in England began to transform agricultural life. As sheep raising became more profitable, much land was converted from tillage to pasturage, and large numbers of peasants were displaced by an emerging entrepreneurial gentry which either bought their land or cheated them out of it. The result was great tumult among the peasantry, as the Webbs were to note:

> When the sense of oppression became overwhelming, the popular feeling manifested itself in widespread organized tumults, disturbances, and insurrections, from Wat Tyler's rebellion of 1381, and Jack Cade's march on London of 1460, to the Pilgrimage of Grace in 1536, and Kett's Norfolk rising of 1549—all of them successfully put down, but sometimes not without great struggle, by the forces which the government could command.

Early in the sixteenth century, the national government moved to try to forestall such disorders. In 1528 the Privy Council, anticipating a fall in foreign sales as a result of the war in Flanders, tried to induce the cloth manufacturers of Suffolk to retain their employees. In 1534, a law passed under Henry VIII attempted to limit the number of sheep in any one holding in order to inhibit the displacement of farmers and agricultural laborers and thus forestall potential disorders. Beginning in the 1550's the Privy Council attempted to regulate the price of grain in poor harvests. But the entrepreneurs of the new market economy were not so readily curbed, so that during this period another method of dealing with labor disorders was evolved.

Early in the sixteenth century, the national government moved to replace parish arrangements for charity with a nationwide system of relief. In 1531, an act of Parliament decreed that local officials search out and register those of the destitute deemed to be impotent and give them a document authorizing begging. As for those who sought alms without authorization, the penalty was public whipping till the blood ran.

Thereafter, other arrangements for relief were rapidly instituted. An act passed in 1536, during the reign of Henry VIII, required local parishes to take care of their destitute and to establish a procedure for the collection and administration of donations for that purpose by local officials. (In the same year Henry VIII began to expropriate monasteries, helping to assure secular control of charity.) With these developments, the penalties for beggary were made more severe, including an elaborate schedule of branding, enslavement, and execution for repeated offenders. Even so, by 1572 beggary was said to have reached alarming proportions, and in that year local responsibility for relief was more fully spelled out by the famous Elizabethan Poor Laws, which established a local tax, known as the poor rate, as the means for financing the care of paupers and required that justices of the peace serve as the overseers of the poor.

After each period of activity, the parish relief machinery tended to lapse into disuse, until bad harvests or depression in manufacturing led again to widespread unemployment and misery, to new outbreaks of disorder, and then to a resuscitation and expansion of relief arrangements. The most illuminating of these episodes, because it bears so much similarity to the present-day relief explosion in the United States, was the expansion of relief during the massive agricultural dislocations of the late eighteenth century.

Most of the English agricultural population had lost its landholdings long before the eighteenth century. In place of the subsistence farming found elsewhere in Europe, a three-tier system of landowners, tenant farmers, and agricultural workers had evolved in England. The vast majority of the people were a landless proletariat, hiring out by the year to tenant farmers. The margin of their subsistence, however, was provided by common and waste lands, on which they gathered kindling, grazed animals, and hunted game to supplement their meager wages. Moreover, the use of the commons was part of the English villager's birthright, his sense of place and pride. It was the disruption of these arrangements and the ensuing disorder that led to the new expansion of relief.

By the middle of the eighteenth century, an increasing population, advancing urbanization, and the growth of manufacturing had greatly expanded markets for agricultural products, mainly for cereals to feed the urban population and for wool to supply the cloth manufacturers. These new markets, together with the introduction of new agricultural methods (such as cross-harrowing), led to large-scale changes in agriculture. To take advantage of rising prices and new techniques, big landowners moved to expand their holdings still further by buying up small farms and, armed with parliamentary Bills of Enclosure, by usurping the common and waste lands which had enabled many small cottagers to survive. Although this process began much earlier, it accelerated rapidly after 1750; by 1850, well over six million acres of common land—or about one-quarter of the total arable acreage—had been consolidated into private holdings and turned primarily to grain production. For great numbers of agricultural workers, enclosure meant no land on which to grow subsistence crops to feed their families, no grazing land to produce wool for home spinning and weaving, no fuel to heat their cottages, and new restrictions against hunting. It meant, in short, the loss of a major source of subsistence for the poor.

New markets also stimulated a more businesslike approach to farming.

Landowners demanded the maximum rent from tenant farmers, and tenant farmers in turn began to deal with their laborers in terms of cash calculations. Specifically, this meant a shift from a master-servant relationship to an employer-employee relationship, but on the harshest terms. Where laborers had previously worked by the year and frequently lived with the farmer, they were now hired for only as long as they were needed and were then left to fend for themselves. Pressures toward short-term hiring also resulted from the large-scale cultivation of grain crops for market, which called for a seasonal labor force, as opposed to mixed subsistence farming, which required year-round laborers. The use of cash rather than produce as the medium of payment for work, a rapidly spreading practice, encouraged partly by the long-term inflation of grain prices, added to the laborer's hardships. Finally the rapid increase in rural population at a time when the growth of woolen manufacturing continued to provide an incentive to convert land from tillage to pasturage produced a large labor surplus, leaving agricultural workers with no leverage in bargaining for wages with their tenant-farmer employers. The result was widespread unemployment and terrible hardship.

None of these changes took place without resistance from small farmers and laborers who, while they had known hardship before, were now being forced out of a way of life and even out of their villages. Some rioted when Bills of Enclosure were posted; some petitioned the Parliament for their repeal. And when hardship was made more acute by a succession of poor harvests in the 1770's, there were widespread food riots.

Indeed, throughout the late eighteenth and early nineteenth centuries, the English countryside was periodically besieged by turbulent masses of the displaced rural poor and the towns were racked by Luddism, radicalism, trade-unionism and Chartism, even while the ruling classes worried about what the French Revolution might augur for England. A solution to disorder was needed, and that solution turned out to be relief. The poor-relief system—first created in the sixteenth century to control the earlier disturbances caused by population growth and the commercialization of agriculture—now rapidly became a major institution of English life. Between 1760 and 1784 taxes for relief—the poor rate—rose by 60 percent; they doubled by 1801, and rose by 60 percent more in the next decade. By 1818, the poor rate was over six times as high as it had been in 1760. Hobsbaum estimates that up to the 1850's, upwards of 10 percent of the English population were paupers. The relief system, in short, was expanded in order to absorb and regulate the masses of discontented people uprooted from agriculture but not yet incorporated into industry.

Relief arrangements evolved more slowly in the United States, and the first major relief crisis did not occur until the Great Depression. The inauguration of massive relief-giving was not simply a response to widespread economic distress, for millions had remained unemployed for several years without obtaining aid. What finally led the national government to proffer aid was the great surge of political disorder that followed the economic catastrophe, a disorder which eventually led to the convulsive voting shifts of 1932. After the election, the federal government abandoned its posture of aloofness toward the unemployed. Within a matter of months, billions of dollars were flowing to localities, and the relief rolls skyrocketed. By 1935, upwards of 20 million people were on the dole.

The contemporary relief explosion, which began in the early 1960's, has its roots in agricultural modernization. No one would disagree that the rural economy of America, especially in the South, has undergone a profound transformation in recent decades. In 1945, there was one tractor per farm; in 1964 there were two. Mechanization and other technological developments, in turn, stimulated the enlargement of farm holdings. Between 1959 and 1961, one million farms disappeared; the three million remaining farms averaged 377 acres in size—30 percent larger than the average farm ten years earlier. The chief and most obvious effect of these changes was to lessen the need for agricultural labor. In the years between 1950 and 1965 alone, a Presidential Commission on Rural Poverty was to discover, "New machines and new methods increased farm output in the United States by 45 percent, and reduced farm employment by 45 percent." A mere 4 percent of the American labor force now works the land, signaling an extraordinary displacement of people, with accompanying upheaval and suffering. The best summary measure of this dislocation is probably the volume of migration to the cities; over 20 million people, more than four million of them black, left the land after 1940.

Nor were all these poor absorbed into the urban economic system. Blacks were especially vulnerable to unemployment. At the close of the Korean War, the national nonwhite unemployment rate leaped from 4.5 percent in 1953 to 9.9 percent in 1954. By 1958, it had reached 12.6 percent, and it fluctuated between 10 and 13 percent until the escalation of the war in Vietnam after 1964.

These figures pertain only to people unemployed and looking for work. They do not include the sporadically unemployed or those employed at extremely low wages. Combining such additional measures with the official unemployment measure produces a subemployment index. This index was first used in 1966—well after the economic downturns that characterized the years between the end of the Korean War and the escalation of the war in Vietnam. Were subemployment data available for the "Eisenhower recession" years, especially in the slum ghettos of the larger central cities, they would surely show much higher rates than prevailed in 1966. In any event, the figures for 1966 revealed a nonwhite subemployment rate of 21.6 percent compared with a white rate of 7.6 percent.

However, despite the spread of economic deprivation, whether on the land or in the cities, the relief system did not respond. In the entire decade between 1950 and 1960, the national AFDC caseload rose by only 17 percent. Many of the main urban targets of migration showed equally little change: the rolls in New York City moved up by 16 percent and in Los Angeles by 14 percent. In the South, the rolls did not rise at all.

But in the 1960's, disorder among the black poor erupted on a wide scale, and the welfare rolls erupted as well. The welfare explosion occurred during several years of the greatest domestic disorder since the 1930's—perhaps the greatest in our history. It was concurrent with the turmoil produced by the civil-rights struggle, with widespread and destructive rioting in the cities, and with the formation of a militant grass-roots movement of the poor dedicated to combating welfare restrictions. Not least, the welfare rise was also concurrent with the enactment of a series of ghetto-placating federal programs (such as the antipoverty program) which, among other things, hired thousands of poor people, social workers, and lawyers who, it subsequently turned out, greatly stimulated people to apply for relief and helped them obtain it. And the welfare explosion, although an urban phenomenon generally, was greatest in just that handful of large metropolitan counties where the political turmoil of the mid- and late 1960's was the most acute.

The magnitude of the welfare rise is worth noting. The national AFDC caseload rose by more than 225 percent in the 1960's. In New York City, the rise was more than 300 percent; the same was so in Los Angeles. Even in the South, where there had been no rise at all in the 1950's, the bulk of the increase took place after 1965—that is, after disorder reached a crescendo. More than 80 percent of the national rise in the 1960's occurred in the last five years of the decade. In other words, the welfare rolls expanded, today as at earlier times, only in response to civil disorder.

While muting the more disruptive outbreaks of civil disorder (such as rioting), the mere giving of relief does nothing to reverse the disintegration of lower-class life produced by economic change, a disintegration which leads to rising disorder and rising relief rolls in the first place. Indeed, greatly liberalized relief-giving can further weaken work and family norms. To restore order in a more fundamental sense the society must create the means to reassert its authority. Because the market is unable to control men's behavior, a surrogate system of social control must be evolved, at least for a time. Moreover, if the surrogate system is to be consistent with normally dominant patterns, it must restore people to work roles. Thus even though obsolete or unneeded workers are temporarily given direct relief, they are eventually succored only on condition that they work. As these adjustments are made, the functions of relief arrangements may be said to be shifting from regulating disorder to regulating labor.

RESTORING ORDER BY RESTORING WORK

The arrangements, both historical and contemporary, through which relief recipients have been made to work vary, but broadly speaking, there are two main ways: work is provided under public auspices, whether in the recipient's home, in a labor yard, in a workhouse, or on a public-works project; or work is provided in the private market, whether by contracting or indenturing the poor to private employers, or through subsidies designed to induce employers to hire paupers. And although a relief system may at any time use both of these methods of enforcing work, one or the other usually becomes predominant, depending on the economic conditions that first gave rise to disorder.

Publicly subsidized work tends to be used during business depressions, when the demand for labor in the private market collapses. Conversely, arrangements to channel paupers into the labor market are more likely to be used when rapid changes in markets or technology render a segment of the labor supply temporarily maladapted. In the first case, the relief system augments a shrunken labor market; in the other, its policies and procedures are shaped to overcome the poor fit between labor demand and supply.

Public work is as old as public relief. The municipal relief systems initiated on the Continent in the first quarter of the sixteenth century often included some form of public works. In England, the same statute of 1572 that established taxation as the method for financing poor relief charged the overseers of the poor with putting vagrants to work. Shortly afterwards, in 1576, local officials were directed to acquire a supply of raw goods—wool, hemp, iron—which was to be delivered to the needy for processing in their homes, their dole to be fixed according to "the desert of the work."

The favored method of enforcing work throughout most of the history of relief was the workhouse. In 1723, an act of Parliament permitted the local parishes to establish workhouses and to refuse aid to those poor who would not enter; within ten years, there were said to be about fifty workhouses in the environs of London alone.

The destitute have also sometimes been paid to work in the general community or in their own homes. This method of enforcing work evolved in England during the bitter depression of 1840–1841. As unemployment mounted, the poor in some of the larger cities protested against having to leave their communities to enter workhouses in order to obtain relief, and in any case, in some places the workhouses were already full. As a result, various public spaces were designated as "labor yards" to which the unemployed could come by the day to pick oakum, cut wood, and break stone, for which they were paid in food and clothing. The method was used periodically throughout the second half of the nineteenth century; at times of severe distress, very large numbers of the able-bodied were supported in this way.

The first massive use of public work under relief auspices in the United States occurred during the 1930's when millions of the unemployed were subsidized through the Works Progress Administration. The initial response of the Roosevelt administration was to appropriate billions for direct-relief payments. But no one liked direct relief—not the President who called for it, the Congress that legislated it, the administrators who operated it, the people who received it. Direct relief was viewed as a temporary expedient, a way of maintaining a person's body, but not his dignity; a way of keeping the populace from shattering in despair, discontent, and disorder, at least for a while, but not of renewing their pride, of bringing back a way of life. For their way of life had been anchored in the discipline of work, and so that discipline had to be restored. The remedy was to abolish direct relief and put the unemployed to work on subsidized projects. These reforms were soon instituted—and with dramatic results. For a brief time, the federal government became the employer of millions of people (although millions of others remained unemployed).

Quite different methods of enforcing work are used when the demand for labor is steady but maladaptions in the labor supply, caused by changes in methods of production, result in unemployment. In such circumstances, relief agencies ordinarily channel paupers directly into the private market. For example, the rapid expansion of English manufacturing during the late eighteenth and early nineteenth centuries produced a commensurately expanded need for factory operatives. But it was no easy matter to get them. Men who had been agricultural laborers, independent craftsmen, or workers in domestic industries (i.e., piecework manufacturing in the home) resisted the new discipline. Between 1778 and 1830, there were repeated revolts by laborers in which local tradesmen and farmers often participated. The revolts failed, of course; the new industry moved forward inexorably, taking the more dependent and tractable under its command, with the aid of the relief system.

The burgeoning English textile industry solved its labor problems during the latter part of the eighteenth century by using parish children, some only four or five years old, as factory operatives. Manufacturers negotiated regular bargains with the parish authorities, ordering lots of fifty or more children from the poorhouses. Parish children were an ideal labor source for new manufacturers. The young paupers could be shipped to remote factories, located to take advantage of the streams from which power could be drawn. (With the shift from water power to steam in the nineteenth century, factories began to locate in towns where they could employ local children; with that change, the system of child labor became a system of "free" child labor.) The children were also preferred for their docility and for their light touch at the looms. Moreover, pauper-children could be had for a bit of food and a bed, and they provided a very stable labor supply, for they were held fast at their labors by indentures, usually until they were twenty-one.

Sometimes the relief system subsidizes the employment of paupers—especially when their market value is very low—as when the magistrates of Lyons provided subsidies to manufacturers who employed pauper children. In rural England during the late eighteenth century, as more and more of the population was being displaced by the commercialization of agriculture, this method was used on a very large scale. To be sure, a demand for labor was developing in the new manufacturing establishments that would in time absorb many of the uprooted rural poor. But this did not happen all at once: rural displacement and industrial expansion did not proceed at the same pace or in the same areas, and in any case the drastic shift from rural village to factory system took time. During the long interval before people forced off the land were absorbed into manufacturing, many remained in the countryside as virtual vagrants; others migrated to the towns, where they crowded into hovels and cells, subject to the vicissitudes of rapidly rising and falling markets, their ranks continually enlarged by new rural refugees.

These conditions were not the result of a collapse in the market. Indeed, grain prices rose during the second half of the eighteenth century, and they rose spectacularly during the Revolutionary and Napoleonic wars. Rather, it was the expanding market for agricultural produce which, by stimulating enclosure and business-minded farming methods, led to unemployment and destitution. Meanwhile, population growth, which meant a surplus of laborers, left the workers little opportunity to resist the destruction of their traditional way of life—except by crime, riots, and incendiarism. To cope with these disturbances, relief expanded, but in such a way as to absorb and discipline laborers by supporting the faltering labor market with subsidies.

The subsidy system is widely credited to the sheriff and magistrates of Berkshire, who, in a meeting at Speenhamland in 1795, decided on a scheme by which the Poor Law authorities would supplement the wages of underpaid agricultural workers according to a published scale. It was a time when exceptional scarcity of food led to riots all over England, sometimes suppressed only by calling out the troops. With this "double panic of famine and revolution," the subsidy scheme spread, especially in counties where large amounts of acreage had been enclosed.

The local parishes implemented the work subsidy system in different ways. Under the "roundsman" arrangement, the parish overseers sent any man who applied for aid from house to house to get work. If he found work, the employer was obliged to feed him and pay a small sum (6 d) per day, with the parish adding another small sum (4 d). Elsewhere, the parish authorities contracted directly with farmers to have paupers work for a given price, with the parish paying the combined wage and relief subsidy directly to the pauper. In still other places, parish authorities parceled out the unemployed to farmers, who were obliged to pay a set rate or make up the difference in higher taxes. Everywhere, however, the main principle was the same: an underemployed and turbulent populace was being pacified with public allowances, but these allowances were used to restore order by enforcing work, at very low wage levels. Relief, in short, served as a support for a disturbed labor market and as a discipline for a disturbed rural society. As the historians J.L. Hammond and Barbara Hammond were to say, "The meshes of the Poor Law were spread over the entire labor system."

The English Speenhamland plan, while it enjoys a certain notoriety, is by no means unique. The most recent example of a scheme for subsidizing paupers in private employ is the reorganization of American public welfare proposed in the summer of 1969 by President Richard Nixon; the general parallel with the events surrounding Speenhamland is striking. The United States relief rolls expanded in the 1960's to absorb a laboring population made superfluous by agricultural modernization in the South, a population that became turbulent in the wake of forced migration to the cities. As the relief rolls grew to deal with these disturbances, pressure for "reforms" also mounted. Key features of the reform proposals included a national minimum allowance of $1,600 per year for a family of four, coupled with an elaborate system of penalties and incentives to force families to work. In effect, the proposal was intended to support and strengthen a disturbed low-wage labor market by providing what was called in nineteenth-century England a "rate in aid of wages."

ENFORCING LOW-WAGE WORK DURING PERIODS OF STABILITY

Even in the absence of cataclysmic change, market incentives may be insufficient to compel all people at all times to do the particular work required of them. Incentives may be too meager and erratic, or people may not be sufficiently socialized to respond to them properly. To be sure, the productivity of a fully developed capitalist economy would allow for wages and profits sufficient to entice most of the population to work; and in a fully developed capitalist society, most people would also be reared to want what the market holds out to them. They would expect, even sanctify, the rewards of the marketplace and acquiesce in its vagaries.

But no fully developed capitalist society exists. (Even today in the United States, the most advanced capitalist country, certain regions and population groups—such as southern tenant farmers—remain on the periphery of the wage market and are only partially socialized to the ethos of the market.) Capitalism evolved slowly and spread slowly. During most of this evolution, the market provided meager rewards for most workers, and none at all for some. There are still many for whom this is so. And during most of this evolution, large sectors of the laboring classes were not fully socialized to the market ethos. The relief system, we contend, has made an important contribution toward overcoming these persisting weaknesses in the capacity of the market to direct and control men.

Once an economic convulsion subsides and civil order is restored, relief systems are not ordinarily abandoned. The rolls are reduced, to be sure, but the shell of the system usually remains, ostensibly to provide aid to the aged, the disabled, and such other unfortunates who are of no use as workers. However, the manner in which these "impotents" have always been treated, in the United States and elsewhere, suggests a purpose quite different from the remediation of their destitution. These residual persons have ordinarily been degraded for lacking economic value, relegated to the foul quarters of the workhouse, with its strict penal regimen and its starvation diet. Once stability was restored, such institutions were typically proclaimed the sole source of aid, and for a reason bearing directly on enforcing work.

Conditions in the workhouse were intended to ensure that no one with any conceivable alternatives would seek public aid. Nor can there be any doubt of that intent. Consider this statement by the Poor Law Commissioners in 1834, for example:

> Into such a house none will enter voluntarily; work, confinement, and discipline will deter the indolent and vicious; and nothing but extreme necessity will induce any to accept the comfort which must be obtained by the surrender of their free agency, and the sacrifice of their accustomed habits and gratifications. Thus the parish officer, being furnished an unerring test of the necessity of applicants, is relieved from his painful and difficult responsibility: while all have the gratification of knowing that while the necessitous are abundantly relieved, the funds of charity are not wasted by idleness and fraud.

The method worked. Periods of relief expansion were generally followed by "reform" campaigns to abolish all "outdoor" aid and restrict relief to those who entered the workhouse—as in England in 1722, 1834, and 1871 and in the United States in the 1880's and 1890's—and these campaigns usually resulted in a sharp reduction in the number of applicants seeking aid.

The harsh treatment of those who had no alternative except to fall back upon the parish and accept "the offer of the House" terrorized the impoverished masses in another way as well. It made pariahs of those who could not support themselves; they served as an object lesson, a means of celebrating the virtues of work by the terrible example of their agony. That, too, was a matter of deliberate intent. The workhouse was designed to spur men to contrive ways of supporting themselves by their own industry, to offer themselves to any employer on any terms, rather than suffer the degraded status of pauper.

All of this was evident in the contraction of relief which occurred in the United States at the close of the Great Depression. As political stability returned, emergency relief and work relief programs were reduced and eventually abolished, with many of those cut off being forced into a labor market still glutted with the unemployed. Meanwhile, the Social Security Act had been passed. Widely hailed as a major reform, this measure created our present-day welfare system, with its categorical provisions for the aged, the blind, and families with dependent children (as well as, in 1950, the disabled).

The enactment of this "reform" signaled a turn toward the work-enforcing function of relief arrangements. This became especially evident after World War II during the period of greatly accelerated agricultural modernization. Millions were unemployed in agriculture; millions of others migrated to the cities, where unemployment in the late 1950's reached extremely high levels. But few families were given assistance. By 1960, only 745,000 families had been admitted to the AFDC rolls. That was to change in the 1960's, as we have already noted, but only in response to the most unprecedented disorder in our history.

That families without jobs or income failed to secure relief during the late 1940's and the 1950's was in part a consequence of restrictive statutes and policies—the exclusion of able-bodied males and, in many places, of so-called employable mothers, together with residence laws, relative responsibility provisions, and the like. But it was also—perhaps mainly— a consequence of the persistence of age-old rituals of degradation. AFDC mothers were forced to answer questions about their sexual behavior ("When did you last menstruate?"), open their closets to inspection ("Whose pants are those?"), and permit their children to be interrogated ("Do any men visit your mother?"). Unannounced raids, usually after midnight and without benefit of warrant, in which a recipient's home is searched for signs of "immoral" activities, have also been part of life on AFDC. In Oakland, California, a public-welfare caseworker, Bennie Parish, refused to take part in a raid in January 1962 and was dismissed for insubordination. When he used for reinstatement, the state argued successfully in the lower courts that people taking public assistance waive certain constitutional rights, among them the right to privacy. (The court's position had at least the weight of long tradition, for the withdrawal of civil rights is an old feature of public relief. In England, for example, relief recipients were denied the franchise until 1918, and as late as 1934 the constitutions of fourteen American states deprived recipients of the right to vote or hold office.)

The main target of these rituals is not the recipient, who ordinarily is not of much use as a worker, but the able-bodied poor who remain in the labor market. It is for these people that the spectacle of the degraded pauper is intended. For example, scandals exposing "welfare-fraud" have diffuse effects, for they reach a wide public—including the people who might otherwise apply for aid but who are deterred because of the invidious connotations of being on welfare. Such a scandal occurred in the District of Columbia in 1961, with the result that half of all AFDC mothers were declared to be ineligible for relief, most of them for allegedly "consorting with men." In the several years immediately before the attack, about 6,500 District of Columbia families had applied for aid annually; during the attack, the figure dropped to 4,400 and it did not rise for more than five years—long after that particular scandal had itself subsided.

In sum, market values and market incentives are weakest at the bottom of the social order. To buttress weak market controls and ensure the availability of marginal labor, an outcast class—the dependent poor—is created by the relief system. This class, whose members are of no productive use, is not treated with indifference, but with contempt. Its degradation at the hands of relief officials serves to celebrate the virtue of all work and deters actual or potential workers from seeking aid.

THE CURRENT CALL FOR REFORM

From our perspective, a relief explosion is a reform just because a large number of unemployed or underemployed people obtain aid. But from the perspective of most people, a relief explosion is viewed as a "crisis." The contemporary relief explosion in the United States, following a period of unparalleled turbulence in the cities, has thus resulted in a clamor for reform. Similar episodes in the past suggest that pressure for reform signals a shift in emphasis between the major functions of relief arrangements—a shift from regulating disorder to regulating labor.

Pressure for reform stems in part from the fiscal burden imposed on localities when the relief rolls expand. An obvious remedy is for the federal government to simply assume a greater share of the costs, if not the entire cost (at this writing, Congress appears likely to enact such fiscal reform).

However, the much more fundamental problem with which relief reform seeks to cope is the erosion of the work role and the deterioration of the male-headed family. In principle, these problems could be dealt with by economic policies leading to full employment at decent wages, but there is little political support for that approach. Instead, the historic approach to relief explosions is being invoked, which is to restore work through the relief system. Various proposals have been advanced: some would force recipients to report regularly to employment offices; others would provide a system of wage subsidies conditional on the recipient's taking on a job at any wage (including those below the federal minimum wage); still others would inaugurate a straightforward program of public-works projects.

We are opposed to any type of reform intended to promote work through the relief system rather than through the reform of economic policies. When similar relief reforms were introduced in the past, they presaged the eventual expulsion of large numbers of people from the rolls, leaving them to fend for themselves in a labor market where there was too little work and thus subjecting them once again to severe economic exploitation. The reason that this happens is more than a little ironic.

The irony is this: when relief is used to enforce work, it tends to stabilize lower-class occupational, familial, and communal life (unlike direct relief, which merely mutes the worst outbreaks of discontent). By doing so, it diminishes the proclivities toward disruptive behavior which give rise to the expansion of relief in the first place. Once order is restored in this far more profound sense, relief-giving can be virtually abolished as it has been so often in the past. And there is always pressure to abolish large-scale work relief, for it strains against the market ethos and interferes with the untrammeled operation of the marketplace. The point is not just that when a relief concession is offered up, peace and order reign; it is, rather that when peace and order reign, the relief concession is withdrawn.

The restoration of work through the relief system, in other words, makes possible the eventual return to the most restrictive phase in the cycle of relief-giving. What begins as a great expansion of direct relief, and then turns into some form of work relief, ends finally with a sharp contraction of the rolls. Advocates of relief reform may argue that their reforms will be long-lasting, that the restrictive phase in the cycle will not be reached, but past experience suggests otherwise.

Therefore, in the absence of economic reforms leading to full employment at decent wages, we take the position that the explosion of the rolls is the true relief reform, that it should be defended, and that it should be expanded. Even now, hundreds of thousands of impoverished families remain who are eligible for assistance but who receive no aid at all.

X

Crime and Justice

In recent years, crime has often been perceived by the public as America's number one social problem—closely matched, since the mid-1980s, by the deeply related problem of drugs. Violent crime, in particular, has made growing numbers of Americans afraid to walk their streets and has generally diminished the quality of urban life in the United States. Moreover, our violent crime rates remain disastrously high—far higher, in fact, than those of other advanced industrial societies—despite dramatic increases in the numbers of criminals who have been put behind bars.

What are the causes of violent crime? Is there a connection between criminal violence and unemployment, as our intuition suggests? Conservative criminologists tend to downplay such an association, arguing that there is only slight evidence linking the crime rate to economic fluctuations. They argue that America experienced relatively little crime during the 1930s Great Depression, while the crime rate rose during the more affluent 1960s and reached a peak in the 1970s. In "Crime and Work," Elliott Currie reviews the evidence and concludes that there is a strong association between unemployment and crime. He argues that those who downplay the relationship make three mistakes. First, subgroups with high crime rates—such as young black males—do experience high unemployment rates, even when overall employment is low. Second, unemployment has a different impact when it portends a lifetime of diminished opportunity. Finally, unemployment statistics do not reflect the *quality* of available work.

Drug crime in the United States has likely risen, and quite dramatically, although it is hard to tell how much from crime statistics, as contained in the Uniform Crime Reports, since these are based on crimes reported to the police. The robbery victim is indeed likely to report the crime to the police. The rape victim may be more hesitant but may tell her story to a

National Victim surveyor attempting to learn how many victims did not report crime to the police. But when a drug seller sells to a buyer, the purchaser is unlikely to report the crime either to the police or to a crime surveyor. In his article, Jerome H. Skolnick concludes that, based on his recent research, drug crimes are overwhelming the American criminal justice system. He argues, moreover, that law enforcement is severely limited in its capacity to undermine the drug trade. Drugs, he argues, are a public health and social problem, while fundamental dilemmas undermine law enforcement's capacity to deal with it.

If drug crime is one part of the crime problem, corporate crime and violence is another. So argues Sierra Club author Russell Mokhiber, who asserts that we seriously undercount the tangible harm to human beings and the environment caused by the excesses of corporate power. In part, Mokhiber reminds us how harmful some of big business excesses have been; the Dalkon Shield intrauterine device, for example, seriously injured tens of thousands of women. [Some of the earlier selections in this book—those dealing with the original Pintos (Selection 1), hazardous chemicals (Selection 27) and the tobacco companies (Selection 2)—make a similar point.]

Mokhiber, however, goes beyond a recounting of corporate abuses to analyze how it is that big corporations are able to engage in such destructive activity without being held responsible as *criminals*, although they may have to pay money damages as convicted defendants in civil court actions. He argues that the severe injury generated by violent corporate misconduct warrants the stigma and penalties associated with the idea of crime.

What are we to do with violent criminals? As crime rose in the 1970s, its rise was accompanied by increasingly heavier penalties and a movement away from a philosophy of rehabilitation to one stressing punishment as the *raison d'être* of the criminal justice system. By 1989, 38 states and the federal government had instituted capital punishment. Since 1976, when capital punishment was reinstated by the U.S. Supreme Court, more than 2,000 convicted criminals have been sentenced to death and more than 100 have been executed, although the United States is the only nation in the Western industrial world employing capital punishment.

David Bruck is a South Carolina lawyer who defends convicted murderers sentenced to death. Bruck opposes the death penalty for several reasons, but perhaps his most compelling reason is that capital punishment is essentially chaotic and arbitrary. Only 3 percent of convicted imprisoned murderers are actually sentenced to die, and it is difficult to distinguish the murders committed by them from those of inmates who are not sentenced to death row.

One statistical pattern seems to account for much of the difference. If the *victim* is white, there is a far greater probability that the murderer will be sentenced to die than if the victim is black. Defendants charged with killing white victims are 4.3 times as likely to receive a death sentence as defendants charged with killing black victims.

In a major Supreme Court case (decided after Bruck's article was written to influence this case), Warren McCleskey, a black man, was convicted of shooting and killing a white policeman during the robbery of a furniture store. The Court acknowledged the validity of the statistical disparity—that those who kill whites are more likely to be sentenced to death than those who kill blacks—but declined to grant it constitutional significance. The Court held that, to prevail in his claim that he was mistreated under the Fourteenth Amendment equal protection clause, a statistical disparity was not enough. McCleskey had the burden of proving "purposeful discrimination" in his *individual* case, rather than empirical documentation of the biases of the death penalty sentencing *system*, which the Court recognized. The dissent disagreed, arguing that racial factors have a pronounced impact on whether or not a convicted murderer will be sentenced to death or to life imprisonment.

37

Crime and Work

Elliott Currie

Toward the end of the sixteenth century, Richard Hakluyt depicted the ominous consequences of England's widespread unemployment. "For all the statutes that hitherto can be devised," he wrote, "and the sharp execution of the same in punishing idle and lazy persons for want of sufficient occasion of honest employment," it had proven impossible to

> deliver our Commonwealth from multitudes of loiterers and idle vagabonds, which, having no way to be set on work . . . often fall to pilfering and thieving and other lewdness, whereby all the prisons of the land are daily pestered and stuffed full of them, where either they pitifully pine away, or else at length are miserably hanged, even twenty at a clap out of some one jail.

The same problem worried American observers three centuries later. In 1878, the economist Carroll D. Wright, Massachusetts Commissioner of Statistics, noted that more than 67 percent of convicts in that state were recorded as "having had no occupation"; of 220 men sentenced to prison one year, "147 were without a trade or any regular means of earning a living." Wright warned of the disquieting implications of this for the "reform" of prisoners:

> Will these men serve their time, and be discharged in their present unfit state to battle with the world? They may go out into society again resolved to do right; but without a reliable means of support they are ill-

prepared to meet the adversities of hard times, or the temptation to gain
by crime what they do not know how to obtain by honest labor.

The connection between crime and the lack of any "regular means of
earning a living" has changed little since Wright's time, or even
Hakluyt's. At the close of the 1970s, nearly 40 percent of state prison
inmates and 55 percent of the inmates of local jails had not been working
full-time in the months before they went behind bars, while those who
did work typically had little to show for it. Only about half of a sample of
"habitual felons" in a Rand Corporation survey of the California prisons
in the late seventies had gained their usual pre-prison income by working;
of those who had, most "had earnings that were not much above a
poverty level." Within this generally deprived sample, moreover, those
prisoners who had been even slightly more successful in the labor market—those the Rand researchers called the *better employed*—committed
crimes, while on the "street," at about one-sixth the rate of the others.
This difference is all the more remarkable given the study's extremely
generous definition of what it meant to be *better employed:* earning all of
$100 a week and working at least 75 percent of their "street" time.

Nor is this all. Later Rand research . . . suggests that unemployment is
one of the most powerful predictors of which inmates among the already
"hardened" prison population are most likely to go on to become *high-rate*
offenders, responsible for much more than their share of serious crime
even in this rather select group.

These findings are no surprise; they fit our commonsense understanding of who goes to prison, and they are compatible with a broad range of
theories of crime, including the "economic" approach favored by many
conservatives. In a society in which work is the indispensable key to most
things—material and otherwise—that our culture considers worth having, it's easy to see why those without work might try other, less legitimate ways to get them. And since work is also one of the most important
ways individuals become integrated into a larger community, it isn't
surprising that those excluded from the world of work will be held less
tightly by the bonds that keep a society together. On the face of it, the
appropriate response seems fairly cut-and-dried; if we want to lower the
crime rate once and for all, we will have to do a much better job of
providing access to work—especially for those groups, like minorities and
the young, who have been most excluded from its benefits.

So far, all this seems fairly obvious; and it has been a staple argument of
liberal criminology for decades. But as it turns out, the relationship
between crime and unemployment is surprisingly controversial. Not
everyone agrees that unemployment has much to do with crime; and of
those who do, not all agree that there is much we can do about it.

For instance, despite the stark evidence supplied by the work histories
of those in prison, James Q. Wilson writes that "contrary to what many
people assert, very little research shows a relationship between economic

factors and crime." For most conservative writers, it follows that improving the prospects for economic security cannot have much effect on the crime rate. More generally, the argument that unemployment is only minimally related to crime serves to focus attention on more "individual" factors—temperament, family practices, perhaps genetic abnormalities— which are presumably less amenable to social intervention. All this is confusing, to say the least, and it contributes greatly to the paralysis that afflicts our public policies toward crime.

It is also misleading. The relationships between unemployment and crime are real; we won't be able even to begin an attack on crime that is both humane and effective if we do not confront them. But these relationships are more complicated than they might seem at first glance, and they deserve careful analysis.

One line of argument dismisses the connections between unemployment and crime on the grounds that there is no good evidence that the crime rate responds strongly to economic *fluctuations*. Conservatives point especially to rising crime in the prosperity of the 1960s and its apparent decline in the Depression of the 1930s. And it's true that formal research on crime and economic fluctuations presents a mixed picture.

The connections between crime rates and the ups and downs of the economy were studied by several noted American scholars in the twenties, and the coming of the Great Depression in the thirties gave the issue new urgency. Many of these early studies were so poorly designed that, as the University of Pennsylvania criminologist Thorsten Sellin concluded in a well-known monograph for the Social Science Research Council in 1937, it was "difficult to arrive at any generalizations" from their results. But two of the most sophisticated efforts in that period—Dorothy S. Thomas's 1927 "Social Aspects of the Business Cycle" and Emma Winslow's study of crime and employment in Massachusetts, commissioned as part of the work of the National Commission on Law Observance and Enforcement in 1931—found strong associations between economic downturns and some kinds of crime, especially what Thomas called "crimes against property with violence"—robbery, housebreaking, and burglary.

Interest in the effect of "hard times" on crime waned in the prosperous postwar era; it was revived only in the gloomier seventies, most notably by the sociologist M. Harvey Brenner of Johns Hopkins University. In a series of studies covering a variety of countries and time periods, Brenner has consistently found chillingly precise correlations between changes in the overall unemployment rate and several measures of crime, including national homicide rates and admissions to state prisions. Thus in 1970, according to Brenner, an increase in the American unemployment rate of one percentage point accounted for nearly 4 percent of that year's homicides, almost 6 percent of its robberies, and close to 9 percent of narcotics arrests. Brenner attributes these tragic effects of unemployment only partly to the pressures of income loss suffered by those out of work; equally important is what Brenner calls the *compound-interest effect* of unemployment on crime rates. Unemployment aggravates two other social pathologies that everyone agrees are closely related to both violent and property crimes: drug and alcohol abuse. Losing a job leads to drug abuse, and drug abuse leads to property crime. Alcohol consumption, Brenner argues, also rises dramatically during economic slumps, and drinking in turn is closely associated with serious violent crime. Moreover, unemployment disrupts family ties by forcing the jobless to migrate in search of work; and this, too, in Brenner's view, leads to higher crime rates.

Brenner has made the strongest recent argument for a clear-cut relationship between national unemployment rates and crime. Other studies in the past two decades have been less confident. On balance, the studies provide what the economist Robert Gillespie, in a 1975 review of the evidence, called "general, if not uniform, support" for the commonsense belief that unemployment rates are related to crime. The kernel of truth in the conservative argument—and it is an important one—is that many careful scholars have found at best what the economists Thomas Orsagh and Ann Dryden Witte call "weak" associations between national-level changes in unemployment rates and crime. Why?

Part of the problem involves technical, methodological difficulties inherent in this kind of research . . . : it is very sensitive to the specific assumptions that are made about what other factors might influence crime rates. Depending on how such factors as age distribution or sentencing policies are entered into the equation, researchers of equal honesty and scrupulousness may well come up with strikingly different conclusions.

But the deeper and more crucial issues involve several ambiguities in the relationship between unemployment and crime itself. These do not disprove the importance of the connection between crime and work; indeed, they strengthen it. But they do mean that we have to view that connection through a more refined lens. The ambiguities fall under three general headings:

1. Unemployment itself appears to have *contradictory* effects on crime.
2. The official unemployment rate alone (on which most of this research has been based) is a poor guide to the true significance of the relationships between employment and crime.
3. Those relationships are affected by a number of intervening factors, including public policies and the level of community support, that do not generally show up in quantitative research.

The first complexity is that, while unemployment tends to increase crime in some ways, it may tend to decrease it in others. In particular, it may restrict the *opportunities* for some kinds of crime, even while increasing the motivation to commit them. Thus, as Lawrence Cohen, Marcus Felson, and Kenneth Land have argued, increases in unemployment may reduce the chances of being robbed by keeping potential victims at home, out of "transit" areas—areas between home and the workplace. By the same token, the fact that unemployed workers spend more time at home restricts opportunities for residential burglary. Looking at rates of robbery, burglary, and auto theft from the late 1940s to the early 1970s, Cohen, Felson, and Land found a "modest" but noticeable association between increases in unemployment and decreases in these crimes. (A somewhat similar argument was made in the late fifties by the sociologists Daniel Glaser and Kent Rice to explain their finding that high levels of unemployment seemed to go hand in hand with increased crime among adults but decreased crime among juveniles. In times of high unemployment, they reasoned, unemployed parents would spend more time at home—and thus give more time and attention to the behavior of their children.) It follows that the same mechanisms probably work in the other direction as well: widespread economic prosperity can increase crimes like robbery and burglary by multiplying the opportunities to commit them.

Another, still more crucial, set of complications arises from the clumsiness of our standard measures of unemployment. At first glance there might seem to be few things simpler than to determine what it means to be unemployed; but in fact, as critics have long pointed out, the conventional definition of unemployment embodied in the official rates obscures more than it reveals. To begin with, it lumps together what are actually widely different experiences among people with very different propensities toward serious crime. In terms of its effects on crime rates, for example, unemployment clearly means one thing in the case of a forty-year-old machinist with three children, a mortgage, and a twenty-year work history who has just lost his job, and another if we're talking about an eighteen-year-old inner-city dropout who has never held a job for more than three months, may never in the future, and knows it. The official rate tells us nothing by itself about the differences between the pain of being out of work for six months and the demoralization of a lifetime with minimal prospects for work. Similarly, because the rate is *national*, it obscures differences at the level of local communities, where, arguably, they count the most. National changes in unemployment may have little effect on the job situation in communities that face persistently high unemployment through good times and bad. When we do focus on specific neighborhoods, the connections between crime and unemployment emerge dramatically. A recent study by Robert Sampson and Thomas Castellano, for example, found that victimization rates were 80 percent higher for crimes of theft and 40 percent higher for crimes of violence in urban neighborhoods with high unemployment than in those with low.

Most important, the strength of the unemployment-crime relationship is obscured by what the official definition of unemployment leaves out. In the first place, it omits great numbers of people who do not have jobs. We count as "unemployed" only those who describe themselves as "looking for work." But if we want to know how the lack of work affects the crime rate, this is misleading. It's logical, after all, that those of the jobless who are still sufficiently hopeful and attached to the world of legitimate work to be actually looking for jobs are *less* likely to be involved in serious crime than those uncounted others who have given up the search for a job—or who have never begun it.

Thus research that has broadened its focus to include people who are both jobless and not in search of work—those who, in economic language, are not "participating in the labor force"—has come up with stronger associations between joblessness and crime than research using the official category of "unemployment" alone. In one of the most careful of these studies, the economists Llad Phillips and Harold Votey of the University of California at Santa Barbara tried to determine how much of the dramatic rise in youth crime in the sixties could be attributed to changes in the labor-market opportunities open to youth. Much had been made (and still is) of the supposed "paradox" of increasing crime in the face of declining *overall* unemployment rates in the sixties. But Phillips and Votey pointed out that despite the *general* improvement in the national unemployment rate, another crucial trend was a simultaneous rise in the unemployment rate for youths—particularly nonwhites—and an even more precipitous drop in their labor-force participation. In 1952, for example, the official unemployment rate for nonwhite men aged eighteen and nineteen was about 10 percent; by 1967 it had reached 20 percent. This took place even though the unemployment rate for the country as a whole was about 3 percent in both years. Measured by their participation in the labor force, the position of youth was even worse; the proportion of nonwhite youths either at work or actively looking for work dropped from nearly 80 percent in 1952 to just 63 percent in 1967. Part of this shift is explainable by the fact that a greater proportion were in school, but not all of it. The harsh fact was that by the late sixties, more youths, especially blacks, were neither working, looking for work, nor pursuing an education. How did that change affect the crime rate?

According to Phillips and Votey, very strongly indeed—so strongly, in fact, that these changes in the labor market were *by themselves* "sufficient to explain increasing crime rates for youths" in the sixties. The most powerful associations between joblessness and youth crime, they found, emerged when they divided their sample into youths who were in the labor force (either working or looking for work) and those who were out of it—those who neither had jobs nor sought them. This distinction was a more accurate predictor of youth crime rates than the more conventional contrast between youths who were working and those who were not. In short, what seemed most closely related to crime among youths was not just being out of work but being so *far* out of work that they had ceased to look for it. To Philips and Votey, this suggested that what principally influenced youth crime was not the *current* state of the economy so much as the long-term experience of fundamentally constricted economic opportunities, an experience that had convinced many urban minority youths that not much was to be gained by looking for a job.

Clearly, then, we need to broaden the focus of investigation beyond the conventional measure of unemployment to include other forms of joblessness. But we need to broaden the terms of our discussion in another way as well; for what the narrow emphasis on the unemployment rate ignores is the larger, ultimately more crucial, issue of how the *quality* of work affects the crime rate. One of the most consistent findings in recent research is that *un*employment is less strongly associated with serious crime than *under*employment—the prospect of working, perhaps forever, in jobs that cannot provide a decent or stable livelihood, a sense of social purpose, or a modicum of self-esteem. As the economist Ann Dryden Witte puts it, "It is not so much individual unemployment per se which causes crime, but rather the failure to find relatively high-wage, satisfying employment." What is at issue, Witte concluded after reviewing the evidence in the late seventies, is "economic viability, rather than just employment per se."

The idea that crime might be linked with the larger problem of inadequate and unstable work, not just the absence of work altogether, is not new. "The kind of labor which requires the most skill on the part of the workman to perform," Carroll D. Wright argued in 1878, "insures the laborer most perfectly against want and crime." Furthermore, he wrote, the benefits of skilled work were passed down across the generations through their elevating effects on family life. "The occupation of the parents has a wonderful effect upon the character and tendencies of their children." The character of work, in other words, shaped the character of individuals in enduring ways; and to Wright, the implication was "so self-evident that it is to my own mind axiomatic in nature." The upgrading of labor—that "elevating process which would make self-supporting citizens out of the unfortunate and criminal classes"—would "conduce to the relief and protection of the community, the alleviation of the condition of the poor and helpless, the judicious punishment of the wicked, and the practical reformation of the vagrant and criminal." "Employers should remember," Wright insisted,

> that if conditions become ameliorated, if life becomes less of a struggle, if leisure be obtained, civilization, as a general rule, grows up. If these conditions be reversed, if the struggle for existence tends to occupy the whole attention of each man, civilization disappears in a measure, communities become dangerous. . . . The undue subjection of the laboring man must tend to make paupers and criminals, and entail a financial burden upon wealth which it would have been easier to prevent than to endure.

Wright's central point—that an economy that condemns many to "drudgery" as well as to frequent unemployment will be neither just nor safe—still holds true today. It is the condition of being locked into what some economists call the "secondary labor market"—low-level, poorly paying, unstable jobs that cannot support a family and that offer little opportunity for advancement—that is most likely to breed crime. Curiously enough, the same conservatives who continually point to the studies that suggest weaker connections between unemployment and crime rates have not usually gone on to acknowledge that the same research also confirms that *inadequate* employment does matter—and matters a lot.

Some of the most revealing findings come from research at New York's Vera Institute of Justice. In one study, the Vera researchers interviewed a sample of men released from the Riker's Island prison in New York City in the late seventies. These were mainly young, minority men who had been convicted of a variety of misdemeanors, mostly crimes against property, and had usually served time before. Most were also poorly educated: less than a third had a high-school diploma or its equivalent, another third never got past the ninth grade. Some had fairly solid job histories, but most didn't; a few had never worked in their lives. Of those who *had* worked, only about half had ever held a job for more than a year; a third had never kept a job for longer than six months. And even those who had had a reasonably solid connection with the labor market in the past had often lost it well before their current spells in prison. Only 16 percent had been working immediately before the arrest that had put them behind bars.

Not only did these men have a decidedly loose relation to the world of work, but with few exceptions the jobs they did hold were "low level and paid poorly": two-thirds of the jobs paid less than $125 a week, in a year when it took almost that amount just to reach the federal poverty level; just 14 percent paid more than $175.

The Vera researchers expected that the careers of these men would exhibit fairly clear-cut and direct connections between unemployment and crime. Instead, as interviews with the men over the space of several months revealed, things were more complicated.

For some of these offenders, work and crime seemed indeed to be, as the Vera researchers put it, mutually exclusive activities; they either worked or stole. "If you're working and you see something you want," one interviewee told them, "you wonder how you're going to save enough to buy it. If you're not working and you see something you want, you wonder how you're going to take it." Some felt that losing a job had been directly responsible for their turning to crime—either because of the loss of income or indirectly, because it led to depression, idleness, and drug use. Others both worked and stole at the same time, but stole much more when they were out of work. All these patterns fit, in one way or another, the researchers' initial expectations. But other patterns also turned up. For a few of the men, working actually *encouraged* their criminality. Some used their jobs as a cover for drug sales. One worked in order to buy enough drugs to resume a career as a dealer. Another, in a truly complex pattern, worked at casual labor in order to buy enough heroin so that he would feel well enough to go out and steal at night. Others simply stole whatever they could from the places they worked. Thus, another respondent, one of the few who had found work since release, claimed he "never had a job where he did not steal."

> When he worked in a hospital, he stole baby socks, sheets, and embalming fluid (which he sold to marijuana dealers to enhance "bad reefer"). When he worked in a bank training program, he stole $50 as soon as he had the chance. His heaviest offense, for which he served four years in an upstate prison, came when he committed an armed robbery at the office building where he worked, having observed when the greatest amount of cash would be out of the safe. He claimed to have worked thirty days since his release cleaning floors at a large discount store, where he reports stealing four television sets, ten tennis outfits, and six pairs of sneakers.

A more common pattern was to alternate between legitimate work and small-scale crime. Men would take jobs for as long as they could handle the boredom, harassment, and low pay that usually came with them, or as long as they felt constrained against replacing petty work with petty crime by the risks of arrest. But these jobs could not hold them for long, and they soon moved back into street crime. What comes out most clearly in Vera's interviews with these men is the relative attractiveness of crime—even the small-time property crimes most of them engaged in—when balanced against the inadequacy of the work available. "If the job pays good, I'll go to the job," one respondent acknowledged; "if the street is good, I'll go back to the street." Over and over, the interviews show how thoroughly the tenuous, unsatisfying work roles available to these men are simply outclassed by the potential rewards of the street. "That's one thing I don't like about jobs," another respondent told the interviewers. "Out on the street . . . I can make close to $300 a night if I were to stay out there 5 or 6 hours . . . whereas if I was working I would make close to $200 in two weeks."

Revealingly, the Vera respondents were "generally far more animated when discussing successful criminals and crime fantasies than they were when defining the kind of job they would 'most like to have'"; they "could more easily envision themselves in grander roles in crime than their daily lives in the legitimate world of work allowed." "Apparently," the Vera researchers conclude, "at least in imagination, there are fewer barriers to upward mobility in crime than in employment."*

---

*That inability even to envision clearly what kind of work they would *like* to do fits a pattern I have seen in conducting interviews with hard-core drug-addicted offenders in California. It was hard to talk with these men and women for very long without realizing that they simply did not think in positive terms, even on the level of fantasy, about what

It's understandable that these poor expectations for decent work might breed the patterns of alternating low-level work and petty property crime documented in the Vera study. But there is also considerable evidence that the same alienated relationship to productive work is deeply implicated in *violent* crime as well. This connection emerges starkly in interviews conducted by researchers at the URSA Institute in San Francisco, who were particularly interested in any characteristics that distinguished violent delinquents from other young offenders. They interviewed sixty-three youths in juvenile prisons in four cities; each was guilty of a violent felony and had been convicted of at least one similar crime in the past. They concluded that "youth employment per se does not reduce delinquency"; but that the *quality* of work—its "status, skills, promotions, wages"—strongly affects all kinds of delinquent behavior, especially serious violence. "Where working youths perceive growth, benefits, and tangible rewards from their employment," the study concludes, "they commit fewer of each type of offense." And "work quality" was precisely what was most lacking in the communities from which these youths came; indeed, these young men "identified few lifestyle choices in their neighborhoods other than criminal activity or idleness."

One reason why this narrowing of choices so conduces to violence is that it makes *illicit* work—like selling drugs—relatively attractive, as the comments in the Vera study suggest. And since disputes over markets or "turf" in illegal occupations cannot be resolved through legal means, force and violence are typically used instead. Deadly weapons have always been a hallmark of illegal work, a fact that helps account for the appearance of peaks in American homicide rates in the twenties—during Prohibition—and from the late sixties onward, when hard drugs spread virulently in American cities. (Close to a third of the homicides in Oakland, California, in 1983 and 1984 were related to drug dealing; most of the victims were young black men—or innocent bystanders.) Reducing the central role of drug dealing in the subterranean economy of the inner cities would surely lower the violent crime rate; but it has proven hard to do (despite heavy penalties . . .) when legitimate labor markets have offered so few attractive alternatives.

The accumulating evidence, then, tells us that it is not just the fact of having or not having a job that is most important, nor is the level of crime most strongly or consistently affected by fluctuations in the national unemployment rate. The more consistent influence is the *quality* of

---

"straight" life had to offer. They could complain about the shortcomings of the jobs they sporadically held and discourse at length about both the benefits and the pains of street life, but if you asked them what they would do if they could do what they wanted—what kind of work they would like to do, what they would like to learn—they had great trouble thinking of anything and often barely understood the question.

work—its stability, its level of pay, its capacity to give the workers a sense of dignity and participation, the esteem of peers and community. In our society these fundamental needs are virtually impossible to satisfy without a job—but they are all too often difficult even *with* a job, and nearly impossible in many of the kinds of jobs available in America today, especially to the disadvantaged young. Whether work can avert crime, in short, depends on whether it is part of a larger process through which the young are gradually integrated into a productive and valued role in a larger community. Similarly, whether unemployment leads to crime depends heavily on whether it is a temporary interruption of a longer and more hopeful trajectory into that kind of role, or represents a permanent condition of economic marginality that virtually assures a sense of purposelessness, alienation, and deprivation.

Obviously, this has more than theoretical relevance. It suggests . . . that efforts to force the young, the marginal, and the deprived into *any* kind of work, however ill rewarded and demeaning, are likely to be futile at best and destructive at worst. If we wish to build a less volatile and violent society, we will need to concentrate on improving the long-term prospects for stable and valued work for those now largely excluded from it.

38

Crack Dilemmas in Search of an Answer

Jerome H. Skolnick

Public anger about drug dealers, street crime, and violence is justifiable. But outrage will take us only so far. Unfortunately, the Bush-Bennett "War on Drugs," which calls for an "unprecedented" expansion of police, prosecutors, courts, and prisons, in addition to military force and interdiction, seems more an expression of outrage than a sound appreciation of the limits of law enforcement. Mr. Bennett and President Bush seem to believe that we have been losing the war on drugs because of a lack of resolve, but I believe the reasons are more fundamental and that it is not fair to ask law enforcement to take responsibility for solving the drug problem in our society.

Why can't we ask law enforcement to shoulder the responsibility? Because, in thinking about what might work and what won't, we need to appreciate the conundrums law enforcement officers face when they are trying to combat crimes involving the sale of an illegal and highly addictive product. The Bennett-Bush *National Drug Control Strategy* (the red book that the president held up in his address to the nation on drug policy, along with the now famous bag of crack) acknowledges that "Despite interdiction's successful disruptions of trafficking patterns, the supply of illegal drugs entering the United States has, by all estimates, continued to grow." Why should that have happened? No matter how hard federal, state, and local police officers try, they encounter frustrating dilemmas. What are some of those dilemmas?

Adapted from Jerome H. Skolnick, "A Critical Look at the National Drug Control Strategy," Yale Law and Policy Review, vol. 8, No. 1, 1990.

THE DEMAND-SUPPLY DILEMMA

Demand generates supply—for drugs just as for video cassette recorders. United States and European demand for drugs has contributed to a rise in the number of producers from a variety of producing countries. Some of these are political allies; others are not. Key is the fact that demand has generated multiple drug producers, followed by a rise in production, with a subsequent drop in price. As Edmundo Morales has observed in his splendid book, *Cocaine: White Gold Rush in Peru*, "Unquestionably, drug production and traffic in Peru have addicted thousands of people to illegal sources of hard cash."[1] Price reduction in turn further invigorates demand, which stimulates the whole cycle over again.

THE DARWINIAN TRAFFICKER DILEMMA

Mr. Bennett and the president acknowledge that "As we have expanded our interdiction efforts we have seized increasing amounts of illegal drugs. Stepped up interdiction has also forced drug traffickers to make significant operational changes. . . . Every time we disrupt or close a particular trafficking route, we have found that traffickers resort to other smuggling tactics that are even more difficult to detect."[2]

This is undoubtedly true, but it seem to argue against, rather than for, the stepped up interdiction advocated by the *National Drug Control Strategy*. As we develop increasingly sophisticated tactics for reducing both narcotic production and smuggling, only the stronger and more efficient producers and smugglers survive. This in turn heightens supply and lowers cost. As this occurs, suppliers seek wider markets, particularly in distressed populations, just as segments of the alcohol and tobacco industries do.

THE BORDERS-ARE-A-SIEVE DILEMMA

Can the borders be sealed? Not according to Rand Corporation economist Peter Reuter, who studied the question for the Department of Defense. The Mexican border is especially permeable. There are few barriers from the south to bringing drugs into that country, and the drugs can be "brought across by small plane, private vehicle, or even by boat."[3] A Mexican-American California narcotics agent made a similar observation to me in an interview in 1989: "Four hundred thousand of my people cross the border every year. How can you stop a much smaller number who are carrying a kilo or two of cocaine on their back?"

THE IRRELEVANCE-OF-SMUGGLING-COSTS DILEMMA

Interdiction is supposed to reduce street sales by increasing production and smuggling costs—in effect, taxing these—and thus raising the street price. This assumes that production and smuggling costs constitute a significant percentage of street price. But that simply is not true. It is relatively cheap to produce and refine a kilo of cocaine: perhaps around $1,000 for a kilo that might eventually, when broken down into quarter or even eight-gram units, retail for $250,000.

Smuggling costs might amount to an additional few percentages of the retail price. Most of the retail price is divided among those who distribute it on this side of the border. Rand Corporation economist Peter Reuter writes, "Fully 99 percent of the price of the drug when sold on the streets in the United States is accounted for by payments to people who distribute it."[4] Thus, a doubling or tripling of smuggling costs would have a negligible impact on street price. As we know, street prices of cocaine have dropped dramatically, by 60–75 percent since the Reagan administration introduced its "War on Drugs" in 1982, headed by then Vice-President Bush. The evidence suggests that interdiction has had little, if any, positive effects and that these can be outweighed by unanticipated side effects.

THE DRUG HARDENING PARADOX

When the Nixon administration succeeded in reducing the supply of low-potency Mexican marijuana to California in the early 1970s, agriculturally skilled drug entrepreneurs developed a high-potency marijuana (sensimilla) industry in northern California, generating a market for a drug five or more times as potent. The paradox is this: the more successful law enforcement is at cutting off supply, the more incentive drug dealers have for hardening drugs, for developing varieties that are more potent, portable, and dangerous. The recent crackdown by state narcotics agents on California marijuana fields has reduced the supply. But crack cocaine is presently less expensive and more available on California streets than marijuana. In sum, law enforcement tactics may create more severe public health problems by generating demand for, and production of, more profitable and dangerous drugs.

Contemporary interdiction policy, and its expansion as advocated by the Bush-Bennett strategy, is grounded in an assumption of the stability of drug preference among those who enjoy faster living through chemistry. We know from history that drug preference, the epidemiology of drug use, is less related to the intrinsic properties of a drug than to the social definition of a particular substance as the drug of choice. Twenty or 30 years ago, heroin was the "problem" drug in American society. Today it is crack cocaine.

But suppose we actually could destroy the Peruvian, Bolivian, and Colombian cocaine fields? Lurking in the background are a variety of manufactured drugs. It is likely that underground chemists could design and manufacture what addicts would consider the ideal drug—one with the kick of crack and the longevity of crank (methamphetamine). If we succeed in destroying agricultural drugs, we could find ourselves looking at a designer drug problem more potent and destructive than anything we have yet seen. Indeed, a powerful new drug, a colorless and odorless form of crystal methamphetamine—street name "ice"—is said to be sweeping Hawaii and is threatening to invade the West Coast ports of San Francisco, Los Angeles, and Portland. Should that happen, it would only be a matter of time before the drug found its way across the country to replace crack as the drug of choice during the 1990s. The only good news "ice" will bring is its economic challenge to the Medellin cartel, but it is doubtful that the distributors of the new drug will prove more concerned with public health than the cocaine producers.

THE OFFICIAL GREED DILEMMA

Whatever the latest fashion in drug use, manufacturers, smugglers, and distributors can operate more efficiently by corrupting public officials. Law enforcement corruption is not discussed in the *National Drug Control Strategy*, although "turf battles" among federal enforcement agencies are. That discussion is acceptable because agency rivalry is a normal and acceptable aspect of bureaucratic processes. Corruption is, by contrast, an unmentionable. But it has to be a serious side effect of expanded law enforcement efforts. As we attempt to put pressure on foreign producers, we will have to work with authorities in such countries as Colombia, Bolivia, Panama, and Peru. The bribe is a familiar part of law enforcement in these countries. Thus, the State Department's Bureau of International Narcotics Matters finds that Jorge Luis Ochoa, a major Colombian drug trafficker "was able to buy his freedom through the intimidated and vulnerable Colombian judicial system." And Tina Rosenberg observes in *The New Republic:*

> In general, the closer an institution gets to the traffickers, the more cor-
> rupt it becomes. Cocaine's new income opportunities for judges have
> been well documented. Prosecutors are less corrupt, but it is a matter of
> logistics, not morals: it is simply easier to win cases by bribing judges,
> or the police. . . . Policemen, the infantry in the war on drugs, are usu-
> ally young men from slum neighborhoods with third grade educations—
> exactly the profile of a drug dealer, and the line between the two tends
> to blur on the job.[5]

What of our urban police? Unfortunately, we are all too familiar with the legendary narcotics scandals that have bedeviled the police in various cities. Perhaps the most famous have occurred in New York City, beginning with the Knapp Commission investigations, including not only narcotics, but other forms of vice as well. Patrick V. Murphy was recruited as a reform police commissioner in New York in the wake of the scandal uncovered by the Knapp Commission. In his autobiography he writes:

> [W]e ultimately discovered that the narcotics units under the previous police administration had made major contributions to the city's drug traffic. It was this area of corruption more than anything else which most shocked me.[6]

Narcotics corruption is not confined to New York City or to the East Coast. Deputies in the Los Angeles County Sheriff's Department were recently involved in what *The Los Angeles Times* called "one of the worst corruption cases" in the Department's history. A videotape shows one deputy hurriedly taking three $10,000 bundles of $100 bills from a dealer's shoulder bag and putting them into his partner's leather briefcase. Although the possibilities of corruption obtain in any form of vice enforcement, only in drug enforcement do we encounter large sums of cash and drugs held by perpetrators who are in no position to complain about being ripped off by police.

By no means am I suggesting that all narcotics police are corrupt. On the contrary, any number of aware police managers, for whom Patrick Murphy has served as an example of the thoughtful and honest police executive, struggle with the potential problem. The Los Angeles deputies were caught in a sting operation conducted by Sheriff Sherman Block. I am suggesting that it is difficult to uncover narcotics corruption, particularly when a small number of individuals are involved; that whatever is discovered has to be the tip of the corruption iceberg; and that corruption needs to be counted as one of the anticipated costs of an unprecedented expansion of drug law enforcement.

THE LOCK-EM-UP DILEMMA

State and federal prison populations have virtually doubled in the 1980s and have tripled since the 1960s. Overcrowded jails and prisons are bulging with newly convicted criminals and also with criminals whose probation and parole were revoked largely because they failed their drug tests when they were released into the community. California, for example, had a 3,200 percent increase of parole violators returned to prison between 1978 and 1988. By the end of 1989, more than 1 million of our fellow Americans will be behind bars. Projected from Department of Justice figures by The Sentencing Project of Washington D.C., the total will include 731,978 in federal and state prisons, and 341,851 in local jails—1,073,829 altogether.

But, as our advanced drug-testing technology consigns more parolees and probationers to prison, we find we cannot continue to convict and impose longer sentences without building new prisons. Mr. Bennett and President Bush recognize the critical lack of prison space as we expand law enforcement. They acknowledge that "Most state prisons are already operating far above their designed capacity."[7] And they also recognize that "many states have been forced under court order to release prisoners before their terms have been served whenever a court-established prison population limit has been exceeded."[8] Their solution? That state governments should persuade their citizens to support the building of new prisons. "The task of building [prisons]" they write, "remains with state governments, who poorly serve their constituents when prison construction is stalled or resisted."[9]

But there is not a word in *The National Drug Control Strategy* about how to finance, staff, and pay for the continuing and rising expense of maintaining prisons. Unfortunately, most citizens have read the president's lips. But perhaps they have misread them. Evidently, the slogan "No New Taxes" applies only to the federal government. But, if state governments are to serve their citizens, as President Bush and Mr. Bennett exhort, they will have to raise taxes.

Even those citizens who demand longer and more certain sentences are reluctant to pay for prisons and understandably are even more reluctant to live next door to them. Highly publicized plans for a 700-bed prison to house convicted Washington, D.C., drug dealers at Fort Meade, Md., were withdrawn—with embarrassment—the day after they were announced, *The New York Times* reported, because "There was too much public resistance."[10]

THE PRISON NETWORKING DILEMMA

Even if we could build new prisons, imprisonment is neither necessarily stigmatic nor entirely foreboding for those who sell drugs. My students and I have been for the past year and one-half interviewing imprisoned California drug dealers. Imprisonment may offer a kind of "homeboy" status, especially for gang youth, for whom the prison can become an alternative neighborhood. Moreover, imprisonment often motivates prisoners in their troublesome ways. Consigned to the margins of society anyhow, in prison they join gangs, use drugs, and make useful connections for buying and selling drugs. The penitentiary was perhaps once a place for experiencing penance. Today's correctional institutions, overcrowded as they are with short-term parole violators (many of whom have failed their court-mandated drug tests), often serve functions similar to those that conventions perform for academics and business people—as an opportunity for networking.

THE FELIX MITCHELL PARADOX

This dilemma is named in honor of the West Coast's formerly most infamous drug distributor. In the mid-1980s, a Federal Strike Force, with considerable assistance and dogged investigation by an incorruptible Oakland police vice squad, succeeded in convicting and imprisoning the East Bay's three leading drug dealers. Among these was the legendary Felix Mitchell, who was later killed in Leavenworth federal prison and was a hero to the thousands who turned out for his funeral. Theoretically, Oakland's streets should have been cleansed of drugs. Did that happen? Hardly. The main result was a drop in price and a rise in street homicides and felonious assaults by gang members as they challenged each other for market share. As territorial arrangements have stabilized, so has the homicide rate, but the street price of crack has remained about the same or has declined.

POLICE STRATEGIES

Is there *anything* law enforcement can do to impair the crack cocaine trade? There is little evidence to support the effectiveness of the law enforcement initiatives the Bush administration proposes. Several of my colleagues at the Center for the Study of Law and Society and I recently evaluated such an initiative in Alameda County (Oakland), California. The sharp rise in drug selling and violence there persuaded the legislature and the governor to provide $4 million from 1985 to 1987 to bolster and expand prosecution, probation, and the courts—just the sort of expansion advocated by the *National Drug Control Strategy*. Following an ethnographic and statistical evaluation, we concluded that all of the law enforcement agencies carried out their mandate thoroughly and professionally, and that the intermediate goals of more prosecutions, more convictions, and more probation violations were met. That was the good news. The bad news was that it didn't seem to much matter. Crime, and narcotics crime in particular, continued to increase. So we concluded that, contrary to popular mythology, "The rise in narcotics crime in Alameda County cannot be attributed to inefficient courts, prosecutors, probation officers or police."

Still, of all the law enforcement initiatives, the least effective will be those aimed at military interdiction, and the most satisfying—at least initially—will be those involving the community and local police. The *National Drug Control Strategy* argues that "The first challenge facing our criminal justice system is to help reclaim neighborhoods that have been rendered unsafe by drugs."[11] In a recent National Institute of Justice publication, Mark Kleiman, a proponent of street level drug enforcement, points to two special threats that street drug dealing poses: that children may become users and that street dealing may become disruptive or violent.

There is much disagreement, however, about the effectiveness of neighborhood police crackdowns. In the same publication, prosecutor Kevin Burke favors street level enforcement, arguing that "[W]hen balanced against the environment of an open drug market, a visible, active police presence is not a tremendous intrusion and therefore not a significant cost of a street-level operation."[12] Thus, although initiatives like New York City's Tactical Narcotics Team's, Operation Pressure Point street-oriented law enforcement are limited in their effectiveness, at least they are directly responsive to citizen calls for assistance. Of course, drug dealers may displace their operations in response to police initiatives, but a police presence may be valuable in reducing fear of crime, if not crime itself.

At the same time, some law enforcement officials are skeptical about the positive effects of crackdowns. Minneapolis Police Chief Anthony Bouza writes:

> Focused, saturation street enforcement will clean up an area, but it is costly and inefficient. It robs other areas of their fair share of scarce resources and it does not eliminate the intractable problem of drug dealing, merely displaces it. It also focuses, inefficiently, on the lowest level of the criminal chain and is sure to lead to abuses and repression, with sweeps and round-ups.[13]

So it is not clear how to repair the damage drug dealing imposes on local communities and what the costs are of an expanded police effort in this direction. Still, so long as demand remains, local law enforcement initiatives are at least responsive to the complaints of law-abiding residents whose neighborhoods are undercut by street dealers and crack houses. Since public safety and civility should be law enforcement's highest priority, that's where I'd put my restricted law enforcement funds. At the same time, we need to understand that law enforcement is merely a holding operation and that we need to address the underlying causes of drug selling and addiction in our society before we can hope for a solution.

Millions of Americans have tried using illegal drugs. Although marijuana use declined in the 1980s, according to NIDA's 1985 National Survey on Drug Abuse, an estimated 61.9 million people over age 12 had used marijuana at least once in their lifetime, and about 18.2 million were current users, perhaps because they found it difficult to distinguish the harmful effects of illegal drugs from those of the legal variety. Moral arguments would surely have more force if, as a nation, we expressed consistent messages about health. Robert Wadman is the chief of police of Omaha, Nebraska, one of a string of heartland American cities where drugs are a daily police problem. "We adults," he observed to a *New York Times* interviewer, "are staggering around with a vodka in one hand and a government-subsidized cigarette in the other, telling our kids they shouldn't use mind altering substances that are bad for their health. Now what's the lesson you would draw from that?"[14]

CRACK COCAINE

The contemporary concern with drugs, the war-on-drugs rhetoric, has escalated partly in conjunction with street violence and partly with the relatively recent invention of the infamous distillate, crack cocaine. The two are doubtless related. Crack cocaine is purified, heat stable cocaine that is suitable for smoking. "Absorbed across the pulmonary vascular bed," write the neurologists Golbe and Merkin, "it produces a more intense euphoria and more precipitous withdrawal than Cocaine HCL (powder cocaine) and is therefore more addictive. It has come into widespread use since 1984."[15]

Crack cocaine is an underground drug designer's method of safely freebasing by a simple process of adding baking soda and heating. Freebasing is not a new technology, but it used to be accomplished by heating the cocaine with volatile chemicals. That can be very dangerous, as Richard Pryor discovered when, in a widely publicized incident, he set himself afire preparing free-base cocaine with ether.

Heat stable cocaine is a superior commercial product because it is relatively pure, is easier to handle than a powder, is safer than free-basing with ether, and is cost effective, offering a bigger bang for the buck because it is more quickly absorbed by smoking. By contrast, nasal ingestion limits the drug's impact because cocaine constricts small blood vessels and slows absorption to the brain.

Last summer, when my students and I interviewed imprisoned drug dealers about gangs, the organization of street crack cocaine dealing, and drug enforcement, we were also interested in amplifying the description of effects one finds in the medical journals with the perceptions of the street user. One of our respondents, who used to free-base, graphically described the attractions of crack. He said:

> It's not addicting like your body craves it. You're not going to get sick and shit by not smoking. Only thing that craves crack is your mind. It's like an illusion. You hit the pipe, you are whatever you want to be. You're into basketball, you *are* Magic Johnson. You're into music, you are Michael Jackson.

In sum, crack cocaine is a compelling, psychologically, but not physiologically, addicting drug, which transports users from where they are to where they fantasize they want to be. We may speculate that the more satisfied and engaged people are with their lives, the less likely it is that they will use the drug. This speculation is supported by one of our most surprising findings. This was the reported absence of crack cocaine use by dealers, who, after all, have the most access to the drug. A California dealer I interviewed told me:

> I never use (crack) cocaine; it's not real when they say that a person that
> sells ends up using his drugs; that's not true, he's like an out-
> cast . . . you get beat up, dogged out; nobody respects you anymore, it
> turns you scandalous; the shit will make you steal from your mama.

Terry Williams, in his impressive ethnographic account of teenage drug dealers in New York City, makes a similar observation. Successful crack dealers virtually all use marijuana, and some use powder cocaine but consider use of crack cocaine a business impediment.

So drug dealers, who have as much access to the drug as anyone, are able to defer its gratifications in the interests of the entrepreneurial imperative. In sum, although crack cocaine is surely a compelling drug, those who are addicted to hard cash are able to forego its pleasures. The *National Drug Control Strategy* entirely misses this point and its implications for the relation between drug dealing and economic opportunity.

LEGALIZATION

Ultimately, the *National Drug Control Strategy* is a political document, and no politician can be criticized for taking a tough attitude toward drugs. If anything, President Bush and Mr. Bennett's political opponents have criticized them for barking louder than they bite. At the other end of the spectrum are numbers of thoughtful people—legislators, city officials, police, prosecutors, scholars—who despair of controlling drugs through criminal law enforcement. For them, legalization is increasingly being proposed as an alternative. Would it be a good one? It might, but we need to think through how legalization would play out if it were implemented, whether we are talking about all drugs or only some, what the benefits and costs would be and to whom, and whether legalization can be reconciled with a positive moral message.

Let's consider two possible legalization models. Under the least restrictive, the free-market model, all psychoactive drugs would be freely available. This model would treat such substances as we treat aspirin, alcohol, and other over-the-counter drugs. Supermarkets could sell—and anyone could purchase—unlimited supplies. Considerable benefits would flow: since all drugs would be licit, we could reasonably speculate that nobody would be interested in buying street corner drugs. At one stroke, we could eradicate smuggling, organized drug gangs, street sales, street violence, and, since drug prices would presumably be reduced, most crimes motivated by purchasing drugs.

An alternative legalization model implies much more formal control. Drugs would be regulated as we currently supervise the content and sale of alcoholic beverages. Administrators might try to monitor purity, potency, and age of buyers. The more controls there are, however, the more incentives there would be for illegal markets. If we prohibited cocaine or crack sales to minors but made the drugs freely available to adults at low prices, we would stimulate an illegal cocaine-crack market for minors. Thus, regulation predictably reduces some of the benefits of decriminalization. Legalization advocates assume that benefits would outweigh costs. But how do we measure costs and to whom? Would these be equitably distributed, or would some communities be "taxed" more than others? To be persuasive, legalization advocates will have to convince skeptics that easier availability of drugs will neither trigger significantly more drug use nor stimulate more intensive use by current users.

We can only speculate about what would really happen. On one theory, drugs are presently so easily available that anyone who wants to use them already does and would not be interested in using significantly larger amounts. Curiously, Mr. Bennett affirms that perception. He writes, "Finally, undeniably, the fact remains that here in the United States, in every State—in our cities, in our suburbs, in our rural communities—drugs are potent, drugs are cheap, and drugs are available to everyone."[16] If drugs are already cheap and available to everyone, why not legalize them?

In actuality, every part of the Bennett assertion is an overstatement. Some drugs are potent; others are less so. Drugs vary in price, so that marijuana is presently more expensive on the street than crack, and drugs still aren't as available as they would be if they were legalized. Indeed, in arguing against legalization, Mr. Bennett makes a good observation that there are deterrent risks to using illegal drugs—purchase price, the time it takes to search them out, unreliable quality of street drugs, and legal sanctions—which would disappear if drugs were legalized. But when he talks about legalizing "drugs" he doesn't distinguish among the risks. He offers an economic analysis of the pricing structure of crack cocaine that may not apply to other drugs and certainly doesn't apply to marijuana.

If we distinguish among drugs, it could be argued that drug legalization would most benefit the 1960s generation of affluent and educated drug users. There are, of course, plenty of them, but their drugs of choice are alcohol, cigarettes, marijuana, and nasal cocaine. Fewer of them are choosing to use any drugs, and, when they do use them, they are choosing to use them more moderately. Legalization might be less likely to increase use among the affluent, educated population than among the less affluent, who don't read the health column of *The New York Times*.

Crack, heroin, and phencyclidine (PCP) are inner-city favorites. Those who speak on behalf of this constituency fear the actual and symbolic consequences of legalizing drugs. They are concerned that legalization will generate a sharp rise in drug use among the truly disadvantaged and especially teenagers who face tough lives and bleak futures. Since they are not saying "no" to expensive illegal drugs, the argument proceeds, why shouldn't they say "yes" to less expensive legal pharmaceuticals?

On the other hand, crack cocaine and PCP are easily available and fairly cheap in the inner-city drug-selling areas I have observed as part of ongoing research on drug enforcement, although they are not as easily available as they would be under a legalization regime. How legalization would affect the incidence, quantity, and frequency of use among inner-city youngsters, should legalization occur, is difficult to predict. If we thought that drug ingestion—and especially addiction—would rise by 50 percent, most of us would oppose legalization; if by 5 percent, many of us would support it. Because the incidence of use is presently decreasing, it is plausible to believe that, if crack were made easily available, relatively few would try it who are not already inclined to do so. That assumes of course that law enforcement is relatively uninfluential in determining crack use initiation.

Mr. Bennett counts among the possible costs of legalization the following: a rise in crime as addicts seek money to buy drugs; a rise in violence associated with cocaine paranoia; and a rise in the need for overburdened treatment facilities. As to the first, addicts already commit crimes in order to buy drugs; if drugs were legal and cheaper, it is hardly clear that they would commit more crimes, and they might commit less. The second and third points assume that there would be a far greater number of cocaine addicts, which may not be true. More importantly, although the argument may apply to crack cocaine addiction, it clearly doesn't apply to marijuana or heroin. A cheap supply of heroin should reduce heroin addict crime, and nobody today seriously claims an association between marijuana use and crime, particularly violent crime.

The big benefit of legalization to the inner city is not accounted for in Mr. Bennett's argument against legalization. Affluent users rarely commit crimes to buy drugs, don't sell drugs on street corners, and don't fire off Uzi's in housing projects. Those who fear a surge of inner-city drug use might concede, as Mr. Bennett does, that drugs are already widely and cheaply available. And they might be moved by an equally plausible prediction of a sharp reduction in crime and violence as illegal drug organizations no longer fight over territory or enforce illegal contracts with violence or the threat of violence. One cannot sue for breach of contract in an underground economy. Thus, legalization could dramatically heighten the safety of the inner city.

Finally, Mr. Bennett does not count the unprecedented expansion of law enforcement as a cost, either to our sensibilities or to our civil liberty. Nor does he count as a cost the increasing involvement of inner-city youngsters as criminals in the drug trade; their predictably progressive contribution to the population of our jails and prisons as penalties for drug selling and use rise; and the cost to society of having an increasingly larger population of former felons who have been hardened by the tough prison regimes advocated in the *National Drug Control Strategy*.

What about the symbolic meaning of *decriminalization*? Legalization of "vice" is often equated with a third model—approval, even promotion, of the formerly forbidden activity. We allow advertising of alcohol and cigarettes, even as medical authorities decry their use. When governments have legalized gambling—lotteries, casinos, and off-track betting—they have also condoned and shamelessly promoted gambling. But decriminalization need not imply approval. When the British legalized casinos in 1968, their purpose was to control organized crime. Not only do they forego promotion of their London casinos, but also they don't permit the casino to advertise at all, not even on matchbooks or in ads in the yellow pages.

Similarly, if drugs are to be legalized, advocates must insure that the purpose will not be to pump money into state treasuries but, rather, to *control* a major social and public health problem. It won't be enough simply to advocate legalization on the basis of a cost-benefit calculation. To be acceptable, legalization will need to be grounded in a larger moral purpose—to reduce crime, to enhance public health and safety, and to invigorate a sense of community. To serve this purpose, legalization will need to be part of a bigger package, including social programs for the truly disadvantaged, strict licensing of sellers, increased enforcement against those who sell to the young (even at the risk of losing some of the decriminalization benefits) major antidrug education programs, massive antidrug advertising, and adequate resources for rehabilitation of users. Proposals for decriminalization that are decontextualized, that fail to advocate a powerful antipoverty, antidrug strategy, will likely be rejected—and should be.

CONCLUSION: A PUBLIC HEALTH–SOCIAL PROBLEMS APPROACH

Is there a middle ground between the "unprecedented" expansion of prisons advocated by the Bush administration and legalization? I suggest there is. We could address the drug problem primarily as a public health and social problems (PHSP) issue rather than primarily as a law enforcement responsibility, with our resources directed mainly toward the former. The *National Drug Control Strategy* considers a PHSP approach to be the equivalent of legalization. It moves directly from a discussion of "a massive shift of emphasis away from drug enforcement and toward, instead, treatment for addicts and for students" into a discussion of legalization, stating that the latter is a starker and "more extreme" version of the former.[17] But of course PHSP and legalization are *qualitatively* different.

The legalization of drugs is a major legal and public relations change, both practically and symbolically on a different plane from a public health–social problems approach—as different as cutting the military budget by 20 percent is from pacifism. One involves a difference in degree; the other, in kind. PHSP does not necessarily suggest that we cut down our prisons; only that we don't expand the criminal justice system with "unprecedented" funding. And, of course, we have already experienced an unprecedented expansion of our prison population in the last decade. In contrast to a policy grounded mainly in enforcement, with increased support for military intervention, interdiction, and expansion of prisons, PHSP stresses intermediate sanctions, counseling, economic opportunity, therapy, education, and a consistent attitude toward health values.

PHSP implies that we provide accurate, not exaggerated, drug information to the young. We made the error in the sixties of overstating the dangers of marijuana. Instead of discouraging use, we encouraged the widespread and erroneous inference that marijuana posed no dangers. Similar erroneous inferences were made about powder cocaine in the 1970s. We often couch our health message in terms of a false polarity. Drugs are either harmless or instantly addictive, when in fact drug effects are complicated by various factors—the drug, its dosage, the means of ingestion, and the life circumstances of the user.

Abstinence messages regarding drugs are especially tricky and can backfire. I found in my alcohol research in the 1950s that individuals who reported the highest rate of alcohol problems had been reared in Protestant sects that preached total abstinence. Nevertheless, in conformity with our culture, these persons used alcoholic beverages. Such persons invariably initiated drinking outside the ambit of a moral community, in a bar or behind a barn. They grew up learning that to drink is to drink hedonistically and often excessively. One drinks to get drunk. "Just say 'no' " is a positive message if it works. But it can be a dangerous message for those who say "yes." And, for young people, alcohol can be a gateway drug to other drug experiments.

Public policy conclusions are very complex in this area. There is now developing a revisionist history of the Volstead Act, which points out, quite correctly, that although prohibition was a law enforcement disaster, it was a public health success. The incidence of alcohol-connected illness, such as cirrhosis of the liver, declined appreciably. Cirrhosis death rates for men were 29.5 per 100,000 in 1911 and 10.7 in 1929. Arrests for public drunkenness and disorderly conduct also declined, and there was no rise in violent crime.

So, if we were to recalculate the costs and benefits of Prohibition, a better case could be made for alcohol prohibition. Still, as we discovered during Prohibition, law enforcement costs predictably rise, because many of us like our wine and whiskey well enough to buy it on the black market. Imagine the black market if we totally outlawed cigarette sales? Choice values are also important. Should everyone in the society be legally required to abstain from alcohol use because some proportion of users abuse the substance? The law enforcement costs of prohibiting alcohol, as well as the burdens to choice values, outweigh the public health benefits. But, even if we could make a stronger case for prohibition on health and public order grounds, it scarcely seems possible to make a case for the nonprohibition model we now embrace—one permitting stimulation of demand for alcohol and cigarettes through advertising, promotion, and relatively low taxation.

Finally, in contrast to a call for legalization, a public health–social problems approach incorporates a moral message every bit as compelling as Mr. Bennett's punitive one. This approach envisions public health in broad terms, as a social and economic opportunity issue as well as a medical one. It does not suggest drugs on demand but, rather, a reordering of priorities. These include community regeneration and a massive investment in antidrug advertising, severe limits on alcohol and cigarette promotion, and educational programs and therapy. It also implies a consistent, nonstimulating and honest approach to understanding the complexity of the effects of substances that alter our perceptions and feelings and that are subject to abuse. Just as there are significant links between public health and the integrity of the "infrastructure"—sewage systems, water supply, bridge construction—there are important connections between crack cocaine addiction and poverty and inequality.

One connection is fairly obvious: the classic connection between delinquency and the lack of alternative opportunity. The California drug dealers my students and I interviewed were rationally materialistic. Drug selling represented a singular economic opportunity in an environment where they perceived few, if any, others. Terry Williams observes that, in addition to the immediate rewards of money and drugs, cocaine offered his New York City Dominican "kids" the opportunity "to show family and friends that they can succeed at something."[18] And Philippe Bourgeois, who studied crack dealers in New York's Spanish Harlem, challenges the assertion of culture-of-poverty theorists that the poor are socialized out of the mainstream and have different values. He concludes that

> On the contrary, ambitious, energetic, inner-city youths are attracted to the underground economy precisely because they believe in the rags-to-riches American dream. . . . Without stretching the point too much they can be seen in conventional terms as rugged individualists on an unpredictable frontier where fame and fortune are all just around the corner.[19]

The risks presented by the criminal justice system are not as salient to them as the violence and threat of violence in the underground economy.

Can we possibly offer economic opportunities to compete with the economic benefits of the drug trade? I think we can. First, we have to distinguish between upper-level, multiple-kilo dealers and youngsters who deal in the streets. A recent article offers a depressing picture of the lower rungs of the crack business, describing it as a "modern, brutalized version of a 19th century sweatshop."[20] And, it continues,

> Despite the popular notion that crack sellers all drive Mercedes-Benzes, wear gold jewelry and get rich quick, most of the people in the business work round the clock, six to seven days a week, for low real wages in an atmosphere of physical threat and control.
>
> Their pay is often docked if they arrive late; they may even be shot or maimed if they are even perceived as trying to cheat their employers, and many fall into such debt to them they have to go into hiding.[21]

So, the drug trade has a down side recognized by many of those who engage in it; although it is advertised as attractive and remunerative, it is also risky, violent, and dangerous. The down side is clearly most recognizable to those who are at its margins, kids who sell on the street and who move in and out of the drug trade, rather than to the higher ups who are well connected and tightly committed. But even those higher up are not entirely content. One higher dealer whom I interviewed told me:

> About selling dope, it's money, you have a good life. But the worst thing about it is buying it. When you sitting up there in a little motel room and everybody got guns, holding guns, and counting money, you sweatin'. No windows open—nothin' can be open 'cause you got all that dope. And you're talkin' about price. You don't want to look weak and he don't want to look weak. All that tension. If I could ever find a way where I didn't have to buy nothing, I'd never buy again.

Let me fantasize. Suppose, as an alternative to boot camps, we considered paying youngsters in disadvantaged communities for playing sports, or a combination of sports and schooling, and moved the idea of "scholarships" into high school or grade school. Suppose we developed an industrial program that subsidized the rebuilding of the inner cities and paid youngsters to work in these programs. True, we could never pay enough to compete with the drug profits of the highest level dealers, but we could compete with the lower levels of the trade.

This is a very different policy vision from the one presented by the Bush-Bennett *National Drug Control Strategy*. Under the heading of "Community Action," the *National Drug Control Strategy's* rhetoric is couched in terms of "combat" and of communities "fighting back." One proposed alternative to "combat" is religion: drug use is consistently characterized as a "moral" rather than a social problem. And, if drug use is a moral problem, it is presumably sufficient to rely on "volunteers" who will "work in drug treatment clinics, schools, hospitals, and community and social service organizations."[22] Moreover, if moral imperfection is the fundamental cause of drug use and dealing, we don't need to consider social and economic conditions as causes.

Users ingest drugs, particularly crack cocaine, for reasons other than moral imperfection: crack makes one feel good, takes one out of life circumstances, and, however fleetingly, puts one's mind in a place that fulfills fantasies. Dealers, whose economic circumstances are better, say they abstain. They don't live in a fantasy world. So economic and social conditions—poverty, disadvantage, neglect, joblessness—generate feelings of pessimism, hopelessness, low self-esteem, despair, which motivate drug use, particularly crack cocaine use.

No recognized antidote to cocaine addiction is presently available. But there can be treatment of the mind. Therapists who work with cocaine-addicted patients try to get their patients to achieve total abstinence. Our interviews with therapists suggest that success varies with social class. Therapists at the Haight-Ashbury Free Clinic in San Francisco told us that, the more the addict can count on social sustenance—friends, family, job, therapy group—the more likely will abstinence be achieved. Poor people usually don't enjoy this kind of neighborhood and familial underpinning.

Addicts who are far gone ultimately experience symptoms comparable to those of clinical depression—anhedonia, an incapacity to take pleasure in anything, such as food, sex, the world series—and craving. They think only about obtaining the drug. But they live in a world—often a housing project—that continually cues their craving because drugs are being used and sold all around them. There are no Betty Ford clinics for the desperately poor, so, once hooked, they are likely to stay hooked.

Young women who live in poverty sell their bodies to obtain the drug. That's bad enough. But they also are susceptible to, and spread, AIDS and give birth to addicted and sometimes HIV-infected babies—an outcome that we will increasingly and depressingly observe in the years ahead.

So how should we address the drug conundrum? Exhortation to drug users or sellers, whether by religious figures or moralistic drug czars, scarcely seems promising. Can Mr. Bennett really believe that those who use or sell drugs will be persuaded by his message? He is far too intelligent to expect that. Rather, he likely anticipates that, by drafting his report in these terms, key policymakers will be persuaded to support his policy recommendations, his emphasis on an unprecedented expansion of law enforcement, interdiction, military intervention, along with ameliorative tactics such as treatment and education.

Mr. Bennett sees the reclamation of neighborhoods as a "criminal justice" challenge, while I see it as a social problem and a public health challenge. A more promising national drug strategy would implicate a long-term understanding of the drug problem and its underlying causes. It would recognize and be responsive to the connection between social disadvantage and street drug selling, the price we are paying for years of neglect of disadvantaged communities, and of the serious limits and costs of an "unprecedented" expansion of law enforcement.

Finally, although the *National Drug Control Strategy* concedes that there are no quick fixes to the drug problem, its basic strategic assumption is questionable. It rests on the idea that each segment of the plan—military intervention, interdiction, unprecedented enlargement of law enforcement, casual user sanctions, treatment, and education—will reinforce the others. But will it, or will it result mainly in expansion of law enforcement facilities and resources, in some rise in treatment and education, and in virtually no attention or resources being addressed to the underlying causes of drug selling and addiction?

NOTES

1. Morales Edmundo *Cocaine: White Gold Rush in Peru* at 174 (1989).
2. *Strategy,* supra note 1, at 73.
3. Reuter, Peter, "Can the Borders be Sealed?" *Public Interest,* Summer 1988.
4. Id.
5. Rosenberg, "The Kingdom of Cocaine: A Report from Colombia" *New Republic,* Nov. 27, 1989, at 28.
6. P. Murphy & T. Plate, *Commissioner: A View from the Top of American Law Enforcement* 245 (1977).
7. *Strategy,* supra note 1, at 26.
8. Id.
9. Id.
10. *N.Y. Times,* April 18, 1989, at A16, col. 4. Mr. Bennett has attributed the halting progress of the War on Drugs to state officials who are reluctant to use state funding for new prison construction. *Wall St. J.,* Nov. 30, 1989, at A16, col. 1.
11. *Strategy.*
12. Burke, "Comments on Street-Level Drug Enforcement" *Street-Level Drug Enforcement: Examining the Issues,* supra note 67, at 53.
13. Bouza, Id. at 49
14. *N.Y. Times,* Oct. 2, 1989, at B10, col. 6.
15. Golbe & Merkin, "Cerebral Infarction in a User of Free-Base Cocaine (Crack)" 36 Neurology 1602 (1986). (footnotes omitted)
16. *Strategy,* supra note 1, at 2.
17. Id. supra note 1, at 6.
18. T. Williams, supra note 96, at 11.
19. Bourgeois, "Just Another Night on Crack Street" *N.Y. Times Magazine,* Nov. 12, 1989, at 63.
20. *N.Y. Times,* Nov. 26, 1989, at 1, col. 1.
21. Id.
22. *Strategy,* supra note 1, at 54.

39

Corporate Crime and Violence

Russell Mokhiber

Name a crime.

Outside of the context of this book, many would respond "burglary" or "robbery" or "murder." Few would respond "monopoly" or "knowingly marketing unsafe pharmaceuticals" or "dumping of toxic wastes."

Name an act of violence.

Similarly, many would respond with examples of violent street crimes, such as assault. Few would respond with examples of violent corporate crime, such as the marketing of a dangerous automobile or the pollution of a community's water supply.

People respond this way despite a near universal consensus that all corporate crime and violence combined, both detected and undetected, prosecuted and not prosecuted, is more pervasive and more damaging than all street crime. The electrical price fixing conspiracy of the early 1960s alone cost American consumers $2 billion, more than all the burglaries in America in one year. According to the Federal Bureau of Investigation, there were 19,000 victims of street murder and manslaughter in 1985. Compare that one-year total with the numbers of victims of corporate crime and violence in the United States today:

- One hundred and thirty Americans die every day in automobile crashes. Many of those deaths are either caused by vehicle defects or preventable by available vehicle crashworthiness designs.
- Almost 800 Americans die every day from cigarette-induced disease.

From Russell Mokhiber, *Corporate Crime and Violence*, San Francisco, Sierra Club Books, 1988. Reprinted by permission.

- Over the next 30 years, 240,000 people—8,000 per year, one every hour—will die from asbestos-related cancer.
- The Dalkon Shield intrauterine device seriously injured tens of thousands of women who used it.
- An estimated 85,000 American cotton textile workers suffer breathing impairments due to cotton dust (brown lung) disease.
- 100,000 miners have been killed and 265,000 disabled due to coal dust (black lung) disease.
- One million infants worldwide died in 1986 because they were bottle-fed instead of breast-fed.
- In 1984, 2,000 to 5,000 persons were killed and 200,000 injured, 30,000 to 40,000 of them seriously, after a Union Carbide affiliate's factory in Bhopal, India, released a deadly gas over the town. . . .

Why is it that despite the high numbers of victims, when people think of crime, they think of burglary before they think of monopoly (if they think of monopoly at all), of assault before they think of the marketing of harmful pharmaceuticals, of street crime before they think of corporate crime? And what can be done to curb corporate crime and violence?

WHY DO PEOPLE THINK OF STREET CRIME BEFORE THEY THINK OF CORPORATE CRIME?

Many corporate executives assume that preventable violence is a cost of doing business, a cost that we as a society must accept as the price of living in an industrial America. With advertising campaigns aimed at molding public opinion and policy, some corporations have covered their violent behavior with a veneer of misinformation and distortion in an attempt to make acceptable what in any other context would be morally repugnant. A case in point is the advertisement run by Monsanto on the heels of many chemical disasters during the late 1970s with the theme "Without Chemicals, Life Itself Would Be Impossible."

Furthermore, in the United States, corporate lawbreakers double as corporate lawmakers. Corporate America has saturated the legislatures with dollars in order to promote laws making legal or non-criminal what by any common standard of justice would be considered illegal and criminal, and to obstruct legislation that would outlaw the violent activity. For example, the tobacco and automobile industries have, over the years, blocked attempts to ban or curb the marketing of tobacco, and to require that automobiles be manufactured with life-saving passive restraints.

When public pressure does produce legislation curbing corporate excesses, corporations then lobby, often successfully, to weaken the constraint. When Congress passed the auto safety law, for example, auto industry lobbyists on Capitol Hill defeated an effort to add criminal sanctions to the bill for knowing or willful violations.

The result is a legal system biased in favor of the corporate violator and against its victims. Because the higher standards of proof in criminal trials are more difficult to meet, and because of finely tuned corporate methods of delay and obfuscation most federal prosecutions of corporations seek civil, not criminal, sanctions; few serious acts of corporate violence are criminally prosecuted. Moreover, most of the penalties that are imposed in civil cases are mere slap-on-the-wrist settlements known as consent decrees.

Even when the criminal prosecution of a corporation is successful, the imposed sanctions are rarely effective. When, for example, General Motors was convicted in 1949 of conspiracy to destroy the nation's mass transit systems, surely one of the more egregious corporate crimes in U.S. economic history, the judge fined the company $5,000.

There are many corporate wrongdoers allowed to go free and many street criminals punished harshly for minor violations. Not one corporate executive went to jail, nor was any corporation criminally convicted for the marketing of thalidomide, a drug that caused severe birth defects in 8,000 babies during the early 1960s, but Wallace Richard Stewart of Kentucky was sentenced in July 1983 to ten years in prison for stealing a pizza. No Ford Motor Company executive went to jail for marketing the Pinto automobile, with its deadly fuel tank, nor was the company convicted of criminal charges (although in one case it was indicted, tried, and found not guilty of reckless homicide). Not one Hooker Chemical executive went to jail, nor was Hooker charged with a criminal offense, after the company exposed its workers and Love Canal neighbors to toxics, but under a Texas habitual offenders statute William Rummel was given life in prison for stealing a total of $229.11 over a period of nine years.

"Crime is a sociopolitical artifact, not a natural phenomenon," Herbert L. Packer wrote in 1968 in *The Limits of the Criminal Sanction*. "We can have as much or as little crime as we please, depending on what we choose to count as criminal." By setting up a system of civil fines, consent decrees, recalls, and other non-criminal controls on corporations, we have chosen to have very little corporate "crime," in Professor Packer's sense of the word, and by so choosing, we have insulated the corporation from the effective sanctions and stigma of the criminal process. In addition, we have sent the outnumbered and underfunded police who investigate corporate crime—euphemistically known as regulators—up against some of the most powerful lawbreakers in society without access to meaningful sanctions. . . .

SIDESTEPPING THE CRIMINAL JUSTICE SYSTEM

Professor Christopher Stone, of the University of Southern California Law School, has observed that up until the nineteenth century, the law was paying increasing attention to the individual, and less to the group.

During this period, according to Stone, laws, rules, and concepts were being developed to deal with what motivated, what steered, and what was "possible, just and appropriate in the case of individual human beings." Corporations did not move to center stage until late in the nineteenth century, and when they did, the criminal law, developed to bring justice to individuals, was not equipped to answer the question: what motivated, what steered, and what was possible, just, and appropriate in the case of corporations?

At the turn of the century, as corporations became increasingly wealthy and powerful, legislatures moved to protect the public from corporate abuses. In 1890, Congress passed the Sherman Antitrust Act, which forbade monopolizing or attempting to monopolize trade and made illegal "every contract, combination . . . or conspiracy in restraint of trade." The act was aimed at busting the corporate monopoly makers that were threatening the competitive economic system. Violation of the act was a criminal offense, punishable by a fine not exceeding $5,000 or by imprisonment up to a year, or both.

But the Sherman Act and a host of subsequent laws aimed at controlling corporate wrongdoing were different in one crucial respect from the criminal laws that governed the noncorporate citizenry. In a radical departure from the historical development of criminal law, legislatures gave prosecutors of corporate crime the option of seeking a *civil injunction* to enforce a law with *criminal sanctions.*

Rather than charging the corporation with a criminal violation and then prosecuting the case in open court before a jury of citizens who would determine guilt or innocence, prosecutors choose instead, in the overwhelming number of cases, to go to civil court and seek to enjoin the corporation from further violations of law. Today, this civil injunction against crime has become the option of choice for federal "regulators."

By relying on the civil injunction, federal police avoid branding the defendant corporation with the symbols of crime, thus crippling the intended punitive and deterrent effects of the criminal sanction. "The violations of these laws are crimes," commented Edwin Sutherland, who formulated this concept of corporate crime, in his ground-breaking 1949 book *White-Collar Crime,* " . . . but they are treated as though they were not crimes, with the effect and probably the intention of eliminating the stigma of crime."

A second radical departure—or "clever invention," to use a Sutherland phrase—from the traditional criminal procedure came in the guise of the abovementioned consent decree. A consent decree is essentially a compromise between two parties in a civil suit, the exact terms of which are fixed by negotiation between the parties and formalized by the signature of a judge.

Thus while the civil injunction against crime removed the corporate defendant from the criminal sphere, the consent decree provided further insulation by moving the legal process from the open courtroom to behind closed doors. Although the defendant corporation invariably emerged from behind those closed doors consenting to an injunction against further violations of the law, it did so without admitting or denying the allegations.

Most federal cases brought against corporations are settled in this manner. The "neither admit nor deny" clause is understandably relished by corporate defendants because it precludes the use of the decree as an admission of guilt in subsequent court proceedings, be they civil or criminal. In many cases, this clause is worth millions of dollars to corporations; without it, private plaintiffs could use the decree as evidence of law violation in private damage actions. Corporate defendants cite numerous other reasons for agreeing to consent decrees (prompt resolution of the case to avoid expensive and protracted litigation, and opportunity to negotiate the language of the consent decree and of the allegations of the complaint), but the "neither admit nor deny" clause is itself the primary motivation for a defendant to settle a case. Once the consent is signed, the public perception is that the corporate defendant is not a lawbreaker, not a criminal, not a crook. The defendant is merely "enjoined."

Sutherland proffered three reasons for this "differential implementation of the law as it applied to large corporations." Most important was the status of businessmen in the United States. According to Sutherland,

> Those who are responsible for the system of criminal justice are afraid to antagonize businessmen; among other consequences, such antagonism may result in a reduction in contributions to the campaign funds needed to win the next election. . . . Probably much more important than fear, however, is the cultural homogeneity of legislators, judges, and administrators with businessmen. Legislators admire and respect businessmen and cannot conceive of them as criminals; businessmen do not conform to the popular stereotype of "the criminal." The legislators are confident that these respectable gentlemen will conform to the law as a result of very mild pressures. The most powerful group in medieval society secured relative immunity by "benefit of clergy" and now our most powerful group secures immunity by "benefit of business," or more generally, "high social status."

Secondly, Sutherland recognized a shift away from implementation of penal sanctions in general, with the shift occurring "more rapidly in the area of white collar crimes than of other crimes." And finally, Sutherland believed that the more gentle treatment of corporate criminals was due in part to "the relatively unorganized resentment of the public toward white collar crimes." This, he explained, was because the violations of laws by businessmen are "complex and their effects diffused," and because

> [T]he public agencies of communication do not express the organized moral sentiments of the community as to white collar crimes, in part because the crimes are complicated and not easily presented as news, but probably in the greater part because these agencies of communication

are owned or controlled by businessmen and because these agencies are themselves involved in the violations of many of these laws.

This two-track prosecutorial setup—a criminal system for individuals and a civil system for corporations—works to undermine the effectiveness of the criminal justice system. Individuals convicted by the criminal justice system must carry not only the burden of the penal sanction, but also the stigma of crime. The corporation is relieved of both. When a corporation signs a consent decree, little public shame attaches because the corporation "neither admits nor denies" violating the law. . . .

CRIMINALS IN THE USUAL SENSE: LAYING THE GROUNDWORK FOR DECRIMINALIZATION OF CORPORATE LAW

"Most criminals in antitrust cases are not criminals in the usual sense." That statement, quoted above, of Wendell Berge, who was assistant to the head of the Justice Department's Antitrust Division in 1940, epitomizes the view of a group of academics, including the likes of Richard Posner and Sanford Kadish, and politicians, such as Ronald Reagan, who believe that criminal sanctions should not be applied to corporate wrongdoing, or should be applied only as a last resort. Many in this camp are adherents to the view that a corporate polluter is not a criminal in the sense that an individual burglar is a criminal, that a corporate price fixer is not a criminal in the sense that an individual robber is a criminal, and that a white-collar criminal is not a criminal in the sense that a street criminal is a criminal.

The academic who argues for decriminalization is not as direct as . . . Mr. Berge, in arguing that price fixers are not "criminals in the usual sense." Instead, the academics present a utilitarian argument for decriminalization that goes something like this:

Because of the heavy reliance on civil remedies and the complementary disuse of the criminal remedies, the criminal law governing corporations is in such an underdeveloped state that corporate criminal sanctions should be effectively scrapped in favor of exclusive reliance on civil monetary penalties, supplemented by equitable remedies such as injunctions and consent decrees. Furthermore, the only significant goal of corporate criminal law is deterrence, and deterrence can be adequately attained through civil monetary penalties and other civil sanctions without reliance on criminal sanctions.

Thus, this school advocates the effective crippling of corporate criminal law, the moral equivalent of throwing the baby out with the bathwater. Brent Fisse, a noted Australian legal scholar, has powerfully argued against such abolition and for a reconstruction of the corporate criminal law to control socially harmful corporate behavior. Fisse notes that "modern corporate criminal law owes its origin and design more to crude borrowings from individual criminal and civil law than to any coherent assessment of the objectives of corporate criminal law and of how those objectives might be attained."

Embarking on such an assessment, a growing number of legal scholars have joined Fisse in reacting strongly against those who would prefer to condemn corporate criminal law to windowdressing in perpetuity. The academic dispute intensified when the *Harvard Law Review*, one of the most respected law journals, published a commentary by its editors in 1979 titled "Developments in the Law—Corporate Crime," which came down on the side of decriminalization by advocating a civil-fine model to control corporate wrongdoing. The Harvard commentary rested on the proposition that although deterrence, rehabilitation, and incapacitation are the traditional aims of the criminal law as applied to individuals, deterrence is the only aim that is important in the realm of the corporate criminal law. From this proposition, the Harvard commentary suggested that since successful deterrence of corporate crime requires the threat of substantial monetary penalties, "one must wonder whether the same or a higher level of deterrence could be better achieved through civil [as opposed to criminal] penalties."

That suggestion takes insufficient account of the deterrent value resulting from the stigma of criminal conviction and punishment. Herbert Packer argued that "there is very little evidence to suggest that the stigma of criminality means anything very substantial in the life of the corporation. John Doe has friends and neighbors; a corporation has none. And the argument that the fact of criminal conviction may have an adverse effect on a corporation's economic position seems fanciful." Millions of dollars spent since then on corporate image advertising by large multinationals argue against Packer's view. A recent study of the effects of adverse publicity on 17 corporations found the loss of corporate prestige was a significant concern of executives in 15 of the cases.

The laissez faire school focuses on the financial motives of corporate executives, ignores other well-documented motivations. A strictly monetary scheme to control corporate wrongdoing addresses the corporation's drive for profits, not a corporate executive's urge for power, nor his or her desire for prestige, creative urge, need to identify with the group, desire for security, urge for adventure, or desire to serve others. As Fisse has noted, "deterring unwanted corporate behavior may require sanctions which, unlike monetary exactions, would be unconstitutional if characterized as civil. Preventive orders and formal publicity orders would be needed to inflict loss of corporate power and prestige directly." . . .

SANCTIONS AGAINST THE INDIVIDUAL WHITE-COLLAR CRIMINAL

If a corporation engages in socially undesirable behavior, the odds are that neither the corporation nor its executives will ever face a sentencing judge. In some cases, the law will not prohibit the corporation's antisocial behavior, as when auto manufacturers knowingly market dangerously constructed or designed vehicles. If such behavior is covered, law enforcement officials may be looking the other way, as with many Reagan administration "regulators." If laws cover such behavior and law enforcement agencies are conscientious about their enforcement responsibilities, corporation-induced political pressures may force a cut of monetary or political support to hamper those agencies.

If an unlucky corporation makes it to the sanctioning stage, the chances are that the corporation and its executives will be treated with kid gloves, especially when compared with individual street criminals.

Street criminals, mostly poor and black, get long prison terms for minor property crimes, yet corporate and white-collar criminals, in the words of Braithwaite, "can fix prices, defraud consumers of millions, and kill and maim workers with impunity, without prison." When General Electric was convicted of price fixing in the early 1960s, the company was fined $437,000. As Lee Loevinger, former chief of the Justice Department's Antitrust Division, put it, the fine was no more severe than "a three-dollar ticket for overtime parking for a man with a $15,000 a year income."

In 1978, the Olin Corporation was convicted of false filings to conceal illegal shipments of arms to South Africa. The company was fined $40,000 and no Olin executive went to jail. In July 1984, Elizabeth McAllister, a peace activist, was sentenced to three years in jail for participating in an antinuclear demonstration at an upstate New York U.S. Air Force Base.

The Clinard corporate crime study found that serious violations by corporations generally receive minor sanctions, with only administrative penalties given in approximately two-thirds of the cases identified as serious violations. The Clinard study also found that 16 executives of 582 companies studied were sentenced to a total of 594 days of actual imprisonment. Three hundred and sixty of those days were accounted for by two officers who received six months each in the same case.

Professor Stone alleges that jailings do not guarantee significant changes in corporate direction since "the very nature of bureaucracy is to make the individual dispensable." But prison sentences for corporate executives are an efficient deterrent mechanism, in terms of both specific deterrence (against the convicted individual) and general deterrence (against those other executives observing the proceedings), available to sentencing judges. Jail sentences in the electrical equipment conspiracy cases had both specific and general deterrent effects. Clarence Burke, a former GE general manager, told a congressional committee after the convictions, "I would starve before I'd do it again." A second GE manager told a senator, "the way my family and myself have been suffering, if I see a competitor on one side of the street, I will walk on the other side, sir."

Gordon Spivack, former assistant chief in charge of field operations for the Justice Department's Antitrust Division, discussing the general deterrent effect of the electrical price fixing prison sanctions, believed that "similar sentences in a few cases each decade would almost completely cleanse our economy of the cancer of collusive price fixing, and the mere threat of such sentences is itself the strongest available deterrent to such activity."

However, there appears to be a general belief among judges that white-collar criminals, no matter what the crime, don't deserve prison. This despite the fact that judges believe in the deterrent effect of imprisonment and have no confidence that fines or other nonincarcerative sanctions would be as effective. One federal judge is quoted as saying that he would not "penalize a businessman trying to make a living when there are felons out on the street." A second judge is of the opinion that "all people don't need to be sent to prison. For white-collar criminals, the mere fact of prosecution, pleading guilty—the psychological trauma of that is punishment enough. They've received the full benefit of punishment."

In one of the few empirical studies of sentencing judges' attitudes toward white-collar criminals, Yale Law School's research program on white-collar crime found that although judges take a serious view of white-collar crime, several factors lead them to find what the authors of the study call "a non-incarcerative disposition," that is, judges don't like to throw white-collar criminals in jail. The authors attribute judges' reluctance to imprison white-collar criminals partly to their belief that such defendants are "more sensitive to the impact of the prison environment than are non-white-collar defendants." One judge put it this way:

> I think the first sentence to a prison term for a person who up to now
> has lived and has surrounded himself with a family, that lives in terms
> of great respectability and community respect and so on, whether one
> likes to say this or not I think a term of imprisonment for such a person
> is probably a harsher, more painful sanction than it is for someone who
> grows up somewhere where people are always in and out of prison.
> There may be something racist about saying that, but I am saying what
> I think is true or perhaps needs to be laid out on the table and faced.

The Yale study also found judges wanting to avoid eliminating the contribution to community and family that white-collar offenders make in the normal course of their lives. One judge described this feeling in the following manner:

> Usually the defendant is one who looks as though he can resume his
> place, if indeed not just continue on his place, in society, as a valuable
> and contributing member of society. Almost always he is a husband and
> a father. Almost always he has children who are in the process of be-
> coming what we like to think children ought to be—well brought up,
> well educated, nurtured, cared for—usually he is a member of the kinds
> of civic organizations in the community who value his services and de-
> rive value from his services. . . . As a result you are up against this
> more difficult problem in degree in the so called white-collar criminals
> as to whether you are not going to inflict a hurt on society by putting
> such person in a prison and making him cease to be a good father and
> a good husband and a good worker in the community.

Finally, the judges felt that white-collar defendants' ability to make restitution to their victims militated against the argument for prison sentences. The judges also felt that community service orders were better suited to white-collar prisoners than was prison.

If judges are not throwing convicted corporate executives in jail, then how are they punishing them? With fines and community service orders whose deterrent effect is questionable. The Clinard study found that the average fine levied against individual officers was $18,250, a pittance compared with the large salaries and bonuses granted corporate executives. In addition to inadequacy, other factors mitigate the effectiveness of the fine as a sanction against criminal activity. First, many corporations indemnify an executive who is found to be acting for the benefit of the corporation if he had no reasonable cause to believe that what he was doing was criminal. Secondly, in some states, notably Delaware, a corporation can take out insurance against fines levied against its executives. One federal judge complained that "one jail sentence is worth 100 consent decrees and that fines are meaningless because the defendant in the end is always reimbursed by the proceeds of his wrongdoing or by his company down the line."

Community service orders, which have grown in popularity over the years, can be seen as a mechanism by which judges try to "do something" to fill the void created by the widespread reluctance to throw white-collar criminals in jail. The most notable of the recent community service orders was U.S. District Court Judge Charles Renfrew's order in the paper label price fixing case. Five individual defendants convicted of price fixing were fined between $5,000 and $15,000 apiece and were put on probation. As a condition of their probation, each was ordered to "make an oral presentation before twelve civic or other groups about the circumstances of his case and his participation therein. . . . " Robert Herbst has labeled Renfrew's sentence "a joke . . . no deterrent threat at all."

In other cases, convicted white-collar criminals have been ordered to:

- give speeches about their violations to business and civic groups;
- work in programs designed to aid the poor;
- help former street criminals participate in community groups and secure job pledges for them from business concerns;
- work 40 hours a week in a drug treatment center for five months and eight hours a week for one additional year;
- work 25 hours a week for five months and 10 hours a week for an additional year in an agricultural school that he had founded;
- make a community service film. The film, about the dangers of PCP, so impressed the judges that he reduced the conviction to a misdemeanor.

There is little evidence that these community service orders have any deterrent effect, either against the individual convicted criminal or generally against those observing the sanctioning process. Judges imposing these sentences further undermine the nation's system of justice. "To keep coming up with alternative sentences," charged Thomas Cahill, former Chief Assistant U.S. Attorney, "in the public's image makes it look like it's a technical violation. It's not. . . . It's a crime and should be treated as a crime." Second, if community service orders are going to be used to displace prison sentences, they should be used to displace prison sentences across the board, for street as well as for corporate criminals. The current system of jail for street thugs and speeches for corporate thugs creates an inequality of justice that undermines respect for the law.

SANCTIONS AGAINST THE CORPORATION

The *Harvard Law Review* commentary on corporate crime rejected retribution as a goal of corporate criminal sanctions, and focused on deterrence as the sole goal. It concluded that corporations cannot be punished in a stigmatic manner; that if stronger deterrents are needed, they should come in the form of heavier fines; and that since criminal fines have no advantage over civil fines, they should come in the form of heavier civil fines.

But the overwhelming evidence from scholars, prosecutors, and judges is that fines, often small and well below authorized ceilings, do not deter corporate crime. Criminologist John Braithwaite has called them "license fees to break the law." Fines in the typical antitrust case rarely reach the authorized ceiling. W. Breit and K. Elzinger, in a study of antitrust violations between 1967 and 1970, found that the Justice Department recommended imposing the maximum fine in less than one-third of the cases where it obtained convictions. Braithwaite, in a recent study of law enforcement in the mine safety area, found that about 90 percent of the mine operators stated that civil penalties assessed or paid did not affect their production or safety activities. "Penalty dollar amounts were not considered of sufficient magnitude to warrant avoidance of future penalties and improvements in safety procedure," he observed. Operators contemptuously classified the fines as a "cost of doing business" or as a royalty paid to the government to continue in business. Producers who were fined saw no connection between penalties and safety.

Christopher Stone's study of laws governing corporations, *Where the Law Ends,* came to similar conclusions. "The overall picture," according to Stone, "is that our strategies aimed to control corporations by threatening their profits are a very limited way of bringing about the internal changes that are necessary if the policies behind the law are to be effectuated." The trouble with using fines to control corporate crime, according to Clinard, is that the amount paid is more than offset by the financial gain from the offense. In his study of more than 500 major U.S. corporations, Clinard found that four-fifths of the penalties levied against corporations were $5,000 or less, 11.6 percent were between $5,000 and $50,000, 3.7 percent were between $50,000 and $1,000,000, and 0.9 percent were over $1,000,000.

A major criticism of using fines to control corporate crime has been described by New York University Law School Professor John C. Coffee, Jr. and others as "the deterrence trap." The corporation contemplating the commitment of a crime will be deterred only if the expected punishment cost of the illegal activity exceeds the expected gain. Coffee gives the following example: If the expected gain were $1 million and the risk of arrest were 25 percent, then the penalty would have to be $4 million in order to make the expected punishment cost equal to the expected gain. Coffee observes that "the maximum meaningful fine that can be levied against any corporate offender is necessarily bound by its wealth." For example,

> if a corporation having $10 million of wealth were faced with an opportunity to gain $1 million through some criminal act or omission, such conduct could not logically be deterred by monetary penalties directed at the corporation if the risk of apprehension were below 10%. That is, if the likelihood of apprehension were 8%, the necessary penalty would have to be $12.5 million (i.e., $1 million times 12.5, the reciprocal of 8%). Yet such a fine exceeds the corporation's ability to pay. In short, our ability to deter the corporation may be confounded by our inability to set an adequate punishment cost which does not exceed the corporation's resources.

Since corporate crimes are easy to conceal and all indications are that rates of apprehension are exceedingly low, most major corporations will not be deterred by the types of fines that federal sentencing officials currently are imposing.

A second practical objection to using fines to control corporate crime is that the costs of any given corporate crime and the corresponding retributive fine may be far larger than the amount a corporation is able to pay. This "retribution trap" is a barrier to effective control of corporate crime. Braithwaite makes the point by asking:

> [C]an we imagine any penalty short of revoking the corporation's right to sell drugs which would be commensurate to the harm caused by the fraud and deceit of a thalidomide disaster? Given what we know about how disapproving the community feels toward corporate crime, there may be many situations where the deserved monetary or other punishments bankrupt the company. The community then cuts its nose to spite its face.

In addition, threatening the corporation as a monolithic "black box" ignores the possible role of individual motivations in directing corporate actions. Stone and others have observed that there may be a fundamental lack of congruence between the aims of the individual and the aims of the firm. A corporate executive may engage in criminal activity to further his own ends, not necessarily those of the firm. Coffee gives the hypothetical example of an executive vice president who is a candidate for promotion to president and may be willing to run risks that are counterproductive to the firm as a whole because he is eager to make a record profit for his division or to hide an error of judgment. In such situation a fine aimed at the corporation won't deter the perpetrator and will probably fail in controlling illegal conduct. Thus when a criminal sanctioning system aims at the "black box" of the corporation instead of the individual decision makers within the black box, it may prove irrelevant to certain kinds of misconduct. Coffee argues that

> the most shocking safety and environmental violations are almost exclusively the product of decisions at lower managerial levels. . . . The directive from the top of the organization is to increase profits by fifteen percent but the means are left to the managerial discretion of the middle manager who is in operational control of the division. . . . The results of such a structure are predictable: when pressure is intensified, illegal or irresponsible means become attractive to a desperate middle manager who has no recourse against a stern but myopic notion of accountability that looks only to the bottom line of the income statement.

Thus in firms where there is a strong "bottom line" ethic, one that loosens legal, moral, and ethical constraints, fines against the organization will fail to have the deterrent effect upon which the entire structure of fines is premised.

Even when fined, criminals tend not to pay. From 1977 to 1983 the federal government collected only about 55 percent of all criminal fines imposed. Since 1968, the dollar volume of criminal fines has increased by a factor of twelve; at the same time, collection rates have fallen from around 80 percent to less than 40 percent. At the end of fiscal year 1982, the amount of delinquent debt owed to the federal government was a staggering $38 billion. This failure to pay fines has the effect of severely undercutting the deterrent and punitive effects of the sanction. As Senator Charles Percy stated in opening Senate hearings in 1983 on the subject, "the collection of criminal fines goes beyond mere fiscal responsibility. Five of every six fines are levied on criminals who do *not* go to prison. Half of the time, they are not even on probation. Therefore, in many cases, when these fines are not paid, these criminals go unpunished. It is as simple as that."

Braithwaite, in his study of coal mine safety enforcement, found that at the time of the Buffalo Creek waste tip disaster, in which over 125 people lost their lives, the operator had been assessed fines exceeding $1.5 million, "not a cent of which was paid." In another case, a coal company had been assessed fines totaling $76,330 for 379 violations, 178 of them for electrical or trolley wire standards. Less than half of the amount had been paid at the time of a coal disaster at the company's

Blacksville mine, in which a fire triggered by a trolley wire ignition caused the death of nine men.

The failure of fines as deterrents of corporate crime has led to a call for the imposition of more effective and varied criminal sanctions. Discussions of sanctions against the corporation have traditionally focused on a narrow field of civil sanctions, specifically fines and injunctive orders. This focus has been broadened in recent years by a number of Australian corporate criminologists who seek to expand the goals of criminal law and to elevate retribution as a legitimate goal of corporate criminal law. This broadened perspective brings into play sanctions that many consider inappropriate or ineffective in punishing or deterring street crime—such as incapacitation and execution—but may work well in the corporate criminal context.

Although individual corporate executives can be incapacitated for crimes against society, corporations willing to continue to flout the laws will merely substitute one executive for another. Thus, if a product safety control manager comes under an incapacitative order forbidding him or her from serving in such a position for three years, the corporation may merely substitute a manager of like mind in place of the exiled manager.

To overcome this substitution problem, legislatures and courts may turn to issuing incapacitation orders against the corporate entity. Courts may order companies to cease operating in areas where the company has shown repeated criminal conduct. In extreme cases, courts may impose an execution order, or death sentence. Since a corporation is a creation of the state, there is no reason why, in cases of egregious conduct, courts may not order the dissolution of the corporate entity. In 1983, for example, the Attorney General of Virginia asked the state's Corporation Commission to dissolve the charter of Croatan Books Inc., a firm reportedly convicted 69 times in five years for possessing obscene films or magazines. The dissolution was moved for on the grounds that the corporation had "continued to exceed or abuse the authority conferred upon it by law."

It is generally agreed that rehabilitation has failed as an approach to controlling street crime. However, there is a growing consensus that it must be examined carefully as a way of gaining control of the corporate crime problem. As Fisse and Braithwaite have observed, it may be difficult to reorganize or rehabilitate a human psyche, but it is much easier to rearrange a corporation's standard operating procedures, defective control systems, inadequate communication mechanisms, and in general its internal structure. Australian investigators who have conducted most of the empirical research in this area conclude that rehabilitation works in the corporate sphere. Hopkins's study of the rehabilitation of corporate criminals in Australia found that most companies prosecuted under the consumer protection provisions of the Australian Trade Practices Act introduced at least some measures to ensure that the offense did not recur. And Fisse and Braithwaite found similar patterns in their study of adverse publicity. Rehabilitation can be demanded by police agencies, through consent decrees and probation orders, as a condition of a suspended sentence or as a contingency of settlement. The police or the courts may thereby order a number of changes within the corporate organization, including changes in how information is exchanged and how decisions are made, as well as the creation of an internal ombudsman and accounting groups.

Court-sanctioned adverse publicity has great potential for bringing corporate criminal conduct under control. The recent quantitative study by Fisse and Braithwaite of 17 corporations involved in publicity crises found that large corporations care greatly about their reputations. The study concluded that corporations fear the sting of adverse publicity more than they fear the law itself.

Corporate antisocial conduct is brought to the attention of the public through a number of channels, including consumer activist groups, investigative reporters, federal police agency enforcement actions, official inquiries, governmentally mandated disclosures, and international boycotts. In some instances a corporation is ordered to publicize its misdeeds as part of the sanction for a violation of law. In the J.P. Stevens case, for example, the company was ordered to give notice of anti-union violations by mail to its employees in North and South Carolina. In a securities case, a defendant was required to send its shareholders copies of the court's decision against it. And, in an FTC case against ITT Continental Baking, in which the company was accused of deceptive advertising for its Profile brand bread, the company agreed to a consent decree that required it to allocate 25 percent of its advertising budget for one year to a disclosure stating that "Profile is not effective for weight reduction."

These instances involved civil and administrative proceedings, but there is a strong case to be made for court-ordered use of formal publicity orders as a sanction for convicted corporations. A 1970 draft of the U.S. National Commission on Reform of Federal Criminal Law (the Brown Commission) recommended:

> When an organization is convicted of an offense, the court may, in addition to or in lieu of imposing other authorized sanctions . . . require the organization to give appropriate publicity to the conviction by notice to the class or classes of persons or sector of the public interested in or affected by the conviction, by advertising in designated areas or by designated media, or otherwise. . . .

Fisse and Braithwaite suggest two ways of implementing this recommendation: first, that publication of the details of an offense be made available as a court-ordered sentence against corporate offenders, and second, that pre-sentence or probation orders against corporate offenders should be used to require disclosure of organizational reforms and disciplinary action undertaken as a result of the offense.

Still, some argue that corporations cannot be stigmatized by adverse publicity despite strong evidence and common sense suggesting the opposite. Surely corporate heads would turn and listen more attentively to law enforcement agents if, for example, Hooker Chemical Company were required to buy television ads to tell the nation about its pollution activities, or if the Ford Motor Company were required to run television ads informing the nation about how it marketed the unsafe Pinto, or if Grunenthal were required to tell the world about how it marketed thalidomide and how thalidomide affected its consumers. To use adverse publicity sanctions not just in remedial orders, but as punitive and educational measures, is one of the more effective and efficient ways of shaming corporate America out of its antisocial behavior and bringing it back within the bounds of legal commerce.

Another alternative corporate sentence is the equity fine. Professor John Coffee, dismayed by the failure of cash fines to effectively sanction corporate wrongdoing, has suggested that the corporation be fined not in cash, but in the equity securities of the corporation. Under Coffee's equity fine proposal, the convicted corporation would be required to authorize and issue such number of shares to a state's victim compensation fund as would have an expected market value equal to the cash fine necessary to deter illegal activity. The fund would then be able to liquidate the securities in whatever manner best maximized its return.

Coffee's equity fine proposal overcomes a number of the problems associated with cash fines. First, the equity fine better aligns the self-interest of managers with the interests of the corporation. When the corporation issues the shares designated for the victims' compensation fund, the per share market value would decline, thus reducing the value of stock options and other compensation available to the executives. Second, Coffee argues that a large block of marketable securities would make the corporation an inviting target for a takeover. Third, stockholders would have greater incentive to take a longer term view of the profit goals of the corporation and to insist on keeping operations within legal bounds. Fourth, the equity fine proposal overcomes the unfairness of cash fines in that the corporation would be less able to pass on the cost of the equity fine to workers and consumers. Finally, the deterrence trap problem associated with cash fines is overcome since the market value of the corporation exceeds its cash reserves. Under equity fines, much larger fines can be levied, fines large enough to deter giant companies from illegal behavior.

Although community service orders against individual white-collar violators have attracted widespread attention and condemnation, little attention has been paid to the potential of community service orders in controlling corporate crime. As Fisse has observed, community service orders against the corporation can be invoked in a wide variety of legal settings: as a condition of probation, as a condition of mitigation of sentence, and as a condition of non-prosecution.

In the Allied Chemical/Kepone case, U.S. District Court Judge Robert Merhige fined Allied $13.24 million after the company pleaded no contest to 940 counts of water pollution. The amount of the fine was reduced to $5 million when the company agreed to spend $8,356,202 to establish the Virginia Environmental Endowment, a nonprofit group that would "fund scientific research projects and implement remedial projects and other programs to help alleviate problems that Kepone has created . . . and . . . enhance and improve the overall quality of the environment in Virginia."

In *United States v. Olin Mathieson,* the corporate defendant, Olin, pleaded no contest to a charge of conspiring to ship 3,200 rifles to South Africa in violation of the trade embargo. U.S. District Court Judge Robert Zampano fined Olin Mathieson $45,000 after the company agreed to give $500,000 to set up the New Haven Community Betterment Fund, a nonprofit group "to promote the general welfare of the greater New Haven area with gifts or grants to charitable organizations."

Another notable example came in 1980, when FMC Corporation pleaded guilty to lying to the federal police (EPA) in 1975 and 1976 by reporting that it was discharging about 200 pounds per day of carbon tetrachloride into the Kanawha River in West Virginia when in reality it knew that the actual discharge was ten times that amount. As part of the plea agreement with U.S. police agents, FMC agreed to pay $1 million into the Virginia Environmental Endowment that had been created by the court order in the Allied/Kepone case.

The community service sanctions in the Allied, Olin, and FMC cases were deductible, whereas fines are not—an advantage regarded favorably by corporate criminals. Fisse suggests making these sanctions expressly a sentence of punishment, thus disallowing tax deductibility and any patent or copyright protection from any product of a project of the community service. But, by redirecting money fines to environmental, consumer, and other community and citizen action groups, judges can leverage the money, money usually lost in the shuffle at state and federal treasury departments, to assist the victims of the corporate criminal activity. Automobile corporate criminals could be directed to pay money to the auto safety groups, pharmaceutical corporate criminals could be directed to pay money to support health groups, and chemical corporate criminals could be directed to support environmental action groups. The deterrent and punitive effects of forcing companies to support their public policy adversaries cannot be overestimated.

And judges need not be limited to redirecting money fines to citizen groups. In the thalidomide case, Fisse suggests that the German manufacturer Grunenthal could have been required to set up production facilities to produce and supply artificial limbs, robotic devices, and other special aids. In the Pinto case, Ford could have been required to set up regional burn treatment centers. Ralph Nader has suggested that "making a coal executive work in a coal mine for two years is better than putting him in a cushy jail." The only limits to imaginative and effective community service orders are those binding the minds of legislators and sentencing judges.

40

Decisions of Death

David Bruck

There are 1,150 men and 13 women awaiting execution in the United States. It's not easy to imagine how many people 1,163 is. If death row were really a row, it would stretch for 1.3 miles, cell after six-foot-wide cell. In each cell, one person, sitting, pacing, watching TV, sleeping, writing letters. Locked in their cells nearly twenty-four hours a day, the condemned communicate with each other by shouts, notes, and hand-held mirrors, all with a casual dexterity that handicapped people acquire over time. Occasionally there is a break in the din of shouted conversations—a silent cell, its inhabitant withdrawn into a cocoon of madness. That's what death row would look like. That's what, divided up among the prisons of thirty-four states, it does look like.

This concentration of condemned people is unique among the democratic countries of the world. It is also nearly double the number of prisoners who were on death row in 1972 when the Supreme Court, in *Furman v. Georgia*, averted a massive surge of executions by striking down all the nation's capital punishment laws.

But in another sense, death row is very small. If every one of these 1,163 inmates were to be taken out of his or her cell tomorrow and gassed, electrocuted, hanged, shot, or injected, the total of convicted murderers imprisoned in this country would decline from some 33,526 (at last count) to 32,363—a reduction of a little over 3 percent. Huge as this country's

David Bruck, "Decisions of Death" from *The New Republic*, December 12, 1983. Reprinted by permission of *The New Republic*, © 1983, The New Republic, Inc.

death row population has become, it does not include—and has never included—more than a tiny fraction of those who are convicted of murder.

It falls to the judicial system of each of the thirty-eight states that retain capital punishment to cull the few who are to die from the many who are convicted of murder. This selection begins with the crime itself, as the community and the press react with outrage or with indifference, depending on the nature of the murder and the identity of the victim. With the arrest of a suspect, police and prosecutors must decide what charges to file, whether to seek the death penalty, and whether the defendant should be allowed to plea-bargain for his life. Most of these decisions can later be changed, so that at any point from arrest to trial the defendant's chances of slipping through the death penalty net depend on chance: the inclinations and ambitions of the local prosecutor, the legal and political pressures which impel him to one course of action or another, and the skill or incompetence of the court-appointed defense counsel.

In the courtroom, the defendant may be spared or condemned by the countless vagaries of the trial by jury. There are counties in each state where the juries almost always impose death, and counties where they almost never do. There are hanging judges and lenient judges, and judges who go one way or the other depending on who the victim's family happens to be, or the defendant's family, or who is prosecuting the case, or who is defending it.

Thus at each stage between arrest and sentence, more and more defendants are winnowed out from the ranks of those facing possible execution: in 1979, a year which saw more than eighteen thousand arrests for intentional homicides and nearly four thousand murder convictions throughout the United States, only 159 defendants were added to death row. And even for those few who are condemned to die, there lies ahead a series of appeals which whittle down the number of condemned still further, sparing some and consigning others to death on the basis of appellate courts' judgments of the nuances of a trial judge's instructions to the jury, of whether the court-appointed defense lawyer had made the proper objections at the proper moments during the trial, and so on. By the time the appeals process has run its course, almost every murder defendant who faced the possibility of execution when he was first arrested has by luck, justice, or favor evaded execution, and a mere handful are left to die.

This process of selection is the least understood feature of capital punishment. Because the media focus on the cases where death has been imposed and where the executions seem imminent, the public sees capital punishment not as the maze-like system that it is, but only in terms of this or that individual criminal, about to suffer just retribution for a particular crime. What we don't see in any of this now-familiar drama are hundreds of others whose crimes were as repugnant, but who are jailed for life or less instead of condemned to death. So the issues appear simple. The prisoner's guilt is certain. His crime is horrendous. Little knots of "supporters" light candles and hold vigils. His lawyers rush from court to court raising arcane new appeals.

The condemned man himself remembers the many points of his procession through the judicial system at which he might have been spared, but was not. He knows, too, from his years of waiting in prison, that most of those who committed crimes like his have evaded the execution that awaits him. So do the prosecutors who have pursued him through the court system, and the judges who have upheld his sentence. And so do the defense lawyers, the ones glimpsed on the TV news in the last hours, exhausted and overwrought for reasons that, given their client's crimes, must be hard for most people to fathom.

I am one of those lawyers, and I know the sense of horror that propels those last-minute appeals. It is closely related to the horror that violent crime awakens in all of us—the random kind of crime, the sniper in the tower or the gunman in the grocery store. The horror derives not from death, which comes to us all, but from death that is inflicted *at random*, for no reason, for being on the wrong subway platform or the wrong side of the street. Up close, that is what capital punishment is like. And that is what makes the state's inexorable, stalking pursuit of this or that particular person's life so chilling.

The lawyers who bring those eleventh-hour appeals know from their work how many murderers are spared, how few are sentenced to die, and how chance and race decide which will be which. In South Carolina, where I practice law, murders committed during robberies may be punished by death. According to police reports, there were 286 defendants arrested for such murders from the time that South Carolina's death penalty law went into effect in 1977 until the end of 1981. (About a third of those arrests were of blacks charged with killing whites.) Out of all of those 286 defendants, the prosecution had sought the death penalty and obtained final convictions by the end of 1981 against 37. And of those 37 defendants, death sentences were imposed and affirmed on only 4; the rest received prison sentences. What distinguished those 4 defendants' cases was this: 3 were black, had killed white storeowners, and were tried by all-white juries; the fourth, a white, was represented at his trial by a lawyer who had never read the state's murder statute, had no case file and no office, and had refused to talk to his client for the last two months prior to the trial because he'd been insulted by the client's unsuccessful attempt to fire him.

If these four men are ultimately executed, the newspapers will report and the law will record that they went to their deaths because they committed murder and robbery. But when so many others who committed the same crime were spared, it can truthfully be said only that these four men were *convicted* because they committed murder: they were *executed* because of race, or bad luck, or both.

If one believes, as many do, that murderers deserve whatever punishment they get, then none of this should matter. But if the 1,163 now on death row throughout the United States had actually been selected by means of a lottery from the roughly 33,500 inmates now serving sentences for murder, most Americans, whatever their views on capital punishment as an abstract matter, would surely be appalled. This revulsion would be all the stronger if we limited the pool of those murderers facing execution by restricting it to blacks. Or if we sentenced people to die on the basis of the race of the *victim*, consigning to death only those—whatever their race—who have killed whites, and sparing all those who have killed blacks.

The reason why our sense of justice rebels at such ideas is not hard to identify. Violent crime undermines the sense of order and shared moral values without which no society could exist. We punish people who commit such crimes in order to reaffirm our standards of right and wrong, and our belief that life in society can be orderly and trusting rather than fearful and chaotic. But if the punishment itself is administered chaotically or arbitrarily, it fails in its purpose and becomes, like the crime which triggered it, just another spectacle of the random infliction of suffering—all the more terrifying and demoralizing because this time the random killer is organized society itself, the same society on which we depend for stability and security in our daily lives. No matter how much the individual criminal thus selected for death may "deserve" his punishment, the manner of its imposition robs it of any possible value, and leaves us ashamed instead of reassured.

It was on precisely this basis, just eleven years ago, that the Supreme Court in *Furman v. Georgia* struck down every death penalty law in the United States, and set aside the death sentences of more than six hundred death row inmates. *Furman* was decided by a single vote (all four Nixon appointees voting to uphold the death penalty laws), and though the five majority justices varied in their rationales, the dominant theme of their opinions was that the Constitution did not permit the execution of a capriciously selected handful out of all those convicted of capital crimes. For Justice Byron White and the rest of the *Furman* majority, years of reading the petitions of the condemned had simply revealed "no meaningful basis for distinguishing the few cases in which [death] is imposed from the many in which it is not." Justice Potter Stewart compared the country's capital sentencing methods to being struck by lightning, adding that "if any basis can be discerned for the selection of these few to be sentenced to die, it is on the constitutionally impermissible basis of race." Justice William O. Douglas summarized the issue by observing that the Constitution would never permit any law which stated

> that anyone making more than $50,000 would be exempt from the death penalty . . . [nor] a law that in terms said that blacks, those that never went beyond the fifth grade in school, those who made less than $3,000

a year, or those who were unpopular or unstable would be the only people executed. *A law which in the overall view reaches that result in practice has no more sanctity than a law which in terms provides the same.* [Emphasis added.]

On the basis of these views, the Supreme Court in *Furman* set aside every death sentence before it, and effectively cleared off death row. Though *Furman v. Georgia* did not outlaw the death penalty as such, the Court's action came at a time when America appeared to have turned against capital punishment, and *Furman* seemed to climax a long and inexorable progression toward abolition. After *Furman*, Chief Justice Warren E. Burger, who had dissented from the Court's decision, predicted privately that there would never be another execution in the United States.

What happened instead was that the majority of state legislatures passed new death sentencing laws designed to satisfy the Supreme Court. By this year, eleven years after *Furman*, there are roughly as many states with capital punishment laws on the books as there were in 1972.

In theory the capital sentencing statutes under which the 1,163 prisoners now on death row were condemned are very different from the death penalty laws in effect prior to 1972. Under the pre-*Furman* laws, the process of selection was simple: the jury decided whether the accused was guilty of murder, and if so, whether he should live or die. In most states, no separate sentencing hearing was held: jurors were supposed to determine both guilt and punishment at the same time, often without benefit of any information about the background or circumstances of the defendant whose life was in their hands. Jurors were also given no guidelines or standards with which to assess the relative gravity of the case before them, but were free to base their life-or-death decision on whatever attitudes or biases they happened to have carried with them into the jury room. These statutes provided few grounds for appeal and worked fast: as late as the 1950s, many prisoners were executed within a few weeks of their trials, and delays of more than a year or two were rare.

In contrast, the current crop of capital statutes have created complex, multi-tiered sentencing schemes based on lists of specified "aggravating" and "mitigating" factors which the jury is to consider in passing sentence. Sentencing now occurs at a separate hearing after guilt has been determined. The new statutes also provide for automatic appeal to the state supreme courts, usually with a requirement that the court determine whether each death sentence is excessive considering the defendant and the crime. The first of these new statutes—from Georgia, Florida, and Texas—came before the Supreme Court for review in 1976. The new laws were different from one another in several respects—only Georgia's provided for case-by-case review of the appropriateness of each death sentence by the state supreme court; Florida's permitted the judge to sentence a defendant to death even where the jury had recommended a life sentence; and the Texas statute determined who was to be executed on the basis of the jury's answer to the semantically perplexing question of whether the evidence established "beyond a reasonable doubt" a "probability" that the defendant would commit acts of violence in the future. What these statutes all had in common, however, was some sort of criteria, however vague, to guide juries and judges in their life-or-death decisions, while permitting capital defendants a chance to present evidence to show why they should be spared. Henceforth—or so went the theory behind these new laws—death sentences could not be imposed randomly or on the basis of the race or social status of the defendant and the victim, but only on the basis of specific facts about the crime, such as whether the murder had been committed during a rape or a robbery, or whether it had been "especially heinous, atrocious and cruel" (in Florida), or "outrageously or wantonly vile, horrible or inhuman" (in Georgia).

After considering these statutes during the spring of 1976, the Supreme Court announced in *Gregg v. Georgia* and two other cases that the new laws satisfied its concern, expressed in *Furman*, about the randomness and unfairness of the previous death sentencing systems. Of course, the Court had no actual evidence that these new laws were being applied any more equally or consistently than the ones struck down in *Furman*. But for that matter, the Court had not relied on factual evidence in *Furman*, either. Although social science research over the previous thirty years had consistently found the nation's use of capital punishment to be characterized by arbitrariness and racial discrimination, the decisive opinions of Justices White and Stewart in *Furman* cited none of this statistical evidence, but relied instead on the justices' own conclusions derived from years of experience with the appeals of the condemned. The *Furman* decision left the Court free to declare the problem solved later on. And four years later, in *Gregg v. Georgia*, that is what it did.

It may be, of course, that the Court's prediction in *Gregg* of a new era of fairness in capital sentencing was a sham, window dressing for what was in reality nothing more than a capitulation to the mounting public clamor for a resumption of executions. But if the justices sincerely believed that new legal guidelines and jury instructions would really solve the problems of arbitrariness and racial discrimination in death penalty cases, they were wrong.

Before John Spenkelink—a white murderer of a white victim—was executed by the state of Florida in May 1979, his lawyers tried to present to the state and federal courts a study which showed that the "new" Florida death penalty laws, much like the ones which they had replaced, were being applied far more frequently against persons who killed whites than against those who killed blacks. The appeals courts responded that the Supreme Court had settled all of these arguments in 1976 when it upheld the new sentencing statutes: the laws were fair because the Supreme

Court had said they were fair; mere evidence to the contrary was irrelevant.

After Spenkelink was electrocuted, the evidence continued to mount. In 1980 two Northeastern University criminologists, William Bowers and Glenn Pierce, published a study of homicide sentencing in Georgia, Florida, and Texas, the three states whose new death penalty statutes were the first to be approved by the Supreme Court after *Furman*. Bowers and Pierce tested the Supreme Court's prediction that these new statutes would achieve consistent and even-handed sentencing by comparing the lists of which convicted murderers had been condemned and which spared with the facts of their crimes as reported by the police. What they found was that in cases where white victims had been killed, black defendants in all three states were from four to six times more likely to be sentenced to death than were white defendants. Both whites and blacks, moreover, faced a much greater danger of being executed where the murder victims were white than where the victims were black. A black defendant in Florida was thirty-seven times more likely to be sentenced to death if his victim was white than if his victim was black; in Georgia, black-on-white killings were punished by death thirty-three times more often than were black-on-black killings; and in Texas, the ratio climbed to an astounding 84 to 1: Even when Bowers and Pierce examined only those cases which the police had reported as "felony-circumstance" murders (i.e., cases involving kidnapping or rape, and thus excluding mere domestic and barroom homicides), they found that both the race of the defendant and the race of the victim appeared to produce enormous disparities in death sentences in each state.

A more detailed analysis of charging decisions in several Florida counties even suggested that prosecutors tended to "upgrade" murders of white victims by alleging that they were more legally aggravated than had been apparent to the police who had written up the initial report, while "downgrading" murders of black victims in a corresponding manner, apparently to avoid the expensive and time-consuming process of trying such murders of blacks as capital cases. Their overall findings, Bowers and Pierce concluded,

> are consistent with a single underlying racist tenet: that white lives are
> worth more than black lives. From this tenet it follows that death as
> punishment is more appropriate for the killers of whites than for the
> killers of blacks and more appropriate for black than for white killers.

Such stark evidence of discrimination by race of offender and by race of victim, they wrote, is "a direct challenge to the constitutionality of the post-*Furman* capital statutes . . . [and] may represent a two-edged sword of racism in capital punishment which is beyond statutory control."

This new data was presented to the federal courts by attorneys for a Georgia death row inmate named John Eldon Smith in 1981. The court of

appeals replied that the studies were too crude to have any legal significance, since they did not look at all the dozens of circumstances of each
case, other than race, that might have accounted for the unequal sentencing patterns that Bowers and Pierce had detected.

The matter might have ended there, since the court's criticism implied
that only a gargantuan (and extremely expensive) research project encom-
passing the most minute details of many hundreds of homicide cases
would be worthy of its consideration. But as it happened, such a study
was already under way, supported by a foundation grant and directed by
University of Iowa law professor David Baldus. Using a staff of law
students and relying primarily on official Georgia state records, Baldus
gathered and coded more than 230 factual circumstances surrounding
each of more than a thousand homicides, including 253 death penalty
sentencing proceedings conducted under Georgia's current death penalty law. Baldus's results, presented in an Atlanta federal court hearing
late last summer, confirmed that among defendants convicted of murder-
ing whites, blacks are substantially more likely to go to death row than are
whites. Although blacks account for some 60 percent of Georgia homicide
victims, Baldus fround that killers of black victims are punished by death
less than one-tenth as often as are killers of white victims. With the
scientific precision of an epidemiologist seeking to pinpoint the cause of a
new disease, Baldus analyzed and reanalyzed his mountain of data on
Georgia homicides, controlling for the hundreds of factual variables in
each case, in search of any explanation other than race which might
account for the stark inequalities in the operation of Georgia's capital
sentencing system. He could find none. And when the state of Georgia's
turn came to defend its capital sentencing record at the Atlanta federal
court hearing, it soon emerged that the statisticians hired by the state to
help it refute Baldus's research had had no better success in *their* search
for an alternative explanation. (In a telephone interview after the Atlanta
hearing, the attorney general of Georgia, Michael Bowers, assured me
that "the bottom line is that Georgia does not discriminate on the basis of
race," but referred all specific questions to his assistant, who declined to
answer on the grounds that the court proceeding was pending.)

The findings of research efforts like Baldus's document what anyone
who has worked in the death-sentencing system will have sensed all
along: the Supreme Court notwithstanding, there is no set of courtroom
procedures set out in lawbooks which can change the prosecution practices of local district attorneys. Nor will even the most elaborate jury
instructions ever ensure that an all-white jury will weigh a black life as
heavily as a white life.

At bottom, the determination of whether or not a particular defendant
should die for his crime is simply not a rational decision. Requiring that
the jury first determine whether his murder was "outrageously or wan-

tonly vile, horrible, or inhuman," as Georgia juries are invited to do, provides little assurance that death will be imposed fairly and consistently. Indeed, Baldus's research revealed that Georgia juries are more likely to find that a given murder was "outrageously or wantonly vile, horrible, or inhuman" when the victim was white, and likelier still when the murderer is black—hardly a vindication of the Supreme Court's confidence in *Gregg v. Georgia* that such guidelines would serve to eliminate racial discrimination in sentencing.

At present, 51 percent of the inhabitants of death row across the country are white, as were seven of the eight men executed since the Supreme Court's *Gregg* decision. Five percent of the condemned are Hispanic, and almost all of the remaining 44 percent are black. Since roughly half the people arrested and charged with intentional homicide each year in the United States are white, it would appear at first glance that the proportions of blacks and whites now on death row are about those that would be expected from a fair system of capital sentencing. But what studies like Baldus's now reveal is how such seemingly equitable racial distribution can actually be the product of racial discrimination, rather than proof that discrimination has been overcome.

The explanation for this seeming paradox is that the judicial system discriminates on the basis of the race of the *victim* as well as the race of the defendant. Each year, according to the F.B.I.'s crime report, about the same numbers of blacks as whites are arrested for murder throughout the United States, and the totals of black and white murder victims are also roughly equal. But like many other aspects of American life, our murders are segregated: white murderers almost always kill whites, and the large majority of black killers kill blacks. While blacks who kill whites tend to be singled out for harsher treatment—and more death sentences—than other murderers, there are relatively few of them, and so the absolute effect on the numbers of blacks sent to death row is limited. On the other hand, the far more numerous black murderers whose victims were also black are treated relatively leniently in the courts, and are only rarely sent to death row. Because these dual systems of discrimination operate simultaneously, they have the overall effect of keeping the numbers of blacks on death row roughly proportionate to the numbers of blacks convicted of murder—even while individual defendants are being condemned, and others spared, on the basis of race. In short, like the man who, with one foot in ice and the other in boiling water, describes his situation as "comfortable on average," the death sentencing system has created an illusion of fairness.

In theory, law being based on precedent, the Supreme Court might be expected to apply the principles of the *Furman* decision as it did in 1972 and strike down death penalty laws which have produced results as seemingly racist as these. But that's not going to happen. *Furman* was a product of its time: in 1972 public support for the death penalty had been dropping fairly steadily over several decades, and capital punishment appeared to be going the way of the stocks, the whipping post, and White and Colored drinking fountains. The resurgence of support for capital punishment in the country over the last decade has changed that, at least for now. Last summer the Supreme Court upheld every one of the four death sentences it had taken under consideration during its 1982–83 session, and in November the Court heard arguments by California in support of its claim that the states should not be required to compare murder sentences on a statewide basis in order to assure fairness in capital sentencing. The justices may have given an indication of their eventual decision on California's appeal when, just three hours before they heard that case, they lifted a stay of execution in a Louisiana case where a condemned prisoner named Robert Wayne Williams had been attempting to challenge the very limited method of comparison used by the Louisiana courts: as a result, Williams may well be dead by the time the California decision is handed down this spring. When in 1972 the Supreme Court was faced with a choice between fairness and the death penalty, it chose fairness. This time the odds are all with the death penalty.

Even with the Court's increasingly hard-line stance on capital appeals, there will probably not be any sudden surge of executions in the next year or two. One of the unreckoned costs of the death penalty is the strain it places on the state and federal judicial systems. Any large number of imminent executions would overload those systems to the point of breakdown. A great deal is being said nowadays about the need to speed up capital appeals: Justice Lewis Powell even added his voice to the chorus last spring at the very moment that the Supreme Court had the question of stays of execution under consideration in a pending case. But this attitude tends to moderate the closer one gets to a specific case. No judge wants to discover after it's too late that he permitted someone to be executed on the basis of factual or legal error, and for that reason alone the backlog of death row prisoners can be expected to persist.

Still, the pace of executions is going to pick up to a more or less steady trickle: possibly one a month, possibly two, maybe more. In September Mississippi's William Winter became the first governor since Ronald Reagan to permit an execution by lethal gas: Jimmy Lee Gray died banging his head against a steel pole in the gas chamber while the reporters counted his moans (eleven, according to the Associated Press). A month later, J. D. Autry came within minutes of dying by lethal injection in Texas, only to have Supreme Court Justice Byron White reverse his decision of the day before and stay the execution. Now Autry is reprieved until the Supreme Court decides whether California (and by implication Texas) must compare capital sentences to ensure some measure of fairness: if the

Court rules that they don't have to, Autry will in all likelihood be executed next year.

So far, the power of the death penalty as a social symbol has shielded from scrutiny the huge demands in money and resources which the death sentencing process makes on the criminal justice system as a whole. Whatever the abstract merits of capital punishment, there is no denying that a successful death penalty prosecution costs a fortune. A 1982 study in New York state concluded that just the trial and first stage of appeal in a death penalty case under that state's proposed death penalty bill would cost the taxpayers of New York over $1.8 million—more than twice as much as imprisoning the defendant for life. And even that estimate does not include the social costs of diverting an already overburdened criminal justice system from its job of handling large numbers of criminal cases to a preoccupation with the relative handful of capital ones. But the question of just how many laid-off police officers one execution is worth won't come up so long as the death penalty remains for most Americans a way of expressing feelings rather than a practical response to the problem of violent crime.

It is impossible to predict how long the executions will continue. The rise in violent crime in this country has already begun to abate somewhat, probably as a result of demographic changes as the baby boom generation matures beyond its crime-prone teenage and early adult years. But it may well turn out that even a marked reduction in the crime rate won't produce any sharp decrease in public pressure for capital punishment: the shift in public opinion on the death penalty seems to have far deeper roots than that. The death penalty has become a potent social symbol of national resolve, another way of saying that we're not going to be pushed around anymore, that we've got the will-power and self-confidence to stand up to anyone, whether muggers or Cubans or Islamic fanatics, that we're not the flaccid weaklings that "they" have been taking us for. The death penalty can only be understood as one of the so-called "social issues" of the Reagan era: it bears no more relationship to the problem of crime than school prayer bears to the improvement of public education. Over the past half-century, executions were at their peak during the Depression of the 1930s, and almost disappeared during the boom years of the 1950s and early 1960s. The re-emergence of the death penalty in the 1970s coincided with the advent of chronic inflation and recession, and with military defeat abroad and the decline of the civil rights movement at home. Given this historical record, it's a safe bet that whether the crime rates go up or down over the next several years, public support for executions will start to wane only as the country finds more substantial foundations for a renewal of confidence in its future.

In the meantime we will be the only country among all the Western industrial democracies which still executes its own citizens. Canada abolished capital punishment in 1976, as did France in 1981: England declined to bring back hanging just this summer. By contrast, our leading companions in the use of the death penalty as a judicial punishment for crime will be the governments of the Soviet Union, South Africa, Saudi Arabia, and Iran—a rogues' gallery of the most repressive and backward-looking regimes in the world. Just last week Christopher Wren reported in the *New York Times* that the total number of executions in the People's Republic of China may reach five thousand or more this year alone.

It's no accident that democracies tend to abolish the death penalty while autocracies and totalitarian regimes tend to retain it. In his new book, *The Death Penalty: A Debate*, John Conrad credits Tocqueville with the explanation for this, quoting from *Democracy in America:*

> When all the ranks of a community are nearly equal, as all men think and feel in nearly the same manner, each of them may judge in a moment the sensations of all the others; he casts a rapid glance upon himself, and that is enough. There is no wretchedness into which he cannot readily enter, and a secret instinct reveals to him its extent. . . . In democratic ages, men rarely sacrifice themselves for one another, but they display general compassion for the members of the human race. They inflict no useless ills, and they are happy to relieve the griefs of others when they can do so without much hurting themselves; they are not disinterested, but they are humane. . . .

Tocqueville went on to explain that his identification of America's democratic political culture as the root of the "singular mildness" of American penal practices was susceptible of an ironic proof: the cruelty with which Americans treated their black slaves. Restraint in punishment, he wrote, extends as far as our sense of social equality, and no further: "the same man who is full of humanity toward his fellow creatures when they are at the same time his equals becomes insensible to their affliction as soon as that equality ceases."

In that passage, written 150 years ago, Tocqueville reveals to us why it is that the death penalty—the practice of slowly bringing a fully conscious human face to face with the prospect of his own extinction and then killing him—should characterize the judicial systems of the least democratic and most repressive nations of the world. And it reveals too why the vestiges of this institution in America should be so inextricably entangled with the question of race. The gradual disappearance of the death penalty throughout most of the democratic world certainly suggests that Tocqueville was right. The day when Americans stop condemning people to death on the basis of race and inequality will be the day when we stop condemning anyone to death at all.

XI

National Security

The search for security is a legitimate and necessary concern of any nation. The U.S. Constitution authorizes Congress "to raise and support armies" and "to provide and maintain a navy." But to say that national security is a legitimate concern does not ensure that it will not also be a problematic one. Obviously, the technology of eighteenth-century armies and navies had little in common with the sophisticated and destructive weapons systems of contemporary military forces. Thus, the question for today is not whether the United States should have military forces but what policies we should follow in determining the role of the military.

Always urgent and controversial, these questions moved into the forefront of public discussion in the 1990s with the historic shifts in relations between the United States and the Soviet Union. The waning tensions between the worlds' superpowers have made it possible to rethink our approach to national security in ways that would have seemed Utopian only a few years before.

Such a rethinking is crucially important today, in the face of the continuing American military presence overseas—in Central America and elsewhere—and of the social effect of our still enormous military budget, which absorbs such a large portion of our economic resources.

The articles in this chapter explore the assumptions that have guided our approach to national security up to now, focusing especially on our conception of America's international military role, the process of military production, and our attitudes toward nuclear weapons. On the whole, the writers are critical—arguing that our approach to national security has failed to take into account several extraordinary political and technological changes in recent years.

Richard J. Barnet, for example, points to four "revolutionary factors of contemporary life" that have transformed international politics and considerations of strategy—the power of the atom, the collapse of colonialism, the worldwide diffusion of nuclear technology, and the skyrocketing costs of advanced weapons systems. Taken together, he argues, these factors demand fundamental reconsideration of traditional national security assumptions, with special regard for their impact on the integrity of our human resources. To the extent that military spending undercuts support for schools, science, cities, and cultural activities, we undermine our most fundamental sources of national strength. In sum, the search for national security should not be conceived narrowly, as a military problem, but more broadly, as a social problem.

The failure to take changing military needs into account is also a main theme of the Center for Defense Information's discussion of "wasteful weapons." Increasingly, we are buying weapons we do not need—and spending much more than we can afford. One reason is that we are still operating on assumptions rooted in the Cold War era, when the dominant idea was the need to prepare for a potential nuclear war with the Soviet Union. In addition, the American defense industry has a built-in stake in producing weapons that are too costly, too complex, and often poorly designed and tested. And the industry's undue influence over Congress and other officials allows this situation to continue. The result is that we are producing weapons that are both intolerably expensive and "irrelevant to our military needs."

Phillip Berryman's article takes up a similar theme: the costs of overestimating threats to national security. For many years, the United States has been deeply involved in supporting dictatorial governments, and trying to forestall revolutionary change, in Central America. Berryman argues that our self-defeating brand of intervention has been based on a grave overestimation of the threat that popular movements in Central America present to the United States—and also on myopic lack of understanding of what Central American revolutionaries truly want, which, on closer inspection, turns out to be just about what ordinary people in most countries want—the chance for peace and for real prosperity, equitably shared. The political situation has changed considerably in Panama and Nicaragua since this article was written. But the assumptions Berryman challenges about the needs of developing countries—and our resulting military posture toward them—are still very much with us.

The ultimate threat to national security—in the United States and every other country in the world—is nuclear war. Like military spending in general, our steady buildup of nuclear weapons has been predicated on the presumed threat of aggression from abroad. The perceived urgency of that threat has kept us from taking a hard look at the possible consequences of the use of those weapons. Some of these are spelled out in Carl Sagan's chilling summary of a report by leading United States scientists on the impact of nuclear war and the use of "strategic" nuclear weapons. The study, though discomforting, is nevertheless essential reading for the contemporary student of American social problems. Nuclear war, even "limited" nuclear war, would inflict calamitous death and destruction on the United States and the whole world. The "nuclear winter" following a nuclear weapons exchange—given the megatonnage of contemporary weapons—would "constitute a global climatic catastrophe." Its genetic impact would destroy the future of the entire human race. Nuclear war is thus the ultimate social problem of our era.

41

The Search for National Security

Richard J. Barnet

The real debate over national security in the United States is between those who believe that the nation has insufficient military power to create a world hospitable to American goods, American values, and the servicing of American needs and those who believe that the objective cannot be achieved with any quantity of military power but, if it is to be achieved, must be achieved in other ways. It is obvious that the world is dangerous, unsettled, violent, and maddeningly unpredictable. The taking of our people as hostages, the gratuitous insults to us in the United Nations, the monumental ingratitude of some of our petty clients, and the heavy-handed, often puzzling behavior of the Soviet Union all foster an impulse to reach for the gun. Yet when we do reach for the gun the threat does not seem to work the way it used to. Is this because something has happened to the American spirit, as the advocates of "get tough" policies insist, or is it because the world has changed?

When Albert Einstein observed, at the dawn of the nuclear age, that "the unleashed power of the atom has changed everything save our modes of thinking," he was identifying only one of the revolutionary factors of contemporary life which have transformed politics. At least three others have contributed to the change in the relationship between force and power. The first is the transformation over the last two generations of billions of people who were previously objects rather than subjects of international politics. With the collapse of the old colonial empires

Richard J. Barnet, "The Search for National Security," from *Real Security: Restoring American Power in a Dangerous Decade,* by Richard J. Barnet. Copyright © 1981 by Richard J. Barnet. Reprinted by permission of Simon & Schuster, Inc.

and the creation of scores of new nations, it is no longer possible for the fate of people in Asia, Africa, and Latin America to be settled in a few chancelleries of Europe. International politics, which was once a drawing-room drama, has become an extravaganza with a cast of thousands—not just the new nations but dissident groups and terrorist organizations that also have the power to make their presence felt. The rules for using violence have been changing—not the treaties regulating the use of force but the unspoken dictates that actually guide political leaders. On to center stage have come ancient religious and tribal rivalries that make it exceedingly difficult for the most powerful nations to organize global battle lines. Thus, arming Pakistan to fight the Russians in Afghanistan—a plausible, if dangerous, Cold War strategy—must be ruled out, because the Pakistanis and the Afghans cannot agree on their border in a region whose allegiance has long been a source of contention. In the Middle East, Saudi Arabia, like Iran, cannot be an effective surrogate wielder of military power, because of old scores in the region which have not yet been settled. When these ancient tensions and rivalries did not matter (because the people who cared passionately about them had no international visibility), it was fairly easy for the great powers, in their rivalries with one another, to ignore local conflicts—or, indeed, to exploit them.

In the early postwar years, when the decolonization process had just got under way, it was a relatively simple matter to organize the American security system on the principle of anti-Communism. Despite the precipitous decline in the appeal of Communism over the last twenty years—or perhaps because of it—an international security system based on anti-Communism is unrealizable. For most people in the world, the writings of Marx and Lenin, the virtues and deficiencies of the Soviet central-planning system, and the betrayed dreams of a classless society are not the issues that define reality. Hitlerism was an easy target, because there was only one Hitler and he gave every evidence of being a mad conqueror who had to be stopped. But in the past five years some of the bloodiest wars have been between nations calling themselves Communist—between Cambodia and Vietnam, between Vietnam and China—and some observers believe that the most likely spark for a world war is renewed fighting between the Soviet Union and China.

The enormous complexity of the contemporary world makes a simple security strategy obsolete. Violence, as Hannah Arendt put it in her extraordinary study "On Revolution," is politically effective only to the extent that its use is thought of as legitimate. Indeed, when it is seen as legitimate it does not need to be used much. And, as Britain found in India, once opposition grows to the point at which a colonial power must fight a war instead of conducting a low-level police operation, the use of violence becomes illegitimate and ultimately ineffective. Modern war achieves its political purpose through its psychological impact. *Schrecklichkeit*, as the early German theorists of modern warfare called it, creates the power to regulate the political behavior of masses of people by intimidating their leaders. For the strategy to work, there must be effective command and control; that is, the leaders who are to be intimidated must have the ability to surrender docile populations to the conqueror. The present situation in Iran is but an extreme case of a more general condition—the inability of political leaders, even under severe threat, to control popular passions or to pacify their own territory. In such a situation, the use of force from outside is ineffective for achieving political purposes. In international relations, it may still be legitimate to "punish" an adversary but not to "punish" leaderless crowds.

A second revolution has occurred in military technology. The spread of nuclear weapons is an accomplished fact. As early as 1975, the United States Arms Control and Disarmament Agency estimated that there would be enough weapons-grade nuclear material moving about the planet in 1985 to make twenty thousand nuclear weapons of the class that destroyed Hiroshima. South Africa and Israel—each a nation that will be involved in a potential life-and-death struggle over the next two decades—are presumed by many intelligence agencies to have nuclear weapons already. We now live in what the military historian Harvey A. DeWeerd calls a "Balkanized world"—a world of small, poor, but over-militarized states struggling for power. It is, he says, an "unmanageable" world, and a dangerous one for the United States, because a local conventional war can suck in the great powers. Emphasizing the familiar point that the generals are always preparing for the last war that was fought, DeWeerd notes that future wars are not likely to be either replays of the Second World War in Europe, to which most of our conventional forces are now addressed, or military expeditions in the desert. They will be small wars, and the belligerents will be exceedingly hard for outside powers to control. Modern weapons of all sorts are now readily available on the international market. Since the Second World War, the United States itself has sold, lent, or given away more than a hundred billion dollars' worth of armaments. Of the fifty largest American industrial companies, thirty-two make or export arms.

The purpose of arms shipments has been, as former Defense Secretary James Schlesinger put it in 1975, "to maintain influence." In defending huge arms shipments to the Shah of Iran and other Persian Gulf leaders, he declared, "The degree of influence of the supplier is potentially substantial, and, typically, those relationships are enduring." But the spread of military technology has had exactly the opposite effect. Instead of making the recipients dependent, it has turned out to be something of an equalizer. Poor, weak countries, though they may be hopelessly in debt and have populations that are starving, can and do conduct formidable military operations against their neighbors, and even against their own people. There is little that the great powers can do about this. Recent advances in military technology mean that bigger is not necessarily safer.

The cruiser and the aircraft carrier—the modern vehicles for international swaggering—are vulnerable to shore-launched missiles of the sort that many Third World countries now have. The first thirty years of the postwar era were remarkably stable, largely because the United States had something approaching a monopoly of military power. It had most of the world's nuclear weapons, and it had the only fighting force that could be dispatched to distant corners of the globe. Today, in part because of the Soviet buildup, in part because of a worldwide arms buildup (to which the United States has been by far the largest contributor), the world is much less amenable to being managed by American military power. This reality is reflected in the schizophrenic reaction of certain Persian Gulf states, which privately urge the United States to take a tougher military role in their area but refuse to allow the United States to have a base on their territory. In Saudi Arabia, for example, the royal family knows that a base would arouse political opposition, domestic and foreign, and could not save their regime. The Reagan Administration, determined to have a presence in the Middle East, is proposing a string of military bases—in the Egyptian port of Ras Banas; on the island of Masirah, off Oman; at Mombasa, in Kenya; at Berbera, in Somalia; and on the island of Diego Garcia, in the Indian Ocean. How these bases would help stabilize this highly volatile area has not been explained.

The third transformation in the relationship between force and power has come about because of an upsurge in the cost of military might. As weapons have become more complex, they have become more expensive. They require esoteric metals and esoteric skills to produce. The nature of warfare itself and the development of democratic consciousness have combined to drive up manpower costs astronomically. In an all-out war to save their country from attack, men can be drafted and paid twenty-one dollars a month, as they were in 1940. In a war for more obscure goals, soldiers expect to be better paid—especially if the war appears to be a more or less permanent fixture. In a democratic society, the choice is either a draft that bows in the direction of universal service or a volunteer professional army. Since Vietnam, the United States has chosen the latter, and the taxpayer has been paying heavily for it, even though, with inflation, the pay is often inadequate. Ironically, the cost of maintaining politically effective military forces has gone up, even as the cost of mass destruction has gone down. In terms of cost effectiveness, atomic bombs are a bargain.

In the early nineteen-fifties, the United States tripled its military budget in about eighteen months to make the point urged so passionately in N.S.C. 68. The Korean War was the political occasion, but most of the buildup occurred in Europe, as a symbol of American global commitment. (No military leader at the time actually expected a Soviet attack.) As the French strategist Raymond Aron has pointed out, in the nineteen-eighties it would be impossible to repeat this feat. The Reagan budget calls for the

United States to spend about a trillion and a half dollars in five years. The impact of military spending on the American economy has, oddly, never been subjected to a full-scale examination by the National Security Council or the Council of Economic Advisers. But there are increasing indications that the economic costs of military power weaken the economy in specific ways and, to that extent, damage national security.

In the nineteen-fifties, conservative Republicans, like Treasury Secretary George Humphrey, believed that excessive military spending would sap America's economic power, and in 1940 leading American industrialists had opposed Roosevelt's rearmament plans, because they were convinced that a big military sector would distort production. It was the New Dealers who believed that military spending, far from being harmful, would actually stimulate the economy. After the war, Leon Keyserling, the chairman of Harry Truman's Council of Economic Advisers, thought that as much as twenty percent of the gross national product could go for defense with no ill effects. Pump-priming through military contracts became the economic underpinning of Cold War strategy. Curiously, fiscal conservatives who today favor radical cuts in government spending in every other area to combat inflation call for sharp increases in military spending.

"The Johnson Administration was justly criticized for increasing defense spending without raising taxes," the economist Otto Eckstein notes. The Reagan Administration is raising military expenditures at rates approaching those of the Vietnam buildup, but it is also proposing a large tax cut. As Seymour Melman, a professor of industrial engineering at Columbia, has pointed out, there are compelling reasons that military spending is particularly inflationary. Cost-plus contracts drive prices up well beyond what they would be in a competitive market. The beneficiaries of military contracts are, for the most part, highly skilled engineers, scientists, technicians, and managers, whose services are removed from the civilian economy. (As much as half the nation's scientists and engineers work directly or indirectly for the Pentagon.) Personnel costs are bid up. And, what is more serious, the civilian economy is starved of innovative technical and managerial talent. The United States now lags behind every other industrial nation in the percentage of its gross national product which is devoted to research and development for the civilian economy. A consequence of this neglect is the competitive advantage now enjoyed by West Germany, Japan, and other smaller nations that can produce important classes of sophisticated goods for export more cheaply and more efficiently than the United States can.

The uncoupling of economic power and military power is a phenomenon of the past fifteen years. It used to be that the nations that could afford the largest armies and navies—Britain under Queen Victoria, Germany under the Kaiser—were also the most dynamic industrial countries. (Czarist Russia, with an enormous military machine and a relatively

primitive industrial economy, was always an anomaly.) In fact, a spectacular army and navy were intended to symbolize great economic power.
Only the richest could afford them. But in our time a nation with a modest
military force, at least compared with that of either superpower, and a
nation with hardly any military force were ascendant economic powers.
West Germany and Japan are creating serious economic problems for the
United States by virtue of their competition in the export war to which all
the industrial nations of the West are committed. Exactly because they
have a modest defense burden, they are able to invest heavily in their
civilian production. The Soviet Union, conversely, is becoming a more
formidable military power, but at an increasing economic sacrifice. As
Myron Rush, a professor of government at Cornell, has noted, the heavy
military expenditures are at the expense of future growth. Like the United
States, the Soviet Union has been shortchanging its civilian production
machine. For the United States, the consequence has been a slow-growth
economy. For a smaller and weaker economy, the consequence is stagnation.

The traditional debate over guns and butter somehow misses the point.
The wish to spend scarce resources on schools, health care, the restoration of decayed cities, and clean air rather than on bombs and tanks is
understandable—President Eisenhower once said that to spend resources
on guns and warships when people were going hungry was "theft"—but
those who advocate a shift of investment from military spending to
spending for social services have been silenced by the notion that protection from enslavement is the most important social service a government
can provide. Yet excessive military spending now produces some of the
same consequences as military defeat; that is, it gives foreign governments greater control over the life of the country. Take the energy crisis.
The decision to invest a trillion and a half dollars in the military rather
than in a crash energy-development program to reduce America's dependence on foreign oil is a prime example of the way the nation's
vulnerability is increased by the act of piling up hardware. The hardware
cannot produce energy; it consumes energy. Nor can it assure access to
energy; there is no military strategy that can effectively assure the flow of
oil through a system vulnerable to sabotage. Useless military forces pre-
empt investment funds, public and private, that could be spent on developing alternative national-security strategies appropriate to the new century that we are soon to enter.

National security cannot be achieved by a nation unwilling to invest in
its own future. By abandoning our schools, our cities in the Northeast and
the Middle West, our small farmers, even our police and firemen, by
failing to find an appropriate industrial base, and by refusing to deal
adequately with the overwhelming security threats—inflation and resource mismanagement—we are cutting deeply into the sources of national strength. Increasingly, national power comes out of innovative

minds rather than out of the barrels of guns. The nation best able to confront the unprecedented problems of advanced industrial civilization, to recognize the limits of national power in an interdependent world, and to create a legitimate social order within the confines of a slow-growth economy is the one that is likely to emerge as No. 1.

42

Wasteful Weapons

Center for Defense Information

T he United States weapons industry is the biggest in the world. The Pentagon spends about $6 Billion per week and executes about 56,000 contracts per working day. But over the past several decades the weapons bought by the Pentagon have become increasingly unrelated to the nation's military needs.

More and more, **the U.S. is buying weapons it does not need and is spending too much for the weapons it does buy.**

For example, the Pentagon buys costly and deadly weapons such as super-accurate nuclear missiles, binary chemical artillery shells, and $600 million Stealth bombers for use in a war nobody could win.

Since World War II six major governmental commissions have examined how the Pentagon buys weapons. All have found serious flaws resulting in enormous waste. Their criticisms included issues such as a lack of professionalism in the management of weapons contracts and conflicts of interest involving those who leave government jobs to work for the same companies they previously supervised. But these commissions failed to take into account basic policies which have perpetuated many of the problems we now face. Consequently, past reform efforts proved unsuccessful because they only tinkered at the margins of the problem and ignored the root causes prompting the Pentagon to buy unneeded weapons in the first place.

From Center for Defense Information, *Defense Monitor*, January 1989. Reprinted by permission.

OBSOLETE GOALS

Weapons should be bought to meet clear and important military goals. If the goals change, the old weapons often become obsolete. The fundamental fault with our current weapons-buying decisions is the Pentagon's reluctance to recognize that our military needs have changed. The goals dictating which weapons we buy today were developed in the Cold War era after World War II.

Since the 1950s weapons have been produced by private companies on a scale previously unimaginable. The idea took hold that in order to intimidate and contain the Soviet Union the U.S. needed to keep its armed forces at something close to a wartime level indefinitely. Today, the prospect of going to war against the Soviet Union around the world appears to be receding.

The Pentagon has very ambitious and expensive military goals. Because of this, there is an inevitable gap between what the military wants to do (or thinks it is required to do) and the resources which are available.

Currently the U.S. builds nuclear weapons to fight and prevail in a nuclear war. The military trains to fight in every corner of the world, from the arctic to the tropics. The Navy seeks to control all the world's oceans. The U.S. plans to provide military aid to 114 countries. The U.S. promises to preserve the world military "balance," a term that has never been defined with any precision.

The U.S. has military agreements with some 60 foreign governments and has long supported anticommunist insurgencies around the world. Thus, we find ourselves in a situation similar to that which Frederick the Great, the eighteenth-century Prussian monarch, warned against when he said, "He who attempts to defend too much defends nothing."

The U.S. seeks to buy complex weapons that allegedly allow it to accomplish these goals. Yet buying increasingly complex weapons at ever higher costs cannot achieve the goal of being able to fight and win at any time and place. This pursuit means the U.S. gets weapons that often do not work and are inappropriate for real world needs.

TRYING TO DO EVERYTHING

Since the end of World War II the U.S. has prepared to fight under all sorts of circumstances, ranging from prolonged nuclear war to conventional war in Europe to intervention in developing nations. The current call for U.S. military forces to interdict drugs is just the latest example of "we can do everything" thinking. Planning to fight everywhere, the Pentagon's solution has been to ask for money to buy complex and costly weapons of all kinds. Since it is unable to devise clearly defined military goals, **the U.S. has opted for an approach in which national security is measured in**

terms of how much money the military spends. But this ignores more crucial questions such as: Is there a valid military need for the weapons, or, if there is, can they be produced at acceptable costs?

Currently, the U.S. and the Soviet Union are conducting negotiations to reduce their nuclear weapons on long-range missiles and bombers. The Soviet Union is beginning to restructure its conventional military forces to reduce their size and offensive capabilities and to make them less well-suited for a surprise attack. In December 1988 Soviet President Mikhail Gorbachev announced the decision to unilaterally reduce Soviet troop strength by 500,000. Some of the world's regional conflicts are being resolved. Soviet troops have withdrawn from Afghanistan, Vietnamese troops have withdrawn from Cambodia, and Cuban troops have been leaving Angola. Furthermore, our allies are no longer the weak, poor countries they were at the end of World War II.

Thus, it is no longer sensible for the "business-as-usual" Cold War assumptions which governed the weapons buying decisions for the past 40 years to drive today's weapons procurement. These assumptions were based on the premise that the Soviet Union was an expansionist state bent on world domination and that the U.S. had to be the world's policeman. At a time when Soviet forces have left Afghanistan, when a Soviet bloc nation such as Poland votes its Communist government out of office, and when the Berlin Wall has been opened, such a proposition cannot be accepted.

MONEY, MONEY, MONEY

There has been an overemphasis on money as a way to increase military strength. **To an alarming degree during the 1980s the U.S. has focused on how much money could be spent, not how well it is spent.** Attention has been paid to what portion of the Gross National Product (GNP) should be devoted to the military or what the annual percentage increases should be, not whether more money is necessary or would significantly contribute to the nation's security.

The Reagan Administration spent a total of $2.2 Trillion dollars on the military. Even taking inflation into account, the 1984 military budget was greater than the 1969 military budget, the peak spending year of the Vietnam War. Never before had the U.S. military budget experienced a 50 percent increase during peacetime. By fanning fears of American military weakness, the Reagan Administration was able to persuade Congress to provide these huge sums of money to the military.

In the 1980s money was spent in haste and without a coherent plan, resulting in inevitable and predictable waste. John Tower, the chairman of the Senate Armed Services Committee in the early 1980s, now states "I regret my part in front-loading the budget."

"IN EVERY CORNER"

The Pentagon still wants to do too much. As recently as 1987 Defense Secretary Caspar Weinberger said, "In every corner of the globe, America's vital interests are threatened by an evergrowing Soviet military threat." He gave first priority to increasing the Pentagon's budget, largely leaving decisions over what to buy and how much to pay to the services. Even those increases, however, proved insufficient to pay for the ambitious military goals of the Reagan Administration. The Joint Chiefs of Staff argued they would need an additional $750 Billion to carry out the missions specified by the Administration, over and above the $1.6 Trillion requested by the Secretary of Defense for the military in the 1984–1988 5-year defense plan. The results are that **Americans pay far too much to the military and receive too little security in return.**

Clearly, the Pentagon cannot expect the sort of money it received during the Reagan Administration. Nor should it, since spending is still at a peacetime high. **According to the Pentagon's latest calculations, the total program cost of 98 major weapons programs currently in production is approximately $819 Billion,** a sum that is higher than the GNP of almost every country in the world. Military officials have yet to appreciate that the unrestricted military spending of the Reagan years is over. In 1989 the General Accounting Office (GAO) found that President Bush's 5-year defense plan is at least $100 Billion short of the money needed to buy weapons already started. In large part this is due to the desire of the services to buy more weapons than the military budget provides. Chronic gaps between plans and reality are a built-in source of inefficiency and waste.

BURDENSOME WEAPONS

During the past 20 years a disturbing situation has developed. The U.S. military shows reduced interest in already-proven conventional weapons. In many respects an already-proven weapon is preferable to a new technologically complex one due to the inherent reliability and lower cost of maintenance and support. Such weapons also make rapid production by a contractor easier if more weapons are needed.

Today's weapons, such as aircraft carriers, take so long to produce and have become so expensive that their protection becomes the foremost priority.

A little-recognized consequence of overreliance on technology is the effect on military troops. Even if complex weapons work as promised, their potential will not be realized unless military personnel are up to the task of operating and maintaining them. Currently we buy weapons developed by Ph.D.s and expect them to be operated by high school

Top ten reasons for wasteful weapons

1. Buying unneeded weapons in pursuit of **obsolete military goals** such as preparing to fight and win a nuclear war.
2. Pursuit of **unachievable military goals** such as preparing to fight wars in all parts of the world at the same time.
3. Assuming that **spending more money** on weapons in itself enhances the security of the United States.
4. Allowing weapons buying decisions to be **influenced by job and profit considerations.**
5. **Failure to test weapons** under realistic combat conditions and starting production before completing adequate testing.
6. Unreasonable demands for **complex high-tech weapons,** regardless of cost.
7. **Improper influence by defense contractors** on the Congress and military officials, including deliberate underbidding to win contracts.
8. **Faulty management** of weapons programs by military officials due to inadequate business skills and "revolving door" conflicts of interest.
9. **Interference by the Congress** in the weapons production process.
10. **Unrealistic planning** by the Pentagon, resulting in understating the cost of weapons.

                                Prepared By Center For Defense Information

graduates. A 1985 study by the Army Research Institute concluded, "**the Army is not developing weapons systems that work well when they get into the field. These problems are going to worsen because weapons are becoming more complex while the supply of capable soldiers is decreasing.**"

WRONG CHOICES

Service traditions cause the development of new and unnecessary weapons. The Navy's tradition of carrying the fight to the enemy has caused the Pentagon to produce bigger and extremely expensive aircraft carriers. They are used frequently for intervening overseas. Yet, in the nuclear missile age, carriers represent extremely vulnerable targets.

In addition, according to current Navy strategy, carrier aircraft would be used to attack targets in the Soviet Union. The high vulnerability of our carriers resulting from such a plan is pointed out by many senior naval officers who question whether any rational military commander would ever risk their loss in such attacks. Such vulnerability makes it questionable whether we need more carriers, let alone the 15 the Navy has currently. The cost of buying just one carrier and the additional warships and aircraft to protect it is about $18 Billion.

The Air Force plans to buy 132 Stealth bombers to add to the B-1B and B-52 bombers during the 1990s and eventually replace them. In the age of nuclear-armed missiles which can destroy the Soviet Union in 30 minutes, the role of the manned bomber is obsolete if not dead. The desire to have more bombers really reflects the traditional importance the Air Force gives to manned strategic bombing. But $72 Billion for Stealth bombers is a high price to pay for an outmoded tradition.

SERVICE COMPETITION

Competition between different military services is yet another reason why we buy unnecessary weapons. The U.S. does not have one air force, it has four: one each for the Air Force, Army, Navy, and Marine Corps. The U.S. has at least half a dozen different ways to attack the Soviet Union with nuclear weapons. Since the end of World War II there have been continuous struggles between the different branches of the military over which services would control which tasks. This has led to duplication and waste in weapons development as the services fight for control of a specific job by seeking to outdo rival services in developing weapons for that task.

POLITICAL SPENDING

Of course, responsibility for decisions to procure unnecessary weapons does not lie only with the military. Another factor is the pressure by contractors who manufacture them and from members of Congress who promote systems built in their districts and states. The motivation of the contractors is easily understood. In many cases the ability of a military contractor to make big profits depends on receiving a contract from the Pentagon. Without one, it may lose money and face financial difficulties.

The Pentagon wants to preserve the vast array of contractors and subcontractors who collectively produce the huge quantities of equipment needed to fight around the world. A contract is often awarded to a particular company to ensure that it stays in business. The awarding of the M-1 tank production contract to the Chrysler Corporation in November 1976 was such a case. This can be expected in **a system where the major motivation for building weapons is profit.**

MILITARY-INDUSTRIAL COMPLEX

The top 20 contractors have annual sales to the Pentagon exceeding a Billion dollars each and cumulatively capture about 50 percent of the total Pentagon spending on weapons each year. In turn, some of these firms monopolize the production of a specific type of weapon. The percentages of business done by the top four firms are: nuclear submarines (99%), fighter aircraft (97%), attack aircraft (97%), helicopters (93%).

Since the Pentagon generally finds the loss of any major contractor unacceptable, due to concern over maintaining an industrial production base for wartime production, contracts are parceled out selectively to firms. Buying weapons primarily to preserve a bloated "defense industrial base" for war with the Soviet Union seems outmoded, particularly as any U.S.-Soviet war would be a short nuclear war.

General Dynamics was awarded the F-111 aircraft contract in 1962 immediately following cancellation of production of its B-58 bomber and was awarded the F-16 in 1974 when F-111 production was ending. McDonnell Douglas was awarded the F-15 fighter aircraft contract in 1970 as the F-4 program was being phased down. Production of the C-5A transport aircraft began at Lockheed as C-141 production ended. For 30 years, Lockheed has provided all of the Navy's submarine ballistic missiles—moving from the Polaris to the Poseidon to the Trident I and now to the Trident II—all on an essentially noncompetitive basis.

PORK BARREL WEAPONS

Members of Congress often press for new weapons or continuing production of old weapons out of concern for jobs in their districts. Fearing their constituents will be angry if a contractor in their district starts laying off workers, many congressmen go to great lengths to ensure that local companies obtain contracts. Rockwell had 5,200 subcontracts in 48 states, a fact it used to great effect to gain support for the B-1B bomber in Congress.

More recently, legislators from Long Island have lobbied to continue production of the F-14D fighter made by Grumman, while legislators from Pennsylvania and Texas have fought to save the V-22 tilt-rotor aircraft made by Bell Helicopter/Textron, aircraft the Secretary of Defense recommended canceling.

Congressmen frequently accept political action committee (PAC) contributions and other favors from defense contractors. They are also extensively lobbied by contractors' representatives. **These three—the congressman, the contractor, and the military service—form a powerful trinity that brings tremendous pressure to bear to ensure that money for building new weapons keeps flowing.**

Also, the Pentagon promises to deploy new weapons to military bases in the states of its supporters. The B-1B was deployed to Dyess Air Force Base in Texas in part to reward former Senate Armed Services chairman John Tower for his past support. The B-1B was also stationed at McConnell Air Force Base in Kansas to ensure the support of Sen. Robert Dole, who was Senate majority leader. In purely military terms, other sites were more suitable.

Although contractor selection is supposed to be insulated from outside pressures, the pattern of awards has shown a definite tendency to favor firms with political clout. Besides making PAC contributions, firms gain influence by paying honoraria to members of Congress for speeches and by arranging to farm out work to as many subcontractors as possible in key districts and states.

Restoring money for weapons that even the Pentagon does not want is a traditional practice. In 1981 the Defense Department requested no funds for the Cobra/TOW helicopter, but the delegation from Texas where the helicopters were made restored 17 of them to the budget at a cost of $44.5 million. That same year the Administration requested no money for the A-6E attack plane, made by Grumman on Long Island, but the New York delegation saw to it that 12 planes were included in the budget at a cost of $186.7 million. These aircraft were then produced with astonishing inefficiency, the A-6E at the rate of one per month and the Cobra at the rate of 1.5 per month, which pushed costs per weapon to new highs.

In 1989 the Northrop Corporation, with the cooperation of the Pentagon, issued a news release defending the B-2 bomber as a jobs program, stating, "The U.S. Air Force's B-2 program is supported nationwide by tens of thousands of men and women at prime contractor Northrop Corporation, key subcontractors Boeing, LTV, General Electric and Hughes, and other suppliers and subcontractors in 46 states." Buying $600 million aircraft to create jobs is a gross waste of tax dollars.

WEAPONS TESTING

Even if the government buys an unnecessary weapon, one would expect it to test weapons rigorously to ensure that they perform properly in combat. Unfortunately, this has not been the case. Far too frequently the Pentagon relies heavily on laboratory testing. This sort of testing is done to determine how well various systems and parts meet theoretical requirements, but such testing does not address the critical question of how well it will perform in combat. Speaking about tests designed to show the "lethality" of Star Wars weapons, Dr. Roger Hagengruber of Sandia National Laboratory, said, "These demonstrations have the potential to be what we call strap-down chicken tests, where you strap the chicken down, blow it apart with a shotgun, and say shotguns kill chickens. But that's quite different from trying to kill a chicken in a dense forest while it's running away."

To determine combat capabilities, one must conduct operational testing. Such testing is done in the field under conditions which realistically reflect the harsh demands of the battlefield.

Frequently, weapons testing is flawed in two ways: it is not realistic, and it is not finished before production decisions are made. Because the Pentagon is obsessed with gaining congressional funding for new weapons it often objects to subjecting its weapons to operational tests for fear of being embarrassed by the results. The embarrassments are avoided by rigging the tests or manipulating the test results.

As a result, the Pentagon often starts producing weapons before it has finished developing and testing them. This results in long-term problems that cost big bucks to fix. The B-1B bomber was produced in that fashion and as a result the U.S. has a bomber plagued by numerous performance problems. The Congressional Budget Office (CBO) and the GAO estimate that it might cost up to another $7 or $8 Billion to fix existing problems. The B-2 Stealth bomber program is also being produced in this fashion.

In addition, if the final design is not determined before a weapon is put into production, one cannot predict how much the final product will cost. By putting such weapons into production, huge cost increases become almost inevitable.

When operational testing is done the results are of great importance. A recent GAO report found that tests showed the combat effectiveness of the Advanced Medium Range Air-to-Air Missile (AMRAAM) had not been demonstrated and recommended the Pentagon not proceed with production until serious problems were fixed. Another GAO report found that the military is not realistically testing its aircraft against bird collisions.

When operational testing is not done properly, the result can be disastrous. The Sergeant York Division Air Defense (DIVAD) gun, which was supposed to protect ground forces against aerial attack, was never operationally tested, which helps explain why it was ultimately canceled in 1985. The tests that were performed were highly unrealistic and unfavorable results of those tests were hidden from superior officers who continued to promote DIVAD.

Recently, Senator David Pryor (D-Arkansas) charged the Pentagon with a coverup with regard to the Airborne Self-Protection Jammer (ASPJ). This is a new joint Navy-Air Force system for jet fighters intended to deceive and jam enemy radar. Sen. Pryor noted that production approval was given for the $4.8 Billion program despite the fact that ASPJ failed many of its operational tests.

Many managers are reluctant to test new weapons realistically. If the results show a weapon is unreliable, the manager is likely to risk having money for the weapon cut off and find his chances for career advancement ended.

WEAPONS LIMITATIONS

The high cost of weapons often means not enough are available for training. This unavailability is compounded by the complexity of many weapons which often generate high training costs and require a longer training time to allow operators to learn to maintain and employ them properly. One example is the B-1B bomber, which costs $21,000 per flying hour to operate. Also, such weapons often need additional support, requiring more money to be spent for operating and maintenance purposes, and may be out of service for repair more often.

The turbine engine of the M-1 tank has limited the tank's mobility by frequently breaking down. In 1986 operational testing of the M-1E1 tank revealed it malfunctioned once every 58 miles. The Army considers one combat day to be 120 miles. That means the tank broke down twice a day. It also costs three and a half times as much per mile to maintain than its predecessor, the M-60.

Because it takes longer to develop and produce complex weapons, there is a greater risk of leaving troops short of the equipment they need. In turn, because of the delay in replacing equipment lost due to normal wear and tear of the inventory, the average age of the force increases.

ILLEGAL MEANS

Getting a major weapons contract is very profitable and the competition for many contracts is extremely fierce. Thus, at times contractors will resort to illegal means to try to gain an edge in bidding for a contract. This too often results in an unqualified company winning a contract. Consequent delays and attempts to fix problems caused by their own inadequacies increase the price. The trafficking in inside information by defense consultants revealed in the Ill Wind investigation made public in 1988 is a recent example. So far, there have been 2 indictments and 24 guilty pleas from this one investigation.

UNREALISTIC PLANNING

The Pentagon frequently puts forward a low estimate of the price of a weapon in order to win congressional approval and arranges contracts in order to build support for the weapon. If people knew how much weapons were really going to cost they might not buy them. The current debate over the B-2 Stealth bomber is a case in point. A GAO report found that underestimating weapons costs is a major factor in the creation of greatly unrealistic cost projections for military programs.

For controversial weapons, the Pentagon sometimes inflates its own requests as a form of insurance to allow for inevitable congressional cuts. The Strategic Defense Initiative (SDI) is typical of this practice. Each year, Administration officials complain Congress is cutting the SDI budget, but up until FY 1990 money for SDI had gone up every year since its inception.

GOLDPLATING

One of the most serious problems facing the U.S. in attempting to produce useful weapons at reasonable prices is that achievable goals are not set. The problem starts at the very outset of the process, when the military seeks new weapons capable of fighting many kinds of wars all around the world. Congress is not provided the information it needs to judge the need for such weapons. Military contractors make big money by pushing the most expensive, high-tech weapons and aid the military in lobbying Congress to buy new weapons.

This often leads to a process known as "goldplating," **the incorporation into a weapon of the newest and most expensive technologies regardless of their battlefield effectiveness or cost.** It was this inclination which led to the fiasco of the DIVAD, a system that was so flawed that former Defense Secretary Weinberger was forced to cancel its production after an expenditure of $1.8 Billion. Norman Augustine, a defense industry official and former Assistant Secretary of the Army, has said, "The last ten percent of performance sought generates one-third of the cost and two-thirds of the problems."

Another weapon which has been afflicted by the "goldplating" syndrome is the Bradley infantry fighting vehicle. The Bradley was to replace the Army's M-113 personnel carrier and was conceived as a motorized infantry combat vehicle which would allow troops to fight while inside. The design kept changing after development began. The TOW antitank missile was attached and a complex turret was added. As a result, the weight rose, causing problems with the vehicle's power train and reducing its ability to ford streams. The TOW turret leaves less room for infantrymen, forcing a reduction in squad size to 7 rather than the 9 soldiers judged necessary. The armor is made of aluminum, which is a reactive metal. When it is hit by an antitank round the aluminum vaporizes, becoming chemical fuel for the explosion and intensifying the deadly blast effects.

UNDERSTATED COSTS

When a new weapon finally receives approval from Congress, the promised capabilities for the program are often highly overstated and the costs are greatly understated. This is due in large part to powerful political pressures. Understating costs enables a contractor to submit an artificially low bid in the hope of winning a contract, subsequently making his profits through price increases, spare parts, training programs, and repair programs. The 1986 Reagan-appointed Packard Commission reported that military planners pursue unneeded weapons capabilities. The Commission noted that this tendency "has led to overstated specifications, which have led to higher equipment costs. Such so-called 'goldplating' has become deeply embedded in our system today."

After a design is approved, the next step is allowing firms to compete for contracts for the weapon. Contractors are discouraged from requesting modifications of or pointing out problems with the design. Since a contractor must promise that it will fully satisfy the blueprint, the competition is based mainly on the contractor's optimism. To make a profit, the contractor always remains optimistic. In order to sell their products they often resort to standard marketing techniques: they advertise, they exaggerate, and they criticize their competitors. Yet a low bid is required to win the contract. The usual result is that the company bids low to win the contract and comes back later asking for more.

United Technologies promised to deliver Black Hawk helicopters to the Army for only $2.6 million apiece in the late 1970s, but jacked up the price to $4.7 million each when the deliveries started. Predictably, a major weapon takes too long to produce (10–15 years) and has many cost overruns.

Wasteful weapons

- **Bradley Fighting Vehicle System.** Army personnel carrier which suffers numerous defects due to goldplating. (**$12 Billion**)
- **B-2 Stealth Bomber.** An obsolete penetrating bomber for fighting a nuclear war with the Soviet Union. (**$72 Billion**)
- **New aircraft carriers.** DOD wants two more vulnerable nuclear powered aircraft carriers. (Each new carrier task force costs **$18 Billion**)
- **MX ICBM.** Intercontinental ballistic missile for fighting a nuclear war with the Soviet Union. (**$23.4 Billion**)
- **Division Air Defense (DIVAD) Gun.** Anti-air cannon that suffered severe defects because it was not realistically tested. (Cancelled after **$1.8 Billion** was spent on it)
- **Midgetman ICBM.** With 12,000 strategic weapons the U.S. does not need a new expensive missile. (**$28 Billion**)
- **Strategic Defense Initiative.** An enormously expensive project to develop a shield against nuclear attack. (A total of **$21 Billion** has been spent between fiscal years 1984 and 1990)
- **Anti-Satellite Weapons (ASAT).** The Pentagon seeks to develop a weapon to destroy Soviet satellites, risking setting off an arms race in space. (**$94.5 Million** was requested in FY 1990)
- **F-14D.** A naval aircraft Congress insisted on buying more of, against the Pentagon's wishes, in order to provide jobs for constituents. (**$1.1 Billion** for fiscal year 1990)

Congress can also drive up costs by calling for cuts in the overall quantity of a particular weapon as a way of dealing with budget limitations. A CBO report noted that stretching out production of weapons over a longer period of time adds to the total cost by preventing manufacturers from producing efficiently and introducing cost-saving manufacturing innovations. The report also noted that stretch-outs often occur because the military services seek to develop and acquire too many different weapons simultaneously.

The Pentagon understands that **Congress will rarely stop a major weapon program once a large amount of money has already been spent** on research and development. For example, since approximately $23 Billion has already been spent on the B-2 bomber, it is probable the program will continue despite current congressional criticism. Senator Dan Quayle, later to become Vice-President, said in 1985, "From a political point of view, Congress cannot and does not cut procurement programs; it is what is known as the camel's-nose-under-the-tent syndrome, and it is adroitly practiced by military planners."

FAULTY MANAGEMENT

Yet another problem with the way we buy our weapons is that **the people charged with buying weapons are often unqualified.** Despite the fact that procurement involves extraordinarily complex technologies and Billions of dollars, the personnel are not considered "professionals" by the Office of Personnel Management. Thus, they are not required to have the same degree of administrative skills found in their counterparts in the private sector. As a result there are far too many people involved in buying weapons who do not have the necessary technical or management skills. Only half of the contract specialists have business-related college degrees.

The Packard Commission found that "lasting progress in the performance of the acquisition system demands dramatic improvements in our management of acquisition personnel at all levels within the Department of Defense."

Too many people in the military involved in this area see it as a dead-end job. The GAO found in a 1986 survey that the average tenure of a program manager, including his time as a deputy program manager, was just over 2 years. Thus, during the 8–12 years of its development, a weapon system is likely to have 4 or 5 different military officers as program managers, an extremely inefficient way to run a business.

The lack of incentives for those military and civilian personnel involved in buying weapons to pay the lowest prices and obtain the most reliable product is one reason why there has been such a serious conflict of interest, also known as the "revolving door," in the military-industrial sector. Many military officers in charge of buying weapons face retirement by the time they reach their early forties. At this time they have children going to college and mortgages to pay and cannot afford a big cut in income. It is usually at this time that a representative of a military contractor pays a visit and says that a job will be available after retirement. If an officer stands up and makes a fuss about the overruns and lack of quality of a weapon being produced there will be no job offer.

The GAO reported that more than 30,000 senior military and civilian employees left the DOD in 1983 and 1984. More than 6,000 of these later held industrial security clearances and approximately 5,700 were thought to be working for companies contracting with the Pentagon.

WHAT TO DO

The U.S. cannot tolerate a "business-as-usual" approach toward military spending any longer. Changing international conditions, constraints on money, growing technological complexity, and the drive for profits have all combined to produce weapons that are becoming irrelevant to our military needs.

Without appropriate military goals, it is unlikely the Pentagon will buy the weapons truly needed for defending the country. Buying weapons to fight nuclear wars or to defend countries capable of defending themselves does not contribute to the defense of the U.S.

To help ensure that the U.S. buys the weapons it needs and does not pay too much for them we should **eliminate the present piecemeal oversight of military affairs by Congress.** The military sections of different congressional support agencies—such as the General Accounting Office, Congressional Budget Office, Office of Technology Assessment, and the Congressional Research Service—could be pulled together into a Congressional Office of Defense Appraisal (CODA) with a clear mandate to help Congress assess defense needs and monitor the military. An immediate task for CODA would be to reassess American military strategy and the force levels needed to carry it out in a world of rapidly changing conditions.

The U.S. would be more likely to buy truly necessary weapons if decisions were not distorted by the desire of contractors to make huge profits from government contracts. To help achieve that, consideration should be given to **making it illegal for contractors to contribute money to members of Congress.**

EFFECTIVE WEAPONS

No matter how technologically complex a weapon is, its effectiveness is only as good as its ability to operate under actual battlefield conditions. U.S. soldiers and sailors should not have to risk their lives operating a weapon whose reliability is based on a contractor's advertising. To ensure combat effectiveness, the military should not produce any weapons until they have been fully tested. This means testing out in the field by the same troops who would actually operate them, not computer tests done in some antiseptic laboratory.

In the past decade the Pentagon bought weapons that were not needed because the military and defense contractors had more money than they could spend effectively. In the future it is likely the U.S. will be reducing both its military spending and the size of its armed forces. This will have at least two very positive effects. **Smaller military budgets will hopefully restore a sense of discipline in spending taxpayers' dollars.** As the U.S. moves to a leaner military force the Pentagon should be able to pay service members more and train them better to operate today's and tomorrow's weapons.

43

Inside Central America

Phillip Berryman

SECURITY THREATS

The most persistent justification for U.S. policy in Central America has been that revolutionary governments or movements there jeopardize U.S. security. The assumption is that these movements are connected to the Soviet Union through Cuba and that their taking power must represent a victory for the USSR and a defeat for the United States.

Arguments along the following lines are often advanced:

1. Nicaragua, backed by Cuba, is already supporting subversion in neighboring countries; other revolutionary governments would only extend subversion and widen the threat.
2. Revolutionary governments in Central America linked to the Soviet Union and Cuba would force the United States for the first time to deploy defense forces to protect its southern flank, thus reducing its ability to project its power elsewhere in the world.
3. U.S. sea lanes in the Caribbean and the Panama Canal would be made more vulnerable by additional revolutionary governments in the region. Even now, the USSR has a greater capacity to interdict U.S. shipping than did the Nazis.
4. Communist takeovers will send a tidal wave of refugees to the United States, reaching perhaps into the millions, putting even greater pressure on U.S. jobs and communities.
5. Finally, there is the question of credibility. If the United States cannot prevail in an area as close as Central America, its ability to influence events elsewhere in the world will be impaired.

Phillip Berryman, "Central American Revolutions," from *Inside Central America*, by Phillip Berryman. Copyright © 1985 by Phillip Berryman. Reprinted by permission of Pantheon Books, a Division of Random House, Inc.

The first point is perhaps the most crucial insofar as it involves the nature of revolution itself and how revolution occurs. Some use physical analogies—"dominoes," "cancer," "prairie fire"—that emphasize geographical contiguity. Secretary of State Haig spoke of a Soviet "hit list" as though the course of all revolutions were determined from the Kremlin. Those who see revolution as the result of small conspiratorial groups assiduously trace connections to a world-wide terrorist network.

Revolution, however, does not occur as a result of the handiwork of a conspiratorial elite. Rather, it begins when social change—indeed, social breakdown—is affecting large numbers of people, so that they become committed to struggle, and when the power structure is weakened or delegitimized. (We are, of course, speaking of genuine revolutions and not barracks coups.) Revolutionary organizations have an undeniable role, but by themselves they cannot create revolutions.

. . . [R]evolutionary conditions did appear in El Salvador, Guatemala, and Nicaragua; and revolutionary organizations arose as well. However, for other nations in the region, this is not the case. Such conditions did not appear in Honduras and Costa Rica, nor have they to this day. Ordinary Costa Ricans feel they have a stake in their society because their economy and the government's social welfare programs have worked for most people. Relatively speaking, Costa Rican egalitarianism and prosperity are deeply rooted because ordinary farmers shared in the coffee prosperity of the nineteenth century. In Honduras the oligarchy appeared late and is underdeveloped; moreover, the country's relative underpopulation means that Honduran peasants have access to more land than do those in El Salvador. In principle, Honduras and Costa Rica could deal with their development problems in an evolutionary, reformist way. To the extent U.S. policy militarizes them, however, it will be cutting off avenues for peaceful change. Should that happen, revolutionary conditions could indeed develop, especially in Honduras.

Structurally, Panama is the most unrevolutionary country in Latin America. It is not primarily an agroexport country; its economy revolves around its "transit function"—the canal, the free zone, and U.S. military bases. Since the 1960s, it has become a leading finance center, with foreign deposits far outstripping domestic deposits. Today, Panama's economic stability depends on its remaining a safe haven for foreign depositors and for the many "paper" companies incorporated there. The slightest hint of genuine instability would deplete its banks. It was perhaps this underlying structural requirement for stability that enabled General Torrijos (1968–1982) to flirt with rhetorical revolution. In practice his programs were no more than populist. Panama cannot afford to become revolutionary, no matter what happens to other countries in the region. Furthermore, any terrorists wishing to destroy the canal locks could do so today from Panama itself with no need of a revolutionary country as a springboard.

Some people fear that Mexico's extremes of wealth and poverty make it a potential revolutionary target. It is true that Mexico's development has left large numbers of people, especially peasants and Indians in the south, in poverty. However, Mexico has a diversified economy and its population of 70 million is spread over a large territory in which conditions vary widely. Even though the present economic crisis affects all, its impact is different in the slums of Mexico City, the border towns of the north, and the coastal tropical areas. Until now the Mexican army has suppressed occasional peasant unrest, while most of the population remained unaware. If an economic crisis were to affect people everywhere in a drastic way, and if organizers could create a unified national movement, something like a revolution might occur. That, however, would be a result of internal conditions. Revolution in Central America would be only a distant influence. It should be noted that the Mexican government's good relations with Cuba over the last twenty-five years—it was the only Latin American government that refused to follow the U.S. lead in breaking relations—have had no appreciable spillover into domestic politics.

Other governments in the region, such as Colombia, Venezuela, and Panama, do not see leftist governments in Central America as a threat to their security. They understand revolutions to be the product of particular social circumstances and organized movements; they do not need to drag in misleading physical analogies and notions of international intrigue.

Those who focus on the security threat tend to see revolutionaries as part of a monolithic global communist movement. In fact, however, revolutionary organizations vary greatly among themselves. Many, if not most, Marxists are independent of Moscow. The Central American revolutionaries are, by and large, Marxists but they do not link their fates to the Soviet Union. This is partly a result of their experience and partly a function of their nationalistic ideology. In other words, they want to be nonaligned.

The notion that revolutionary governments threaten U.S. security should be looked at with a sense of proportion and a degree of common sense. Clearly, an offensive Soviet deployment in the Western hemisphere—in Nicaragua for instance—would be a dangerous escalation in an arms race that is already out of control. Even now, however, Soviet submarines are poised off U.S. shores with nuclear weapons able to reach their targets in minutes. Moreover, for a tiny Central American country to accept Soviet missiles would be suicidal, since it would immediately become a nuclear target.

The argument that Soviet-linked revolutionary regimes in Central America threaten vital U.S. sea lanes assumes a peculiar situation in which: (a) the United States is engaged militarily with the Soviet Union (b) in a confrontation that is both prolonged and non-nuclear and (c) in which the USSR and its Central American ally judge they can attack U.S. shipping without provoking an all-out attack against the ally or a dangerous escalation against the USSR.

In reality, any military confrontation between the United States and the

USSR, even if it began with conventional weapons, would be almost certain either to escalate rapidly or to move toward negotiations. Again, it would be suicidal for a tiny Central American country to make itself a target for the United States.

Those whose main focus is U.S. security argue that a Central American country might allow the USSR to install naval facilities that would enhance its Caribbean presence, but it is hard to see what that would add to what the USSR has had in Cuba for two decades.

Despite its inherent irrationality, the possibility that a revolutionary country might provide the Soviet Union with some offensive military capability, in return for military protection, economic aid, or trade, cannot be utterly excluded. After all, that is what Cuba did in the early 1960s. Preventing such an outcome should be an ultimate consideration for the United States. Hence, one aim of a negotiated approach should be to remove Central American conflicts from the arena of East-West confrontation.

Some here in the United States assert that Marxist governments in Central America will generate hordes, perhaps millions, of "feet people," refugees fleeing totalitarianism, and that they will head for the United States. First it should be noted that already an estimated 300,000 Salvadorans and Guatemalans have come to the United States—fleeing not Marxism, but the violence of their own governments.

Some Nicaraguans fled the Sandinista revolution either with Somoza or later. Most of those who arrived in the United States are not properly refugees but expatriates—they chose to leave Nicaragua because they anticipated that their standard of living could decline under the revolution. Some poor Nicaraguans also fled, particularly Miskito Indians who escaped to Honduras. Should a revolutionary government come to power in El Salvador, no doubt some people will flee, either because they believe their standard of living will fall or because they fear the consequences of their ties to the army or government.

It is not the advent of revolutionary governments that is most likely to generate large numbers of refugees, however. Rather, it is an ever more protracted and destructive war that will uproot people from their land and destroy their country's economy. The resolution to the refugee problem would be an end to the wars. It is interesting to note that most refugees who fled the attacks of Somoza's National Guard in Nicaragua returned when the war ended.

The credibility argument—that is, that Central America is a test of U.S. resolve and power which has grave implications elsewhere—is dangerous and pernicious. Over the long run, neither of the superpowers can permanently impose its will on other nations. Security must be grounded not in military might but in respect for the rights of others, for self-determination, and for pluralism and diversity. American citizens should not be made to feel that their sense of self-worth depends on their government's ability to "prevail" in tiny countries almost a thousand miles from their border.

No one doubts that the United States is technologically capable of turning Central America into a smoking wasteland. What is really in question is whether it will have the wisdom to seek solutions that can end the causes of strife and rebellion. This sort of credibility has ramifications that go beyond Central America.

WHAT DO THE REVOLUTIONARIES WANT?

According to a prevalent sterotype, those who lead revolutions are power-hungry, ruthless, even bloodthirsty people, whose aim is to take over their countries in order to establish totalitarian regimes subordinate to the imperial aims of the Soviet Union. In that view, revolutions are irrational, a collective plunge into the abyss. They can be "understood" only as pathology.

The starting point here, on the contrary, is that Central American revolutions make sense—at least to those who have taken part in them. In many ways, revolutionaries themselves are as rational as corporation executives. They carefully calculate and weigh various options as they pursue their ends with single-minded determination. If their proposals and the means by which they would carry them out are better understood, then it will be much clearer to what extent their aims may be compatible with U.S. interests.

Assuming that Central American revolutionary movements embody proposals for meeting the aspirations of the population (whether they will work is a separate question), we shall examine the outlines of what these proposals entail on the basis of Sandinista government programs, documents of the Salvadoran and Guatemalan revolutionary movements, and analyses by Central American social scientists.

An end to violence

Out of a concern to address the political and economic issues, the number one aspiration of people in Central America might be overlooked: peace. The basic reason for violence in Central America today is resistance to change on the part of those holding economic and political power. Many Central Americans have joined the guerrillas out of what they see as a need for self-defense: for them the army is the aggressor.

Not only must the murders and massacres be ended, but people must feel that their lives are secure. Despite the undeniable military buildup in Nicaragua, most citizens see the Sandinista army and police not as a repressive force but as supportive of the revolution they are seeking to build. Their insecurity comes from the U.S.-backed *contras*. A first aspiration is peace and security.

A new economic model

All observers recognize that any solution in Central America must entail economic change. What the United States has proposed, however, is largely an infusion of aid in massive amounts. To the extent that there is any notion of a new approach to development, it is that Central America and Caribbean countries should encourage export industries, such as those in Puerto Rico or Taiwan. As in those countries, corporations would be attracted by the comparative advantage of cheap labor. However, because they are so keyed to the export market, such industries are not too dissimilar to the banana plantations of old. They do little for genuine internal development. Moreover, the world economy has room for only a few Taiwans and Puerto Ricos, and Central America's present instability will make outside investors wary for quite some time.

Over the last twenty years, Latin American economists and social scientists have developed a critique of existing models of development. This whole body of sometimes conflicting theories (dependence, world-systems, modes of production) is essentially negative. It explains why development is not working for the bulk of the population, but says little about what should be done. Since no Latin American country has undertaken serious structural reform between the 1973 coup in Chile and the Nicaraguan revolution, this is hardly surprising.

With the advent of the Nicaraguan revolution, social scientists from Central America and the Caribbean countries have been stimulated to seek an alternative model of development, one that would begin to meet the basic needs of the population—in their words, one where the economy would follow the "logic of the majorities." Like many Latin American intellectuals, these scholars are sympathetic to Marxism. Nevertheless, they have had to recognize that classical Marxist theory offers relatively little help for the real situations in their countries. Both Russia and China, the two classical cases of attempted transition to socialism, have huge populations and vast natural resources. They were able to turn inward and attempt sweeping experiments within their own borders. Whatever one may think of the results, they have little to say to the tiny nations of Central America and the Caribbean. Hence, these social scientists began by analyzing the peculiar features of their region and their countries.

All these countries have small open agroexport economies. They do not produce capital goods and will not be able to do so, given their size. Machinery for industrialization can become available only with foreign exchange earned through agroexports. Their real interests will best be served if they can remain part of the Western economic system in order to have both the widest markets for their products and access to Western machinery and technology.

An adequate development strategy must first seek to meet the basic needs of the population. Yet it must also lay the groundwork for rational industrialization by finding a new model of saving and of investment in capital goods for further development.

Food self-sufficiency must be part of the starting point. In recent decades, the landholding elites have expanded agroexports at the expense of the production of basic foods such as corn and beans. Nicaragua has made strides toward self-sufficiency in basic foods, but it is also finding that increasing the real income of the poor increases demand even for those basic food items.

Basic grains like corn and beans are produced by individual peasants working small tracts of land. While a doctrinaire application of Marxist theory might point toward collectivization, the experience of socialist countries shows that this does not lead to efficient agriculture. Moreover, Central American peasants expect not grandiose schemes but control over the land they work and fair prices for what they produce, although they are quite willing to work together and to try new techniques and new methods of organization.

Similarly, an industrialization strategy should emphasize the production of articles for the daily use of the majority instead of luxury items that only a few people can afford—for example, affordable soap instead of expensive scented varieties with foreign brand names. At present, much manufacturing takes place in small artisan shops. It might make sense to stimulate this artisan production and integrate it into overall national plans.

Until now, most of the profits from the mainspring of their economy, agroexports, have gone to foreign investors or to national oligarchies for their own luxury consumption or into their foreign bank accounts; only to some extent have profits been reinvested in the countries themselves. In the 1960s the agroexport class used its profits to become partners of the multinationals that were attracted to the Central American Common Market. A new economic model must center on a new kind of accumulation—that is, on generating savings for investment in solid development that will benefit the majority of the population. With this in mind, Nicaragua, even while it has sought to become self-sufficient in basic food production, is also expanding and modernizing agroexport production—for instance, it is building new sugar mills to bring in needed foreign exchange.

Until now, each of the small countries of the Carribbean and Central America has related bilaterally to its trading partners in North America and Europe. They have competed with each other in marketing the same tropical products. A key component in a new development strategy would make their economies more complementary and increase intra-regional trade. (A political corollary is that diverse kinds of governments should find ways of working together toward common development aims.)

All of this implies a strong state role in the economy, especially in controlling strategic sectors such as banking, finance, and foreign trade. It does not necessarily entail a state-owned economy. The decisive question is not ownership but rather the thrust of the economy and whose interests are served. When a relatively small group—an oligarchy—effectively controls a country's economy by means of its institutions and its veto power over the government, it can determine what is produced and for whom.

A concept from conventional economics will illustrate the point. Economists speak of "consumer sovereignty," meaning that people "vote" when they spend their money, buying one brand instead of another, or simply choosing from among countless other ways to use their money. However, if 2 percent of the population receives twice as much income as the whole bottom half of the population, it can easily "outvote" the majority—for instance, by importing Mercedes-Benz automobiles—while the bulk of the population scarcely has the economic votes to demand subsistence rations of corn and beans. Strong state support of the efforts of the poor to organize can begin to rectify this imbalance and move toward greater equity.

The Sandinistas and other Central American revolutionaries say they intend to maintain a "mixed economy"—that is, one made up of private, state, and cooperative sectors. Some might see here a tactical ploy to allay fears and to hide an intention of eventually instituting an entirely state-owned and -run economy. However, it should be noted that what is frequently regarded as the private sector—that is, the larger plantations and businesses—is only part of the story. The whole private sector extends from small peasant tracts and village stores through medium-sized enterprises to large private operations. In Nicaragua, small and medium-sized enterprises do not feel threatened by the revolution. It is only the owners of larger enterprises (actually quite modest by U.S. standards) who feel that the revolution is unfair—primarily because their profits are now limited and they no longer set the rules. Some businesses do decline in a revolution, primarily luxury imports. On the other hand, some owners of large plantations worth millions of dollars have quietly continued to produce within the context of the revolution.

One other observation may help put the question of the state's role in the economy into perspective. Even if the Nicaraguan government were to take possession of the country's entire economy, its total gross national product of $2.4 billion in 1982 would put it far below the fiftieth largest industrial corporation in the United States—Monsanto, whose sales totaled $6.9 billion. It would even stand slightly below McDonald's, whose sales reached $2.5 billion. In a world economy dominated by giant multinational corporations, it is only logical that Third World countries would want to acquire some muscle through strong state participation in the economy. In both capitalist Mexico and Brazil, state enterprises are major economic actors.

In sum, based on a growing body of research and analysis, Central American revolutionaries hope to foment a new kind of mixed economy with strong state participation that will reorient production toward meeting basic needs (especially food self-sufficiency) and at the same time lay the groundwork for further integrated development.

Political participation

Strictly speaking, the political systems of sovereign countries are internal matters—except where gross violations of human rights become a concern of the international community. Thus, in principle, which political forms a revolutionary government adopts should not be of direct concern to U.S. policy. Nevertheless, since much of the debate in Central America pits "democratic" El Salvador and Honduras against "totalitarian" Nicaragua, some discussion of the political aims of revolutionary groups is necessary.

The carrying out of revolutionary change requires power and an effective revolutionary party and state. It also demands the active participation of the population. In fact, it is in this active participation in changing social and economic structures and building a new kind of society that revolutionaries see as the essence of democracy. For them, politics is a matter of ongoing popular involvement. A prime example of this is Nicaragua's 1980 literacy crusade. At that time some 60,000 students left their classrooms and went into the countryside for five months to teach peasants to read and write, while some 35,000 more taught in their own areas. Some 500,000 peasants learned to read and write, thus lowering the illiteracy rate from 52 percent to 13 percent. At the same time, the students came face-to-face with the real Nicaragua by living in peasant huts, sharing simple food, and sometimes going hungry.

Seen from this angle, it is electoral politics that appears undemocratic. If the central political act is voting periodically for candidates preselected by parties controlled by dominant elites, then democracy is not served. Although, in principle, voting allows people to "throw the rascals out" in such countries as El Salvador, the real rascals in the military and oligarchy are beyond the reach of the electoral process. Institutions such as political parties and congresses primarily provide an arena in which elites can struggle over secondary issues and seemingly legitimize the overall power arrangements in society.

This is not to argue that the revolutionary concept is superior. Certainly, the historical record of "people's democracies" reveals a great deal of hypocrisy, deceit, and crime. Within them, the most critical issues, especially regarding foreign policy, are argued only in closed party chambers. Without genuine public opposition, revolutionary parties can cease to be accountable to the people whom they ostensibly serve.

On the other hand, shopfloor democracy seems to function in some socialist countries. In Yugoslavia, for example, both factory and office workers have an integral role in management decisions.

The point here is modest. While the aspiration for democracy is broad, no particular form is finished or perfect. Indeed, democracy is unfinished business around the world. We might recall that one of the demands of the Solidarity Movement in Poland was that workers be involved in the hiring and firing of supervisors. Such a demand would seem utterly alien to most Americans, and yet people in Solidarity saw it as a logical democratic aspiration.

By the same token, revolutionary political forms may make sense to people in revolutionary countries. The crucial question for U.S. policy should be not whether such forms are congruent with U.S. notions of democracy, but whether they enjoy sufficient legitimacy from their own people.

Nonalignment

The Sandinistas and the revolutionary opposition movements in El Salvador and Guatemala see themselves as part of the Third World and would describe their approach to foreign policy as "nonalignment." However, both the U.S. government and the U.S. public find it difficult to accept nonalignment. The feeling that those who are not completely with us are against us runs deep, and the low esteem (and even contempt) shown for the United Nations in the United States seems to reflect a feeling that it is primarily a forum for upstart nations to berate this country.

This difficulty is compounded when former client states assert their independence. Some might see Nicaragua as following a Soviet line in international forums. In fact, such votes are actually following a world-wide pattern. All Third World countries tend to vote against the United States to a greater or lesser extent. Of all votes cast in the Thirty-Eighth General Assembly of the United Nations, the average rate of agreement with the United States for all Third World countries was 18.9 percent—while Nicaragua voted with the United States 14.1 percent of the time.

In seeking a modus vivendi in Central America, the United States would have to acknowledge the right to genuine nonalignment, including the right to maintain trade and diplomatic relations with socialist countries.

ACCOMMODATION WITH THE UNITED STATES

This discussion has tried to make a reasonable case. To what extent, however, can one assume that revolutionaries are reasonable? Upon taking power, will they not show their true colors—say, by forcing out the civilian politicians whom they have used to front for them? First, it should be recalled that the opposition movements are broad and diverse. Moreover, engaging in guerrilla warfare for years is not a preparation for organizing an economy, carrying out land reform, managing state enterprises, reorganizing health care, increasing literacy, reforming educational systems and curricula, dealing with other governments, or negotiating with banks and multinational corporations. All these tasks demand large numbers of qualified people. Most will not be Marxists, even if they agree with the overall aims of the revolution and employ some Marxist terminology.

To take an example from Nicaragua, successive economic plans have been the product of a continued and intense discussion between government technocrats and Sandinista leaders, taking into account complex issues such as whether the agricultural wage should be raised (with the consequent risk of inflation) and what to do about the enormous inherited foreign debt. Many of these technocrats were managers in the private sector before the revolution. These discussions have amounted to an ongoing course in economics and business management for people who have spent their previous years in the mountains. Some "moderates" who have left the government, like Arturo Cruz, former ambassador to the United States, have received considerable media attention; what goes unnoticed is that many moderates have been working in the Sandinista government for five years and continue to do so. Indeed, the Sandinista government sends administrators to a training institution in Managua run by the Harvard Business School.

Just as revolutionary movements acknowledge their need for civilian expertise and broad-based coalitions to carry out the reforms they envision, they are pragmatic enough to recognize that they are located in what the United States has long regarded as its backyard. Their economies are tied to those of the West. The United States has been the largest market for the region's agroexports and the primary source of its imports. In many cases, it would be too costly to switch to other kinds of equipment or technology. Even if they should desire to diversify their economic relations, it would be in their interest to remain within the Western economic system.

Moreover, the Soviet Union is clearly not willing to offer Nicaragua or any other Central American nation the large amounts of aid it would need to break away from the Western economic system. The Soviet Union may strain to support Cuba, but there is little reason to believe it could adopt other such clients. Because they would want to remain nonaligned, Central American revolutionary governments would no doubt establish relations with the Eastern bloc, but they could expect no more than modest aid.

Finally, it would in no sense be in their interest for Central American revolutionary governments to face the active hostility of the United States. The resources employed against the Sandinistas are a negligible part of the U.S. budget, and yet they force the Nicaraguan government and people to bring major development efforts to a standstill and to shift to a defense-and-survival economy.

To conclude the point: Central American revolutionary movements, should they take power, would have every reason to reach an accommodation with the United States.

There is no inherent reason why the United States could not reach an accommodation with revolutionary movements in Central America. To do so, of course, the United States would have to distinguish between its own long-range interests as a whole and the interests of particular parties who fear the consequences of any revolution. It would have to recognize that it is dealing with small agroexport countries that pose no genuine security threat to the hemisphere, and it would have to be sophisticated enough to take a pragmatic (rather than an ideological) approach to relations with these countries.

A final objection should be considered. Some might believe that an accommodation with revolutionary movements in Central America would encourage revolutionary movements in other Latin American countries where U.S. interests are much greater (such as Mexico, Brazil, and Chile). Although it is never stated, this fear may be the real bottom line in economic terms. The United States' investment in Central America is only a minuscule 2.5 percent of its total investment in Latin America. But just as the Chilean coup was a devastating reminder to many Latin Americans that basic change may take many years, even generations, the Nicaraguan revolution has energized many with a sense of hope. Its demonstration effect is real.

However, it is ethically repugnant to think that Central Americans should have to continue to die in large numbers simply to send a message about U.S. determination. Central America belongs to Central Americans—properly speaking, the United States cannot lose it all. Revolutions can come only from within a people. An outside demonstration effect can at most help people overcome psychological barriers and enable them to believe that victory is possible, but it will not supply any of the basic conditions for revolution. If U.S. policymakers or local elites are concerned about further revolutions, the lesson of Central America should impel them to examine whether similar structural conditions exist elsewhere and whether people's basic aspirations are being frustrated in a similar manner.

44

Nuclear War and Climatic Catastrophe: Some Policy Implications

Carl Sagan

It is not even impossible to imagine that the effects of an atomic war fought with greatly perfected weapons and pushed by the utmost determination will endanger the survival of man.

> —*Edward Teller, Bulletin of the Atomic Scientists,* February 1947

The extreme danger to mankind inherent in the proposal by [Edward Teller and others to develop thermonuclear weapons] wholly outweighs any military advantage.

> —*J. Robert Oppenheimer, et al., Report of the General Advisory Committee, AEC,* October 1949

The fact that no limits exist to the destructiveness of this weapon makes its very existence and the knowledge of its construction a danger to humanity. . . . It is . . . an evil thing.

> —*Enrico Fermi and I. I. Rabi, Addendum, ibid.*

A very large nuclear war would be a calamity of indescribable proportions and absolutely unpredictable consequences, with the uncertainties tending toward the worse. . . . All-out nuclear war would mean the destruction of contemporary civilization, throw man back centuries, cause the deaths of hundreds of millions or billions of people, and, with a certain degree of probability, would cause man to be destroyed as a biological species . . .

> —*Andrei Sakharov, Foreign Affairs,* Summer 1983

Carl Sagan, "Nuclear War and Climatic Catastrophe: Some Policy Implications," excerpted from *Foreign Affairs,* Vol. 62 (Winter 1983–84). Reprinted by permission of the author.

Apocalyptic predictions require, to be taken seriously, higher standards of evidence than do assertions on other matters where the stakes are not as great. Since the immediate effects of even a single thermonuclear weapon explosion are so devastating, it is natural to assume—even without considering detailed mechanisms—that the more or less simultaneous explosion of ten thousand such weapons all over the Northern Hemisphere might have unpredictable and catastrophic consequences.

And yet, while it is widely accepted that a full nuclear war might mean the end of civilization at least in the Northern Hemisphere, claims that nuclear war might imply a reversion of the human population to prehistoric levels, or even the extinction of the human species, have, among some policymakers at least, been dismissed as alarmist or, worse, irrelevant. Popular works that stress this theme, such as Nevil Shute's *On the Beach*, and Jonathan Schell's *The Fate of the Earth*, have been labeled disreputable. The apocalyptic claims are rejected as unproved and unlikely, and it is judged unwise to frighten the public with doomsday talk when nuclear weapons are needed, we are told, to preserve the peace. But, as the above quotations illustrate, comparably dire warnings have been made by respectable scientists with diverse political inclinations, including many of the American and Soviet physicists who conceived, devised and constructed the world nuclear arsenals.

Part of the resistance to serious consideration of such apocalyptic pronouncements is their necessarily theoretical basis. Understanding the long-term consequences of nuclear war is not a problem amenable to experimental verification—at least not more than once. Another part of the resistance is psychological. Most people—recognizing nuclear war as a grave and terrifying prospect, and nuclear policy as immersed in technical complexities, official secrecy and bureaucratic inertia—tend to practice what psychiatrists call denial: putting the agonizing problem out of our heads, since there seems nothing we can do about it. Even policymakers must feel this temptation from time to time. But for policymakers there is another concern: if it turns out that nuclear war could end our civilization or our species, such a finding might be considered a retroactive rebuke to those responsible, actively or passively, in the past or in the present, for the global nuclear arms race.

The stakes are too high for us to permit any such factors to influence our assessment of the consequences of nuclear war. If nuclear war now seems significantly more catastrophic than has generally been believed in the military and policy communities, then serious consideration of the resulting implications is urgently called for.

It is in that spirit that this article seeks, first, to present a short summary, in lay terms, of the climatic and biological consequences of nuclear war that emerge from extensive scientific studies conducted over the past two years, the essential conclusions of which have now been endorsed by a large number of scientists. These findings were presented in detail at a special conference in Cambridge, Mass., involving almost 100 scientists on April 22–26, 1983, and were publicly announced at a conference in Washington, D.C., on October 31 and November 1, 1983. They have been reported in summary form in the press, and a detailed statement of the findings and their bases will be published in *Science*. The present summary is designed particularly for the lay reader.

Following this summary, I explore the possible strategic and policy implications of the new findings. They point to one apparently inescapable conclusion: the necessity of moving as rapidly as possible to reduce the global nuclear arsenals below levels that could conceivably cause the kind of climatic catastrophe and cascading biological devastation predicted by the new studies. Such a reduction would have to be to a small percentage of the present global strategic arsenals.

The central point of the new findings is that the long-term consequences of a nuclear war could constitute a global climatic catastrophe.

The immediate consequences of a single thermonuclear weapon explosion are well known and well documented—fireball radiation, prompt neutrons and gamma rays, blast, and fires. The Hiroshima bomb that killed between 100,000 and 200,000 people was a fission device of about 12 kilotons yield (the explosive equivalent of 12,000 tons of TNT). A modern thermonuclear warhead uses a device something like the Hiroshima bomb as the trigger—the "match" to light the fusion reaction. A typical thermonuclear weapon now has a yield of about 500 kilotons (or 0.5 megatons, a megaton being the explosive equivalent of a million tons of TNT). There are many weapons in the 9-to-20-megaton range in the strategic arsenals of the United States and the Soviet Union today. The highest-yield weapon ever exploded is 58 megatons.

Strategic nuclear weapons are those designed for delivery by ground-based or submarine-launched missiles, or by bombers, to targets in the adversary's homeland. Many weapons with yields roughly equal to that of the Hiroshima bomb are today assigned to "tactical" or "theater" military missions, or are designated "munitions" and relegated to ground-to-air and air-to-air missiles, torpedoes, depth charges and artillery. While strategic weapons often have higher yields than tactical weapons, this is not always the case. Modern tactical or theater missiles (e.g., Pershing II, SS-20) and air support weapons (e.g., those carried by F-15 or MiG-23 aircraft) have sufficient range to make the distinction between "strategic" and "tactical" or "theater" weapons increasingly artificial. Both categories of weapons can be delivered by land-based missiles, sea-based missiles, and aircraft; and by intermediate-range as well as intercontinental delivery systems. Nevertheless, by the usual accounting, there are around 18,000 strategic thermonuclear weapons (warheads) and the equivalent number of fission triggers in the American and Soviet strategic arsenals, with an aggregate yield of about 10,000 megatons.

The total number of nuclear weapons (strategic plus theater and tactical) in the arsenals of the two nations is close to 50,000, with an aggregate yield near 15,000 megatons. For convenience, we here collapse the distinction between strategic and theater weapons, and adopt, under the rubric "strategic," an aggregate yield of 13,000 megatons. The nuclear weapons of the rest of the world—mainly Britain, France and China—amount to many hundred warheads and a few hundred megatons of additional aggregate yield.

No one knows, of course, how many warheads with what aggregate yield would be detonated in a nuclear war. Because of attacks on strategic aircraft and missiles, and because of technological failures, it is clear that less than the entire world arsenal would be detonated. On the other hand, it is generally accepted, even among most military planners, that a "small" nuclear war would be almost impossible to contain before it escalated to include much of the world arsenals. (Precipitating factors include command and control malfunctions, communications failures, the necessity for instantaneous decisions on the fates of millions, fear, panic and other aspects of real nuclear war fought by real people.) For this reason alone, any serious attempt to examine the possible consequences of nuclear war must place major emphasis on large-scale exchanges in the five-to-seven-thousand-megaton range, and many studies have done so. Many of the effects described below, however, can be triggered by much smaller wars.

The adversary's strategic airfields, missile silos, naval bases, submarines at sea, weapons manufacturing and storage locales, civilian and military command and control centers, attack assessment and early warning facilities, and the like are probable targets ("counterforce attack"). While it is often stated that cities are not targeted "per se," many of the above targets are very near or colocated with cities, especially in Europe. In addition, there is an industrial targeting category ("countervalue attack"). Modern nuclear doctrines require that "war-supporting" facilities be attacked. Many of these facilities are necessarily industrial in nature and engage a work force of considerable size. They are almost always situated near major transportation centers, so that raw materials and finished products can be efficiently transported to other industrial sectors, or to forces in the field. Thus, such facilities are, almost by definition, cities, or near or within cities. Other "war-supporting" targets may include the transportation systems themselves (roads, canals, rivers, railways, civilian airfields, etc.), petroleum refineries, storage sites and pipelines, hydroelectric plants, radio and television transmitters and the like. A major countervalue attack therefore might involve almost all large cities in the United States and the Soviet Union, and possibly most of the large cities in the Northern Hemisphere. There are fewer than 2,500 cities in the world with populations over 100,000 inhabitants, so the devastation of all such cities is well within the means of the world nuclear arsenals.

Recent estimates of the immediate deaths from blast, prompt radiation, and fires in a major exchange in which cities were targeted range from several hundred million to 1.1 billion people—the latter estimate is in a World Health Organization study in which targets were assumed not to be restricted entirely to NATO and Warsaw Pact countries. Serious injuries requiring immediate medical attention (which would be largely unavailable) would be suffered by a comparably large number of people, perhaps an additional 1.1 billion. Thus it is possible that something approaching half the human population on the planet would be killed or seriously injured by the direct effects of the nuclear war. Social disruption; the unavailability of electricity, fuel, transportation, food deliveries, communications and other civil services; the absence of medical care; the decline in sanitation measures; rampant disease and severe psychiatric disorders would doubtless collectively claim a significant number of further victims. But a range of additional effects—some unexpected, some inadequately treated in earlier studies, some uncovered only recently—now make the picture much more somber still.

Because of current limitations on missile accuracy, the destruction of missile silos, command and control facilities, and other hardened sites requires nuclear weapons of fairly high yield exploded as groundbursts or as low airbursts. High-yield groundbursts will vaporize, melt and pulverize the surface at the target area and propel large quantities of condensates and fine dust into the upper troposphere and stratosphere. The particles are chiefly entrained in the rising fireball; some ride up the stem of the mushroom cloud. Most military targets, however, are not very hard. The destruction of cities can be accomplished, as demonstrated at Hiroshima and Nagasaki, by lower-yield explosions less than a kilometer above the surface. Low-yield airbursts over cities or near forests will tend to produce massive fires, some of them over areas of 100,000 square kilometers or more. City fires generate enormous quantities of black oily smoke which rise at least into the upper part of the lower atmosphere, or troposphere. If firestorms occur, the smoke column rises vigorously, like the draft in a fireplace, and may carry some of the soot into the lower part of the upper atmosphere, or stratosphere. The smoke from forest and grassland fires would initially be restricted to the lower troposphere.

The fission of the (generally plutonium) trigger in every thermonuclear weapon and the reactions in the (generally uranium-238) casing added as a fission yield "booster" produce a witch's brew of radioactive products, which are also entrained in the cloud. Each such product, or radioisotope, has a characteristic "half-life" (defined as the time to decay to half its original level of radioactivity). Most of the radioisotopes have very short half-lives and decay in hours to days. Particles injected into the stratosphere, mainly by high-yield explosions, fall out very slowly—characteristically in about a year, by which time most of the fission products, even when concentrated, will have decayed to much safer levels. Particles injected into the troposphere by low-yield explosions and fires fall out more rapidly—by gravitational settling, rainout, convection, and other processes—before the radioactivity has decayed to moderately safe levels. Thus rapid fallout of tropospheric radioactive debris tends to produce larger doses of ionizing radiation than does the slower fallout of radioactive particles from the stratosphere.

Nuclear explosions of more than one-megaton yield generate a radiant fireball that rises through the troposphere into the stratosphere. The fireballs from weapons with yields between 100 kilotons and one megaton will partially extend into the stratosphere. The high temperatures in the fireball chemically ignite some of the nitrogen in the air, producing oxides of nitrogen, which in turn chemically attack and destroy the gas ozone in the middle stratosphere. But ozone absorbs the biologically dangerous ultraviolet radiation from the Sun. Thus the partial depletion of the stratospheric ozone layer, or "ozonosphere," by high-yield nuclear explosions will increase the flux of solar ultraviolet radiation at the surface of the Earth (after the soot and dust have settled out). After a nuclear war in which thousands of high-yield weapons are detonated, the increase in biologically dangerous ultraviolet light might be several hundred percent. In the more dangerous shorter wavelengths, larger increases would occur. Nucleic acids and proteins, the fundamental molecules for life on Earth, are especially sensitive to ultraviolet radiation. Thus, an increase of the solar ultraviolet flux at the surface of the Earth is potentially dangerous for life.

These four effects—obscuring smoke in the troposphere, obscuring dust in the stratosphere, the fallout of radioactive debris, and the partial destruction of the ozone layer—constitute the four known principal adverse environmental consequences that occur after a nuclear war is "over." There may be others about which we are still ignorant. The dust and, especially, the dark soot absorb ordinary visible light from the Sun, heating the atmosphere and cooling the Earth's surface.

All four of these effects have been treated in our recent scientific investigation. The study, known from the initials of its authors as TTAPS, for the first time demonstrates that severe and prolonged low temperatures would follow a nuclear war. (The study also explains the fact that no such climatic effects were detected after the detonation of hundreds of megatons during the period of U.S.-Soviet atmospheric testing of nuclear weapons, ended by treaty in 1963: the explosions were sequential over many years, not virtually simultaneous; and, occurring over scrub desert, coral atolls, tundra and wasteland, they set no fires.) The new results have been subjected to detailed scrutiny, and half a dozen confirmatory calculations have now been made. A special panel appointed by the National Academy of Sciences to examine this problem has come to similar conclusions.

Unlike many previous studies, the effects do not seem to be restricted to northern mid-latitudes, where the nuclear exchange would mainly take place. There is now substantial evidence that the heating by sunlight of atmospheric dust and soot over northern mid-latitude targets would profoundly change the global circulation. Fine particles would be transported across the equator in weeks, bringing the cold and the dark to the Southern Hemisphere. (In addition, some studies suggest that over 100 megatons would be dedicated to equatorial and Southern Hemisphere targets, thus generating fine particles locally.) While it would be less cold and less dark at the ground in the Southern Hemisphere than in the Northern, massive climatic and environmental disruptions may be triggered there as well.

In our studies, several dozen different scenarios were chosen, covering a wide range of possible wars, and the range of uncertainty in each key parameter was considered (e.g., to describe how many fine particles are injected into the atmosphere). Five representative cases are shown in Table 1, . . . ranging from a small low-yield attack exclusively on cities, utilizing, in yield, only 0.8 percent of the world strategic arsenals, to a massive exchange involving 75 percent of the world arsenals. "Nominal" cases assume the most probable parameter choices; "severe" cases assume more adverse parameter choices, but still in the plausible range.

Predicted continental temperatures in the Northern Hemisphere vary after the nuclear war according to the curves shown in Figure 1. . . . The high heat-retention capacity of water guarantees that oceanic temperatures will fall at most by a few degrees. Because temperatures are moderated by the adjacent oceans, temperature effects in coastal regions will be less extreme than in continental interiors. The temperatures shown in Figure 1 are average values for Northern Hemisphere land areas.

Even much smaller temperature declines are known to have serious consequences. The explosion of the Tambora volcano in Indonesia in 1815 led to an average global temperature decline of only 1°C, due to the obscuration of sunlight by the fine dust propelled into the stratosphere; yet the hard freezes the following year were so severe that 1816 has been known in Europe and America as "the year without a summer." A 1°C cooling would nearly eliminate wheat growing in Canada. In the last thousand years, the maximum global or Northern Hemisphere temperature deviations have been around 1°C. In an Ice Age, a typical long-term temperature decline from preexisting conditions is about 10°C. Even the most modest of the cases illustrated in Figure 1 give temporary temperature declines of this order. The Baseline Case is much more adverse. Unlike the situation in an Ice Age, however, the global temperatures after nuclear war plunge rapidly and take only months to a few years to recover, rather than thousands of years. No new Ice Age is likely to be induced by a Nuclear Winter.

Because of the obscuration of the Sun, the daytime light levels can fall to a twilit gloom or worse. For more than a week in the northern mid-latitude target zone, it might be much too dark to see, even at midday. In Cases 1 and 14 (Table 1), hemispherically averaged light levels fall to a few percent of normal values, comparable to those at the bottom of a dense overcast. At this illumination, many plants are close to what is called the compensation point, the light level at which photosynthesis can barely keep pace with plant metabolism. In Case 17, illumination, averaged over the entire Northern Hemisphere, falls in daytime to about 0.1 percent of normal, a light level at which plants will not photosynthesize at all. For Cases 1 and especially 17, full recovery to ordinary daylight takes a year or more (Figure 1).

As the fine particles fall out of the atmosphere, carrying radioactivity to the ground, the light levels increase and the surface warms. The depleted ozone layer now permits ultraviolet light to reach the Earth's surface in increased proportions. The relative timing of the multitude of adverse consequences of a nuclear war is shown in Figure 2. . . .

Perhaps the most striking and unexpected consequence of our study is that even a comparatively small nuclear war can have devastating climatic consequences, provided cities are targeted (see Case 14 in Figure 1; here, the centers of 100 major NATO and Warsaw Pact cities are burning). There is an indication of a very rough threshold at which severe climatic consequences are triggered—around a few hundred nuclear explosions over cities, for smoke generation, or around 2,000 to 3,000 high-yield surface bursts at, e.g., missile silos, for dust generation and ancillary fires. Fine particles can be injected into the atmosphere at increasing rates with only minor effects until these thresholds are crossed. Thereafter, the effects rapidly increase in severity.

As in all calculations of this complexity, there are uncertainties. Some factors tend to work towards more severe or more prolonged effects; others tend to ameliorate the effects. The detailed TTAPS calculations described here are one-dimensional; that is, they assume the fine particles to move vertically by all the appropriate laws of physics, but neglect the spreading in latitude and longitude. When soot or dust is moved away from the reference locale, things get better there and worse elsewhere. In addition, fine particles can be transported by weather systems to other locales, where they are carried more rapidly down to the surface. That would ameliorate obscuration not just locally but globally. It is just this transport away from the northern mid-latitudes that involves the equatorial zone and the Southern Hemisphere in the effects of the nuclear war. It would be helpful to perform an accurate three-dimensional calculation on the general atmospheric circulation following a nuclear war. Prelimi-

nary estimates suggest that circulation might moderate the low temperatures in the Northern Hemisphere predicted in our calculations by some
30 percent, lessening somewhat the severity of the effects, but still leaving
them at catastrophic levels (e.g., a 30°C rather than a 40°C temperature
drop). To provide a small margin of safety, we neglect this correction in
our subsequent discussion.

There are also effects that tend to make the results much worse: for
example, in our calculations we assumed that rainout of fine particles
occurred through the entire troposphere. But under realistic circumstances, at least the upper troposphere may be very dry, and any dust or
soot carried there initially may take much longer to fall out. There is also a
very significant effect deriving from the drastically altered structure of the
atmosphere, brought about by the heating of the clouds and the cooling of
the surface. This produces a region in which the temperature is approximately constant with altitude in the lower atmosphere and topped by a
massive temperature inversion. Particles throughout the atmosphere
would then be transported vertically very slowly—as in the present stratosphere. This is a second reason why the lifetime of the clouds of soot and
dust may be much longer than we have calculated. If so, the worst of the
cold and the dark might be prolonged for considerable periods of time,
conceivably for more than a year. We also neglect this effect in subsequent
discussion.

Nuclear war scenarios are possible that are much worse than the ones
we have presented. For example, if command and control capabilities are
lost early in the war—by, say, "decapitation" (an early surprise attack on
civilian and military headquarters and communications facilities)—then
the war conceivably could be extended for weeks as local commanders
make separate and uncoordinated decisions. At least some of the delayed
missile launches could be retaliatory strikes against any remaining adversary cities. Generation of an additional smoke pall over a period of weeks
or longer following the initiation of the war would extend the magnitude,
but especially the duration of the climatic consequences. Or it is possible
that more cities and forests would be ignited than we have assumed, or
that smoke emissions would be larger, or that a greater fraction of the
world arsenals would be committed. Less severe cases are of course
possible as well.

These calculations therefore are not, and cannot be, assured prog-
nostications of the full consequences of a nuclear war. Many refinements
in them are possible and are being pursued. But there is general agreement on the overall conclusions: in the wake of a nuclear war there is likely
to be a period, lasting at least for months, of extreme cold in a radioactive
gloom, followed—after the soot and dust fall out—by an extended period
of increased ultraviolet light reaching the surface.

. . . Every American and Soviet leader since 1945 has made critical
decisions regarding nuclear war in total ignorance of the climatic catastro-

phe. Perhaps this knowledge would have moderated the subsequent course of world events and, especially, the nuclear arms race. Today, at least, we have no excuse for failing to factor the catastrophe into long-term decisions on strategic policy.

Since it is the soot produced by urban fires that is the most sensitive trigger of the climatic catastrophe, and since such fires can be ignited even by low-yield strategic weapons, it appears that the most critical ready index of the world nuclear arsenals, in terms of climatic change, may be the total *number* of strategic warheads. (There is some dependence on yield, to be sure, and future very-low-yield, high-accuracy burrowing warheads could destroy strategic targets without triggering the nuclear winter, as discussed above.) For other purposes there are other indices— numbers of submarine-launched warheads, throw-weight (net payload deliverable to target), total megatonnage, etc. From different choices of such indices, different conclusions about strategic parity can be drawn. In the total number of strategic warheads, however, the United States is "ahead" of the Soviet Union and always has been.

Very roughly, the level of the world strategic arsenals necessary to induce the climatic catastrophe seems to be somewhere around 500 to 2,000 warheads—an estimate that may be somewhat high for airbursts over cities, and somewhat low for high-yield groundbursts. The intrinsic uncertainty in this number is itself of strategic importance, and prudent policy would assume a value below the low end of the plausible range.

National or global inventories above this rough threshold move the world arsenals into a region that might be called the "Doomsday Zone." If the world arsenals were well below this rough threshold, no concatenation of computer malfunction, carelessness, unauthorized acts, communications failure, miscalculation and madness in high office could unleash the nuclear winter. When global arsenals are above the threshold, such a catastrophe is at least possible. The further above threshold we are, the more likely it is that a major exchange would trigger the climatic catastrophe.

Traditional belief and childhood experience teach that more weapons buy more security. But since the advent of nuclear weapons and the acquisition of a capacity for "overkill," the possibility has arisen that, past a certain point, more nuclear weapons do not increase national security. I wish here to suggest that, beyond the climatic threshold, an increase in the number of strategic weapons leads to a pronounced *decline* in national (and global) security. National security is not a zero-sum game. Strategic insecurity of one adversary almost always means strategic insecurity for the other. Conventional pre-1945 wisdom, no matter how deeply felt, is not an adequate guide in an age of apocalyptic weapons.

If we are content with world inventories above the threshold, we are saying that it is safe to trust the fate of our global civilization and perhaps our species to all leaders, civilian and military, of all present and future major nuclear powers; and to the command and control efficiency and technical reliability in those nations now and in the indefinite future. For myself, I would far rather have a world in which the climatic catastrophe cannot happen, independent of the vicissitudes of leaders, institutions and machines. This seems to me elementary planetary hygiene, as well as elementary patriotism.

Something like a thousand warheads (or a few hundred megatons) is of the same order as the arsenals that were publicly announced in the 1950s and 1960s as an unmistakable strategic deterrent, and as sufficient to destroy either the United States or the Soviet Union "irrecoverably." Considerably smaller arsenals would, with present improvements in accuracy and reliability, probably suffice. Thus it is possible to contemplate a world in which the global strategic arsenals are below threshold, where mutual deterrence is in effect to discourage the use of those surviving warheads, and where, in the unhappy event that some warheads are detonated, there is little likelihood of the climatic catastrophe.

To achieve so dramatic a decline in the global arsenals will require not only heroic measures by both the United States and the Soviet Union—it will also require consistent action by Britain, France and China, especially when the U.S. and Soviet arsenals are significantly reduced. Currently proposed increments in the arsenals at least of France would bring that nation's warhead inventory near or above threshold. I have already remarked on the strategic instability, in the context of the climatic catastrophe only, of the warhead inventories of these nations. But if major cuts in the U.S. and Soviet arsenals were under way, it is not too much to hope that the other major powers would, after negotiations, follow suit. These considerations also underscore the danger of nuclear weapons proliferation to other nations, especially when the major inventories are in steep decline.

It is widely agreed—although different people have different justifications for this conclusion—that world arsenals must be reduced significantly. There is also general agreement, with a few demurrers, that at least the early and middle stages of a significant decline can be verified by national technical means and other procedures. The first stage of major arms reduction will have to overcome a new source of reluctance, when almost all silos could be reliably destroyed in a sub-threshold first strike. To overcome this reluctance, both sides will have prudently maintained an invulnerable retaliatory force, which itself would later move to sub-threshold levels. (It would even be advantageous to each nation to provide certain assistance in the development of such a force by the other.)

As arsenals are reduced still further, the fine tuning of the continuing decline may have to be worked out very carefully and with additional safeguards to guarantee continuing rough strategic parity. As threshold inventories are approached, some verifiable upper limits on yields as well as numbers would have to be worked out, to minimize the burning of cities if a nuclear conflict erupted. On the other hand, the deceleration of the arms race would have an inertia of its own, as the acceleration does; and successful first steps would create a climate conducive to subsequent steps.

In summary, cold, dark, radioactivity, pyrotoxins and ultraviolet light following a nuclear war—including some scenarios involving only a small fraction of the world strategic arsenals—would imperil every survivor on the planet. There is a real danger of the extinction of humanity. A threshold exists at which the climatic catastrophe could be triggered, very roughly around 500–2,000 strategic warheads. A major first strike may be an act of national suicide, even if no retaliation occurs. Given the magnitude of the potential loss, no policy declarations and no mechanical safeguards can adequately guarantee the safety of the human species. No national rivalry or ideological confrontation justifies putting the species at risk. Accordingly, there is a critical need for safe and verifiable reductions of the world strategic inventories to below threshold. At such levels, still adequate for deterrence, at least the worst could not happen should a nuclear war break out.

National security policies that seem prudent or even successful during a term of office or a tour of duty may work to endanger national—and global—security over longer periods of time. In many respects it is just such short-term thinking that is responsible for the present world crisis. The looming prospect of the climatic catastrophe makes short-term thinking even more dangerous. The past has been the enemy of the present, and the present the enemy of the future.

The problem cries out for an ecumenical perspective that rises above cant, doctrine and mutual recrimination, however apparently justified, and that at least partly transcends parochial fealties in time and space. What is urgently required is a coherent, mutually agreed upon, long-term policy for dramatic reductions in nuclear armaments, and a deep commitment, embracing decades, to carry it out.

Our talent, while imperfect, to foresee the future consequences of our present actions and to change our course appropriately is a hallmark of the human species, and one of the chief reasons for our success over the past million years. Our future depends entirely on how quickly and how broadly we can refine this talent. We should plan for and cherish our fragile world as we do our children and our grandchildren: there will be no other place for them to live. It is nowhere ordained that we must remain in bondage to nuclear weapons.

XII

Epilogue:
Options and Strategies

Between World War II and the 1960s, the United States enjoyed a period that the sociologist C. Wright Mills called the "American celebration"—a time when the stability of American institutions seemed assured, prosperity was virtually taken for granted, and the American way of life was held up as a shining example for other, less fortunate countries to follow.

As we've seen throughout this book, all of that seems very distant now. American society is changing rapidly—not always for the better—and those changes are, in turn, reflections of our changing role in the wider world. One result is that many of our traditional approaches to social problems have outlived their usefulness. What worked in the rapidly expanding economy of the past—and in a world where American economic and political dominance was virtually unchallenged—no longer works today.

On that point, there would be little disagreement. But exactly what new strategies we should put into place instead is another, much more controversial, story. Each of the articles in this chapter takes up that question, exploring some alternative social and economic options open to us as we move toward the twenty-first century. The specifics vary considerably, but there are common themes.

Some of those themes are set out in the statement on economic justice by the bishops of the Catholic church in the United States. The bishops find much that is inspiring and encouraging in contemporary America, but also much "unfinished business." In particular, they find it both irrational and unjust that millions of Americans are unable to be fully "active and productive participants in the life of society." One of the most formidable barriers to that participation is unemployment, and in the

575

excerpt in this chapter the bishops outline strategies to move us closer to full employment—strategies based on the fundamental moral principle that all citizens have a *right* to decent work.

The bishops argue that the challenge of building an economy that is more just, more equitable, and more productive is as important and as difficult as the political challenge faced by America's founders. To make such a reformed economy possible, we will need the coordination of all sectors of society—business, labor, the general public, and government. As we noted in the introduction to this book, there has been much recent criticism of what many people see as government's excessive role in American society. The bishops reject the argument that government intervention to serve social goals is necessarily a bad thing, and so do Gar Alperovitz and Jeff Faux, who tackle that argument head-on. They note that government has always been involved in the American economy, often in productive and indeed indispensable ways. And, contrary to what many believe, for several years already we have been allowing government's role in American society to expand—but often in destructive or unproductive ways and rarely with a clear sense of what we want government to do. Alperovitz and Faux call for a more conscious use of government to guide economic activity—especially in directions that strengthen local communities and build full employment.

Since the close of World War II, many of the kinds of social and economic initiatives suggested by the bishops and by Alperovitz and Faux have been put on hold, in part, because of the diversion of American resources to support an enormous military. In "Planning for Economic Conversion," Seymour Melman and Lloyd J. Dumas argue that the lessening of the threat of war between the United States and the Soviet Union has now made it both possible and urgently necessary to carry out long delayed civilian agendas for economic and social reconstruction. They stress that shifting our economy from military to civilian purposes won't happen automatically; it will require careful planning. Huge sections of the American economy, from the defense industries themselves to the universities, are now dependent wholly or partly on military spending, and the transition will not be easy. But a rationally planned conversion of resources now absorbed by defense is, they argue, the best hope for reversing America's domestic and international economic decline.

Robert Heilbroner's article takes up one aspect of that decline more specifically: the erosion of America's infrastructure—the roads and bridges, research centers, airports, and other public facilities that undergird our economic and social life. The steady deterioration of that foundation, resulting from our commitment to military spending, our reluctance to raise taxes, and our fear that the necessary public spending will increase the deficit, has contributed importantly to our economic decline relative to more farsighted industrial societies. Rebuilding the infrastructure will cost vast amounts of money, but the costs of *not* doing so are much greater, and Heilbroner, like Melman and Dumas, argues that reduced super-power tensions now allow us to shift resources from the military to this most urgent civilian priority.

45

Economic Justice for All

Catholic Bishops of the United States

THE U.S. ECONOMY TODAY: MEMORY AND HOPE

6. The United States is among the most economically powerful nations on earth. In its short history the U.S. economy has grown to provide an unprecedented standard of living for most of its people. The nation has created productive work for millions of immigrants and enabled them to broaden their freedoms, improve their families' quality of life and contribute to the building of a great nation. Those who came to this country from other lands often understood their new lives in the light of biblical faith. They thought of themselves as entering a promised land of political freedom and economic opportunity. The United States *is* a land of vast natural resources and fertile soil. It *has* encouraged citizens to undertake bold ventures. Through hard work, self-sacrifice and cooperation, families have flourished; towns, cities and a powerful nation have been created.

7. But we should recall this history with sober humility. The American experiment in social, political and economic life has involved serious conflict and suffering. Our nation was born in the face of injustice to native Americans, and its independence was paid for with the blood of revolution. Slavery stained the commercial life of the land through its first 250 years and was ended only by a violent civil war. The establishment of women's suffrage, the protection of industrial workers, the elimination of child labor, the response to the Great Depression of the 1930s and the civil

rights movement of the 1960s all involved a sustained struggle to transform the political and economic institutions of the nation.

8. The U.S. value system emphasizes economic freedom. It also recognizes that the market is limited by fundamental human rights. Some things are never to be bought or sold. This conviction has prompted positive steps to modify the operation of the market when it harms vulnerable members of society. Labor unions help workers resist exploitation. Through their government the people of the United States have provided support for education, access to food, unemployment compensation, security in old age and protection of the environment. The market system contributes to the success of the U.S. economy, but so do many efforts to forge economic institutions and public policies that enable *all* to share in the riches of the nation. The country's economy has been built through a creative struggle; entrepreneurs, business people, workers, unions, consumers and government have all played essential roles.

9. The task of the United States today is as demanding as that faced by our forebears. Abraham Lincoln's words at Gettysburg are a reminder that complacency today would be a betrayal of our nation's history: "It is for us, the living, rather to be dedicated here to the unfinished work they have thus far nobly advanced." There is unfinished business in the American experiment in freedom and justice for all. . . .

15. Several areas of U.S. economic life demand special attention. Unemployment is the most basic. Despite the large number of new jobs the U.S. economy has generated in the past decade, approximately 8 million people seeking work in this country are unable to find it and many more are so discouraged they have stopped looking. Over the past two decades the nation has come to tolerate an increasing level of unemployment. The 6 percent to 7 percent rate deemed acceptable today would have been intolerable 20 years ago. Among the unemployed are a disproportionate number of blacks, Hispanics, young people, or women who are the sole support of their families. Some cities and states have many more unemployed persons than others as a result of economic forces that have little to do with people's desire to work. Unemployment is a tragedy no matter whom it strikes, but the tragedy is compounded by the unequal and unfair way it is distributed in our society.

16. Harsh poverty plagues our country despite its great wealth. More than 33 million Americans are poor; by any reasonable standard another 20 million to 30 million are needy. Poverty is increasing in the United States, not decreasing. For a people who believe in "progress," this should be cause for alarm. These burdens fall most heavily on blacks, Hispanics and native Americans. Even more disturbing is the large increase in the number of women and children living in poverty. Today children are the largest single group among the poor. This tragic fact seriously threatens the nation's future. That so many people are poor in a nation as rich as ours is a social and moral scandal that we cannot ignore.

17. Many working people and middle-class Americans live dangerously close to poverty. A rising number of families must rely on the wages of two or even three members just to get by. From 1968 to 1978 nearly a quarter of the U.S. population was in poverty part of the time and received welfare benefits in at least one year. The loss of a job, illness or the breakup of a marriage may be all it takes to push people into poverty.

18. The lack of a mutually supportive relation between family life and economic life is one of the most serious problems facing the United States today. The economic and cultural strength of the nation is directly linked to the stability and health of its families. When families thrive, spouses contribute to the common good through their work at home, in the community and in their jobs, and children develop a sense of their own worth and of their responsibility to serve others. When families are weak or break down entirely, the dignity of parents and children is threatened. High cultural and economic costs are inflicted on society at large.

19. The precarious economic situation of so many people and so many families calls for examination of U.S. economic arrangements. Christian conviction and the American promise of liberty and justice for all give the poor and the vulnerable a special claim on the nation's concern. They also challenge all members of the church to help build a more just society. . . .

70. *Distributive justice requires that the allocation of income, wealth and power in society be evaluated in light of its effects on persons whose basic material needs are unmet.* The Second Vatican Council stated: "The right to have a share of earthly goods sufficient for oneself and one's family belongs to everyone. The fathers and doctors of the church held this view, teaching that we are obliged to come to the relief of the poor and to do so not merely out of our superfluous goods." Minimum material resources are an absolute necessity for human life. If persons are to be recognized as members of the human community, then the community has an obligation to help fulfill these basic needs unless an absolute scarcity of resources makes this strictly impossible. No such scarcity exists in the United States today.

71. Justice also has implications for the way the larger social, economic and political institutions of society are organized. *Social justice implies that persons have an obligation to be active and productive participants in the life of society and that society has a duty to enable them to participate in this way.* This form of justice can also be called "contributive," for it stresses the duty of all who are able to help create the goods, services and other nonmaterial or spiritual values necessary for the welfare of the whole community. In the words of Pius XI, "It is of the very essence of social justice to demand from each individual all that is necessary for the common good." Productivity is essential if the community is to have the resources to serve the well-being of all. Productivity, however, cannot be measured solely by its output in goods and services. Patterns of production must also be measured in light of their impact on the fulfillment of basic needs, employ-

ment levels, patterns of discrimination, environmental quality and sense of community.

72. The meaning of social justice also includes a duty to organize economic and social institutions so that people can contribute to society in ways that respect their freedom and the dignity of their labor. Work should enable the working person to become "more a human being," more capable of acting intelligently, freely and in ways that lead to self-realization.

73. Economic conditions that leave large numbers of able people unemployed, underemployed or employed in dehumanizing conditions fail to meet the converging demands of these three forms of basic justice. Work with adequate pay for all who seek it is the primary means for achieving basic justice in our society. Discrimination in job opportunities or income levels on the basis of race, sex or other arbitrary standard can never be justified. It is a scandal that such discrimination continues in the United States today. Where the effects of past discrimination persist, society has the obligation to take positive steps to overcome the legacy of injustice. Judiciously administered affirmative-action programs in education and employment can be important expressions of the drive for solidarity and participation that is at the heart of true justice. Social harm calls for social relief.

74. Basic justice also calls for the establishment of a floor of material well-being on which all can stand. This is a duty of the whole of society, and it creates particular obligations for those with greater resources. This duty calls into question extreme inequalities of income and consumption when so many lack basic necessities. Catholic social teaching does not maintain that a flat, arithmetical equality of income and wealth is a demand of justice, but it does challenge economic arrangements that leave large numbers of people impoverished. Further, it sees extreme inequality as a threat to the solidarity of the human community, for great disparities lead to deep social divisions and conflict.

75. This means that all of us must examine our way of living in light of the needs of the poor. Christian faith and the norms of justice impose distinct limits on what we consume and how we view material goods. The great wealth of the United States can easily blind us to the poverty that exists in this nation and the destitution of hundreds of millions of people in other parts of the world. Americans are challenged today as never before to develop the inner freedom to resist the temptation constantly to seek more. Only in this way will the nation avoid what Paul VI called "the most evident form of moral underdevelopment," namely greed.

76. These duties call not only for individual charitable giving but also for a more systematic approach by businesses, labor unions and the many other groups that shape economic life—as well as government. The concentration of privilege that exists today results far more from institutional

relationships that distribute power and wealth inequitably than from differences in talent or lack of desire to work. These institutional patterns must be examined and revised if we are to meet the demands of basic justice. . . .

OVERCOMING MARGINALIZATION AND POWERLESSNESS

77. These fundamental duties can be summarized this way: *Basic justice demands the establishment of minimum levels of participation in the life of the human community for all persons.* The ultimate injustice is for a person or group to be actively treated or passively abandoned as if they were nonmembers of the human race. To treat people this way is effectively to say that they simply do not count as human beings. This can take many forms, all of which can be described as varieties of marginalization or exclusion from social life. This exclusion can occur in the political sphere: restriction of free speech, concentration of power in the hands of a few or outright repression by the state. It can also take economic forms that are equally harmful. Within the United States, individuals, families and local communities fall victim to a downward cycle of poverty generated by economic forces they are powerless to influence. The poor, the disabled and the unemployed too often are simply left behind. This pattern is even more severe beyond our borders in the least-developed countries. Whole nations are prevented from fully participating in the international economic order because they lack the power to change their disadvantaged position. Many people within the less-developed countries are excluded from sharing in the meager resources available in their homelands by unjust elites and unjust governments. These patterns of exclusion are created by free human beings. In this sense they can be called forms of social sin. . . .

95. The economic challenge of today has many parallels with the political challenge that confronted the founders of our nation. In order to create a new form of political democracy they were compelled to develop ways of thinking and political institutions that had never existed before. Their efforts were arduous and their goals imperfectly realized, but they launched an experiment in the protection of civil and political rights that has prospered through the efforts of those who came after them. *We believe the time has come for a similar experiment in securing economic rights: the creation of an order that guarantees the minimum conditions of human dignity in the economic sphere for every person.* . . .

136. Full employment is the foundation of a just economy. The most urgent priority for domestic economic policy is the creation of new jobs with adequate pay and decent working conditions. We must make it possible as a nation for everyone who is seeking a job to find employment within a reasonable amount of time. Our emphasis on this goal is based

on the conviction that human work has a special dignity and is a key to achieving justice in society.

137. Employment is a basic right, a right which protects the freedom of all to participate in the economic life of society. It is a right which flows from the principles of justice which we have outlined above. Corresponding to this right is the duty on the part of society to ensure that the right is protected. The importance of this right is evident in the fact that for most people employment is crucial to self-realization and essential to the fulfillment of material needs. Since so few in our economy own productive property, employment also forms the first line of defense against poverty. Jobs benefit society as well as workers, for they enable more people to contribute to the common good and to the productivity required for a healthy economy.

138. Joblessness is becoming a more widespread and deep-seated problem in our nation. There are about 8 million people in the United States looking for a job who cannot find one. They represent about 7 percent of the labor force. The official rate of unemployment does not include those who have given up looking for work or those who are working part time but want to work full time. When these categories are added, it becomes clear that about one-eighth of the work force is directly affected by unemployment. The severity of the unemployment problem is compounded by the fact that almost three-fourths of those who are unemployed receive no unemployment insurance benefits.

139. In recent years there has been a steady trend toward higher and higher levels of unemployment, even in good times. Between 1950 and 1980 the annual unemployment rate exceeded current levels only during the recession years of 1975 and 1976. Periods of economic recovery during these three decades brought unemployment rates down to 3 percent and 4 percent. Since 1979, however, the rate has generally been above 7 percent.

140. Who are the unemployed? Blacks, Hispanics, native Americans, young adults, female heads of households and those who are inadequately educated are represented disproportionately among the ranks of the unemployed. The unemployment rate among minorities is almost twice as high as the rate among whites. For female heads of households, the unemployment rate is over 10 percent. Among black teen-agers unemployment reaches the scandalous rate of more than one in three.

141. The severe human costs of high unemployment levels become vividly clear when we examine the impact of joblessness on human lives and human dignity. It is a deep conviction of American culture that work is central to the freedom and well-being of people. The unemployed often come to feel they are worthless and without a productive role in society. Each day they are unemployed our society tells them: We don't need your talent. We don't need your initiative. We don't need *you*. Unemployment takes a terrible toll on the health and stability of both individuals and

ask whether our nation will ever be able to modernize our economy and achieve full employment if we continue to devote so much of our financial and human resources to defense-related activities.

149. These are some of the factors that have driven up the rate of unemployment in recent years. Although our economy has created more than 20 million new jobs since 1970, there continues to be a chronic and growing job shortage. In the face of this challenge, our nation's economic institutions have failed to adapt adequately and rapidly enough. For example, failure to invest sufficiently in certain industries and regions, inadequate education and training for new workers and insufficient mechanisms to assist workers displaced by new technology have added to the unemployment problem.

150. Generating an adequate number of jobs in our economy is a complex task in view of the changing and diverse nature of the problem. It involves numerous tradeoffs and substantial costs. Nevertheless, it is not an impossible task. Achieving the goal of full employment may require major adjustments and creative strategies that go beyond the limits of existing policies and institutions, but it is a task we must undertake.

GUIDELINES FOR ACTION

151. We recommend that the nation make a major new commitment to achieve full employment. At present there is nominal endorsement of the full-employment ideal, but no firm commitment to bringing it about. If every effort were now being made to create the jobs required, one might argue that the situation today is the best we can do. But such is not the case. The country is doing far less than it might to generate employment.

152. Over the last decade, economists, policy-makers and the general public have shown greater willingness to tolerate unemployment levels of 6 percent to 7 percent or even more. Although we recognize the complexities and tradeoffs involved in reducing unemployment, we believe that 6 percent to 7 percent unemployment is neither inevitable nor acceptable. While a zero unemployment rate is clearly impossible in an economy where people are constantly entering the job market and others are changing jobs, appropriate policies and concerted private and public action can improve the situation considerably, if we have the will to do so. No economy can be considered truly healthy when so many millions of people are denied jobs by forces outside their control. The acceptance of present unemployment rates would have been unthinkable 20 years ago. It should be regarded as intolerable today.

153. We must first establish a consensus that everyone has a right to employment. Then the burden of securing full employment falls on all of us—policy-makers, business, labor and the general public—to create and implement the mechanisms to protect that right. We must work for the

States have also added to the size of the labor force. These demographic changes, however, cannot fully explain the higher levels of unemployment.

145. Technological changes are also having dramatic impacts on the employment picture in the United States. Advancing technology brings many benefits, but it can also bring social and economic costs, including the downgrading and displacement of workers. High technology and advanced automation are changing the very face of our nation's industries and occupations. In the 1970s, about 90 percent of all new jobs were in service occupations. By 1990, service industries are expected to employ 72 percent of the labor force. Much of the job growth in the 1980s is expected to be in traditionally low-paying, high-turnover jobs such as sales, clerical, janitorial and food service. Too often these jobs do not have career ladders leading to higher-skilled, higher-paying jobs. Thus the changing industrial and occupational mix in the U.S. economy could result in a shift toward lower-paying and lower-skilled jobs.

146. Increased competition in world markets is another factor influencing the rate of joblessness in our nation. Many other exporting nations have acquired and developed up-to-the-minute technology, enabling them to increase productivity dramatically. Combined with very low wages in many nations, this has allowed them to gain a larger share of the U.S. market and to cut into U.S. export markets. At the same time many corporations have closed plants in the United States and moved their capital, technology and jobs to foreign affiliates.

147. Discrimination in employment is one of the causes for high rates of joblessness and low pay among racial minorities and women. Beyond the normal problems of locating a job, blacks, Hispanics, native Americans, immigrants and other minorities bear this added burden of discrimination. Discrimination against women is compounded by the lack of adequate childcare services and by the unwillingness of many employers to provide flexible employment or extend fringe benefits to part-time employees.

148. High levels of defense spending also have an effect on the number of jobs in our economy. In our pastoral letter "The Challenge of Peace," we noted the serious economic distortions caused by the arms race and the disastrous effects that it has on society's ability to care for the poor and the needy. Employment is one area in which this interconnection is very evident. The hundreds of billions of dollars spent by our nation each year on the arms race create a massive drain on the U.S. economy as well as a very serious "brain drain." Such spending on the arms race means a net loss in the number of jobs created in the economy, because defense industries are less labor-intensive than other major sectors of the economy. Moreover, nearly half of the American scientific and engineering force works in defense-related programs, and over 60 percent of the entire federal research and development budget goes to the military. We must

families. It gives rise to family quarrels, greater consumption of alcohol, child abuse, spouse abuse, divorce and higher rates of infant mortality. People who are unemployed often feel that society blames them for being unemployed. Very few people survive long periods of unemployment without some psychological damage even if they have sufficient funds to meet their needs. At the extreme, the strains of job loss may drive individuals to suicide.

142. In addition to the terrible waste of individual talent and creativity, unemployment also harms society at large. Jobless people pay little or no taxes, thus lowering the revenues for cities, states and the federal government. At the same time, rising unemployment requires greater expenditures for unemployment compensation, food stamps, welfare and other assistance. It is estimated that in 1986, for every one percentage-point increase in the rate of unemployment, there will be roughly a $40 billion increase in the federal deficit. The costs to society are also evident in the rise in crime associated with joblessness. The Federal Bureau of Prisons reports that increases in unemployment have been followed by increases in the prison population. Other studies have shown links between the rate of joblessness and the frequency of homicides, robberies, larcenies, narcotics arrests and youth crimes.

143. Our own experiences with the individuals, families and communities that suffer the burdens of unemployment compel us to the conviction that as a nation we simply cannot afford to have millions of able-bodied men and women unemployed. We cannot afford the economic costs, the social dislocation and the enormous human tragedies caused by unemployment. In the end, however, what we can least afford is the assault on human dignity that occurs when millions are left without adequate employment. Therefore, we cannot but conclude that current levels of unemployment are intolerable, and they impose on us a moral obligation to work for policies that will reduce joblessness.

UNEMPLOYMENT IN A CHANGING ECONOMY

144. The structure of the U.S. economy is undergoing a transformation that affects both the quantity and the quality of jobs in our nation. The size and makeup of the work force, for example, have changed markedly in recent years. For a number of reasons, there are now more people in the labor market than ever before in our history. Population growth has pushed up the supply of potential workers. In addition, large numbers of women have entered the labor force in order to put their talents and education to greater use and out of economic necessity. Many families need two salaries if they are to live in a decently human fashion. Female-headed households often depend heavily on the mother's income to stay off the welfare rolls. Immigrants seeking a better existence in the United

165. Jobs that are created should produce goods and services needed and valued by society. It is both good common sense and sound economics to create jobs directly for the purpose of meeting society's unmet needs. Across the nation, in every state and locality, there is ample evidence of social needs that are going unmet. Many of our parks and recreation facilities are in need of maintenance and repair. Many of the nation's bridges and highways are in disrepair. We have a desperate need for more low-income housing. Our educational systems, day-care services, senior-citizen services and other community programs need to be expanded. These and many other elements of our national life are areas of unmet need. At the same time, there are more than 8 million Americans looking for productive and useful work. Surely we have the capacity to match these needs by giving Americans who are anxious to work a chance for productive employment in jobs that are waiting to be done. The overriding moral value of enabling jobless persons to achieve a new sense of dignity and personal worth through employment also strongly recommends these programs.

166. These job-creation efforts will require increased collaboration and fresh alliances between the private and public sectors at all levels. There are already a number of examples of how such efforts can be successful. We believe that the potential of these kinds of partnerships has only begun to be tapped.

Examining new strategies

167. In addition to the actions suggested above, we believe there is also a need for careful examination and experimentation with alternative approaches that might improve both the quantity and quality of jobs. More extensive use of job sharing, flex time and a reduced work week are among the topics that should continue to be on the agenda of public discussion. Consideration should also be given to the possibility of limiting or abolishing compulsory overtime work. Similarly, methods might be examined to discourage the overuse of part-time workers who do not receive fringe benefits. New strategies also need to be explored in the area of education and training for the hard-to-employ displaced workers, the handicapped and others with special needs. Particular attention is needed to achieve pay equity between men and women, as well as upgrading the pay scale and working conditions of traditionally low-paying jobs. The nation should renew its effort to develop effective affirmative-action policies that assist those who have been excluded by racial or sexual discrimination in the past. New strategies for improving job-placement services at the national and local levels are also needed. Improving occupational safety is another important concern that deserves increased attention.

168. Much greater attention also needs to be devoted to the long-term task of converting some of the nation's military production to more peaceful and socially productive purposes. The nation needs to seek more

needed for a dynamic and productive economy. Investment in a skilled work force is a prerequisite both for sustaining economic growth and achieving greater justice in the United States. The obligation to contribute to this investment falls on both the private and public sectors. Today business, labor and government need to coordinate their efforts and pool their resources to promote a substantial increase in the number of apprenticeship programs and to expand on-the-job training programs. We recommend a national commitment to eradicate illiteracy and to provide people with skills necessary to adapt to the changing demands of employment.

160. With the rapid pace of technological change, continuing education and training are even more important today than in the past. Businesses have a stake in providing it, for skilled workers are essential to increased productivity. Labor unions should support it, for their members are increasingly vulnerable to displacement and job loss unless they continue to develop their skills and their flexibility on the job. Local communities have a stake as well, for their economic well-being will suffer serious harm if local industries fail to develop and are forced to shut down.

161. The best medicine for the disease of plant closings is prevention. Prevention depends not only on sustained capital investment to enhance productivity through advanced technology, but also on the training and retraining of workers within the private sector. In circumstances where plants are forced to shut down, management, labor unions and local communities must see to it that workers are not simply cast aside. Retraining programs will be even more urgently needed in these circumstances.

162. *(2) We recommend increased support for direct job-creation programs targeted on the long-term unemployed and those with special needs.* Such programs can take the form of direct public-service employment and also of public subsidies for employment in the private sector. Both approaches would provide jobs for those with low skills less expensively and with less inflation than would general stimulation of the economy. The cost of providing jobs must also be balanced against the savings realized by the government through decreased welfare and unemployment-insurance expenditures and increased revenues from the taxes paid by the newly employed.

163. Government funds, if used effectively, can also stimulate private sector jobs for the long-term unemployed and for groups particularly hard to employ. Experiments need to be conducted on the precise ways such subsidies would most successfully attract business participation and ensure the generation of permanent jobs.

164. These job-generation efforts should aim specifically at bringing marginalized persons into the labor force. They should produce a net increase in the number of jobs rather than displacing the burden of unemployment from one group of persons to another. They should also be aimed at long-term jobs and should include the necessary supportive services to assist the unemployed in finding and keeping jobs.

formation of a new national consensus and mobilize the necessary political will at all levels to make the goal of full employment a reality.

154. Expanding employment in our nation will require significant steps in both the private and public sectors, as well as joint action between them. Private initiative and entrepreneurship are essential to this task, for the private sector accounts for about 80 percent of the jobs in the United States, and most new jobs are being created there. Thus a viable strategy for employment generation must assume that a large part of the solution will be with private firms and small businesses. At the same time, it must be recognized that government has a prominent and indispensable role to play in addressing the problem of unemployment. The market alone will not automatically produce full employment. Therefore, the government must act to ensure that this goal is achieved by coordinating general economic policies, by job creation programs and by other appropriate policy measures.

155. Effective action against unemployment will require a careful mix of general economic policies and targeted employment programs. Taken together, these policies and programs should have full employment as their No. 1 goal.

General economic policies

156. The general or macro-economic policies of the federal government are essential tools for encouraging the steady economic growth that produces more and better jobs in the economy. *We recommend that the fiscal and monetary policies of the nation—such as federal spending, tax and interest-rate policies—should be coordinated so as to achieve the goal of full employment.*

157. General economic policies that attempt to expand employment must also deal with the problem of inflation. The risk of inflationary pressures resulting from such expansionary policies is very real. Our response to this risk, however, must not be to abandon the goal of full employment, but to develop effective policies that keep inflation under control.

158. While economic growth is an important and necessary condition for the reduction of unemployment, it is not sufficient in and of itself. In order to work for full employment and restrain inflation, it is also necessary to adopt more specific programs and policies targeted toward particular aspects of the unemployment problem.

Targeted employment programs

159. *(1) We recommend expansion of job-training and apprenticeship programs in the private sector administered and supported jointly by business, labor unions and government.* Any comprehensive employment strategy must include systematic means of developing the technical and professional skills

effective ways to retool industries, to retrain workers and to provide the necessary adjustment assistance for communities affected by this kind of economic conversion.

169. These are among the avenues that need to be explored in the search for just employment policies. A belief in the inherent dignity of human work and in the right to employment should motivate people in all sectors of society to carry on that search in new and creative ways. . . .

363. Confronted by this economic complexity and seeking clarity for the future, we can rightly ask ourselves one single question: How does our economic system affect the lives of people—*all* people? Part of the American dream has been to make this world a better place for people to live in; at this moment of history that dream must include everyone on this globe. Since we profess to be members of a "catholic" or universal church, we all must raise our sights to a concern for the well-being of everyone in the world. Third World debt becomes our problem. Famine and starvation in sub-Saharan Africa become our concern. Rising military expenditures everywhere in the world become part of our fears for the future of this planet. We cannot be content if we see ecological neglect or the squandering of natural resources. In this letter we bishops have spoken often of economic interdependence; now is the moment when all of us must confront the reality of such economic bonding and its consequences, and see it as a moment of grace—a *kairos*—that can unite all of us in a common community of the human family. We commit ourselves to this global vision.

46

More Government, Not Less

Gar Alperovitz and Jeff Faux

I s government inherently bureaucratic, wasteful, clumsy and burdened by red tape? Do private corporations automatically develop
and manage a nation's resources better than public enterprises? Is the free
market invariably more efficient than careful planning in guiding and
directing a nation's economic destiny?

Unfashionable as it is to say so in the midst of the "Reagan revolution,"
the answer to all these questions is an emphatic no. In fact, it is almost
certain that we will one day look back on the current period of anti-
government sentiment in the United States as a brief interlude before a
new era of efficient, enlightened and—yes—expanded involvement of
federal, state and local government in the economy.

It is pure nostalgia to think that our post-industrial society will be run in
the future as if it were a semi-developed, agricultural nation in mid-19th
century. There is a worldwide trend toward more government, and not
even America under Ronald Reagan has been immune to it.

Contrary to common opinion, federal spending as a percentage of
Gross National Product has risen, not fallen, during the Reagan administration. In the Jimmy Carter years, federal spending averaged just over
22 percent of GNP; under Reagan it has averaged 24.2 percent.

This president, like others before him, has openly used the power of
government to manage the economy. He continued the Chrysler bailout.
His Agriculture Department handed over $21 billion of surplus commodi-

A Twentieth Century Fund study of public authorities in states and cities found that, with some exceptions, "the present system . . . has been generally successful at producing good management and effective operations." The major criticism was that public organizations were too conservative in their operations and tended to reflect the interest and biases of businessmen who dominate their boards.

To be sure, during the recent slowdown in economic growth there is some evidence that the relative productivity of public enterprises in Western Europe declined in late 1970s. But that seems, in large part, to have resulted from the greater freedom of private managers to lay off workers in recessions. In effect, private companies shifted the costs of unemployment to the public (which paid increased welfare and unemployment costs), while public firms tended to absorb these costs themselves.

This is a point that is too often side-stepped by enthusiastic supporters of the free market and the private sector. While it is all very well to extol the efficiency of private enterprise, it is easy to ignore the costs of this efficiency to taxpayers and communities. In our current, relatively unplanned economy, taxpayers subsidize major corporate investment decisions, which, in turn, often wreak havoc on communities and their tax bases.

Any accountant looking at the overall costs from the taxpayers' point of view of a company's decision to pull up stakes and move would evaluate the "efficiency" of such a move very differently from the company's own bookkeepers.

At present, communities have little power to control the flight of companies and capital. They are caught up in a competition for capital that is ultimately destructive to all. The Sunbelt may be benefiting temporarily from a wave of business investment at the expense of the North and Midwest, but the benefits may only be shortlived. At some point, companies are likely to shut down and move elsewhere to take advantage of cheaper labor, more ample water and other factors, leaving communities to pick up the tab for schools, highways and other services.

This is where planning comes in. Only a comprehensive approach at both the national and local level can define investment goals that protect communities, jobs and, ultimately, taxpayers.

Since 1978, legislation has been introduced at the local, state, and federal level to require advance notice of plant closings and to aid firms owned by their workers or their communities.

A serious strategy for safeguarding local economic stability would include technical assistance, loans and loan guarantees to build up community-based enterprises. The federal government has a role to play here. A firm should always be free to move if it so desires; but there is no reason for it to receive tax incentives, grants for training programs and research favored public ownership of utilities, railroads and other industries that were not competitive. This highly respected conservative teacher of Milton Friedman declared that "every industry should be either effectively competitive or socialized."

Government-owned, or partially owned, railroad, airline, aircraft, electrical, and automobile companies have been responsible for good deal of France's industrial innovation and, in the case of aircraft and autos, for a significant part of her manufacturing exports. Government-owned Renault, for example, has been highly successful in competition with private firms. And European governments, working together, built the successful commercial aircraft Airbus.

In Western Europe public enterprises account for 8 to 12 percent of total employment and 15 to 30 percent of total capital investment. Six of the largest 12, and 15 of the largest 50, Western European industrial firms are wholly or substantially owned by governments. For example, West German, Canadian, French, Italian and British governments are major shareholders in their respective oil and gas industries.

Current economic difficulties in Europe have aroused new interest in U.S.-style free enterprise and entrepreneurism. In England, some public enterprises have been sold back to the private sector. However, on balance, the changes in Europe as a whole have been relatively modest. French President Francois Mitterand has brought more banks into the public sector.

Despite our anti-government ideology, the record of public agencies in this country is quite different from what the conventional wisdom holds. During World War II the federal government created a variety of efficient businesses—aluminum industries on the West Coast, steel mills and an oil pipeline from Texas to the East Coast, all of which were later purchased by the private sector. The federal government currently operates civilian airports, builds ships in Navy shipyards, manages a third of the nation's land and administers the world's largest pension system, Social Security.

The state of Wisconsin runs the State Life Insurance Fund, created by Republican populist Gov. Robert LaFollette in 1917. State Life is solvent and unsubsidized. Moreover, it sells life insurance for 10 to 40 percent less than its private competitors.

State governments operate liquor stores, hotels, resorts and lotteries. South Dakota makes and sells cement, and Nebraska produces and sells hog cholera serum. Hundreds of localities efficiently run their own water companies.

Comparing the efficiency of public and private enterprises is no easy matter. Public utility companies, for example, often have the disadvantage of serving unprofitable rural areas. On the other hand, they don't pay taxes and can offer investors tax-free bonds. Several studies have found public utilities to be more efficient producers and distributors of electric power, even when their tax advantages are eliminated.

ties to farmers as part of a Payment-in-Kind program. His administration "informally" limited imports of Japanese automobiles and restricted imports of steel, sugar and motorcycles. Not only has the government taken over Continental Illinois National Bank—the nation's eighth largest—but it has virtually guaranteed all large banks that it will not permit them to fail.

The Reagan administration has supported government programs that aid the defense and nuclear power industries. And that is to say nothing of indirect government action, such as the 1981 tax bill that heavily favored big manufacturing industries over small business and the service sector.

The administration's actual record, if not its rhetoric, is part of a trend with a long history. Over the years, the federal government has subsidized regions of the United States with military bases and aerospace projects; an interstate highway system; billion-dollar water projects; rural electrification; ports and waterways. It has promoted American agriculture with price supports for corn, export subsidies for wheat and an elaborate system of allotments, quotas and marketing orders that help growers of tobacco, cotton, sugar, peanuts, oranges, apples and dozens of other commodities.

Federal investment in canals and turnpikes, and vast subsidies to railroads, helped "open the West." Government policies that subsidized the development of new labor-saving technologies in agriculture encouraged the mass migration of rural blacks to northern and midwestern cities after World War II.

There is nothing unusual about any of this, much as it goes against the grain of America "free enterprise" mythology. In every nation in the world, governments are deeply involved in planning, subsidizing, financing and in some cases operating major sectors of the economy. Such private-public cooperation helps countries compete internationally, avoids wasteful duplication of research efforts, safeguards employment and maintains the stability of communities.

The expansion of the Japanese steel industry, which contributed to the devastation of U.S. steel companies, was the result of an economic strategy designed by the Japanese government.

There is no iron law of economics that says private enterprise is innately superior to public enterprise. Big corporations are as vulnerable as big government to the ills of size, bureaucracy and monopoly.

Real conservatives are the first to acknowledge this. The late Henry C. Simons, founder of the Chicago school of economics, came to believe that many corporations (as opposed to individual entrepreneurs) had outlived their usefulness.

Simons recognized the need for restraints on corporate practices. He advocated strong antitrust laws and federal chartering of corporations. He

47

Planning for Economic Conversion

Seymour Melman and Lloyd J. Dumas

I t's time to start planning the conversion of America's defense economy to civilian work. By conversion we mean political, economic and technical measures for assuring the orderly transformation of labor, machinery and other economic resources now being used for military purposes to alternative civilian uses. The political impetus for conversion is gaining momentum as a result of the relaxation of cold war tensions. Another stimulus to action is America's deteriorating competitive position in the world economy.

A major factor in America's decline to the status of a second-class industrial power has been the voracious appetite of the military-industrial complex, which employs 6.5 million civilian and military personnel in more than 135,000 factories, laboratories and bases. From 1947 to 1989 this country diverted to military purposes resources whose value exceeded the fixed reproducible, tangible wealth of the entire civilian economy. Tens of thousands of factories became virtual wards of the Pentagon; sheltered from the discipline of the marketplace, they adopted inefficient and costly methods. An indirect consequence of the larger share of tax dollars funneled into the military establishment was a diminution of public investment in the infrastructure and its resulting decay. The debilitating effect of all those developments on American industrial strength is readily apparent.

Labor productivity, a key indicator of long-term efficiency, has significantly declined. Between 1968 and 1988 labor productivity (measured by cost and benefits of corporate investment decisions. This requires increasing the scope and competence of government planning.

Arguments have been made that a more coherently planned economy would make it harder for this country to compete internationally. In fact, the opposite is the case.

As things now stand, the closing of out-moded factories in declining industries is so threatening to jobs and community welfare that corporations, communities and unions all team together to fight for protection. This only postpones the day of reckoning, perpetuating inefficiency and lack of competitiveness.

But if communities and workers were assured alternative jobs, the impasse could be broken, allowing the modernization to go forward more rapidly.

Planning does not do away with politics; it puts politics out in the open. It forces special-interest groups to stand up and be counted. Cozy alliances between political leaders and economics interests are bought to light. In a more planned economy, there are still deals and compromises, but they can be labeled and evaluated openly.

At present, the expansion of government is carried on behind a smokescreen of free-enterprise rhetoric that confuses the public and makes rational decision-making impossible. A sensible U.S. economic policy would recognize the need to build up a coherent planning capacity at both the national and local level. It would accept the fact that only government is capable of assessing the total costs and benefits of economic decisions to the taxpayer and the nation. It would put community well-being at the center of national planning for full employment. And it would reap the benefits of an economy that mixed public and private enterprises in ways that took advantage of the special contributions of each.

Only such an economic policy allows a satisfactory answer to the question, "What's in it for me?" The answer cannot be that we will beat the Japanese to 40 percent of the world's computer business, but you will lose your job or your business in the process.

and development funds from federal, state and local governments if its move throws excessive numbers of people out of work and makes them dependent on public welfare and unemployment funds. In that case, the total costs far outweigh the total benefits.

The closing of a plant by an absentee conglomerate does not necessarily mean that the plant is unprofitable. Rather, it means that the plant is not profitable enough for the liking of the conglomerate. Local owners however, might be willing to settle for a smaller profit, because of the jobs and other economic benefits from keeping the plant running.

The experience of Herkimer, N.Y., a small city not far from Syracuse, illustrates the broader returns that are possible from emphasizing economic stability strategies.

The nation's largest manufacturer of library furniture, a Sperry Rand subsidiary named the Library Bureau, was located in Herkimer. In 1975 the parent company decided to close the plant because it was not producing the 22 percent return on investment that Sperry Rand required of its subsidiaries. Closing the 250-worker plant would have devastated the little community, so after several futile efforts to change Sperry Rand's mind, the workers and small businessmen in the town decided to buy the firm and run it themselves.

A group headed by John Ladd, a local businessman with a flair for politics, formed a corporation and sold $1.5 million worth of stock in $1 and $2 shares to workers and local residents. They borrowed $2 million from local banks, another $2 million from the U.S. Department of Commerce, and bought the plant. When the dust settled, the employees owned some 30 to 40 percent of the shares, and their neighbors in Herkimer owned the rest.

During the first full year of operation, the worker- and community-owned company earned 17 percent on its investment—not enough for the multinational Sperry Rand Corp., but plenty for the people and workers of Herkimer, who saved their jobs and their town.

The impact on local communities of unexpected new investment is not always positive, either. In California's "Silicon Valley," the cost of an average house has jumped dramatically, and large numbers of new houses are awaiting basic service hookups. By the year 2000, Houston's population is expected to have grown sixfold from its 1950 level, resulting in congestion, pollution, water shortages, overcrowded schools and hospitals and a huge run-up in real estate values. Because of excessively rapid growth, a city industrial and real estate commission took the almost unheard-of step of recommending that large industrial corporations be encouraged to locate outside the county, since new tax revenue from industry was not adequate to offset the costs of growth.

If we are to reduce these costly and inefficient patterns of boom and bust, we must face up to the need for a comprehensive assessment of the

the dollar value of output per hour of workers in the nonagricultural business sector) rose by 24 percent, approximately one-third of the gain between 1948 and 1968.

In every year between 1894 and 1970 the United States ran a trade surplus—exporting more goods than it imported. In 1971 these surpluses turned into deficits. By 1987 the foreign trade deficit hit a peak of $170 billion, more than 160 percent above the record level set only four years earlier. "Made in the U.S.A." once meant well-made, high-quality, reasonably priced goods produced by industrial workers earning the highest wages in the world. Now U.S. trade deficits reflect in part a decline in quality and productive efficiency.

In 1982 the American economy plunged into its worst economic downturn since the Great Depression. By the end of the 1980s, however, the unemployment rate fell to more tolerable levels. Inflation remained well below the double-digit rates of the late 1970s. And the real gross national product grew more than 25 percent between 1982 and the third quarter of 1988, when it passed the $4 trillion mark. Supposedly, the country is in the midst of the strongest economic recovery since World War II.

But that is an illusion. We have merely pumped up the economy with a huge infusion of public and private debt. This facade of prosperity is not based on the efficient production that drove the economy's remarkable growth throughout much of America's industrial history—an expansion whose benefits were spread among the population rather than going to one small segment of it at the expense of all the rest.

Between fiscal 1980 and fiscal 1989 the national debt more than tripled, from $914 billion to $2.8 trillion. In less than three years after 1985, the federal government added nearly $780 billion in debt, an amount equal to more than 85 percent of the *total* national debt as of 1980. State and local government debt, and the private debt of households and nonfinancial institutions, soared from nearly $3 trillion in 1980 to more than $6 trillion by September 1988. Between 1980 and 1987 the United States went from being the world's largest creditor nation, to whom $106 billion was owed, to being the world's largest debtor nation, with a net international debt approaching $400 billion.

All that borrowing served temporarily to paper over deep-seated economic problems, giving us a fleeting reprieve. But it has also created a "bubble of debt" on top of a steadily eroding economic base, adding the possibility of a sudden collapse to the continuing long-term deterioration in American economic performance.

THE FORCES OF REAL RECOVERY

Despite these very serious problems, the end of the 1980s has brought some cause for optimism. Three powerful political forces have begun to develop that may just push the United States in the direction it needs to go to turn this downbeat picture around: the growing pressure to balance the federal budget, the increasing prominence of the competitiveness issue and the extraordinary opportunities created by *perestroika* and *glasnost* in the Soviet Union and Eastern Europe.

Balancing the budget

The enormous increase in the national debt between 1980 and 1989 was clearly the result of the Reagan Administration's tax cuts combined with a military spending binge. Had the borrowing been in support of a major program of public investment in infrastructure, education and the like, it would not have been a great problem. Productive investment would have eventually generated more than enough additional wealth to pay back the borrowed money with interest. But unproductive use of the money for military expansion means that it must now be paid back out of existing wealth—and that will be painful.

Annual military budgets more than doubled during that period, and this accelerated spending accounted for more than 50 percent of the increase in national debt. The military-driven debt, in turn, led to a near tripling of the annual net interest on that debt, from $53 billion to $152 billion. Looked at differently, without this explosive increase in the national debt, the interest savings alone would have taken us two-thirds of the way to balancing the federal budget.

In the 1987 fiscal year, spending on the military and interest on the national debt accounted for almost 90 percent of all the federal income tax revenues collected from both individuals and corporations. . . . In the absence of draconian tax increases or slashes in social programs greater than the public was willing to accept from the previous administration, significant cuts in the military budget are highly likely. Without them it will be impossible to balance the federal budget in the foreseeable future. This is not a question of ideology or political preference. It is simply a matter of fiscal reality.

Competitiveness

The fiscal pressures for cutbacks in military spending reinforce demands for the changes that are needed to rebuild American industrial competitiveness. More than forty years of high military spending has diverted from civilian industry the resources that are critical to efficient, competitive production, including roughly 30 percent of the nation's engineers and scientists and a comparable portion of its capital. Engineers and scientists trained to design and produce for cost-minimizing in civilian industry are the key to developing technology for better product designs and more efficient methods of production; capital allows these innovations to be put into use on the factory floor. The long-term drain of these resources has undermined the ability of U.S.-based factories to maintain

Department and to administering major research institutions, like the Lawrence Livermore and Los Alamos nuclear weapons laboratories, for the Pentagon. At the same time the departments of universities that might be expected to have some connection with civilian production, the engineering and business schools, have become less production-oriented during the long cold war period. Some schools are beginning to make an effort to reestablish the importance of civilian production in their curriculums, but the emphasis is small compared with the military-oriented research activities. The universities also contain large departments and schools—such as political science and international relations—whose faculties and curriculums have focused on training cold war technicians, researchers and administrators.

For all the personnel of the military-serving institutions it is significant that the knowledge for performing their tasks comprises their intellectual capital and work skills. Therefore a change to a civilian economy entails the obsolescence of intellectual capital and the necessity for learning new skills.

Alongside these direct economic ties to the military at the universities there are a number of ideological commitments that play an important part in sustaining support for military institutions. Among economists, for example, it is generally accepted that money equals wealth, that the proper measure of economic product is in money terms, that the money value of an economic activity denotes its value independent of the usefulness of the product. Military goods and services are thus counted as additions to real wealth despite the fact that they do not contribute to the central purpose of the economy—to provide the material standard of living. They add neither to the present standard of living (as do ordinary consumer goods) nor to the future standard of living by increasing the economy's capacity to produce (as do industrial machinery, equipment and the like).

Since the Great Depression, economists, and indeed the larger society, have defined the central problem of the U.S. economy as the maintenance of proper levels of market demand, and thereby of income and employment. From this perspective, expenditures that generate market demand are critical, regardless of the nature of the product. A consensus formed that military spending is the best way to accomplish this effect. Thus, most economics textbooks do not differentiate between firms producing military goods and civilian enterprises.

From these assumptions it is a short step to the idea that the United States is uniquely capable of affording guns *and* butter for an indefinite period of time. This belief has facilitated the acceptance of sustained negative trade balances and spreading incompetence in U.S. manufacturing. Large subsidies to the American standard of living in the form of trade imbalances are therefore considered normal, while the role of the military economy in causing a collapse of production competence is world and performs the same functions as similar offices in large corporations.

Furthermore, the management of the Pentagon's central office controls the largest block of finance capital in the hands of any single American management. Every year since 1951 the new capital made available to the Defense Department has exceeded the combined net profits of all U.S. corporations. The top managers in the Pentagon and their subordinates are endowed with the usual managerial imperative to maintain and enlarge their decision-making power. Accordingly, they have consistently opposed all proposals for economic conversion planning in the United States.

This managerial opposition to conversion planning is not specific to any particular social structure, political ideology or management technique. Thus the managers of the U.S. military economy perform their command function via allocation of money resources, while those of the Soviet Union perform the command function by direct physical resource pre-emption and allocation. The results in each case are similar: pre-emption of major resources from civilian production and powerful pressures for operating in an unproductive, cost-maximizing way.

The work force and surrounding communities of factories, bases and laboratories that serve the military are another institutional barrier to economic conversion. In the United States 3.5 million men and women work in the military industry. An additional 1 million are employees of the Pentagon, including civilian workers on bases, and there are 2 million in the armed forces. For these 6.5 million people and their families and surrounding communities, the military-serving facilities have been the principal sources of jobs for most of their lives. The skills they have developed and the relationships with which they are familiar are powerful incentives to continue working for the military. The people in such enterprises know that even the appearance of an interest in the idea of economic conversion would bring the disfavor of the Pentagon's top managers.

The nation's organized engineering societies include large numbers of engineers beholden to the military economy. This has a significant effect on the contents of society meetings, the subject matter of journals and learned papers, and the network of contacts available for employment opportunity. At this writing no single engineering society has ventured to propose contingent conversion planning for its members as a way of coping with the possible reversal of military budget growth. In its November 1989 issue *Spectrum*, a journal of the Institute of Electrical and Electronics Engineers, published a special report titled "Preparing for Peace," a serious, courageous attempt to survey the military engineers' prospects during a subsiding cold war.

Finally, there are the universities, particularly the larger ones, which have grown accustomed to receiving major R&D grants from the Defense competitive position, especially relative to those nations (Japan and Germany, for example) whose commercial industries are only lightly burdened by that drain.

To revitalize the competitiveness of American industry we must attack the structural causes of inefficiency. This can be accomplished in a solid, long-term way only by an infusion of capital and technical talent. That means redirecting a significant fraction of these critical resources from military to civilian research and production.

Perestroika and glasnost

The remarkable changes in the Soviet Union and Eastern Europe offer great promise of substantial arms reduction. We have seen only a beginning, but it is a hopeful one. The prospect of a 50 percent reduction in strategic nuclear arsenals—even talk of the total elimination of nuclear weapons within a decade or two—has moved from the realm of an impossible dream to the real world of negotiations. Progress toward reduction of conventional forces has begun.

Each of the three forces we have been discussing has its counterpart in the Soviet Union, which has finally admitted that it too is plagued by out-of-control budget deficits. The military's diversion of critical resources from the country's civilian industrial base has played no small part in rendering those industries hopelessly inefficient. At the same time, the attention of the nations of Western Europe has turned increasingly to economic integration rather than military adventurism. As far as the Soviet Union is concerned, this surely diminishes the threat to their security.

The convergence of these three forces in both the United States and the Soviet Union has made large-scale demilitarization an increasingly practical, attainable goal. And large-scale demilitarization is just what is needed to free sufficient resources for building healthy, growing economies in both nations.

OBSTACLES TO CONVERSION

Nevertheless, there are strong institutional and ideological barriers to implementation of economic conversion. The most prominent of these are the managements in central government offices and the private firms that are dependent on the military economy. Government departments are ordinarily viewed as "bureaucracies"; however, the central management in the Defense Department that controls the operations of 35,000 prime contracting establishments is, functionally, a central administrative office. This central administrative office is probably the largest such entity in the up detailed technical and economic plans for shifting to viable alternative civilian activity. Funds would be provided for services such as income support, continued health insurance and pension benefits during any actual transition resulting from military cutbacks.

There are two reasons why military-industry workers should be specially protected, even though workers in other industries are not. First, such protection is vital to breaking the hold of the politically powerful "jobs" argument, which raises the specter of lost jobs to constituents and thus damage to the political careers of representatives who vote against any military programs. The second is that the special obstacles to conversion of military industry must be overcome to allow the infusion of resources into civilian activity that will ultimately revitalize the whole of U.S. industry, and not just the prospects of converted defense workers and firms.

By moving military-sector resources into profitable civilian activity through a carefully planned process of economic conversion, the nation can break its decades-long addiction to military spending and build a stronger and more secure economic base. Without such a revitalization of civilian production, it is difficult to see how America can climb out of the deep hole of production incompetence, deficit and debt it dug for itself in the 1980s and reverse the deterioration of its economic performance and competitive position in the global marketplace.

CONVERSION TO WHAT?

What could the 6.5 million employees of the military-serving institutions do for a living beyond their work for the Pentagon? There are three major areas of work that could be done by these people. The first is repairing the American infrastructure. This includes building and repairing roads, railroads and bridges; constructing waste disposal plants; cleaning up toxic and nuclear wastes; erecting new housing to make up for the enormous shortfall in construction and repair during the past decades; refurbishing libraries, public school buildings, university facilities and so on. In New York City alone there are 1,000 public school buildings, of which 83 percent require major repairs. Bridges and highways have been crumbling for want of proper maintenance, and the country's railroads are more like the Toonerville Trolley of cartoon fame than modern high-speed facilities. The cost of repairing the infrastructure could amount to more than $5 trillion. The work to be done would surely extend over several decades.

House Resolution 101 includes a provision for a Cabinet-level council that would be charged with encouraging state, city and county governments to prepare capital budgets for renovating the public works and services under their jurisdiction. If carried out, this would set in motion a than the other. The point is that they are very different. It is simply not reasonable to expect a manager used to operating in one of these worlds to perform efficiently in the other without undergoing substantial retraining and reorientation. That takes time and will not happen automatically. Civilian firms may well prefer to hire inexperienced civilian managers instead of facing the costs involved in retraining an experienced military manager for civilian work. The same consideration holds for engineers and scientists—the other main component of the military-serving labor force—who would require substantial retraining and reorientation.

The products of military industry are notorious for their poor reliability, despite requirements that only components meeting stringent military specifications be used. These components are not only remarkably costly but also certified to withstand extraordinary extremes of shock, temperature and so on. Poor reliability is an unavoidable consequence of the increasing complexity of military weaponry. Thus sophisticated military aircraft have been in repair a third or more of the time. That's bearable when the cost of maintenance is not a limiting factor. But city transportation systems cannot accept vehicles that are "not mission capable" a third of the time. Hence, the retraining of military-experienced engineers and managers is an essential aspect of economic conversion. Of course, the physical facilities and equipment of military industry will require modification as well.

PLANNING FOR CONVERSION

Advanced contingency plans for moving into alternative civilian-oriented activity could help carry the nation smoothly through the transition to a demilitarized economy and protect militarily dependent communities against the considerable economic disruption they will otherwise experience. The transformation of a facility and its work force to civilian production must be planned locally, by those who know them best—not by distant "experts." Even at its best such a planning process will be lengthy. A great many details must be worked through to insure that the transition is smooth and that the resulting facility and work force are properly restructured to be an efficient civilian producer, able to operate profitably without continuing subsidies. It is long past time to get this process under way.

A bill now before Congress, House Resolution 101, would institutionalize a nationwide system of highly decentralized contingency planning for economic conversion at every military facility in the United States. The resolution, called the Defense Economic Adjustment Act, sponsored by Representative Ted Weiss, would require the establishment of labor-management Alternative Use Committees at every military facility with 100 or more people. These local committees would be empowered to draw ignored. Nevertheless, domestic economic problems and international political changes compel attention to the feasibility of economic conversion.

THE PROCESS OF ECONOMIC CONVERSION

The ideology of the free-market economy argues that the labor and facilities no longer needed in the military-serving sector will flow smoothly and efficiently toward an expanding civilian sector once military spending is cut. The market will take care of the transition. There is no need for special attention and certainly no need for advance preparation.

But this isn't true. The world of military industry is very different from the world of commercial industry. For one thing, military-serving firms do not operate in anything like a free-market environment. In the military production system, the nature, quantity and price of output are not determined by impersonal market forces. They are set by the interaction of the Pentagon's central planners and the managers of the military-industrial firms. Military industry, unlike any civilian industry, has only one customer—the Defense Department. Even when military firms sell to other nations, they typically sell products initially designed and produced to satisfy the needs of the Defense Department and can sell abroad only with its permission. Furthermore, the vast majority of defense contracts are negotiated rather than awarded through true price-competitive bidding.

More important, competition in the civilian commercial marketplace provides a crucial element of cost discipline that is largely absent in military industry. In practice, most major military contractors operate on a cost-plus basis, being reimbursed for whatever they have spent plus a guaranteed profit. In such an environment, there are no real penalties for inefficient production. In fact, company revenues can be increased by jacking up costs. Such cost escalation would spell bankruptcy for firms operating in a free market.

The sales function of a typical civilian company involves dealing with large numbers of potential customers, ranging from perhaps a few dozen for firms purveying industrial products to millions for consumer goods producers. For military firms the sales function means knowing the Armed Services Procurement Regulations, developing contacts within the Defense Department and being adept at lobbying. The most crucial job of managers in civilian industries is keeping costs down while producing good quality products. Managers in defense firms need pay relatively little attention to cost, but they must try to manufacture products capable of operating under extreme conditions while delivering every possible increment of performance.

It is not a question of one kind of management being easier or harder thoroughly decentralized set of nationwide planning operations for projects that would have employment needs beyond the size and capabilities of the existing work force.

The second area of new work for the converted military labor force would involve producing in the United States many of the products that are now imported. There is no law of nature or economics that prevents factories in the United States from once again becoming competent producers of shoes, for example; we now import 80 percent of our supply. An infusion of fresh investment and talent into the machine-tool industry could restore our former ability to produce high-quality machinery. The United States now buys 50 percent of its new machine tools from Japan, Germany and South Korea.

The third area is new ideas, a sphere in which American engineers and technicians once excelled.

A uniquely large proportion of engineers and administrators are employed in the military-serving industries. For those occupations some special conversion prospects will surely be in order. Teachers of mathematics and the sciences are in notoriously short supply in American high schools and junior colleges. The major teachers colleges could design appropriate programs for training some of these men and women to teach the young, an activity that would have long-range benefits for society. Many engineers could be retrained as civil engineers to work in American communities. The addition of an engineer to a city's or a town's staff would mean a substantial improvement in the ability of local governments to cope with the array of public works that are their responsibility.

COLLECTING THE PEACE DIVIDEND

Apart from the planning of economic conversion, its actual execution will be heavily dependent on the timing and the size of the peace dividend that would result from the reduction of military budgets. Savings can be expected from two sources: first, and early on, reduction of certain military activities (such as base closings and elimination of marginal weapons programs) at the initiative of the federal government; second, de-escalation of military spending and the size of the military-serving institutions as a result of international agreements setting in motion a programmed reduction of the arms race. The first of these approaches could yield possible savings of several billion dollars annually. *The New York Times* editorialized on March 8 in favor of weapons and force cuts starting with $20 billion per year and reaching $150 billion annually after ten years. That would bring down annual military spending to a level comparable to that in President Carter's budgets. But a thoroughgoing military de-escalation would require international disarmament agreements.

A program for reversing the arms race was laid out by President Kennedy in April 1962 in a document called "Outline of Basic Provisions of a Treaty on General and Complete Disarmament in a Peaceful World." This plan called for a ten-year period to accomplish a significant reversal of the arms race among nations and the parallel establishment of international institutions for inspecting the disarmament process, for coping with international conflict by nonmilitary means and for developing an international peacekeeping force. If this blueprint is implemented, a ten-year cumulative peace dividend of $1.5 trillion is within reach. That is the magnitude of resources needed to start serious economic conversion and to rebuild the infrastructure and industry of the country.

for concern" because it can adversely affect the growth of the private sector.

Thus the neglect of the national infrastructure has been an unmitigated disaster. No one has gained: all have lost. That is why I argue that of all the means of reestablishing our place, the most important is to rebuild the embankment on which the economy runs—indeed to expand it to the size consonant with our present-day social and economic needs. Paradoxically, this is also the cheapest way of regaining our momentum—indeed, as we shall see, it could be thought of as costing nothing.

I will turn in a moment to that opportunity. First, however, it is important to understand how we got where we are. How could a state of disrepair clearly injurious to our individual as well as our national interests have been permitted to come about?

There are three reasons, and everyone knows the first. We have been unwilling to impose the taxes—on income, consumption, or even on sin—to pay for public improvements. This is not because our tax structure is so high: in 1985 Sweden's tax revenues amounted to 51 percent of its gross domestic product, France's came to 46 percent, Germany's and England's each to 38 percent. Our revenue—federal plus state and local—was 29 percent of our gross product. Among advanced industrial capitalisms only Japan's was lower—28 percent.

I do not point this out to deplore (although I do deplore it), but to locate the first reason for our inadequate stock of public capital. It has simply been our refusal to pay for a more adequate one—a refusal as evident in the state legislatures as it is on Capitol Hill. The American public has made clear its distaste for taxes, even though opinion polls have again and again indicated the public's dissatisfaction with the existing state of the environment, public facilities, the schools, and the like. However self-defeating and paradoxical this frame of mind, it is a fact of political life that must be reckoned with.

The second reason that we have allowed our infrastructural base to erode has been our fear of deficits. Even though adamantly opposed to paying more taxes, we could still have built roads and bridges, financed education, undertaken housing programs or carried on bold programs of public research and development, if we had been willing to pay for them by borrowing. That is, after all, the way in which the private sector typically finances its capital undertakings. Corporate America does not pay for its own infrastructure—that is, for its investment outlays—by writing checks against its earnings. It finances capital expenditures by issuing new bonds or new stock, which it will "service" from the enhanced earnings that its new capital projects are expected to produce.

Precisely such an avenue of finance is open to the government. Public investment, like private investment, typically yields its payback over a ing on infrastructure absorbed 6.9 percent of the nonmilitary federal budget. Irregularly, but with increasing momentum, this share has been declining ever since. During the 1970s it plummeted to an average of 1.5 percent. During the 1980s the share dropped still further to 1.2 percent. Thus a smaller and smaller fraction of government spending has gone into reinforcing or extending the public foundation of the economy. To drive across the Queensboro Bridge in New York is to know at first hand the meaning of allowing our infrastructure to decay.

Where there is longstanding current neglect, catch-up costs become large. The United States Department of Transportation tells us that it will now take $50 billion to repair the nation's 240,000 bridges. To bring our highways up to their condition in 1983 will take ten years and $315 billion in current dollars. Air traffic control is in desperate need of funds for expansion and modernization—at least $25 billion by the year 2000. According to the Department of Housing and Urban Development, it will cost $20 billion to rehabilitate the nation's stock of public housing, and rehabilitation does not mean adding to the current, shamefully inadequate stock. There is no official tally of the total expenditures needed to repair and maintain the infrastructure over the next ten years. The Congressional Budget Office estimates the amount at about $60 billion per year. The Association of Public Contractors puts it at $118 billion per year. The nation's contractors are hardly a disinterested source, but in this case their estimates may be closer to reality.

These totals, moreover, include only "hard" investment—the public counterpart of private spending for plant and equipment. But some public spending for "soft" purposes is also properly included in infrastructure because it contributes to economic growth. One obvious such candidate is expenditure on education, whose economic consequence is the improvement of the skills and productivity of our citizenry.

This "soft" portion of our infrastructure is also badly neglected. Spending on elementary and secondary education reached 4.4 percent of GNP in the 1970s. It has fallen by 10 percent during the present decade. At the same time, investment in higher education has not risen since the 1970s. This is an important part of the reason that the quality of our labor force is deteriorating both at the bottom and at the top—and thus part of the reason that we are falling behind.

Economists of all political colorations agree that our ramshackle and rotting infrastructure constitutes a serious obstacle to vigorous economic growth. For example, David Aschauer of the Chicago Federal Reserve Bank has calculated that a dollar of public investment is today productive of more output than a dollar of private investment, and that private profitability would rise by two percentage points—that is, from, say 10 to 12 percent—if infrastructure investment were merely brought back to its 1981 levels. The final report of President Reagan's Council of Economic Advisers also notes the fall in federal investment spending as "a matter

48

Seize the Day

Robert Heilbroner

America is falling behind. I do not mean only that we are losing ground against Europe and Japan. I mean that we are falling behind with respect to our own capacities. We are not the country we once were, or the country we could be.

I do not need to document this sorry assertion. I want to write about what I think we can do to catch up. For we now have a unique chance to become the country we could be if we lived up to our possibilities. It lies within our grasp to overcome the single most difficult obstacle we face in trying to recover our momentum. That obstacle is the inadequacy of our infrastructure, the public underpinnings without which a society cannot be healthy or an economy prosperous.

Infrastructure is the public capital of a nation—the network of roads and water mains, harbors and air navigation systems, public health research facilities and public waste disposal facilities, on which we all depend for much of the quality of our individual lives. We also depend on it for much of our collective efficiency. Just as a train cannot exceed the limits of its roadbed, an economy cannot exceed those of its infrastructure.

American infrastructure is in a state of near collapse. For nearly twenty-five years we have virtually ceased to improve our public capital. Following World War II, we set out to build up interstate highways, airports, research and development laboratories and the like, until by 1952 spend-

tunities. If we let this one slip through our fingers, we will have passed over the greatest and most nourishing free lunch we are likely ever to enjoy.

Of course that lunch is not really free. It is true that we can rebuild our infrastructure without either paying added taxes or suffering the consequences of additional borrowing, but it is also true that we could use the cut in military spending to reduce our taxes or to cut back the amount that the government borrows. Thus the real cost of taking advantage of the chance to rebuild the country's infrastructure is the private gain we will have to forgo—lower taxes, less public borrowing, with its interest costs— in order to achieve a long-denied public gain.

Nevertheless, if the money is spent effectively, it will feel like a free lunch. The proviso is important. The Pentagon has no monopoly on waste. Free or not, the lunch will not be nourishing if we use the peace dividend to buy ourselves a gigantic pork barrel.

That sobering consideration does not argue against seizing the unique chance to make up for past neglect. Rather, it alerts us to the need to find appropriate ways to monitor an opportunity of such extraordinary importance. Perhaps a newly organized bipartisan committee, along the lines of the much respected Congressional Budget Office, or entirely outside the structure of government, should watch over the performance of our public investment effort as we bring it up to the level that will be necessary.

In that case, we would see a change in the quality of life, as the numbers of school dropouts decline, the air gets cleaner, and the economy becomes more productive, the society more decent. We may even remember with disbelief what a ride across the old Queensboro bridge was like. Some may still declare that they would rather have had a tax cut, or a reduction in the national debt, but I suspect that most of us will simply be thankful that America has finally stopped falling behind and has begun to ready itself for whatever place it deserves in the scheme of things.

number of years, which is the rationale behind borrowing to pay for it, rather than paying the bill immediately. Moreover, just as private investment brings added earnings, so public investment brings a larger national income. The private corporation uses its additional earnings to pay the dividends or interest on its newly issued securities; the government uses the enhanced tax revenues that flow from a larger national income to pay interest on its new debts.

So why have we not used government borrowing to build public capital, as we have so often done in the past? Part of the answer is that, at least during the last few years, the opposition of the public to more taxes seems to have been matched by its opposition to more deficits. In late 1988, 44 percent of a nation-wide poll of voters chose "reducing the deficit" as the single most pressing issue facing the incoming Bush administration— more than twice the percentage of the next most worrisome issue (protecting U.S. workers against foreign competition). Perhaps the fear of deficits reflects the failure of politicians to explain the resemblance of government borrowing for infrastructure to corporate borrowing for plant and equipment. Perhaps it reflects the failure of economists to explain the similarity to politicians. Whatever the explanation, the fear of deficits is clearly another reason why infrastructure did not get built. We were afraid that we might bankrupt ourselves if we built it. That, too, is a state of mind not likely to change in the near future.

There is one last reason why we have so neglected our public capital. It is that while our public capital expenditures for roads and housing and transportation and education have been declining, our spending for military purposes has been growing. Between 1980 and 1989, military spending doubled from $143 billion to over $300 billion. If we had managed to reduce military spending in 1989 to its inflation-corrected level in 1980, we would have been able to "find" some $50 to $60 billion for infrastructural repairs. But that option was not open to us. As long as the existence of a Soviet threat was the unchallengeable assumption on which American foreign policy was based, the claims of the military might have been whittled away, but could not be radically slashed.

The extraordinary events in Europe have challenged this assumption. There is no longer any question that the Pentagon budget will be sharply cut. Savings on the order of $50 billion ought to be visible within a year or two. If military spending decreases over the next three to five years to perhaps half its present level, which seems possible, $150 billion or more will be pared from the Pentagon budget. Moreover, these are annual savings, available each year from the budgets of the future.

Applied to the improvement of our infrastructure, these funds would approximately restore its level to that of the 1960s. Moreover, that tremendous restoration could take place without incurring a penny of new taxes or a dime of new borrowing. History does not offer many such oppor-